T5-BQA-027

It All Began with Stratigraphy and Chronology

Çiğdem Maner, Mark Weeden,
Masako Omura, Kimiyoshi Matsumura (Eds.)

It All Began with Stratigraphy and Chronology

Archaeology in Central Anatolia

Festschrift Dedicated to Sachihiro Omura on his 77th Birthday

2025

Harrassowitz Verlag · Wiesbaden

Cover illustration: Aerial Photograph of Kaman-Kalehöyük © JIAA

Publication of this book was funded by the Japanese Institute of Anatolian Archaeology, affiliated with the Middle Eastern Culture Center in Japan

Bibliografische Information der Deutschen Nationalbibliothek
Die Deutsche Nationalbibliothek verzeichnet diese Publikation in der Deutschen Nationalbibliografie; detaillierte bibliografische Daten sind im Internet über https://www.dnb.de abrufbar.

Bibliographic information published by the Deutsche Nationalbibliothek
The Deutsche Nationalbibliothek lists this publication in the Deutsche Nationalbibliografie; detailed bibliographic data are available on the Internet at https://www.dnb.de

For further information about our publishing program consult our website http://www.harrassowitz-verlag.de

Kreuzberger Ring 7c–d, 65205 Wiesbaden, produktsicherheit.verlag@harrassowitz.de

Printed on permanent/durable paper.
Printing and binding: Esser printSolutions, Göttingen
Printed in Germany

ISBN 978-3-447-12202-3
eISBN 978-3-447-39568-7

Contents

Foreword by Her Imperial Highness Princess Akiko of Mikasa

I would like to cordially congratulate Dr. Sachihiro Omura on the publication of his 77 year commemorative collection of work.

I had the pleasure of first meeting Dr. Omura in the summer of my second year of Gakushuin Girls' Senior High School. My father had a strict policy of only allowing trips abroad if there was some significant meaning to the visit; travel simply for the sake of sightseeing or tourism was denied. The first trip I was allowed to take was to Turkey. When my father was leaving to attend the inaugural ceremony at the Institute of Anatolian Archaeology, I begged to accompany him. "Grandpa worked on that site," I pleaded. "I want to see what he did."

My father's response was: "This is to be an official visit. Schedule will be restricted." However, he made up for the refusal by arranging for me to take a separate trip to Turkey during my summer vacation. It was Dr. Omura who accompanied me and served as my guide throughout.

We went around to all sorts of places, such as Ankara, Cappadocia, Kaman-Kalehöyük, Troy, Pergamon, and Istanbul. I was moved by the remains of Troy, having read and enjoyed Greek mythology. And the magnificent scene that nature, wind and rain had created over tens of thousands of years at Cappadocia made me feel very small indeed.

Furthermore, I was especially struck by the mysteries of Kaman-Kalehöyük. The process of trying to unravel what had occurred there over tens of thousands of years was the main purpose of our trip. I recall being drawn in by Dr. Omura's twinkling eyes like a little boy, betraying his own fascination as he explained the importance of this site and the artefacts that had been excavated. The midsummer sun was beating down on us all the while. It was there that I came to know the deep allure of this world that is Archaeology.

After that, of course, I read history at Gakushuin University and completed my dissertation on tartans and how it influenced the national identity of the Scottish people. Dr. Omura learned of my dissertation and invited me to present my research at the Middle Eastern Culture Center. I tried to beg off, arguing that there was no linkage between Scotland and the Middle East, and also that I was still too inexperienced in academics. However, Dr. Omura responded very strictly that too many young researchers are, conversely, overspecialized, so it is important to listen to many other research presentations. In the end, I decided to accept his persuasion.

This was my first experience of talking outside my research field and at another university. I remember very well how nervous I was and I took a great deal of time preparing for it. The presence of my grandfather, His Imperial Highness Prince Mikasa added to the tension. After I had completed my presentation and responded to a few queries, the prince raised his hand from the back of the room and posed a most difficult question that I had never even thought of. I was not able to answer him. This was the first setback I experienced as a researcher and it also left me determined to become the same sort of capable academic that the prince clearly was. I realise I owe a great deal to Dr. Omura for the lessons of that day. They have made me the researcher that I am now.

I hope that Dr. Omura will continue to do his work with those same twinkling eyes and to keep sharing his passion with many more followers. Allow me to say in closing that I also wish that Dr. Omura's research will continue to unravel the historical secrets that lie sleeping in the Anatolian Plateau.

Groundbreaking Ceremony "鍬入れ式" by H. I. H. Prince Takahito Mikasa at Kaman-Kalehöyük (1986).

Inauguration Ceremony of JIAA (2005). From the left, former prime minister and current President of the Republic of Türkiye Recep Tayyip Erdoğan, H. I. H. Princess Akiko of Mikasa and H. I. H. Prince Tomohito of Mikasa.

Inauguration of Tahsin Özgüç Conference Hall (2008).
H. I. H. Princess Akiko of Mikasa and Prof. Halil Bülent Özgüç.

Bibliography – Sachihiro Omura

I. Books and Monographs

Omura, S.

- 1978 *Unknown Ancient Kingdom* (in Japanese), Tokyo, JTB Publishing.
- 1981 *The Iron Empire: Excavation of the Hittite* (in Japanese), Tokyo, NHK Publishing Inc.
- 2000 *Journey to the World history – Turkey* (in Japanese), Tokyo, Yamakawa Shuppansha Ltd.
- 2001 *Cappadocia: Cave Monastery and Underground City* (in Japanese), *ASIA* series, Tokyo, Shueisha Inc.
- 2004 *A Chronicle of Anatolian Archaeological Excavation: 20 years at Kaman-Kalehöyük* (in Japanese), NHK Publishing Inc.
- 2014 *A Truth of Troy: A Real Image of H. Schliemann Seen from the Excavation Sites in Anatolia* (in Japanese), Tokyo, Yamakawa Shuppansha Ltd.
- 2018 *Wind of Anatolia: Archaeology and International Contribution* (in Japanese), Tokyo, Lithon.

Omura, S. and C. Shinohara

- 2022 *Captivated by Hittite: A Manga Artist Interviews an Archaeologist* (in Japanese), Tokyo, Yamakawa Shuppansha Ltd.

II. Books Edited

Omura, S. (ed.)

- 1991 *The World of the King Midas: The Painted Potteries from the 1st Millennium B.C. at Kaman-Kalehöyük* (in Japanese), Tokyo, The Middle Eastern Culture Center in Japan.
- 2024 Kaman Kalehöyük Arkeoloji Müzesi Kataloğu/Kaman Kalehöyük Archaeological Museum Catalogue/カマン·カレホユック考古学博物館, Kaman/Kırşehir, Japanese Institute of Anatolian Archaeology.

Omura, S., Y. Nagata and M. Naito (eds.)

- 2012 *53 Chapters for Learning Turkey*, Tokyo, Akaishi Publishing.

III. Articles

Omura, S.

- 1989a "1987 Yılı Kaman-Kalehöyük Kazıları," *KST* X/I, pp. 353–368.
- 1989b "1987 Kırşehir İli Sınırları İçinde Yapılan Yüzey Araştırmaları," *AraST* VI, pp. 555–570.
- 1991a "1989 Yılı Kaman-Kalehöyük Kazıları," *KST* XII/I, pp. 427–442.
- 1991b "1989 Yılı Kırşehir, Yozgat, Nevşehir, Aksaray İlleri Sınırları içinde yürütülen Yüzey Araştırmaları," *AraST* VIII, pp. 69–89.
- 1991c "Painted Pottery Collected from the Basin of the Delice River in Central Anatolia," in by M. Mori, H. Ogawa, and M. Yoshikawa (eds.), *Near Eastern Studies: Dedicated to H. I. H. Prince Takahito Mikasa on the Occasion of His Seventy-Fifth Birthday* (BMECCJ 5), Wiesbaden, pp. 279–292.
- 1992a "1990 Yılı Orta Anadolu'da Yürütülen Yüzey Araştırmaları," *ArST* 9, pp. 541–560.
- 1992b "1990 Yılı Kaman-Kalehöyük Kazıları," *KST* XIII/I, pp. 319–336.
- 1993a "1991 Yılı İç Anadolu'da Yürütülen Yüzey Araştırmaları," *ArST* 10, pp. 365–386.
- 1993 "1991 Yılı Kaman-Kalehöyük Kazıları," *KST XIV/I*, pp. 307–326.
- 1994a "1992 Yılında İç Anadolu'da Yürütülen Yüzey Araştırmaları," *AraST XI*, pp. 311–336.
- 1994b "1992 Yılı Kaman-Kalehöyük Kazıları," *KST XV/I*, pp. 271–293.
- 1994c "1985–1992 Kaman-Kalehöyük Kazıları," *1993 Yılı Anadolu Medeniyetleri Müzesi Konferanslar*, pp. 46–57.
- 1995a "1993 Yılında İç Anadolu'da Yürütülen Yüzey Araştırmaları," *AraST XII*, pp. 215–244.
- 1995b "1993 Yılı Kaman- Kalehöyük Kazıları," *KST XVI/I*, pp. 313–330.
- 1995c "Preliminary Report on the Ninth Excavation at Kaman-Kalehöyük (1994)," *AAS* 4, pp. 1–48.
- 1995d "A Preliminary Report on the Archaeological Survey in Central Anatolia (1994)," *AAS* 4, pp. 49–108.
- 1996a "A Preliminary Report of Ninth Excavations of Kaman-Kalehöyük (1994)," in H. I. H. Prince Takahito Mikasa (ed.), *Essays on Ancient Anatolia and Syria in the Second and Third Millennium B.C.* (BMECCJ 9), Wiesbaden, pp. 87–134.

- 1996b "A Preliminary Report of the General Survey in Central Anatolia (1994)," in H.I.H. Prince Takahito Mikasa (ed.), *Essays on Ancient Anatolia and Syria in the Second and Third Millennium B.C.* (BMECCJ 9), Wiesbaden, pp. 135–192.
- 1996c "1994 Yılı Kaman-Kalehöyük Kazıları," *KST XVII/I*, pp. 189–207.
- 1996d "1994 Yılı İç Anadolu'da Yürütülen Yüzey Araştırmaları," *AraST* XIII/II, pp. 243–272.
- 1996e "A Preliminary Report on the Tenth Excavation at Kaman-Kalehöyük (1995)," *AAS* 5, pp. 1–70.
- 1996f "A Preliminary Report on the Archaeological Survey in Central Anatolia (1995)," *AAS* 5, pp. 71–130.
- 1997a "1995 Yılı Kaman-Kalehöyük Kazıları," *KST XVIII/I*, pp. 201–212.
- 1997b "1995 Yılı İç Anadolu'da Yürütülen Yüzey Araştırmaları," *AraST XIV/II*, pp. 283–302.
- 1997c "A Preliminary Report on the Eleventh Excavation at Kaman-Kalehöyük (1996)," *AAS* 6, pp. 1–66.
- 1997d "A Preliminary Report on the Archaeological Survey in Central Anatolia (1996)," *AAS* 6, pp. 67–108.
- 1998a "1996 Yılı Kaman-Kalehöyük Kazıları," *KST XIX/I*, pp. 311–322.
- 1998b "1996 Yılı İç Anadolu'da Yürütülen Yüzey Araştırmaları," *AraST XV*, pp. 41–50.
- 1998c "A Preliminary Report on the Twelfth Excavation at Kaman – Kalehöyük (1997)," *AAS 7*, pp. 1–84.
- 1998d "A Preliminary Report on the Archaeological Survey on Central Anatolia (1997)," *AAS 7*, pp. 85–128.
- 1998e "An Archaeological Survey of Central Anatolia (1995)," in H.I.H Prince Takahito Mikasa (ed.), *Essays on Ancient Anatolia in the Second Millennium B.C., (BMECCJ 10)*, Wiesbaden, pp. 78–113.
- 1999a "The Eleventh Excavation in Kaman-Kalehöyük 1996," in H.I.H. Prince Takahito Mikasa (ed.), *Essays on Ancient Anatolia, (BMECCJ 9)*, Wiesbaden, pp. 51–93.
- 1999b "A Preliminary Report On the Archaeological Survey in Central Anatolia (1998)," *AAS* 8, pp. 1–78.
- 1999c "A Preliminary Report on the Thirteenth Excavation at Kaman-Kalehöyük (1998)," *AAS* 8, pp. 1–78.
- 2000a "1998 Yılı İç Anadolu Yüzey Araştırması," *AraST XVII*, pp. 25–30.
- 2000b "1998 Yılı Kaman-Kalehöyük Kazıları," *KST* XXI/1, pp. 217–228.
- 2000c "Preliminary Report on the 14th Excavation at Kaman-Kalehöyük (1999)," *AAS* 9, pp. 1–36.
- 2000d "Preliminary Report of the General Survey in Central Anatolia (1999)," *AAS* 9, pp. 37–96.
- 2001a "Preliminary Report on the 15th Excavation Season at Kaman-Kalehöyük (2000)," *AAS* 10, pp. 1–36.
- 2001b "Preliminary Report of the General Survey in Central Anatolia (2000)," *AAS* 10, pp. 37–49.
- 2001c "1999 Yılı Kaman-Kalehöyük Kazıları," *KST XXII/I*, pp. 327–336.
- 2001d "1999 Yılı İç Anadolu'da Yürütülen Yüzey Araştırmaları," *AraST XVIII/II*, pp. 83–88.
- 2002a "2000 Yılı Orta Anadolu'da Yürütülen Yüzey Araştırmaları," *AraST* XIX/II, pp. 303–307.
- 2002b "2000 Yılı Kaman-Kalehöyük Kazıları," *KST XXIII/I*, pp. 389–396.
- 2002a "Preliminary Report on the 16th Excavation at Kaman-Kalehöyük (2001)," *AAS* 11, pp. 1–44.
- 2002b "Preliminary Report of the General Survey in Central Anatolia (2001)," *AAS* 11, pp. 45–112.
- 2002c "Field Course on Archaeology at Kaman-Kalehöyük," *AAS* 11, pp. 113–116.
- 2003a "2001 Yılı Kaman-Kalehöyük Kazıları," *KST XXIV/I*, pp. 11–17.
- 2003b "2001 Yılı İç Anadolu'da Yürütülen Yüzey Araştırmaları," *AraST XX/II*, pp. 271–275.
- 2003c "Preliminary Report on the 17th Excavation at Kaman-Kalehöyük 2002," *AAS 12*, pp. *1–36*.
- 2003d "Preliminary Report of the General Survey in Central Anatolia 2002," *AAS 12*, pp. 37–88.
- 2004 "Preliminary Report on the 18th Excavation at Kaman-Kalehöyük 2003," *AAS* 13, pp. 1–36.
- 2004b "Preliminary Report of the General Survey in Central Anatolia 2003," *AAS* 13, pp. 37–86.
- 2004c "The Engraved Earthenwares in Central Anatolia (in Japanese)," in *Festschrift for H.I.H. Prince Takahito Mikasa on the Occasion of His Eighty-Eight Birthday*, Publishing Society for the Festschrift, Tokyo, Tosui Shobo Publishers & Co.Ltd., pp. 121–139.

- 2005a "Preliminary Report on the 19th Excavation at Kaman-Kalehöyük (2004)," *AAS* 14, pp. 1–54.
- 2005b "Preliminary Report of the 2004 General Survey in Central Anatolia," *AAS* 14 (2005), pp. 55–84.
- 2006a "Preliminary Report on the 19th Excavation at Kaman-Kalehöyük (2005)," *AAS* 15, pp. 1–62.
- 2006b "Preliminary Report of the 2005 General Survey in Central Anatolia," *AAS* 15, pp. 63–102.
- 2007a "Preliminary Report on the 20th Excavation at Kaman-Kalehöyük (2006)," *AAS* 16, pp. 1–43.
- 2007b "Preliminary Report of the General Survey in Central Anatolia (2006)," *AAS* 16, pp. 45–84.
- 2007c "2003–2006 yılında İç Anadolu'da yapılmış olan Yüzey Araştırmaları," *AraST* XXV, pp. 213–224.
- 2008a "Preliminary Report on the 22nd Excavation Season at Kaman-Kalehöyük in 2007," *AAS* 17, pp. 1–43.
- 2008b "2003–2006 Yıllarında İç Anadolu'da Yapılmış Olan Yüzey Araştırmaları," *AraST* XXV/II, pp. 213–224.
- 2008c "2003–2006 Yılı Kaman-Kalehöyük Kazıları," *KST* XXIX/III, pp. 1–16.
- 2008d "Issues in the 'Cultural Chronology' of Anatolian Archaeology: With Reference to Excavations at Kaman-Kalehöyük (in Japanese)," *Tohogaku (Eastern Studies)* 115, pp. 158–168.
- 2009a "2007 Yılı Kaman-Kalehöyük Kazıları," *KST* XXX/III, pp. 197–206.
- 2009b "Did the Hittite Have High Quality Iron? (in Japanese)," *Kagaku* 79 No. 10, pp. 1130–1140.
- 2011a "2009 Yılı Kaman-Kalehöyük Kazıları," *KST* XXXII/IV, pp. 421–426.
- 2011b "The Construction of a "Cultural Chronology" for Kaman-Kalehöyük (Turkey) and Burnt Layer (in Japanese)," *Tohogaku (Eastern Studies)* 122, pp. 119–130.
- 2011c "Kaman-Kalehöyük Excavations in Central Anatolia," in S. Steadman and R.G. McMahon (eds.), *The Oxford Handbook of Ancient Anatolia: (10,000–323 B.C.E)*, Oxford, Oxford University Press, pp. 1095–1111.
- 2012 "2010 Yılı Kaman-Kalehöyük Kazıları," *KST* XXXIII/IV, pp. 447–462.
- 2013 "The Round Silos at Kaman-Kalehöyük from the Second Millenium B.C.," in M. Alparslan and M.D. Alparslan (eds.), *Hittites – An Anatolian Empire*, İstanbul, Yapı Kredi Yayınları, pp. 290–295.
- 2014a "2013 Yılı Kırşehir İlinde Yapılan Yüzey Araştırmaları," *AraST* XXXII/II, pp. 503–512.
- 2014b "Kaman-Kalehöyük Kazıları 2013," *KST* XXXVI/III, pp. 623–632.
- 2016a "2014 Yılında Kırşehir İlinde Yapılan Yüzey Araştırmaları," *AraST* XXXIII/II, pp. 157–164.
- 2016b "2014 Yılı Kaman-Kalehöyük Kazıları Japon anadolu Arkeoloji Entitüsü," *KST* XXXVII/III, pp. 381–390.
- 2016c "Kaman-Kalehöyük Kazıları," in *Kırşehir-Arkeoloji ve Paleoantropoloji* Çalışmaları, Kırşehir, T.C. Kırşehir ve Turizm Müdürlüğü, pp. 7–27.
- 2016d "2011–2014 Yıllarında Kırşehir İlinde Yapılan Arkeolojik Yüzey Araştırmaları," in *Kırşehir-Arkeoloji ve Paleoantropoloji* Çalışmaları, T.C. Kırşehir ve Turizm Müdürlüğü, pp. 143–184.
- 2017a "2015 Yılı Kaman-Kalehöyük Kazıları," *KST XXXVIII/III*, pp. 527–536.
- 2017b "2015 Yılı Kırşehir, Yozgat İllerinde Yapılan Yüzey Araştırmaları," *AraST* XXXIV/II, pp. 611–616.
- 2017c "The Early Iron Age in Central Anatolia: With Reference to Excavations at Kaman-Kalehöyük (in Japanese)," *Tohogaku (Eastern Studies)* 134, pp. 122–135.
- 2019 "The Large Architectural Remains of the 2nd Millennium B.C. Unearthed at Kaman-Kalehöyük in Central Anatolia," in I. Nakata *et al.* (eds.), *Prince of the Orient: Ancient Near Eastern Studies in Memory of H. I. H. Prince Takahito Mikasa*, Society for Near Eastern Studies in Japan, pp. 47–66.

IV. Joint Articles

Anderson, C.P., L. Atıcı, and S. Omura
- 2018 "Conflict at Kaman-Kalehöyük: The End of the Middle Bronze Age at a Rural Settlement in Central Anatolia," *American Journal of Physical Anthropology* 165, pp. 10.

Damgaard, P.B. and S. Omura *et al.*
- 2018 "The First Horse Herders and the Impact of Early Bronze Age Steppe Expansions into Asia," *Science*, DOI 10.1126/science.aar7711.

Ertepınar, P., C.G. Langereis, A.J. Biggin, L.V. de Groot, F. Kulakoğlu, S. Omura, and A. Süel

- 2016 "Full Vector Archaeomagnetic Records from Anatolia Between 2400 and 1350 BCE: Implications for Geomagnetic Field Models and the Dating of Fires in Antiquity," *Earth and Planetary Science Letter* 434, pp. 171–186.

Fairbairn, A., and S. Omura

- 2005 "Archaeological Identification and Significance of ÉSAG (agricultural storage pits) at Kaman-Kalehöyük, Central Anatolia," *Anatolian Studies* 55, pp. 15–23.

Fenwick, R. S. H., and S. Omura

- 2015 "Smoke in the Eyes? Archaeological Evidence for Medicinal Henbane Fumigation at Ottoman Kaman-Kalehöyük, Kırşehir Province, Turkey," *Antiquity* 89, no. 346, pp. 905–921.

Henderson, J., S. Chenery, S. Omura, K. Matsumura and E. Faber

- 2018 "Hittite and Early Iron Age Glass from Kaman-Kalehöyük and Büklükale, Turkey: Evidence for Local Production and Continuity?," *AAS* XXI, pp. 70–84.

Kristiansen, K., B. Hemphill, G. Barjamovic, S. Omura, S. Y. Şenyurt, V. Moiseyev and A. Gromov *et al.*

- 2018 "Archaeological Supplement A," In *Archaeology of the Caucasus, Anatolia, Central and South Asia 4000–1500 B.C.E*, Damgaard *et al.* (eds.), DOI 10.5281/zenodo.1243933.

Mikami, T. and S. Omura

- 1987 "1985 Kaman-Kalehöyük Yüzey Araştırmaları," *AraST* IV, pp. 227–237.
- 1988a "1986 Kaman – Kalehöyük Kazıları," *KST* IX/II, pp. 1–16.
- 1988b "1986 Kırşehir İli Sınırları İçinde Yapılan Yüzey Araştırmaları," *AraST V/II*, pp. 123–156.
- 1991a "General survey of Kaman-Kalehöyük in Turkey (1985)," in H. I. H Prince Takahito Mikasa (ed.), *Essays on Ancient Anatolian and Syrian Studies in the 2nd and 1st Millenium B.C. (BMECCJ 4)*, Wiesbaden, pp. 62–86.
- 1991b "A preliminary report on the first excavation at Kaman-Kalehöyük in Turkey (1986)," in H. I. H Prince Takahito Mikasa (ed.), *Essays on Ancient Anatolian and Syrian Studies in the 2nd and 1st Millennium B.C.*, (*BMECCJ 4*), Wiesbaden, pp. 87–130.
- 1992 "A Preliminary Report on the Second Excavation at Kaman-Kalehöyük in Turkey (1987)," in H. I. H Prince Takahito Mikasa (ed.), *Essays on Ancient Anatolia and its Surrounding Civilizations* (*BMECCJ*. 6), Wiesbaden, pp. 23–59.
- 1993 "A Preliminary Report on the third Excavation at Kaman-Kalehöyük in Turkey (1988)," in H. I. H Prince Takahito Mikasa (ed.), *Essay on Anatolian Archaeology (BMECCJ 7)*, Wiesbaden, pp. 43–74.

Mori, M., and S. Omura

- 1990a "1988 Kaman-Kalehöyük Kazıları," *KST* XI/I, pp. 335–354.
- 1990b "1988 Kırşehir; Yozgat ve Nevşehir İlleri Yüzey Araştırmaları," *AraST* VII, pp. 295–310.
- 1995 "A preliminary report on the excavations at Kaman-Kalehöyük in Turkey (1989–1993)," In *Essays on Anatolian Archaeology* (*BMECCJ*. 8), edited by H. I. H Prince Takahito Mikasa, Wiesbaden, pp. 1–42.

Nakai, I., Y. Abe, K. Tantrakarn, S. Omura, and S. Erkut

- 2008 "Preliminary Report on the Analysis of an Early Bronze Age Iron Dagger Excavated from Alacahöyük," *AAS* 17, pp. 321–323.

Nakai, I., Y. Abe, K. Tantrakarn, K. Matsumura and S. Omura

- 2018 "An Analysis of Glass Artefacts found in the 16th century B.C. layer at Büklükale, Turkey – One of the Oldest Glass Vessels Excavated in the Near East," *AAS* XXI, pp. 61–69.

Nakai, I., K. Tantrakarn, Y. Abe, and S. Omura

- 2013 "Study on Western Asiatic Cast Ribbed Rectangular Beads from Kaman-Kalehöyük, Turkey, by Using Portable X-ray Fluorescence," *Open Journal of Archaeometry* 1, no. 1, pp. 109–114.

Omura, S. and K. Kashima

- 2002 "The Geo-archaeological Program at Kaman Kalehöyük and its Surroundings," *ArkST* XVII, pp. 119–126.
- 2003 "The Geo-Archaeological Research Project at Kaman-Kalehöyük and Surroundings in 2001" *ArkST* XVIII, pp. 69–75.

Paterakis, A. B. and S. Omura

- 2014 "Gold Cloisonné from the Assyrian Colony Period in Central Anatolia," in O. Kaelin, R. Stucky, and A. Jamieson (eds.), *Proceedings of the 9th International Congress on the Archaeology of the Ancient Near East, 9–13 June 2014, Basel, Vol.* 3, Wiesbaden, pp. 293–300.

Paterakis, A. B., S. Omura, and E. van Bork

- 2015 "An Unusual Example of Gold Cloisonné from Central Anatolia," *STAR Science & Technology of Archaeological Research* 1, no. 2, pp. 106–114.

Conferences and Lectures

Omura, S. 2013 "Excavation Research at Kaman-Kalehöyük, 2013." Research Debrief Session in 2013 and 24th Conference on Survey in Turkey, 22 December, Tokyo.

- 2014 "Kaman-Kalehöyük excavations in Central Anatolia, Turkey." The Meeting of Arts and Science in the History of Ironmaking – International Organized Session, The Iron and Steel Institute of Japan. Tokyo Institute of Technology, 23 March, Tokyo.
- 2014 "Japon Anadolu Arkeoloji Enstitüsü Kazı ve Konsevasyon Çalışmaları." 23. Müze Kurtarma Kazıları Sempozyumu ve Müzecilik Çalıştayı, T.C. Kültür ve Turizm Bakanlığı, Erdoba Elegance Hotel, 4–7 May, Mardin.
- 2014 "2013 Yılında Kırşehir İli'nde Yürütülen Yüzey Araştırmaları." T.C. Kültür ve Turizm Bakanlığı, Kültür Varlıkları ve Müzeler Genel Müdürlüğü, 03 June, Zeugma Mozaik Müzesi, Gaziantep.
- 2014 "Japan and Turkey: Where Did We Come From? Where Are We Going." Activities in the Framework of the 90th Aniversary of Turkey-Japan Diplomatic Relations Joint Symposium, 22 September.
- 2015 "Excavation Research at Kaman-Kalehöyük, 2014." Research Debrief Session in 2014 and 25th Conference on Survey in Turkey, 11 February, Tokyo.

Paterkis, A.B. and S. Omura 2015. "The influence of East and West on Bronze Objects found in Central Anatolia: Small Bronze Finds from Kaman-Kalehöyük." XIXth International Congress on Ancient Bronzes: Getty Bronze Congress, 13–17 October, Los Angeles.

Masubuchi, M. and S. Omura, 2015. "Modification of the Iron Culture before and after the Destruction of the Hittite according to the Iron Objects from Kaman-Kalehöyük in Central Anatolia." 20th Meeting of the Japanese Society for West Asian Archaeology at Nagoya University, 13th June, Nagoya.

- 2016 "Excavation Research at Kaman-Kalehöyük, 2015." Research Debrief Session in 2015 and 26th Conference on Survey in Turkey, 28 February, Tokyo.
- 2016 "Activities of the Japanese Institute of Anatolian Archaeology (2015)." *Research Debrief Session in 2015 and 26th Conference on Survey in Turkey*, 28 February, Tokyo.
- 2016 "Takahashi Y., A. Sekimoto, K. Matsumura, S. Omura and I. Nakai, "Provenance Study of Wheel made Pottery from Kaman-Kalehöyük, Turkey Using Heavy Mineral Analysis and Chemical Compositional Analysis." Poster-session of the 33th Meeting of Japan Society for Scientific Studies on Cultural Properties, 4–5th June, Nara University.
- 2016 Otsuka, A., K. Abe, I. Nakai, K. Matsumura and S. Omura, "Scientific Classification and Phase Identification of the Black/Brown pigment used for the Painted Pottery from Kaman-Kalehöyük, Turkey using Nondestructive Analysis." Postersession of the the 33th Meeting of Japan Society for Scientific Studies on Cultural Properties, 4–5th June, Nara University.
- 2017 "Excavation Research at Kaman-Kalehöyük, 2016." Research Debrief Session in 2016 and 27th Conference on Survey in Turkey, 4 March 2017, Tokyo.
- 2017 "Activities of the Japanese Institute of Anatolian Archaeology (2016)." Research Debrief Session in 2016 and 27th Conference on Survey in Turkey, 4 March 2017, Tokyo.
- 2018 "Excavation Research at Kaman-Kalehöyük, 2017." Research Debrief Session in 2017 and 28th Conference on Survey in Turkey, 25 March 2018, Tokyo.
- 2018 "Kaman-Kalehöyük Kazıları." *Japon Anadolu Arkeoloji Enstitüsü Kazı Çalışmaları*, 5 Mayıs, Kaman, Turkey.
- 2018 "Activities of the Japanese Institute of Anatolian Archaeology (2017)." Research Debrief Session in 2017 and 28th Conference on Survey in Turkey, 25 March, Tokyo.
- 2019 "Excavation Research at Kaman-Kalehöyük, 2018." Research Debrief Session 2018

and 29th Conference on Survey in Turkey, 25 March, Tokyo.
2019 "Activities of the Japanese Institute of Anatolian Archaeology (2018)." Research Debrief Session 2018 and 29th Conference on Survey in Turkey, 25 March, Tokyo.
2019 "Excavation Research at Kaman-Kalehöyük, 2018." Research Debrief Session 2018 and 29th Conference on Survey in Turkey, 25 March, Tokyo.

Kazı Sonuçları Toplantısı and Araştırma Sonuçları Toplantısı

1988 "1987 Yılı Kaman-Kalehöyük Kazıları." 10. Uluslararası Kazı, Araştırma ve Arkeometri Sempozyumu, Ankara.
1988 "Kırşehir İli Sınırları İçinde Yapılan Yüzey Araştırmaları". 10. Araştırma ve Arkeometri Sempozyumu, Ankara.
1990 "1989 Yılı Kaman-Kalehöyük Kazıları." 12. Uluslararası Kazı, Araştırma ve Arkeometri Sempozyumu, Ankara.
1990 "1989 Yılı Kırşehir, Yozgat, Nevşehir, Aksaray İlleri Sınırları içinde yürütülen Yüzey Araştırmaları." 12. Uluslararası Kazı, Araştırma ve Arkeometri Sempozyumu, Ankara.
1991 "1990 yılı Orta Anadolu'da Yürütülen Yüzey Araştırmaları." 13. Uluslararası Kazı, Araştırma ve Arkeometri Sempozyumu, Çanakkale.
1991 "1990 yılı Kaman-Kalehöyük Kazıları." 13. Uluslararası Kazı, Araştırma ve Arkeometri Sempozyumu, Çanakkale.
1992 "1991 yılı İç Anadolu'da Yürütülen Yüzey Araştırmaları." 14. Uluslararası Kazı, Araştırma ve Arkeometri Sempozyumu, Ankara.
1992 "1991 Yılı Kaman-Kalehöyük Kazıları." 14. Uluslararası Kazı, Araştırma ve Arkeometri Sempozyumu, Ankara.
1993. "1992 Yılında İç Anadolu'da Yürütülen Yüzey Araştırmaları." 15. Uluslararası Kazı, Araştırma ve Arkeometri Sempozyumu, Ankara.
1993 "1992 Yılı Kaman-Kalehöyük Kazıları." 15. Uluslararası Kazı, Araştırma ve Arkeometri Sempozyumu, Ankara.
1994 "1993 Yılında İç Anadolu'da Yürütülen Yüzey Araştırmaları." 16. Uluslararası Kazı, Araştırma ve Arkeometri Sempozyumu, Ankara.
1994 "1993 Yılı Kaman- Kalehöyük Kazıları." 16. Uluslararası Kazı, Araştırma ve Arkeometri Sempozyumu, Ankara.
1995 "1994 Yılı Kaman-Kalehöyük Kazıları." 17. Uluslararası Kazı, Araştırma ve Arkeometri Sempozyumu, Ankara.
1995 "1994 Yılı İç Anadolu'da Yürütülen Yüzey Araştırmaları." 17. Uluslararası Kazı, Araştırma ve Arkeometri Sempozyumu, Ankara.
1996 "1995 Yılı Kaman-Kalehöyük Kazıları." 18. Uluslararası Kazı, Araştırma ve Arkeometri Sempozyumu, Ankara.
1996 "1995 Yılı İç Anadolu'da Yürütülen Yüzey Araştırmaları. 18. Uluslararası Kazı, Araştırma ve Arkeometri Sempozyumu, Ankara.
1997 "1996 Yılı Kaman-Kalehöyük Kazıları." 19. Uluslararası Kazı, Araştırma ve Arkeometri Sempozyumu, Ankara.
1997 "1996 Yılı İç Anadolu'da Yürütülen Yüzey Araştırmaları." 19. Uluslararası Kazı, Araştırma ve Arkeometri Sempozyumu, Ankara.
1999 "1998 Yılı İç Anadolu Yüzey Araştırması." 21. Uluslararası Kazı, Araştırma ve Arkeometri Sempozyumu, Ankara.
1999 "1998 Yılı Kaman-Kalehöyük Kazıları." 21. Uluslararası Kazı, Araştırma ve Arkeometri Sempozyumu, Ankara.
2000 "1999 Yılı Kaman-Kalehöyük Kazıları." 22. Uluslararası Kazı, Araştırma ve Arkeometri Sempozyumu, Izmir.
2001 "2000 Yılı Orta Anadolu'da Yürütülen Yüzey Araştırmaları." 23. Uluslararası Kazı, Araştırma ve Arkeometri Sempozyumu, Ankara
2001 "2000 Yılı Kaman-Kalehöyük Kazıları." 23. Uluslararası Kazı, Araştırma ve Arkeometri Sempozyumu, Ankara.
2002 "2001 Yılı Kaman-Kalehöyük Kazıları." 24. Uluslararası Kazı, Araştırma ve Arkeometri Sempozyumu, Ankara.
2002 "2001 Yılı İç Anadolu'da Yürütülen Yüzey Araştırmaları." 24. Uluslararası Kazı, Araştırma ve Arkeometri Sempozyumu, Ankara.
2004 "2003–2006 Yıllarında İç Anadolu'da Yapılmış Olan Yüzey Araştırmaları." 29. Uluslararası Kazı, Araştırma ve Arkeometri Sempozyumu, Kocaeli.
2004 "2003–2006 Yılı Kaman-Kalehöyük Kazıları." 29. Uluslararası Kazı, Araştırma ve Arkeometri Sempozyumu, Kocaeli.
2008 "2007 Yılı Kaman-Kalehöyük Kazıları." 30. Uluslararası Kazı, Araştırma ve Arkeometri Sempozyumu, Ankara.

2010 "2009 Yılı Kaman-Kalehöyük Kazıları." 32. Uluslararası Kazı, Araştırma ve Arkeometri Sempozyumu, Istanbul.

2011 "2010 Yılı Kaman-Kalehöyük Kazıları." 33. Uluslararası Kazı, Araştırma ve Arkeometri Sempozyumu, Malatya.

2012 "General Survey at Kırşehir 2011." 34. Uluslararası Kazı, Araştırma ve Arkeometri Sempozyumu, 29 May, Çorum.

2012 "Kaman-Kalehöyük Excavations 2011." 34 Uluslararası Kazı, Araştırma ve Arkeometri Sempozyumu. 29 May, Çorum.

2013 "General Survey at Kırşehir 2012." 35. Uluslararası Kazı, Araştırma ve Arkeometri Sempozyumu, 28 May, Muğla Sıtkı Koçman University, Muğla.

2013 "Kaman-Kalehöyük Excavations 2012." 35. Uluslararası Kazı, Araştırma ve Arkeometri Sempozyumu. 28 May, Muğla Sıtkı Koçman University, Muğla,.

2014 "2013 Yılında Kırşehir İli'nde Yürütülen Yüzey Araştırmaları." T.C. Kültür ve Turizm Bakanlığı, Kültür Varlıkları ve Müzeler Genel Müdürlüğü, 03 Haziran, Zeugma Mozaik Müzesi, Gaziantep.

2014 "2013 Yılı Kaman-Kalehöyük Kazıları." 36. Uluslararası Kazı, Araştırma ve Arkeometri Sempozyumu, T.C. Kültür ve Turizm Bakanlığı, Kültür Varlıkları ve Müzeler Genel Müdürlüğü, 03 Haziran, Zeugma Mozaik Müzesi Gaziantep.

2015 "Kaman-Kalehöyük Excavations in 2014." 37th Uluslararası Kazı, Araştırma ve Arkeometri Sempozyumu, 11–15 May, Atatürk University, Erzurum.

2015 "Archaeological Survey in Kırşehir Province, 2014." 37th Uluslararası Kazı, Araştırma ve Arkeometri Sempozyumu, 11–15 May, Atatürk University, Erzurum.

2016 "2015 Yılında Kırşehir ve Yozgat İllerinde Yürütülen Yüzey Araştırmaları." 38. Uluslararası Kazı, Araştırma ve Arkeometri Sempozyumu, 25 Mayıs 2016, Trakya Üniversitesi, Edirne.

2016 "2015 Yılı Kaman-Kalehöyük Kazıları." 38. Uluslararası Kazı, Araştırma ve Arkeometri Sempozyumu, 25 Mayıs, Trakya Üniversitesi, Edirne.

2018 "Kaman-Kalehöyük Excavation 2017." 40th International Symposium of Excavations, Surveys and Archaeometry, 08 May, Onsekiz Mart Üniversitesi, Çanakkale.

2019 "Kaman-Kalehöyük Excavation 2018." 41th Uluslararası Kazı, Araştırma ve Arkeometri Sempozyumu, June, Dicle Üniversitesi, Diyarbakır.

2023 "2022 Yılında Kaman-Kalehöyük Kazıları." 43. Uluslararası Kazı, Araştırma ve Arkeometri Sempozyumu, Hacı Bayram Veli Üniversitesi, Ankara.

2024 "2023 Yılında Kaman-Kalehöyük Kazıları." 44. Uluslararası kazı, Araştırma ve Arkeometri Sempozyumu. Hacı Bektaş Üniversitesi, Nevşehir.

Invited Lectures

2012 "Eski Tunç Çağında Kaman-Kalehöyük." in *Early Bronze Age Workshop in 2012 – Japanese Institute of Anatolian Archaeology*, 22–23 September, Kırşehir.

2013 "Arkeoloji Açısından Anadolu'nun Önemi." 7 May, Ahi Evran University, Kırşehir.

2013 "Çeyrek Yüzyıl Işığında Kaman-Kalehöyük Kazıları ve Japon Anadolu Arkeoloji Enstitüsü 1985–2013" in 2nd *Conference of Japanese Studies in Turkey*, 14 June, *Boğaziçi University*, İstanbul.

2013 "İç Anadolu'da Kaman-Kalehöyük'ün Yeri ve Önemi" 8th October, Adnan Menderes University, Aydın.

2013 "Kızılırmak Havzası Arkeolojisi" 12 December, Kırıkkale University, Kırıkkale.

2014 "Keynote: Turkey and Japan observed from the Archaeological Excavation Field," Symposium for the 90th Anniversary of the Diplomatic Relation between Turkey and Japan, 1st Session – Relation between Japan and Turkey: Music, Language, Art and History, 22nd Sep. 2014, Ankara.

2014 "Iron Empire: Hittite Excavations (in Japanese)," The Meeting of Arts and Science, 16th March, Tokyo University of Arts, Tokyo.

2014 "Japon Anadolu Arkeoloji Enstitüsü Kazı ve Konservasyon Çalışmaları," 23. Müze Kurtarma Kazıları Sempozyumu ve Müzecilik Çalıştayı, 4–7 May, T.C. Kültür ve Turizm Bakanlığı, Mardin.

2014 "Kaman-Kalehöyük excavations in Central Anatolia, Turkey (in Japanese)." The Meeting of Arts and Science in the History of Ironmaking – International Session, The Iron and Steel Institute of Japan. 23 March, Tokyo Institute of Technology, Tokyo.

2014 "Excavations of Ancient Sites in Turkey and International Contributions." Mitaka Global Citizen Lecure, 25th March, Mitaka Network University, Tokyo.

2014 "Why does Japan excavate in Turkey?." at Kitakyushu Museum of Natural History & Human History, 15th March, Kitakyushu.

2015 "Hitit İmparatorluğun Ekonomik Kaynağı." 9th Gıda Mühendisliği Kongresi, 12–14 Kasım, Selçuk, İzmir,.

2015 "Is Archaeology able to make international contributions? (in Japanese)." 24th May, International Christian University, Tokyo.

2016 "Archaeological General Survey in Central Anatolia 1986–2015." Culture and Communication in Anatolia held at Atılım University, June 15, Ankara.

2024 "Kaman-Kalehöyük'te tespit edilen M.Ö. 2. bine ait Silolar." Hititlerin İzinde, Yeni Bilgiler ve Perspektifler, May 8, Çorum.

A Life Dedicated to Anatolian Archaeology and the Foundation of the Japanese Institute of Anatolian Archaeology (JIAA) in Kaman

*Çiğdem Maner**

A long, visionary and idealistic planning period and several years of research and excavation predated the foundation of the Japanese Institute of Anatolian Archaeology at Çağırkan in Kaman (district of Kırşehir) in 1998. The Japanese Institute of Anatolian Archaeology, abbrevated as JIAA, was established as an affiliated institute of the Middle Eastern Culture Center in Japan (MECCJ). The main aim of Dr. Sachihiro Omura for the foundation of JIAA, was, that he wanted to leave something behind after many years of excavation in Türkiye. "We have excavated for many years in Kaman-Kalehöyük, Büklükale and Yassıhöyük and I want to leave this research institute for the next generations of archaeologists" he said during a conversation we had (Fig. 1). I had joined Kaman-Kalehöyük in 1997 as a graduate student for the first time and between the years of 2016–2021 I was assistant director of the excavation. During several conversations over a long time span I have asked Dr. Sachihiro Omura (Omura San or Omura Bey as his colleagues and students call him) questions on his life, education, dreams, accomplishments and the foundation of the institute, which have created the ground for this short essay.

"*What are you doing*?"

Omura San remembers his father asking him this sentence, when he was digging up the backyard as a little boy.

He was only five years old and replied with a proud voice:

"*I am excavating*!"

Omura San's passion for archaeology started at a very young age. From the minute his father caught him digging, his father and also his teacher gave him books, stones and pottery to study and to quench his thirst for archaeology. It was clear from the early days on, that he would become a dedicated and passionate archaeologist.

Who would have thought that these early excavations and passion would lead to a great vision and the foundation of the Japanese Institue of Anatolian Archaeology in Çağırkan, a village of Kaman (Kırşehir) in Türkiye?

The Omura family had been living in Northeast China, in Manchuria. After Japan had lost the war with China, they moved from Manchuria to Japan and Sachihiro Omura was born in Japan. He was born on 7th September 1946 in Morioka (Iwate Prefecture) in northern Japan and he is the youngest of four siblings (he has one sister and two brothers). "We still have a house in Manchuria. My brother went there, visited it and took a foto of the house" he told me. His parents were both school teachers. Omura went to a local school, trying to read as much as possible on archaeology and excavations and to dig.

In 1972 he graduated from the Institute of Archaeology at Waseda University and in the same year he enrolled at the University of Ankara. While he was a student at Waseda and Ankara Universities, he joined the excavation

* Koç Üniversitesi, Department of Archaeology and History of Art, cmaner@ku.edu.tr

mission at Malqata in Luxor (Egypt) between 1972–75 and 1979–80 and at Fustat between 1981–83. During the excavation at Malqata in 1973, His Imperial Highness Prince Takahito Mikasa visited the excavation site. Prince Takahito was an archaeologist himself and very much interested in ancient world heritage. During this visit, the heat, water and food made the Prince feel ill, and he was forced to rest in the excavation house for a few days. The director of the excavation asked Omura to stay with His Imperial Highness Prince Takahito Mikasa and to cook for him some rice and to take good care of him. After Prince Takahito Mikasa felt healthier, he departed from the excavation, but gave Omura a card, and said that he could call and write whenever he would need something.

"It is still like a dream" says Omura San.

This is an important encounter and moment because Prince Takahito Mikasa would later on support the excavations at Kaman-Kalehöyük, invitations of Turkish academics to Japan, exhibition on Anatolian Civilizations in Japan, publications and the foundation of JIAA and the Kaman-Kalehöyük Museum. Omura was not planning to continue to work on Egyptian civilization, and that's why he never took a photo in Egypt. He wanted to work in Türkiye specifically on the Hittites.

Omura was intrigued by the Hittite civilization, because they were known as the first civilization, which produced and used iron tools and he was planning to research on this topic. He signed up for an exchange program to study at Ankara University and enrolled in 1972 in the Department of Hittitology as a graduate student at Ankara University. He had received a scholarship from the Turkish government to study in Türkiye. He got a plane ticket to fly with Pan Am (Pan American Airlines) to Ankara. The journey started in Tokyo and had five stopovers: Hongkong-Bankok-Delhi-Teheran-Istanbul. He arrived in Ankara on 19th September 1972 at 7.50 am. The journey had taken 2 days and the ticket price for an economy seat was 2000 USD. Before coming to Ankara he had read several books about Türkiye and also learned some Turkish words. He was well prepared, excited for his stay in Ankara and for this new chapter in his life (Fig. 2).

The plan was, that he would study at the Department of Ancient Near Eastern Archaeology (Proto ve Ön Asya Arkeolojisi) at Dil ve Tarih-Coğrafya Fakültesi at Ankara University. However, due to an unsolvable administrative problem, he was enrolled in the graduate program in the Department of Hittitology. His advisor at Ankara University was the Hittitologist Prof. Sedat Alp, with whom he excavated several seasons (1973–1980) at Konya Karahöyük (Fig. 3–5). In 1978 Omura submitted his Master thesis on "Hitit Döneminde Hayat Ağacı/Life Tree in the Hittite Period".

The stipend of his scholarship was never enough to sustain his life in Ankara, hence Omura was writing short texts for Japanese publications and newspapers about Türkiye and he was selling postcards in Sıhhiye around the university campus with his friends. For the texts he wrote he earned 100 USD, which paid for his rent. He remembers that the years between 1972–1981 were not easy at all. Luckily, he could have lunch with his friend Sedat Erkut at the cantine of the Türk Tarih Kurumu (Turkish Historical Society), where Erkut's father was working. This deep and dear friendship with Sedat Erkut, who became one of the leading Professors in Hittitology, would continue until he passed away in 2016. Upon the request of the Ministry of Culture and Tourism of the Turkish Republic in 2012, that all foreign excavations should have a Turkish assistant director, Prof. Sedat Erkut was appointed as assistant director of the Kaman-Kalehöyük excavations, which he continued until he passed away (Fig. 6).

Omura attended several excavations while he was at Ankara University. In 1973 he joined four excavations in Türkiye: Korucutepe with Prof. Hayri Ertem, Patnos and Haraba excavations with Prof. Baki Öğün and Ancoz and Konya Karahöyük with Prof. Sedat Alp (Fig. 7–9). He continued to join the excavations at Korucutepe until 1978 and the excavations at Konya Karahöyük until 1980. These excavations were in Central and Eastern Anatolia and laid the ground for ideas for his own projects and the foundation of the institute.

In 1977 Omura reached out to His Imperial Highness Prince Takahito Mikasa. He wanted to invite his Professors Sedat Alp and Tahsin Özgüç to Japan for conferences and a budget for their plane tickets and stay in Japan was necessary. "I called the number on the card, but I wasn't sure if the secretary would put me through to speak with Prince Mikasa. However, I was connected right away and the Prince remembered me very well and agreed to support the invitation of my Professors". A few years later Prince Takahito Mikasa visited the excavations at Kültepe (Fig. 10) and Prof. Tahsin Özgüç was invited again to Japan in 2004 for a conference (Fig. 11).

While Omura was studying in Ankara, he was also one of the main contact persons for Japanese students and academics, who came to Türkiye (Fig. 12). In 1979 he met Masako Tanji, an archaeologist interested in the Prehistory of Anatolia. She was also an exchange student from Japan, and was planning to study Çatalhöyük and the prehistory of Anatolia. Originally from Osaka, she had studied archaeology at Osaka University. In April 1984 they got married in Morioka, Japan and in 1987 their daughter Sachiko was born.

After Omura obtained his Masters degree he switched to the Department of Near Eastern Archaeology at Ankara University, where he finished his PhD in 1990 under the supervision of Prof. Kutlu Emre (Fig. 13). His thesis was on Alishar III pottery (Anadolu'da III. Alişar Seramiği), which explains also his interest in the Early Bronze Age. Masako Omura started a PhD on reused seals in the Old Assyrian Trading Colony Period with Prof. Nimet Özgüç, which she finished in 1998 (Fig. 14).

Omura returned to Japan in 1981, where he became first Researcher and then Chief Researcher in 1984 at the Middle Eastern Culture Center in Japan (MECCJ), a position he still holds today. His position at MECCJ was followed by an invitation as Guest Professor to the International Research Center for Japanese Studies in 1991. While he was chief researcher at MECCJ he organized and initiated an unforgettable exhibition on the heritage of Türkiye in 1985. 430 objects from Prehistory to the Ottoman period arrived in Tokyo for the "Land of Civilizations, Turkey – Uygarlıklar Ülkesi Türkiye" exhibition at the Idemitsu Museum of Art in Tokyo. This is the first time, that such a large exhibition on the heritage of Türkiye had been exhibited in Japan. Prof. Dr. Tahsin and Prof. Dr. Nimet Özgüç came to Japan for the inauguration of the "Land of Civilizations, Turkey" exhibition and conferences (Fig. 15).

The "Archaeological General Survey in Central Anatolia" known also as the "General Survey" was initiated in 1985. The idea to conduct a survey in Central Anatolia encompassing several cities evolved from the wish to establish a diachronic chronology for Central Anatolia. The survey covered the cities of Ankara, Kayseri, Konya, Kırşehir, Yozgat, Nevşehir and Niğde and continued until 2017. The results help to establish an enourmous dataset of archaeological sites in Central Anatolia and its chronology. During the General Survey an intensive survey had been conducted at Kaman-Kalehöyük, which laid the ground for the excavations at the site and excavations started in 1986.

"It all began with stratigraphy and chronology" Omura said, when I had asked him why he started excavating Kaman-Kalehöyük (Fig. 16). One of the frequent visitors were Prof. Tahsin Özgüç and his wife Prof. Nimet Özgüç (Fig. 17–18). Through the excavations at Kaman-Kalehöyük it is possible to establish a solid stratigraphy for the Ottoman, Iron Age, Hittite, Colony and Early Bronze Age periods at the site. Especially the Iron Age stratigraphy of Kaman-Kalehöyük supports the understanding of the Iron Age Period of Central Anatolia and also beyond. To have a deeper understanding of the Hittite, Colony and Early Bronze Age periods excavations were initiated at Yassıhöyük (led by Dr. Masako Omura) and Büklükale (led by Dr. Kimiyoshi Matsumura) by the JIAA in 2009.

During the first season at Kaman-Kalehöyük the mission stayed in Çağırkan village. However, the conditions were not suitable to create a sustainable and healthy excavation camp. Omura asked the Turkish state for appropriation of land to built an excavation camp in 1986, which he was granted. An orchard with dozens of almond and pear trees is the home of the JIAA. The jucy pears and sweet almonds are a healthy snack for researchers who work in the camp. In 1987 prefabricated houses were built not far away from Kaman-Kalehöyük. The camp consisted at the beginning of 8 rooms, study and library, conservation labs and a dining hall. Within the years this camp was expanded and became larger and developed into a major hub for international research, conservation, analysis, study and collaboration. In 2002 constructions started for the new permanent guest-house, institute and museum, which were finished in 2009 and inaugurated in 2010. Kaman-Kalehöyük is a significant educational excavation not only for Japanese students, who want to specialise in Ancient Anatolia and the Ancient Near East, but for students from all around the globe. Hundreds of students and researchers from the whole world have been either trained or conducted research there.

A major concern for Omura was to establish facilities for conservation and analyses. Within a short time, an extremely well-equipped lab was established and in 1988/89 an X-ray mashine was brought from the United States of America. Especially the equipment, analysis, geophysical prospections and research in the conservation lab, turned Kaman-Kalehöyük into the most modern excavation at its time in Türkiye and the Near East. A second concern of Omura is to share knowledge and in 1993 the first conservation course at the camp was held. These courses on conservation continue and new courses on archaeobotany, archaezoology, anthropology, museology, paleoenvironment, and heritage conservation have been added in recent years. Omura states, that sharing knowledge with all stakeholders, will support sustainable heritage protection and create awareness. He spends most of his time taking researchers, interested people around the sites, museum and the institute (Fig. 19). Every Saturday during excavation season at Kaman-Kalehöyük, local workers and team members get special training on excavation methods, stratigraphy, recent topics in archaeology and analysis (see Ilkay İvgin in this volume).

The idea of creating a Japanese garden next to the camp developed in 1989. Prince Takahito Mikasa had the idea to create a small garden for the inhabitants of the region. The garden was built between 1990–93 and a variety of Japanese trees and in 2010 fish called "Koi" in Japanese for the pond were brought from Japan. At that time Japanese landscape architects and gardeners have created the first Japanese garden in Türkiye. Çağırkan, which is in Kaman a district of Kırşehir, is one of the driest and most treeless regions of Türkiye. The meaning of *kır* in English would probably be prairie. It is a couragous idea to create a lush green garden in this region without water. An underground irrigation pipe system was built to water the garden. Today, when one drives from Kaman to Çağırkan, the Prince Mikasa Memorial Garden is the only green spot on the hill and one feels already home just seeing it from far away. Specifically, during Spring, Summer and Fall newly-wed couples choose this garden to have their memorial pictures.

The first camp set the ground for the foundation of the JIAA. In one of our conversations Omura said: "I was invited for dinner at the Palace in Tokyo. There was a very long table, and I was sitting at the other end of this table. Prince Mikasa asked about my new plans and I told him that I would like to establish an institute for research on Anatolian archaeology in Kaman". The Prince agreed and supported the project until the end of his life. On May 5th 1998, the JIAA was inaugurated as an affiliated institute of the MECCJ. For the inauguration Prince Tomohito Mikasa (son of Prince Takahito Mikasa) wrote on a wooden rectangular shaped board "Institute" in Japanese (Fig. 20). This is still hanging outside the entrance to the Institute today. Omura was elected Director of the Japanese Institute of Anatolian Archaeology of MECCJ in 1998 and in 2013 member of the board of MECCJ. H. I. H. Prince Tomohito Mikasa, chairman of the JIAA, greatly supported the construction of the permanent institute through major fundraising acitivities (see foreword by Her Imperial Highness Princess Akiko). In September 2005 the research wing and in 2007 the library and conference wing and in 2009 the museum and the guesthouse were completed and inaugurated in 2010 (Fig. 21). Today JIAA consists of the three excavation sites, the institute, guesthouse and the Kaman-Kalehöyük archaeological museum. In 2017 the Prince Mikasa foundation was established, where Omura continues to serve as the chairman of the board of directors.

Publications are an important part of JIAA. The research journal *Anatolian Archaeological Studies* (AAS) was first published in 1992. The journal is published annually and is a medium to share research results, reports and news of the JIAA. In Honor of Prince Mikasa a book series was published by Harrassowitz between 1984 and 1999. The "Bulletin of the Middle Eastern Culture Center in Japan" (BMCCJ) was an important venue for publications on a variety of topics related to Anatolian archaeology. Education and improvement of educational conditions are a concern of Omura. A few years after the dig at Kaman-Kalehöyük had started, Omura started to support successful students from Çağırkan village. At the beginning these scholarships were paid from his private funds and the amount of money provided was little, however he wished that the students would buy a book every month and would be able to buy lunch and use local transportation to reach their schools. In 1990 H. I. H. Prince Tomohito and also H. I. H. Prince Takahito donated some funds to support the students and in 1998 the *Mikasanomiya Fund Scholarship* was inaugurated. Through these donations it was possible to sustain the scholarships and since then the *Mikasanomiya Fund* provides 3–5 scholarships each year to students in Çağırkan. These scholarships have inspired other institutions and donors to support the scholarships as well. In 2004, a donation was received to create a special scholarship only for female students from Çağırkan. *The Soroptimist International of Kyoto Scholarship for Female Students* supports 3–5 female students each year. In 2007 a donation from the *Tokyo Japanese-Turkish Women's Club* was received. Six female students for the academic year of 2024–25 are supported with these scholarships. Until now approximately 150 students from Çağırkan Village benefitted from these scholarships.

Other than archaeology, Omura has a great passion for nature, food, karaoke, dogs and lately his grandson. He is a passionate and very good cook. One can find him in the kitchen cooking a good Japanese curry. "I could not survive without Turkish cuisine and especially *mercimek çorbası*" he says. "I also love Japanese Ramen, but my doctor doesn't allow me to eat Ramen in these days" he laments. An obligation for everyone researching at Kaman-Kalehöyük are the karaoke nights (Fig. 22). Omura convinced everyone to sing, even the state representatives and unforgettable cheerful memories were created in the dining hall.

Omura's love for dogs started even before his passion for archaeology and cooking. He remembers sleeping with his favorite dog, even before he could walk. Hundreds of dogs have lived at the institute since 1986. Every dog could find shelter, food and water and many puppies were born here. One of his favorite dogs was Hana, a smart and lovely Kangal dog from Sivas who passed away in 2022 (Fig. 23).

Omura San enjoys the Prince Mikasa Memorial Garden every day and listens to the sound of the trees, flowers and grass. From his bungalow he can walk directly to the museum and tour in the garden. "When I walk, I have many new ideas" he says. And he has several new ideas he would like to accomplish as soon as possible. One is a center for archaeological science and analysis and an educational archaeology centre for children (Fig. 24).

Fig. 1. Team of Kaman-Kalehöyük field season 2012 (JIAA archive).

Fig. 2. At the entrance of Dil ve Tarih–Coğrafya Fakültesi (DTCF) at Ankara University (1973) (JIAA archive).

Fig. 3. Excavation mission at Konya Karahöyük (1974) (JIAA archive).

Fig. 4. In front of a tent with the bekçi (guard) of the Konya Karahöyük excavation (1974/75) (JIAA archive).

Fig. 5. Excavating at Konya Karahöyük (1974) (JIAA archive).

Fig. 6. Dr. Sachihiro Omura with Prof. Dr. Seyhan Doruk (left) and Prof. Dr. Sedat Erkut (right) on 28.08.2010 at JIAA (JIAA archive).

Fig. 7. Bekçi's tent at Ancoz (Adıyaman) (1977) (JIAA archive).

Fig. 8. Exploring Anatolia with mates from Ankara University (1975) (JIAA archive).

Fig. 9. Study session at Ancoz (Adıyaman) (1977) (JIAA archive).

Fig. 10. Visit of His Imperial Highness Prince Takahito Mikasa at Kültepe in 1993. H. I. H. Prince Mikasa pointing to the ground, Prof. Dr. Tahsin Özgüç pointing to the site, in the back left Dr. Sachihiro Omura (Foto courtesy: Prof. Dr. Tayfun Yıldırım).

Fig. 11. H. I. H. Prince and Princess Mikasa at a welcome party at the Turkish restaurant "Harem" in Tokyo on the 21st of April 2004 . Front left: Prof. Dr. Tahsin Özgüç, right: Dr. Sachihiro Omura (JIAA archive).

Fig. 12. With Shigeru Katsuda bey, Honorary Professor, University of Osaka, at Ihlara Vadisi in Cappadocia (1973) (JIAA archive).

Fig. 13. At Sıhhiye Meydanı with university colleagues (1974) (JIAA archive).

Fig. 14. Prof. Dr. Nimet Özgüç with Dr. Masako Omura (right), Dr. Kimiyoshi Matsumura (left) and Dr. Sachihiro Omura in the library of JIAA (2012) (JIAA archive).

Fig. 15. "Land of Civilization, Turkey" exhibition inaugural lecture. Front line: His Imperial Highness Prince Takahito Mikasa, Prof. Dr. Nimet Özgüç (left) and Prof. Dr. Tahsin Özgüç (right) (1985) (JIAA archive).

Fig. 16. Discussion on the stratigraphy of the North Sector with one of the head-workman (Zinnuri Çöl) at Kaman-Kalehöyük (2015) (JIAA archive).

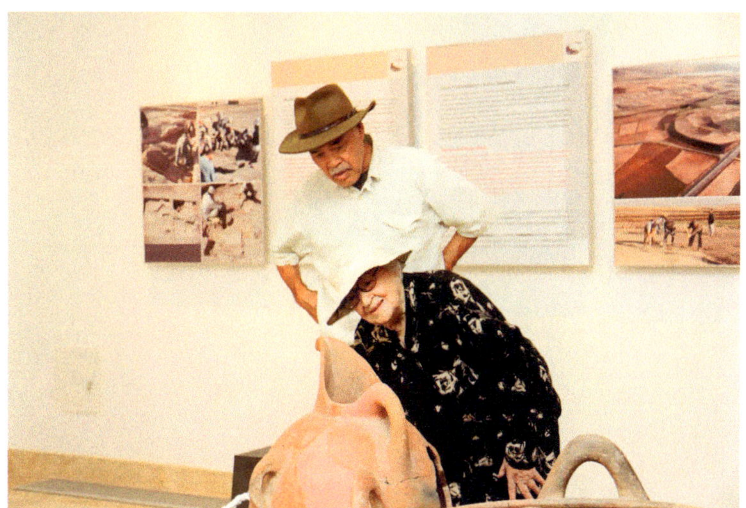

Fig. 17. Prof. Dr. Nimet Özgüç examining a jar at the Kaman-Kalehöyük Museum (2012) (JIAA archive).

Fig. 18. Prof. Dr. Tahsin Özgüç's visit of the Kaman-Kalehöyük excavations. During a chat with Dr. Sachihiro Omura and Çiğdem Maner (1998) (JIAA archive).

Fig. 19. Tour of the Kaman-Kalehöyük Museum (2010) (JIAA archive).

Fig. 20. Panel written by Prince Tomohito Mikasa outside the main entrance of the first Institute (1988) (JIAA archive).

Fig. 21. Prince Mikasa Memorial Garden, Kaman-Kalehöyük Museum, JIAA and Kaman-Kalehöyük faraway (2010) (JIAA archive).

Fig. 22. Karaoke night in the dining hall. Dr. Sachihiro Omura with the ministry representative and university colleague Ömer Özden (2007) (JIAA archive).

Fig. 23. Hana's kiss (2014) (JIAA archive).

Fig. 24. Archaeology day for local school children in the Kaman-Kalehöyük museum (2015) (JIAA archive).

Hittite Royal Administrative Concept and Its Representation in Cultic Texts: The Implementing of Cosmic Order

Ada Taggar Cohen *

Abstract

The concept of administration prevailing during the existence of the Hittite kingdom has been defined as manifested by the royal patriarchal family, which maintained power in the hands of an elite that supported itself – as was common in the entire Ancient Near East – on the divine world's benevolence. However, as we look at various genres of the Hittite cultic texts we can get insight into understanding the status of the royals vis-a-vie the divine world. I will hereby offer a short interpretation of the way in which the Hittite king related himself to the goddess with the Hittite term ^{LÚ}*ara-* to be understood in the administrative context as "colleague of the same class", or even more as "colleague in the same task-force". The concept of administration in a hierarchical formation, as is revealed from their texts, bestowed on the Hittite kings, and with them the royal family, an important cultic status, related directly to the state administration.

Öz

Hitit Krallığı'nın varlığı sırasında hakim olan yönetim anlayışı, tüm eski Yakın Doğu'da olduğu gibi, tanrısal dünyanın gücü üzerinde kendini destekleyen elit bir toplumun elinde iktidarı sürdüren ataerkil kraliyet ailesi tarafından ortaya konan bir kavram olarak tanımlanmıştır. Ancak Hitit kült metinlerinin çeşitli türlerine baktığımızda, kraliyet ailesinin ilahi dünya karşısındaki konumunu konusunda fikir sahibi olunabilir. Makalede, Hitit kralının kendisini tanrıçayla ilişkilendirme şeklinin, idari bağlamda "aynı sınıftan meslektaş" hatta daha çok "aynı görev gücü"olarak anlaşılması için Hititçe ^{LÚ}*ara-* terimiyle ilgili kısa bir yorum sunacağım. Metinlerden de anlaşılacağı üzere hiyerarşik bir oluşum içinde olan yönetim anlayışı Hitit krallarına ve onlarla birlikte önemli bir kültü statüsü olan kraliyet ailesine bahşedilmiştir ve devlet yönetimiyle doğrudan ilişkilidir.

I am glad to dedicate the following reflections to a great colleague, a scholar of Anatolian history and archaeology, to whom I am grateful for making a wonderful and precious research visit to the Museum of Anatolian Cultures in Ankara possible.

Introduction

Trevor Bryce starts his description of Hittite kingship by taking a look at Ḫattušili I's speech at the installation of his heir Muršili I, in the text "The Testament of Ḫattušili I" (CTH 6, Bryce 2002: p. 11ff.). In its essence this text describes the status of the king within the royal family and the council that supported his actions, from the early time of the consolidation of the kingdom during the 17th century B.C. This text speaks very clearly on two aspects of kingship: one is the king's position within his country based on his character, which enables him to rule well and the other relates to the fact that the royal line prevailing within the family is decided on by the living king. According to this text the heir to the throne is proclaimed by the current king, who by his decision could replace the one previously announced. In this regard

* Professor at the Graduate School of Theology, Doshisha University, Kyoto Japan, acohen@mail.doshisha.ac.jp

the council, named in Hittite *panku-*, meaning a royal body, was there with the king to support his declaration as a legal decree (Beckman 1982). This legal decree of installation of Muršili as heir to the throne is accompanied by a speech containing wisdom advice from Ḫattušili I to Muršili I, as well as his council, closing with instructions regarding total loyalty to the king and also to the gods through service to them (Taggar Cohen 2019: 52–53). The concept of correct service, delivered from the top by legal decrees (=laws), together with the demand for total loyalty is at the core of the hierarchical formation of the Hittite administration. The idea of loyalty, i.e. the fulfillment of the rules imposed by the king, is manifested in the Hittite texts which are categorized in their colophons, or within the text itself, by the term *išḫiul-* as well as the obligation to take an oath (*lingai-*) as part of the procedure (Miller 2013). The formation of echelons within the administration, basically the elite ruling class, created a royal authoritative force, starting in the late 15th century B.C. and evolving into a traditional one during the empire period. A class of people partly from the royal family and partly married to or related to it, was the bureaucracy that ran the kingdom.[1]

The maintenance of the hierarchical elite was based on direct and in a sense personal loyalty to the king as is revealed in these oath and instructions texts (CTH 251–275), which are witnessed to in the monthly taking of the oath.[2] The creation of this elite, as can be seen in early periods, was through land donations[3] and the division of spoils by the king himself,[4] as well as his installation of family members in different roles and locations, within the kingdom. The land donations would have created a class of wealthy landowners, while the receivers were also part of the extended family.

In the following, I will draw a picture of this royal formation with its hierarchical structure, which was held through trust and loyalty, specifically pointing to the fact that this administrative concept starts with the king and the gods and is implemented via cultic activity, which is reflected in the mythological accounts in the rituals.

A.

For the Hittites, the mundane world was a combination of divine and human. Although there is not a clear story of creation in the Hittite texts, some texts offer a view of the world in which they lived as being intertwined with the deities who belonged to heaven and the underworld, but were strongly involved in human activities on earth, for the very reason that human-beings served them and expected their support in response. As pointed out by Mary Bachvarova (2014) there are the Hurro-Hittite myths of the birth of the gods but they do not include the creation of mankind. A possible creation myth found among the Hittite texts comes from the ritual text CTH 434.1 as suggested by Susanne Görke (2019: 166). The text says thus: "When the gods established[5] heaven and earth, they split up heaven and earth for themselves. The

1 In the words of Pecchioli Daddi 2005: 600 "the politico-administrative texts are the legal tools to regulate the relationships of subordination in the kingdom, they constitute a homogeneous *corpus* as far as function and reference point are concerned; instead, from a formal, typological and content standpoint, there are substantial differences, of which the Hittite scribes were aware."

2 Wondering whether indeed these oaths were taken monthly, I suggest referring back to the cultic management where such activity may have been conducted during the festival of the month which we know was supposed to be celebrated systematically.

3 For a summary of this issue see the recent work of Bilgin 2018: 387f. with previous studies, especially Rüster and Wilhelm 2012. The most important legal sentence concerning land donation is: LUGAL.GAL *išši-ma ana* mPN ARAD-*di-šu ana* NÍG.BA-*šu iddin* "The Great King took (it), and gave (it) as his gift to his subject".

4 The very personal involvement of the king is seen in the corpus of the Maşat letters of the Middle Hittite period, Hoffner 2009: 91–97.

5 The verb *dair-* Pl. prt. 3 can also be the verb *dai-* "to place, to put, to establish" when not accompanied with -za. I therefore suggest the possible translation of

upper gods took heaven for themselves, the lower gods took the nether world for themselves. And each one took all for himself."[6] In the continuation of the text, the two goddesses of the riverbank – GULŠ (faith-goddess) and MAH (Mother goddess) are termed as "those who create human beings".[7] These texts, however, lead us to understand that it was the gods who controlled the universe. Moreover, the gods are understood to be themselves tied in a family relationship, of which the human family was a copy (Beckman 2004: 309f.). Thus, these powerful entities residing above and below the human world controlled it with a steward – their representative – the king.[8]

The king was at the top of the human hierarchy, having a special relationship with the divine world. His family, too, was granted special attention from the gods. There are two descriptions of these relationships in the Hittite texts. First, there is evidence of local Anatolian Ḫattian concepts in the texts from the old Hittite period with rituals recited in the Ḫattian language as well as mention of the names of Ḫattian deities. Secondly, starting in the early Empire period, there are texts showing the influence of Mesopotamian concepts of kingship.[9] A still older stratum of the Ḫattian mythological accounts seems to be at the foundation of Hittite kingship concepts, even though other influences are evident through the ages. The text CTH 414 is an important reflection of the founding relationships between the gods and the king in which the deities played a supporting role to the king. This text belongs to the older stratum of Hittite religion, but nevertheless lasted until the end of the empire.[10]

The text is a combination of a ritual that includes dramatic mythological depictions that reflect on the understanding of the king and the royal family's relations with the deities. The foundation and building of the king's palace needed to receive permission from the gods. As correctly indicated by Charles W. Steitler (2017: 133) "the building activity itself was considered a fitting expression of reverence towards the Sun-goddess and the Storm-god." One has to ask, though, why does a palace require divine approval?[11] If we are speaking of the founding of a temple, the answer is easier, since the one who resides in it should approve of it – a practice well-known from other texts in the Ancient Near East – the god must approve of the building (Boda and Novotny. 2010), but with regard to the Hittite king's palace, there is a need for explanation.

There are three gods in the main part of the text: The Sun-goddess, the Storm-god and the goddess Ḫalmaššuitt, who is a representation of the Throne, and to whom the king speaks here directly. He requests her permission to cut down the trees for building the house; the goddess gives him permission saying that the Sun-goddess and the Storm-god have already approved it (via oracle). In his request to the goddess the king uses the following words:

---

it here as "established". See Hoffner-Melchert 2008: 22 note 48.

6 For the text see F. Fuscagni (ed.) hethiter.net/: CTH 434.1 (2012). Obv. i, 8': *kuwapi nepiš tēkan dair/ nu=za* DINGIR^{MEŠ}*arḫa šarrir/ nu=za šarāzziuš* [DINGIR^{MEŠ}] *nepiš dāir/ katterieš=ma=za* DINGIR^{MEŠ} *[d]aganzipan katterr=a* KUR-*e/ nu=za kuišša kuitta dāš*. A correlation to this idea exists in the Mesopotamian "Story of the Flood" in Atra-Ḫasis tablet I lines 11–17 (Lambert and Millard 1999: 43).

7 Fuscagni' ibid, Obv. i, 17'*antuḫšan kuiēš šamnieškanzi*.

8 This has been discussed in length in Mouton and Görke 2014, Mouton and Gilan 2014, with references.

9 This picture has already been drawn by Popko 1995 and Hass 1994; and more recently summarized by Taracha 2009.

10 CTH 414 transliteration and translation into German of at least six copies dating from Old Hittite (KUB 29.3) to late Hittite period (HT 39), does point to its importance for the royal scribes. See S. Görke (ed.), hethiter.net/: CTH 414.1. For a recent study and translation into English see Beckman 2011: 72–75, 452.

11 Steitler 2017: 132 n. 398, noting other scholars as well, indeed supports the fact that this ritual is for a royal palace, based on KUB 29.1 rev. iii,13 (§ 34) *mān kuwapi kuwapi* URU-*ri* É.GAL-*LAM wetezzi* "When (the King) builds a palace in a town anywhere." I discuss this further below.

Obv. i, 10–13 (§ 3) [Then the King] says to the Throne: "Come, let us go! [You], step behind the mountains. You shall not become my man. You shall not become my in-law. Be my partner, indeed, be my colleague!"
[*nu* LUGAL-*u*]š GIŠDAG-*ti tezzi ehu pāiwani* [*zigg*]=*a* HUR.SAGMEŠ-*aš* EGIR-*an tīya* LÚ-*aš=miš lē kišta gāinaš=miš lē kišta araš=miš arāš=miš eš*

Obv. i, 33–34 (§ 10) Now I, the Labarna, have united myself to you.
And I called the Throne-goddess my colleague
kinuna=šmaš=za LUGAL-*uš l*[*aba*]*rnaš ulanun*
nu GIŠDAG-*an aram=man halzihhu*[*n*]

An important concept arising from this speech regarding the status of the king in relation to the gods is the fact that he sees himself as requesting to be part of the divine "task-force". The term *ara-* used by the king instead of being taken plainly as "friend" could also mean "one who is part of a class / a team of officials / a group of professionals".[12] A survey of the term LÚ*ara-* reveals that this meaning in the majority of cases appears in the context of administrative texts and ritual texts.[13] The term indicates a member of a class of officials, or workers, such as in CTH 255.1.A iv, 38–45 speaking of a colleague within the royal courtiers of Tudḫaliya IV (cf. Miller 2013: 304–307 §§ 32"-33"). CTH 258.1.B a decree of Tudḫaliya I to officials uses the term LÚ*ara-šiš* "his fellow worker/colleague", and once the combination LÚ*maniyahhandaša* LÚḪA.LA-*ŠU* "his administrative partner/ colleague" once in the same context (KBo 27.16 iii, 4'–6', in Miller 2013: 138 § 11").[14] Professionals such as cultic functionaries are also termed as LÚ*ara-* whether they are part of the priesthood i.e. LÚSANGA, or temple personnel as ENMEŠ TU$_7$ DINGIR MEŠ "kitchen supervisors of the gods" (Taggar-Cohen 2006: 60/80–81=CTH 264, iii, 77, 81) or the female practitioners and members of the cult MUNUSŠU.GI (CTH 744=KBo 24.105) or singers (CTH 772.7=KUB 53.15+41.15 i, 17'–18'), as well as other functionaries.

The second concept arising from the text is the hierarchy between the three deities: The Storm-god and the Sun-goddess were higher than the Throne goddess. The first two gave the king kingship – the rule over the land(s), and secured it for him by giving him years of long life. The Throne goddess, on the other hand, brought the king the insignia, the symbols with which kingship was seen, and then received the king's request to help him in obtaining the trees necessary for building. The fact that the Throne goddess, Ḫalmaššuitt, was the active figure, supports an interpretation of the king's request that this goddess would agree to him becoming part of her "task force", whose aim was to build a dwelling place. In contrast, the Storm-god and the Sun-goddess were considered as "Father and Mother" by the king, and had a higher status than that of the Throne goddess to whom the king appealed with a wish to be her i.e. the Throne goddess' colleague as part of the lower level of the divine world.

B.

The divine world had its hierarchy but also its family relations which seem to be reflected in the royal family. Thus, in regard to the

12 Puhvel *HED* 1: 116–121. HW² I: A: 221–224. LÚ*ara* is written in Akkadograms LÚ*TAPPÛ* and Sumerograms LÚ HA.LA meaning in Akkadian "partner, colleague, companion, friend"; see *CAD* T:184ff.

13 Such are the instructions-texts (*išḫiul and lingai*), which indicate the way members in the class of officials i.e. LÚMEŠ GAL, LÚMEŠ *MEŠEDI* LÚMEŠ *BELMADGALTI*, or class of professionals such as cultic figures LÚMEŠ SANGA, etc. should obey the rules of conduct of their class. This is true for old Hittite and empire period texts.

14 ḪA.LA appears already in OA *zittu* in the meaning of "share in jointly owned property, income, collective work" (CAD Z:144, 2. a). It appears in the combination LÚḪA.LA-*ŠU* in Hittite as shareholder/partner in the laws for example § 53 § 192; see Hoffner 1997: 64–65, 151.

building texts, in CTH 413 as pointed out by Gary Beckman, the gods themselves were the builders of the house, in quite a fascinating way.[15] The king and queen were thus a reflection of the Storm-god and the Sun-goddess.[16] Regarding this, the higher echelon administratively controlling the cosmos is the level of the gods. The king and queen identify themselves as their servants, the second level after the gods. But on the other hand, we also find the king hoping to unite with the divine in the physical and spiritual sense as the following texts state. The first is from the main text concerning the building of a house, and the second is from an incantation ritual:

> 1)
> "Unite it! Make it one! Carry it to the heart of the man. Let the soul of the king unite with his heart too!" Let the Sun-goddess and the Storm-god decide for the king's treaty (*ták-šu-li-ši-it*[17]) And let their word (=decree) be one! Sun-goddess and Storm-god, re-entrust (for ruling *ma-ni-aḫ-tén*) the land to the king!" They renewed his years. They renewed his awesomeness (*na-aḫ-ša-ra-at-ta-an*). (CTH 414.1 § 28–9/ KUB 29.1 ii, 44–48)[18]

> 2)
> "O Sun-god of the Gods, as (the drink) *marnuwan* and beer are blended and their essence and contents become one, may the soul and the interior of the Sun-god of the Gods and of the Labarna hereby become one! O [Storm-god of the Gods], as (the drink) *walḫi* and fine beer are blended and their essence and contents become [one], may the soul and interior of the Storm-god of Heaven and the Labarna [become] one!"
> CTH 458.10.1.A = KUB 41.23 ii 18'-21'// KUB 57.86.[19]

Thus, the Hittite king wished to become part of the divine world in his essence, and building a house for himself and his entire family, was actually building a house for the gods as becomes clear from the second part of the ritual in CTH 414. In this part a description of the installation of the hearth takes place. The hearth was considered a divine entity, but was also the center of a Hittite temple, and was always mentioned in rituals as the place of libation. The gods were seated next to the hearth together with the family – the king and the queen and the secondary wives, the daughters of the household, the paternal brothers, and there was a direct speech of the Hearth: "This is good for me" (Beckman 2010: 75 § 43–45). The scene shows that the

15 Beckman's translation (2010: 86): § 7 "This temple that we have just built for you, O deity (she calls by name the deity for whom they built it)—it was not we who built it, (but) all of the gods (who) built it." § 8 "The male gods built it as carpenters. Telipinu laid the foundations. Thereupon Ea, King of Wisdom, built the walls. All the mountains brought the wood and stone. The goddesses brought mud plaster." § 9 "They laid down the foundation stones of silver and gold."

16 As indicated by Görke (2019: 164) and following her joint contribution with G. Torri (2014), there are three texts CTH 726, 725 and 414 which include mythological accounts that "present the creation of kingship in Hattusa". According to her CTH 726 speaks of the gods building a palace, 725 "the gods share the country and establish the royal power", and 414 "The king describes how he received his power from the gods and how he will protect the palace and the royal kingship". The conclusion is "as the gods build their palace and kingdom, the king likewise builds his palace and kingdom on earth." The group of texts on buildings includes the following CTH numbers: 413, 414, 415, 725 and 726.

17 I have translated *takšulšet dandu* "let them decide his treaty" in comparison with the usage of *takšul-* in KUB 40.106 ii? 4: *[l]ukatti-ma* ^{URU}Takkuptan *ták-šu-li da-a-i* "tomorrow he will decide/make the treaty/ peace at the town of Takkuptan" see CHD Š3 p. 440. This word here stands in correlation with the OH benediction in KUB 21.22, 43–45: "The mother of the Storm-god came down for the second time. For the Storm-god she is his mother, but for the Labarna she is his binding (*išḫiešša-ššit*)." The *takšul- and išḫi-ul-* are to be understood as the servitude status of the king to the divine world.

18 Kellerman 1978: 203–204; Beckman 2010: 74.

19 Beckman 2012: 608. Transliteration: Theo van den Hout, 1995: 569.

gods dwelled in this palace together with the royal family, while in the full ritual mention is made of the fact that the gods renewed his years and his rule and, in a sense, re-created him (Beckman 2010: 74 § 29–30). The fact that the entire family was assembled at the hearth of the house shows the importance of the family unit, even if the king was considered the most important as the head of the family.

C.

The use of the term ^{LÚ}*ara-* in the legal texts shows that the one who is titled as such was considered part of the administrative classes, that he worked in collaboration with others, and thus received his own authoritative powers and duties from his superiors. Outside of the instructions-texts we also find the title appearing in international treaties. Such an example found in the treaty between Šuppiluliuma II and Talmi-Teššub (CTH 122.2), includes a sentence regarding the relations between the authoritative lord and the lower levels: "May your dear colleague not be in separation with your lord."[20]

More than that, the make-up of the elite is understood to be composed of the following "members": the "lord", who was the person at the top of the indicated class, person who was member of the class, his wife, his brother, his sister, his relative and his "colleague" (^{LÚ}*ara-*). The lower class would be considered the subject(s). An example of a list such as this can be found in the *išḫiul-* for all men, probably declared by Tudḫaliya I:

> CTH 259 =KUB 13.20 i, 32–35:
> The provincial legal cases that you judge, you must judge well. No one shall do it for the administering of bread and beer[21] **for his (own) estate, for his brother, his wife, his kin, his entire (family), his in-law, (or) his colleague** (^{LÚ}*ara-*). You must not make a superior case inferior, neither shall you make an inferior case superior.[22]

The list clearly shows the nuclear family first, adding close relatives and in-laws, and last in line is the ^{LÚ}*ara-*. Nevertheless he was part of that ruling group and thus held power within the administration.[23]

D.

During the early Hittite empire period, religious thought from Mesopotamia and North Syria including the influence of the Hurrian religion and concepts of kingship were absorbed by the Hittites (Steitler 2017: 430–431). This influence was largely seen in textual activity and rather less in iconography, although the appearance of the Hittite king in the attire of the Sun-god points to Mesopotamian influence. However, as Charles W. Steitler (2017: 435) claims, this god was also important during the

20 Hittite: ^{LÚ}*araš=ta aššuwanza IŠTU* EN-*KA arḫaiyan le ešzi*. Cf. Beckman 2019: 36–37. Another example comes from a Hittite letter KUB 40.1 rev. 24–31: "May my colleagues not seek? any further to call attention to me [...] and when I bring back the results of the command to Your Majesty, the Sun Goddess of Arinna will treat (me) graciously for the sake of Your Majesty, my lord, (so that it will be said:) "Nothing has been done which should be considered a crime"." Transliteration and translation with commentary see Hoffner 2009: 360.

21 "Bread and wine" stand for any bribe or gift received for the distortion of justice.

22 Hittite: *DI-NAM*$^{\text{HI.A}}$ KUR-*TI ku-e ḫa-an-ni-iš-ket*$_9$*-te-e-ni na-at* SIG$_5$*-in ḫa-an-ni-iš-ke-et-tén na-at-za-kán a-pí-e-el ŠA* É-*ŠU* ŠA ŠEŠ-*ŠU* DAM-*ŠU ḫa-aš-ša-an-na-aš-ši pa-an-ku-na-aš-ši* ^{LÚ}*ka-e-na-an-ti* ^{LÚ}*a-ri-eš-ši ŠA* NINDA KAŠ *ma-a-ni-ia-aḫ-ḫi-ya-at-ti le-e ku-iš-ki i-ya-zi nu ša-ra-a-az-zi* DI- *le kat-te-er-ra-aḫ-te-e-ni kat-te-er-ra-ma ha-an-ne-eš-šar le-e ša-ra-a-az-zi-ya-aḫ-te-ni*. cf. Miller 2013: 150–151.

23 See similarly in the rules for Frontier Governors CTH 261.I.B = KUB 13.2 iii, 25'-28'(Miller 2013: 228–229): "He shall not, however, do it for a lord, nor shall he do it for a brother, his sister or his colleague. And let no one accept a bribe. He shall not make a superior case inferior; he shall not make the inferior superior. You shall do what is just!" The three categories are "*BE-LIM* lord", "ŠEŠ brother", "NIN sister", and ^{LÚ}*ara-* colleague. See for the Hittite family construction Pringle 1993: 218, especially interesting is KBo 7.28+(CTH 371.1).

Old Hittite kingdom. The important place of the Sun-god was in the context of a legal and administrative role. As such, we can see the relationship between the king and the Sun-God.

Irene Winter, in a paper from a conference published in 2008 titled "Touched by the Gods", on the divine statues of Mesopotamian kings, speaks in some detail of the status of Hammurabi in relation to the gods, in his iconographic scenes together with the gods. On the Law Stele she writes: "Hammurapi is depicted making direct eye contact with (the image of) the deity as he receives the authority to promulgate his laws. [...] It thus corresponds well to the verbal references to the king in the prologue." Hammurabi was chosen and given the power to rule and fight wars by the gods. She goes further to say:

> The social and political implications of being favored by/beloved by deity (Sumerian ki-ág, Akkadian *râmu*) have been discussed recently by [Margaret] Jaques (2006:123–45), suggesting that the term is used to demonstrate not only an emotional relationship, but also – conjoined with or independent of emotion – **one of partnership** (my emphasis). At the same time as this partnership has implications of obedience, loyalty, and cultic service on the part of the recipient of (divine) love, it nonetheless serves to mark the beloved as one of special standing. (Winter 2008: 83)

This idea should be taken into consideration in understanding of the role of the Hittite king when his administrative function is described. Philip Jones (2005) discussing the question of divine kingship in the Ancient Near East, emphasizes the fact that kingship in the Old Babylonian period was seen as part of establishing cosmic balance against the unpredicted conduct of the deities. The position held by the king contributed to human order. He thus became part of the cosmic order, and in time in Mesopotamia was even imagined to be divine. For this reason, the king was attached to the Sun-god, the one who was responsible for law and order.[24]

The Hittite prayers of the empire period bear witness to a specific connection between the king and his gods. These prayers, as noted by scholars, are structured on Sumero-Akkadian prayers which were imported from Mesopotamia.[25] The group of prayers titled by Singer (2002: 30f.) "Prayers to the Sun-god for Appeasing an Angry Deity" includes the "Prayer of a Mortal" CTH 372, which was shown to be an adaptation from Mesopotamia in early Hittite scholarship, and recently Metcalf came back to it (2011: 168–176). The part of the prayer that relates to the relations between the god and the king is as follows:

> In the circumference of heav[en] and [e]arth, you alone,
> O Sun-god, you are the (source of) light //
> O Sun-god, mighty king
> Son of Nikkal! The land's custom, (and) law (*išḫiul-*),
> you alone keep establishing // O Sun-god, Mighty king,
> among the gods, you alone are widely worshiped //
> and the strong 'bond' (*išḫiya-*) to you alone is given //
> A just lord of governance you are,
> You are father (and) mother to the 'dark' lands.[26] (CTH 372: A i 14–21)

The prayer contains of the words: "and the strong 'bond' to you alone is given // A just lord of governance you are" suggesting the Sun-god

24 One of the repeated achievements of the Mesopotamian kings in the law collections was that they established order. Laws of Urnamma (Roth 1995: 17, A iv, 169–170); Lipit-Ištar (Roth 1995: 25 i 20–37); Hammurabi (Roth 1995: 81 v, 14–24) and more.

25 For a recent illuminating detailed description of the structures adopted, and the contents adapted from those prayers see Rieken 2019: 149–162.

26 Translation follows Schwemer 2015: 374–393. For *riksu* or *markasu* see CAD R: 352(b), 354(8); CAD M: 283–4 (4) respectively. Schwemer reads in line 19: *išh[i]šša* for *išhišša(r)* "bond"; see also Puhvel 1984, 399.

as holding/having the "bond" in Hittite *išḫi-ya-* which correlates with the Akkadian *riksu* or *markasu*. This is the bond of the universe that allows the god to rule. This term appears also in the prayer of Kantuzili which is one of the group of prayers (CTH 373=KUB 30.10 obv. 7) translated by Daniel Schwemer 2015: 356 thus:

> O my god, since my mother gave birth to me, you, my god, have raised me. Only you, my god, are [my name] and my bond (*išḫišša=mitt=a*), Only you, [my god] joined me up with good people, and only you, my god, taught me doing (well) in a strong place. My god, you have called [me], Kantuzili, servant of your body (and) your soul.

These two passages imply that the king was a human being, under the protection of the deity, through a special *išḫiya-* that basically refers to what we have already mentioned as the Hittite concept of administration through *išḫiul-* texts of loyalty and oaths. The king was part of the group of administrators below the gods. Whereas in the Ḫattian tradition he strove to be part of the divine "task force", in the later tradition he was nurtured and educated by the deity in order to be of service to it. The Hittite king was thus a mirror image of the gods; the gods were allotted their lands/cities in the mythological tale, as the king was allotted Ḫattuša. KUB 30.29 obv. 9–15 describes the places allotted to the Ḫattian gods:[27] "Allotments are given to the gods. The Sun-god sat down in the city of Arinna. The goddess Ḫalmaššuitt in the city of Ḫarpisa likewise...". The Hittite king received the city of Ḫattuša as his domain.[28] The king then built dwelling places for the gods and served them by fulfilling their laws as part of a special class of human beings, that were connected to the gods through a "task".[29]

In this regard the title of the Hittite king LUGAL.GAL interpreted as the "great(est) of king(s)" would fit very well this concept.[30] The idea of a hierarchy going from the divine world to humans, places the Hittite king as a member of a class of the lower gods, one of which he will become after his death. In the Ḫattian traditions he seems to be closer to the gods, but in the later traditions he is more of an implementer of duties that are strongly connected with mundane life.

Whether of Ḫattian tradition or Mesopotamian origin, the need of the kings to be at one with the gods seems to be part of the human wish to be part of a united group striving to work for a better world. The Hittite king is part of the cosmic order, but unlike the gods he is mortal and has only a certain number of years on earth given by the gods. Whereas during the Old Hittite period the king strived to assume a closer place to the divine, as a "colleague" in joint activities, in the Empire period, under Mesopotamian influence, the king's position of servitude to the gods, as part of a functioning system in which the king fulfills the gods' law, is evident.

Acknowledgments

Research for this paper was supported by a grant from the Japan Society for the Promotion of Science for the years 2017–2020 (17K02234).

27 F. Fuscani (ed.), hethiter.net/: CTH 430.1.

28 IBoT 1.30 "May the Tabarna, the king, be dear to the gods! The land belongs to the Storm-god alone. Heaven, earth and the population belong to the Storm-god alone. He has made the Labarna, the king, his administrator and given him the land of Ḫattuša." (with duplicates HT 67 rev. 1–7, KUB 48.13 rev. 9–16) See Gilan and Mouton 2014:106.

29 For the concept of divine law for the Hittites see Taggar Cohen 2020.

30 Yakubovich 2014: 46–47.

Bibliography

Bachvarova, M.

- 2014 "Hurro-Hittite Stories and Hittite Pregnancy and Birth Rituals," in M.W. Chavalas (ed.), *Women in the Ancient Near East: A Sourcebook*, New York, pp. 272–299.

Boda, M.J. and J. Novotny (eds.)

- 2010 *From the foundations to the Crenellations: Essays on Temple Building in the Ancient Near East and Hebrew Bible*, Münster.

Beckman, G.

- 1982 "The Hittite Assembly," *JAOS* 102, pp. 435–442.
- 2004 "Pantheon. II. Bei den Hethitern," *Reallexikon der Assyriologie* 10, Berlin, pp. 308–316.
- 2011 "Temple Building among the Hittites." In M.J. Boda and J. Novotny (eds.) *From the Foundations to the Crenellations: Essays on Temple Building in the Ancient Near East and Hebrew Bible*, Münster, pp. 71–90, 451–455.
- 2012 "The Horns of Dilemma, or on the Divine Nature of the Hittite King," in G. Wilhelm (ed.), *Organization, Representation, and Symbols of Power in the Ancient Near East*, Winona Lake, pp. 605–610.
- 2019 "Hatti's Treaties with Carchemish," in N. Bolatti Guzzo and P. Taracha (eds.), *A Tribute to Massimo Poetto on the Occasion of His 70th Birthday*, Warsaw, pp. 32–42.

Bilgin, T.

- 2018 *Officials and Administration in the Hittite World*, SANER 21, Berlin-Boston.

Bryce, T.

- 2002 *Life and Society in the Hittite World*, Oxford.

Gilan, A. and A. Mouton

- 2014 "The Enthronement of the Hittite King as Royal Rite of Passage," In A. Mouton and J. Patrier (eds.), *Life, Death, and coming of Age in Antiquity: Individual rites of passage in the Ancient Near East and Adjacent regions*, Leiden, pp. 99–117.

Görke, S.

- 2019 "Mythological Passages in Hittite Rituals," In S. Blakely and B.-J. Collins (eds.), *Religious Convergence in the Ancient Mediterranean*, Atlanta, pp. 163–171.

Görke, S. and A. Mouton

- 2014 "Royal Rites of Passage and Calendar Festivals in the Hittite World," In A. Mouton and J. Patrier (eds.), *Life, Death, and coming of Age in Antiquity: Individual rites of passage in the Ancient Near East and Adjacent Regions*, Leiden, pp. 117–146.

Haas, V.

- 1994 *Geschichte der hethitischen Religion*, Leiden.

Hoffner, H.A. Jr.

- 1997 *The Laws of the Hittites: A Critical Edition*, Leiden-NY-Köln.
- 2009 *Letters from the Hittite Kingdom*, Atlanta.

Hoffner, H.A. Jr. and C.H. Melchert

- 2008 *A Grammar of the Hittite Language* 1, Winona Lake.

Jones, P.

- 2005 "Divine and Non-Divine Kingship," In D.C. Snell (ed.), *A Companion to the Ancient Near East*, Malden-Oxford-Victoria, pp. 331–342.

Kellerman, G.

- 1978 "The King and The Sun-God in The Old Hittite Period," *Tel Aviv* 5: 199–208.

Lambert, W.G. and A.R. Millard

- 1999 *Atra-Hasīs: The Babylonian Story of the Flood*, Winona Lake.

Miller, J.L.

- 2013 *Royal Hittite Instructions and Related Administrative Texts*, Atlanta: SBL.

Pecchioli Daddi, F.

- 2005 "Classification and New Edition of Politico-Administrative Texts," *ICH 5*, pp. 599–611.

Popko, M.

- 1995 *Religions of Asia Minor*, Warsaw.

Pringel, J.M.

- 1993 *Hittite Kinship and Marriage: A Study Based on the Cuneiform Texts from 2nd Millennium Bogazköy*, PhD Dissertation, School of Oriental and African Studies, University of London.

Rieken, E.

- 2019 "Hittite Prayers and their Mesopotamian Models," In S. Blakely and B-J. Collins (eds.), *Religious Convergence in the Ancient Mediterranean*, Atlanta, pp. 149–162.

Roth, M.T.

- 1995 *Law collections from Mesopotamia and Asia Minor*, Atlanta.

Schwemer, D.

- 2015 "Hittite Prayers to the Sun-God for Appeasing an Angry Personal God: A Critical

Edition of CTH 372–374," In M. Jacques (ed.), *Mon dieu, qu'ai-je fait?: les diĝir-šà-dab(5)-ba et la piété privée en Mésopotamie*, Friebourg-Göttingen, pp. 349–393.

Steitler, C. W.

– 2017 *The Solar Deities of Bronze Age Anatolia: Studies in Texts of the Early Hittite Kingdom*, Wiesbaden.

Taggar-Cohen, A.

– 2006 *Hittite Priesthood*, Heidelberg.

– 2019 "Biblical Wisdom Literature and Hittite Didactic Texts in the Ancient Near Eastern Literary Context," *JISMOR* 14, pp. 45–64.

– 2020 "Ritual as Divine Law: The Case of Hittite Royal Cultic Performance and its biblical Correspondence," *Orient* 55: 13–27.

Taracha, P.

– 2009 *Religions of Second Millennium Anatolia*, Wiesbaden.

– 2017 *Two Festivals Celebrated by a Hittite Prince (CTH 647.I and II–III): New Light on Local Cults in North-Central Anatolia in the Second Millennium B.C.*, Wiesbaden.

Torri, G and Görke, S.

– 2014 "Hittite Building Rituals Interaction Between Their Ideological Function and Find Spot," In A. Mouton and J. Patrier (eds.), *Life, Death, and Coming of Age in Antiquity: Individual Rites of Passage in the Ancient Near East and Adjacent Regions*, pp. 287–300.

Van den Hout, T.

– 1995 "Tudḫalija IV. und die Ikonographie hethitischer Grosskönige des 13. Jhs.," *BiOr* 52: 545–575.

Winter, I. J.

– 2008 "Touched by the Gods: Visual Evidence for the Divine Status of Rulers in the Ancient Near East," In N. Brisch (ed.), *Religion and Power: Divine Kingship in the Ancient World and Beyond*, Chicago, pp. 75–101.

Yakubovich, I.

– 2014 "The Luwian Title of the Great King," In A. Mouton (ed.), *Hittitology Today: Studies on Hittite and Neo-Hittite Anatolia in Honor of Emmanuel Laroche's 100th Birthday*, Istanbul, pp. 39–50.

Hittite Rituals at Samuha: The Archaeological Record

Andreas Müller-Karpe *

Abstract

By means of texts from Boğazköy some Hittite figurines from Kayalıpınar / Samuha are interpreted as relicts of purification rituals with donkeys or mules as 'scapegoats'. Other terracotta objects might indicate activities of diviners.

Öz

Kayalıpınar/Samuha kazısında bulunan bazı eşek ya da katır şeklindeki Hitit figürinleri Boğazköy çivi yazılı metinleri aracılığıyla arınma ritüellerindeki günah keçisi olarak yorumlanmaktadır. Diğer pişmiş toprak objeler kâhinlerin faaliyetlerine işaret etmektedir.

Since the early times of Hittitology Samuha is known as one of the most important cities in 2nd millennium Anatolia. But for a long time, this knowledge came from the cuneiform archives in Boğazköy and Kültepe exclusively. Scholars wrote a series of articles concerning Samuha, especially its religious importance, and a monograph was even published decades before Samuha was discovered and identified as an archaeological place and then excavated (Lebrun 1976).

This unusual situation changed in 2014 when some tablets were found at Kayalıpınar in Sivas province, proving this very findspot to be the Samuha that scholarship had been searching for for such a long time (Rieken 2014). Excavations started at Kayalıpınar already in 2005, but the crucial tablets were discovered nine years later. These tablets belong to a small archive, containing exclusively religious texts from the second half of the 13th century B.C. (Rieken 2019). Some meters South-East of the archive (the main concentration of the fragments of the tablets) a pit was excavated, filled up with rubbish of the late Empire Period: Pottery, animal bones, ashes and dark earth derived from decomposed organic materials (Fig. 1, 2). Such a pit is not very surprising in a settlement. Most of the material seemed to be normal kitchen waste but also some curious objects were discovered in between: A series of small cups, often called 'votive cups', miniature jars, fragments of terracotta figurines and some amorphous terracotta objects (Müller-Karpe and Müller-Karpe 2019: 235–237).

The so-called votive cups are very common in Hittite contexts. Two main types can be distinguished: 1. A very small one, obviously without any practical use, produced only for ritual purposes (Fig. 3.4–7, 4.20f.,23f., type N5: Müller-Karpe 1988: 126, Pl. 41), 2. A slightly bigger one, which might be also useful in normal domestic contexts. The second type shows a great variation of forms, mainly thick-walled, simple conical cups (Fig. 3.9,15f., 4.1f., 6.10–12,14,17, type N2) and forms with thinner walls and a rounded body (Fig. 3.10–14,17, 4.3–5,7–9,18, type N1). The second type with its two main variants can be found nearly everywhere in Hittite settlements, however concentrations of findspots in a 'sacred pond' and in temples, especially in and around adyta, prove their use (also) in rituals (Müller-Karpe 1988: 124; Parzinger and Sanz 1992: 29f., 75–77). Many examples were found in Boğazköy, Kuşaklı and other sites, but in most cases their forms are rather standardised. Usually the

* Vorgeschichtliches Seminar der Philipps-Universität Marburg / Germany.

votive cups from any of the archaeological contexts are very similar to each other. The pit near the archive in Kayalıpınar shows a different picture: hardly two or three cups have exactly the same profile. Some examples have quite unusual forms: Fig. 3.10f., 4.2,9,19. This variability indicates a different origin, and might reflect different local productions. A possible explanation could be: Visitors to a sanctuary came from outside bringing their own votive cups with their offerings. Not only official priests and the urban inhabitants took part in ceremonies, but also people from villages and hamlets of a wider region. If this interpretation is correct, these votive cups reflect personal piety and folk religion in contrast to the "state cult", which most of the tablets are dealing with[1].

Some small votive jars from the 'archive pit' show unusual forms as well. One of them has a singular horizontal knob instead of a handle (Fig. 4.26). But most of the pottery from this pit represents 'normal' Hittite kitchen ware, like the trefoiled jar and bowls (Fig. 3.1–3, 4.13,16). It is a simple, coarse, but well-done domestic pottery, typical for this period. On the contrary the votive cups and -jars are generally very sloppily produced as one-way-articles for single use. This is quite astonishing: Not precious, thin-walled dishes with polished surfaces were commonly used for sacrificial offerings, but cheap, roughly modelled pottery. The usually flat bottoms of the votive cups aren't flat in some cases but so bumpy, that the cups cannot stand horizontally on a table. In all likelihood religious people at this time were very well aware of the fact, that the gods did not really need or use their offerings, even though Hittite texts give another impression. The ritual itself was important, the symbolic act and the symbolic offering.

Other objects from this pit also have to be interpreted within the context of religious symbolism, first of all fragments of animal figurines. Like the votive cups, the modelling of the figurines is quite careless. We can recognise a four-legged animal, the species of which is impossible to determine (Fig. 5.4, Müller-Karpe and Müller-Karpe 2019: 237). Potentially cuneiform texts from Boğazköy may help to solve this question. Several texts describe a special role of donkeys and mules made of clay in religious ceremonies. One of the best examples is the Hittite 'Ritual of [f]*Allī* of the land of Arzawa' (CTH 402). § 1: "Thus says [f]Allī, the woman of Arzawa: If a man is bewitched (= sick) I treat him as follows: Five figurines of clay, ... one donkey of clay ... three small cups of clay. She places them ..." (There follows a detailed description how the evil is eliminated using the figurines as substitutes for the sick person, for instance:) § 29: "When it becomes morning, she removes the figurines from under (the bed). She unties the linen ribbon(s) and lays them on top of the figurines. She takes a *dalappa-* of pistachio-"dust" and presses it against him, and says: "In the same way as this 'dust' thoroughly purifies, so may it purify this man (in) all (his) members! May it also purify his house, his altar, his threshing floor including wife, husband and children!" (Hoffner 1972: 86).

Rituals of Mesopotamian origin were used in Hittite Anatolia as well. An Akkadian text from Boğazköy proves this (KUB 29, 58): "In order to release the ... disease: take urine from a live donkey, tuft and hair of its tail, then mix the urine from a donkey with the clay from the tablet house, pour (it) out (and) make two donkey figurines. You place the tail tuft (of the living donkey) on the tail tuft (of donkey figures) (and) the hair of the tail (of the living donkey) on the hair of its (i.e. donkey figures) tail. You make a seat (and) an *agālu* donkey from ordinary clay (and) put a substitute figure on the *agālu* donkey.

(For the making) of a substitute figure, you mix urine of that man who has been seized by the Namtar demon (the sick person), hair from his armpit, hair from his breast and parings of his nail with clay and make a substitute figurine. ... You set the substitute figure which is riding on the *agālu* donkey, onto the donkey figurine.

1 Singer 2002: 311: "... we know practically nothing about the ways the commoners supplicated their gods."

You install the donkey figurines before Šamaš (the sun) on the roof and scatter date flour ... before Šamaš ..." (Bacskay 2018: 171).

Real donkeys could be used in rituals as well[2], but the cheaper version for poor people was a terracotta figurine of a donkey, as we learn from a Hittite Ritual of the diviner *Dandanku* (CTH 425.2): "As follows Dandanku, the augur: When there is a dying in the middle of the army camps, this ritual is performed. As soon as eating and drinking is finished, the ritual lord rises. (Then) you bring a donkey. If (the ritual lord) is a poor man, then you make a donkey out of clay. One turns one's eyes to the land of the enemy (and) one says as follows: "You have done evil in this land and in the camp; this donkey shall take it (and) bring it into the land of the enemy."[3] These three examples show the role of such figurines as 'carriers of the evil'. In other religions often goats were used in rituals to play this role, which became an idiom in English[4] as 'scapegoats'. The first mention is known from Ebla in the 24th century (Zatelli 1998). Also in Mesopotamia and in the Bible (Leviticus 16,8–21, goat of 'ăzāzêl, ritual at Yom Kippur) goats are vehicles to eliminate evils (Rutherford 2020, 130, 135–140). But as donkeys and mules were the main means of transport, these animals were preferred in Anatolia as 'scapegoats'[5]. Even though the terracotta figurine (Fig. 5.4) from the pit in Kayalıpınar does not look like a donkey at first sight, it might be used in this way like the purification ritual mentioned above. Its body is hollow with an opening at its back. Unlike animal-shaped rhyta (*BIBRU*), there is no spout at the mouth. This figurine had no function for liquids to be filled in at the back and poured out through the mouth. But it could perfectly be used as a container of dust or flour as purifying substances or symbolising 'the evil'.

Much better identifiable as an equid (donkey, mule or horse) are three terracotta figurines from Kayalıpınar, found during the first season of excavations in 2005 (Fig. 7). The findspot is the western corner of the only partially preserved eastern room of the so-called House of Tamura from the Early Hittite (kārum) Period (Level 5a)[6].

In contrast to the hollow modelled figurine from the 'archive pit' they are solid, but they have an opening at the back as well. These openings might be filled with substances, needed for the ritual. They could also be used to insert and fix a human figurine, like the description in the Akkadian text tells us[7]. One of the equid figurines has a very interesting detail: It shows blinkers, one of the oldest representations of this element of harness. Terracotta figurines of equids are very common in the Iron Age, but not in the Bronze Age. The most recent study is from Çiğdem Maner (2020: 129), she discusses examples from Tell Atchana, Karkemish, Tell Munbaqa and Tell Tayinat.

Beside pottery and fragments of figurines some strange terracotta objects were found in the 'archive pit'. They are made of coarse clay and fired in a mostly reducing atmosphere (Fig. 6). Subsequently their colour changes from grey to black, only the longish object is more reddish-brown (Fig. 6.1). Their forms seem to be accidental, but fingerprints and traces of mod-

2 At Tell Brak six skeletons of donkeys "apparently ritually interred" were found in an Akkadian context. "They ended their lives at more or less the same time, as sacrifices to a demanding god who could not be appeased with the one aged male and two aged females but required, as well, a young male and a young female donkey in the prime of life": Clutton-Brock 2001: 327, 338.

3 Fuscagni), hethiter.net/: CTH 425.2.

4 Similar expressions are known in other languages, like 'Sündenbock' (German), bouc émissaire / Tête de Turc (! French).

5 In Hittite purification rituals also humans (a man and a woman), a bull, sheep, and a ram are mentioned as substitutes (Haas 1994: 910). Further discussion: Bremmer 1983; Wright 1987: 15–74.

6 When the objects were discovered, the architectural and stratigraphic context was not clear yet. Hence the preliminary report has to be revised (Müller-Karpe, V. 2006; Müller-Karpe, A., Müller-Karpe, V. and Kryszat 2014: 14).

7 Models of horses and wagons made of clay are also mentioned in another Hittite ritual as well: Haas 1994: 879.

elling prove that they were made intentionally. Comparable objects were found in Ebla. Nicolò Marchetti published a deposit of 18 different terracotta objects from the Middle Bronze Age in 2009, and interprets them convincingly as clay models for divination activities: whole or fragmentary models of livers, intestines and malformed animal figurines. They "are covered with a thin coating of red paint, perhaps in order to imitate the colour of entrails" (Marchetti 2009, 281). The examples from Kayalıpınar are not exact parallels to the Ebla finds, but the idea might be the same. The flat object could be a fragment of a liver model (Fig. 7.2), the longish object a part of intestine, and the thick, ovoid one a heart or lung (Fig. 7.3). All these organs were usually examined by diviners (Haas 2008, 56–61).

Especially liver models are known from numerous sites all over the Ancient Near East (Meyer 1984; 1987; de Vos 2013). Models of other organs are not so frequent. But if not inscribed and broken, they can hardly be recognised at excavations. Concerning the diviner an observation of the intestine like: "to the back a cysticercus of a tapeworm."[8] may have been very important, but a clay model of such a diagnostic finding will hardly be noticed by any archaeologist.

Bibliography

Bácskay, A.
- 2018 *Therapeutic prescriptions against fever in ancient Mesopotamia*, AOAT 447, Münster.

Bremmer, J.
- 1983 "Scapegoat Rituals in Ancient Greece," *Harvard Studies in Classical Philology* 87, pp. 299–320.

Clutton-Brock, J.
- 2001 "Ritual Burials of a Dog and Six Domestic Donkeys," in D. Oates, J. Oates and H. McDonald (eds.), *Excavations at Tell Brak. 2: Nagar in the Third Millennium B.C.*, Oxford, pp. 327–336.

Haas, V.
- 1994 *Geschichte der hethitischen Religion, Handbuch der Orientalistik I,15*, Leiden, New York, Köln.
- 2008 *Hethitische Orakel, Vorzeichen und Abwehrstrategien*, Berlin, New York.

Hoffner, H. A. Jr.
- 1972 "Note on "Texts and Fragments (62)"," *JCS* 24, pp. 84–86.

Lebrun, R.
- 1976 *Samuha. – Foyer Religieux de l'Empire Hittite. Publications de l'Institut Orientaliste de Louvain 11*, Louvain-la-Neuve.

Maner, Ç.
- 2020 "Terracottas and other clay objects," in: K. A. Yener, M. Akar, and M. T. Horowitz.(ed.) *Tell Atchana, Alalakh 2, The Late Bronze II City, 2006–2010 Excavation Seasons*, İstanbul, pp. 127–133.

Marchetti, N.
- 2009 "Divination at Ebla during the Old Syrian Period: The Archaeological Evidence," in J. Schloen and J. David (ed.) *Exploring the Longue Durée : Essays in Honor of Lawrence E. Stager*, pp. 279–296

Meyer, J.-W.
- 1984 „Einige Aspekte zur Bearbeitung unbeschrifteter Tonlebermodelle," *MDOG* 116, pp. 119–30.
- 1987 *Untersuchungen zu den Tonlebermodellen aus dem Alten Orient*, AOAT 39, Kevelaer – Neukirchen-Vluyn.

Meier, G.
- 1939 "Ein akkadisches Heilungsritual aus Boğazköy," *ZA 45* [NF 11], pp. 195–215.

Müller-Karpe, A.
- 1988 *Hethitische Töpferei der Oberstadt von Hattuša. Ein Beitrag zur Kenntnis spät-großreichszeitlicher Keramik und Töpferbetriebe. Marburger Studien zur Vor- und Frühgeschichte 10*, Marburg.

Müller-Karpe, V.
- 2006 „Pferdeterrakotten aus dem Bereich des Gebäudes B," in A. Müller-Karpe *et al.*, „Untersuchungen in Kayalıpınar 2005," *MDOG* 138, pp. 224–227.

Müller-Karpe, A., V. Müller-Karpe and G. Kryszat
- 2014 „Untersuchungen in Kayalıpınar 2013 und 2014," *MDOG* 146, pp. 11–41.

8 *ziḫḫum* Haas 2008: 102.

Müller-Karpe, A. and V. Müller-Karpe
– 2019 „Untersuchungen in Kayalıpınar 2017 und 2018. Mit Beiträgen von Mert Özbilgin, Daniel Scherf und Riko Süssenguth," *MDOG* 151, pp. 219–70.
– 2019 (ed.), *Keilschrifttafeln aus Kayalıpınar 1. Textfunde aus den Jahren 1999–2017*, DAAM 1, Wiesbaden.

Otten, H.
– 1973 "Das Ritual der Allī aus Arzawa," *ZA* 63, pp. 76–82. [ZA 63 = NF 29].

Parzinger, H. and R. Sanz
– 1992 *Die Oberstadt von Ḫattuša: Hethitische Keramik aus dem zentralen Tempelviertel. Funde aus den Grabungen 1982–1987. Boğazköy – Ḫattuša 15*, Berlin.

Rieken, E.
– 2014 „Ein Kultinventar für Šamuḫa aus Šamuḫa und andere Texte aus Kayalıpınar," *MDOG* 146, pp. 43–54.

Rutherford, I.
– 2020 *Hittite Texts and Greek Religion*, Oxford.

de Vos, A.
– 2013 *Die Lebermodelle aus Boğazköy. Studien zu den Boğazköy-Texten, Beiheft 5*, Wiesbaden.

Wright, D. P.
– 1987 *The Disposal of the Impurity: Elimination Rites in the Bible and in Hittite and Mesopotamian Literature* , Atlanta.

Zatelli, I.
– 1998 "The Origin of the Biblical Scapegoat Ritual: The Evidence of Two Eblaite Texts," *Vetus Testamentum* 48, pp. 254 – 263.

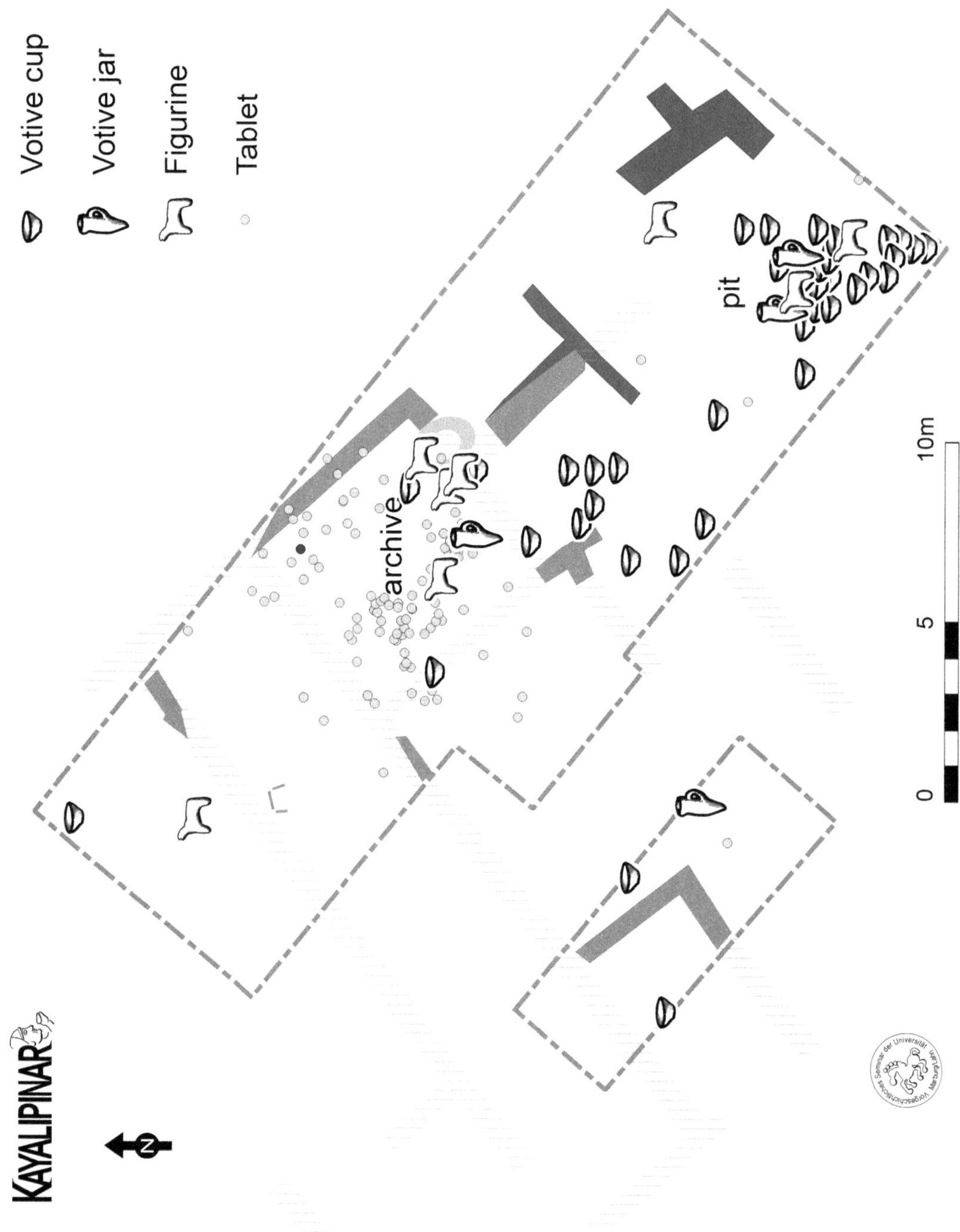

Fig. 1. Kayalıpınar / Samuha, area of the 'archive excavation' in 2015 and 2017 with relicts of rituals.

Fig. 2. Kayalıpınar / Samuha, 'archive excavation' pottery in situ.

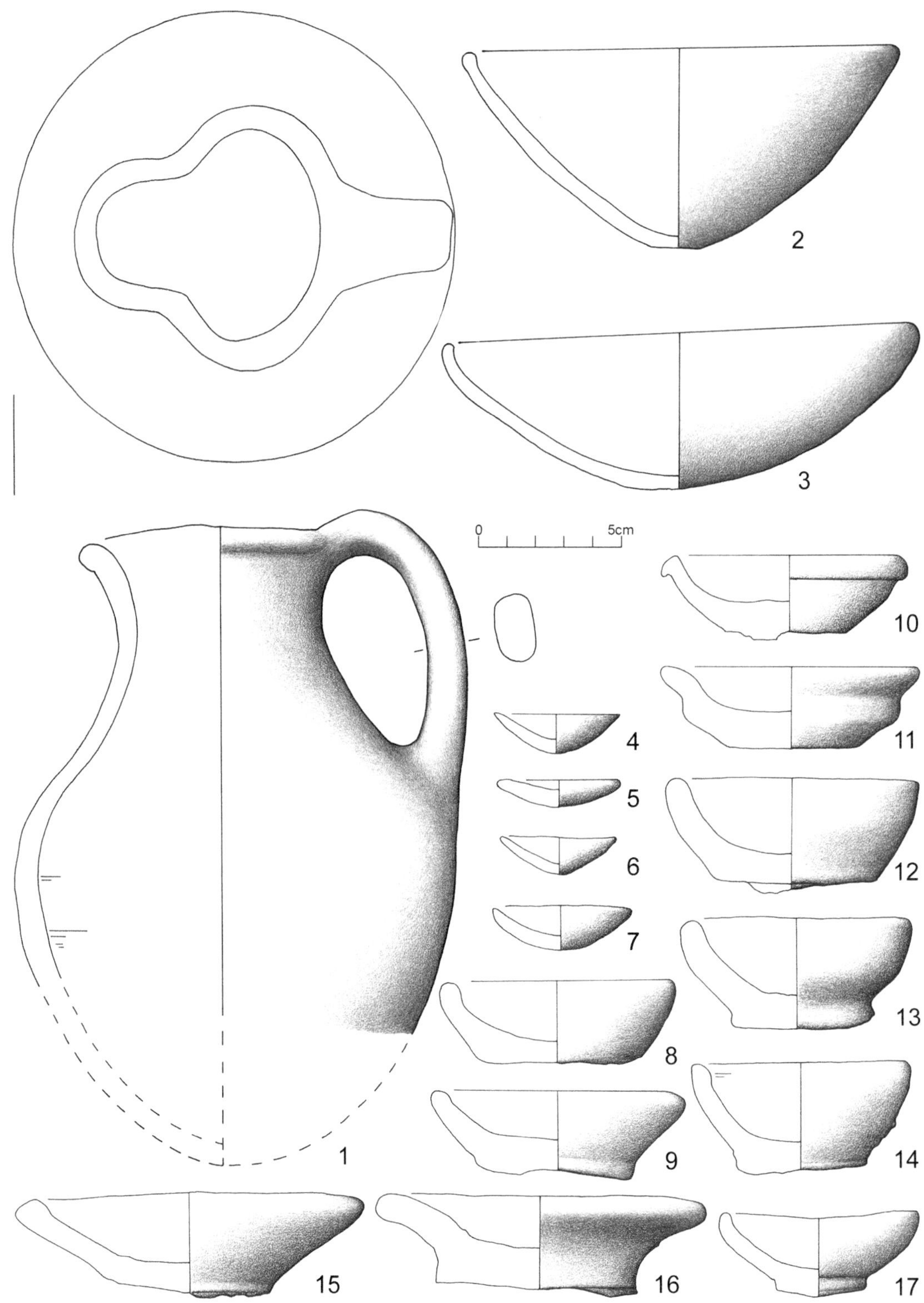

Fig. 3. Hittite pottery from the 'archive pit' in Kayalıpınar / Samuha.

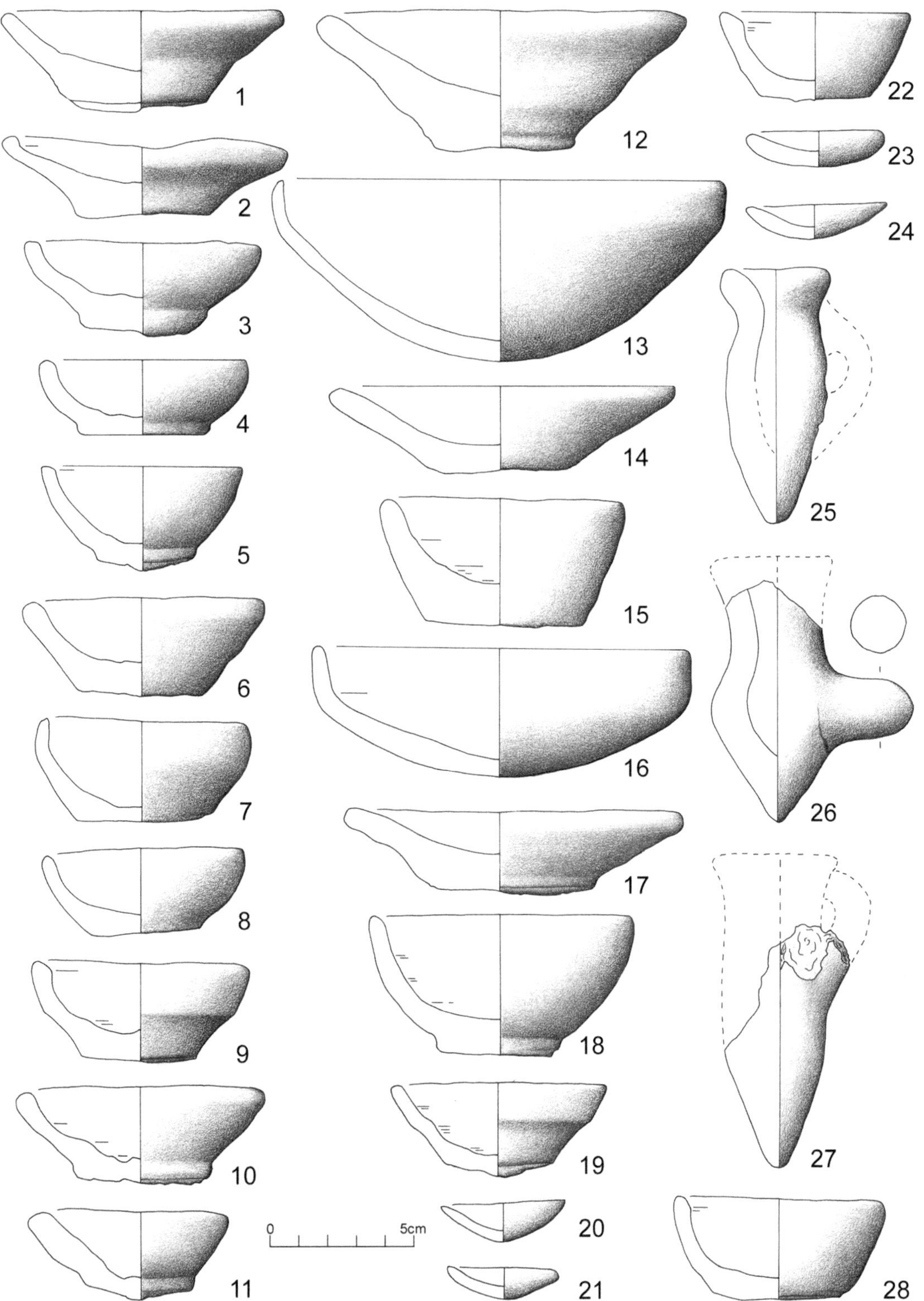

Fig. 4. Hittite pottery from the 'archive pit' in Kayalıpınar / Samuha.

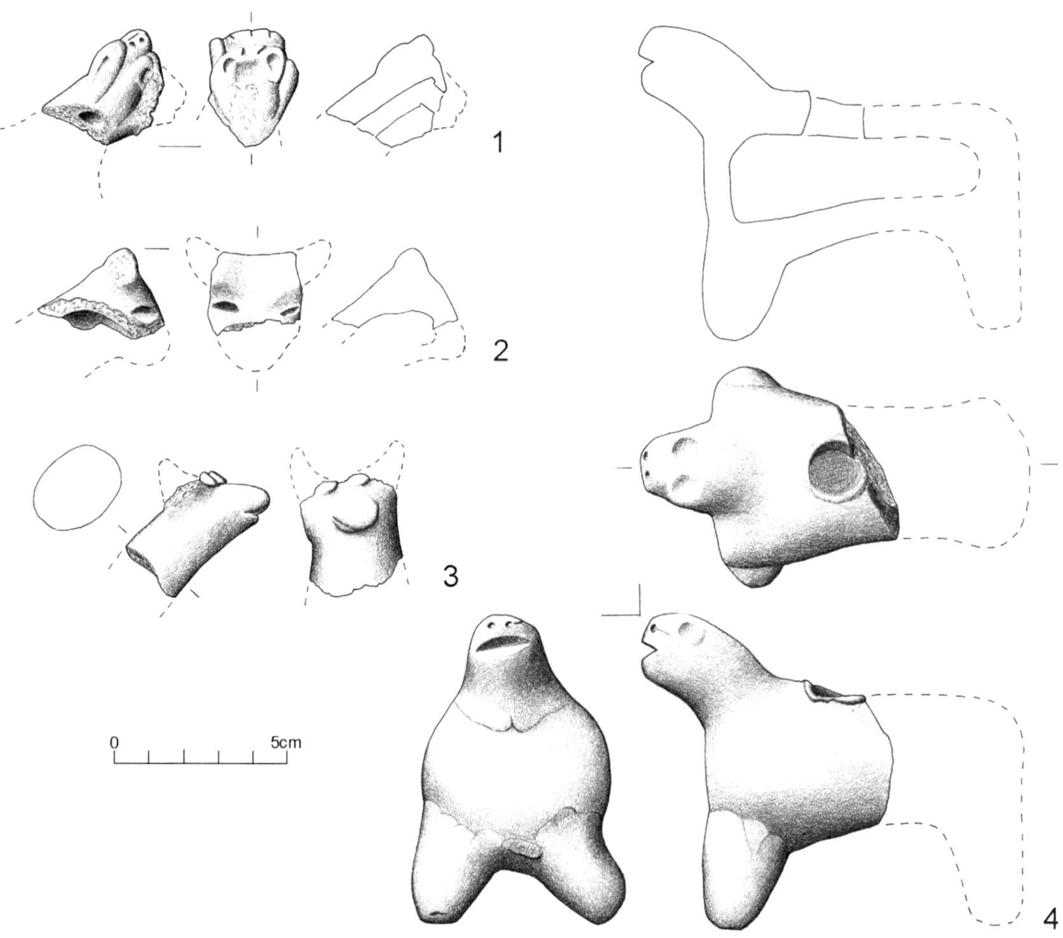

Fig. 5 Zoomorphic figurines from the Hittite 'archive pit' in Kayalıpınar / Samuha.

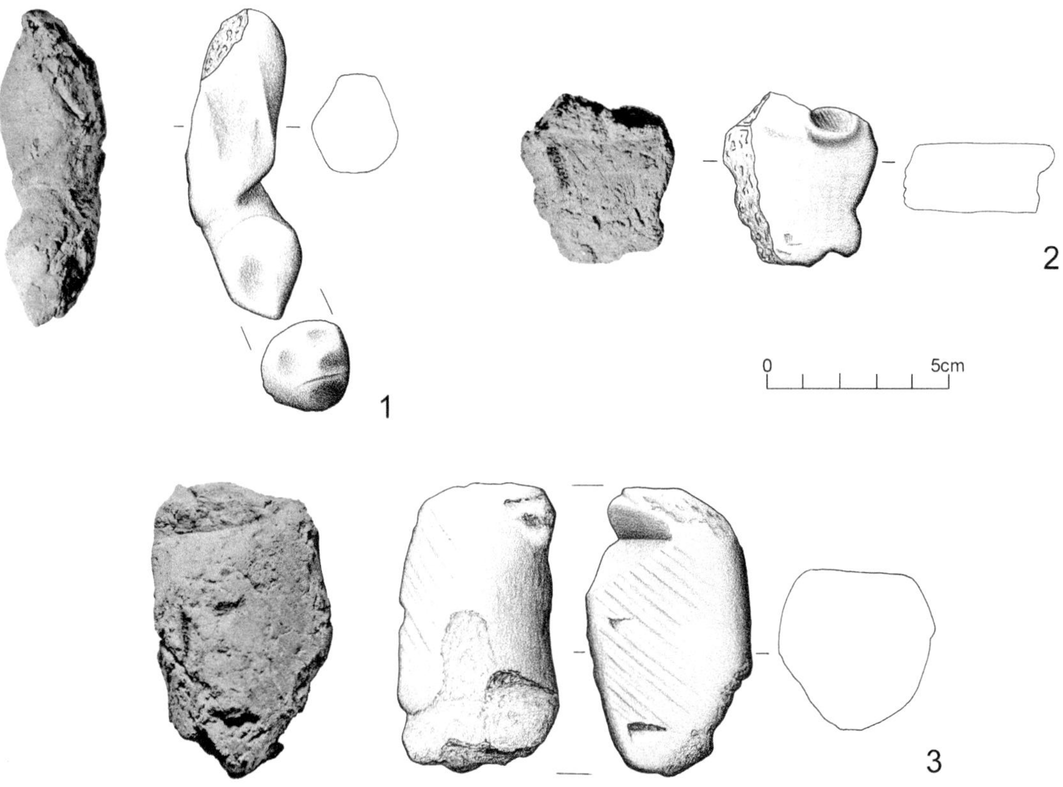

Fig. 6. Potential models of organs from the Hittite 'archive pit' in Kayalıpınar / Samuha (Kp 17/201).

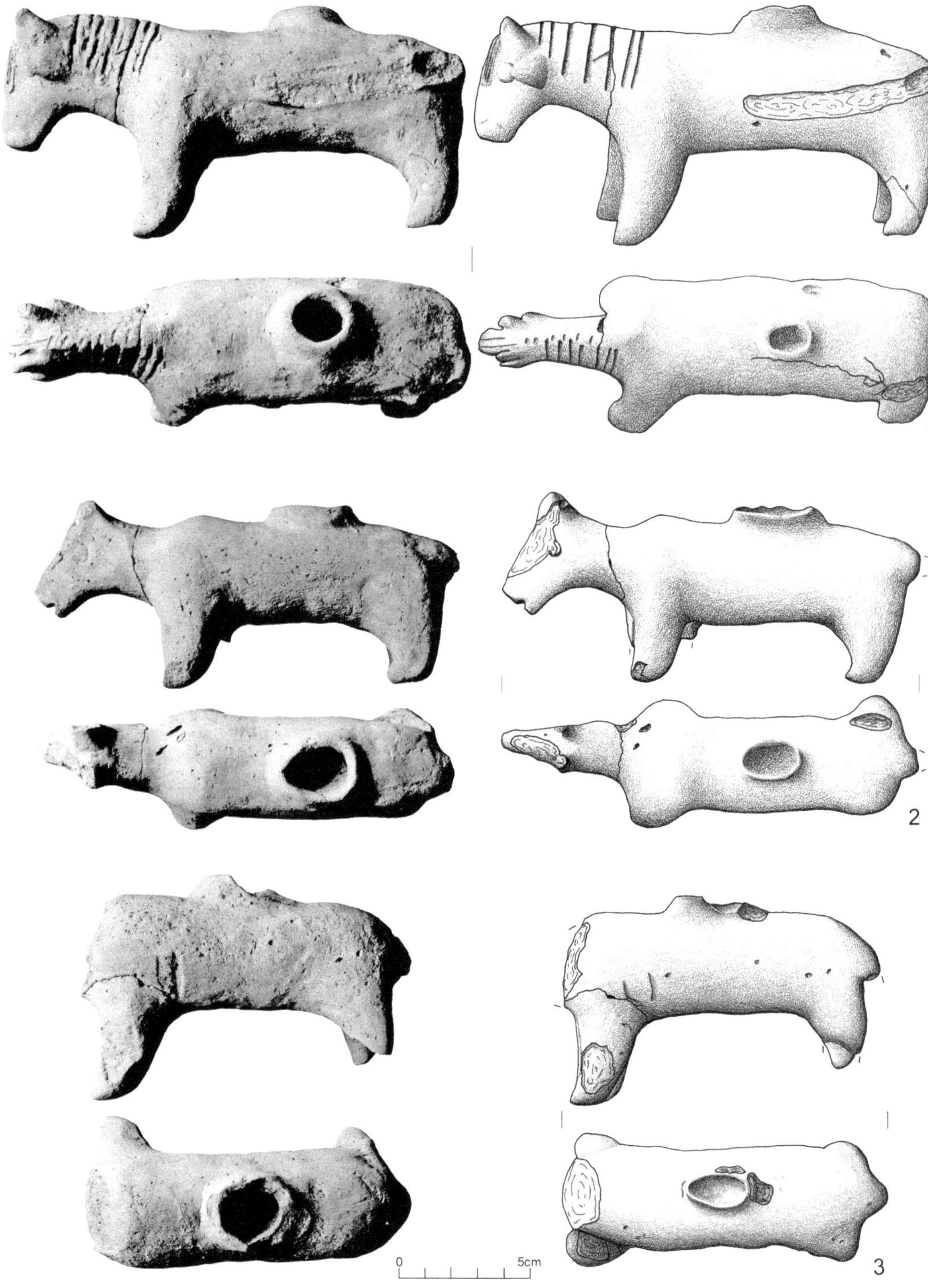

Fig. 7. Figurines of an equid from the 'House of Tamura' level 5a in Kayalıpınar / Samuha (Kp 05/147. 148. 125).

All Change in the Land(scape) of a Thousand Gods: Beyond the Beyşehir Occupation Phase in Central Anatolia

Andrew Fairbairn, Nathan Wright and Mark Weeden *

Abstract

The end of the second millennium B.C. saw a reordering of the Mediterranean political world with the end of several important Bronze Age polities, including the Hittite Kingdom based in Central Anatolia's high plateau. Often referred to as 'the land of a thousand gods', the Hittite Kingdom had a complex pantheon of deities connected to places, events and atmospheric phenomena that invested the king with power. Wood charcoal analysis from Kaman Kalehöyük in the central plateau, demonstrates a long history of woodland exploitation through the Bronze and Iron Ages, including clear evidence for unsustainable woodland exploitation in the LBA and a dramatic shift towards pine exploitation at the end of the second millennium, concurrent with the end of centralised Hittite power in the region. The mid to later second millennium B.C. also saw the emergence of the Beyşehir Occupation Phase in Anatolian pollen diagrams, which signals the start of obvious anthropogenic impact on vegetation, including forest composition. Archaeobotanical evidence points to increasing human impact and modification of Anatolia's native forests during this period. Drawing on these data, combined with historical evidence of religious and other practices, we argue while these changes can be seen as destructive and extractive, they also suggest evidence for resistance to forest use and its preservation. The most parsimonious explanation for such practices in the Bronze Age is the deliberate preservation of some regions as a result of Hittite beliefs in the divine qualities of places and their links to kingly power.

Öz

M.Ö. ikinci binyılın sonu, Orta Anadolu'nun yüksek platosunda bulunan Hitit Krallığı da dahil olmak üzere birçok önemli Tunç Çağı devletinin sona ermesiyle Akdeniz siyasi dünyasının yeniden düzenlenmesine tanık olmuştur. Genellikle 'bin tanrılı ülke' olarak anılan Hitit Krallığı, krala güç veren yerler, olaylar ve atmosferik fenomenlerle bağlantılı karmaşık bir tanrılar panteonuna sahipti. Orta Plato'daki Kaman-Kalehöyük'te yapılan odun kömürü analizleri, Tunç ve Demir Çağları boyunca uzun bir ormanlık alan kullanımı geçmişi olduğunu göstermektedir; buna, Geç Tunç Çağı'nda sürdürülemez ormanlık alan kullanımına dair açık kanıtlar ve ikinci binyılın sonunda, bölgedeki merkezi Hitit iktidarının sona ermesiyle eşzamanlı olarak çam kullanımına doğru dramatik bir kayma da dahildir. MÖ ikinci binyılın ortalarından sonlarına doğru Anadolu polen diyagramlarında Beyşehir Yerleşim Evresi'nin ortaya çıkışı, orman oluşumu da dahil olmak üzere bitki örtüsü üzerindeki belirgin antropojenik etkinin başlangıcına işaret etmektedir. Arkeobotanik kanıtlar, bu dönemde Anadolu'nun doğal ormanlarında artan insan etkisine ve değişikliğine işaret etmektedir. Bu verilere dayanarak, dini ve diğer uygulamalara ilişkin tarihsel kanıtlarla birlikte, bu değişiklikler yıkıcı ve sömürgeci olarak görülürken aynı zamanda orman kullanımına karşı çıkma ve ormanın korunmasına dair kanıtlar sunduğunu savunuyoruz. Tunç Çağı'ndaki bu tür uygulamalar için en makul açıklama, Hititler yerlerin ilahi nitelikleri ve krallık gücüyle alakalı inançların bir sonucu olarak bazı bölgeleri korumuşlardır.

* University of Queensland, School of Social Science, Brisbane, Australia – University of New England, Department of Archaeology, Classics and History, Armidale, Australia – UCL, Department of Greek and Latin, London, UK

Introduction

In recent decades, Anatolia's long and complex landscape and economic histories have been increasingly understood as the result of more methodologically refined and widespread archaeological and palaeoenvironmental investigations, including archaeobotanical and zooarchaeological analyses. Under the leadership of Dr. Sachihiro Omura, the Japanese Institute of Anatolian Archaeology has been vital in introducing and supporting these new archaeological approaches in Turkey, serving both to expand the knowledge base through its long-term commitment to science-based archaeology during excavation while building capacity and expertise as a result of its training programs for students new to the field. In the case of plant use, which was poorly known outside the Neolithic in Central Anatolia, Kaman-Kalehöyük now has the key regional archaeobotanical sequence spanning the mid-third to late first millennium B.C. (e.g. Nesbitt 1994; Fairbairn 2002; Wright *et al.* 2015; Üstünkaya 2015) and, after a settlement hiatus, into the Ottoman Period (Fenwick 2015; Fenwick *et al.* 2017). A combination of seed analysis, wood charcoal analysis (anthracology) and, more recently, phytolith analysis (Turnbull 2020) has resulted from decades of careful field practice and supporting work in the JIAA's laboratory at Çağırkan. An identical approach applied to Büklükale and Yassıhöyük excavations has already provided unique information on the region's economic history (Fairbairn *et al.* 2019), with further research and integration from the three sites providing exciting opportunities for further understanding the history of landscape change.

While the Dr. Omura's support for science-based techniques has been essential for understanding landscape histories, equally important has been the development of the JIAA as a place for broad-based discussion between specialists from the many fields with a shared interest in the past. This paper is the result of just such a discussion between a seed archaeobotanist, an anthracologist and a philologist, focused on understanding a curious change in landscape use apparent in the wood charcoal data from Kaman-Kalehöyük, namely the 'pine-shift', which occurred at the end of the Second Millennium B.C. concurrent with the end of the Hittite Kingdom (Wright *et al.* 2015). Linking changes in human behaviour reflected in archaeological datasets, especially those that imply changing landscape practices, to political or cultural causes is replete with pitfalls, especially when drawing on diverse sources that vary in spatial and temporal resolution to explain them. Here we draw on archaeobotanical, palynological and historical sources to provide an explanation for this phenomena centred on the changing political ecology of landscape use and how it affected woodland exploitation in the Anatolian landscape. Very few archaeological excavations could have produced the opportunity for this kind of collaborative research and we offer this paper both in honour of Dr. Omura's enduring contribution to Anatolian archaeology and in thanks for his unwavering support of our work over the decades.

Anthracology and Kaman-Kalehöyük's Pine-Shift

Anthracology is the study of wood charcoal, that is the partially burnt remains of tree trunk, branch and root wood left when these materials are exposed to fire, found in archaeological sites, aiming to understand the palaeoenvironmental, economic and cultural histories of wood exploitation through time and space (Asouti and Austin 2005). As the major fuel of the pre-industrial age, wood was commonly burnt in the past and it is the most abundant and widely preserved form of archaeological plant remains found in sites around the world. The basic premise in anthracology is that wood charcoals found in archaeological sites form evidence for past wood use, allowing insights into both human activity in ancient settlements and providing a record of wood availability in the landscape Kabukcu and Chabal 2020). At Kaman-Kalehöyük, as at most sites, the majority of wood charcoal was derived from fuel wood, burnt in fire installations and recovered from them or from hearth-cleanings deposited in middens/rubbish dumps. Analysis has demonstrated that the charcoal assemblages deposited in Kaman-Kalehöyük's numerous pits was identical to those found in fire installations/hearths, providing support for the taphonomic assumption that agricultural pits were re-used at the end of their lives as middens and thus provide a cross section of artefacts and ecofacts from everyday life (Wright *et al.* 2017). The same research demonstrated that these assemblages differed from charcoal remans found in burnt buildings, which were dominated by the remains of construction material such as wooden beams, roofing etc. Thus, the analysis of wood charcoals from a variety of depositional contexts in archaeological sites, provides information for which to reconstruct a variety of activities from fuel use to construction technology.

Anatomical study of charcoals allows the type of tree – in scientific terms the taxon, such as species, family etc – to be identified and in some cases the part of the tree exposed to fire, such as the tree-trunk, root or twig (dendroecological analysis or dendrology) (Wright 2017). Quantitative study of changing taxon and element abundance, as well as features such as diameter, presence of decay etc, allows economic and cultural histories to be reconstructed via the analysis of wood use in general and wood fuel selection in particular (Euba *et al.* 2016; Moskal-del Hoyo *et al.* 2010). Wood fuel use is to a greater or lesser extent a reflection of wood availability, including the presence and abundance of trees in the local environment, determined by climate, tree species environmental preferences and human management/deforestation (Kabukcu 2018). It also reflects access to those tree resources, which would have been conditioned by social and economic practices and rights, as well as the suitability of different species for fuel, construction etc. It also reflects access to those tree resources, which would have been conditioned by social and economic practices and rights, as well as the suitability of different species for fuel, construction and other activities. Distinguishing human and environmental factors in patterning woodland structures, abundance and change can be difficult when approached through palynology alone. This is especially the case in Anatolia, where pollen cores are widely spaced, may be subject to considerable time-averaging and distant from excavated settlements. However, the analysis of charcoal data in concert and contrast to other environmental and cultural data provides an invaluable source for reconstructing detailed landscape histories of management and change at an otherwise unreachable temporal and spatial resolution.

Anthracological research at Kaman-Kalehöyük from c. 2000–300 B.C. shows a considerable change in landscape practices and management over the whole period and one very different to the denuded landscape seen today (Wright *et al.* 2015; 2017; Wright 2016; 2017). Analysis of mixed rubbish/pit assemblages shows that oak was the dominant fuel species over the whole period of occupation, its use showing the persistence of open oak woodland cover near to the site through the whole period (Wright *et al.* 2015). In areas that are heavily deforested, as in Kaman's immediate vicinity today, fuel needs are traditionally met by secondary fuels, traditionally dung (Miller 1994) and more recently coal and gas, or wood from fast growing plantation species, such as poplar. Kaman shows neither of these trends through most of its excavated history, with high quality oak wood fuel being mixed with other species from river valleys, forest edge and other disturbed habitats (minor species in Wright *et al.* 2015), and, in the Iron Age, significant exploitation of pine forests. The shift to pine, which is a minor component of <10 % abundance throughout the Middle and Late Bronze Age, is stark in the Iron Age, where it comprises 20–40 % abundance (Fig. 1).

This 'pine-shift' is not the only temporal pattern seen at the site, with a significant decline in the number of tree species (taxon richness or nTaxa) from a peak in the early 2nd Millennium B.C. (MBA I–III, c. 2000–1650 B.C.) to a low point in the Late Bronze Age by c. 1200 B.C., which was sustained through the Early and Middle Iron Age (Fig. 1). While the high nTaxa seen in the MBA I–III suggests a landscape that had already seen deforestation, river valley and minor species were maintained and dendroanthracology data indicate that smaller oak branch and twig wood was harvested, not significantly affecting the long-term survival of the source trees. Very low nTaxa in the LBA suggests that continued harvesting and removal of trees led to the development of a depauperate landscape with significant pressure on trees and wood supply, with loss of most tree species from the river valleys and depression of minor taxa. Interestingly there is no clear switch to poorer quality fuels in the LBA, such as dung, to make up for this pressure on fuel, but rather a focus on harvesting larger trees, including their root boles, indicated by ring curvature and other data (Wright 2017). This unsustainable practice would have rapidly led to the loss of established oak woodland. In the Iron Age, the pattern of low nTaxa continues until the Late Iron Age, which at Kaman-Kalehöyük corresponds with the Persian Empire, during which taxon richness increases, perhaps signalling new approaches to wood fuel management or the advent of plantations. From the Early Iron Age, a major change in wood fuel use is seen in the sudden increase in the use of pine wood as fuel.

Explaining the Pine Shift: Is it Just the BOP or Climate Change?

Palynology has identified a major phase of anthropogenic impact on woodland cover in Anatolia lasting from approximately 1500 B.C.-600 AD, known as the Beyşehir Occupation Phase (hereafter BOP) after the region in which it was first identified (Van Zeist *et al.* 1975; Eastwood *et al.* 1998). The BOP sees an increase in crops, open country plants and arboriculture species indicating both vegetation disturbance and increasing plant cultivation. Interestingly, the BOP data show that pine pollen steadily increases from the EBA onwards with, what could be termed, a dip in pollen abundance in the EIA (Fig. 2, black arrows). This indicates that pine was broadly available in the landscape during the Bronze Age. In fact, according the BOP data, pine pollen accounts for 75 % of arboreal pollen and 50 % of total pollen by the LBA while other pollen catchments such as Eski Acıgöl and the more distant lake Van show a consistent and almost unchanging presence of pine across the landscape (Fig. 2) Litt *et al.* 2009; Roberts *et al.* 2001; Wick *et al.* 2003, Woldring and Bottema 2002). So, while available, pine was not used in the Bronze Age and the increase in wood fuel at Kaman in the EIA correlates well with the reduction in pollen abundance in cores of the same period, which would be expected if harvesting increased.

Kaman-Kalehöyük's pine shift and longer-term pattern of vegetation impact, including declining taxon richness and a change to less sustainable harvesting methods, fits within this broader regional pattern of accumulating anthropogenically driven vegetation change. It suggests that the expanding power of territorial states in the Late Bronze Age went hand-in-hand with increasing anthropogenic modification of habitats. This may well signal the increasing demands for food in an increasingly urban and connected world, with efforts to extract more from the environment accelerated by increasing aridity over the period and the taxation and tribute demanded by powerful centralised states, such as the Hittite Empire.

Yet, it is hard to characterise the pine-shift as merely a local variant of the BOP. As noted earlier, MBA I–III data from Kaman-Kalehöyük shows that woodland cover near the site was already experiencing human impact well before the 1500 B.C. initiation of the BOP, with the most extreme evidence for anthropogenic forest impact in the LBA. Deforestation and significant anthropogenic change in woodland had occurred for at least 800 years when the pine shift occurred. The key factor is the sudden increased use of pine. Was the pine-shift due to an increase in pine in the environment at the end of the second millennium B.C. as a result of climate change? Evidence suggests not. As noted above, the pollen evidence from Eski Acıgöl and Beyşehir Gölü indicates that pine was present in the region's woodland in significant quantities through the second millennium B.C. In fact, the wood charcoal evidence from Kaman-Kalehöyük shows that pine was occasionally used as a fuel from the MBA IV, but only in modest quantities. Furthermore, while pine is a strong coloniser of open ground, it is neither more competitive nor more drought tolerant than oak at low to mid altitudes (Richardson 2000). Oak itself responds well to intensive harvesting via methods such as coppicing, which increases pollen production – and may possibly be seen for the first time in the EIA BOP data, and colonises open areas aggressively (Asouti and Kabukcu 2014; Eastwood *et al.* 1998). Thus, it seems unlikely that pine was colonising open ground at the expense of oak. A more likely scenario is that pine was simply under-used through the Bronze Age and local stands, probably on the high mountain slopes of Baran Dağ and adjoining ridges 2km to the south of Kaman-Kalehöyük, were used extensively during the Iron Age for the first time as a routinely gathered everyday fuel.

Changing Times, Changing Attitudes

With climate change and environmental factors unlikely to provide the answer to the pine-shift, a political alternative has been suggested, namely that the mountains on which pine is likely to grow were protected by Hittite authority and exploitation was opened when the Hittite state collapsed (Wright *et al.* 2015: 227–228). The correspondence of increasing pine fuel use and the end of Hittite authority is certainly very clear in the Kaman-Kalehöyük data, though pine was occasionally used as fuel in the LBA and was also used on occasion as a construction timber. It is possible that the two were connected, with the modest fuel wood coming from the leftovers of construction activity or from the burning of old structural timbers for fuel. Interestingly the room fill data for the EIA (Fig. 1) show that the increase in pine is not from construction use, in fact this period shows the least amount of pine use for construction out of any of the periods analysed. Pine was now being used primarily for fuel and not for construction as in previous and subsequent periods. There is a decline in the amount of pine being used for construction from the MBA III to the MBA IV all the way through to the EIA, with a rebound in the MIA, though in the latter it is still an important fuel.

It is worth commenting on the broader archaeological changes that are seen at the end of the LBA at Kaman-Kalehöyük. Occupied throughout the second millennium B.C., the settlement has evidence for defensive walls, phases of destruction in the MBA I–III and the development of a probable administrative role during the Hittite period, including the imposition of a large central masonry building and huge grain stores (Omura 2011; Fairbairn and Omura 2005). Beyond an increasing focus on pine use, the Iron Age occupation evidences significant change in many aspects of life, including ceramic styles and production techniques, trade networks and in the settlement itself, where the architecture changes to include semi-subterranean dwellings indicative of changing domestic cultures. With the demise of the Hittite Kingdom, new local polities also emerged.

Was part of the change in the human world a change in attitude to the landscape itself? Landscapes are cultural creations, in which the social, political and economic desires and conventions are manifest in a series of human actions that pattern and shape the natural world. While cultivation of crops and feeding of animals, the collection of fuel and mining of raw materials in part shape the physical world, cultural beliefs and social practises are significant in providing rules about when such activities are appropriate, allowable and who might take advantage of them. It is easy to assume, following a backward projection of Judeo-Christian belief in the primacy of humans as masters of the natural world, mixed with modern market-based and libertarian ideologies, that in the past people were free to do as they pleased to extract and use resources. Ample evidence shows that this was not the case. From the Hittite world, we have good historical sources that demonstrate that land and resource rights were complex, with the world owned by the gods, whose human proxy – the king – had authority to allot them as he deemed fit (see below). Estates were awarded to the great and good depending on political requirements and temples, as well as the palace itself, had landholdings over which they could exert influence and extract resources (see Bryce 2002).

As noted above, one possibility for the pine shift is that the local mountain Baran Dag was itself protected and thus the trees upon it. There is some evidence, however, that trees themselves were given direct protection. One of the clearest examples of a Hittite sensitivity towards arboreal ecology is presented by a ritual. The Hittite foundation ritual CTH 414 (Görke 2015) is preserved on manuscripts dating to the Old-Middle Hittite periods (16th-mid 15th-centuries) as well as to the New Hittite period, more specifically the 13th century B.C. The content of the ritual is likely to be quite old, as it contains a number of Hattic deities, as well as other clearly Hattic content, meaning that its frame of reference is likely to be the cultural world encountered in central Anatolia in the earlier phase of Hittite state-formation (Klinger 1996: 136–141). In fact, the central Anatolian area is likely to have been partly bilingual Hattic-Hittite during much of this earlier period (Goedegebuure 2008). Very broadly speaking, the Hattic elements of Hittite ritual decline throughout Hittite history, as does the understanding of the Hattic language, but this ritual seems to have remained popular and meaningful, as indicated by its 13th century copies.

The ritual starts off (Görke 2015 § 1): "when the king builds a palace somewhere, [if they roof (it)] with wood, then they speak these words...." The ritual is preceded by a narrative involving the king and the throne, in which the king seems to be asking the throne to intercede on his behalf with the trees for them to allow him to cut them down in order to use them as palace-timbers. Presumably the throne is eminently qualified for this role, as it is made of wood. The text is quite bizarre for a modern audience, but seems fairly clear:

> "and the king speaks to the throne: come let's go, you stand behind the mountains, you should not be my man, you should not be my kinsman, be my companion, my companion. Come, let us go to the mountain, and I the king will give you a zapziki, and we will eat from a zapziki, and you look after your mountain. The divine sun-god and the storm-god assigned to me the land and my house, and I the king will also look after my land and my house. You should not come into my house, and I will not come into your house... " (Görke 2015 §§ 4–7) and the king asks the storm-god for the trees, which the rains have made bushy and made grow: "You grew green under the heaven, the lion slept under (you), the panther slept under you, and the bear mounted you, and my father the storm-god put evil beyond you. The ox grazed under you, the sheep grazed under you, and now the king, Labarna, I have united with you and I have called my companion, the throne. Are you not the companion of the king? Assign to me this tree, so I can cut it. And the throne speaks back to the king, saying 'cut it, cut, the sun-goddess and the storm-god have assigned it to you. (To the trees) now, go up from this country, the storm-god has assigned you to the king, and they will put decorations over you, and they will hoist you up, and they will pronounce spells over you'" (Görke 2015 §§ 9–12; see also Sir Gavaz this volume, Taggar-Cohen this volume, with slightly different translations).

This ritual interlude, whether it was narrated or somehow acted out, establishes a clear chain of command and ownership. The country belongs to the storm-god and the sun-goddess, but they have assigned it to the king, as well as the right to have a house or palace. The king needs to look after his domain, and the throne, being made of wood, looks after its domain, which is on the mountain. Nevertheless, it appears that the king has to assure the trees on the mountains through the intercession of the throne that they are going to be treated well if they are cut down. On the one hand this is direct evidence, if it were needed, for trees being cut down in order to build palaces. On the other it seems to suggest that simply going to the mountain and cutting down a tree was not appropriate, especially if the tree's primary use was not for important structures or ceremonies but rather, simply for fuel. It may indicate that there was some sort of taboo against procuring trees from mountains without performing the appropriate rituals. Unfortunately, the text does not indicate which trees are being cut down here.

In a further ritual text, this time nothing to do with foundation rituals (CTH 329 manuscript P; Glocker 1997: 84–87), a mountain is asked for permission to cut down an *eya*-tree. A man is sent to cut the tree down on mount Sidduwa, and makes a bread offering, asking the mountain to eat. He says "Mt Sidduwa, we are carrying away this *eya*-tree for the storm-god (of Kuliwisna), for decoration and for clothing" (KUB 12.19 iii 18'-24'; see also Sir Gavaz, this volume). It is not entirely clear what is meant by this, possibly the tree's wood or foliage is to be used as decoration in the temple of the storm-god. But again we see that it is not possible simply to go to the mountain and chop a tree down. The identity of the *eya*-tree is debated. Most scholarly opinion holds it to be an oak (e.g. Haas 2003: 291–293), but it has also been supposed to be a tall juniper (Fairbairn *et al.* 2019: 338), pine (Sir Gavaz this volume), or yew (Kloekhorst 2008: 233), which are all more likely than oak due to the fact that mountain oak tends to be scrubby and not good for use in construction. It can be very difficult to identify ancient tree-names with modern taxa, but at the least we have another case here where permission needs to be asked. This time it is the divine mountain that seems to need to be appeased before a tree can be removed.

In spite of the difficulties we have in understanding these ancient texts with their obscure expressions, it does seem from the above that trees on mountains were protected and are likely to have been throughout the history of the Hittite state. However, mountains continued to be venerated in the period after the collapse of the central Hittite power, as we know from Iron Age Hieroglyphic Luwian inscriptions in central Anatolia, and the cults of mountain and other ecological deities such as the stag-god continued as well. It is also unclear how culturally specific such compensatory rites for cutting down trees are. With a practice that has numerous cross-cultural parallels, it is difficult to know just how to interpret the fact that we do not have evidence for this specific ritual activity after the Late Bronze Age, especially when we have so much less evidence anyway due to the absence of cuneiform archives in Central Anatolia.

Conservation or Inadvertent Consequence?

In an earlier paper (Wright *et al.* 2015) it was suggested that the Kaman-Kalehöyük pine-shift was the result of the disappearance of formal Hittite protection of mountains, on which pine forest is most likely to thrive near Kaman, with the end of the Hittite Empire. Further research suggests that protection could be afforded to the trees themselves, under the protection of the Storm God and/or of the mountains on which they resided, and appropriate rituals were required to obtain the requisite permission to cut them down. Putting the archaeological, palynological and historical evidence together, there is evidence for the action of a powerful set of proscriptions, applying even to the Hittite king, which provided effective protection to certain groups of trees in the landscape. In fact, this provides the most parsimonious explanation for lack of exploitation available pine during the Bronze Age and the sudden increase in pine fuel use at Kaman-Kalehöyük during the Early Iron Age when such controls disappeared.

While we cannot with certainty identify the trees referred to in the historical records, CTH 414 suggests that those harvested were to be used to construct a palace roof. Where large roofs have been sampled, including the JIAA excavation of EBA Yassıhöyük and MBA Büklükale as well as Gordion and Kültepe the species identified include pine, oak , juniper and, at Kaman-Kalehöyük maple, all of whose straight, tall trunks provide strong, long and durable architectural elements (Fairbairn and Wright 2017; Marston 2009; 2012; Miller 2010; Wright 2016). There seems to be a preference for juniper and pine for beams and oak for posts which fit with the structural properties of these timbers (Wright 2017). Thus, the limited archaeological evidence does not conflict with pine being one of those protected tree species.

The fact that CTH 414 refers to palace construction and the CTH 326 to the decoration of a temple, suggests that access to trees was for individuals or institutions of high state, religious, secular or both. It also suggests that large trees used for construction etc during the Hittite period were of considerable value and were not open to general foraging and harvest. This is evidence for socially ranked resource access, controlled to some extent by religious practice. Such control could have been exercised in the rules of access granted by the king to landowners and grandees, and in the title of temples over their landed estates, and its presence at Kaman could indicate such estates in the immediate area. In this scenario, the change in pine use in the EIA is indicative of not simply a change in political system, but a re-ordering of the concepts about which landscape access and ownership were structured. Pine, which was a restricted resource and rarely made into the fuel or construction supply of the Late Bronze Age, became a commonly harvested fuel and a part of the everyday experience of people at the settlement (see Fig. 2). Whether this reflected changing rights to collect the wood or an opening up of access to the mountains and their pine forests, previously proscribed, is uncertain but the restrictions limiting its use were gone.

This raises a larger question about whether the Hittite avoidance of pine represents active conservation of the trees and habitat for their own value or whether it was an inadvertent consequence of abstract religious practice? The reason for permission being required to cut down trees in the two texts quoted here is the protection of those trees afforded by divinities – the Storm God and a mountain. Directly interpreted, that suggests that protection was a simple ownership issue. Conservation in the modern sense does not seem to be present here and the unsustainable harvesting of oak, combined with the long-term depletion of riverine and minor species, suggests that destructive levels of resource exploitation were not beyond the people of Kaman-Kalehöyük in the Hittite period. However, the texts are few and lack detail about the reasoning behind protection; perhaps this was a blanket protection on all high mountains or particularly large or distinctive trees. However it was justified, the practice certainly conserved the pine forests of Kaman for several hundred years and added diversity to an otherwise an anthropogenically damaged woodland landscape. Such inadvertent protection would have been important for maintenance of biodiversity and also may well have created anthropogenically selected reserves which may well have enhanced the presence of some species and ages of trees in specific geographical regions. One of the characteristics of the palynological record of this period – exemplified in the BOP – is that it becomes more regionally varied; perhaps the protection of some populations of trees added to this complexity.

The increase in pine fuel exploitation in the Early Iron Age is evidenced in the pollen diagram at Beyşehir Gölü, suggesting that the increase in exploitation of pine may have been more widespread than at Kaman-Kalehöyük's locale. With religious and social controls loosened, the focus on pine as a major fuel makes sense if it was present due to the diminution of river and minor tree species in the wider landscape. As seen today in central Anatolia, in heavily used landscapes, once removed or harvested, many tree species can struggle to recruit saplings due to the pressure of grazing and browsing livestock. The charcoal data suggest that remedial action to improve taxonomic diversity, including perhaps landscape proscriptions and plantations, did not emerge following the Hittite Kingdom in the Kaman-Kalehöyük catchment until the Persian period (Wright *et al.* 2015).

Concluding Comments: Archaeobotany and the Political Ecology of Ancient Landscapes

In recent years, archaeobotanists have begun to more actively engage with the political ecology of the past, investigating the landscape and its use beyond resource procurement and starting to tease apart the social, political and cultural consequences and agency of landscape interactions (Morrison 2018; Rosenzweig 2018; Rosenzweig and Marston 2018). Rather than being a neutral backdrop to the human past, or simply a body of useful things, the landscape is an active place in which human affairs are enacted but which can be deployed to achieve political ends and whose use and construction inevitably has political outcomes.

While often regarded as a means of reconstructing woodland and environment, anthracological research at Kaman-Kalehöyük, when combined with historical evidence and broader consideration of archaeological context, has opened a door on an unexpected episode of woodland preservation, driven by religious belief and linked to creation and maintenance of Hittite power structures. As well as the protection of some mountains, as previously discussed, historical evidence indicates the protection of trees themselves, providing an element of landscape preservation in the face of otherwise significant woodland impact. The end of this system, with the fall of the Hittite Kingdom in the central plateau, led to a period of significant change in access to woodland fuels that locally saw a sustained period of low woodland diversity, only restored under the Persian Empire. While we cannot see this as a deliberate conservation ethic in the modern sense of the word, the proscription on trees recorded in historical documents is the best explanation for the sudden rise in pine fuel exploitation in the Iron Age. This example perhaps provides a case where the politically imposed rules of state inadvertently caused the conservation of specific trees and landscapes and provided a respite for an environment increasingly affected by the ever-increasing needs of the urban world. Ironically, the lack of access to the pine woods may have contributed to the even less sustainable wood harvesting seen at the same time in Kaman-Kalehöyük's oak and riverine forests.

While aspects of this story must remain speculative, the combination of archaeological sources derived from thirty-five years of archaeological enquiry at Kaman-Kalehöyük and the collaborative discussions between a variety of scholars that have been fostered by Dr. Omura, have provided an intriguing example of landscape management that demonstrates the potential for high resolution work of this kind for furthering our understanding the ancient world. The potential for future insights as the JIAA continues its mission is considerable and we look forward to exploring them as ever more data is generated.

Acknowledgements

This research was supported by the Japanese Institute of Anatolian Archaeology, the Australian Research Council (DP0987316 and FT130101702 awarded to AF), and for NW the Australian Institute of Nuclear Science and Engineering travel scholarship, the Australian Postgraduate Award Scheme and The University of Queensland Graduate School GSITA.

Bibliography

Asouti, E. and P. Austin
- 2005 "Reconstructing woodland vegetation and its exploitation by past societies, based on the analysis and interpretation of archaeological wood charcoal macro-remains," *Environmental Archaeology* 10, pp. 1–18.

Asouti, E. and C. Kabukcu
- 2014 "Holocene semi-arid oak woodlands in the Irano-Anatolian region of Southwest Asia: natural or anthropogenic?," *Quaternary Science Reviews* 90, pp. 158–182

Bryce, T.
- 2002 *Life and society in the Hittite world*, OUP, Oxford.

Euba, I., E. Allue and F. Burjachs
- 2016 "Wood uses at El Mirador cave (Atapuerca, Burgos) based on anthracology and dendrology," *Quaternary International* 414, pp. 285–293.

Eastwood, W.J., N. Roberts and H.F. Lamb
- 1998 "Palaeoecological and archaeological evidence for human occupance in southwest Turkey: the Beyşehir occupation phase," *Anatolian Studies* 48, pp. 69–86.

Fairbairn, A.
- 2002 "Archaeobotany at Kaman Kalehöyük 2001," *Anatolian Archaeological Studies* 11, pp. 201–212.

Fairbairn, A.S. and N. Wright
- 2017 "Grinding burning and trading at Kültepe: Archaebotanical evidence for economic differences between settlements in Anatolia's Middle Bronze Age," in F. Kulakoğlu and G. Barjamovlc (eds), *Movement, Resources, Interaction: Proceedings of the 2nd Kültepe International Meeting Kültepe, 26–30 July 2015* (= Subartu XXXIX), Brepols, Turnhout, pp. 9–27.

Fairbairn, A.S., N. Wright, M. Weeden, G. Barjamovic, K. Matsumura and R. Rasch
- 2019 "Ceremonial plant consumption at Middle Bronze Age Büklükale, Kırıkkale Province, central Turkey," *Vegetation History and Archaeobotany* 28, pp. 327–346.

Glocker, J.
- 1997 *Das Festritual für den Wettergott von Kulliwišna, Textzeugnisse eines lokalen Kultfestes im Anatolien der Hethiterzeit, Eothen 6*, LoGisma, Firenze.

Goedegebuure, P.
- 2008 "Central Anatolian Languages and Language Communities in the Colony Period: A Luwian-Hattian Symbiosis and the Independent Hittites," in J. Dercksen (ed.), *Anatolia and the Jazira During the Old Assyrian Period (PIHANS 111)*, NINO, Leiden, pp. 137–180.

Görke, S.
- 2015 *Ein Palastbauritual (CTH 414.1)* hethiter.net/: CTH 414.1 (ExPl. A, 11.06.2015).

Haas, V.
- 2003 Materia Magica et Medica Hethitica. Ein Beitrag zur Heilkunde im Alten Orient, Berlin – New York

Kabukcu, C. and L. Chabal
- 2020 "Sampling and quantitative analysis methods in anthracology from archaeological contexts: Achievements and prospects," *Quaternary International*, https://doi.org/10.1016/j.quaint.2020.11.004

Kabukcu, C.
- 2018 "Wood charcoal analysis in Archaeology," in E. Pişkin, A. Marciniak and M. Bartkowiak (eds), *Environmental Archaeology: Current Theoretical and Methodological Approaches*, Springer, Cham, pp. 133–154.

Klinger, J.
- 1996 *Untersuchungen zur Rekonstruktion des hattischen Kultschicht*, StBoT 37, Harrassowitz, Wiesbaden.

Kloekhorst, A.
- 2008 *Etymological Dictionary of the Hittite Inherited Lexicon*, Brill, Leiden.

KUB = *Keilschrifturkunden aus Boghazköy*

Litt, T., S. Krastel, M. Sturm, R. Kipfer, S. Örcen, G. Heumann, S.O. Franz, U.B. Ülgen and F. Niessen
- 2009 "Lake van drilling Project "PALEOVAN," International Continental Scientific Drilling Program (ICDP): Results of a Recent Pre-Site Survey and Perspectives," *Quaternary Science Reviews* 28, pp. 1555–1567.

Marston, J.M.
- 2009 "Modelling Wood Acquisition Strategies from Archaeological Charcoal Remains," *Journal of Archaeological Science* 36, pp. 2192–2200.
- 2012 "Agricultural Strategies and Political Economy in Ancient Anatolia," *AJA* 116, pp. 377–403.

Miller, N.F.
– 2010 *Botanical Aspects of Environment and Economy at Gordion*, Turkey, University of Pennsylvania Press, Philadelphia.

Morrison, K.D.
– 2018 "Empires as Ecosystem Engineers: Toward a Nonbinary Political Ecology," *Journal of Anthropological Archaeology* 52, pp. 196–203.

Moskal-del Hoyo, M., M. Wachowiak and R.A. Blanchette
– 2010 "Preservation of Fungi in Archaeological Charcoal," *Journal of Archaeological Science* 37, pp. 2106–2116.

Richardson, D.M.
– 2000 Ecology and biogeography of Pinus, CUP, Cambridge.

Roberts, N., J.M Reed, M.J. Leng, C. Kuzucuoğlu, M. Fontugne, J. Bertaux, H. Woldring, S. Bottema, S. Black, E. Hunt and M. Karabıyıkoğlu
– 2001 "The Tempo of Holocene Climatic Change in the Eastern Mediterranean Region: New High-Resolution Crater-Lake Sediment Data from Central Turkey," *The Holocene* 11, pp. 721–736.

Rosenzweig, M.S.
– 2018 "Assessing the Politics of Neo-Assyrian Agriculture," *Archaeological Papers of the American Anthropological Association* 29, pp. 30–50.

Rosenzweig, M.S. and J.M. Marston
– 2018 "Archaeologies of Empire and Environment," Journal of Anthropological Archaeology 52, pp. 87–102.

Turnbull M.
– 2020 *Pit Storage Technologies and Agricultural Risk Minimisation in Central Anatolia: A Phytolith Analysis of Kaman-Kalehöyük's Bronze and Iron Age Pits*, Unpublished Honours Thesis, The University of Queensland, Brisbane.

Üstünkaya, M.C.
– 2015 *Investigating Climate Related Agricultural Stress Patterns at Bronze and Iron Age Kaman-Kalehöyük: The Integration of Botanical Stable Carbon and Nitrogen Isotope Values, Grain Weight Values, and Seed Analysis*, Unpublished PhD Thesis, The University of Queensland, Brisbane.

Wick, L., G. Lemcke and M. Sturm
– 2003 "Evidence of Late glacial and Holocene climatic change and Human Impact in Eastern Anatolia: High-Resolution Pollen, Charcoal, Isotopic and Geochemical Records from the Laminated Sediments of Lake Van, Turkey," *The Holocene* 13, 665–675.

Woldring, H. and S. Bottema
– 2002 "The Vegetation History of East-Central Anatolia in Relation to Archaeology: The Eski Acigöl Pollen Evidence Compared with the Near Eastern Environment," *Palaeohistoria* 44, 1–34.

Wright, N.J., A.S. Fairbairn, J.T. Faith and K. Matsumura
– 2015 "Woodland Modification in Bronze and Iron Age Central Anatolia: An Anthracological Aignature for the Hittite state?" *Journal of Archaeological Science* 55, pp. 219–230.

Wright, N.J., A.S. Fairbairn, M.C. Üstünkaya and J.T. Faith
– 2017 "Explaining Changing Patterns of Wood Presence Across the Bronze and Iron Age at Kaman-Kalehöyük, Central Anatolia," *Quaternary International* 431, pp. 90–102.

Wright, N.J.
– 2016 "Ancient Woodland and its Management in Central Anatolia: An Anthracological Study of the Bronze and Iron Ages at Kaman-Kalehöyük, Turkey," Unpublished PhD Thesis, The University of Queensland, Brisbane.
– 2017 "Examining Dendrological Features of Oak as Possible Signals of Systematic Woodland Management in the Central Anatolian Bronze and Iron Ages," *Quaternary International* 463, pp. 298–311.

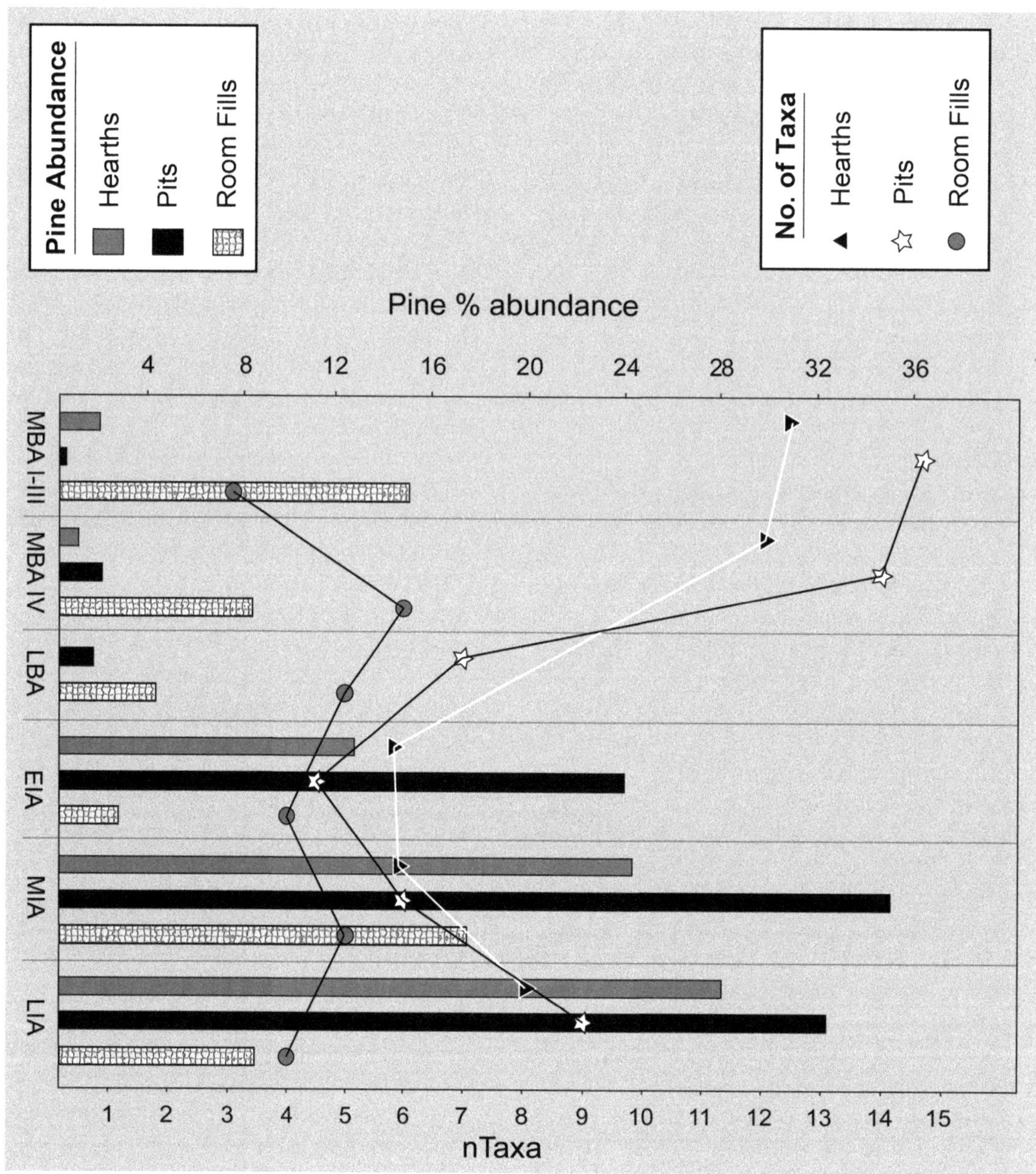

Fig. 1. Variation in wood charcoal data by occupation phase in % pine abundance and the number of taxa (nTaxa) for different depositional contexts at Kaman-Kalehöyük (data in Wright *et al.* 2015).

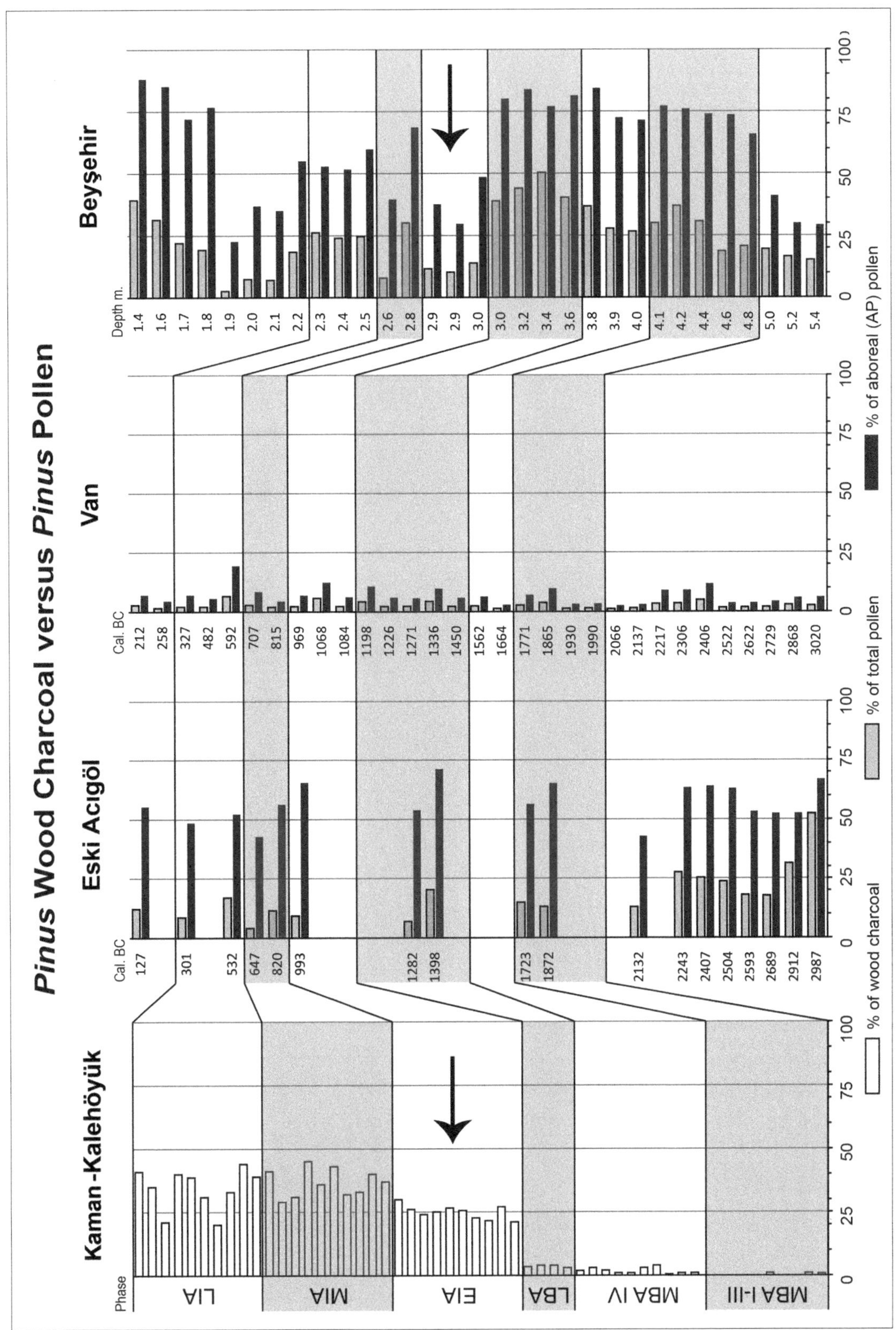

Fig. 2. Kaman pine data compared to BOP, Eski Acıgöl and Lake Van pollen data, with a 'dip' marked with arrows (data derived from: Litt *et al.* 2009, Roberts *et al.* 2001, Wick *et al.* 2003, Woldring and Bottema,2002; Wright 2015).

The Terrace Building at Gordion: An Iron Age Industrial District

*C. Brian Rose**

Abstract

This article summarizes the excavation results of one of Gordion's best preserved and most idiosyncratic structures, the Terrace Building, which was constructed in the late 9th century B.C. The complex featured two long buildings 105 m long that were primarily devoted to textile production and food processing. They rank among the longest in Anatolia, second only to those in the Hittite capital at Hattusa. The most striking material uncovered within them includes a set of horse trappings with ivory frontlets and blinkers, jewelry of electrum, gold, and silver, several bronze animal figurines, and bronze cauldrons. All of these are likely components of diplomatic gift exchange ca. 800 B.C., which was a period of major transition at Gordion. An extensive fire had destroyed many of the buildings, and the monumental fortification walls went out of use during the construction of a new and enlarged citadel.

Öz

Bu makalede Gordion'un en iyi korunmuş ve en kendine has yapılarından biri olan, M.Ö. 9. yüzyılın sonlarına tarihlenen Teras Yapısı'nın kazı sonuçları özetlenmektedir. Yapı esasen tekstil ve yiyecek üretimine ayrılmış 105 metre uzunluğunda iki uzun binadan oluşmaktadır. Hitit başkenti Hattuşa'dakilerin ardından ikinci en uzun binalar olarak Anadolu'nun en uzun binaları arasına girmektedirler. Burada ortaya çıkarılan en çarpıcı malzemeler arasında alın bağları ve göz siperleri fildişinden olan bir at koşum takımı; elektrum, altın ve gümüş takılar, birkaç bronz hayvan figürini ve bronz kazanlar bulunmaktadır. Tüm bunlar Gordion'da büyük bir değişim dönemi olan yaklaşık M.Ö. 800 civarında muhtemel diplomatik hediye takaslarının parçası olmuştur. Geniş çaplı bir yangın binaların birçoğunu yok etmiştir ve yeni ve daha büyük bir şehrin kurulması ile anıtsal sur duvarları kullanım dışı kalmıştır.

Attempting to untie the knots in the chronology of the Anatolian Iron Age has been the focus of most of Sachihiro Omura's scholarly life, especially at the site of Kaman-Kalehöyük. Such an endeavor has never been and never will be straightforward, as the 100-year shift in Gordion's Destruction Level from 700 B.C. to 800 B.C. has amply demonstrated. Nevertheless, we now have a far clearer knowledge of that chronology as a consequence of Prof. Omura's excavations and research at Kaman, which puts all of us who address similar problems in his debt. In this article I offer a synopsis of one of Gordion's best preserved and most idiosyncratic structures, the Terrace Building, since the assemblages uncovered within it have provided such a multi-faceted perspective on industrial activity, especially textile production, in 9th century B.C. central Anatolia.

Gordion received a new wave of immigrants from southeastern Europe in the second half of the twelfth century B.C., as did Troy, and it is these settlers who would eventually be labeled as Phrygians in the Greek literary tradition (DeVries 1990: 371–372, 390–391; Henrickson and Voigt 1998: 101; 2000: 46; Sams 1988; 1994: 8–9; Vassileva 2005; Aslan and Hnila 2015) (Fig. 1). It is not unlikely that the new Thracian arrivals at Gordion crossed at the Bosphorus while those who traveled to Troy moved into Asia via the Dardanelles. They did so, in all likelihood, because the collapse of the Hittite Empire prompted the opening of a commercial corridor stretching from southeastern Europe to central Anatolia, thereby facili-

* Mediterranean Section, Penn Museum, 3260 South St., Philadelphia, PA 19104, USA, roseb@upenn.edu

tating contact between Thrace and Anatolia. New handmade wares appear at both Troy and Gordion at roughly the same time, and there are enough similarities in shape, decoration, and technology to suggest that the migrants were tied to the same cultural traditions of Thrace.[1]

The new Phrygian inhabitants were not prodigious builders from what we can tell, so for the next 250 years, Gordion appears to have been not much more than a village. And then, in the Early Phrygian period, everything changed (Fig. 2). The radiocarbon dates for the transition to Early Phrygian, 912 to 862 B.C., are later than many had suspected, so we need to imagine a scenario in which a monumental citadel was built during the first half of the 9th century, completely reconfigured ca. 850 B.C., and significantly revised again ca. 825 B.C. with the construction of the Terrace Building, which was Gordion's industrial quarter (Kealhofer 2019: 17–18). By 800 B.C., at the time of a major conflagration in and around the Terrace Building, the citadel was being rebuilt on a level approximately 5 m higher than the earlier one (Figs. 3, 4). This is a tremendous amount of construction to have occurred in less than a century, but the radiocarbon dates are clear. Such a high level of activity during such a relatively brief period raises questions about both the power brokers in control of the settlement and about the labor force they commanded, which I address at the end of this section.[2]

Phase 1 of this period (ca. 900–875 B.C.) witnessed the fortification of the citadel and the construction of a monumental gate at the northeast. The latter structure, referred to by Young as the Early Phrygian Building or EPB, was continually modified during four phases of construction lasting less than fifty years (Fig. 5).[3] The initial gate featured a square court, approximately 7.5 m wide, and flanked by towers at north and south (Young 1966: 274–275; Sams 1994: 8). The portal, at least in its initial phase, had a width of 5.20 m, and the unroofed corridor that led to it was probably 45 m long, ultimately connecting to the citadel fortifications at the east.

One new feature was the size of the wall stones: those on either side of the gate passage were built with low blocks of gray sandstone, some of which were 2 m in length (Young 1966: 273; DeVries 1990: 372, Fig. 2). This is a highly unusual measurement for wall stones of any period in antiquity, and they are unique at Gordion. One has the distinct sense that the builders were unfamiliar with monumental stone masonry and were exploring different options as they proceeded. They were clearly, and not surprisingly, concerned about security. The south wall of the gate was 5.40 m thick, and the width of the corridor narrowed as it approached the gate per se, from 9 to 8.5 m.

Around the middle of the 9th century B.C. there was yet another dramatic change in the citadel's topography, even more revolutionary than what had occurred between ca. 875 and 850 B.C. (Fig. 6). Spacious megarons with double-pitched roofs would now occupy a series of walled courts devoted to administration and industry, all of which were protected by massive stone fortifications (Voigt 2013: 186–194; Rose 2017: 137–142). Some of the new roofing systems featured beams over 10 m in length with no internal supports, which is, as far as we know, a more daring feat of engineering than one would have found in roughly contemporary Assyrian palaces, including the Nimrud throne room of Assurnasirpal II (Liebhart 1988). New mortuary customs were introduced as well, with monumental tumuli covering wooden

1 Aydıngün and Aydıngün 2013: 65–78. Handmade pottery occurs also at Daskyleion and Kaman-Kalehöyük (Matsumura 2001; Kealhofer et al 2008). For the handmade pottery from Gordion, see Sams 1994: 19–29.

2 One can get a sense of the energetics associated with such a project by examining the infrastructure of the City Wall reconstruction at Hattusa between 2003 and 2005: Seeher 2007, 211–224.

3 The primary sources for the EPB Gate are Young 1966: 273–275; DeVries 1990: 373–374; Sams 1994: 8–10; Notebooks 143: 126–199; 147: 60–79; 150: 34–96.

tomb chambers that held bronze cauldrons and bowls associated with elite feasting.

The impetus for this radical transformation is unclear, but it certainly looks as if a new power broker had appeared in the region, one who was capable of quickly mobilizing labor and resources for a building campaign unlike anything that Gordion had experienced before. There is no way of determining whether this new configuration was prompted by local/regional initiative or outside intervention, but in later Phrygian tradition, the shift in the city's fortunes was linked to the arrival of an outsider named Gordias or Midas, whose cart featured the legendary Gordian Knot.[4]

The large free-standing megarons derive from LBA western Anatolia, and the tumulus tradition perhaps from the Balkans, but the bronze cauldron attachments and carved stone orthostats are tied to traditions in the Neo-Hittite cities of North Syria.[5] Nevertheless, unlike the North Syrian centers there were no monumental statues of rulers and gods, nor any identifiable temples. In other words, the power broker(s) responsible for the construction of the Early Phrygian citadel chose elements from both east and west while choosing to identify exclusively with neither. As I mentioned earlier, we are not in a position to say whether the brokers in question emerged from the surrounding area or from another region, but the changes in the appearance and character of the site developed in less than a quarter century.[6]

Also unclear is how a sufficient labor force was acquired and trained so quickly. A project of this magnitude would have required leveling, draining, and terracing a massive area. Stone would have to be quarried, timber would have to be felled, and both would have to be transported to the Citadel Mound where masons and carpenters would prepare the materials for use. The mudbrick fabrication industry would have been yet another component. The number of bricks needed cannot, of course, be determined, but Altan Çilingiroğlu has estimated that a minimum of 8 million would have been required to build the citadel of Urartian Ayanis (Çilingiroğlu 2013: 84). The water supply would have been yet another obstacle to construction in that there were no wells on the Citadel Mound, and the Sakarya River lay at least 130 m to the east. Water from the river must have been carried to the citadel whenever it was needed, which would have made the construction process even more complicated (Young 1964: 286; Marsh 2012).

The Terrace Phase: 825–800 B.C.

During the late 9th century, ca. 825–800 B.C., yet another major building campaign on the citadel occurred, one that again involved the transport of enormous quantities of stone to the citadel and entailed the complete reconfiguration of the area to the west of the Inner and Outer Courts (Fig. 7).[7] This zone would now become the Terrace Building Complex, which featured two long buildings 105 m long that were primarily devoted to textile production and food processing (Fig. 8).[8] Rodney S. Young excavated nearly all of the building on the northeast side, simply referred to as the Terrace Building, which features eight adjoining megarons numbered from south to north, so TB-1 is the furthest to the south and TB-8 at the north-

4 The sources are collected in Roller 1984.

5 Megarons: Warner 1979; tumuli: Agre 2016; orthostats: Sams 1989; cauldron attachments: Young et al 1981. For further discussion of the origins of the tumulus type, see Rose 2017, 171–72. The use of wooden beams in stone foundations is a standard feature of Gordion's architecture during the 9th and 8th centuries B.C., but such a technique was used at sites both East and West during the Late Bronze and Early Iron Age: at Troy, Hattusa, and in North Syria (Karatepe-Arslantaş; Ugarit): Naumann 1971, 86–87; Özyar 2013, 124–125.

6 For Urartu, see Çilingiroğlu 2013.

7 Terrace Building: Young 1960: 240–242; Young 1966: 269–272; Young 1968: 238–241; DeVries 1990: 374–77.

8 DeVries 1990: 385–86; Burke 2005: 71, Fig. 6–2; Holzman 2019. In one of the CC (Clay-Cut) Terrace Buildings, the sifted barley found on the floor was probably intended for beer production (DeVries 1990: 386).

ern end. On the other side of a 23 m wide court is a parallel building with a seemingly identical plan, although only three of the units have been excavated. This is traditionally called the CC (or Clay-Cut) Building, and Young plausibly assumed that it too contained eight adjacent megarons, for a total of 16.

We can therefore conclude that at some point in or around 825 B.C., a decision was reached to organize the citadel's food and textile production more systematically, which meant that the spaces in which those activities occurred needed to be reconfigured. As they had done in the past, the rulers of Gordion chose to proceed with a monumental complex of workshops that would rank among the longest in Anatolia, second only to those in the Hittite capital at Hattusa. The footprint occupied by the new complex was over 140 × 90 m, and its elevation 1–2 m above the Inner and Outer Courts at the east endowed it with even greater prominence. Creating a terrace of this magnitude required the transport and deposition of enormous quantities of stone rubble: at least 2 m were deposited over the now abandoned Megarons 7 and 8, and nearly 4 m was set below TB-6, a slice of which was discovered during the sondage there in 2014 (Rose 2017: 154–157) (Fig. 9). In other words, the ground level on this side of the mound appears to have been very uneven prior to the new construction.

One would expect that such extensive deposits of stone must have been robbed from earlier buildings, but they evince no finished surfaces, so they must have been quarried especially for the terrace construction. Many of them clearly came from the limestone deposits at Kızlarkayası, 5 m away from Gordion, which would have entailed an especially large infrastructure. Carts would have been needed to transport the rubble, trees needed to be felled to supply the timber for the roofs, a variety of metal objects such as nails, shovels, and axes would have to be produced, as well as spinning frames for the rope, and the list goes on. By this point Gordion was no stranger to such massive construction projects, and both labor and equipment may well have been easy to mobilize, but the scope of work, even for 9th century Gordion, is striking.

Unlike the megarons, each of the Terrace Building units was identical in size, with the interior space of each unit (vestibule and main room) measuring 21 × 11.50 m, which made them slightly larger than most of the megarons. The 1.30 m thick walls were bedded on wooden beams and featured masonry faces with rubble filling. The length of each building is close to twice its width, so each group of two represents a nearly perfect square, and the interior encompasses approximately the same space as the megarons at Mycenae, Pylos, and Tiryns. Each of the units shared a party wall with its neighbors, although there was no secondary access within the units; each was treated as an independent building. The back walls of units 2, 4, 6, and 8 project .30-.35 m beyond those of its neighbors, thereby providing greater stability to an extraordinarily long wall, but each of the walls is bonded to the others. The walls are of red, grey, and white stone covered with plaster, so there was no attempt to exploit the color of the stone as in the nearby and nearly contemporary Polychrome Gate House (Notebook 100: 160).

All of the units featured a horseshoe-like arrangement of evenly spaced interior supports for both the upper galleries and the roof, and nearly all featured a hearth in the main room that was between 1 m and 1.5 m in diameter (Fig. 8). The width of the gallery was 2.5 m, supported by four posts on each side and a single one at the back of the main room; most of these measure .12 by .20 m, although the corner posts were larger and L-shaped, and the column at the back was also often larger in size.

There is no evidence that would indicate how the buildings were roofed. Certainly most if not all of the megarons in the Outer and Inner Courts has double pitched roofs, and the same type of roofs have been restored on the units of the Terrace Building in the Early Phrygian model prepared by Gareth Darbyshire and Christopher Ray (Darbyshire and Ray 2014) (Fig. 10). There is no evidence for such double-pitched roofs in Mycenaean Greece or in LBA Anatolia, but architectural drawings on stone dated to ca. 850 B.C. and excavated in Gordion's Outer Court do feature double-pitched roofs, so those at Gordion may be the earliest so far attested (Roller 2009, 54–57, nos. 9a, b). If such roofs were in fact used, then we need to reconstruct a gutter between each of them, undoubtedly made of wood, which would have channeled the water into the wide court separating the two lines of buildings. It would then have traveled to the west side, which was lower in elevation, and would then presumably have been evacuated in the low-lying area between the eastern and western mounds (Rose 2017: 138, 171).

The proposed wooden gutters would not have survived the fire, of course, and very little of the area between the two lines of buildings has been excavated; Young dug only the area between TB-5 and CC-1. The water systems therefore cannot yet be reconstructed, and neither can the roofs with any certainty. Nevertheless, the benefits of double-pitched roofs with regard to water control would have been clear from the buildings in the Outer and Inner Courts, and it is difficult to believe that the technique would not have been repeated in later monumental construction.

Nearly all of the units of the Terrace Building Complex were similarly equipped, with a grinding stand and multiple grinding stones against the back of the main room (Fig. 11). Positioned around the three sides of the main room were large numbers of vessels for cooking and the storage of liquids, some of which had clearly fallen from the galleries at the time of the fire. Judging by the find spots of the weaving equipment, it looks as if textile production occurred in both the main room and anteroom of most units.

The two exceptions to this pattern of organization are units 1 and 2, where excavation yielded jewelry of electrum, gold, and silver, as well as bronze figurines, ivory horse fittings, and at least five bronze cauldrons, one of which featured bull protomes (DeVries 1980: 38–39; Young 1962: 166–67). Such assemblages would be more appropriate for treasure houses than workshops, which suggests that the function of this area may have been more multi-faceted that one might have expected.

All of these objects were in use or in storage at the time of the fire, and there is no evidence of foraging for valuables in any of the units after the ashes had cooled, as there was in Megaron 4, nor for any disturbance of the destruction deposits. There is also no indication that anyone died in the fire, even though the units were clearly in operation when it occurred; the cause of the fire, in fact, is likely to have been an oven or hearth in the Terrace Building judging by the areas that were burned. If Keith DeVries was right in his estimation of as many as 300 workers in the complex during an average workday, then the question arises as to how all of them could have been quickly evacuated at the time of the fire in 800 B.C.

Some would certainly have been able to exit via the portals at the south and north, but since both appear to have been built with crowd control in mind, large numbers of people could not have used them for escape. One can only conclude that there must have been at least one and probably more exits from the Terrace complex, most likely located at the west and leading into the inter-mound area, which is only now beginning to be understood (Rose 2017: 171).

There is one additional issue that has never been addressed: with approximately 300 people working simultaneously, there would have been a need for latrines somewhere in the area, and they must have been in close proximity to the units themselves so that the flow of work was not disrupted. The presence of chamber pots in the units is unlikely given the high level of food preparation in both main room and anteroom, so the location must have been exterior. Moreover, the ground level in the complex slopes down from north to south, toward the CC buildings, which lay above a significant depression in the center of the mound.

We should consequently except a latrine-like facility somewhere in the CC area, probably coupled with some sort of drainage system, although any rainfall would have cleaned the area due to the sloping ground. There was also undoubtedly some provision for collecting and reusing the urine, since it surely would have been used in the textile dying process. It is also worth remembering that a latrine lay directly in front of the EPB citadel gate ca. 850 B.C., which is the last place one would have expected it to be (Sams 1994: 9).

Terrace Building 2

Most of the Terrace Buildings featured cooking and weaving facilities, but not all were identical. Both TB-1 and the adjacent unit TB-2 lacked any traces of ovens or mudbrick platforms, so food processing and cooking were not among the activities carried out here (Young 1962: 165–167; Notebook 70: 131–132; NB89: 166–196; NB100: 59–74, 91–94). Nevertheless, there were nearly 600 loomweights in TB-2: 500 in the main room and 87 in the anteroom, so the storage of weaving components was one of the TB-1's main functions at the time of the fire. Twenty of the weights were discovered in two lines along the eastern side of the anteroom, and were once no doubt attached to a warp weighted loom in this area (Voigt 1994: 272). Nearby was a long-toothed wooden comb with unwoven warp threads on one side and woven textile on the other (Voigt 1994: 272 (SF 89–583); Burke 2010: 132–133). First name? Burke has suggested that its narrow width of 6 cm would have made it suitable for the production of small decorated bands, which reminds one of the frequent references to "garments of multi-colored trim" in the descriptions of Assurnasirpal II's war booty from Syria (Grayson 1976: 122–142).

Those colors would have been applied with plant as well as mineral pigments, as in the goethite-dyed textiles from the Tumulus MM tomb chamber, or the ornamented trim of King Warpalawa's tunic and cloak at Ivriz, and it is noteworthy that Mary Voigt discovered a jar of such pigments in the TB-2 anteroom.[9] Among the other commodities stored in the anteroom were seeds in jars, including barley, wheat, lentils, bitter vetch, and flax (Holzman 2019: 531). The latter commodity is especially noteworthy given the extensive evidence for weaving in this complex.

The main room of TB-2 was even richer in discoveries, both in terms of type and material, especially by comparison to those in the other units of the complex. Lying on the floor, having fallen from the gallery, was a bronze object with a short handle attached to a circular plate 0.21 m in diameter (Notebook 89: 189; B1443). It was called a "saucepan" at the time of excavation, although it is surely one of the "bronze casseroles" that figure so prominently in descriptions of booty in the Assyrian annals. Assurnasirpal II received 100 bronze casseroles in tribute from Bit-Zamani, near modern Diyarbakır, and Karkemish sent as many as a thousand of them to Shalmanesar III (859–824 B.C.) as part of their tribute (Grayson 1991: 211). These were high status vessels that were used in feasts, many of which no doubt formed part of the triumphal celebrations that were tied to such booty.

The most unique assemblage within the room lay in the northeast sector, where excavation yielded a range of objects in gold, silver, electrum, and ivory, including jewelry and horse trappings, as well as seven large spherical glass beads (G267 a–b) that were found with a set of bronze tweezers (B1336). A miniature silver fibula (J132) occupied the same group (Notebook 89: 190–191).

In the middle of the back (north) wall were six bronze animal figurines, varying in height from 6–9 cm, that were likely stored in a cloth bag that had been set within a bronze cauldron (Vassileva 2012), The figurines include a wild sheep or mouflon (B1328); an animal on a plinth, perhaps a deer (B1327); a bridled animal, perhaps a horse (B1329); two double headed horses on a single plinth (B1326a); two horse heads similar to the previous example (B1326b); a goat or mouflon (B1330); and a silver bird (ILS 332).

9 Ballard 2012 (goethite); Holzman 2019: 528, 544, Fig. 11 (Warpalawa); Voigt 1994: 272 (pigments).

The most striking material involves a set of horse trappings that included iron snaffle bits and ivory frontlets and blinkers (Fig. 12). All of these were discovered near the northeast corner, along the east wall, and therefore in close proximity to the bronze animal figurines, the glass beads, and the gold.

It is worth considering what the nature of this elite assemblage can tell us about Gordion's relations with other areas of Anatolia at the end of the 9th century B.C. Phoebe Sheftel and Irene Winter have argued persuasively that the style and iconography of the ivory horse gear point to North Syria as the site of production, and very likely Karkemish.[10] The parallels for the fibulae, however, come primarily from western Anatolia, especially Lydia, and the source of the electrum is almost certainly the Pactolus River (Young *et al* 1981: 243, 247; Caner 1983: 41-42, 52). More difficult to analyze are the bronze animal figurines, which have been linked at different times to western Iran (Luristan), North Syria, and Thrace (Vassileva 2012).

In any event, all of the above are likely components of diplomatic gift exchange ca. 800 B.C., perhaps stored here at the outset of the "Unfinished Project" that would lead to the construction of the Middle Phrygian citadel (Voigt 2012). In a state as complex and powerful as Phrygia, gift exchange would undoubtedly have been a standard feature of political life throughout the 9th and 8th centuries B.C. But around 800 B.C. the practice would have become increasingly important, in that Gordion's imposing citadel walls that had offered such security went out of use during the construction of the new and enlarged citadel. Securing and maintaining peaceful relations with other Anatolian powers would have been more essential than ever before, and Gordion's conferral of gifts on those states would have prompted reciprocal gifts, some of which may be represented by the elite assemblage in TB-2.

10 These are discussed in full in chapter 3a of Phoebe Sheftel's 2023 manuscript on the ivories from Gordion.

All of this evidence, when viewed together, yields an unusually nuanced portrait of life in the complex. Grain was brought into the building for grinding and sieving and then transported to the ovens in the anterooms. At the same time, beer may have been brewing and fermenting in both rooms, as large animals were being prepared for butchery (McGovern 2009: 111–114). It seems logical to assume that the animals were slaughtered in another location and then brought into the TB-units. With so much space allotted to textile and food preparation, there was limited space for animal processing, and a recalcitrant victim could easily have upset the adjacent activities, not to mention the profusion of blood that would need to be regularly washed away.

During the periods in which the food was baking, which could require a lengthy period, the workers could turn to spinning and weaving so that no time would be wasted, although it is also conceivable that there were separate teams specializing in each activity, as in the Hittite kingdom (Hoffner 1974; Pecchioli 1982; Beccelli *et al* 2014; Vigo 2018). Since water had to be carried into the complex from the rivers, a steady stream of workers must have focused on that task to ensure a consistent supply, while others would have tended the fires in the hearths and ovens with wood and chaff.

The range of smells must have been particularly rich, with a mixture of wheat, barley, beer, wool, raw and roasting meat, and burning wood perpetually in the air, while the voices of approximately 25 workers would have echoed in the high-roofed halls.[11] Supervisors must have monitored the raw material that entered each unit as well as the finished products that emerged from it, as other administrators distributed those products to targeted areas of the settlement, which surely included the citadel's megarons. We look forward to the excavation of similar industrial complexes, especially at Kaman, in the hope that we can further clarify the networks of central Anatolian food and textile production during the Iron Age.

11 The number derives from DeVries 1980: 40.

Bibliography

Agre, D.
- 2016 "On the Untraditional Use of Mounds in Thrace During the Late Iron Age," in O. Henry and U. Kelp (eds.), *Tumulus as Sema: Space, Politics, Culture and Religion in the First Millennium B.C.*, Berlin, pp. 233–242.

Aslan, C. C. and P. Hnila
- 2015 "Migration and Integration at Troy from the End of the Late Bronze Age to the Iron Age," in N. Stampolidis, Ç. Maner, and K. Kopanias (eds.), *NOSTOI: Indigenous Culture, Migration and Integration in the Aegean Islands and Western Anatolia during the Late Bronze and Early Iron Ages*, Istanbul, pp. 185–209.

Aydıngün, Ş. and H. Aydıngün
- 2013 "Erken Demirçağ'da "İstanbul Boğazı" Üzerin Trak/Frig Kavimlerinin Anadolu'ya Geçişine Ait İlk Bulgular," *Arkeoloji ve Sanat* 142, pp. 65–78.

Baccelli, G., B. Bellucci, and M. Vigo
- 2014 "Elements for a Comparative Study of Textile Production and Use in Hittite Anatolia and in Neighboring Areas," in: M. Harlow, C. Michel and M. L. Nosch (eds.), *Prehistoric, Ancient Near Eastern and Aegean Textiles and Dress. An Interdisciplinary Anthology*, Oxford – Philadelphia, pp. 97–141.

Ballard, M., B. Burke, and E. Simpson
- 2012 "Gordion Textiles," in T. Sivas and H. Sivas (eds.), *Phrygians: In the Land of Midas, In the Shadow of Monuments (Frigler: Midas'ın ülkesinde, anıtların gölgesinde)*, Istanbul, pp. 360–375.

Burke, B.
- 2005 "Textile production at Gordion and the Phrygian economy," in L. Kealhofer (ed.) *The Archaeology of Midas and the Phrygians*, Philadelphia, pp. 69–81.
- 2010 *From Minos to Midas: Ancient Cloth Production in the Aegean and in Anatolia*, Oxford and Oakville.

Caner, E.
- 1983 *Fibeln in Anatolien* I. Prähistorische Bronzefunde XIV 8, München.

Çilingiroğlu, A.
- 2013 "The Urartian City and Citadel of Ayanis: An Example of Interdependence," in S. Redford and N. Ergin (eds.), *Cities and Citadels in Turkey: From the Iron Age to the Selcuks*, Leuven, pp. 81–96.

Darbyshire, G., and C. Ray
- 2014 "Modelling Gordion's Citadel," *Expedition* 56, pp. 22–23.

DeVries, K.
- 1980 "Greeks and Phrygians in the Early Iron Age," in K. DeVries (ed.) *From Athens to Gordion: The Papers of a Memorial Symposium for Rodney S. Young*, Philadelphia, pp. 33–50.
- 1990 "The Gordion Excavation Seasons of 1969–1973 and Subsequent Research," *AJA* 94, pp. 371–406.

Grayson, A. K.
- 1976 *Assyrian Rulers of the Early First Millennium B.C. (1114–859 B.C.*,. Toronto.

Henrickson, R. and M. M. Voigt
- 1998 "The Early Iron Age at Gordion: The Evidence from the Yassıhöyük Stratigraphic Sequence," in N. Tuna, Z. Aktüre, and M. Lynch (eds.), *Thracians and Phrygians: Problems of Parallelism. Proceedings of an International Symposium on the Archaeology, History, and Ancient Languages of Thrace and Phrygia, Ankara, 3–4 June 1995*, Ankara, pp. 79–106.

Hoffner H. A.
- 1974 *Alimenta Hethaeorum. Food Production in Hittite Asia Minor* (AOS 55), New Haven.

Holzman, S.
- 2019 "A Patterned Textile from Phrygian Gordian and its Relation to 9th-Century Painted Pottery and Mosaics," *Hesperia* 88.3, pp. 527–556.

Kealhofer, L., P. Grave, B. Marsh and K. Matsumura
- 2008 "Analysis of Specialized Iron Age Wares at Kaman-Kalehöyük," *Anatolian Archaeological Studies* XVII, pp. 201–224.

Kealhofer, L., P. Grave, and M. M. Voigt
- 2019 "Dating Gordion: the Timing and Tempo of Late Bronze and Early Iron Age political Transformation," *Radiocarbon* 61.2, pp. 495–514.

Liebhart, R. F.
- 1988 *Timber Roofing Spans in Greek and Near Eastern Monumental Architecture during the Early Iron Age*, Ph.D. thesis, University of North Carolina – Chapel Hill.

Marsh, B.
- 2012 "Reading Gordion Settlement History from Stream Sedimentation," in *The Archaeology of Phrygian Gordion, Royal City of Midas*, ed. C. B. Rose, Philadelphia, pp. 39–46.

Matsumura, K.
- 2001 "On the Manufacturing Techniques of Iron Age Ceramics from Kaman-Kalehöyük (II); The Cultural Influence of Phrygia at Kaman-Kalehöyük," *Anatolian Archaeological Studies* X, pp. 101–110.

McGovern, P.
- 2009 *Uncorking the Past: The Quest for Wine, Beer, and Other Alcoholic Beverages*, Berkeley.

Pecchioli D. F.
- 1982 *Mestieri, professioni e dignità nell'Anatolia ittita*, (Incunabula Graeca 79), Rome.

Naumann, R.
- 1971 *Architektur Kleinasiens von ihren Anfängen bis zum Ende der hethitischen Zeit*, Tübingen.

Özyar, A.
- 2013 The Writing on the Wall: Reviewing Sculpture and Inscriptions on the Gates of the Iron Age Citadel of Azatiwataya (Karatepe-Aslantaş), in S. Redford and N. Ergin (ed.), *Cities and Citadels in Turkey: From the Iron Age to the Selcuks*, Leuven, pp. 115–135.

Roller, L. E.
- 1984 "Midas and the Gordian Knot," *ClAnt* 3, pp. 256–271.
- 2009 *The Incised Drawings from Early Phrygian Gordion*. Gordion Special Studies 4, Philadelphia.

Rose, C. B.
- 2017 "Fieldwork at Phrygian Gordion, 2013–2015," *AJA* 121, pp. 135–178.
- 2021 "Midas, Matar, and Homer at Gordion and Midas City," *Hesperia* 90.1.

Sams, G. K.
- 1988 "The Early Phrygian Period at Gordion: Toward a Cultural Identity," in ed. O. W. Muscarella (ed.), *Phrygian Art and Archaeology*, special issue of *Source: Notes in the History of Art* VII, New York, pp. 9–15.

Sams, G. K.
- 1989 "Sculpted Orthostates at Gordion," in K. Emre, M. J. Mellink, B. Hrouda and N. Özgüç (eds.) *Anatolia and the Ancient Near East: Studies in Honor of Tahsin Özgüç*, Ankara, pp. 447–454.
- 1994 *The Gordion Excavations, 1950–1973: Final Reports, Vol. IV: The Early Phrygian Pottery*, Philadelphia.

Seeher, J.
- 2007 *A Mudbrick City Wall at Hattusa. Diary of a Reconstruction*, Istanbul.

Sheftel, P.
- 2023 *The Bone and Ivory Objects from Gordion*, Philadelphia.

Vassileva, M.
- 2012 "Bronze Animal Figurines from Gordion," in: *Anatolian Iron Ages 7: the proceedings of the Seventh Anatolian Iron Age Colloquium held at Edirne, 19–24 April 2010.* Ancient Near Eastern Studies. Supplement (39), Leuven, pp. 317–332.

Vigo, M.
- 2018. "On the Terminology of Some (Job) Titles in Hittite Texts," *AOAT* 440, pp. 271–314.

Voigt, M. M.
- 1994 "Excavations at Gordion 1988–89: The Yassıhöyük Stratigraphic Sequence," in A. Çilingiroğlu and D. H. French (eds.), *Anatolian Iron Ages 3: The Proceedings of the Third Anatolian Iron Ages Colloquium held at Van, 6–12 August 1990,* Ankara, pp. 265–293.
- 2012 "The Unfinished Project of the Gordion Early Phrygian Destruction Level," in C. B. Rose (ed.) *The Archaeology of Phrygian Gordion, Royal City of Midas*, Philadelphia, pp. 67–100.
- 2013 "Gordion as Citadel and City," in S. Redford and N. Ergin (eds.), *Cities and Citadels in Turkey: From the Iron Age to the Seljuks*, Leuven, pp. 161–228.

Voigt, M. M., and R. C. Henrickson
- 2000. "Formation of the Phrygian State: The Early Iron Age at Gordion," *Anatolian Studies* 50, pp. 37–54.

Warner, J.
- 1979 "The Megaron and Apsidal house in Early Bronze Age Western Anatolia: New Evidence from Karataş," *AJA*, *83*(2), pp. 369–385.

Young, R. S.
- 1960 "Gordion campaign of 1959: Preliminary report," *AJA* 64, pp. 227–244.
- 1962 "The 1961 Campaign at Gordion," *AJA* 66, pp. 53–168.
- 1964 "The 1963 Campaign at Gordion," *AJA* 68, pp. 279–292.
- 1966 "The Gordion Campaign of 1965," *AJA* 70, pp. 267–278.
- 1981 *Gordion Excavations Reports, Vol. I: Three Great Early Tumuli*, Philadelphia.

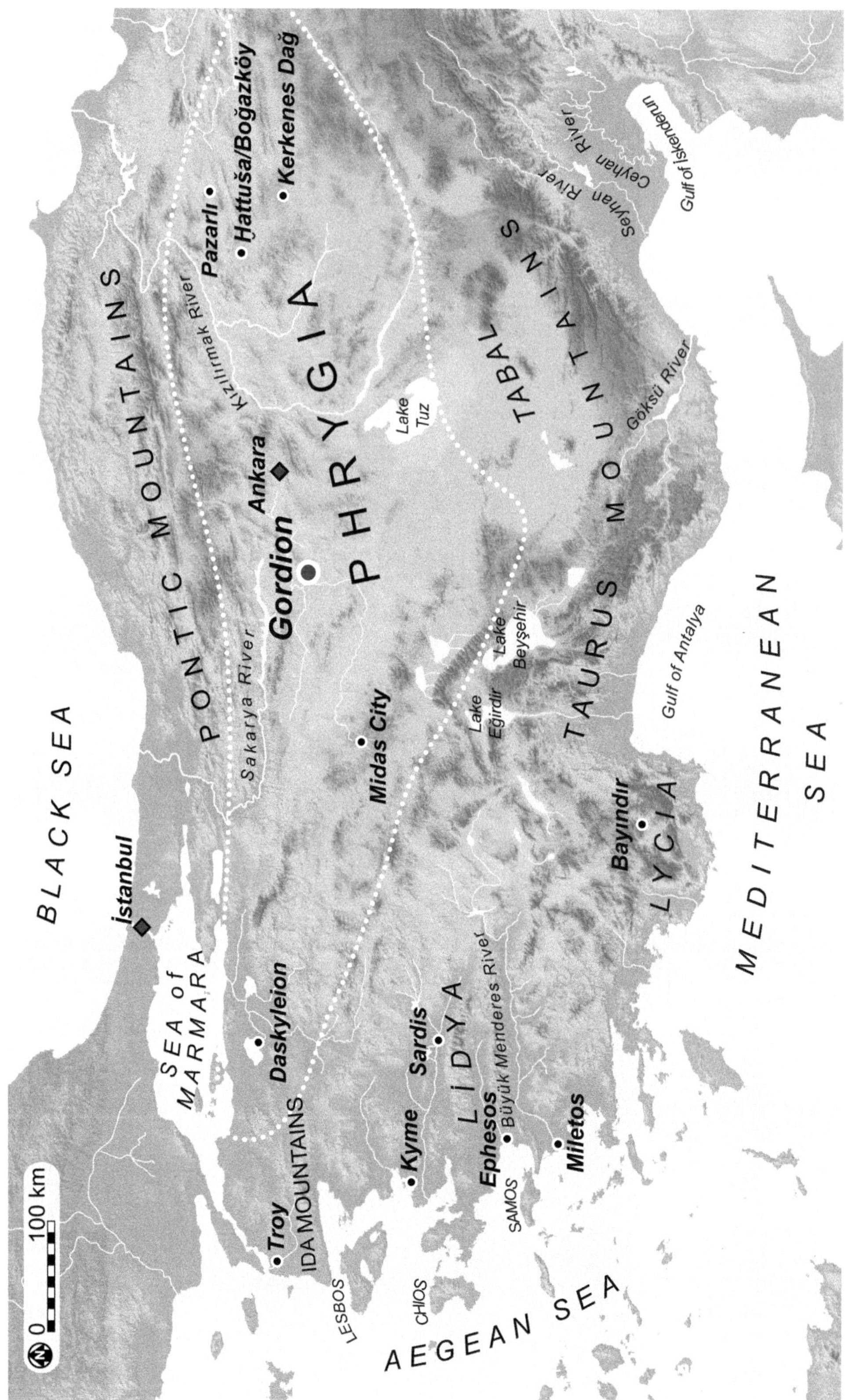

Fig: 1. Map of Anatolia with a reconstruction of the area under Phrygian control during the 8th century B.C. G. Darbyshire, A. Anderson and G. Pizzorno; courtesy Penn Museum, Gordion Project Archives.

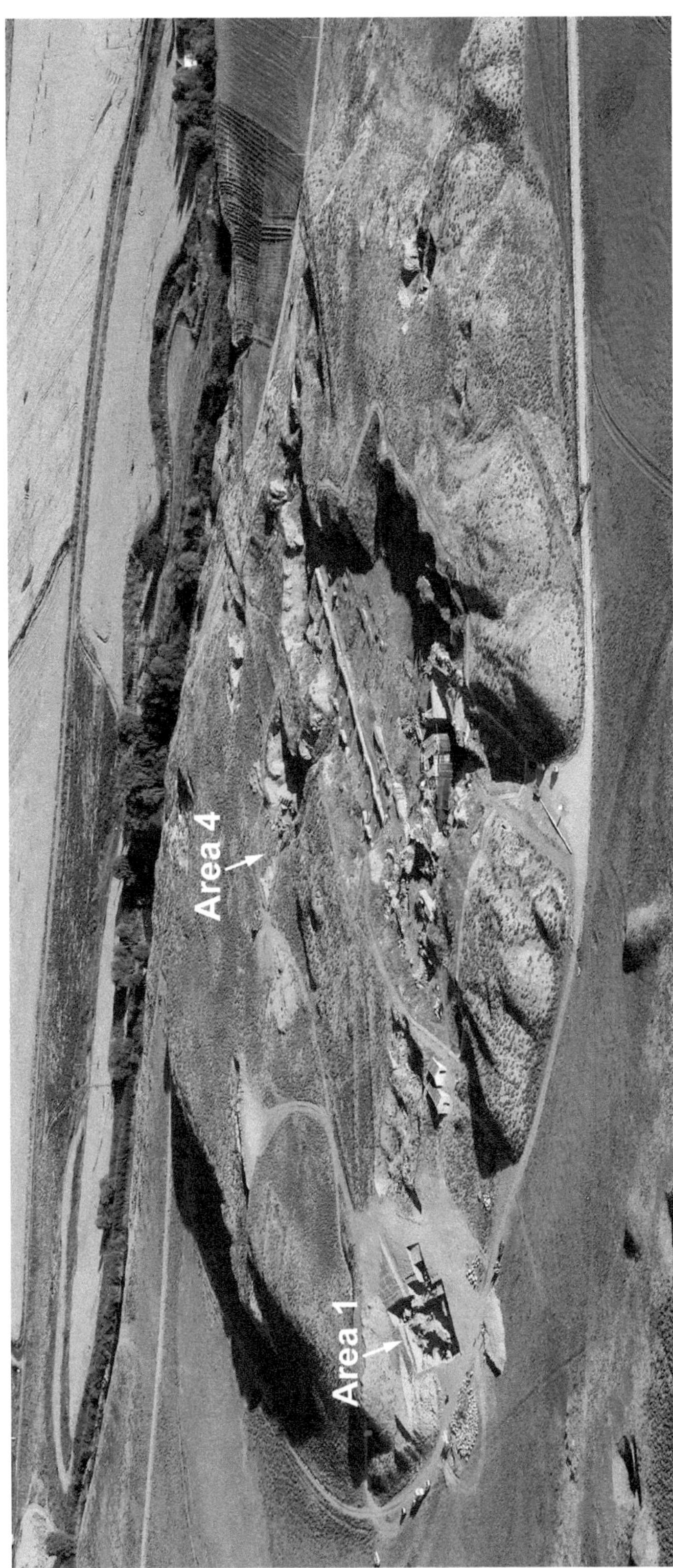

Fig: 2. Aerial view of Gordion's citadel, from east. The Sakarya River (modern course) is visible immediately beyond the Citadel Mound. Courtesy Penn Museum, Gordion Project Archives.

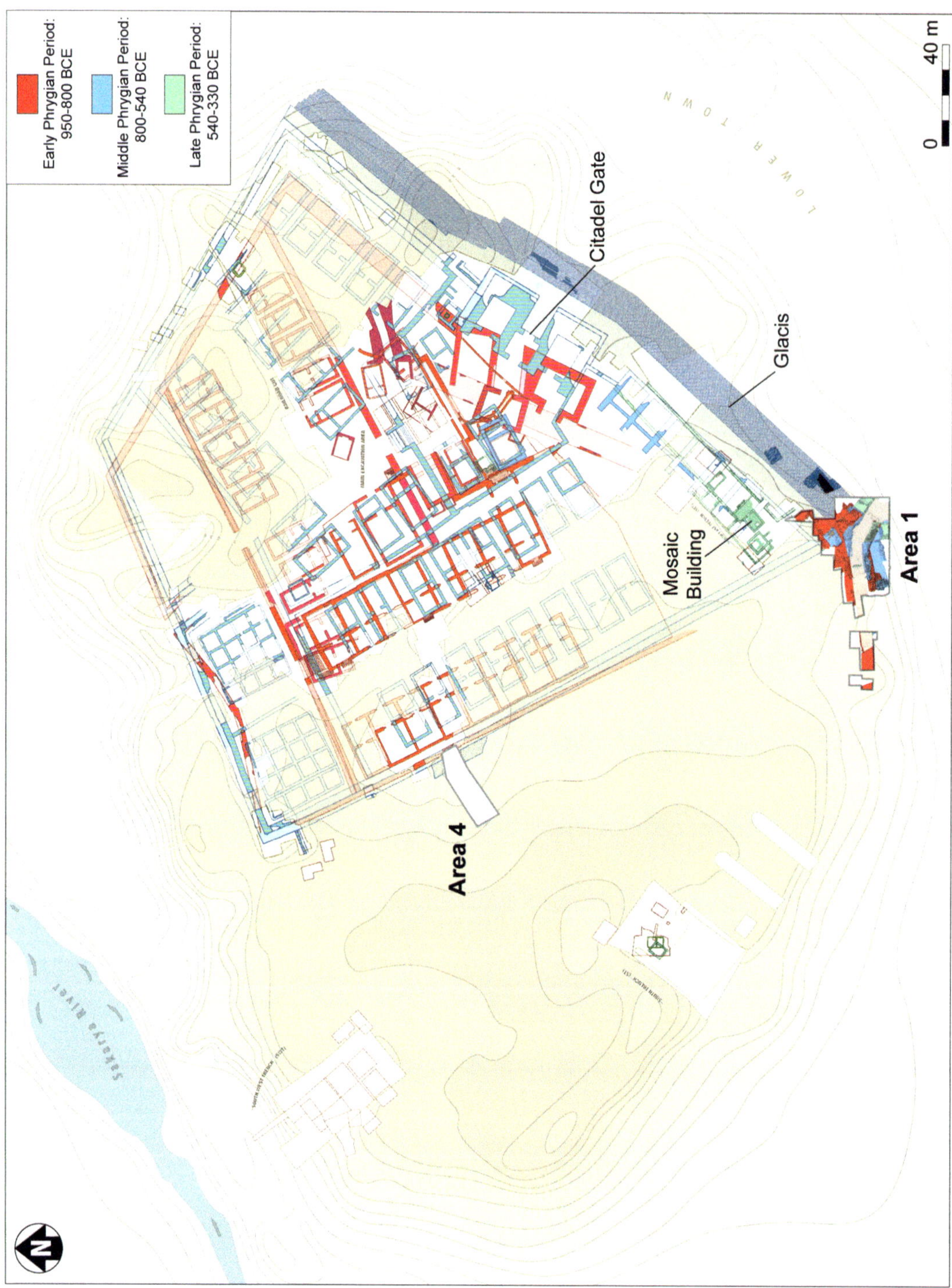

Fig: 3. Plan of the Citadel Mound at Gordion showing the Early, Middle, and Late Phrygian phases of habitation. The Sakarya River appears in its current position at upper left. G. Darbyshire, A. Anderson and G. Pizzorno; courtesy Penn Museum, Gordion Project Archives.

Fig: 4. Aerial view of the Terrace Building Complex at Gordion, looking northwest. Photo by Giese and Huebner, Inc.; courtesy Penn Museum, Gordion Project Archives, image no. 13-GGH-5948.

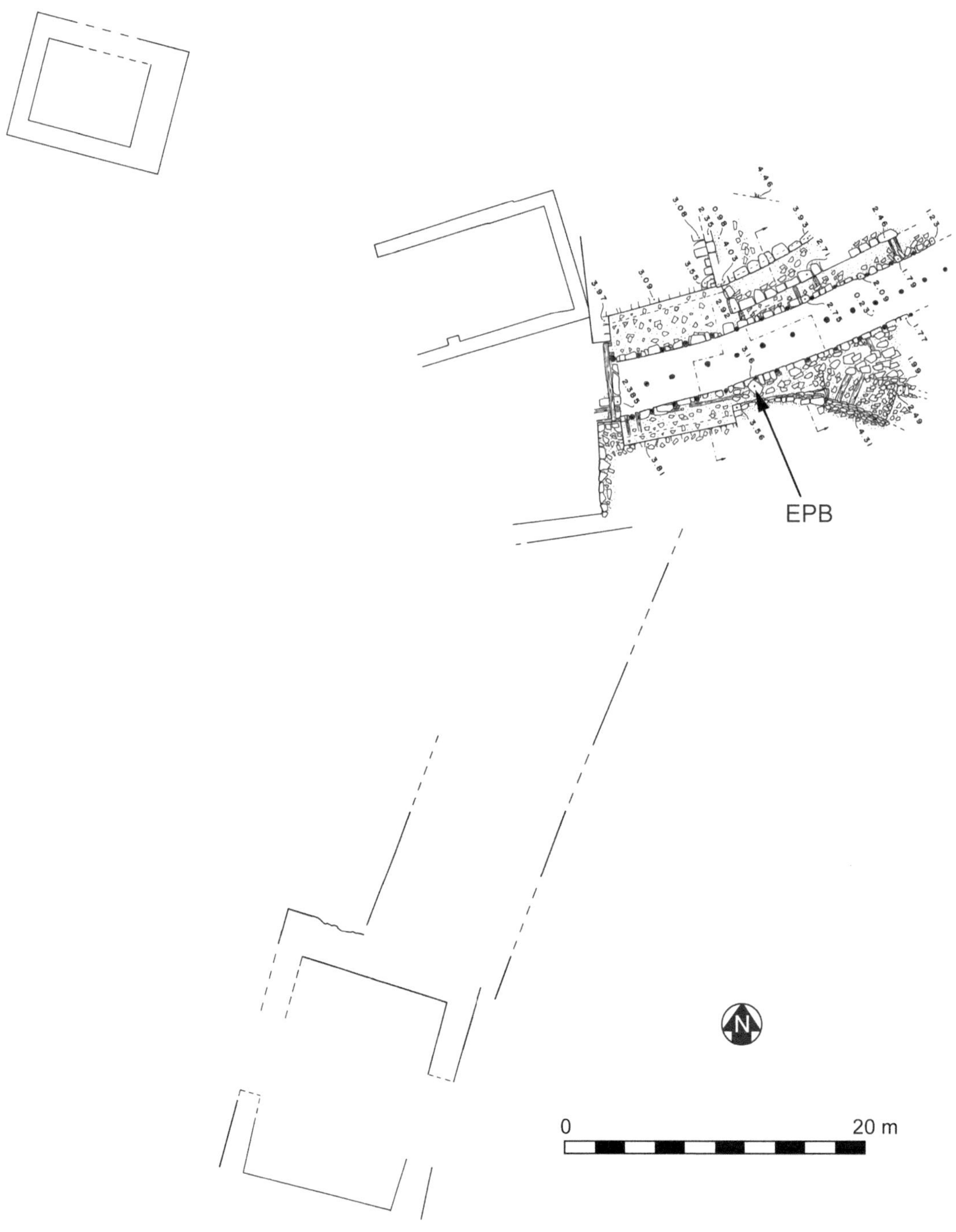

Fig: 5. Plan of the Early Phrygian Building (EPB), ca. 875 B.C.
Courtesy Penn Museum, Gordion Project Archives, image no. 1969-18 / 100510.

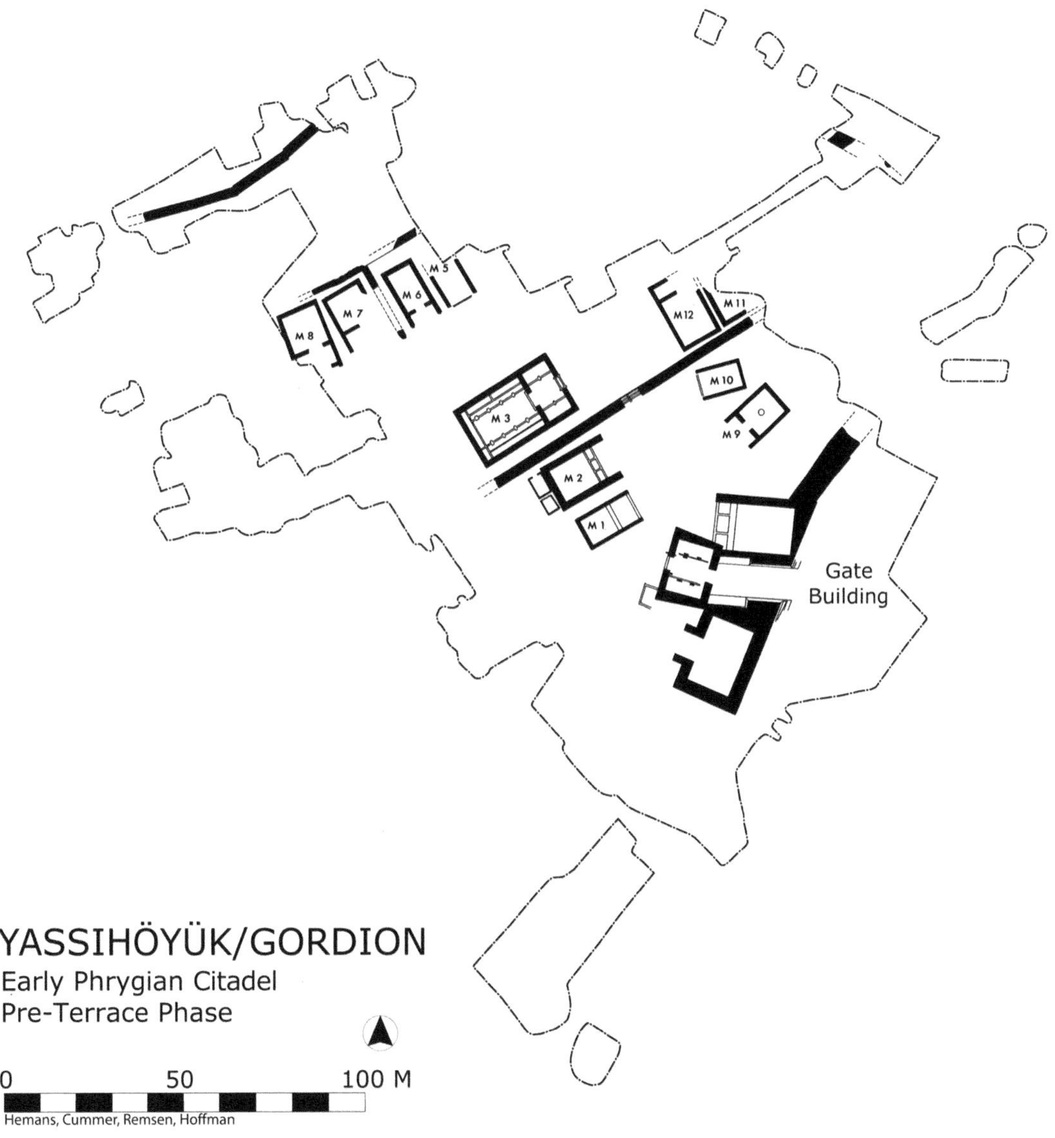

Fig: 6. Plan of Early Phrygian Gordion, ca. 850 B.C.
Courtesy Penn Museum, Gordion Project Archives, image no. 141167.

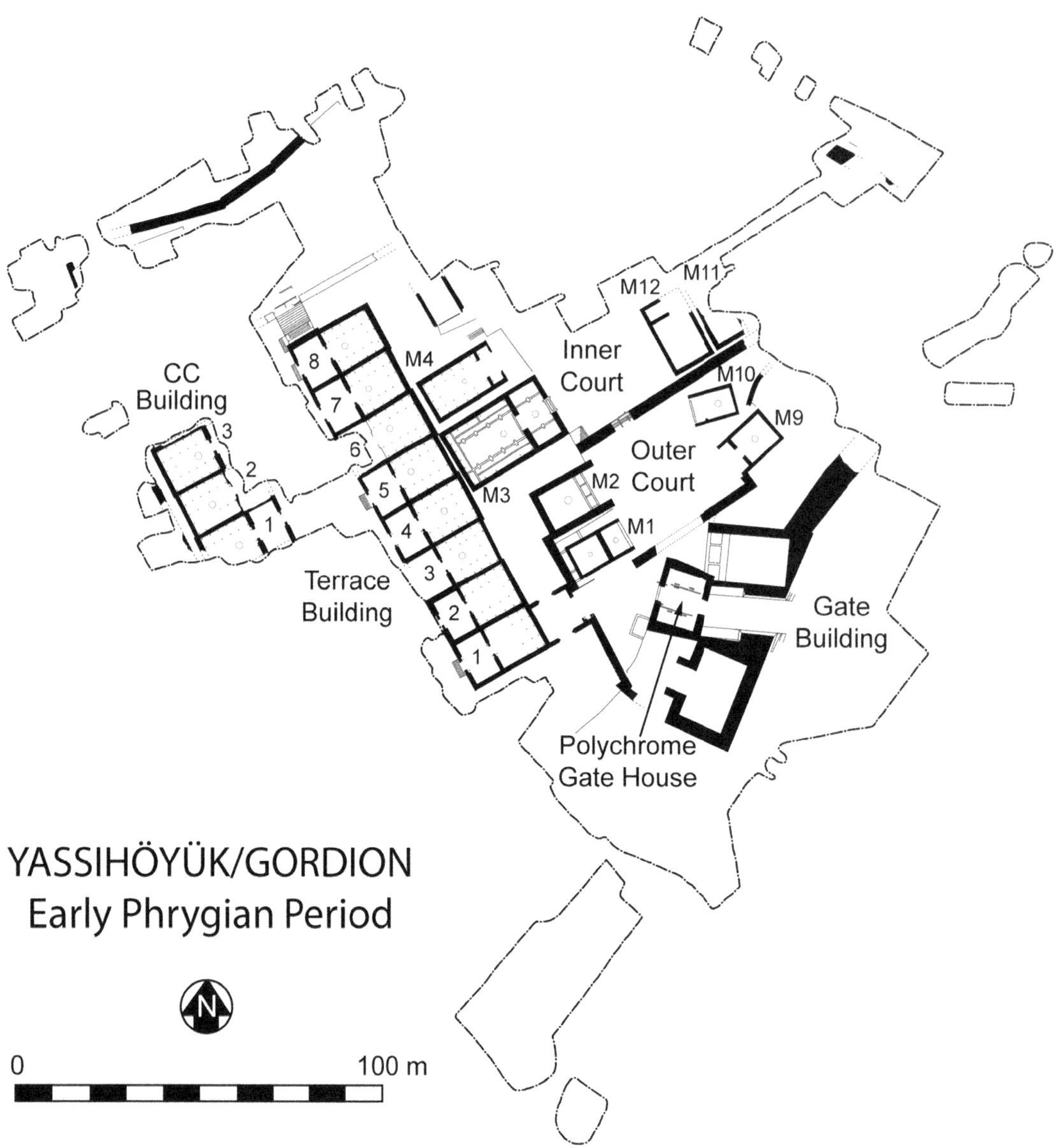

Fig: 7. Plan of Early Phrygian Gordion, ca. 825 B.C.
Courtesy Penn Museum, Gordion Project Archives, image no. 1988-1 / 140245 / v2.

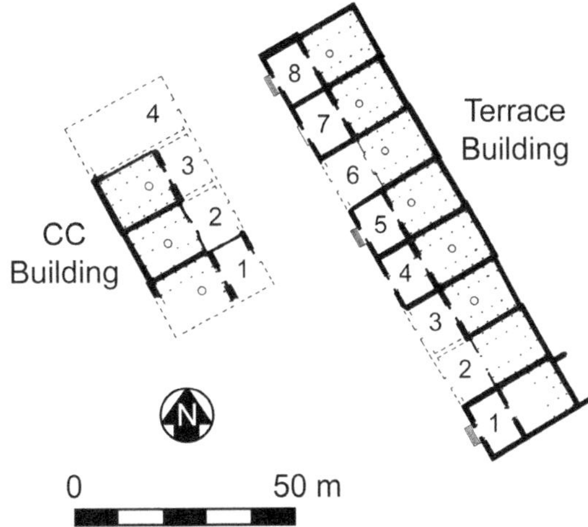

Fig: 8. Plan of Terrace Building, ca. 825 B.C.
Courtesy Penn Museum, Gordion Project Archives, image no. 1979-7 / 102701.

Fig: 9. Excavation beneath the rubble fill supporting the Terrace Building, looking west.
Courtesy Penn Museum, Gordion Project Archives, image no. 2014_4142.

Fig: 10. Reconstruction of the eastern side of the Citadel Mound in the Early Phrygian period, ca. 825 B.C., looking west. Modeled by C. Ray and G. Darbyshire. Courtesy Penn Museum, Gordion Project Archives.

Fig: 11. Grinding stand in main room of CC-2, Terrace Building Complex.
Courtesy Penn Museum, Gordion Project Archives, image no. R548-37.

Fig: 12. Ivory horse frontlet (9th c. B.C.) from Terrace Building 2.
Courtesy Penn Museum, Gordion Project Archives, image no. R556-5.

Investigating Changing Agricultural Management Practices at Kaman-Kalehöyük Using Grain Weight Analysis

*M. Cemre Üstünkaya, Elizabeth A. Stroud and Andrew S. Fairbairn**

Abstract

Kaman-Kalehöyük, occupied continuously from at least the Early Bronze Age to the end of Iron Age, provides a great opportunity for archaeologists to understand this critically important period since the first survey of the site started in 1981. Integration of several sub-disciplines-archaeobotany, zooarchaeology, osteoarchaeology etc.- from this site has given archaeologists a plethora of information on the past human societies that occupied Anatolia. Collection of archaeobotanical material from Kaman-Kalehöyük from the outset has provided one of the most continuous archaeobotanical collections within the region, if not across the globe. This paper will use that extensively collected archaeobotanical material from Kaman- Kalehöyük to test use of grain weight analysis in exploring the impact of genetics, environmental factors and agricultural management strategies in agricultural production at the settlement from the EBA to Late Iron Age.

Öz

En azından İlk Tunç Çağı'ndan Demir Çağı'nın sonuna kadar sürekli iskân edilen Kaman-Kalehöyük'te 1981 yılında ilk araştırmaların başlamasından bu yana arkeologlara bu kritik önemdeki dönemi anlama konusunda eşsiz bir fırsat sunmaktadır. Arkeobotani, zooarkeoloji, osteoarkelo gibi gibi birçok alt disiplinin araştırmalara entegre edilmesi araştırmacılara Anadolu'da yaşamış geçmiş insan toplulukları hakkında geniş bir bilgi yelpazesi sunmaktadır. Bu makalede, Kaman-Kalehöyük'ten kapsamlı bir şekilde toplanan arkeobotanik malzemeyi, İlk Tunç Çağı'ndan Geç Demir Çağı'na kadar olan yerleşimdeki tarımsal üretimde genetiğin, çevresel faktörlerin ve tarımsal yönetim stratejilerinin etkisini araştırmak amacıyla tahıl ağırlık analizini kullanımı test edilecektir.

Introduction

Farming is often considered the economic foundation of complex human societies and under the direction of Dr. Sachihiro Omura, the JIAA has supported this important research direction into the development of ancient agriculture, especially through the archaeobotany program at Kaman-Kalehöyük. The Kaman-Kalehöyük project provides one of the most holistic approaches to Anatolian archaeology with extensive collections and study of a wide range of archaeological remains since the start of excavations in 1986, in line with Dr. Omura's vision of bringing together experts in different disciplines to understand the past. As a result, political, architectural, technological, agricultural and socio-economic changes are well understood across multiple archaeological periods, including several important phases of change, such as the Early Iron Age "Dark Age", which is represented at only a few sites in Anatolia and nowhere as extensively as at Kaman-Kalehöyük. Prehistoric and historic periods have been well-recorded and sampled over the last 35 years of excavations and the near continuous occupation of the site, from at least the Early Bronze Age, has generated significant

* Institut Català d'Arqueologia Clàssica, Tarragona, Spain, mcu22@cantab.ac.uk – University of Oxford, Oxford, United Kingdom– The University fo Queensland, Brisbane, Australia

outcomes not only for the Anatolian prehistory but also for the Old World Archaeology at large (Atıcı 2003, 2005; Bong *et al.* 2010; Bradley 2008; Fairbairn 2002, 2004, 2006; Fairbairn, Longford, and Griffin 2007; Fairbairn and Omura 2005; Fenwick 2013; Hongo 1996, 1997, 2003; Kealhofer *et al.* 2008; Matsumura 2008; Omura 1992, 2000; Omori and Nakamura 2006; Stroud 2007; Wright 2017). The site has among the highest number of recorded radiocarbon dates across Anatolia and has contributed significantly to resolving outstanding problems in Anatolian and Southwest Asian chronology (Manning *et al.* 2001; Omori and Nakamura 2007, 2006).

This paper is offered in honour of Dr. Omura and investigates the long-term development of agriculture at Kaman-Kalehöyük using grain weight analysis (GW hereafter). GW is the mass of a single grain after harvesting and can be used to understand average grain yield at the end of growth season. It is one of the main measurements used to evaluate the quality of crops in modern agronomic studies. GW reflects grain yield and thus, if reconstructed archaeologically, allows investigation of economic gain/loss through time. In early societies founded on agriculture, GW provides a means of understanding the significance of changing agricultural yield in relation to collapse, resilience and climate change. Hence, the integration of GW analysis into archaeology allows us to gain further insights into the history of socio-economic change in past societies. There are difficulties in using GW from archaeological sites, but Kaman-Kalehöyük provides the perfect opportunity to evaluate its utility due to the long settlement history, extensive archaeobotanical sampling and integration of several disciplines to understand the landscape, material culture and chronology of the site (e.g. Fairbairn *et al.* this volume). The aim of this paper is to use GW of crop remains to investigate changes in agricultural practices at Kaman-Kalehöyük from the EBA until the end of the Iron Age and evaluate the potential of the method at the site.

Grain weight analysis in archaeology

While GW is a useful measure in modern agronomic studies, its method is not directly applicable to archaeobotanical crop remains, as they are mostly preserved by charring, which removes mass from the grains, making it difficult to make a direct comparison. Ferrio *et al.* (2004) used modern grains to model and test the possibility of creating a formula to calculate GW in archaeological crops. The experimental approach utilised measurements of principal dimensions; length (L), breadth (B) and thickness (T) as shown in Fig. 1; of two common economic crops; barley (*Hordeum vulgare* L.) and wheat (*Triticum aestivum* L.); before and after charring to ascertain the changing relationship between the dimensions before and after charring (Ferrio *et al.* 2004). Modelling has shown that it is possible to calculate GW within a statistically confident range from the principal dimensions of charred grains allowing archaeobotanists to reconstruct relative changes in ancient grain yields (Ferrio *et al.* 2004).

While the Ferrio *et al.* (2004) study allows calculation of GW, it does not provide any information on the causation behind variations in GW. Changes in GW for barley and wheat can be caused by varying environmental conditions, such as soil fertility, water availability, temperature etc., but also genetics and the variety of crop accessions used. Genetics have a strong influence on GW and more experiments are necessary to understand how different accessions act under different environmental conditions (Ferrio *et al.* 2006; Lightfoot *et al.* 2020; Tambussi *et al.* 2005).

Accessions are a group of related plants from a single species collected at one time from a specific location in order to capture the diversity in a given population. Hence, while accessions include the same species, they have enough genotypic and phenotypic heterogeneity to produce different grain sizes and/or grain yield, being adapted to specific geographical environments. Hence, a species that is adapted to grow well in Central Anatolian conditions does not always grow well in other places. A number of agricultural studies have investigated how different wheat and barley accessions work under conditions of water stress (Bagues *et al.* 2019; Saad *et al.* 2014). However, there are not many studies taking into account the possibility of accessions in archaeological record being the/a source of variation in GW.

Similar to genetics, environmental factors play a significant role in GW, especially during the grain filling period; which changes based on the geographical location but mostly is in the spring season for the Northern hemisphere (Gooding *et al.* 2003). Gooding *et al.* (2003) showed that temperature and water availability are important factors affecting the grain filling period and hence the final GW. Yet, these are not the only environmental factors that can influence GW. Modern agronomic studies are filling the gap on how nitrogen and salt levels in soil as well as length of daylight all have different effects on GW and grain numbers and thus impacting the final grain yield (Cossani, Slafer, and Savin 2009, 2011, 2012; Erda *et al.* 2005; Marino, Tognetti, and Alvino 2009; Ugarte, Calderini, and Slafer 2007). Gooding *et al.* (2003) showed that a decrease in water availability and/or increase in temperature over 20°C during the grain filling period causes a significant drop in GW and affects grain quality. Furthermore, genetics can at times drive the impact of environmental factors on grain filling (Lightfoot *et al.* 2020; Tambussi *et al.* 2005).

Hence, effective interpretation of GW results both within archaeology and agricultural studies requires the recognition of field conditions such as water availability within the landscape and nutrient levels along with the possibility of genetics on the outcome of GW (Acreche and Slafer 2006). Study of GW change in agriculture and archaeobotany can provide a better explanation for the impact of genetic and environmental factors (Acreche and Slafer 2006; Cossani, Slafer, and Savin 2009, 2011, 2012; Ferrio *et al.* 2004; Ferrio *et al.* 2006; Gooding *et al.* 2003; Marino, Tognetti, and Alvino 2009; Misra *et al.* 2010; Ugarte, Calderini, and Slafer 2007). While, disentangling the impact of genetics from environmental factors completely may not be possible, understanding how these two agents influence GW can be deduced.

Methods

GW was reconstructed for Kaman-Kalehöyük using the two most common crops preserved there: hulled barley (*Hordeum vulgare*) and free-threshing wheat (*Triticum aestivum/durum*) allowing comparison of GW between crops that have distinctive responses to field conditions. Hulled barley is known to have a greater tolerance to low water availability compared to wheat crops (Cossani, Slafer, and Savin 2012; Tambussi *et al.* 2005). Samples were selected from each Kaman- Kalehöyük phases which are IV-Early Bronze Age, IIIC-Middle Bornze Age, IIIB-the Old Hittite Period (Middle Bronze Age), IIIA-Hittite Empire (Late Bronze Age), IID-Early Iron Age (Anatolian Dark Age), IIC-Middle Iron Age and IIA-Late Iron Age (Persian Empire) periods (Table 3). Selection for use in the study was based on the preservation level of grains, with those included that preserved complete length, breadth and thickness measurements (Fig. 1). The site strata varied in grain preservation, meaning that the number of grains measured varied from assemblage to assemblage and period to period. The chronological periods are represented in the analysis by aggregated samples from multiple contexts and represent generalised values for periods of one or more centuries.

Grain Weight Analysis

Following the Ferrio *et al.* (2004) study, well-preserved wheat (*Triticum aestivum/durum*) and barley (*Hordeum vulgare*) were selected for measurements from the EBA to the end of Iron Age. All selected grains were photographed, and length (L), breadth (B), and thickness (T) measurements collected as shown in Figure 1 (Stroud 2007; Üstünkaya 2015). The following formulae, developed by Ferrio *et al.* (2004) was used to calculate the GW values from the morphological measurements as follows:

Table 1. Kruskal-Wallis analysis; raw p values for free-threshing wheat GW

	IV	IIIC	IIIB	IIIA	IID	IIC	IIA
IV		**8.50E-21**	**2.24E-14**	**0.0001513**	**2.89E-11**	**2.03E-05**	**1.34E-19**
IIIC	**8.50E-21**		0.574	0.5408	*0.09341*	0.1238	0.9786
IIIB	**2.24E-14**	0.574		0.451	*0.06837*	*0.08878*	0.6253
IIIA	**0.0001513**	0.5408	0.451		0.8008	0.3854	0.5164
IID	**2.89E-11**	*0.09341*	*0.06837*	0.8008		0.5854	0.1037
IIC	**2.03E-05**	0.1238	*0.08878*	0.3854	0.5854		*0.09906*
IIA	**1.34E-19**	0.9786	0.6253	0.5164	0.1037	*0.09906*	

– Wheat:

$$GW = -15.4 + [2.47 \times (L \times B)]$$
$$GW = -15.1 + [2.98 \times (L \times T)]$$

– Barley:

$$GW = 0.21 \times (L \times B)^{1.60}$$
$$GW = 0.78 \times (L \times B)^{1.28}$$

Ferrio *et al.* (2004) provided two formulae for both barley and free-threshing wheat in order to increase the robustness of the GW estimation. GW is calculated with both formula once and average of these two GW values are used in analysis.

Statistical Analysis

Statistical investigation of the results compared the GW results between the settlement phases at Kaman-Kalehöyük to identify significant changes in GW through time. A Kruskal-Wallis analysis was used as the sample set was not normally distributed. Kruskal-Wallis evaluates whether statistically significant difference exits between multiple datasets using the median values, which is more robust in non-normally distributed data.

Results

A total of 1348 (466 barley and 882 wheat) grains was measured. Descriptive statistics for wheat and barley in different Kaman settlement phases showed that mean values range 9 mg to 20 mg and 10 mg to 27 mg, respectively (Table 3). Boxplots for reconstructed GW of wheat and barley comparing Kaman-Kalehöyük phases are given in Fig. 2 and Fig. 3.

Free-threshing wheat GW values showed that IV (EBA) period has lower GW values than the rest of the Kaman-Kalehöyük periods (Fig. 2) and the difference in values is statistically significant (Table 1 in **bold**), with p-values of <0.05. Other Bronze Age median values and ranges are similar, with Late Iron Age values (IIA) similar to those of the Bronze Age, and those from the Early to Middle Iron Age higher. While the Kruskall-Wallis results do not meet the <0.05 p-value significance threshold, they are very low, suggesting the trend could be worth further investigation (Table 1 in *italics*). Especially since this trend clearly separates the MBA IIIC and IIIB from the Iron Age IID (Dark Age period which occurs right after the Late Bronze Age collapse). There is no such separation between the Iron Age IID samples and the Late Bronze Age IIIA or the Late Bronze Age IIIA and the Middle Bronze Age IIIC and IIIB samples suggesting that most major changes occurred earlier and continued through to the Late Bronze Age. The subtlety of this trend needs further nuanced investigation.

Barley GW values are quite high and very similar from the EBA (phase IV) to the Old Hittite Period (phase IIIB) but drop significantly during the IIIA-LBA period ($p<0.01$) (Table 2 in **bold**). While the LBA sample is small, the fact that no values fall within the interquartile range of other phases suggests this

Table 2. Kruskal-Wallis analysis; raw p values for barley GW

	IV	IIIC	IIIB	IIIA	IID	IIC	IIA
IV		0.335	0.6198	**9.18E-05**	0.6598	0.1067	**0.0002164**
IIIC	0.335		0.5113	**8.54E-05**	0.4057	0.1087	**0.02995**
IIIB	0.6198	0.5113		**0.0001798**	0.5326	*0.08626*	**0.001743**
IIIA	**9.18E-05**	**8.54E-05**	**0.0001798**		**0.001235**	**0.04533**	**9.29E-05**
IID	0.6598	0.4057	0.5326	**0.001235**		0.2276	**0.02696**
IIC	0.1067	0.1087	*0.08626*	**0.04533**	0.2276		**0.008475**
IIA	**0.0002164**	**0.02995**	**0.001743**	**9.29E-05**	**0.02696**	**0.008475**	

could be a reliable indicator of GW for the period. Values for the Early and Middle Iron Age (IID and IIC) rebound and show no statistical difference to the IV-IIIB samples, though the sample sizes are small. GW from the IIA-Late Iron Age shows a statistically significant difference compared to other periods, with the largest values in the assemblage ($p<0.01$).

Descriptive statistics also showed that wheat maximum values increased over time with IV-EBA starting at 17.96 mg and changing to 32.68 mg by end of the Late Iron Age (Table 3). However, we cannot say the same for barley GW values. The barley GW maximum starts quite high (46.09 mg), unlike wheat GW. However, we can see the maximum value falls by the LBA to 13.82 mg. During the Iron Age both barley maximum and minimum GW values increases while the range starts narrowing. On the other hand, wheat range does not show a pattern in terms of changes in minimum/maximum range.

Discussion

Modern agronomic studies showed that the GW values of wheat and barley in Europe do not drop under 30 mg for wheat grains and 40 mg for barley grains even in adverse climate conditions (Peltonen-Sainio *et al.* 2008). Similarly, GW values for modern Central Anatolian varieties of wheat and barley do not drop under 36 mg and 41 mg, respectively (Akdeniz *et al.* 2004; Gul *et al.* 2012). When compared to these modern figures, Kaman-Kalehöyük's ancient wheat grains are similar in size to modern counterparts but have a wide range of GW values. On the other hand, ancient barley grains are smaller and more variable in size. Differences in GW values between modern and archaeological crops not only reflect the higher degree of selection and genetic uniformity in modern crop varieties but also the change in modern agricultural techniques (i.e. modern machinery use, better genetic selection, better irrigation and accumulated knowledge of cultivation).

A more archaeologically meaningful comparison between ancient grains is shown in Table 3, where Kaman-Kalehöyük's GW mean values and ranges are compared to ancient Spanish GW data for the same time periods. Spanish GW values have a narrower range compared to Anatolian grains for both wheat and barley. Spanish grains show similar trends to Kaman-Kalehöyük's grains in terms of change. There is no significant change in free-threshing wheat values from MBA to the IA, as at Kaman-Kalehöyük where we see significant difference from the EBA to MBA. Furthermore, a similar trend of decrease in barley GW during the LBA can be detected at both sites.

The differences between the GW values for Spanish and Anatolian grains can be attributed to several factors, including: genetics (as Spanish varieties were probably different to Anatolian varieties), environmental factors and

Table 3. A comparison of minimum and maximum vaulues of Spanish and Anatolian archaeological grains. Kaman-Kalehöyük GW medianvalues are added in brackets

Period	Kaman phases	Ferrio *et al.* (2006)	Current data	Ferrio *et al.* (2006)	Current data
		Free-threshing wheat		Barley	
Iron Age	IIA (LIA)	8.4–22.4	4.15–32.68 (16.71)	9.4–23.2	6.8–29.82 (27.62)
	IIC (MIA)		14.76–28.73 (19.44)		6.8–25.44 (19.11)
	IID (EIA)		1.43–46.76 (18.39)		10.18–37.87 (23.25)
Late Bronze Age	IIIA	17.5–20.2	8.83–26.91 (16.74)	10.9–13.7	6.26–13.82 (10.19)
Middle Bronze Age (I–III)	IIIB	17.0–20.3	4.27–34.36 (15.64)	14.1–21.3	4.97–46.09 (24.06)
	IIIC		0.5–45.54 (16.18)		8.48–52.28 (25.12)
Early Bronze Age	IV	No data	1.51–17.96 (9.31)	No data	7.92–46.09 (22.9)

growth conditions. Similarities between datasets on the other hand, can be due to the global climate patterns.

To begin with, one of the earliest forms of genetic selection that improved grain yield for early agricultural societies was the selection of seed size. By the Early Bronze Age, farming societies were well-established and increasing GW was mostly based on agricultural improvements, such as the introduction of irrigation and manuring (Ferrio *et al.* 2006).

Wild cereals growing in Southwest Asia in recent decades have a GW value ranging between 20 mg to 35 mg (Blumler 1998), which is similar to the Kaman-Kalehöyük sample. This similarity in GW values between wild and domesticated cereals implies that genetic improvements via domestication do not always end up with a significant increase in the GW value (Ferrio *et al.* 2006). However, considering the evidence of early domestication in Anatolia, we expect that most of the crops utilised by ancient populations had mostly reached an optimum grain size by the Bronze Age, we might be able to eliminate genetics as a reason for changing GW values. However, the introduction of new accessions is still a possibility for this period, meaning GW changes may reflect different growth conditions for newly introduced accessions.

Next, we would like to look into what the environmental factors were that affected GW values. While, there are many environmental factors that may play a role in GW values, water stress/availability has been the main factor that is reviewed both in archaeological and agricultural studies (Ferrio *et al.* 2005; Gooding *et al.* 2003; Lelièvre *et al.* 2011; Saad *et al.* 2014). Water availability proxies in Anatolia focus on earlier period, especially on the 4.2k BP event, and data are lacking from MBA to IA periods (Jones, Roberts, and Leng 2007; Jones and Neil Roberts 2008; Roberts *et al.* 2001; Roberts *et al.* 2018; Turner, Roberts, and Jones 2008). The lack of datasets from later periods makes it harder to determine if there is any link between changing water availability and GW values for the Bronze

Age and Iron Age periods. There are broader regional climate proxies that show an increase in aridity at the end of the LBA which might explain the decrease in barley GW values (Roberts *et al.* 2018). On the other hand, a significant sustained increase in GW values for free-threshing wheat from the MBA onwards cannot be explained by regional climate proxies. Similarly, the increase in barley GW at the end of IA does not fit with climate proxy data. Considering growth conditions across Central Anatolia should be quite similar, it is hard to relate changes in GW directly to climate proxies. However, irrigation should be further investigated.

The significant increase in GW of free-threshing wheat from MBA onwards can be attributed to cultural selection, selective breeding and genetic improvements in crops. One explanation might be the adoption of new landraces which are better adapted to Anatolian conditions, since the increase in GW happens during phase IIIC, in which the Assyrian trade network opened central Anatolia to increasing exchange and mobility. Another reason could be a change to more intensive wheat cultivation due to the demands of a centralised government during the Hittite period.

Barley does not show similar trends to wheat, as barley has quite high GW values from the EBA onwards up until the LBA, where there is a significant drop in GW interpreted as a drop in grain yield. While we might be able to connect the drop in GW to climate change, there are other explanations since we expect to see a similar trend in wheat GW following barley. A drop in GW values for barley can also be explained by changing agricultural management practises, for example, less agricultural input to barley cultivation, less irrigation, less manuring or adopting a higher risk agricultural strategy using barley in marginal areas (Stroud 2007). The significant increase in barley during the Late Iron Age may again signal the changing production methods and demands of the Persian Empire, which is also hinted for woodland management at in anthracological data from the site (Wright 2017; Wright *et al.* 2015)

Conclusion

Grain weight analysis of >1300 wheat and barley grains from Kaman-Kalehöyük showed that the approach can be a powerful tool in identifying periods of change in agricultural production, whether it is driven by cultural factors, genetics, changing government or all three. This study showed that Kaman-Kalehöyük's barley and wheat grains followed a different trend in terms of their GW values. While, we can interpret the significant increase in wheat GW values to genetics or the introduction of new accessions at the end of EBA, the decrease in GW values for barley at the end of LBA is harder to interpret. A drop in GW may not be due to genetics unless there is a new accession introduction that did not like the growth conditions in Anatolia. It might be attributed to water stress, perhaps representing a change in agricultural strategy as much as to climate change. This interpretation is supported by some of the regional climate proxies (Roberts *et al.* 2011; Roberts *et al.* 2018).

While disentangling the relationship between genetics, environment and agricultural practices is a complex task and requires further study to understand nuances, Kaman-Kalehöyük's dataset can show how GW is useful in understanding long term changes. Next, we would like to compare concentrated grain remains with remains from generalised assemblages to see if the range between maximum and minimum values are narrower, which might help for us to define accessions. Furthemore, experimental work on Anatolian accessions are necessary to understand how charring impact archaeological records as Spanish modern grains were used for Ferrio *et al.*'s (2004) work and formulae provided may not work in a similar matter to Spanish archaeological grains.

As ever, applying modern agronomic studies to ancient crop assemblages requires ancient specimens to sample and with a strong commitment to ongoing sampling and analysis at the JIAA, Kaman-Kalehöyük and its sister sites promise to be important locations for the analysis of crop histories into the future.

Bibliography

Acreche, M. M. and G. A. Slafer
- 2006 "Grain Weight Response to Increases in Number of Grains in Wheat in a Mediterranean Area," *Field Crops Research* 98: pp. 52–59.

Atıcı, L.
- 2003 "Early Bronze Age Fauna from Kaman-Kalehöyük (Central Turkey): A Preliminary Analysis," *Anatolian Archaeological Studies* 12, pp. 99–101.
- 2005 "Centralized or Decentralized: The Mode of Pastoral Economy at Early Bronze Age Kaman-Kalehöyük," *Anatolian Archaeological Studies* 14, pp. 119–128.

Bagues, M., C. Hafsi, Y. Yahia, I. Souli, F. Boussora and K. Nagaz
- 2019 "Modulation of Photosynthesis, Phenolic Contents, Antioxidant Activities, and Grain Yield of Two Barley Accessions Grown under Deficit Irrigation with Saline Water in an Arid Area of Tunisia," *Polish Journal of Environmental Studies* 28, pp. 3071–3080.

Bong, W. S. K., K. Matsumura, K. Yokoyama and I. Nakai
- 2010 "Provenance Study of Early and Middle Bronze Age Pottery from Kaman-Kalehöyük, Turkey, by Heavy Mineral Analysis and Geochemical Analysis of Individual Hornblende Grains," *Journal of Archaeological Science* 37, pp. 2165–2178.

Bradley, K. M.
- 2008 *Weeds of Change: An Investigation into Bronze Age Agricultural Production at Kaman-Kalehöyük*, Unpublished PhD thesis, University of Queensland.

Cossani, C. Mariano, G. A. Slafer and R. Savin
- 2009 "'Yield and Biomass in Wheat and Barley Under a Range of Conditions in a Mediterranean Site," *Field Crops Research* 112, pp. 205–213.
- 2011 "Do Barley and Wheat (Bread and Durum) Differ in Grain Weight Stability Through Seasons and Water–Nitrogen Treatments in a Mediterranean Location?," *Field Crops Research* 121, pp. 240–247.
- 2012 "Nitrogen and water use efficiencies of wheat and barley under a Mediterranean environment in Catalonia," *Field Crops Research* 128, pp. 109–118.

Erda, L., X. Wei, J. Hui, X. Yinlong, L. Yue, B. Liping and X. Liyong
- 2005 "Climate Change Impacts on Crop Yield and Quality with CO2 fertilization in China," *Philos Trans R Soc Lond B Biol Sci* 360 pp. 2149–2154.

Fairbairn, A.
- 2002 "Archaeobotany at Kaman-Kalehöyük 200," *Anatolian Archaeological Studies* 11, pp. 201–212.
- 2004 "Archaeobotany at Kaman-Kalehöyük 2003 "*Anatolian Archaeological Studies* 13, pp. 107–120.
- 2006 "Archaeobotany at Kaman-Kalehöyük 2005,"*Anatolian Archaeological Studies* 15, pp. 133–137.

Fairbairn, A., C. Longford and B. Griffin
- 2007 "Archaeobotany at Kaman-Kalehöyük 2006," *Anatolian Archaeological Studies* 16, pp. 151–158.

Fairbairn, A and S. Omura
- 2005 "Archaeological Identification and Significance of ÉSAG (Agricultural Storage Pits) at Kaman-Kalehöyük, Central Anatolia," *Anatolian Studies* 55, pp. 15–23.

Fenwick, R.
- 2013 *From Tiny Seeds, Mighty Empires Grow: An Archæological Ottoman Village Site Through a World-Systems Perspective*, Unpublished PhD thesis, University of Queensland.

Ferrio, J. P., N. Alonso, J. Voltas and J. L. Araus
- 2006 "'Grain Weight Changes Over Time in Ancient Cereal Crops: Potential Roles of Climate and Genetic Improvement," *Journal of Cereal Science* 44, pp. 323–332.
- 2004 "Estimating Grain Weight in Archaeological Cereal Crops: A Quantitative Approach for Comparison with Current Conditions," *Journal of Archaeological Science* 31, pp. 1635–1642.

Ferrio, J. P., J. L. Araus, R. Buxó, J. Voltas and J. Bort
2005 "Water Management Practices and Climate in Ancient Agriculture: Inferences from the Stable Isotope Composition of Archaeobotanical Remains," *Vegetation History and Archaeobotany* 14, pp. 510–517.

Gooding, M.J., R.H. Ellis, P.R. Shewry and J. D. Schofield
- 2003 "Effects of Restricted Water Availability and Increased Temperature on the Grain Filling,

Drying and Quality of Winter Wheat," *Journal of Cereal Science* 37, pp. 295–309.

Hongo, H.
- 1996 *Patterns of Animal Husbandry in Cental Anatolia from the Second Millennium B.C. through the Middle Ages: Faunal Remains from Kaman-Kalehoyuk, Turkey*, Unpublished PhD thesis, Harvard University.
- 1997 "Patterns of animal husbandry, environment, and ethnicity in central Anatolia in the Ottoman Empire period: faunal remains from Islamic layers at Kaman-Kalehöyük," *Japan Review*, pp. 275–307.
- 2003 "Continuity or Changes: Faunal Remains from Stratum IId at Kaman-Kalehöyük," in B. Fischer, H. Genz, E. Jean and K. Köroglu (eds.), *From Bronze to Iron Ages in Anatolia and its Neighboring Regions*, Istanbul, pp. 257–269.

Jones, M. D. and C. N. Roberts
- 2008 "Interpreting Lake Isotope Records of Holocene Environmental Change in the Eastern Mediterranean," *Quaternary International* 181, pp. 32–38.

Jones, M. D., C. N. Roberts and M.J. Leng
- 2007 "Quantifying Climatic Change Through the Last Glacial–Interglacial Transition Based on Lake Isotope Palaeohydrology from Central Turkey," *Quaternary Research* 67, pp. 463–473.

Kealhofer, L., P. Grave, B. Marsh and K. Matsumura.
- 2008 "Analysis of Specialized Iron Age Wares at Kaman-Kalehöyük," *Anatolian Archaeological Studies*, p. 17.

Lelièvre, F., G. Seddaiu, L. Ledda, C. Porqueddu and F. Volaire
- 2011 "Water Use Efficiency and Drought Survival in Mediterranean Perennial Forage Grasses," *Field Crops Research* 121, pp. 333–342.

Lightfoot, E., M., C. Ustünkaya, N. Przelomska, T.C. O'Connell, H.V. Hunt, M.K. Jones and C.A. Petrie
- 2020 "Carbon and Nitrogen Isotopic Variability in Foxtail Millet (*Setaria italica*) with Watering Regime," *Rapid Communications in Mass Spectrometry* 34, pp. 1–14.

Manning, S.W., B. Kromer, P.I. Kuniholm and M.W. Newton
- 2001 "Anatolian Tree Rings and a New Chronology for the East Mediterranean Bronze-Iron Ages," *Science* 294, pp. 2532–5.

Marino, S., R. Tognetti and A. Alvino
- 2009 "'Crop Yield and Grain Quality of Emmer Populations Grown in Central Italy, as Affected by Nitrogen Fertilisation," *European Journal of Agronomy* 31, pp. 233–240.

Matsumura, K.
- 2008 "A Note on Anatolian Iron Age Ceramic Chronology: Black Lustrous Ware with Diamond Faceting," *Anatolian Archaeological Studies*, p. 17.

Misra, S.C., S. Shinde, S. Geerts, V.S. Rao and P. Monneveux
- 2010 "'Can Carbon Isotope Discrimination and Ash Content Predict Grain Yield and Water Use Efficiency in Wheat?," *Agricultural Water Management* 97, pp. 57–65.

Omori, T., and T. Nakamura
- 2006 "Radiocarbon Dating of Archaeological Materials Excavated at Kaman-Kalehöyük: Initial Report," *Anatolian Archaeological Studies* 15, pp. 263–268.
- 2007 "Radiocarbon Dating of Archaeological Materials Excavated at Kaman-Kalehöyük: Second Report," *Anatolian Archaeological Studies* 16, pp. 111–123.

Omura, S.
- 1992 "1990 Yılı Kaman-Kalehöyük Kazıları," *KST* XIII (1), pp. 319–336.
- 2000 "Preliminary Report on the 14th Excavation at Kaman-Kalehöyük (1999)," *Anatolian Archaeological Studies* 9 pp. 1–36.

Peltonen-Sainio, P., S. Muurinen, A. Rajala and L. Jauhiainen
- 2008 "Variation in Harvest Index of Modern Spring Barley, Oat and Wheat Cultivars Adapted to Northern Growing Conditions," *Journal of Agricultural Science* 146, pp. 35–47.

Roberts, C. Neil, W.J. Eastwood, C. Kuzucuoğlu, G. Fiorentino and V. Caracuta
- 2011 "Climatic, Vegetation and Cultural Change in the Eastern Mediterranean During the Mid-Holocene Environmental Transition," *The Holocene* 21, pp. 147–162.

Roberts, N., J.M. Reed, M.J. Leng, C. Kuzucuoğlu, M. Fontugne, J. Bertaux, H. Woldring, S. Bottema, S. Black, E. Hunt and M. Karabıyıkoğlu
- 2001 "The tempo of Holocene Climatic Change in the Eastern Mediterranean Region: New High-Resolution Crater-Lake Sediment Data from Central Turkey," *The Holocene* 11, pp. 721–736.

Roberts, N., J. Woodbridge, A. Bevan, A. Palmisano, S. Shennan and E. Asouti
- 2018 "Human Responses and Non-Responses to Climatic Variations During the Last Glacial-Interglacial Transition in the Eastern Mediterranean," *Quaternary Science Reviews* 184, pp. 47–67.

Saad, F., A. A. Abd El-Mohsen, M. A. Abd El-Shafi and I. H. Al-Soudan
- 2014 "Effective Selection Criteria for Evaluating Some Barley Crosses For Water Stress Tolerance," *Advance in Agriculture and Biology* 2, pp. 112–23.

Stroud, E. A.
- 2007 *Continuity or Change in Agricultural Production at Kaman-Kalehöyük: An Investigation using Morphometrics and Grain Weight Methods*, Unpublished PhD thesis, University of Queensland.

Tambussi, E. A., S. Nogués, P. Ferrio, J. Voltas and J. L. Araus
- 2005 "Does Higher Yield Potential Improve Barley Performance in Mediterranean Conditions?," *Field Crops Research* 91, pp. 149–160.

Turner, R., N. Roberts, and M. D. Jones
- 2008 "Climatic Pacing of Mediterranean Fire Histories from Lake Sedimentary Microcharcoal," *Global and Planetary Change* 63, pp. 317–324.

Ugarte, C., D. F. Calderini and G. A. Slafer
- 2007 "Grain Weight and Grain Number Responsiveness to Pre-Anthesis Temperature in Wheat, Barley and Triticale," *Field Crops Research* 100, pp. 240–248.

Üstünkaya, M. C.
- 2015 *Investigating Climate Related Agricultural Stress Patterns at Bronze and Iron Age Kaman-Kalehöyük: The Integration of Botanical Stable Carbon and Nitrogen Isotope Values, Grain Weight Values, and Seed Analysis*, Unpublished PhD thesis, The University of Queensland.

Wright, N.
- 2017 *Ancient Woodland and its Management in Central Anatolia: An Anthracological Study of the Bronze and Iron Ages at Kaman-Kalehöyük, Turkey*, Unpublished PhD thesis, University of Queensland.

Wright, N., A. Fairbairn, M. C. Üstünkaya and J. T. Faith
- 2015 "Explaining Changing Patterns of Wood Presence Across the Bronze and Iron Age at Kaman-Kalehöyük, Central Anatolia," *Quaternary International* 431, pp. 90–102.

Fig. 1. Measurements of breadth, length and thickness as shown on the figure were taken from each barley and free-threshing wheat grain in this study.

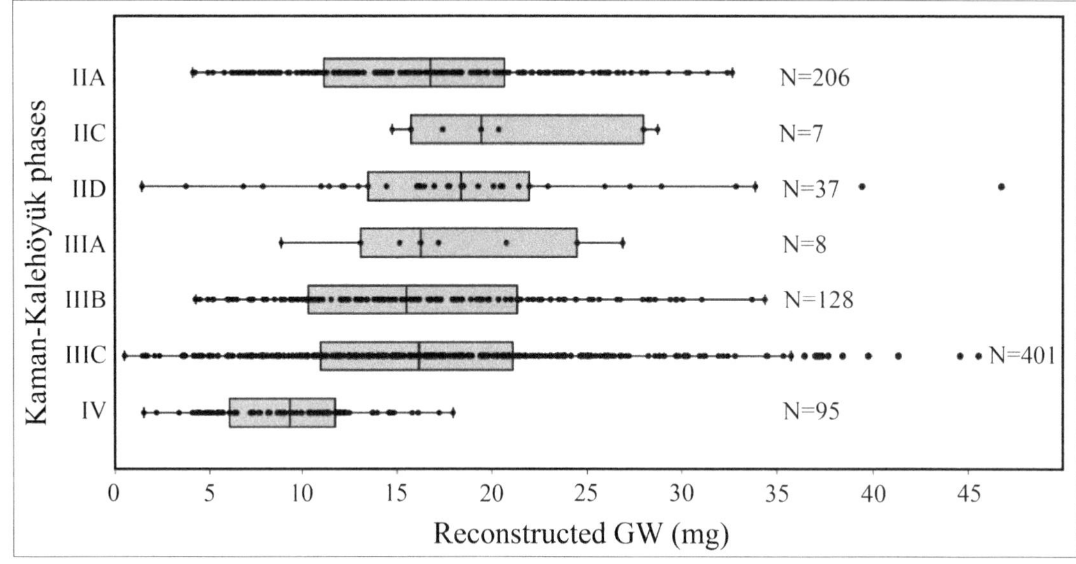

Fig. 2. Boxplot/jitter plot for reconstructed free-threshing wheat GW values based on Kaman phases and population (N) in each phase.

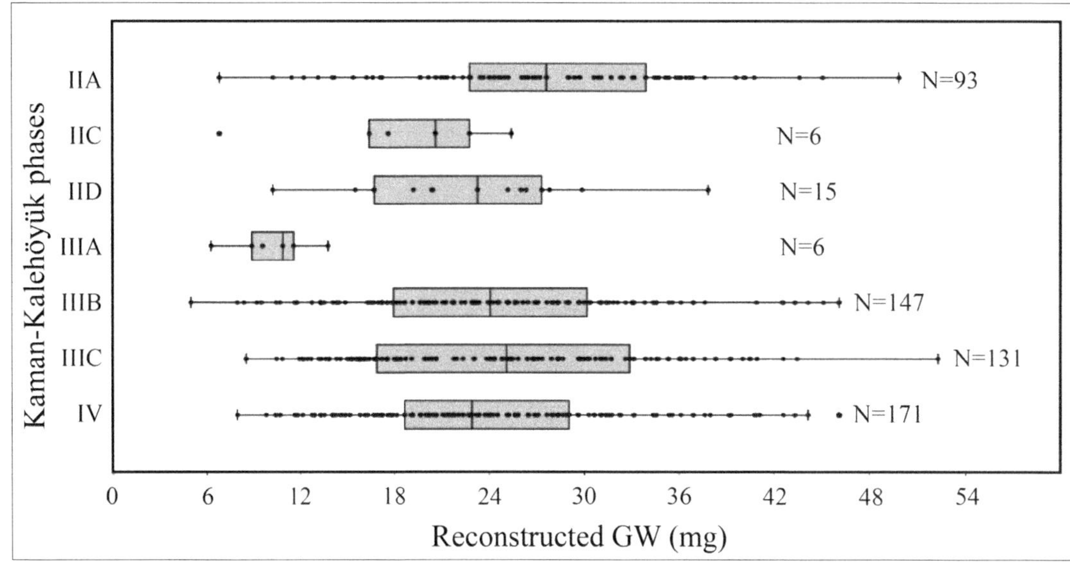

Fig. 3. Box plot/jitter plot for reconstructed barley GW values based on Kaman phases and population (N) in each phase.

Two Hittite Seals with Hieroglyphic Inscriptions from Kaman-Kalehöyük

Daisuke Yoshida *

Abstract

From the numerous Hittite seal materials excavated at Kaman-Kalehöyük, this article focuses on two seals that are characteristic of the empire period. One is a bronze tripod seal, and the other is a biconvex seal. The owner of the tripod seal is Kummayaziti, and the biconvex has a male name on one side and a female name on the other.

Öz

Bu makale Kaman Kalehöyük'te çok sayıda ortaya çıkan Hitit dönemi mühürlerinin arasından Hitit İmparatorluk dönemine tarihlenen ve karakteristik özelliğini taşıyan iki mühüre odaklanmaktadır. Tripod tutamaklı mührün sahibi Kummayaziti, iki yüzü dışbükey mührün bir yüzünde erkek ismi, diğerinde kadın ismi yazmaktadır.

The excavations at Kaman-Kalehöyük (since 1986 under the direction of Dr. Omura) have revealed a considerable number of seals and seal impressions from the Hittite period, which provide us a rich material for the Hittite glyptic. In this modest contribution in honor of Dr. Omura on the occasion of his 77th birthday, two Hittite seals from Kaman-Kalehöyük, which have the seal shapes characteristic of the Hittite empire period (tripod, biconvex), are presented.[1]

Tripod Seal

The tripod seal presented here (KL 89–42, Fig. 1) was found 1989 in the North Sector (VII, Grid: XXXIII-55) of the site (Yoshida 1994: 108 (photo 2), 109–11; 2000: 35, 36 (Fig. 23). Its handle has the shape of three lion paws. They carry a thin round plate on which a small cylindrical, tubular loop is placed. The circular base (seal plate) is disc-shaped and bears an inscription in Anatolian Hieroglyphs. The height of the whole seal is 2.3cm, the diameter of the circular base 2.95cm (0.25cm in thickness).

Seals with tripod handles made of metal (silver, silver alloy or bronze) are well documented[2] and fairly popular throughout the Hittite empire period (14th and 13th centuries B.C.). However, they belong mostly to museums and private collections, so that their provenance is largely unknown, with a few exceptions.[3]

* dsk.yoshida@mbr.nifty.com

1 These two seals have already been reported in Japanese, Yoshida 1994; 2000.

2 Mora 1987: VIb 1.10 (silver); 1.21 (silver or silver alloy); VII 1.3 (silver or silver alloy); 3.2 (silver-plated copper); 4.8 (bronze); 4.10 (bronze); 4.12 (silver); 4.14 (silver or silver alloy); XI 1.5 (silver [base]); 3.11 (whitish-yellow metal [bronze?]); XIIa 2.60 (bronze); 3.1 (silver [base], iron [handle]); XIIb 1.49 (silver); 1.51 (bronze); 1.59 (silver alloy); 1.70 (silver); 1.78 (silver alloy); 1.81 (bronze); 1.82 (bronze); 1.83 (bronze); Boehmer and Güterbock 1987: 238 (bronze); Schachner and Özenir 2006 (silver); Dinçol, A. and B. 2010: three tripod seals from the private collection (silver or silver alloy). Two examples testify that such tripod handles were also used with hemispherical seals. One is made of ivory from the upper city of Boğazköy-Hattusa (Boehmer and Güterbock 1987: 74, Abb. 14; Dinçol, A. and B. 2008: no. 308), the other is made of gold and was found in Tamassos in Cyprus (Mora 1987: V 3.2). Also the famous silver seal of Tarkasnawa King of Mira, known as the Tarkondemos seal (Güterbock 1977; Nowicki 1982; Mora 1987: VIII 3.1; Hawkins and Morpurgo-Davies 1998) probably belongs to this type, although the handle is almost completely lost.

3 Two pieces from sites in the 'Salt Lake' (Tuz Gölü) plain, namely one from Çorca (Güterbock 1939; Mora

According to A. and B. Dinçol (Dinçol, A. and B. 2002: 86; 2008: 4), the oldest example of this type is a seal found in Alacahöyük (Dinçol, B. 1982; Mora 1987: IIb 2.5), which is dated to the late 15th century B.C.

The seal surface is flat and framed by a single line. The inscription, which gives the name of seal owner, consists of PURUS (L.[4] 322) and the combination VIR.*zi/a* (L. 312 – L. 376) for *ziti*. The initial sign PURUS ("pure") is read šuppi- in Hittite and *kumma-/kummi-* in Luwian, and well known as the first element of name Šuppiluliuma (PURUS.FONS-*MI*). The PURUS-sign shows here four vertical lines or bars in the central space, like that on the seals of Šuppiluliuma I.[5] To the right and left of the main group two triangles (L. 370), a star and L. 440 ('Heilszeichen') can be seen.

The phonetic reading Kummayaziti (/Kummiyaziti) for PURUS-VIR.*zi/a* is established by the cuneiform correspondence of the name [m]Kum-ma-ya-LÚ.[6] This name is attested also on seals or seal impressions from other sites:

> Ališar: Gelb 1935: no. 75 (biconvex seal; Mora 1987: XIIb 1.6b).[7]
> Boğazköy: Güterbock 1942: no. 106 (seal impression);
> Boehmer and Güterbock 1987: no. 215 (seal impression);
> Herbordt 2005: nos. 174, 175 (both seal impression);
> Dinçol, A. and B. 2008: nos. 141, 271 (both seal impression).
> Çelebibağ: Güterbock 1937 (biconvex seal; Mora 1987: XIIb 1.10).
> Ras Shamra/Ugarit: Schaeffer *et al.* 1956: pp. 52–3 (Schaeffer), Figs. 78, 79 (p. 56), pp. 153–4 (Laroche) (impression of signet ring on the tablet (RS.17.371 + 18.20); The name is written in cuneiform on the tablet [m]Ku-um-y[a-ziti]. Mora 1987: X 1.2).

Biconvex Seal

Another seal from Kaman-Kalehöyük to be discussed here is a biconvex seal, the most common type of Hittite hieroglyphic seals in the late Hittite Empire period (13th century B.C.).[8] The present biconvex seal KL 96–10 (2.75 cm in diameter, 1.57 cm in thickness; Fig. 2)[9] came to light during the excavations of 1996 in the North Sector (XXX, Grid: XLIX-50). It is made of baked clay[10] (instead of usual stone) and pierced through transversely by a small hole. This perforation runs approximately perpendicular to the inscription on Side A. Both sides of the seal are only slightly convex and framed by a circular boarder. The edge is smooth and without any decoration.[11]

1987: XIIa 3.1) and one from Çardak (Güterbock 1949: 56f., 62f., res. 15.3, 19.1; Mora 1987: XI 3.11), and one piece from Karapınar/Ali Tepesi, about 90 km east of Konya (Schachner and Özenir 2006). In Boğazköy only one badly preserved bronze stamp is known to date (Boehmer and Güterbock 1987: no. 238).

4 Hieroglyphs are identified by their numbers in the sign lists of Laroche 1960 (L. no.).

5 On the other hand, the PURUS-sign on the seals of Šuppiluliuma II. lacks these lines or bars. For this distinction between the seals of Šuppiluliuma I. and II. see Otten 1967: 226–8; see also Neve 1992; Hawkins 1995: 31; 2011: 101; Bawanypeck 2011: 68–9; Klinger 2015: 104–5.

6 Laroche 1966: no. 621; Boehmer and Güterbock 1987: 69; Hawkins *apud* Herbordt 2005: 259, 299, 435.

7 Because of the poor state of preservation, the first sign cannot be clearly identified as PURUS.

8 For the dating of biconvex seals, see especially Gorny 1993. They remain in use even after the fall of the Hittite empire, albeit in a limited way: Boehmer and Güterbock 1987: 65; Gorny 1993: 191; Mora 2016.

9 Yoshida 2000: 35, 37 (Fig. 24). Alp also drew attention to this seal in his study on the biconvex seal from Troy (Alp 2001: 28). A photograph of KL 96–10 is published in *Anatolian Archaeological Studies* 6, 1997 (color page at the beginning of the volume).

10 For biconvex seals made of (baked) clay/terracotta see e.g. Boehmer and Güterbock 1987: nos. 194, 206, 207 (from Boğazköy); Mora 1987: VIa 4.2, 5.1 (both from Arslantepe/Malatya); VIb 1.11; XIIb 1.66; XIIb 3.4 (from Gözlü Kule/Tarsus). Biconvex seals made of metal are also known, albeit only a few, such as those from Boğazköy (Bo 97/28 [bronze], Seeher 1998: 231, 234), Emar (EM 99:38 [silver], Starke 2001) and Troy (E9.573 [bronze], Hawkins and Easton 1996).

11 The edge of biconvex seals is usually decorated with two parallel grooves.

KL 96–10 is an example of 'couple' seals which bear a hieroglyphic inscription with a male name on one side and a female name on the other. The seal owners were very likely members of the same family and presumably man and wife. This type of seal is quite common in Hittite glyptic[12] and attested as early as the 'Middle Hittite' period. The earliest example known to me is a disc-shaped ivory seal from Boğazköy, dated to the first half of the 14th century B.C.[13] This period seems to coincide with the time when the 'Gemeinschaftssiegel' of king and queen came to be used.[14]

Side A. The signs are well preserved and clear. The hieroglyphs of the name in the center of the field can be read from top to bottom as follows: L. 391 (*mi*) – L. 415 (*sa*) – L. 29 (*tá*) – L. 153 (*nu*) = *Mis(a)tanu*. Left and right in the field are the hieroglyphs BONUS$_2$ (L. 370) over VIR$_2$ (L. 386), which identify the owner as a man, and three stars as filling elements.

The name *Mis(a)tanu* is hitherto unattested, but the names ending in *–nu* are well attested (Alp 2001: 28), also often on seals:

Iyarinu[15] (*i(a)+ra/i-nú-u*): Güterbock 1942: no. 138; Herbordt 2005: no. 152 (both seal impression from Boğazköy);
Lalinu (*la-li-nu*): Mora 1987: XIIb 1.50 (biconvex seal);
(M)uwanu (BOS-*nu*): Dinçol, A. and B. 2008: no. 204 (seal impression from Boğazköy);
Nu(n)nu[16] (*nú-nú-u*): Mora 1987: XIIa 2.9 (seal impression from Gözlü Kule/Tarsus);
Tarhu(nta)pihanu[17] (TONITRUS(-[⌜*ta*?⌝])-*pi-ha-nu*): Herbordt 2005: no. 422 (seal impression from Boğazköy);
Walwanu[18] (LEO?-*wa-nu*): Mora VIb 1.44 (biconvex seal);
LINGUA+CLAVUS[19]-*nú*: d' Alfonso 2010 (hemispheroid seal from Kavuşan Höyük in southeastern Turkey);
MAGNUS??-*la-á*?-*nu* (=*Ur(a)lanu*?): Weeden 2010 (biconvex seal from Kaman-Kalehöyük);
... -*nu*: Dinçol, A. and B. 2008: no. 133 (x-*nu*), no. 140 (x-x-*nú*) (both seal impression from Boğazköy); Hawkins and Easton 1996 (x-x-*nu*, cf. Alp 2001: 29 [*Tarhun-tà-nu*]) (bronze biconvex seal from Troy).

The basic words for the names ending in *-nu* include divine names like *Iyarinu*(*Yarri-nu*), geographical/ethnic names like *Kaškanu* (*Kaška-nu*), or appellative like *Walwanu* (*walwa/i* "lion" *-nu*). Analysis and linguistic affiliation of the name *Mis(a)tanu* is unclear.

The sign L. 153 (*nu*), rare in the Empire period, occurs in glyptic almost exclusively in the final position of the name. The only exception

12 Güterbock 1980: 55–7. The shape of 'man and wife' seals is almost exclusively biconvex; Mora 1987: VIa 3.5; VIb 1.29 (?); VII 6.15; XIIa 2.3; XIIa 2.22; XIIa 2.24; XIIa 2.27; XIIa 2.29; XIIa 2.33; XIIa 2.39; XIIa 2.40; XIIa 2.41; XIIa 2.47; XIIa 2.49; XIIa 2.58; XIIa 2.70; XIIb 1.58 (?); XIIb 1.67; XIIb 1.68; XIIb 1.71; XIIb 1.87; Boehmer and Güterbock 1987: nos. 194, 195; Dinçol, A. and B. 2008: no. 175; Beckman 1998: nos. 5, 6; Hawkins and Easton 1996 (biconvex bronze seal from Troy); cf. also a biconvex seal from Kaman-Kalehöyük KL 92-5 (Weeden 2010: 251–2). On two cylinder seal impressions with hieroglyphic inscriptions of male and female names found at Emar see Singer 2000: 84 (Text 8 Seal 5, Pl. XXII); Beyer 2001: A 75 (p. 92–3). However, this type of seal is quite exceptional in Emar.

13 Bo 2005/12, Herbordt 2006: 185–6.

14 The oldest known 'Gemeinschaftssiegel' of king and queen is that of Arunuwanda I and Ašmunikal (also from the first half of the 14th century B.C.), Güterbock 1940: no. 60; Beran 1967: no. 162.

15 Laroche 1966: no. 437; see also Hawkins *apud* Herbordt 2005: 257.

16 Laroche 1966: no. 897.

17 Laroche 1966: no. 1276; cf. mTar-hu-u[n-p]í-ha-nu-uš (Alp 1991: no. 72 obv. 3).

18 The cuneiform correspondence of the name: mWa-al-wa-nu (Alp 1991: no. 56 rev. 21). For the reading of LEO/UR.MAH see especially Hawkins *apud* Herbordt 2005: 293–5.

19 For LINGUA+CLAVUS see e.g. Hawkins *apud* Herbordt 2005: 292; d' Alfonso 2010: 2–3.

known to me is L. 153 in the name of Queen *Tanuhepa* (*ta_x* [L. 42]-*nu* [L. 153]-*ha* [L. 215]-*pa* [L. 334]).[20] On the other hand, L. 395 (*nú*), usual sign for *nu* in the Empire period, takes any position in the name.

Side B. The signs on the side with the female name[21] are well preserved, as are those on side A. The main group for the name also consists of four signs: L. 423 (*ku* ?) – L. 90 (*ti*) – L. 19 (á) – L. 90 (*ti*) = *Ku*[?]*ti*(*y*)*ati*/*Ku*(*wa*)[?]*ti*(*y*)*ati*. The identification of the first sign with L. 423 is uncertain. The outer contour of the first sign looks very similar to L. 423, but the inner markings are placed horizontally, not vertically as would be usual for L. 423.

It is extremely rare for L. 19 (á) to be used inside the name, as in this case. L. 19 otherwise appears either in initial position, or less often in final position.[22] The main group is flanked by BONUS$_2$ (L. 370).FEMINA (L. 79) for a woman's name. Two stars as filling motifs.

The name *Ku*[?]*ti*(*y*)*ati*/*Ku*(*wa*)[?]*ti*(*y*)*ati* is so far unattested. There are, however, many female names ending in -(*t*)*ti*,[23] such as *Aliwanatti*,[24] *Annayati*,[25] *Annitti*,[26] *Aršakiti*/*Arzakiti*,[27] *Hahharti*,[28] *Harapšiti*,[29] *Henti*,[30] *Hurmawanatti*,[31] *I*(*a*)-*la-ti*,[32] *Kapurti*,[33] *Kadduširi*,[34] *Mutamuti*,[35] *Muwatti*,[36] *Na-wa*/*i-ti*,[37] *Nikalmati*,[38] *Paškuwatti*,[39] *Pitati*,[40] *Pu-mu-ti*,[41] *Pušti*,[42] *Šaušgatti* (ᵈ*IŠTAR-atti*),[43] *Taniti*,[44] *Tatiwašti*,[45] *Duttarriyati*,[46] *Tuwa*-FEMINA-*ti* (= *Tuwanatti*),[47] *Utati*,[48] *Uwašunati*,[49] *Wašti*,[50] *Watti*,[51] *Witti*,[52] *Zamuwatti*,[53] *Zuwahallati*.[54]

20 Güterbock 1940: nos. 24–9 (with Muršili); no. 42 (with Muwatalli II); nos. 43–4 (with Urhi-Teššub = Muršili III); Herbordt, Bawanypeck and Hawkins 2011: nos. 46–50 (with Muwatalli II); nos. 51–2 (with Urhi-Teššub); nos. 58–64 (with Muršili); 65 (Tanuhepa alone).

21 For the Hittite women's names see the extensive work by Th. Zehnder (Zehnder 2010).

22 Hawkins *apud* Herbordt 2005: 426.

23 Laroche 1966: 332; Zehnder 2010: 96.

24 Alp 1991: no. 113 obv. 11 (ᶠA-li-wa-na-at-ti-iš); Zehnder 2010: 109.

25 Laroche 1966: no. 60; Zehnder 2010: 114.

26 Laroche 1966: no. 76; Zehnder 2010: 119.

27 Laroche 1966: no. 149; Zehnder 2010: 126, 127.

28 Laroche 1966: no. 240; Zehnder 2010: 138.

29 Laroche 1966: no. 299; Zehnder 2010: 146.

30 Laroche 1966: no. 363; Zehnder 2010: 155.

31 Laroche 1966: no. 407; Zehnder 2010: 166.

32 Mora 1987: IV 1.4 (hemispheroid seal); Zehnder 2010: 175.

33 Laroche 1966: no. 515; Zehnder 2010: 182.

34 Laroche 1966: no. 554; Zehnder 2010: 186.

35 Laroche 1966: no. 827; Zehnder 2010: 226.

36 Laroche 1966: no. 838; cf. also seal impressions in Güterbock 1942: no. 88; Herbordt 2005: nos. 260–70; Dinçol, A. and B. 2008: no. 24; Zehnder 2010: 224–5.

37 Mora 1987: XIIa 2.40b (biconvex seal); Zehnder 2010: 232.

38 Laroche 1966: no. 875; Zehnder 2010: 232–3.

39 Laroche 1966: no. 955; Zehnder 2010: 245.

40 Laroche 1966: no. 1032; Zehnder 2010: 251–2.

41 Mora 1987: XIIb 1.71b (biconvex seal); Zehnder 2010: 254.

42 Laroche 1966: no. 1061; Zehnder 2010: 256.

43 Laroche 1966: no. 1142; Zehnder 2010: 269.

44 Laroche 1966: no. 1242; Zehnder 2010: 22–3, 283.

45 Laroche 1966: no. 1310; Zehnder 2010: 288.

46 Laroche 1966: no. 1388; Zehnder 2010: 297.

47 Mora 1987: XIIa 2.56 (biconvex seal); Zehnder 2010: 294; cf. Ta-FEMINA (Beckman 1998: no. 3B, biconvex seal), and also *Aliwanatti* (Ali-wanatti), *Hurmawanatti* (Hurma-wanatti). On the Luwian word for woman (*wanatti-*) see Starke 1980.

48 Laroche 1981: no. 1455a; Zehnder 2010: 313–5.

49 Laroche 1981: no. 1465a; Zehnder 2010: 305.

50 Laroche 1981: no. 1511a; cf. Wa/i-s(à)-ti (with Pi-ha-TONITRUS prince on cylinder seal impression from Emar [Beyer 2001 A 75]), [Wa/i]-s(a)-ti (on seal impression [Beyer 2001 C 22]); Zehnder 2010: 304.

51 Laroche 1966: no. 1518; Zehnder 2010: 306.

52 Laroche 1981: no. 1522a; Zehnder 2010: 310.

53 Laroche 1966: no. 1531; Zehnder 2010: 316–7.

54 Laroche 1966: no. 1578; Zehnder 2010: 324.

Bibliography

Alp, S.
- 1991 *Maşat-Höyük'te Bulunan Çivi Yazılı Hitit Tabletleri (Hethtische Keilschrifttafeln aus Maşat-Höyük)*, Ankara.
- 2001 "Das Hieroglyphensiegel von Troja und seine Bedeutung für Westanatolien," Studien zu den Boğazköy-Texten 45, Wiesbaden, pp. 27–31.

Bawanypeck, D.
- 2011 see Herbordt, Bawanypeck and Hawkins 2011.

Beckman, G.
- 1998 "Anatolian stamp seals from a California collection," *Studi micenei ed egeo-anatolici* 40, pp. 83–6.

Beran, Th.
- 1967 *Die Hethitische Glyptik von Boğazköy. I. Teil: Die Siegel und Siegelabdrücke der vor- und althetitischen Perioden und die Siegel der hethitischen Grosskönige.* Boğazköy-Ḫattuša V, Berlin.

Beyer, D.
- 2001 *Emar IV: Les sceaux.* Orbis Biblicus et Orientalis, Series Archaeologica 20, Göttingen.

Boehmer, R. M. and Güterbock, H. G.
- 1987 *Glyptik aus dem Stadtgebiet von Boğazköy. Grabungskampagnen 1931–1939, 1952–1978.* Boğazköy-Ḫattuša XIV, Berlin.

d' Alfonso, L.
- 2010 "A Hittite seal from Kavuşan Höyük," *AnatSt* 60, pp. 1–6.

Dinçol, A. and Dinçol, B.
- 2002 "Große, Prinzen, Herren. Die Spitzen der Reichsadministration im Spiegel ihrer Siegel," In *Die Hethiter und ihr Reich, das Volk der 1000 Götter.* Bonn, pp. 82–7.
- 2008 *Die Prinzen- und Beamtensiegel aus der Oberstadt von Boğazköy-Ḫattuša vom 16. Jahrhundert bis zum Ende der Grossreichszeit.* Boğazköy-Ḫattuša XXII, Mainz am Rhein.
- 2010 "Drei hieroglyphische Tripodstempel aus der Perk Sammlung," In Ş. Dönmez (ed.), *Veysel Donbaz'a Sunulan Yazılar DUB.SAR. É.DUB. BA.A (Studies Presented in Honour of Veysel Donbaz)*, Istanbul, pp. 87–89.

Dinçol, B.
- 1982 "Bir Alacahöyük Mührünün Okunuşu hakkında," *Anadolu Araştırmaları* 8, pp. 59–61.

Gelb, I. J.
- 1935 *Inscriptions from Alishar and vicinity.* The University of Chicago Oriental Institute Publications XXVII (Researches in Anatolia VI), Chicago.

Gorny, R. L.
- 1993 "The Biconvex Seals of Alişar Höyük," *AnatSt* 43, pp. 163–91.

Güterbock, H. G
- 1937 "Alaca Höyük civarında ele geçen bir eti mührü (Ein hethitisches Siegel aus der Gegend von Alaca Höyük)," *Belleten* 1, pp. 501–4.
- 1939 "Un cachet hittite de Çorca," *Revue Hittite et Asianique* V/35, pp. 91–2, Pl. 19.
- 1940 *Siegel aus Boğazköy. Erster Teil. Die Königssiegel der Grabungen bis 1938.* Archiv für Orientforschung Beiheft 5, Berlin (Nachdruck Osnabrück 1967).
- 1942 *Siegel aus Boğazköy. Zweiter Teil. Die Königssiegel von 1939 und die übrigen Hieroglyphensiegel.* Archiv für Orientforschung Beiheft 7, Berlin (Nachdruck Osnabrück 1967).
- 1949 "Yeni eti hiyeroglif yazıtları ve mühürleri (Neue hethitische Hieroglypheninschriften und Siegel)," *Türk Tarıh, Arkeologya ve Etnografya Dergisi* 5, pp. 53–65, res. 15–21.
- 1977 "The Hittite Seals in the Walters Art Gallery," *The Journal of the Walters Art Gallery* 36, pp. 7–16
- 1980 "Seals and Sealing in Hittite Lands," In K. DeVries (ed.), *From Athens to Gordion. The papers of a memorial symposium for Rodney S. Young*, Philadelphia, pp. 51–63.

Hawkins, J. D.
- 1995 *The Hieoglyphic Inscription of the Sacred Pool Complex at Hattusa (Südburg). With an Archaeological Introduction by Peter Neve.* Studien zu den Boğazköy-Texten, Beiheft 3, Wiesbaden.
- 2011 see Herbordt, Bawanypeck and Hawkins 2011.

Hawkins, J. D. and Easton, D. F.
- 1996 "A Hieroglyphic Seal from Troia," *Studia Troica* 6, pp. 111–118.

Hawkins, J. D. and Morpurgo-Davies, A.
- 1998 "Of Donkeys, Mules and Tarkondemos," In J. Jasanoff *et al.* (eds.), *Mír Curad. Studies in honor of Calvert Watkins*, Innsbruck, pp. 243–60.

Herbordt, S.
- 2005 *Die Prinzen- und Beamtensiegel der hethitischen Grossreichszeit auf Tonbullen aus*

dem Nişantepe-Archiv in Hattusa. Mit Kommentaren zu den Siegelinschriften und Hieroglyphen von J. David Hawkins. Boğazköy-Ḫattuša XIX, Mainz am Rhein.
– 2006 "Siegelfunde aus den Grabungen im Tal vor Sarıkale 2005," *Archäologischer Anzeiger* 2006, pp. 183–6.

Herbordt, S., Bawanypeck, D. and Hawkins, J. D.
– 2011 *Die Siegel der Großkönige und Großköniginnen auf Tonbullen aus dem Nişantepe-Archiv in Hattusa.* Boğazköy-Ḫattuša XXIII, Mainz am Rhein.

Klinger, J.
– 2015 "Šuppiluliuma II. und die Spätphase der hethitischen Archive," In A. Müller-Karpe *et al.* (eds.), *Saeculum. Gedenkschrift für Heinrich Otten anlässlich seines 100. Geburtstags.* Studien zu den Boğazköy-Texten 58, Wiesbaden, pp. 87–111.

Laroche, E.
– 1960 *Les Hiéroglyphes Hittites,* Paris.
– 1966 *Les Noms des Hittites,* Paris.
– 1981 "*Les Noms des Hittites: Supplément,*" *Hethitica* 4, pp. 3–58.

Mora, C.
– 1987 *La Glittica anatolica del II millennio A. C.: classificazione tipologica. I. I sigilli a iscrizione geroglifica,* Studia Mediterranea 6. Pavia; Primo supplemento 1990.
– 2016 "The Luwian-Hieroglyphic Seal from Troy: an Update and Some Remarks," In H. Marquardt *et al.* (eds.), *Anatolica et indogermanica: Studia linguistica in honorem Johannis Tischler septuagenarii dedicta,* Innsbruck, pp. 213–8.

Neve, P.
– "1992 Šuppiluliuma I. oder II. ?," In H. Otten *et al.* (eds.), *Hittite and other Anatolian and Near Eastern Studies in Honour of Sedat Alp,* Ankara, pp. 401–8.

Nowicki, H.
– 1982 "Zum Herrschernamen auf dem sogenannten „Tarkondemos"-Siegel," In J. Tischler (ed.), *Serta Indogermanica. Festschrift für Günter Neumann zum 60. Geburtstag,* Innsbruck, pp. 227–32.

Otten, H.
– 1967 "Zur Datierung und Bedeutung des Felsheiligtums von Yazılıkaya. Eine Entgegnung," *Zeitschrift für Assyriologie und verwandte Gebiete* 58, pp. 222–40.

Schachner, A. and Özenir, S.
– 2006 "Ein hethitisches Stempelsiegel aus Silber und die Stellung der sogenannten Dreifußsiegel in der hethitischen Grossreichszeit", In A. Erkanal-Öktü et al. (eds.), Hayat Erkanal'a Armağan: Kültürlerin Yansıması (Studies in Honor of Hayat Erkanal: Cultural Reflections), İstanbul, pp. 653–59.

Schaeffer, C. F.-A. *et al.*
– 1956 *Ugaritica III. Mission de Ras Shamra VIII,* Paris.

Seeher , J.
– 1998 "Die Ausgrabungen in Boğazköy-Ḫattuša 1997," *Archäologischer Anzeiger* 1998, pp. 215–41.

Singer, I.
– 2000 "Appendix I: The Hittite Seal Impressions," In J. G. Westenholz *et al., Cuneiform Inscriptions in the Collection of the Bible Lands Museum Jerusalem, The Emar Tablets.* Cuneiform Monographs 13, Groningen, pp. 81–9 with Pls.

Starke, F.
– 1980 "Das luwische Wort für 'Frau,'" *Zeitschrift für Vergleichende Sprachforschung* (= *Historische Sprachforschung*) 94, pp. 74–86.
– 2001 "Ein silbernes, bikonvexes Siegel mit luwischer Hieroglypheninschrift," In U. Finkbeiner *et al.,* Emar 1999 – Bericht über die 3. Kampagne der syrisch-deutschen Ausgrabungen, *Baghdader Mitteilungen* 32, pp. 41–110 (pp. 103–5).

Weeden, M.
– 2010 "A Hittite Seal from Kaman-Kalehöyük," In I. Singer (ed.), *ipamati kistamati pari tumatimis. Luwian and Hittite Studies presented to J. D. Hawkins on the occasion of his 70th Birthday,* Tel Aviv, pp. 249–55.

Yoshida, D.
– 1994 "Hittite Seals with hieroglyphs excavated at Kaman-Kalehöyük," *Anatolian Archaeological Studies* 3, pp. 107–13 (in Japanese).
– 2000 *Writings in Ancient Anatolia,* Tokyo (in Japanese).

Zehnder, Th.
– 2010 *Die hethitischen Frauennamen. Katalog and Interpretation.* Dresdner Beiträge zur Hethitologie 29. Wiesbaden.

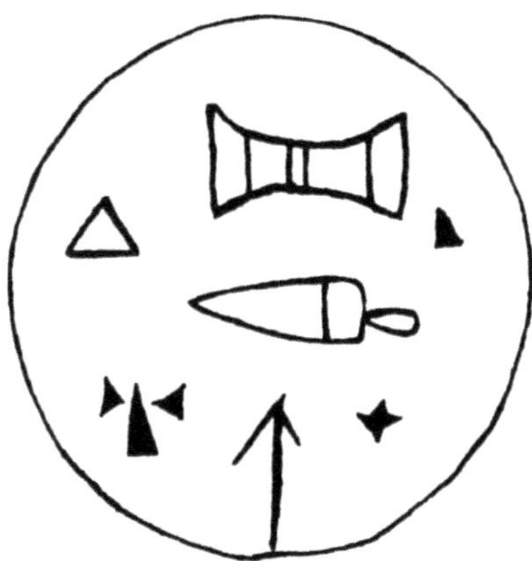

Fig. 1. KL 89-42

Side A

Side B

Fig. 2. KL 96-10

The "Eagle-Man" イーグルマン鷲人

J. David Hawkins †

Dedicated to Sachihiro Omura

The "eagle-man" is a striking but not very common Hieroglyph (L. 133), upper part eagle with forward-pointing wing, lower part human waist and legs. Until recently it was only attested in 4 or 5 inscriptions of Yariri (KARKAMIŠ A6, § 19, 15*b*, § 1 A24*a*5, see Fig. 1.1–3), and TELL AHMAR 1, § 1 (see Fig. 1.4); and (without the legs) KARKAMIŠ A11*a*, § 12 (see Fig. 1.5). Since then it has appeared on KULULU 4, § 3 (Fig. 1.6); and ARSUZ 1, § 10; 2, § 6 (both one-legged, Fig. 1.7–8); 2, § 10 (full, Fig. 1.9). It always shows *+ra/i* except KULULU 4, § 3 (Fig. 1.6). For all these inscriptions, the edition in Hawkins (2000) can be consulted (*ed.*).

Its phonetic value was established as *ara/i* by its alternation with *a+ra/i* in the name *Yariri* (modern readings). A cursive form L. 134 was recognized by the alternations *wa/i-ara/i-*, *wa/i-ra+a-* and *wa/i+ra/i-* in the word *wara-ma* (ASSUR letters *a* and *b*). The cursive form shows a simplified body with two forward-pointing lines representing the wing and an attached *ra/i* (all readings modern).

In fact the "eagle-man" in its Late (ie. Iron Age) form does go back to the Empire period, being found on two MESKENE seals in the names *Saggar-abu* (Beyer 2001: B10) and *Ari-Sarruma* (ibid., B53), where it has the Cun. equivalent Hier. *sà-ka*-L. 133, (also *sà-ka+ra/i-*B6) = Cun. ᴰ30; Hier. L. 133 = Cun. SUM-, thus semi-digraphically *ara/i*. There seems to be no published photograph of B53, but B10 is shown on Beyer, planche 12, in two impressions: neither shows the "eagle-man" particularly clearly, but adequately to see the forward-pointing wing and the attached *+ra/i*; the head can be seen and the outline shape of the undivided legs. Both adequately attest the usage of the "eagle-man" with his later syllabic value *ara/i*.

A different form of eagle with reading *ara/i* appeared on a Boğazköy seal-impression as early as Beran, *Boğazköy* III, no. 14 (Fig. 1.12), and now in NİŞANTEPE nos. 71–74 (Fig. 1.13–14), from at least three different seals (Bittel *et al.* 1957; Herbordt 2005: p. 250, Tafel 6). From the eagle-protome and forward-pointing wing, Laroche was able to identify it as an Empire seal variant of the "eagle-man", and evaluate it also *ara/i* (modern), equating it with the Cun. PN *Arnili* (Laroche 1966 no. 146), though the Hier. form now becomes *Arnilizi*. One NİŞANTEPE example showed a markedly more cursive form of the eagle (no. 73; Fig. 1.13), which allowed me to bring in two Late archaizing forms on SUVASA (D) and TOPADA, § 8 (see Hawkins 2000: p. 460). The last in particular seemed to be a Late linear form of the cursive L.134, yielding the word *zi/a-ara/i*, "here". Subsequent observations have confirmed this.

The trail is revisited by Petra Goedegebuure and Theo van den Hout in their edition of TÜRKMEN-KARAHÖYÜK 1 (Goedegebuure *et al.* 2020: p. 37) tracing a TK 1 line 2 attestation (Fig. 1.17) through SUVASA (Fig. 1.15) and TOPADA (Fig. 1.16) to YALBURT (block 14, § iii), for which they offer an interpretation. This latter form now links with two other Empire attestations, old and new from Boğazköy with which we may conclude, although it cannot be claimed that these are currently intelligible, even giving an *ara/i* reading in their fragmentary contexts.

BOĞAZKÖY 10 (Bo. number unknown, see Fig. 1.18) [...] L. 417(5)-*ma-sa*$_5$ *ara/i* [...: the first 3-sign group recurs on BOĞAZKÖY 9 in the context ASCIA CAPERE L. 417(5)-*ma-sa*$_5$ [... . It seems to be a single word ending phonetically *-masa*, but our ignorance of L. 417(5)(?) does not help.

ara/i [...]: the eagle protome is graphically rendered with its clear forward-pointing wing (Fig. 1.18), but lack of context precludes elucidation.

BOĞAZKÖY 27 *k*i (Bo. 2004/46): unusual fragment with horizontal and vertical dividers splitting it into four "boxes". The lower two (sinistroverse) preserve: ...] *la-mi-n*[*i*?] || *ara/i* DEUS × [...; no coherent sense is available. *ara/i* has an ultra-cursive but identifiable form (Fig. 1.19), comparable to that of YALBURT block 14, § iii; and NİŞANTEPE no.73. This is also found as a Late archaism TOPADA, SUVASA, TÜRKMEN-KARAHÖYÜK line 2.

To summarize, we have seen that the "eagle-man" in striking monumental form has a number of appearances in the Late period (Iron Age), but only in Empire attestation on two MESKENE seal impressions. Otherwise in the Late period it is much more common in its cursive form. On Empire seals from Boğazköy it appears in a rather different form but showing the identifying characteristics (eagle protome, forward-pointing wing and the usual *+ra/i* represented by a trailing crest. One example (NİŞANTEPE no. 73), has the much more cursive linear form found also on Empire YALBURT and two monumental relief fragments from BOĞAZKÖY.

The only reading established for the sign in its various forms is some version of *ara/i*: the PNN *Yariri* and *Ariyahina* (Late) and *Saggarabu*, *Ari-Sarruma* (Meskene) and probably *Arnilizi* (Boğazköy); otherwise the common noun *ari-*, "time, age" (ARSUZ 1+2, in place of the much more common writing with the cursive form.

The purpose of the present note has been to draw together the "eagle-man" in its various forms and common reading and collect the evidence that these have been correctly if somewhat scatteredly recorded.

I take the opportunity here to publish a pencil sketch which I made in the University Museum on my visit to Philadelphia in 1996, of a seal impression on a tablet in the Rosen Collection published by Beckman (1996: p. 69f., RE 51 l. 20 — seal impression not previously published, here by kind permission of Gary Beckman). The piece was already mentioned, Hawkins *apud* Herbordt (2005: p. 250) under 70–74 *Arnilizi*. The very cursive form of *ara/i* (Fig. 1.20) writing *Ari-Sarruma* compared with the "eagle-man" *Ari-Sarruma* serves to pull all forms together. The unmatching epigraph $^{\mathrm{NA4}}$KIŠIB ^{I}*ta-e* ... DUMU *la* is not unusual. See Fig. 2.

It remains only to lay to rest one supposed attestation claimed incorrectly to belong here: KIZILDAĞ 4, § 2c (see Fig. 1.21). The reading of the toponym determined REGIO has caused problems: Meriggi hesitated over the first sign as *mu* or *ma*. Having examined the stone from which I traced my copy on acetate in 1989, I favoured *ma*. The third sign generally accepted as *ka* did look more like an animal head than other forms of the sign. Poetto (1998) with autopsy and an excellent photograph (reproduced Hawkins 2000, plate 29) saw it as an eagle's head, beak, mouth, eye and backward-pointing feather crest, and it is true that these features do appear to be present. Poetto interpreted his reading as *ma-sà* REGIO *ara/i-na*, "the land of Masa forever", which I in a last minute insertion into Hawkins 2000: p. 441 accepted. Since then my doubts had been growing whether a simple eagle head could represent the *ara/i* value of the eagle-man, and these doubts have been resolved by the appearance of TÜRKMEN-KARAHÖYÜK 1, line 1 showing that the 8th century B.C. copyist of 12th century B.C. KIZILDAĞ 4 understood it as *mu-sà-ka-* REGIO, which we should accept as "(conquered) the land Muska".

Bibliography

Beckman, G. M.
- 1996 *Texts from the Vicinity of Emar in the Collection of Jonathan Rosen*, History of the Ancient Near East/Monographs 2, Padova.

Beyer, D.
- 2001 *Emar IV Les Sceaux*, Orbis Biblicus et Orientalis, Series archaeologica 20, Fribourg – Suisse – Göttingen.

Bittel, K. *et al.*
- 1957 *Bogazköy 3 Funde aus den Grabungen 1952–1955*, Abhandlungen der Deutschen Orient-Geselleschaft 2, Berlin.

Goedegebuure, P. *et al.*
- 2020 "TÜRKMEN-KARAHÖYÜK 1: a new Hieroglyphic Luwian inscription from Great King Hartapu, son of Mursili, conqueror of Phrygia," *Anatolian Studies* 70, pp. 29–43.

Hawkins, J. D.
- 2000 *Corpus of Hieroglyphic Luwian Inscriptions Vol. 1 Inscriptions of the Iron Age*, Studies in Indo-European Language and Culture 8.1, Berlin.

Herbordt, S.
- 2005 *Die Prinzen-und Beamtensiegel der hethitischen Grossreichszeit auf Tonbullen aus dem Nişantepe-Archiv in Hattusa*, mit Kommentaren zu den Siegelinschriften und Hieroglyphen von J. David Hawkins, Boğazköy-Ḫattuša 19, Mainz am Rhein.

Laroche, E.
- 1966 *Les noms des Hittites*, Études Linguistiques 4, Paris.

Poetto, M.
- 1998 "Traces of Geography in Hieroglyphic Luwian Documents of the Late Empire and Early Post-Empire Period (BOĞAZKÖY-SÜDBURG and KIZILDAĞ IV): the Case of Maša," in S. Alp and A. Süel (ed.), *III. Uluslararası Hititoloji Kongresi Bildirileri, Çorum 16–22 Eylül 1996 – Acts of the IIIrd International Congress of Hittitology, Çorum, September 16–22, 1996*, Ankara, pp. 496–479

Fig. 1. Attested forms of the Hieroglyph "eagle-man".

Fig. 2. Pencil sketch of a seal impression on a tablet in the Rosen Collection (Beckman RE 51).

Re-Evaluation of Late Bronze Age Chronology of Beycesultan Based on New Excavation Results

Eşref Abay *

Abstract

The chronology of the Late Bronze Age layers (Layers III-I) unearthed in the excavations conducted by the British Institute of Archaeology in Beycesultan settlement based entirely on the relative pottery typology was deemed problematic, and thus, was subject to a great deal of criticism. Critics draw special attention to the similarity between the pottery finds uncovered in the aforementioned cultural layers and the Assyrian Colonial Period and the Old Hittite Period pottery finds unearthed in Central Anatolia. For this reason, the Late Bronze Age layers of Beycesultan were dated to the time interval between the 14th and 11th centuries B.C. by James Mellaart and it has been asserted that they should have been dated to an earlier date. The Late Bronze Age layers (Layers 6–4) have been investigated in a large area of 1400 m² at the Beycesultan excavations, which were restarted in 2007 under my direction, and the excavation work continues to the present. The pottery finds uncovered in these layers and the absolute dating obtained indicate that the Late Bronze Age culture in Beycesultan started 300 years earlier around the 1700s B.C. contrary to what Mellaart had asserted. In view of these data, it is understood that the chronology of Beycesultan and therefore the Central Western Anatolian Late Bronze Age needs to be re-evaluated. Absolute dating obtained from other finds in recent years also reveals that the Late Bronze Age process in the region is in agreement with our suggestion. Carbon-14 dating and relative evaluations obtained from the excavations conducted on the eastern cone of the settlement in recent years currently show that the Late Bronze Age in Beycesultan continued until at least the 13th century B.C.

Öz

Beycesultan yerleşiminde İngiliz Arkeoloji Enstitüsü'nün yapmış olduğu kazılarda açığa çıkarılan Geç Tunç Çağ tabakalarının (Layers III-I) tamamen göreli keramik tipolojisine dayalı olarak yapılmış olan kronolojisi problemli olarak görülüp birçok eleştiri almıştır. Eleştirilerin dikkat çektiği konu, söz konusu kültür tabakaların da tespit edilen keramik buluntuların Orta Anadolu'da Koloni dönemi ve Eski Hitit Dönemi keramik buluntuları ile benzerliğidir. Bu sebeple Beycesultan Geç Tunç Çağ tabakalarının James Mellaart tarafından tarihlendiği M.Ö. 14–11. Yy aralığından daha erkene tarihlenmesi gerektiği iddia edilmiştir. 2007 yılında başkanlığımda tekrar başlatılan ve halen devam eden Beycesultan kazılarında Geç Tun Çağ tabakaları (Tabakalar 6–4) 1400 m² lik geniş bir alanda araştırılmıştır. Söz konusu bu tabakalarda tespit edilen keramik buluntular ve elde edilen mutlak tarihlemeler Beycesultan da Geç Tunç Çağ kültürünün Mellaart' ın iddia ettiğinin aksine 300 yıl daha erken, yaklaşık olarak M.Ö. 1700 lerde başladığını göstermektedir. Bu veriler ışığında Beycesultan ve dolayısı ile İç Batı Anadolu Geç Tunç Çağ kronolojisinin yeniden değerlendirilmesi gerektiği anlaşılmaktadır. Son yıllarda diğer buluntu yerlerinden elde edilen kesin tarihlemeler de bölge de Geç Tunç Çağ sürecinin bizim önerimiz ile benzeştiğini göstermektedir. 2019 yılından bu yana yerleşimin doğu konisi üzerinde yürüttüğümüz kazı çalışmalarından elde ettiğimiz C14 tarihlemeler ve rölatif değerlendirmeler Beycesultan'da Geç Tunç Çağ'ın şimdilik en azından 13.yy a kadar devam ettiğini göstermektedir.

* Ege University, Faculty of Letters, Department of Archaeology, esref.abay@ege.edu.tr

The chronological dating of the Late Bronze Age (Layers III-Ia–b) layers unearthed during the British Institute of Archaeology excavations undertaken across six consecutive seasons between 1954 and 1959 in Beycesultan has been the subject of a series of criticisms (Hachmann 1961: 369; Fischer 1975: 88; Canby 1966: 379). The problematic part of Beycesultan Late Bronze Age chronology, which was developed by Mellaart with relative dating methods based on pottery sequence, predominantly consists of the dating of Beycesultan Layer II to the 13th and early 12th century B.C. Critics, or Rolf Hachmann to be more exact, stated that the pottery unearthed on this layer and some other finds were similar to those found in Boğazköy Büyükkale IVb-a and therefore should be dated to the Old Hittite period. Moreover, Hachmann also asserted that it would be correct to date not only Beycesultan layer II but also layer I to the Old Hittite period based on the data obtained from the excavations in Bogazköy, Alişar and Kültepe (Hachmann 1961: 369). However, Hachmann did not provide any information about what these data were. In his 1955 report on the Beycesultan Excavation, Mellaart stated that there were two imitations of Mycenaean pottery from a layer II vessel dated to LH III-B;[1] however, Hachmann criticized him for not providing any pictures or drawings of the pottery in question, and claimed that it was a mystification rather than a true find (Hachmann 1961: 369). On the other hand, these shards, later published by Mellaart and Ann Murray, represent a paint-decorated ceramic tradition that was observed from the early 16th century B.C. to the 11th century B.C. in Inland Southwest Anatolia, rather than Mycenaean pottery. These shards, which are characterized by red, brown or black paint decorations over gold wash ware, were first discovered at Beycesultan Mound and Aphrodisias followed by a significant recent discovery at Laodikeia Asopos Tepesi excavations and included in the Late Bronze Age repertory to a remarkable degree (Dedeoglu-Konakçı 2017: 191–192). In the meantime, an imported Mycenaean vessel shard, which was claimed to have been discovered in situ at layer III and was also effective in the chronological dating of Beycesultan layer II, was reported in the same publication by Mellaart and Murray (Mellaart and Murray 1995: 94, Fig. P.6. 11). Based on this pottery sherd claimed to be dated to the LH III A or B period (ca. 1360–1240 B.C. or ca. 1300–1260 B.C.), Mellaart asserted that Beycesultan layer III belonged to the 14th century B.C. (Mellaart and Murray 1995: 94–96). In the chronological dating of Beycesultan layer II, the similarity between a few shards of rope-printed pottery as well as types of flasks and bottles found in the last late deposit of this layer and the Bogazköy pottery was taken as criteria and it was stated that it would be proper to date this layer to the 13th B.C. and the early 12th B.C. (Mellaart and Murray 1995: 93, 96). Likewise, as a result of the ceramic comparison, the suitable dates suggested by Mellaart were the 12th B.C. for Beycesultan layer Ib and the 11th century B.C. for layer Ia (Mellaart and Murray 1995: 96).

Although Franz Fischer, who had published the Boğazköy Hittite pottery, did not agree with Hachmann's correlating the Beycesultan layer II phase with the Bogazköy Büyükkale IVb-a phase, he stated that this correlation was remarkable (Fischer 1975: 89, Anm. 80). Fischer, too, refrained from providing any descriptive information on the criteria that were deemed remarkable.

In her book review on Beycesultan Volume II, Jeanny Vorys Canby also drew attention to the resemblance between Beycesultan layer III and II pottery and Central Anatolian Middle Bronze Age pottery (Canby 1966: 379).

A common point of these criticisms is that the Late Bronze Age chronology of Beycesultan is a controversial issue, and even the existence of a settlement in Beycesultan during the Late Bronze Age might be debatable.

1 Mellaart states that the stratigraphic status of this pottery find provides a terminus post quem for the destruction of layer II, and that this destruction must be before 1225 B.C. (Mellaart 1955: 80–81).

Mellaart, who strongly opposed these debates, stood up for the accuracy of his chronological dating; however, he was well aware that the chronology he had postulated contained weaknesses not only owing to the fact that Beycesultan Late Bronze Age pottery displayed a local character and did not allow comparison of specific dating samples, but also to the unavailability of any written documents from these layers and the shortage of data for Carbon 14 chronological dating. Mellaart clearly expressed this assessment in his publication on Beycesultan Vol. III and stated that future excavations in this settlement would deliver a solution for this problem related to chronological dating (Mellaart and Murray 1995: 96). The fact that Mycenaean pottery chronology was taken as a basis in the establishment of the Western Anatolian chronology caused local materials to be pushed into the background. This in turn delayed the establishment of a regional chronology based on the dynamics of the region. It is particularly difficult to establish the Late Bronze Age chronology of Inner West Anatolia considering that the region has a local pottery tradition and unlike coastal regions almost no imported pottery has been unearthed. For this reason, Carbon-14 dating obtained in settlements with uninterrupted stratification is of great importance to establish the Inner West Anatolian chronology.

Excavations at Beycesultan were restarted in 2007 under my direction, and work continues to the present. In the excavations since then, mainly cultural layers dating back to the 2nd millennium B.C. have been investigated. In these studies, conducted on the eastern and western cones, the cultural layers dated to the Late Bronze Age, which was a previous controversial issue, were investigated in large areas and a great deal of Carbon-14 dating data were obtained. Regrettably, in the studies we have conducted so far, no written document has yet been discovered in these layers. The objective of this article is to contribute to the existing debates on chronological dating in the light of new excavation data. It is also remarkable that our work is included in the Festschrift of Dr. Sachihiro Omura, who provided great contributions to the establishment of Anatolian chronology with the systematic excavations he carried out in Kaman-Kalehöyük. I would like to take the occasion to express that it is a great honor for me to contribute an article to this Festschrift prepared in honor of a scientist like Dr. Omura, who has made great contributions to Anatolian Archaeology.

The Results of New Excavations at Beycesultan

Beycesultan is located on Çivril plain in the Province of Denizli in southwest Anatolia (Fig. 1). The objective of the excavations restarted in 2007 was to explore Beycesultan, a key settlement for South-Western Anatolia, using modern excavation methods, and to obtain new data by investigating the cultural phases that currently seem to be problematic in large areas. Along these lines, research has continued in an area of roughly 1400 m^2 after it was started in the N 27 grid square on the western cone of the settlement in 2008 and was later expanded so as to include the O26, O27, M27 and M28 grid squares through the years. Cultural phases covering the periods of the Seljuk/Principality, Byzantine, Late Bronze and Middle Bronze Age were unearthed during the excavation works conducted in this site (Dedeoğlu and Abay 2004: 2, Tab. 1). For the sake of avoiding any confusion, Arabic numerals were used in the new strata denominations instead of the strata nomenclature created with Roman numerals as the result of the British Institute of Archaeology excavations. On the other hand, the post-Late Bronze Age processes that were never included in previous strata are also added to the new stratification. Hence, the New Period excavation stratification covered not only the Seljuk/Principality Period and Byzantine Period but also the Iron Age as it was identified in the First Period excavations, regardless of the fact that it has not yet been identified in the New Period excavations. Accordingly, the layers representing the Late Bronze Age in the new excavations were termed Layer 4, Layer 5 and Layer 6 (see Fig. 2).

The Late Bronze Age data explored in an area of 1400 m^2 were uncovered within a well-defined architectural context (Fig. 4). Data on Layer 5, which covers the early process of the Late Bronze Age, displayed that the said layer had two clearly distinguishable sub-phases (5b-5a). Layer 5b is an earlier layer and reveals a well-developed city plan with 3 m-wide streets extending in an east–west direction. The streets were carefully paved with pebbles. The Carbon-14 dating obtained from this layer, which seems to have ended with a great fire, indicates that layer 5b might be dated to ca. 1700–1595 B.C (Fig. 3). The architectural and archaeological data from this layer reveal that it was contemporary with Layer II, which was uncovered during the British excavations at Beycesultan (Dedeoğlu and Abay 2014: 1–39). Buildings of layer 5b indicate that a two-storey house plan with many rooms prevailed in the settlement (Fig. 5). The houses have their own storage rooms, each of which contains large storage jars, as well as a hearth located in the main room. Within the uncovered rooms, there were many in situ finds because of the abrupt end of the 5b phase caused by a fire. This fire which ruined the layer II was also detected in earlier excavations carried out on the eastern cone of the mound.

Layer 5a indicates that there were many architectural changes in the settlement. The calibrated Carbon-14 dating shows that this phase might belong to a period between 1600 and 1500 B.C. In contrast to the two-storey and multi-room buildings of layer 5b, smaller, single-storey houses consisting of two rooms are seen in layer 5a (Fig. 6). There is only a hearth in these houses, and they do not have any storage rooms. In other words, unlike layer 5b, none of the buildings has its own storage area. The only architectural unit related to storage is a small rectangular clay bin which is located on the corner of the main room. In contrast to the previous layer, no traces of intensive production activity have been encountered in the houses, either. A large building complex is uncovered in this phase. This structure has a rectangular plan, and six of its rooms have already been uncovered. Probably the greater part of the building complex remains in the unexcavated area. This well-planned, multi-roomed complex also indicates the presence of central control in the society of layer 5a. The building complex also contains some ritualistic architectural elements. Particularly, the sacred hearth or altar located in the east part of the building has the characteristics of being part of the domestic cult. The hearth is formed by a rectangular panel with two clay horn-shaped standards rising right in front of this panel and an offering pot partially buried in its platform to the south of the standards. The clay horn-shaped standards were decorated with seal impressions of concentric circles. Six complete vessels, one jar decorated with a symbolic human face and two horn-shaped clay objects or pot supports are among the in situ finds located right around the hearth.

A general evaluation reveals that there is no significant difference between the Layer 5 phases regarding both ware groups and forms, and that they display continuity (Figures 7–8). Most of the ceramics consist of fine ware, medium or well-fired and wheel-made pottery. Other than these examples, a small amount of coarse ware storage vessels may also be mentioned. The ceramics may be classified into some ware groups according to their surface color. Red-Brown or Red Surfaced Ware, Brown Surfaced Ware, Lustrous ware coated with micaceous silver wash, Light Brown or Buff Surfaced Ware and Grey-Black Mottled Surfaced Ware have been identified. The majority of ceramics are those of the Red-Brown or Red Surfaced Ware. These pots generally have a light brown, brick red and red- brown clay color. They mostly have small stone, lime or mica inclusions and are well or medium fired. Only a limited number of examples is underfired. As a slip, mostly red-brown was preferred but also red, brick red and orange colors were used on these pots which are all well slipped. As a surface treatment, burnishing was generally preferred but some examples were not burnished. Bowls (Figure 7: 5–8; Figure 8:5–10), jars (Figure 7:

1–3), fruit plates (Figure 7: 18–21; Figure 8: 14–15), chalices (Figure 7: 14–17; Figure 8: 11–13) and pot stands are among the identified shapes. Regarding the bowl shapes, sharp shouldered bowls with outwardly thickened or everted rims and semi- globular bodied bowls with outwardly thickened rims are rather prevalent. Some examples have a groove decoration made in several lines on the shoulder and pattern burnished decoration on the body (Figure 7: 4, 8 , 10–13 ,17; Figure 8: 9, 17–19). Relief nipple decorations just underneath the rim can also be encountered (Figure 7: 1, 9; Figure 8:1). The conical plates with inverted and everted rims and conical or semi globular dishes with in-turned rims are among the shapes that belong to this group. A ray-like burnish decoration made on the inner and outer surface of the bodies can also appear on some plates. Necked or non-necked jars with o utwardly thickened, everted or flattened rims , and fruit plates, goblets and pot stands are also quite widespread. Half-moon or human face shaped relief decorations, dots, notches, lines and grooves were used on the upper body of jars as decorative elements. Ray-like burnish decoration was often preferred to decorate fruit plates and goblets. The ware group named Brown Surfaced Ware has light brown or reddish-brown colored clay with small stone, lime and mica inclusions. They are represented with well or medium fired, brown slipped and burnished ceramics.

It should be noted that the shapes seen in Layer 5 are not only limited to the ones mentioned above. Almost all of the forms unearthed in Layer II of the Beycesultan Mound were found in this layer too, regarding both the ware group and shape features. Among these are flasks, large storage vessels with seal impressions and pithoi, beak- mouthed pitchers, various shapes and types of rhytons, large jars and miniature vessels.

Due to the fact that Layer 4 was severely affected by construction activities in the Byzantine period, the architectural remains uncovered from this layer are extremely few and the existing ones merely consist of remains of walls and floors that do not display any architectural integrity. Furthermore, no Carbon-14 dating samples could be obtained from this layer. The pottery finds from this phase consist of wheel-made fine wares. Three main groups stand out among the well or medium fired pottery. (These main ware groups can be described based on the color of the exterior: Light Brown or Buff Ware, Red-Brown or Red Ware, Brown Ware.) The most frequent group among the ceramics uncovered until the present day is the Light Brown or Buff Ware. The surfaces of these vessels were left without burnishing. On a limited number of examples, gold and silver wash was applied on the interior and exterior of the vessels. The shapes used for this group are jars, bottles, bowls and plates (Figure 9). While the jars included short-necked small jars with everted or simple rims and short- necked jars with out-turned rims, the bottles consist of single-handled examples with out- turned or flattened rims . The bowls were made with everted rims and sharp shoulders or simple rims and conical bodies whereas the plates had inwardly and outwardly thickened rims. The vessels of this group are generally well- fired and all of them are slipped. Even though red brown is the most used slip color, red and orange can also be seen. The application of buffing can only be seen on a limited number of vessels. Gold and silver wash was used on the interior and exterior of a limited number of examples in this group as well. Among the most common shapes are mostly large and small bowls, but also jars. There are globular bodied examples with everted rims among the jars.

Seals and Sealings from Beycesultan

Several of the artifacts found in Beycesultan are seals and sealings. While neither seals nor bullae were discovered in the new period excavations, two stamp seals and a bulla were discovered at layer II and I during the British excavations (Figs. 10a–b). However, Mellaart had good reason not to take these seals into consideration while dating the layer in which they were found (Mellaart and Murray 1995: pp. 92–96). In view of the possibility that seals were used for a long time after the date they were made, using seals for chronological dating does not always yield reliable results. However, it is quite notable that the comparative dating of these seals and the sealings is compatible with the date we propose for layer 5. Therefore, I believe it is necessary to deal with these seals and the bulla here. One of these is a stamp seal carved from stone (Fig. 10a) (Mellaart and Murray 1995: 123–124, Fig. O33, 292). The seal has a circular stamping face. The end of the seal is shaped into a conical knob. This part is perforated for suspension on a cord (Fig. 10a). On the stamping face is a crouching griffon surrounded by two circles of ladder design. As stated by Mellaart, the closest similar example bearing a griffon motif comes from Boğazköy, (Mellaart and Murray 1995: 123–124; Boehmer and Güterbock 1987, Pl. II, no. 30). Although this clay seal, which is shown among the seal finds of the Kārum period, is cracked, it bears great resemblance to the Beycesultan sample in terms of both motif and form. Another such example of comparison is seen in the Central Anatolian settlement of Alişar. The figure on the Alişar sample resembles more a sphinx (Mellaart and Murray 1995: 123–124, Fig. O33, 292; Von der Osten, 1937, Fig. 249, B. 1478). Similarly, stamp seals with griffon and other animal motifs are also uncovered in layer Ib in Kültepe/Kanis (Özgüç 2003: Fig. 328–330) and in layer I in Konya Karahöyük (Alp 1994: 176–177, (Lev. 78/208, figure 88; Lev. 86/236, figure 98, Lev. 86). /237, Fig. 99). As in the example of Beycesultan, the griffon and animal figures are surrounded by a circular ladder motif. Sedat Alp dated Karahöyük Layer I to the last phase of the Assyrian Trade colonies, to ca. 1750 B.C. (Alp 1994: 258). Based on seal examinations, R. Michael Boehmer indicates that it would be more accurate to date layer I of Karahöyük to about 50 years later than the date suggested by Sedat Alp, i. e. 1700 B.C. (Boehmer 1989: 43; 1996: 17–22).

Another stamp seal made of ivory was discovered in Layer Ib at Beycesultan (Fig. 10b) (Mellaart and Murray 1995: 126–127, Fig. O.41, 343). This stamp seal with a hammerhead handle has a circular stamping face. There are spiral designs on the stamping face. Seals bearing the closest resemblance in terms of both form and design can were discovered in Boğazköy. These types of seals emerged at the end of the Assyrian Colony Period in Boğazköy, and continued to appear until the Old Hittite period (Boehmer R. M. and H. G. Güterbock 1987: Pl. II, no. 21 (bulla); Beran, 1967: Pl. 3, no. 24). About the same dates were given for a similar seal from Alacahöyük (Koşay 195: Pl. 79, 7).

On the clay bulla detected in Beycesultan layer II, there are two seal impressions that seem to have been made with the same stamp seal (Fig. 10c) (Mellaart and Murray 1995: 126–127, Fig. O.20, 208). In the middle of the seal impression, there is no motif other than a simple circular spiral motif. Similar examples bearing similar spiral motifs are also detected in layer I of Konya Karahöyük. There are double-headed eagle motifs or a similar circular S-shaped spiral motif in the middle of the stamping face of the samples found in Karahöyük (Alp 1994: Lev. 73/192, Fig. 81; Lev. 85/234, Fig. 96). Similar S-shaped spiral motifs are seen in Kültepe stamp seals, as well (Özgüç and Tunca 2001: Kt. v/t 41). Unlike the ones in Beycesultan, these seal samples detected in Kültepe Ib have a spiral motif and rosette or a double-headed eagle motif in the center of the seal surface (Özgüç and Tunca 2001: Kt. v/t 22, 43; T. Özgüç 2003: Fig. 325–327).

General Evaluation and Conclusion

Both absolute and relative dating data reveal that the 5b-a Layers of Beycesultan are contemporary with Layers II and Ib in the early period excavations. The differentiation observed in the architectural structuring and settlement understanding, which started in the process called layer 6 in the new period excavations in Beycesultan and Layer III in the first period excavations, continued in layers 5b and 5a. Likewise, we have defined this process as the Early Phase of the Late Bronze Age. Our new data on Layer 6 preceding layer 5, which we have dated to 1700–1600 B.C. by pulling it back about 300 years in the new period excavations, is limited for the time being given the fact that it has not been possible to explore this layer in large areas as yet. At the same time, as we asserted before, this layer (Layer 6) should be accepted as the beginning of the Late Bronze Age process. This layer, which is contemporary with layer III in the early excavations, was dated to the LH III A or B period, i.e. ca. 1360–1240 B.C. or ca. 1300–1260 B.C., by Mellaart and Murray (Mellaart and Murray 1995: 94, Fig. P.6.11) based on a single piece of Mycenaean import pottery (Mellaart and Murray 1995: 94–96). New data from Beycesultan have proven that this chronological dating is completely invalid. One of the two Carbon-14 samples obtained from Layer 6 was dated to 1880–1688 B.C., and the second sample to 1830–1662 B.C. We believe these data indicate that Layer 6 can be dated to approximately 1700 B.C. or just before that date. Against this background, it can be presumed that a single piece of imported Mycenaean pottery, claimed to have been found in layer III during the First Period Beycesultan excavations, may have been mixed in from a more recent layer. Considering a settlement like Beycesultan, where many Byzantine pits destroyed the Late Bronze Age layers, this confusion is highly likely. On the basis of the new excavation data at Beycesultan, Carbon-14 dating data obtained from Western Anatolia in recent years support the chronology we have established (Dedeoğlu, F. and E. Abay 2004). In parallel with Beycesultan, the Troy and Maydos Kilisetepe Carbon-14 dating s (Pavuk 2014: 404, Abb 166; Başaran-Mutlu 2019: 6) pulled back the beginning of the Late Bronze Age in Western Anatolian chronology to an earlier time (Fig. 11). A general evaluation of the data we have obtained in recent years reveals that the last period of Beycesultan layer 5 can be said to be contemporary with Troy VIb/c (Pavuk 2014: 404, Abb 166), Maydos Kilisetepe Vb (Başaran-Mutlu 2019: 6), Çine Tepecik II2b (Günel 2010: p. 28), Limantepe III 1–2 (Aykurt 2013: 53) and Kaymakcı LB 1 (Roosevelt *et al.* 2018: 648). When the Beycesultan Layer 5 pottery tradition is examined, it can be asserted that it largely resembles the Central Anatolian settlements. Considering the Carbon-14 datings obtained, Beycesultan layer 5 may be contemporary with Layer IVc of Boğazköy – Büyükkale (Schachner 2019: pp. 14–17) and likewise Konya Kara Höyük layer I (Alp 1994: 258; Boehmer 1989: 43; 1996: 17–22).

Despite the fact that we currently do not have Carbon-14 dating data for the late phase of the Late Bronze Age (layer 4) of the western cone, where uninterrupted 2nd Millennium B.C. stratigraphy has been defined, the pottery data summarized above indicate that significant differences exist between the late and the early phases of the Late Bronze Age. Among the elements displaying the differences between the two phases of this layer are the gradual replacement of the red and dark brown pottery with buff and light brown ones, and the increase in the use of paint decorated and gold mica coated pottery. It can also be said that the paint decorations applied on the gold wash pottery demonstrated a relative increase in this phase. An evaluation of the forms revealed that a great amount of previously discovered fruit plates, goblets, trefoil and beak mouthed jugs were replaced by plain bowls and pots in this layer and the number of bottles also increased. The most notable point at this point is the significant decrease in the number of goblets and fruit plates and the increase in the number of common everyday vessels instead. The pottery belonging to the Late Bronze Age layers unearthed in the excavations at nearby sites such as Aphrodisias and Asopos Tepesi revealed a picture confirming the changes we have identified in Beycesultan and summarized above. (Şimşek and Konakçı 2013: 1; Joukowsky 1986: 367, 371).

It is yet not clear how long the Late Bronze Age lasted in Beycesultan. Preliminary observations on Carbon-14 data as well as finds unearthed in the excavations we have conducted on the Eastern Cone of the settlement since 2019 currently indicate that the settlement existed in Beycesultan until the late 14th century B.C. and the early 13th century B.C.

Bibliography

Alp, S.

- 1994 *Konya Civarında Karahöyük Kazılarında Bulunan Silindir ve Damga Mühürleri*, Ankara.

Aykurt, A.

- 2013 "An Updated Assessment on Western Anatolian Middle Bronze Age Chronology in Light of Excavations of the Izmir Region," CollAn XII, pp. 37–77.

Başaran-Mutlu, M.

- 2019 "Maydos Kilisetepe Höyüğü M.Ö. 2. Binyıl Yerleşim Özellikleri" *Fırat Üniversitesi Sosyal Bilimler Dergisi* 29/1, pp. 1–16.

Beran, T.

- 1967 *Die hethitische Glyptik von Boğazköy. 1. Teil: Die Siegel und Siegelabdrücke der Vor- und Althethitischen Perioden und die Siegel der hethitischen Grosskönige- Boğazköy Hattusa. Ergebnisse der Ausgrabungen*, Bd. V, Berlin.

Boehmer, R.M. and H.G. Güterbock

- 1987 *Glyptik aus dem Stadtgebiet von Boğazköy: Grabungskampagnen 1931–1939, 1952–1978*, Berlin.

Boehmer, R.M.

- 1989 "Zur Datierung des Karahöyük," in K. Emre, B. Hrouda, M. Mellink and N. Özgüç (eds.) *Anatolia and the Ancient Near East. Studies in Honor of Tahsin Özgüz*, Ankara, pp. 39–44.
- 1996 "Nochmals zur Datierung der Glyptik von Karahöyük Schicht I," *Istanbuler Mitteilungen* 46, pp. 17–22.

Canby, J.V.

- 1966 "Review Work (s): Beycesultan, Vol. II, Middle Bronze Age Architecture and Pottery by Seton Lloyd and James Mellaart," AJA 70 (4), pp. 379–380.

Dedeoğlu, F. and E. Konakçı

- 2015 "Local Painted Pottery Tradition from Inland Southwest Anatolia and Its Contribution to Second Millennium B.C. Chronology," *Mediterranean Archaeology and Archaeometry* 15 (2), pp. 191–214.

Dedeoğlu, F. and E. Abay

- 2004 "Beycesultan Höyük Excavation Project: New Archaeological Evidence from Late Bronze Layers," *Arkeoloji Dergisi* XIX, pp. 1–39.

Fischer, F.

- 1963 *Die Hethitische Keramik von Bogazköy*, 75. Wissenschaftliche Veröffentlichung der Deutschen Orient-Gesellschaft, Berlin.

Günel, S.

- 2010 "Mycenaean Cultural Impact on the Çine (Marsyas) Plain, Southwest Anatolia: The Evidence from Çine-Tepecik," *Anatolian Studies* 60, pp. 25–49.

Hacmann, R.

- 1961 "Die Königsliste von Chorsabad, die assyrischen Abstandsdaten und das Problem der absoluten Chronologie der europäischen Bronzezeit," *V. Internationaler Kongress Vor- und Frühgeschichte, Hamburg 1958*, pp. 366–373.

Joukowsky, M.S.

- 1986 *Prehistoric Aphrodisias, An Account of the Excavations and Artifact Studies. Vol. I: Excavations and Studies*. Providence R.I.

Koşay, H.Z.

- 1951 *Türk Tarih Kurumu tarafından yapılan Alaca Höyük Kazısı: 1937–1939 daki çalışmalara ve keşiflere ait ilk rapor = Les fouilles d'Alaca Höyük entreprises par la Societe d'Historie Turque: rapport preliminaire sur les travaux en 1937–1939*, Ankara.

Mellaart, J.

- 1970 "The Second Millennium Chronology of Beycesultan," *Anatolian Studies* 20, pp. 55–67.

Özgüç, N. and Ö. Tunca

- 2001 *Kültepe-Kaniš, Mühürlü ve Yazıtlı Kil Bullalar, Sealed and Inscribed Clay Bullae*, Ankara.

Özgüç, T.

- *2003 Kültepe Kaniš/Neša, The Earliest International Trade Center and the Oldest Capital City of the Hittites*, İstanbul.

Pavuk, P.

- 2014 *Troia VI Früh und Mitte: Keramik, Stratigraphie, Chronologie*, Bonn.

Roosevelt, C., C. Luke, S. Ünlüsoy, J.M. Marston, P. Pavuk, M. Pieniazek, J. Mokrisova, C. Scott, N. Shin, F.G. Slim

- 2018 "Exploring Space, Economy, and Interregional Interaction at a Second-Millennium B.C.E. Citadel in Central Western Anatolia: 2014–2017 Research at Kaymakçı" *AJA* 122 (4), pp. 645–688.

Schachner, A.

- 2019 *Hattuşa: Efsanevi Hitit* İmparatorluğunun İzinde, İstanbul.

Şimşek, C. and E. Konakçı

- 2013 "Güneybatı Anadolu'da Yeni Bir Prehistorik Yerleşim: Asopos Tepesi," *Arkeoloji Dergisi* XVII, pp. 1–37.

Von der Osten, H.H.

- 1937 *The Alishar Hüyük Seasons of 1930–1932, OIP 28, Part 1*, The University of Chicago Press. Chicago Illinois.

Fig. 1. Map showing the location of Beycesultan.

Old Stratigraphy (According to Lloyd-Mellant)	New Stratigraphy	Period	Relative Dating	Absolute Dating
	1	Seljuk Period/ Early Ottoman Period	13-14th Century AD	
	2a 1-2	Byzantine Period	11-12th Century AD	
	2b			
	Hiatus			
Ia	4a	Late Bronze Age		
Ib	4b			1600-1500 BC
II	5a 5b			1700-1595 BC
III	6	Middle Bronze Age		1880-1688 BC 1830-1662 BC
IV a-c	7			1955-1870 BC 1845-1810 BC 1800-1775 BC
	8			1916-1746 BC 1884-1736 BC
V	9			2026-1882 BC
	10			2130-2080 BC 2060-1940 BC

Fig. 2. Comparative stratigraphy of Beycesultan.

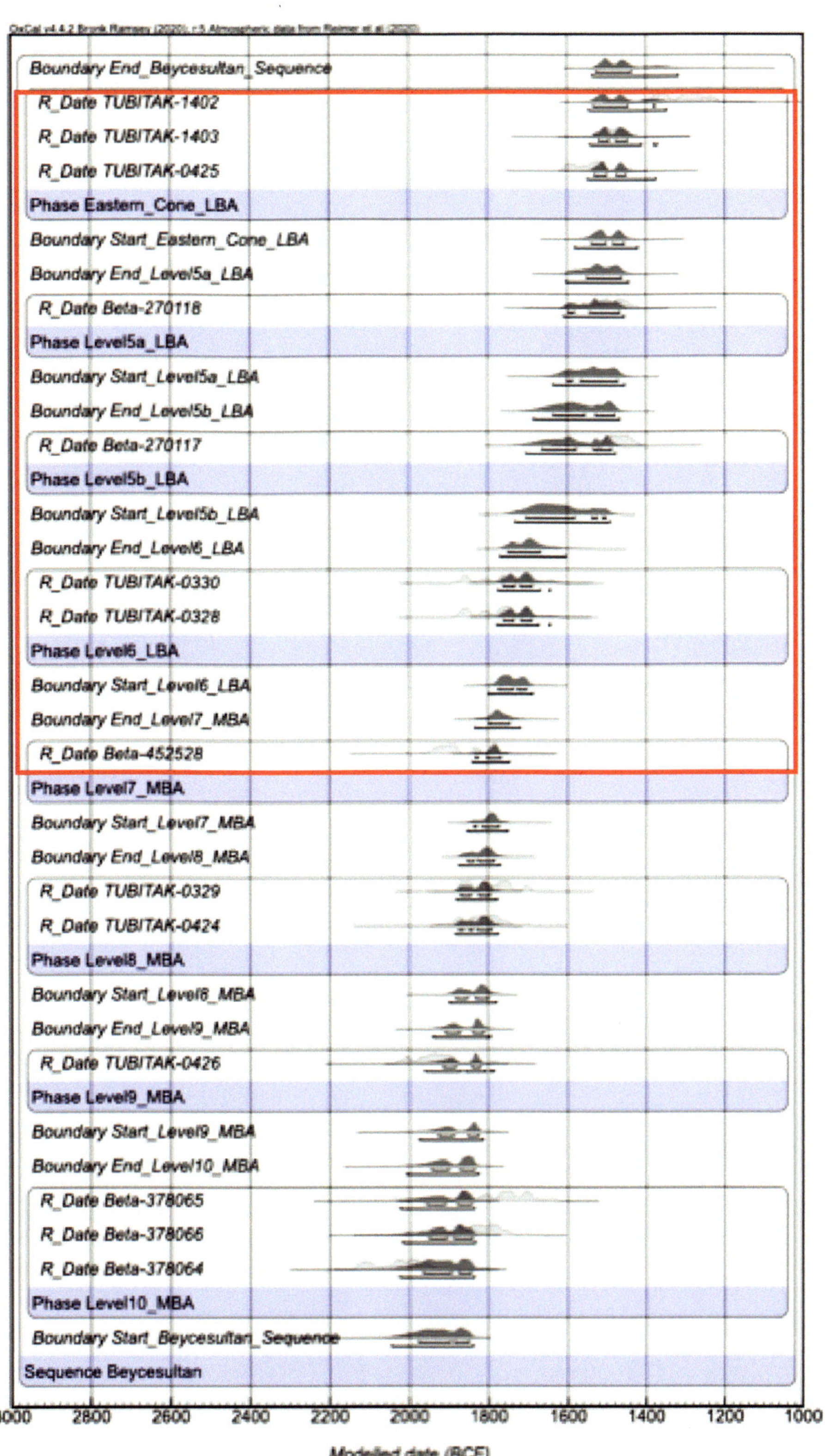

Fig. 3. Radiocarbon results from Layers 4 -10.

Fig. 4. View of Layer 5a (stone walls) and Level 5b architectural remains in trench N27.

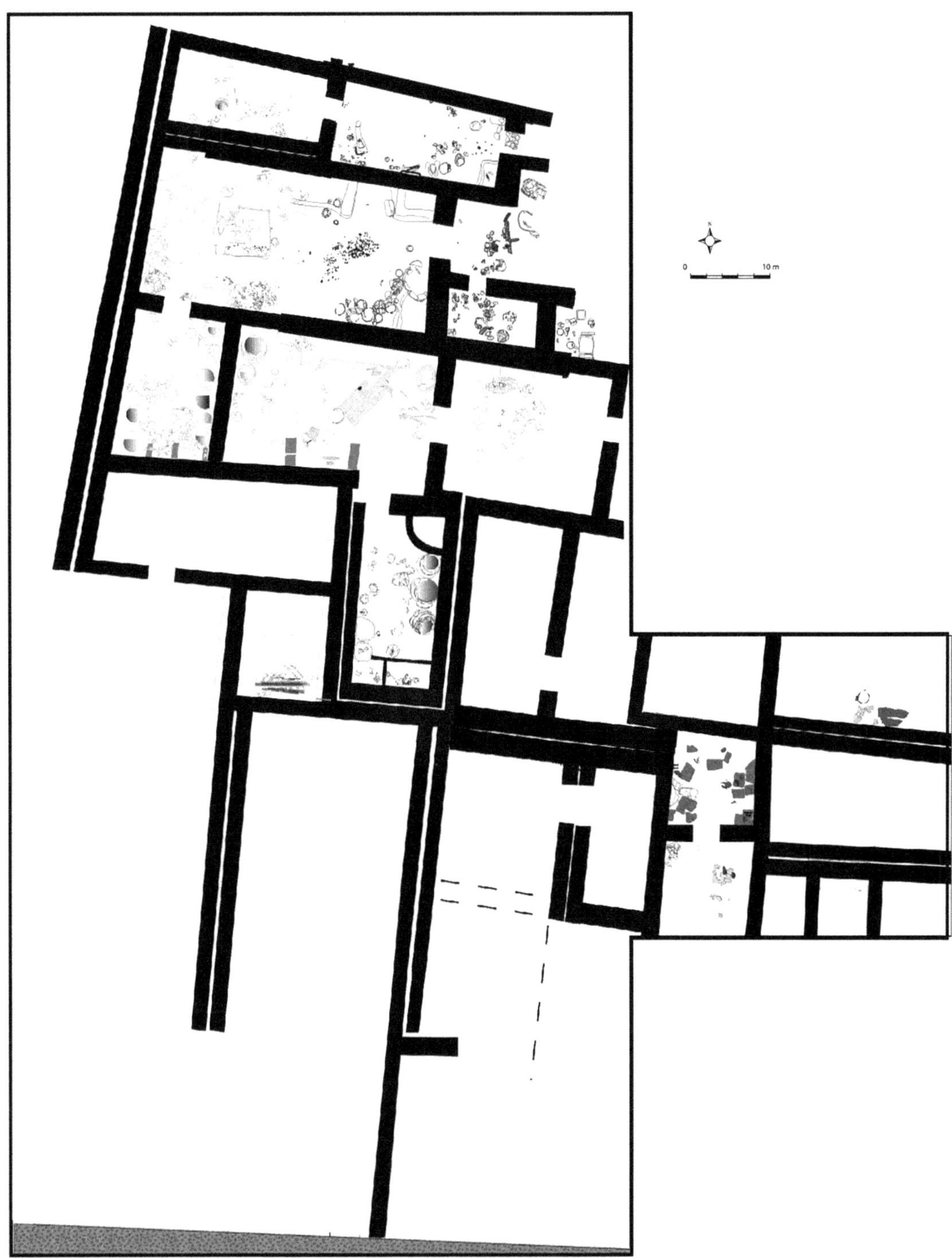

Fig. 5. Plan of Layer 5b architectural remains.

Fig. 6. Plan of Layer 5a architectural remains.

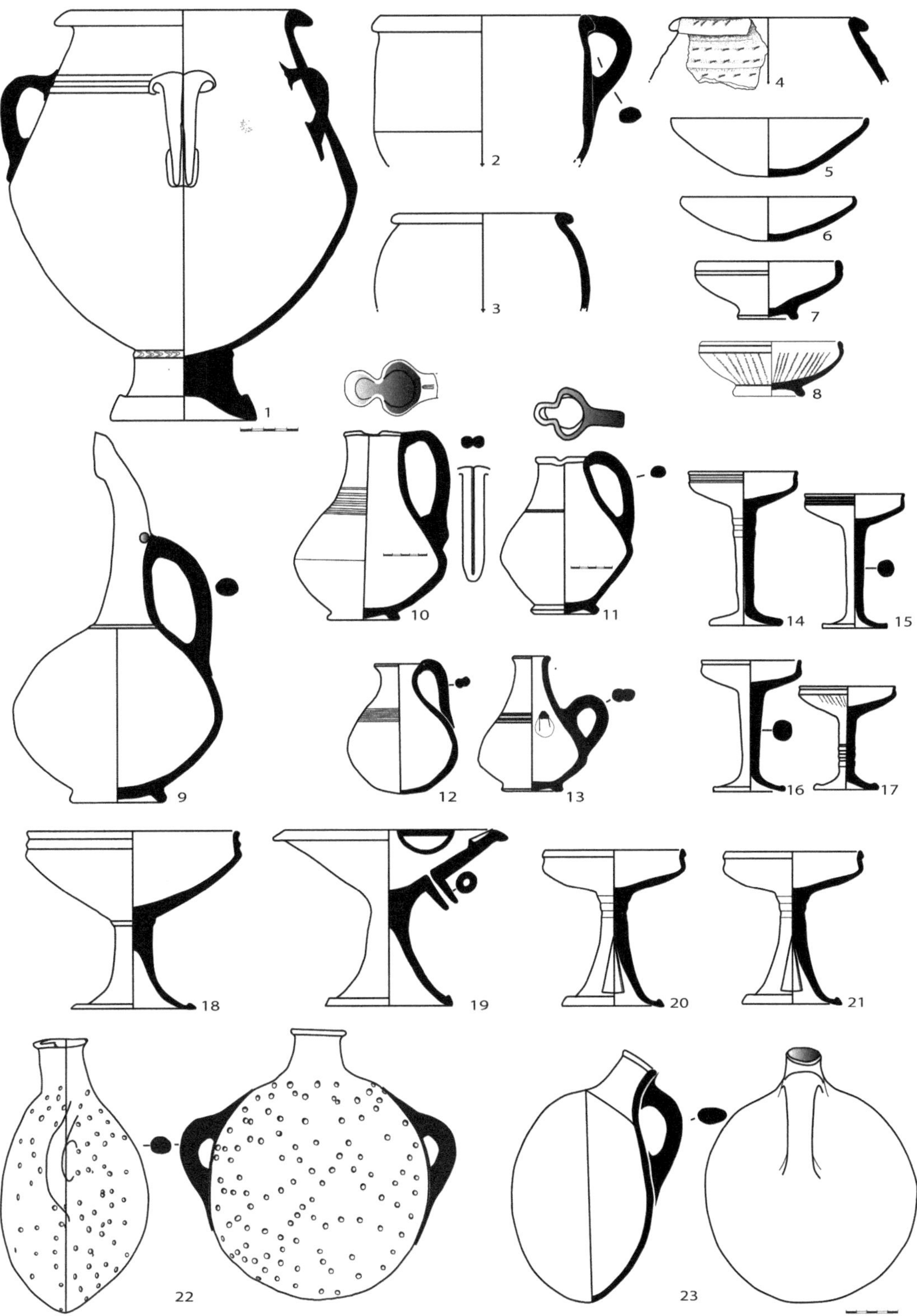

Fig. 7. Pottery samples from Layers 5a–b.

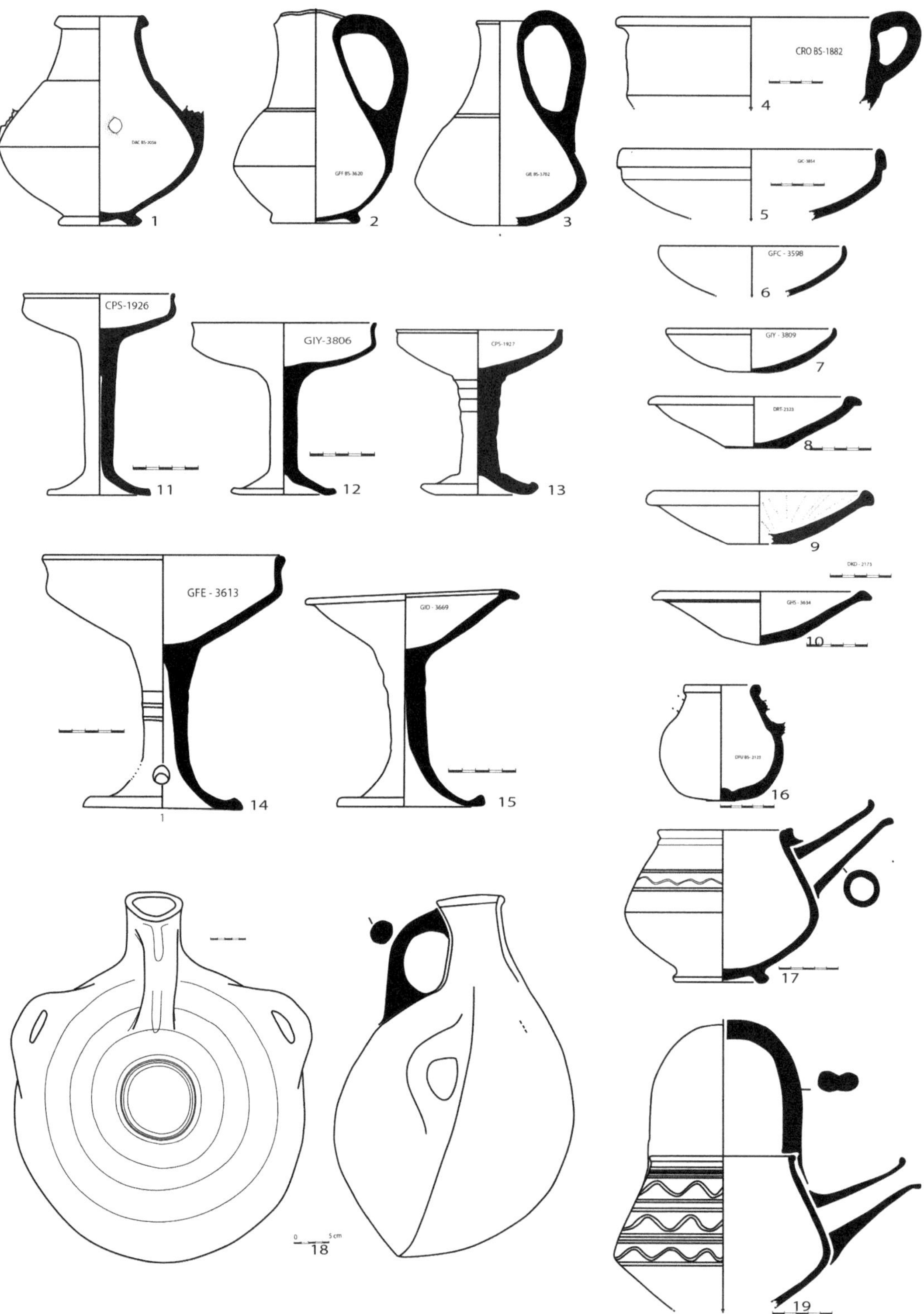

Fig. 8. Pottery sample from Layers 5a–b.

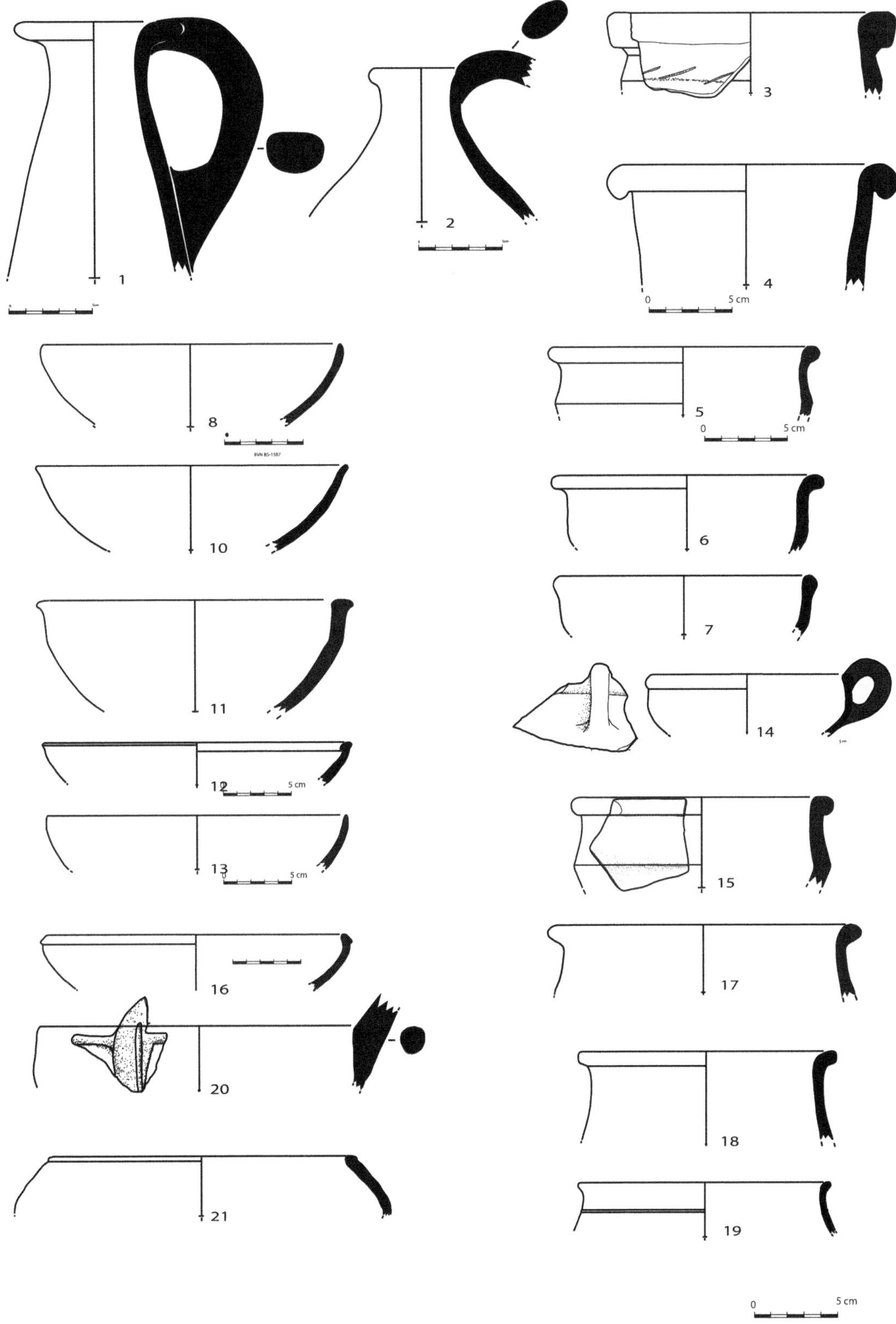

Fig. 9. Pottery sample from Layer 4.

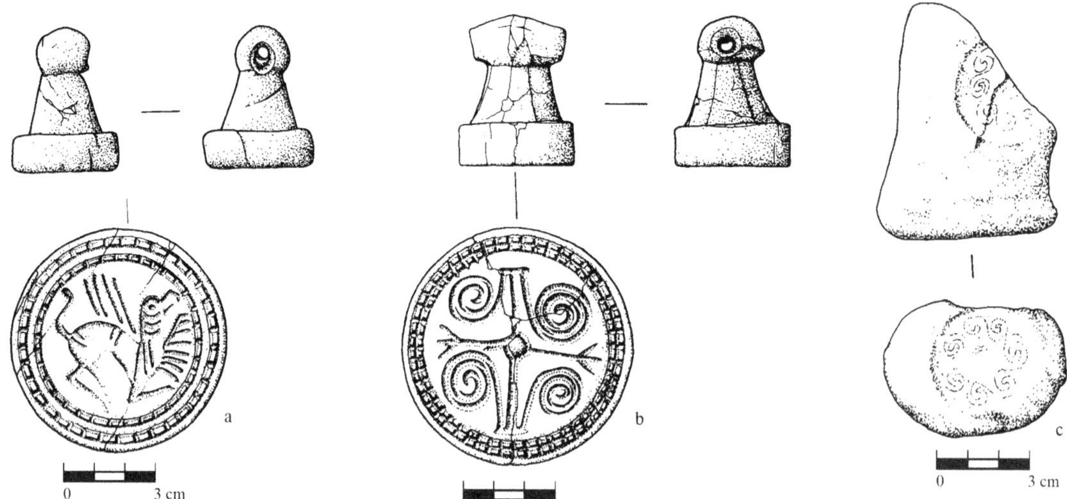

Fig. 10. Seals and Bulla found during British excavations at Layers II and Ib in Beycesultan (after Mellaart and Murray 1995: Figs. O.20, 208; O33, 292; O.41, 343)

BCE	Beycesultan	Troy	Maydos Kilisetepe	Liman Tepe	Seyitömer	Çine Tepecikhöyük	Demirci Hüyük	Gordion	Boğazköy Büyükkale	Kültepe/ Karum	Konya Karahöyük	Miletus
1300												
		VIg-h		II: 3					III			
	4											V
1400			Va					11-10				
									IVa-b			
		VIe-f		?			Surface					
1500			Vb									IVb
	5a					II2a	5					
		VId						13-12 c				
1600				III: 1-2				e				
							4					
	5b								IVc	Ia/Kültepe 6		IVa
			Vc					m				
											I	
		VIb/c						e				
1700	6		VIa		IVA		2 / 3					IIIb
				III: 3				16-14 t				
		VIa							IV d	Ib/Kültepe 7		
								e				
1800	7						1					
			Vb	III: 4								IIIa
						II2b		r				
		V										
								18-17 y	c	II/Kültepe 8	II	
1900	8											
				III: 5	IVB		Bahçehisar ??		IV b			
		IV							a			
			VII									II
2000	9											
					IVC					II-IV/Kültepe 9-10	III	
	10	Proto IV	VIII									
2100												

Fig. 11. Comparative chronological table of Beycesultan and other contemporary settlements.

Notes on the Middle Iron Age Settlement Pattern in the Kızılırmak Basin Based on the Ian A. Todd Survey

Geoffrey D. Summers *

Abstract

This paper is concerned with archaeological evidence pertaining to Middle Iron Age (MIA) settlements and settlement patterns based on geography, topography, excavations and surveys. It offers commentary and interpretation of results from the Central Anatolian Survey conducted by Ian Todd in the 1960s (Todd 1980) together with some very recent discoveries on the Anatolian plateau. Sachihiro Omura's excavations at Kaman-Kalehöyük, together with his Central Anatolian General Survey, are fundamental to our subject.

Öz

Bu çalışma, coğrafya, topografya, kazılar ve yüzey araştırmalarına dayanan Orta Demir Çağı (ODÇ) yerleşimleri ve yerleşim düzenlerine ilişkin arkeolojik kanıtlarla ilgilidir. Ian Todd tarafından 1960'larda yürütülen Orta Anadolu Yüzey Araştırması'nın (Todd 1980) sonuçları ile Anadolu platosundaki bazı yeni keşiflerin yorum ve değerlendirmelerini sunmaktadır. Sachihiro Omura'nın Kaman-Kalehöyük kazıları ve Orta Anadolu Genel Yüzey Araştırması konumuz için temel teşkil etmektedir.

Physical Geography

The area of the Todd survey covered here (Fig. 1) can be divided into two roughly equal portions: firstly, an area to the northeast between the Kızılırmak and the Delice Çayı, the north-western and south-eastern limits coinciding with the old vilayet boundaries with the Seyfe Gölü basin in the eastern sector; secondly, the area south of the Kızılırmak delimited by the borders of Nevşehir and Niğde *vilayets* as they were drawn in the 1960s. The southern area is dominated by two geographic features, the southern portion of the Tuz Gölü basin and the Mendeliz massif. The wide flood plains of both the Kızılırmak and the Delice Çayı might provide explanation for the absence of settlements along their banks.

The Kızılırmak, the longest river in Turkey, rises some 2000 m absl in the mountains near Sivas from whence it sweeps through Central Anatolia in a great bend before flowing northwards through the Pontic Mountains to debouch into the Black Sea. Neither the middle nor lower reaches are navigable, but there does seem to have been some local, presumably seasonal, river transport on the upper reaches in the Bronze Age (Barjamovic 2011). Much of the bend was flooded by construction of the Hirfanlı dam in 1959 without systematic archaeological survey being undertaken. Several more dams have since been constructed. For present purposes there are two consequences; firstly, it is not possible to reconstruct the settlement pattern within the area flooded by Hirfanlı, although no large mounds were reported by early travellers through the area that was subject to regular seasonal flooding; secondly, it is not possible today to judge the extent and timing of seasonally low water in a normal year that would have facilitated fording or crossing on rafts. In flood the river carries much silt, hence its modern name: Kızılırmak (Red River). The Ancient Greek name, Halys, means Salty, reflecting water not favoured for drinking or agriculture (Kaçaroğlu, Değirmenci and Cerit 2001).

* Retired researcher, summersgd@gmail.com

Parameters

The MIA, which for the purposes of this paper is taken to extend from the mid-10th century to the Persian invasion c. 550 B.C. settlement pattern owes little to that of the Hittite Empire because a centralized empire with an exceptionally large capital at Hattusa was replaced in the MIA by a number of principalities. To the west lay Phrygia, not necessarily a unified kingdom before the time of Midas. During the Hittite Empire all roads led to Hattusa (Hawkins in press) while the Kızılırmak seems not to have been a significant boundary or barrier. For Hittite geography we now have Weeden and Ullmann's *Hittite Landscape and Geography* (2017).

Whatever the causes and rapidity of the LBA collapse, it has long been thought to have brought about a 'Dark Age' on the Anatolian Plateau, devoid of urban settlement and written texts. The very recent research at Türkmenkarahöyük associated with the very strange Luwian Hieroglyphic inscription TKH I (Goedegebuure *et al.* 2020; Massa *et al.* 2020; Osborne *et al.* 2020; Hawkins and Weeden 2021)[1] has, however, gone some way towards filling this historical void by affirming the existence of a Great King named K/Hartapu who defeated the land of Muska. This Hartapu I, son of a certain Mursilli, was already known from KIZILDAĞ 4 and it is tentatively proposed that he was an otherwise unknown descendant of Kuruntiya (Hawkins 1992; Hawkins and Weeden 2021). It is thus possible that there were in the Early Iron Age (EIA) so-called rump states in central Anatolia mirroring those in North Syria (Weeden 2013; Osborne 2020). As yet, however, we have no firm archaeological or epigraphic evidence for continuity of urban settlement from the twelfth century to the ninth. Within the bend of the Kızılırmak there is strong evidence for the destruction of Hittites cities followed by some three centuries of non-urban settlement. Regarding the Konya Plain, the KRASP survey team state that they have not found early handmade pottery that is known from Gordion and elsewhere and claim evidence for continuity in the ceramic tradition from the LBA into the EIA (Massa *et al.* 2020). Similar claims were made for Porsuk. Here caution is appropriate. Not a single sherd of this plain early handmade pottery was found amongst the copious material collected by Todd (personal observation), and none is to be seen on the surface of large mounds such as Kaman and Gordion where it has been excavated. As to Porsuk, the EIA date is questionable (Crespin 1999) and remains in doubt. Relevant here is the proposal to identify Türkmenkarahöyük with LBA Tarhuntassa (Massa 2020) and very plausibly with MIA Parzuta mentioned in the TOPADA inscription. Hawkins and Weeden have set out objections to identification with Tarhuntassa to which might it be added that if continuity of urban life from the LBA to the MIA at Türkmenkarahöyük can be demonstrated by ongoing fieldwork the change of name would require explanation.

TKH 1 and KIZILDAĞ 4 inform us of developments in the western Hittite empire, including perhaps arrival of tribes from the Balkans that were possibly implicated in its demise. Archaeological support might be found in EIA levels at Gordion where Voigt has argued for the arrival of newcomers (Voigt 2013, Voigt and Henrickson 2000). At the eastern end of the empire new radiocarbon evidence from Arslantepe (Malatya) is likewise sugges-

1 I am greatly indebted to David Hawkins and Mark Weeden for providing a draft of their paper and, together with Çiğdem Maner, for much enlightening discussion. While I strongly favour the dating and historical suggestions of Hawkins and Weeden, this in no way diminishes my gratitude to Michele Massa for discussing the TKH discoveries with me in Ankara, and to both Michele Masa and James Osborne for providing pre-publication copies of their papers. Michele Massa employed his GIS skills to create the map that appears as Figure 1. Federico Manuelli kindly provided a draft of the paper to appear in *Radiocarbon*. Çigdem Maner and Kimiyoshi Matsumura made many helpful suggestions, the incorporation of which has greatly improved this contribution. Healthy academic discourse means that we are not always in agreement, while errors of fact and interpretation remain entirely my own.

tive of cultural changes, presumably paralleled by political ones, somewhat before the (traditional) date for the abandonment and destruction of Hattusa in the early 12th century B.C. (Manuelli *et al.* in press).

Here, however, my focus is the MIA. No later than the 9th century B.C. some of the area under consideration belonged to Neo-Hittite kingdoms in what the Assyrians were to call the Lands of Tabal. By the 8th century B.C. new kingdoms had been established and archaeological evidence for settlement patterns is sufficiently robust to permit preliminary analysis. Territory on the western side of the Kızılırmak and north of the two lake basins, Tuz Gölü and Konya, was part of Phrygia, its populace, as noted above, perhaps partial descendants of the Muska who presumably arrived at the start of the Iron Age. By the late 8th eighth century B.C. Phrygia may have become a larger polity under the dynasty of Midas, but there are clear regional differences in material culture (Summers 2018a; see also Draycott 2019: 200). Even at its height, with Midas leading a coalition of forces against Assyria, Gordion may not have amounted to anything greater than a kingdom stretching between somewhere around Sivrihisar in the west, the Kızılırmak in the east, c. 200km, and between the southern side of the Pontic mountains at north and a southern border on a line between the Tuz Gölü, Salt Lake, and Afyonkarahisar, c. 100 km. It might be suggested that the population of this area had become phrygianised (van Dongen 2014, Summers 2018a). The Konya basin is roughly equated with the kingdom of Great King Hartapu, very possibly named Parzuta. Harpartu's kingdom lay to the west of our area and most probably to the west of what the Assyrians knew as Tabal (although Tabal may well have included territories of which the Assyrians had little or no direct knowledge). That Hartapu, unlike Midas, does not appear in Neo-Assyrian inscriptions has chronological implications. Of more direct concern to us is the kingdom of Tuwana whose known kings included Warpalawa. Massa *et al.* (2020) convincingly argue that the contemporaneous kingdoms ruled by Hartapu with its sacred landscape that embraced Kızıldağ and Karadağ, and Tuwana with its principle cult centre on Göllüdağ, approached by a sacred way with cultic stations, were of similar size. That would place them within the same general range suggested above for Gordion. These observations might now permit us to look for similar geographies to the east, both north and south of the Kızılırmak.

Territories and Sacred Landscapes

The KRASP team (Massa *et al.* 2020) have identified a sacred landscape associated with Türkmenkarahöyük that they incorporated into a map showing 'spheres of influence'. My purpose here is to elaborate these concepts, underpinned by the hypothesis that by the 9th century B.C. there were fixed borders between polities. Frontiers, if that concept has value, lay either side of a linear border. Such borders, while fixed and well defined, were fluid rather than hard barriers, and fluctuated as a result of conflict and treaties, thus they were borders in theory if less so in practice. They could perhaps be imposed by Assyria, as suggested by Müller-Karpe who identified a towered wall along ridges north of Kuşaklı with Neo-Assyrian control (Müller-Karpe 2009; Weeden 2010: 56 with n.108). Before discussing where such borders may have lain it is worthwhile to consider sacred landscapes.

Hittite cities were frequently associated with sacred mountains that were considered the realm of gods, some having shrines immediately below their peaks. The prime example is Sarissa (Kuşaklı) where both textual and archaeological evidence meld (Müller-Karpe 2015: Wilhelm 2015). Zippalanda (Uşaklı) is probably another example (Archi 2015) where a sacred area with a pool below the tor might now lie buried beneath Iron Age remains on the high southern ridge of Kerkenes Dağ. Both examples are instances of mountains associated with elevated springs and ponds, reinforcing Hittite concepts of mountain gods providing water, as sculpted at Eflatun Pınar (Bachmann and Özenir 2005), while Storm Gods strode over their bowed heads as depicted in Chamber A at Yazilikaya (Seeher 2011).

In the MIA there seem also to have been sacred mountains and associated shrines, but there are substantive differences. I propose that these MIA high mountains were often snow-capped, practically inaccessible. Cultic establishments were situated on elevated peaks that stood out in the landscape looking toward yet loftier mountains. This change for the LBA to the MIA is far more than a mere increase in size and elevation of the god's abodes, it constitutes a significant development whereby each kingdom venerated a single mountain focus from smaller, more accessible, cultic centres. Hartapus I and II, seated at Türkmenkarahöyük, looked to Karadağ from their sacred establishment at Kızıldağ. Karadağ itself was provided with a mountain top shrine, one that would have taken considerable time and effort to reach from Türkmenkarahöyük. The kings of Tuwana, if the hypothesis holds, constructed an impressive cultic centre on the Göllüdağ from where they may have venerated the far less accessible Hasan Dağ. Moving west we come to the kingdom, name unknown, ruled at one time by Wasusarma whose capital (Hawkins and Weeden 2021) may have been at Kululu, but might more plausibly lie beneath the later Achaemenid, Hellenistic and Roman levels of modern Kayseri (Barjamovic 2015). This kingdom is dominated by Erciyes Dağ, the highest peak in Central Turkey. A less elevated, more accommodating, ceremonial centre has yet to be identified. Further eastwards lies Havuzköy, which Weeden (2010: pp. 40–41 with n.20) has plausibly suggested as the seat of king 'Dadilu the Kashkan'. Returning to our focus of interest we have one Kiyakiya of Šinathutu known from a Luwian inscription found near Aksaray. The exceptionally large site of Harmandalı (Fig. 1) is a strong candidate for his capital in view of the very extensive Iron Age occupation reported by Omura (1997: 285). To the north of Harmandalı, equidistant from the Kızılırmak, is the very large site at the centre of Kırşehir where Middle Iron Age levels have now been reached in a small exposure (Adak Adıbelli 2020). These principalities comprised more than city states for each controlled smaller towns, well-known examples of which include Kınık Höyük, Ovaören and Sultanhan.

Iron Age Hieroglyphic Luwian inscriptions between the Kızılırmak and the Delice Çayı number but two. One is the fortress inscription KARABURUN that names a king Sipi, son of Ni (Hawkins 2000: 480–483), both otherwise unknown. The other, unassociated with any settlement, is ÇALAPVERDİ (Hawkins 2000: 497–498).[2] Whether the region between the Kızılırmak and the main Ankara highway that marks both the northern limit of the Todd survey and the edge of the Cappadocian plain was part of Tabal, i. e. was known to the Assyrians, is not the pertinent question (contra Simon 2017). The more important issue is whether there were kingdoms within sacred landscapes like those of Hartapu and Wasusarma or something different. While there are any number of peaks, none rival Hasan Dağ or Erciyes Dağ. A strong candidate for a cultic site is the highly visible Sivri where there are substantial, uninvestigated MIA and other remains within walking distance of Alişar Höyük. By the same token, extensive excavations at both Alişar towards the east and the more westerly Kaman-Kalehöyük have failed to reveal eighth century architecture that appears monumental in scale. Furthermore, no sites north of the Kızılırmak have (yet) produced Iron Age sculpture. One might thus conclude that the region north of the Kızılırmak did not recover from collapse of the Hittite Empire as fast or to the same extent as the Konya plain or Southern Cappadocia. It may not be irrelevant to note that similar north-south discrepancies in prosperity have persisted until modern times.

2 The site of Eskikale (Kaletepehöyük) above Çalapverdi does clearly exhibit occupation as early as the 8th century, see Bossert and Fischer 1998.

Cities, Kingdoms, Boundaries and Rivers

To what extent did Neo-Hittite capitals on the central Anatolian Plateau resemble Syro-Hittite cities? Similarities might be hinted at by Göllüdağ where size, centralized planning, monumentality and sculpture (but not inscriptions) are suggestive of resemblances at the same time as displaying distinctive Anatolian traditions. Tuwana, capital of Warpalawas, presumably resembled Türkmenkarahöyük, surely provided with defences and monumental buildings. Were both city gates and public buildings embellished with relief sculpture? Maybe, but excavations have revealed no vestige apart from the Black Stone (Çınaroğlu 1987) while no sites on the central plateau compare with, for instance, Zincirli or Tayinat unless buried beneath later remains. On the other hand, notable sculpture from Kululu, Sultanhan and Kültepe (Kanesh) could point to differences in preservation or even archaeological visibility. New work at Türkmenkarahöyük will doubtless be informative.

Axiomatic is that, as stated earlier, MIA polities had clearly defined territorial borders. The much later testimony of Herodotus states that the eastern border of Phrygia was at the Kızılırmak. The distribution of MIA Phrygian grey ware and Alişar-related pattern painted wares support the river being a boundary below the bend before a late 7th century B.C. Phrygian expansion eastwards (Summers 1994, 2018). Massa *et al.*, (2020) write about 'spheres of influence' rather than borders, and do not discuss territories because they rightly see these as changing over time. However, thinking about the 8th century B.C. rather than a longer span makes it possible to suggest where borders between the MIA kingdoms might have been drawn. Both the location of the most northeasterly of the inscriptions of Hartapus II and evidence possibly gleaned from the TOPADA inscription suggest that the Mendeliz Çayı could have been a border, as suggested by Weeden (2010). Building on this idea, it is not difficult to envisage that the Kızılırmak, while not a severe physical barrier, could certainly have formed the northern border of Wasusarma's realm.[3] Close examination of Google Earth imagery reveals a plethora of water courses, ridges and topographic features that, frustratingly, make for too many variables for additional guesses to be made.

Evaluation of Evidence from the Ian Todd Survey

A total of 125 sites from which Iron Age pottery was identified amongst the sherds in the BIAA collection are listed in tables 1 and 2 and mapped on Fig. 1. It is not yet possible to integrate this data with that from the more extensive and intensive survey of Central Anatolia conducted by the Japanese Institute of Anatolian Archaeology (henceforth JIAA) that was conceived and directed by Sachihiro Omura. While many of the results have been published in preliminary form, together with some preliminary analysis, detailed descriptions of sites together with analysis of the pottery is not yet available. With the exception of a few sites that have since been destroyed the Japanese team will have re-surveyed the majority of sites listed here and collected greater quantities of ceramics than are housed in the BIAA collections. One area of difficulty is that of names. Generally, Todd named sites according to the nearest village while more recent surveys, including those of the JIAA , have employed local names for sites. Pulling together a concordance of sites from all of the surveys that have been conducted in Central Anatolia, together with records from museums, will be an enormous task that can perhaps best be tackled by taking one discrete area at a time. Working through all of the material in the JIAA is likely to take some considerable time and require significant resources in terms of expertise and technical support. While it is perhaps unlikely that there will be significant changes to the results presented in this paper that are based on little more than the

3 Lead strips with cursive Luwian hieroglyphic writing are letters, thus their findspots are not necessarily indications of territory or place. If they are so considered the picture offered here will require revision.

presence/absence of identifiable IA sherds, the Japanese survey covers a very much larger area of the plateau with highly intensive coverage of certain areas, particularly in the catchment area of Kaman-Kalehöyük. One element still perhaps required is a strategy of systematic hill-walking, slow, strenuous and often unrewarding as it is, to map defensive elements, seasonal camps, burial sites and other cultural remains that will be essential for an integrated approach to landscape archaeology. With regard to the present paper, implications for the definition of territories and borders are obvious enough.

While the Todd survey data requires that interpretation be considered tentative it may nevertheless be thought sufficiently robust for useful observations to be made and pertinent questions asked at this preliminary stage in the progress of archaeological research on the Central Anatolian Plateau. Limitations include a focus on prehistoric mounds either seen from vehicular roads or indicated on 1:200,000 Turkish maps. Many sites, in striking comparison to today, were undamaged resulting in low visibility of sherds, while most were visited only once. It is unnecessary to detail well-known problems in interpreting survey data other than to note that larger and medium-sized mounds may have lower skirts or appended elements that make them bigger than indicated in the tables. Of greater significance is an expectation that more intensive survey will identify smaller fortified hilltop sites, lookout stations, etc. The fortress at Karaburun, mentioned earlier, being a flat-topped hill rather than a mound was not visited by Todd even though Gelb had dug a test trench revealing 3 m depth of occupation (Gelb 1939 : no. 33, p. 32 with Pl. L).

Middle Iron Age Ceramics from the Todd Survey

The MIA is defined by buff wares with patterning in dark paint (Figs. 2–5). One surprise is that only a single Alişar IV animal silhouette sherd was collected.[4] Contemporaneous is Middle Phrygian monochrome pottery, generally grey. Imports are absent, or unrecognised, bar a few fine-line black-on-red pieces that were produced somewhere to the west or southwest (Summers 1992: figs 1–8 with Pl. XLVI(a); Schaus 1992).

As to chronology, in this paper it is posited that the MIA begins perhaps as early as the later 10th century B.C., with Alişar IV style pottery in the east and the first level of monumental Phrygian building at Gordion in the west. It draws to an end in the late 7th century B.C. with the clouded demise of the Neo-Hittites states and the end of hieroglyphic Luwian inscriptions.

At Kaman-Kalehöyük this long MIA period perhaps begins as early as level IId and continues to the end of IIc.[5] These levels are characterised by wheelmade buff wares with patterning in dark paint, principally divided by the introduction of cream slip and improved firing techniques in IIc. At both Kaman IIc and Yassıhöyük (Kırşehir) much of the pottery is handmade (Matsumura 2001; Küçükarslan 2017). This mode of production may be generally the case for this genre of pattern painted ceramics that is not always immediately apparent with slipped and burnished bowl sherds.[6]

4 There must be a bias in the Todd survey since animal style Alişar IV has been excavated, amongst other places, at Kaman-Kalehöyük, Kınık Höyük and Göllüdağ. Its reported abundance at Göllüdağ has been confirmed to me through personal communication from David Hawkins who recalls, having ascended to the excavation on horseback, being shown excellent examples coming directly from the excavations. This presence at Göllüdağ has chronological implications that cannot be addressed here.

5 The JIAA team date Kaman-Kalehöyük IId wheelmade dark on buff ceramics to the EIA on the basis of parallels with the excavated sequence at Porsuk. As noted above, this EIA date for Porsuk is far from secure. All three phases of IId were provided with defences, which may not be compatible with an EIA dating. This not to deny the presence of EIA pottery, including a few sherds of early handmade, from Kaman, but comparisons with EIA levels at both Gordion and Buyukkale (Boğazköy) are weak. It is not clear to me that substantial in situ EIA levels have been excavated at Kaman. For discussion of the dating see Matsumura and Omori 2010.

6 Macroscopic examination of grit tempered sherds in the BIAA collections confirms this general observation, but the data has not been quantified.

The surprising variety of MIA bowl rim forms would be explicable if these vessels were handmade rather than thrown on a fast wheel. In the very basic scheme adopted here no attempt is made to subdivide the MIA simply because it is not possible to recognise such subdivision in the sherds to hand. A high percentage of the bowl fragments in the BIAA collection have painted patterns on the rims, and it may be that most of the plain sherds happen to have broken between patterned elements such as groups of lines across rims.

Middle Iron Age Sites and Settlement Sizes

The first observation is that the MIA settlement pattern (Fig. 1) owes very little to the Hittite Empire. When the centralised Hittite state, with its capital at the mega-site of Hattusa, crumbled and much of its population moved or dispersed, all known Hittite cities within the bend of the Kızılırmak were destroyed and abandoned with no continuity of full urban life. Very recently claims have been made for continuity in Southern Cappadocia (an anachronistic term) and the Konya plain (e.g. d'Alfonso 2020a and 200b), but none have yet been substantiated and perhaps owe more to wishful thinking than to evidence. Within the bend of the Kızılırmak ceramic assemblages from Büyükkaya suggest the arrival of new elements in the population, if not population replacement (Seeher 2010). In the MIA, then, there is evidence for the emergence of a new geopolitical order with multiple centres of power. Nevertheless, restrictions of river crossings and mountain passes, as well as the natural routes by which the Anatolian plateau was traversed, retained their indelible importance. The new capitals, Gordion, Kemerhisar (Tuwana), Türkmen-Karahöyük (Parzuta?) and probably Kayseri (Mazaca), to mention the most obvious, together with a handful of smaller urban centres such as Kınık Höyük, Ovaören, Kaman-Kalehöyük and Alişar, had emerged by the 9th century B.C. This was not a static picture but rather one of frequent, almost continual conflict between Anatolian states themselves, as shown for instance in the TOPADA and TKH I hieroglyphic inscriptions, and with Assyria.

With regard to the Todd survey, a total of 125 sites are seen to have MIA occupation (Table 1). Of these 83.67 %, appear to be 3 ha or less in extent, while no more than 10 % are greater than 7 ha (Table 2). Of the remaining 13 sites, the cultic enclosure on Göllüdağ, at 110 ha, is an exception. One known Neo-Hittite capital within the Todd survey area is Tuwana (modern Kemerhisar, classical Tyana), capital of King Warpalawa. Noted above, the large site at Harmandalı is a possible candidate for the seat of Kiyakiya while Kayseri is suggested for Wasusarma's capital. With regard to Göllüdağ, while much of the enclosed space is steep and devoid of buildings and the surface area includes a crater lake, the monumentality of the public buildings together with a small amount of large-scale stone sculpture perhaps provide a proxy for the capital. If that is correct it would suggest the possibility that Tuwana may not have been so very dissimilar to Syro-Hittite cities. Unexpectedly, perhaps, there is no known hieroglyphic inscription from the mountaintop site itself despite the generally accepted late 8th century B.C. date and the various inscribed stele and other cultic installations that appear to have been set up along the route from Tuwana (Çınaroğlu 1989; d'Alfonso and Mora 2010). Another site that probably attained urban status is Alaaddin Tepe (Niğde), probably Neo-Hittite Nahita, where the size of the MIA site is unknown, but the tepe, perhaps a citadel, is only 9 ha in area. It is instructive to compare additional sites of substance, including Harmandalı (30 ha), Ovaören (Babakonakı) (18+ha) and Porsuk Zeyve Höyük (probably ancient Dunna) without a reported lower town (10 ha). Additionally, there are some large mounds, most notably that in the centre of the modern city of Kırşehir as well as Kaman- Kalehöyük that could very possibly have developed extensive lower towns in the Iron Age. Neo-Hittite inscriptions and Neo-Assyrian texts mention a greater number of un-named 'kings' whose cities, perhaps local centres of power, have not been identified on the ground. From a different perspective, if Kaman-Kalehöyük is considered to have been a Neo-Hittite site of significance it is pertinent to reiterate that no monumental architecture has (yet) been excavated, and no sculpture or inscription fragments recovered. Büklükale, just outside the area of the survey, which controlled an important crossing of the Kızılırmak throughout the 2nd millennium B.C., may not have retained urban proportions in the Neo-Hittite period when occupation the lower town appears sparse (Matsumura 2018). That is not to say that it lost its strategic importance close to the southern border of Phrygia, only that there does not seem to have been an urban population. That site size alone is not a marker of urban settlement is perhaps indicated by Yassıhöyük (Kırşehir) where there is MIA occupation (Küçükarslan 2017) and a lead scroll bearing cursive Anatolian Hieroglyphic text was recovered (Akdoğan and Hawkins 2010), but neither Neo-Hittite architectural monumentality nor what could reasonably be termed urban-scale settlement has (yet) been reported (Omura 2016).

To summarise, the Kingdom of Warpalawas and his dynasty had their capital at Tuwana (Kemerhisar) and a cultic centre on Göllüdağ together with a number of towns such as the two sites currently being excavated, Ovaören and Kınık Höyük. Of the area within the bend of the Kızılırmak covered by the Todd survey there is less that stands out. This may be because the major centres lay to the south of the river, e.g. at Kululu, Sultanhanı, Kültepe (where sculpture was found) and probably Kayseri (perhaps the capital), as well as at Havuzköy near Sivas (portal lions). This distribution might also be a reflection of a border along the Kızılırmak. On the other hand, it is probable that some of the larger mound sites were appended by a skirt and were thus of greater size and importance than recognized in the data available, but this remains conjecture. What is striking is the large number of small sites, presumably villages, many only a single hectare in extent. It is impossible to know how many of these were provided with defences.

The purpose of this paper has been re-examine the MIA settlement data from the Todd survey in the light of new evidence for and ideas about the political geography of Central Anatolia and the Konya plain that have stemmed from the discovery and rapid publication of the Türkmenkarahöyük Anatolian hieroglyphic inscription. Massa's map of 'spheres of influence' (Massa *et al.* 2020: 67 Fig. 14) is based on the KRASP and that of 'southern Cappadocia' by d'Alfonso and his team. There would have been a border, however much it may have fluctuated through time, between these two kingdoms that was very possibly perceived as running from peak to peak along to the length of the Karacadağ. Maner's ongoing Konya Ereğli Survey Project (KEYAR) survey of this region has identified a number of MIA towns that will need to be integrated in a refined and revised model (Maner 2019 with references).

Conclusions

Examination of old survey data taken together with more recent results of ongoing fieldwork and crucial, if frustratingly difficult, hieroglyphic Luwian inscriptions have permitted the plotting of sites on maps with tentative ranking by size. Credible estimates about the size of kingdom territories, in no small part based on the distribution of hieroglyphic inscriptions, with assumptions concerning the coincidence of natural (rivers and ridges) and territorial borders, may permit proposals to be made with regard to 8th century B.C. political geography, perhaps just before or around the time that Midas assumed the throne at Gordion. The restricted area of Todd's survey as well as limitations stemming the ways in which data was collected have dissuaded me from the temptation of drawing borders on the map, a task I leave to bolder minds. Analysis and publication of Sachihiro Omura's Central Anatolian Survey combined with new KRASP data, the results of ongoing work at Türkmenkarahöyük and excavation of Iron Age levels at Kınık Höyük will permit much progress to be made for the entire 1st millennium B.C.

Bibliography

Adak Adıbelli, İ.
- 2020 "Kırşehir Kale Höyük 2018 Yılı Çalışmaları," *41 Kazı Sonuçları Toplantısı* 2. Cilt II, pp. 503–520.

Akdoğan, R. and J. D. Hawkins
- 2010 "The Kırşehir Letter: A New Hieroglyphic Luwian Text on a Lead Strip," in: A. Süel (ed.), *Acts of the VIIth International Congress of Hittitology Corum 25–31 August 2008*, Ankara, pp. 1–16.

Archi, A.
- 2015 "Hittite religious landscapes." in A. D'Agostino, V. Orsi and G. Torri (eds.) *Sacred landscapes of Hittites and Luwians. Proceedings of the international conference in honour of Franca Pecchioli Daddi* (Studia Asiana 9), Firenze, pp. 11–25.

Bachmann, M. and S. Özenir
- 2005 "Das Quellheiligtum Eflatun Pınar," *Archäologischer Anzeiger* 2004/1, pp. 85–122.

Barjamovic, G.
- 2011 *A Historical Geography of Anatolia in the Old Assyrian Colony Period*, Copenhagen.
- 2015 "Kültepe after Kaneš," in F. Kulakoğlu and C. Michel (eds.) *Proceedings of the 1st Kültepe International Meeting* (Subartu 35), Turnhout, pp. 233–242.

Bossert, E-M. and F. Fischer
- 1998 "Çalapverdi: Beobachtungen anlässlich eines Besuchs im Jahre 1960," in G. Arsebük, M.J. Mellink and W. Schirmer (eds.), *Light on Top of the Black Hill: Studies Presented to Halet Çambel*, Istanbul, pp. 177–188

Crespin, A-S.
- 1999 "Between Phrygia and Cilicia: the Porsuk area at the beginning of the Iron Age," *Anatolian Studies* 49, pp. 61–71.

Çınaroğlu, A.
- 1987 "Kemerhisar-Ambartepe 1986 Kazısı," *IX. Kazı Sonuçları Toplantısı I, Kongreye Sunulan Bildiriler*, pp. 351–360.
- 1989 "*New Iron Age Discoveries Around Niğde*, Ankara.

d'Alfonso, L.
- 2019 "War in Anatolia in the Post-Hittite Period: The Anatolian Hieroglyphic Inscription of Topada Revised," *Journal of Cuneiform Studies* 71, pp. 133–152.
- 2020a "Reorganization vs. Resilience in Early Iron Age Monumental Art of Central Anatolia," in M. Cammarosano, E. Devecchi and M. Viano (eds.), *talugaeš witteš: Ancient Near Eastern Studies Presented to Stefano de Martino on the Occasion of his 65th Birthday*, Münster, pp. 81–101.
- 2020b "An Age of Experimentation: New Thoughts on the Multiple Outcomes Following the Fall of the Hittite Empire after the Results of the Excavations at Niğde-Kinik Höyük (South Cappadocia)," in S. de Martino and E. Devecchi (eds.), *Anatolia Between the 13th and the 12th Century B.C.E*, Turin, pp. 95–116.

d'Alfonso, L. and C. Mora
- 2010 "Archaeological Survey in Northern Tyanitis," in P. Matthiae (ed.), *6th International Congress of the Archaeology of Ancient Near East, Vol. 2* (ICCANE 6), Wiesbaden, pp. 123–138.

Draycott, C. M.
- 2019 "Activating the Achaemenid landscape: The Broken Lion Tomb (Yilan Taş) and the Phrygian Highlands in the Achaemenid Period," in G.R. Tsetskhladze (ed.) *Phrygia in Antiquity: From the Bronze Age to the Byzantine Period* (Colloquia Antiqua 24), Leuven, pp. 189–218.

Gelb, I.J.
- 1939 *Hittite Hieroglyphic Monuments*, Chicago.

Goedegebuure, P., T. van den Hout, J. Osborne, M., Massa., C. Bachhuber and F. Şahin.
- 2020 "TÜRKMEN-KARAHÖYÜK 1: A New Hieroglyphic Luwian Inscription from Great King Hartapu, Son of Mursili, Conqueror of Phrygia," *Anatolian Studies* 70, pp. 29–43.

Hawkins, J. D.
- 1992 "The inscriptions of Kızıldağ and Karadağ in the light of the Yalburt Inscription," in H. Otten (ed.) *Hittite and other Anatolian and Near Eastern Studies in honour of Sedat Alp*, Ankara, pp. 259–274.
- 2000 *Corpus of Hieroglyphic Luwian Inscriptions. Volume I: Inscriptions of the Iron Age*. Berlin and New York.
- In Press "Routes in the Hittite Kingdom," in *Pathways of Communication | Roads and Routes in Anatolia*, BIAA.

Hawkins, J. D. and M. Weeden
- 2021 "The New Inscription from Türkmenkarahöyük and its Historical context," *Altorientalische Forschungen* 48 (2) pp. 384–400.

Kaçaroğlu, F., M. Değirmenci and O. Cerit
- 2001 Water quality problems of a Gypsiferous watershed: Upper Kızılırmak Basin, Sivas, Turkey," *Water, Air, Soil & Pollution* 128, pp. 161–180.

Küçükarslan, N.
- 2017 *Middle Iron Age pottery from Yassıhöyük (Kırşehir): A Central Anatolian assemblage.* Unpublished MA Thesis, Ankara, Bilkent University.

Maner, Ç,
- 2019 "Inside Tarḫuntašša: A Systematic Survey of Karapınar, Konya. The 2017–2018 Field Seasons of the KEYAR Survey Project," in S.R. Steadman and G. McMahon (eds.) *The Archaeology of Anatolia Volume III: Recent Discoveries (2017–2018)*, Newcastle upon Tyne, pp. 347–373.

Manuelli, F., C. Vignola, F. Marzaioli, I. Passariello and F. Terrasi
- 2021 "The beginning of the Iron Age at Arslantepe: A 14c perspective," *Radiocarbon* 63(3), pp. 885–903.

Massa, M., C. Bachhuber, F. Şahin, H. Erpehlivan, J. Osborne and A.J. Lauricella,
- 2020 "A landscape-oriented approach to urbanisation and early state formation on the Konya and Karaman plains, Turkey," *Anatolian Studies* 70, pp. 45–75.

Matsumura, K.
- 2001 "On the Manufacturing Techniques of Iron Age Ceramics from Kaman-Kalehöyük (II): the Cultural Influence of Phrygia at Kaman-Kalehöyük." *Anatolian Archaeological Studies* 10, pp. 101–110.
- 2018 "The Glass Bottle and Pendant from Büklükale and Their Dating," *Anatolian Archaeological Studies* 21, pp. 11–29.

Matsumura, K. and T. Omori
- 2010 "The Iron Age Chronology in Anatolia Reconsidered: The Results of the Excavations at Kaman-Kalehöyük," in P. Matthiae, F. Pinnock, L. Nigro and N. Marchetti (eds.) *Proceedings of the 6th International Congress on the Archaeology of the Ancient Near East, May, 5th–10th 2008, "Sapienza" – Università di Roma*, vol. I. Wiesbaden, pp. 443–455.

Müller-Karpe, A.
- 2009 "Auf dem Rücken der Berge: Die kappadokische Mauer in Anatolien," *Antike Welt* 40(4), pp. 17–21.

- 2015 "Planning a Sacred Landscape: Examples from Sarissa and Hattusa," in A. D'Agostino, V. Orsi and G. Torri (eds.) *Sacred landscapes of Hittites and Luwians*, Firenze, pp. 83–92.

Omura, M.
- 2016 "Yassıhöyük Excavations First Five Seasons 2009–2013," *Anatolian Archaeology Studies* 19, pp. 11–72.

Omura, S.
- 1997 "1995 Yılı İç Anadolu'da Yürütülen Yüzey Araştırmaları." XIV. *Araştırma Sonuçları Toplantısı* Cilt II, pp. 283–302.

Osborne, J.F.
- 2020 *The Syro-Anatolian City-states*, Oxford.

Osborne, J.F., M. Massa, F. Şahin, H. Erpehlivan and C. Bachhuber
- 2020 "The city of Hartapu: results of the Türkmen-Karahöyük Intensive survey project, *Anatolian Studies* 70, pp. 1–27.

Schaus, G.P.
- 1992 "Imported West Anatolian Pottery at Gordion," *Anatolian Studies* 42, pp. 151–177.

Seeher, J.
- 2010 "After the Empire: Observations on the Early Iron Age in Central Anatolia," in I. Singer (ed.), *ipamati kistamati pari tumatimis. Luwian and Hittite Studies presented to J. David Hawkins on the Occasion of his 70th Birthday*, Tel Aviv, pp. 220–229.
- 2011 *Gods carved in Stone: The Hittite Rock Sanctuary of Yazılıkaya*, Istanbul.

Todd, I.A.
- 1980 *The Prehistory of Central Anatolia I: The Neolithic Period* (SIMA 160), Göteborg.

Simon, Z.
- 2017 "The Northern Border of Tabal," in A. Mouton (ed.) *Hittitology Today: Studies on Hittite and Neo-Hittite Anatolia in Honor of Emmanuel Laroche's 100th Birthday*, Istanbul, pp. 201–11.

Summers, G.D.
- 1992 "An Aerial Survey of Çevre Kale, Yaraşlı," *Anatolian Studies* 42, pp. 179–206.
- 1994 "Grey Ware and the Eastern Limits of Phrygia," in A. Çilingiroğlu and D.H. French (eds.), *Anatolian Iron Ages 3*, London, pp. 241–52.
- 2018a Phrygians east of the Red River: Phrygianisation, migration and desertion," *Anatolian Studies* 68, pp. 99–118.

– 2018b "Notes on Chronology in the Phrygian Highlands: Cultic Installations, Defenses, and Clamp Cuttings," *Journal of Near Eastern Studies* 77, pp. 67–84.

van Dongen, E.

– 2014 "The Extent and interactions of the Phrygian Kingdom," in S. Gaspa, A. Greco, D. Morandi Bonacossi, S. Ponchia and R. Rollinger (eds.) *From Source to History: Studies on Ancient Near Eastern Worlds and Beyond Dedicated to Giovanni Battista Lanfranchi* (AOAT 412), Münster, pp. 697–711.

Voigt, M. M.

– 2013 "Gordion as Citadel and City," in S. Redford and N. Ergin (eds.) *Cities and Citadels in Turkey: from the Iron Age to the Seljuks*, Leuven, pp. 161–228.

Voigt, M. M. and Henrickson, R.

– 2000 "Formation of the Phrygian State: The Early Iron Age at Gordion," *Anatolian Studies* 50, pp. 37–54.

Weeden, M.

– 2010 "'Tuwati and Wasusarma. Imitating the behaviour of Assyria," *Iraq*, 72, pp. 39–62.

– 2013 "After the Hittites: The Kingdoms of Karkamish and Palistin in Northern Syria," Bulletin of the Institute of Classical Studies 56, pp. 1–20.

Weeden, M. and L. Z. Ullmann (eds.)

– 2017 *Hittite Landscape and Geography* (HbO 121), Leiden.

Wilhelm, G.

– 2015 "The sacred landscape of Sarissa." in A. D'Agostino, V. Orsi and G. Torri (eds.) *Sacred landscapes of Hittites and Luwians* (Studia Asiana 9), Firenze, pp. 93–99.

Site_no	Site_name	Area hectares	2nd mill.	MIA	LIA	Longitude	Latitude
1	Alaeddin Tepesi and Kale	9.0		X		4212888.44	654530.54
4	Altıntepe - Andaval	0.6		X	X	4210097.29	655134.63
5	Aşlama Höyük	3.0		X		4222979.12	678868.80
6	Fertek	4.5		X	X	4202561.83	643595.09
7	Boz Duvarlı	0.8		X		4198371.62	640621.38
13	Gölcük Höyük	1.2	X	X	Z	4233171.95	655617.41
17	Çardak-Çiftlik	2.5	X	X	X	4228541.35	624421.36
19	Karamelendiz Höyük	0.5	X	X	X	4229676.76	625826.48
24	Göllü Dağ	110.0		X		4235702.86	635173.00
27	Agzıkarahan S.W.	0.4		X		4256449.01	599473.97
28	Alayhanı Höyük	0.3		X	X	4264884.59	615354.89
32	Çimeli Yeniköy Höyük	0.2		X	X	4259415.99	578715.35
33	Kocaş Tepe	11.0	X	X	X	4258593.26	573685.27
34	Demirci Höyük Tepesi	0.4	X	X		4249399.00	612014.00
37	Mamasun Barajı Kale	0.1		X	X	4251170.13	598695.86
38	Mamasun Höyük	?	X	X	X	4252316.36	602417.34
39	Gücünkaya Höyük	5.0	X	X	X	4249582.79	598975.15
41	Kavak Tepe	7.0	X	X	X	4250038.14	579351.71
43	Uşak Tepe	1.4	X	X	X	4244335.05	607891.81
44	Künk Höyük	1.5		X	X	4236938.18	574498.87
46	Geyral Höyük	1.5	X	X	X	4256351.78	610673.68
47	Saratlı Höyük	1.0	X	X		4257496.11	605576.86
50	Süleyman Höyük	0.5	X	X		4261202.80	615522.01
51	Çakmak Höyük	1.3		X	X	4253747.64	576144.34
61	Arpalı Höyük	0.8		X	X	4271596.52	567493.89
62	Çardak Höyük	0.5	X	X	X	4275279.89	565968.44
63	Çardak SW Höyük	0.6		X	X	4274668.22	565762.18
67	Hacimahmutuşağı Yayla	1.6	X	X		4277957.45	563134.49
72	Yüksekli Kilise - Gelveri	0.5		X		4236978.00	618131.00
73	Kültepesi Ağaçlı	3.0	X	X		4250901.08	618440.38
75	Bekarsultan E Höyük	4.0		X		4250330.69	620926.82
85	Sülüklü Höyük	0.5	X	X	X	4234955.99	547306.39
86	Şemşettin Höyük	1.2		X	X	4232792.83	552050.01
91	Marıl Höyük	12.0	X	X	X	4223328.68	550313.12
92	Tosun Höyük	1.5	X	X	X	4248645.22	527901.37
98	Buetköy Höyük	3.2	X	X	X	4241444.21	539737.01
100	Dokuz Höyük	2.2		X		4231359.41	571765.11
101	Gözlükuyu Höyük	2.2	X	X	X	4227334.88	593043.13
107	Yılanlı Höyük	3.9		X	X	4248433.51	568289.73

Site_no	Site_name	Area hectares	2nd mill.	MIA	LIA	Longitude	Latitude
110	Pınarbaşı Höyük	3.5		X		4197215.18	633181.72
111	Bayat – Bor / Kınık Höyük	1.7	X	X	X	4199805.38	621280.69
112	Kayı Höyük	0.2		X		4199273.71	627227.81
113	Kızılca Höyük	7.0		X	X	4187782.52	617728.17
115	Kemerhisar Höyük	50.0		X	Z	4187761.27	638099.16
116	Kerhane Höyük	1.3		X		4180417.35	620881.73
117	Kızıl Höyük	1.3		X	X	4180568.26	625727.61
120	Aflak Höyük	1.0		X	X	4289948.64	589815.12
121	Bozkır Höyük	1.3	X	X	X	4293976.36	596255.44
122	Cavarlı Höyük	1.6	X	X	X	4300034.80	587568.21
123	Muradlı Höyük	3.9		X		4304864.84	591162.40
124	Sungurlu Höyük	1.5		X		4280678.36	561337.11
125	Harmandalı	30.0	X	X	X	4312159.43	583080.61
129	Ersele Höyük	1.0		X		4281939.33	605673.28
134	Zeyve - Porsuk	10.0	X	X	Z	4153229.32	639677.30
136	Taş Tepe	2.0		X		4268489.96	631994.31
137	Ağıllı Höyük	5.5	X	X	X	4260138.39	629055.78
141	Cami Höyük	1.4	X	X	X	4295134.03	671102.84
142	Topaklı Höyük	6.0	X	X	X	4319136.35	658146.41
143	Zank Höyük	2.0	X	X		4313004.33	655463.92
144	Bel Höyük	0.6		X	X	4322264.28	666657.41
145	Karayusuf Höyük	0.8	X	X	X	4314858.77	673582.66
147	Yazıhöyük	2.0	X	X	X	4245022.78	643240.74
148	Araplı Höyük	0.8		X	X	4291389.43	638277.98
150	Göstesin - Babakonakı	18.0	X	X	X	4274083.46	612983.48
152	Tuzköy Tepe	1.0	X	X	X	4293786.81	632297.16
153	Maltepe-Yalıntaş / Yakatrla	1.0	X	X	X	4284438.34	617726.56
154	Tekerlik Höyük	5.1	X	X	X	4308584.63	606640.21
155	Yamalı Höyük	0.5	X	X	X	4306124.47	610130.89
156	Avanos Höyük / Kızılözün	1.6	X	X	X	4291341.37	650039.42
157	Cemel Höyük	0.2		X	X	4295257.00	647614.00
159	Gavur Höyük	1.7	X	X	X	4307722.94	622256.47
160	Karahöyük Hacıbektaş	9.5	X	X	X	4312067.44	635292.05
161	Hasanlar Höyük	2.5	X	X	X	4332117.56	643314.70
163	İlicek Höyük	3.8	X	X	X	4319431.30	641338.88
165	Kayaaltı Höyük	1.3		X	X	4324072.09	651957.01
166	Kızılağıl Höyük	0.5	X	X	X	4318414.00	648676.00
167	Kızılağıl S Höyük	0.5		X	X	4318404.32	648567.00
169	Kozaklı Höyük	2.8	X	X	X	4343475.81	657269.50

Site_no	Site_name	Area hectares	2nd mill.	MIA	LIA	Longitude	Latitude
174	Mercimek Höyük	0.8	X	X	X	4349171.35	662374.78
175	Karasınır Höyük	3.2	X	X	X	4352069.34	657346.07
176	Vakıf Höyük	0.5	X	X	X	4346597.78	664594.67
178	Gürüş Höyük	1.6	X	X	X	4363407.40	650682.73
180	Özbek Höyük	1.7	X	X	X	4355205.00,	646915.73
181	Gökçe Höyük	2.5	X	X	X	4347689.15	647772.67
182	Kuşaklı Höyük	0.8		X		4349537.10	637884.63
183	Küllüce Höyük	1.9	X	X	X	4342454.33	646151.70
186	Kırşehir Höyük	4.6	X	X	X	4333614.78	600024.80
187	Boztepe Höyük	7.0	X	X	X	4347726.75	608649.72
191	Özlü Höyük	1.7	X	X	X	4345229.60	613337.60
192	Çamalak Höyük	3.6		X	X	4359421.76	634022.07
193	Yassıhöyük	25.0	X	X	0	4352690.81	592705.83
195	Çiğdeli NW Höyük	1.0		X	X	4361005.23	626300.85
196	Karahöyük-Çiğdeli	0.5		X	X	4359558.00	628860.00
197	Çoğun Höyük	0.7	X	X	Z	4351103.50	596031.97
198	Tataroğlu Höyük	1.3		X	X	4342440.94	590964.34
201	Çavuşlu Höyük	7.0	X	X	X	4306671.08	603970.20
203	Sevdiğin Höyük	4.7	X	X	X	4330331.21	589537.34
204	Kayatuzu Höyük	3.5	X	X	X	4318174.99	608802.25
205	Sulhanlı Höyük	1.0	X	X	X	4301116.06	599854.81
207	Kuru Höyük	0.5	X	X	X	4356435.36	617850.52
208	Hashöyük	5.6	X	X	X	4367644.81	601858.51
209	Huseyinli Höyük	3.1	X	X	X	4358245.47	612377.47
210	Öksüz Höyük	4.0		X	X	4363358.64	617167.83
211	Sarı Höyük	0.6		X	X	4361531.65	620508.41
213	Çiçek Dağı Höyük	4.7	X	X	X	4385042.92	621571.54
214	Avanoğlu Höyük	3.2	X	X	X	4393783.00	581582.00
216	Ayvalı Höyük	2.0	X	X	X	4399056.49	589650.78
217	Güllühüyük	7.6	X	X	X	4382625.20	594847.68
218	Kızılcalı Höyük	0.7		X	X	4397856.27	605959.15
220	Zekere Höyük	0.9	X	X	X	4363924.17	632004.67
221	Kormenli Höyük	1.0		X	X	4361077.71	566484.15
223	Kale / Kaman-Kalehöyük	9.7	X	X	X	4357353.24	567774.62
224	Darözü	2.0	Z	X		4358095.12	566157.08
225	Kurancılı Höyük	0.9	X	X	X	4356018.24	578932.95
226	Meryemkaşı Höyük	2.5	X	X	X	4346944.41	554668.48
228	Budak Höyük	3.0	X	X	X	4333888.46	626396.44
229	Bezirgan Höyük	0.5	X	X	X	4327695.00	609796.00

Site_no	Site_name	Area hectares	2nd mill.	MIA	LIA	Longitude	Latitude
230	Gölhisar Höyük	0.4		X	X	4328745.41	604853.07
232	Karıplı Büyük Höyük	8.7	X	X	X	4341074.49	637040.83
237	Karahöyük (Obruk)	1.3		X	X	4323645.03	628360.02
239	Guru Höyük	0.5		X	X	4336889.53	617927.32
240	Seyfe Höyük	3.3		X	X	4339081.21	617019.19
241	Tataryeğenağa Höyük	1.5	X	X	X	4322588.31	637008.68
242	Yazıkınık Höyük	1.4	X	X	X	4335481.54	621778.36
NA	Karaburun	1.4		X		4304455.00	626147.00

Table 1: Middle Iron Age sites with BIAA numbers surveyed by Ian Todd and other BIAA researchers. Occupation in all three periods probably indicates advantageous locations. It does not indicate continuous occupation, there being no evidence for EIA presence at any site. X = present, Z = probably present.

Est. Area	Site-name	Site-no	Longitude	Latitude
110.0	Göllü Dağ	24	4235702.86	635173.00
50.0	Kemerhisar Höyük	115	4187761.27	638099.16
30.0	Harmandalı	125	4312159.43	583080.61
25.0	Yassıhöyük	193	4352690.81	592705.83
18.0	Göstesin - Babakonakı	150	4274083.46	612983.48
12.0	Marıl Höyük	91	4223328.68	550313.12
11.0	Kocaş Tepe	33	4258593.26	573685.27
10.0	Zeyve - Porsuk	134	4153229.32	639677.30
9.7	Kale / Kaman-Kalehöyük	223	4357353.24	567774.62
9.5	Karahöyük Hacıbektaş	160	4312067.44	635292.05
9.0	Alaeddin Tepesi and Kale	1	4212888.44	654530.54
8.7	Karıplı Büyük Höyük	232	4341074.49	637040.83
7.6	Güllühüyük	217	4382625.20	594847.68
7.0	Kavak Tepe	41	4250038.14	579351.71
7.0	Kızılca Höyük	113	4187782.52	617728.17
7.0	Boztepe Höyük	187	4347726.75	608649.72
7.0	Çavuşlu Höyük	201	4306671.08	603970.20
6.0	Topaklı Höyük	142	4319136.35	658146.41
5.6	Hashöyük	208	4367644.81	601858.51
5.5	Ağıllı Höyük	137	4260138.39	629055.78
5.1	Tekerlik Höyük	154	4308584.63	606640.21
5.0	Gücünkaya Höyük	39	4249582.79	598975.15
4.7	Sevdiğin Höyük	203	4330331.21	589537.34
4.7	Çiçek Dağı Höyük	213	4385042.92	621571.54

Est. Area	Site-name	Site-no	Longitude	Latitude
4.6	Kırşehir Höyük	186	4333614.78	600024.80
4.5	Fertek	6	4202561.83	643595.09
4.0	Bekarsultan E Höyük	75	4250330.69	620926.82
4.0	Öksüz Höyük	210	4363358.64	617167.83
3.9	Yılanlı Höyük	107	4248433.51	568289.73
3.9	Muradlı Höyük	123	4304864.84	591162.40
3.8	İlicek Höyük	163	4319431.30	641338.88
3.6	Çamalak Höyük	192	4359421.76	634022.07
3.5	Pınarbaşı Höyük	110	4197215.18	633181.72
3.5	Kayatuzu Höyük	204	4318174.99	608802.25
3.3	Seyfe Höyük	240	4339081.21	617019.19
3.2	Buetköy Höyük	98	4241444.21	539737.01
3.2	Karasınır Höyük	175	4352069.34	657346.07
3.2	Avanoğlu Höyük	214	4393783.00	581582.00
3.1	Huseyinli Höyük	209	4358245.47	612377.47
3.0	Aşlama Höyük	5	4222979.12	678868.80
3.0	Kültepesi Ağaçlı	73	4250901.08	618440.38
3.0	Budak Höyük	228	4333888.46	626396.44
2.8	Kozaklı Höyük	169	4343475.81	657269.50
2.5	Çardak-Çiftlik	17	4228541.35	624421.36
2.5	Hasanlar Höyük	161	4332117.56	643314.70
2.5	Gökçe Höyük	181	4347689.15	647772.67
2.5	Meryemkaşı Höyük	226	4346944.41	554668.48
2.2	Dokuz Höyük	100	4231359.41	571765.11
2.2	Gözlükuyu Höyük	101	4227334.88	593043.13
2.0	Taş Tepe	136	4268489.96	631994.31
2.0	Zank Höyük	143	4313004.33	655463.92
2.0	Yazıhöyük	147	4245022.78	643240.74
2.0	Ayvalı Höyük	216	4399056.49	589650.78
2.0	Darözü	224	4358095.12	566157.08
1.9	Küllüce Höyük	183	4342454.33	646151.70
1.7	Bayat – Bor / Kınık Höyük	111	4199805.38	621280.69
1.7	Gavur Höyük	159	4307722.94	622256.47
1.7	Özbek Höyük	180	4355205.00,	646915.73
1.7	Özlü Höyük	191	4345229.60	613337.60
1.6	Hacimahmutuşağı Yayla	67	4277957.45	563134.49
1.6	Cavarlı Höyük	122	4300034.80	587568.21
1.6	Avanos Höyük / Kızılözün	156	4291341.37	650039.42
1.6	Gürüş Höyük	178	4363407.40	650682.73
1.5	Künk Höyük	44	4236938.18	574498.87

Est. Area	Site-name	Site-no	Longitude	Latitude
1.5	Geyral Höyük	46	4256351.78	610673.68
1.5	Tosun Höyük	92	4248645.22	527901.37
1.5	Sungurlu Höyük	124	4280678.36	561337.11
1.5	Tataryeğenağa Höyük	241	4322588.31	637008.68
1.4	Karabuyrun	NA	4304455.00	626147.00
1.4	Uşak Tepe	43	4244335.05	607891.81
1.4	Cami Höyük	141	4295134.03	671102.84
1.4	Yazıkınık Höyük	242	4335481.54	621778.36
1.3	Çakmak Höyük	51	4253747.64	576144.34
1.3	Kerhane Höyük	116	4180417.35	620881.73
1.3	Kızıl Höyük	117	4180568.26	625727.61
1.3	Bozkır Höyük	121	4293976.36	596255.44
1.3	Kayaaltı Höyük	165	4324072.09	651957.01
1.3	Tataroğlu Höyük	198	4342440.94	590964.34
1.3	Karahöyük (Obruk)	237	4323645.03	628360.02
1.2	Gölcük Höyük	13	4233171.95	655617.41
1.2	Şemşettin Höyük	86	4232792.83	552050.01
1.0	Saratlı Höyük	47	4257496.11	605576.86
1.0	Aflak Höyük	120	4289948.64	589815.12
1.0	Ersele Höyük	129	4281939.33	605673.28
1.0	Tuzköy Tepe	152	4293786.81	632297.16
1.0	Maltepe-Yalıntaş / Yakatarla	153	4284438.34	617726.56
1.0	Çiğdeli NW Höyük	195	4361005.23	626300.85
1.0	Sulhanlı Höyük	205	4301116.06	599854.81
1.0	Kormenli Höyük	221	4361077.71	566484.15
0.9	Zekere Höyük	220	4363924.17	632004.67
0.9	Kurancılı Höyük	225	4356018.24	578932.95
0.8	Boz Duvarlı	7	4198371.62	640621.38
0.8	Arpalı Höyük	61	4271596.52	567493.89
0.8	Karayusuf Höyük	145	4314858.77	673582.66
0.8	Araplı Höyük	148	4291389.43	638277.98
0.8	Mercimek Höyük	174	4349171.35	662374.78
0.8	Kuşaklı Höyük	182	4349537.10	637884.63
0.7	Çoğun Höyük	197	4351103.50	596031.97
0.7	Kızılcalı Höyük	218	4397856.27	605959.15
0.6	Altıntepe - Andaval	4	4210097.29	655134.63
0.6	Çardak SW Höyük	63	4274668.22	565762.18
0.6	Bel Höyük	144	4322264.28	666657.41
0.6	Sarı Höyük	211	4361531.65	620508.41
0.5	Karamelendiz Höyük	19	4229676.76	625826.48

Est. Area	Site-name	Site-no	Longitude	Latitude
0.5	Süleyman Höyük	50	4261202.80	615522.01
0.5	Çardak Höyük	62	4275279.89	565968.44
0.5	Yüksekli Kilise - Gelveri	72	4236978.00	618131.00
0.5	Sülüklü Höyük	85	4234955.99	547306.39
0.5	Yamalı Höyük	155	4306124.47	610130.89
0.5	Kızılağıl Höyük	166	4318414.00	648676.00
0.5	Kızılağıl S Höyük	167	4318404.32	648567.00
0.5	Vakıf Höyük	176	4346597.78	664594.67
0.5	Karahöyük-Çiğdeli	196	4359558.00	628860.00
0.5	Kuru Höyük	207	4356435.36	617850.52
0.5	Bezirgan Höyük	229	4327695.00	609796.00
0.5	Guru Höyük	239	4336889.53	617927.32
0.4	Agzıkarahan S.W.	27	4256449.01	599473.97
0.4	Demirci Höyük Tepesi	34	4249399.00	612014.00
0.4	Gölhisar Höyük	230	4328745.41	604853.07
0.3	Alayhanı Höyük	28	4264884.59	615354.89
0.2	Çimeli Yeniköy Höyük	32	4259415.99	578715.35
0.2	Kayı Höyük	112	4199273.71	627227.81
0.2	Cemel Höyük	157	4295257.00	647614.00
0.1	Mamasun Barajı Kale	37	4251170.13	598695.86
?	Mamasun Höyük	38	4252316.36	602417.34

Table 2: Middle Iron Age sites ranked by estimated areas in hectares.

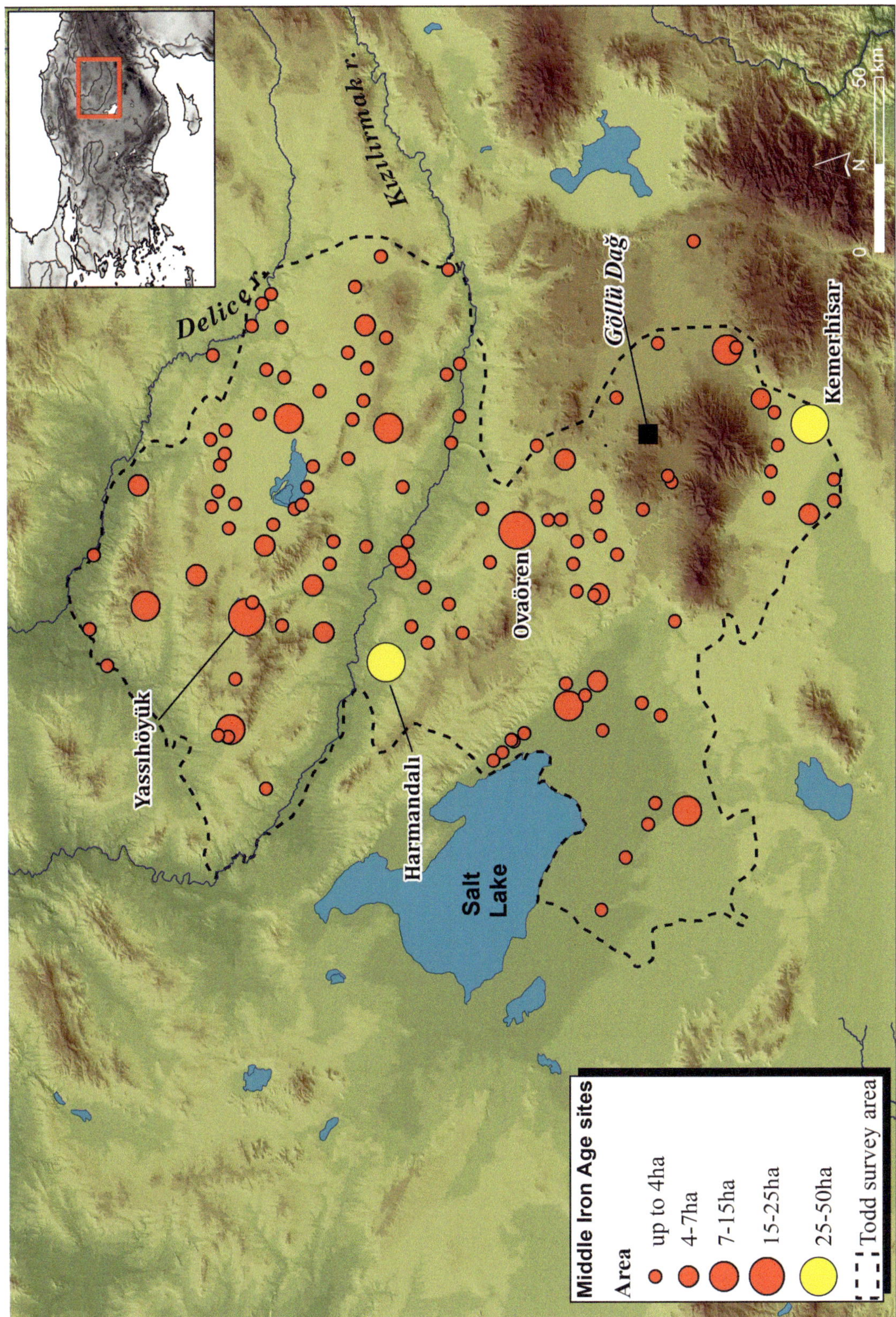

Fig. 1. Map of sites with Middle Iron Age occupation, made by Michele Massa.

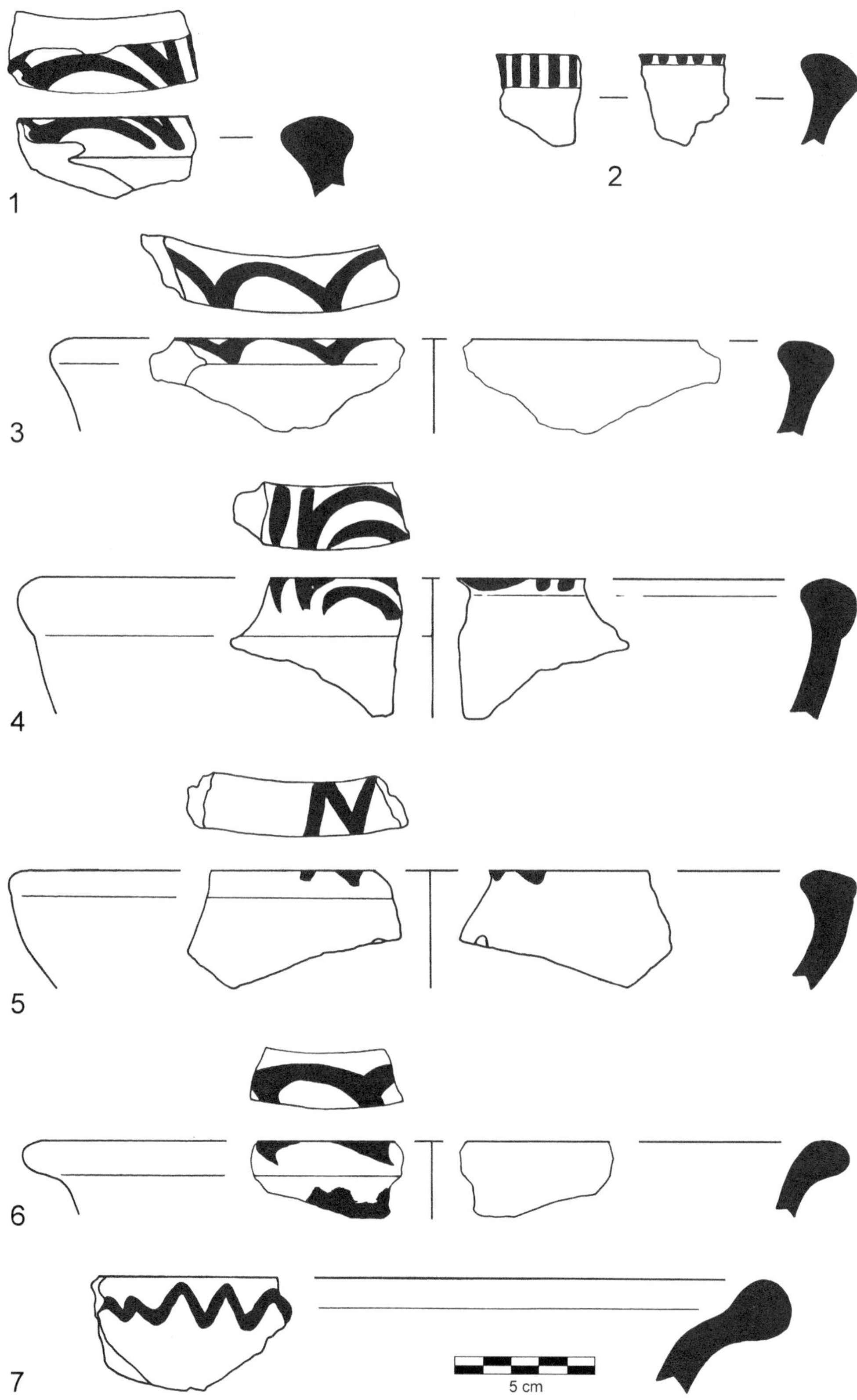

Fig. 2a. Typical Middle Iron Age bowls with a variety of rim forms, 1–6, and a krater, 7. Cream slip with patterning in dark paint.

Fig. 2b. Typical Middle Iron Age bowls with a variety of rim forms, 1–6, and a krater, 7. Cream slip with patterning in dark paint. Koçaş Tepe.

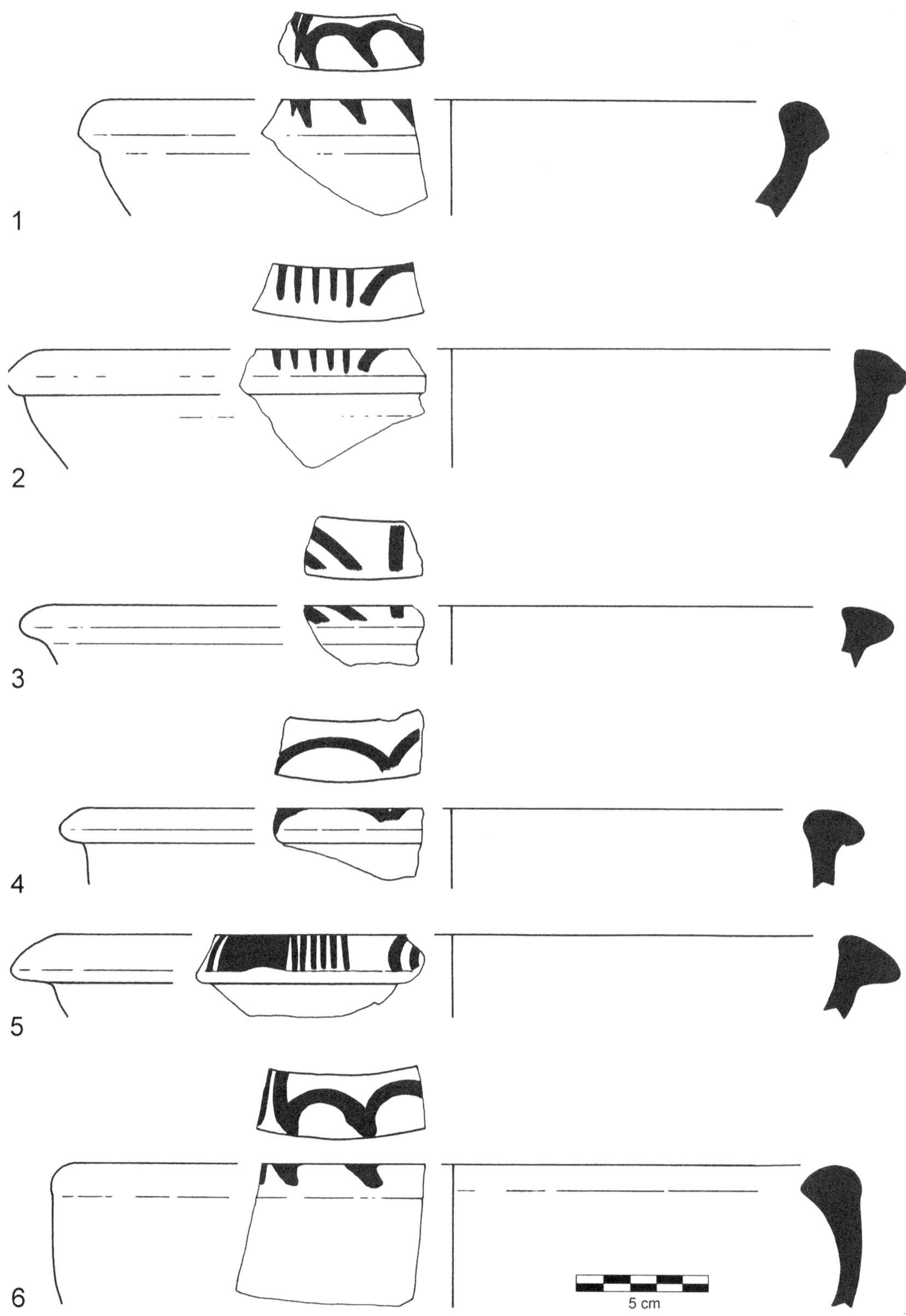

Fig. 3a. Typical Middle Iron Age bowls with a variety of rim forms. Cream slip with patterning in dark paint.

Fig. 3b. Typical Middle Iron Age bowls with a variety of rim forms. Cream slip with patterning in dark paint. Cavarlı 4; Fertek 5; Geyral 2; Kınık 6; Pınarbaşı 1; Sungurlu 3.

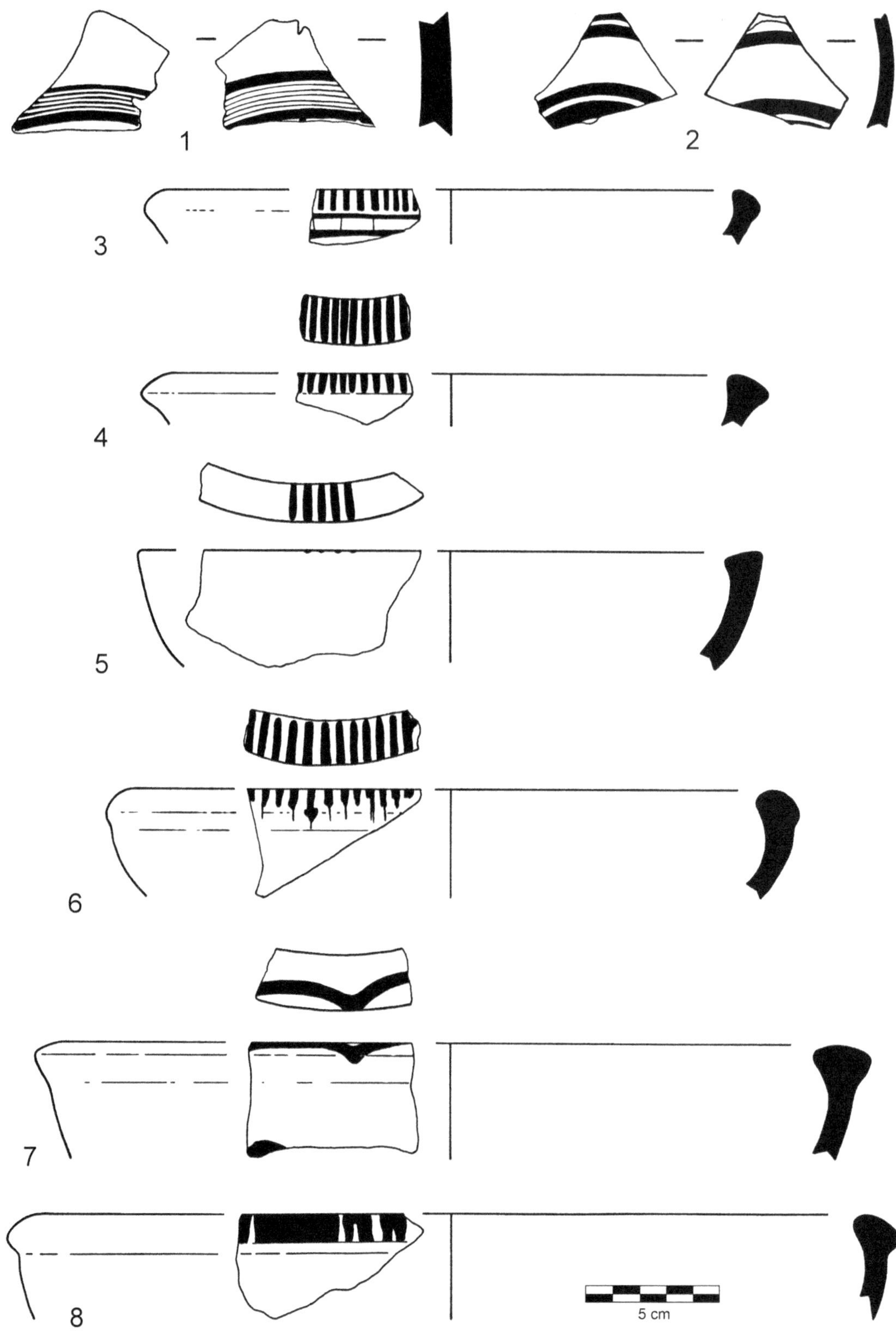

Fig. 4a. Typical Middle Iron Age bowls with a variety of rim forms. Black painted patterning on red.

Fig. 4b. Typical Middle Iron Age bowls with a variety of rim forms. Black painted patterning on red. Geyral 8; Koçaş 2–5; Kültepesi 6; Mamasın 7; Marıl 1.

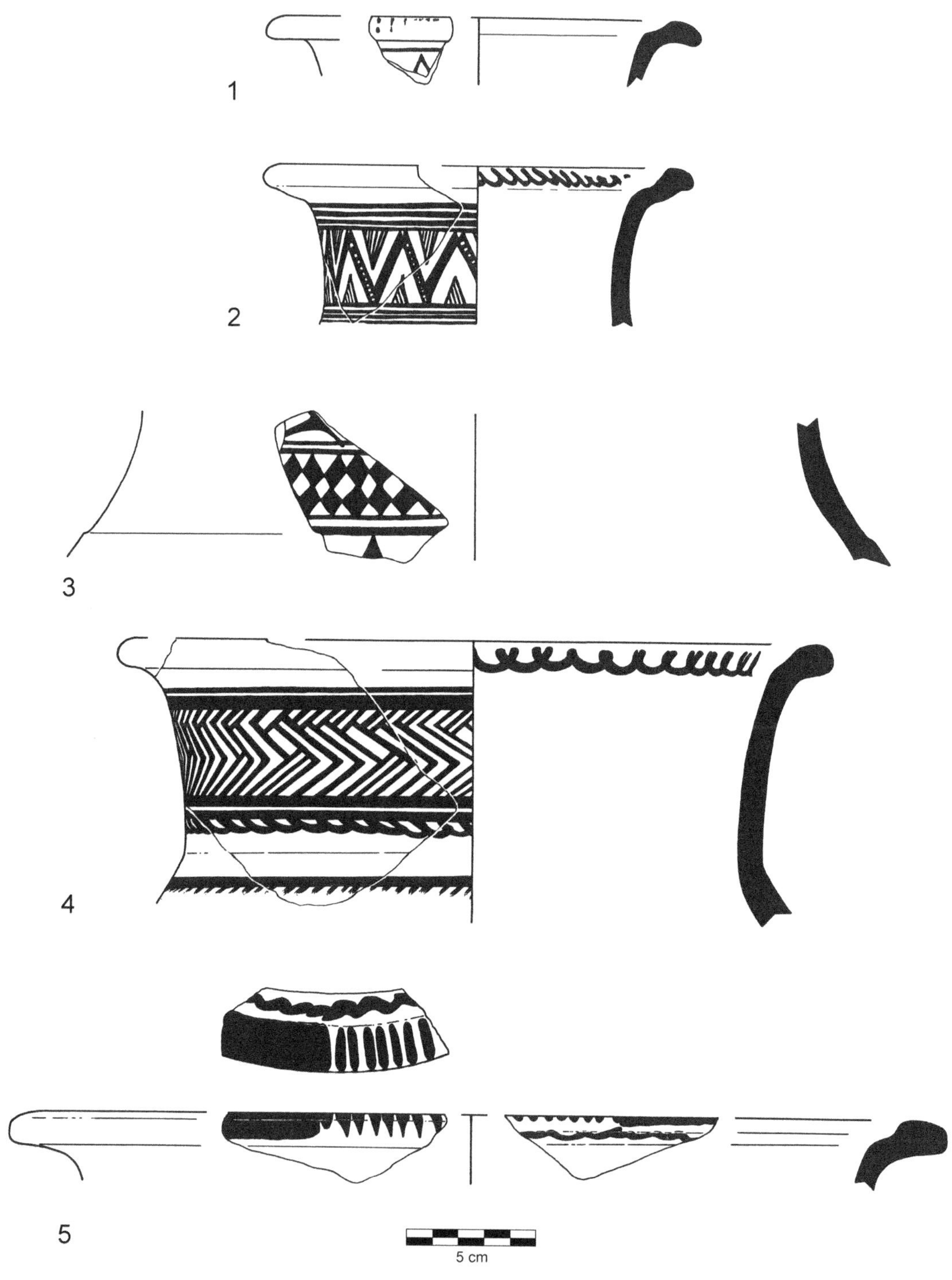

Fig. 5a. Typical Middle Iron Age jars and kraters. Cream slip with patterning in dark paint. Fertek 3, Harmandalı B. K.T. 1, 2, 4, 5.

Fig. 5b. Typical Middle Iron Age jars and kraters.

Examination of the Performance of Crossroads Rituals in Hittite Anatolia

Hajime Yamamoto *

Abstract

This paper discusses the rituals performed at crossroads by the Hittites in Anatolia and their possible relevance for identifying archaeological sites. A fragment of the Palace Chronicle (KUB 26.87) mentions a crossroad in the Hittite city of Nenašša. Hittite religious texts indicate that the Hittites evoked and gave offerings to specific deities at crossroads to ask them to eliminate evils. The texts indicate that such crossroads rituals originated in the Luwian religion. Although we cannot localize Nenašša with the limited information provided in the fragment, based on some historical events and that crossroads rituals originated from the southern Anatolia, we may assume that Nenašša was in the border area of the core land with the western lands.

Öz

Bu çalışma Anadolu'da Hititler tarafından gerçekleştirilen yol ayrımı ritüellerini ele almaktadır. Saray Tarihi'nin bir parçası (KUB 26.87), Maraššantiya Nehri'nin güney kıvrımında yer alan Hitit şehri Nenašša'da bir yol ayrımından bahsetmektedir. Hitit dini metinleri, yol ayrımlarında belirli tanrıları çağırdıklarını ve kötülükleri ortadan kaldırmalarını istemek için onlara adaklar sunduklarını göstermektedir. Metinler, bu tür yol ayrımı ritüellerinin Luvi dininden kaynaklandığını göstermektedir. Parçada verilen sınırlı bilgilerle Nenašša'nın konumunu belirleyemesek de bazı tarihi olaylar ve yol ayrımı ritüellerinin Güney Anadolu kökenli olması sebebiyle kentin yol ayrımı noktasının batıdan gelen bir yol ile kuzeyden güneye giden bir yolun kesiştiği yer olduğunu varsayabiliriz.

Introduction

Büklükale is located approximately 100 km southeast of Ankara, Turkey, at the modern crossing of the Bâla-Kırşehir road on the western bank of Kızılırmak (Hittite Maraššantiya). As pointed out by Kimiyoshi Matsumura and Mark Weeden, the site's location "seems to have been important from a strategic perspective, because it is situated at the narrowest point of Kızılırmak and one of the most important crossing-points through the ages has been here."[1] Cuneiform tablets dating back to the Hittite period have been discovered during the ongoing excavation of the site.[2] Several attempts have been made to identify the site as one of the ancient Hittite cities which were important trading centers during the Assyrian Colony Period.[3] Of these attempts, Massimo Forlanini (2012) identified Büklükale as Durmitta, and Carlo Corti (2017) suggested it was Nenašša. Durmitta and Nenašša were closely linked during the Hittite period. Fragments of cult inventories KUB 48.105 + KBo 12.53 (CTH 529) indicate that Nenašša was a province of Durmitta. Based on this, Forlanini (2012) concludes that Büklükale represents Durmitta.

* Assistant Professor, Yamaguchi University, Faculty of Education, Yamaguchi, 753-8511

1 Matsumura and Weeden (2019: 3). The site has been undergoing excavation since 2009 under the direction of the Japanese Institute of Anatolian Archaeology.

2 For details on the Hittite epigraphic finds from the site, see Weeden (2016; 2017).

3 Barajamovic (2011), Ünal (2018), and Sir Gavaz (2019) proposed that this site might represent the ancient cities of Waḫšušana, Wašḫaniya, and Šalatiwara, respectively.

Forlanini (2009: 52) suggests that Nenašša itself should have been Classical Nyssa (near Harmandalı). Both he and Gojko Barjamovic (2011: 249 and 399) locate the city in the vicinity of the Tüz Gölü. Adam Kryszeń (2016: 376 and n. 869), however, supposed that Nenašša was positioned further north, perhaps as far north as Karakeçili, rather than the traditional region of Tüz Gölü.[4] Corti (2017: 232 and n.144) proposes that Durmitta was located somewhere between the town of Kızılırmak and Kalecik, and that Nenašša was supposedly situated in the south of the province, implying that Büklükale might be the site of this ancient city. In short, the ancient identity of Büklükale is still up for debate. In contribution to the research, this paper focuses on Nenašša from a religious viewpoint that could help connect the culture of the region to a possible location.

Some historical texts mention that, despite constituting the kingdom's core territory, Nenašša was located near the kingdom's borders with enemy lands. Ḫattušili I records in his Annals that on his return from Arzawa he first reconquered Nenašša, which the Hurrians had turned against him (KBo 10.2 i 22–23: CTH 4).[5] Later on, Nenašša became the Hittite–Kaškaean border, probably under the reign of Tudḫaliya III. In the so-called concentric invasion mentioned by Ḫattušili III (KBo 6.28 i 6–7: CTH 88), the Kaškaean enemy made the city of Nenašša his border. Only a few religious texts, such as the texts of the *nuntariyašḫaš* festival and the KI.LAM festival, mention Nenašša.[6] Further, it is recorded that an administrator (AGRIG) from Nenašša was introduced to the king during the KI.LAM festival in Ḫattuša. This indicates that Nenašša was an important administrative center in the kingdom.

Although religious texts do not offer direct insight as to the city's location, details of a religious practice may provide some insights into the culture of Nenašša and its surroundings. This paper examines both the mentions of Nenašša in the Palace Chronicles and descriptions of the crossroads rituals that might have been performed in the city.

Mentions of Nenašša and Crossroads in the Palace Chronicles

Nenašša was an important city in the Hittite core territory. The Proclamation of Telipinu reveals that Nenašša was governed by the royal family. King Telipinu reflected on the earlier reign of one of his predecessors, Labarna as follows:

> KBo 3.67 i 7–12 (CTH 19.II.C)
> He destroyed the lands, one after another, stripped (?) the lands of their power and made them the borders of the sea. When he came back from campaign, however, each (of) his sons went somewhere to a country: The cities of Ḫupišna, Tuwanuwa, Nenašša, Landa, Zallara, Paršuḫanta (and) Lušna, the(se) countries they each governed and the great cities made progress. (van den Hout 2003: 194)

Nenašša was one of the cities that were conquered and entrusted to the princes by Labarna.[7] The Palace Chronicles indicate that Nenašša was once under the control of a man named Pimpira, "son of Nenašša.[8]" Pimpira was a prince (the king's brother or son) and an important subject of Ḫattušili I, who later became the regent of Muršili I, the king's successor. He was probably one of the seven princes who governed the cities mentioned in Telipinu's proclamation (Forlanini 2010: 118 and n.22).

4 For other discussions of Nenašša's location, see Kryszeń (2016: 371–376).

5 When we consider its localization at Büklükale, a pear-shaped glass bottle found at the site might be evidence that the area might be connected with the Hurrians in the early history of the Hittite kingdom (BK100177; Matsumura 2018; 2020: 241). See also n.16.

6 The palace (É.GAL) of Nenašša appears in KUB 10.48 ii 6–8 (CTH 626) and the house (É) of Nenašša in KBo 10.24 iv 31–33 (CTH 627).

7 In this regard, it should be noted that a burnt layer of the Büklükale site was dated to the beginning of the Hittite period (Matsumura and Weeden 2019: 537).

8 KBo 3.34 iii 15'-19' (CTH 8).

A Palace Chronicle fragment (KUB 26.87: CTH 9), possibly a copy in the end of the thirteenth century of the original text (Dardano 1997: 67), indicates that there was an important crossroads in Nenašša:[9]

> KUB 26.87 rev.1'-12' (CTH 9)
> (1') [-z]i-in da-a-ir [
> (2') [ ]x ku-i-e-eš ki-š[a-
> (3') [mKa-a-]ru-wa-an LUGAL-i pa-a[k-nu-an-zi?
> (4') [mK]a-a-ru-wa-an i-da-lu i-ya-a[n-zi?
> (5') [ ] ⸢É?⸣.GAL-az kat-ta pár-aḫ-ta
> (6') [URUN]e-i-na-aš-ši KASKALMEŠ ḫa-at-te-re-eš[-na-aš[10]
> (7') [ ]x na-at DINGIRMEŠ at-ti-mi ša-an-ḫe-er [
> (8') [i-d]a-lu ir-ma-a-an pí-i-e-er [
> (9') [ ]x le-e šar-ra-an-du-m[a
> (10') [ ]x na-ak-ki-ya pé-di ti[-
> (11') [-w]a-an zi-iš-te-e-[ni[11]]
> (12') [ ]x DINGIRMEŠ-iš [
> "(1'-2') ...they took... (3') [they] def[amed Kar]ruwa before the king...(4') they treated Karruwa badly[12]...(5') he chased down from the [pal]ace...(6') at Nenašša, to the cross of the roads...(7') the gods demanded it from my father[13]...(8') they gave [e]vil, the illness... (9') you (pl) shall not transgress...(10') in the place hard to reach...(11') you (pl) cross...(12') the gods..."

According to the fragment, a person named Karruwa was defamed in front of a king[14] and was probably chased away from the palace by him. It also indicates that something happened at a crossroads in Nenašša which fomented the spread of evil and illness. Although we cannot exclude the possibility that this refers to a political event, it is more likely that a certain ritual was performed since some Hittite religious texts relate that rituals were performed at crossroads.

9 Transliteration by Dardano (1997: 67), with some changes shown n.10-n.11.
10 Restoration of CHD-P: 72.
11 Following Kloekhorst 2014: 76–77.
12 For the translation of lines 3–4, see CTH-P: 58.
13 For the translation of line 7, see CHD-M: 219.
14 Karruwa appears in Telipinu's proclamation as the Chief of Treasure Guards (UGULA LÚ.MEŠŠÀ.TAM); however, his identification with the person mentioned in the fragment is uncertain.

Crossroads as Places of Contact with Deities

Crossroads represented a place of contact between gods and human beings and they had an important meaning as the places where offerings are made to gods for the Hittites in Kizzuwatna, the Lower Land and Arzawan lands (Mouton 2008: 94). Hittite texts describe crossroads as places where one could evoke deities – mostly Luwian gods – in order to eliminate evils and purify a ritual client. During evocation rituals (CTH 669), the diviner asked the gods to return to their own temples, looking for them both in heaven and in the netherworld and natural landscapes, including at forks in roads:

> KUB 10.72 (CTH 669.4.A) ii 5'-18'[15]
> He invoked (saying): You turned aside [his eyes elsewhere]. [If] you have gone [to the sky], either to the netherworld, to the mountain or the river, or to the fork in the road (KASKAL-*aš ḫattarešnaš*), valleys, meadows, springs, to the clay(s) of the bank, to the fires, if you left your temple or the ritual client, [no]w I am drawing you back from all (these places). Come back! Care for your temple and ritual client favorably again and turn to them favorably.

The diviner evoked the god in various places requesting the god to return to its own temple to ensure the ritual client's well-being and long life. Hittites also believed that gods could be found at crossroads. Further, Francesco Fuscagni points out that crossroads (KASKAL(.MEŠ)-*aš ḫattarešnaš*) appears in other evocations in purification rituals as the domain of the goddess Ištar in KBo 41.21+KBo 17.32 obv.13' (KASKAL-*ša-aš ḫatta*[*r*]*ešnaš*), preceded by

15 Based on Fuscagni (2010: 138–141) and CHD-P: 72.

mountains and rivers, and in KBo 54.73: 4' (KASKAL.MEŠ-*aš ḫatta[rešnaš]*), preceded by springs and meadows (Fuscagni 2010: 143).[16] The following texts indicate that the Hittites saw crossroads as places of rituals which were attributable to the cultural sphere of southern and western Anatolia.

Birth Rituals

In Kizzuwatnean birth rituals, the *patili*-priest sacrifices two goats at a fork in a road to purify a pregnant woman:

> KUB 9.22 iii 16–23 (CTH 477.A)[17]
> [And] the *patili*-priest gives a jug of wine to the woman, while she hands over to him two young goats. And them the woman "sacrifices" with wine, and the *patili*-priest drives them away.
>
> And when at the crossing of the road he arrives (*n=aš=šan maḫḫan KASKAL-ša-aš ḫatrešnaš [par]ā ari*), then one young goat for the male [deities] of the šinapši he [sac]rifices, and (the other) young goat for the male deities of the city he [sacri]fices.

In order to provide a blood sacrifice for purification, the *patili*-priest sacrifices two young goats at the fork of a road to the male deities of the *šinapši-* and the male deities of the city. The *šinapši-* had a particular function in purification rituals (Beckman 1983: 113); šinapši-deities, including the Kizzuwatnean triad of Teššub, Ḫebat, and Šarruma, "cohabited" with the deceased, and therefore offerings made to these deities were related to deceased spirits (Mouton 2008: 36–38). Further, as discussed later, sacrifices might have been performed at the right and left branches of a fork in the road for the male deities of *šinapši-* and the male deities of the city, respectively.[18]

Ritual of Bappi

Bappi, the priestess of the Luwian goddess Ḫuwaššanna of Ḫupišna in the Lower Land, performed the healing ritual. In this ritual, Bappi placed different types of loaves of bread at a fork in a road for two divine or demonic groups:

> KUB 17.12 ii 1–17 (CTH 431.B)[19]
> She quickly [takes] two *warmanni*-breads, two small baked thick loaves and beer. She carries [them] over to the fork in [the road ([KASKAL]-*aš ḫatarešnaš*)[20]]. And she [break]s them and libates beer. Then she speaks as follows: "What is on the right should eat on the right! This offering shall be good!" Then (she takes) two *warmanni*-breads and two small fresh thick loaves and carries them to the fork in the road (*n=aš* KASKAL-*aš ḫatarniyaḫaš pēdāi*). And she breaks them to the left and speaks as follows: "What pleasantly walks on the left, (his offering) shall be a pleasant for him, and that illness shall be pleasant for that man (i.e., the patient)! Here comes Ḫuwašššanna, my lady! You, terrifying ones, my adversaries, step out of the way!

The beginning of the text states that the patient had been inflicted with evil from the goddess Ḫuwaššanna. The priestess prepared four *warmanni*-bread and four thick loaves, two of which were unbaked (Hutter 2004: 253–254). She gave them to two groups of deities or demons who seemed to be hostile to the patient. One group was expected to accept the offerings

16 It should be noted that the cult for Ištar and Hurrian influence might be inferred from both archaeological evidence from Büklükale such as the round glass pendant (BK100182; Matsumura 2018), a bulla with a winged goddess (BHS2; Weeden 2016: 90–92).

17 Translation by Beckman (1983: 94–95). Further, bird sacrifices seemed to have been performed at crossroads in the following rituals (KUB 9.22 iv 42–44).

18 Ritual offerings for Gulšeš, which probably used the right and left branches of a fork in a road, are described in KBo 11.17 i 1'-15' (CTH 434) and IBoT 3.91 iv? 5' (CTH 470); however, the description in the latter is too fragmented to interpret.

19 Transliteration and translations are based on Görke (2015); further, refer to CHD-P: 72 for lines 9–10 and CHD-M: 242 for lines 11–17.

20 Following its duplicate KUB 54.34 ii 12.

on the right side of the fork and the other was expected to accept those on the left side. The priestess placed baked bread and beer for the beings on the right and two unbaked loaves of bread for the beings on the left. These offerings were intended to attract hostile deities, and so give the goddess space to calm down.[21] Hutter points out that Bappi, despite being "active" in rituals for Ḫuwaššanna alone, performed rituals similar to the ones performed by Wise Woman (MUNUSŠU.GI) (Hutter 2004: 255–256). He also states that Hittite rituals addressing the goddess originated in Luwian rituals connected to the Lower Land including Ḫupišna.

Ritual of Allī of Arzawa

The ritual of Allī, or Wise Woman, indicates the Arzawan tradition. The entire ritual was intended to treat a person who had been bewitched by an "evil tongue." In this ritual, yarn of different colors representing evil elements were wrapped around anthropomorphic figurines to transfer the evil inflicted on the patient to the sorcerer. Once the transfer was completed, Allī buried the ritual objects in the ground. Subsequently, she first offered one unleavened bread and beer to Ariya, a Luwian god, on the right branch of the fork and then to "the gods of the roads" on the left to ensure that the evil would not come back to the patient:

> KUB 24.9 ii 34'-39' + KBo 12.127 ii 4'-6' (CTH 402.A)[22]
> She (= Allī) steps back a little and breaks one unleavened bread for Ariya. Then she places it on the right branch of the fork (*n=at=kan* KASKAL-*ši* ZAG-*naz dāi*). She libates beer and says: "You, take this evil and do not let it go!" She breaks one unleavened bread at the fork in the road and places it on the left branch (1 NINDA.SIG KASKAL-*aš ḫattarišnaš paršiya* KASKAL-*ši* GÙB-*za dāi*). She libates beer and says: "You, the gods of the roads, keep the evil! Do not let it come back!"

This procedure reveals that the offerings were placed on the two branches of the fork to signify the existence of two deities: here, the right branch was for Ariya and the left was for other gods of the roads.[23] Some of the manuscripts of this composition are attested to in the Middle Hittite period (Mouton 2016: 190), which indicates that aspects of Arzawan religious practices had already been accepted in the core area of the kingdom at the time the text was written.[24]

Ritual against pests in the army

There is additional evidence of the presence of Arzawan elements in crossroads rituals. An augur named Dandanku from Arzawa performed a series of rituals to stop an epidemic within the army. The first step in the rituals was to mix yarn of various colors with feed and scatter them across a fork in a road to satisfy the Luwian god Iyarri, who was responsible for the epidemic:

> KUB 7.54 ii 7–24 (CTH 425.2.A)[25]
> Dandanku, the augur, (speaks) as follows: "When death prevails in the midst of the army, they perform this ritual.

21 The beings on the left appear evil deities unlike those on the right; however, as stated in CHD-M: 242–243, the reference need not imply that one deity was evil and the other was good. A text describes a Wise Woman asking the terrifying Ḫeptad to "step off the road" in a ritual for the protective deity of the hunting bag (KBo 17.105 iii 30–32: CTH 433).

22 The transliteration and translations restored with its duplicate KUB 24.11 ii 14'-17' are based on Mouton (2016: 208–211); further, refer to CHD-P: 72 for ii 34'–37'.

23 Offerings and incantations dedicated to other Luwian gods, the deities of Marwainzi, "the dark ones," and the deities of Šalawaneš of the Gate are mentioned in the preceding and following paragraphs, although they were not performed at crossroads.

24 Arzawan traditions might have been introduced to the mainland of Ḫatti even before the subjugation of the lands during the empire period (Yakubovich 2010: 102–103; 278).

25 The translation and transliteration are based on Fuscagni (2016); refer to CHD-P: 151 for lines 13–14.

> Feed mixture is mixed. (Then) they take grain and straw, red wool, blue wool, black wool, and white wool. They mix grain (and) straw together and scatter it across the fork in the road (*n=at* KASKAL-*aš ḫaddareš<šar> pariyan išḫuwanzi*). He speaks as follows:
> "The horse-men (who belong to) you, the god Iyarri, shall give this feed mixture to the horses while the female servants of the god shall take the red wool, blue wool, black wool, green wool, and white wool."

The feed mixture and colorful yarn were scattered across the fork in the road. The feed was taken by "the horse-men" belonging to Iyarri and the yarn was taken by the god's female servants. The two groups were probably expected to take the offerings at the two branches of the fork. This procedure was probably performed to attract the god; for instance, the animal sacrifices mentioned in the following paragraph were probably intended for the Seven Deities (Ḫeptad).[26] At the end of this ritual, the evils causing the epidemic were transferred to a donkey, and the donkey was expected to take them to the enemy lands. Based on Arzawan rituals such as this one, Hutter suggests that "there was obviously some fear of, but also some competence against, pestilence which fostered Luwian beliefs in Arzawa," and that these rituals were popular in the Hittite Empire (Hutter 2003: 236).

The mantalli-ritual

A ritual fragment KUB 39.61 records the so-called *mantalli*-ritual. This ritual also had a connection with Arzawan tradition. It aimed to break the magical bond between the patient and his deceased parent.[27] In this ritual, the ritual materials and offerings of food and drink were brought to a fork in the road:

> KUB 39.61 i 8–14 (CTH 470.93)[28]
> Here are his ritual materials: one vessel of beer, one pitcher (of) wine, one pitcher of beer, one pitcher of *tawal*, one pitcher of *walhi*, one cheese, one rennet, one female kid, nine breads of soldiers, twice seven unleavened breads [...] one dried sheep limb, one fillet, one ... , a small [...] cucumber, greenery, wheat, iron anklet [...] and he/she will determine how (to prepare) all this [...] bring [...] to the [fo]rk [in the road] ([KASKAL-*aš ḫat*]⸢*ta*⸣*rešnaš peda*(-)[ ]).

In this ritual, a fork in the road appears to be the place for making offerings. The following paragraphs indicate that at the fork, a lamb was sacrificed to the Sun goddess of the Earth and something was offered to Ḫilašši (i 15–17). Subsequently, it seems as though some drink was poured into a hole for deities residing in the netherworld (ii 1–6).

There seem to have been different versions of the *mantalli*-ritual, including the Hittite and Arzawan versions, as described in the oracle inquiry. According to KUB 5.6 + KUB 18.54 iii 17–37 (CTH 570), "Until Masḫuiluwa and Zaparti-ŠEŠ come down from the ritual and until they perform *mantalli* rituals in Hittite and Arzawa fashion together with His Majesty, they will come (and) treat the deity and His Majesty again for a second time" (van den Hout 1998: 5). These rituals indicate that ritual practitioners used crossroads or forks in a road to contact deities or deceased spirits, give offerings (such as food, drink, and animal sacrifices), ask them to take away evils and illnesses, and purify patients. They often addressed two kinds of deities: main deities, who were pleaded with on the right path, and other deities, who were seen at the left path in the rituals of Bappi and Allī and, perhaps, the ritual of the *patili*-priest. Whereas deities hos-

26 For the translation for ii 20–24 and details on the animal sacrifice made in this ritual, see Collins (2006: 181–182).

27 The *mantalli*-rituals were intended to break the magical bond usually between a living person and a dead person, through magic or curses, and often involved offerings and the pleading of the living's case to the wrathful deceased being (van den Hout 1998: 5; Mouton 2007: 78).

28 Based on the translation by Mouton (2007: 152–154).

tile to patients were expected to step away, the addressed deities were attracted to or calmed down by the ritual performances, welcomed to the path, and asked to be benevolent to the patient, as seen in the rituals of Bappi, Allī, and Dandanku. Since these rituals were designed to satisfy Luwian gods, this element of the rituals may have originated from the Luwian religion. Hence, they may represent the cult based on the southwestern Anatolian tradition, which is well-represented in Arzawan cults.

Forks in roads were probably chosen as the sites of ritual performances because they were not only considered to be divine places but also believed to have caught divine attention. Even though religious texts do not mention their specific locations and forms, we may reasonably interpret that significant crossroads were intersections of large streets or roads where people traveled to and from every direction. As a result, Hittites may have believed that the gods could use these intersections to view human activities, including their speeches and offerings, from afar.[29] The Hittites considered crossroads to be divine places (e.g., CTH 669), since they might have reminded them of links to a different world. Further, they might have associated the divergence of roads with the image of deposition of evils to enemy lands.

Crossroads of Nenašša in KUB 26.87

Although we can assume from KUB 26.87 rev.6' that some rituals were performed at the crossroads in Nenašša, we do not know what type of rituals were performed there. The text does not clarify the gods addressed by the ritual, the offerings made to the gods, or the ritual's practitioner or purpose. We can at least understand there was divine involvement in this matter (KUB 26.87 rev.7'). After Karruwa was chased away from the palace, something happened at the crossroads of Nenašša. Subsequently, the gods demanded something to "my father," probably the king's father, or the gods avenged him on some issue, which resulted in the spread of evil and illness.[30] This anecdote probably attempted to prevent that situation among later generations as an admonition. This suggests that Nenašša was perceived by the readers or audience as a place connected to lands beyond the kingdom, which were perhaps places that were difficult to reach or were forbidden to the Hittites. The words "transgression" and "the place hard to reach" (KUB 26.87 rev. 9'–10') imply that a certain divine punishment was inflicted on the land because of a violation of territorial borders or the gods' places of residence. Therefore, there is a possibility that some ritual was conducted in Nenašša and later needed atonement.

Regarding its geographical features, Nenašša constituted the kingdom's core territories but was located near its borders, since it was the first city to be reconquered on the king's return from his expedition to the Arzawan lands and might have once been the kingdom's border with the Kaškaeans. The city should have been the point connecting the core territory and the outside lands. We cannot localize Nenašša with the limited information provided in the fragment KUB 26.87. However, due to some historical events and that the crossroads rituals seem to have been originated from the Luwian religion deduced from the rituals discussed above[31], we may assume that important roads stretching to the west and to the north-south were within or in the vicinity of the city[32].

29 We can find religious connotations of crossroads in literature other than the religious texts of the Ancient Near East, for example, in the legend of Hekate in Greek mythology (Beckman 1983: 113).

30 For details on the verb *šanḫ-*, see CHD-Š: 162–171.

31 The connection of crossroad rituals and southern Anatolia is also suggested by Mouton (2008: 94), and Hutter (2003: 236) points out that Arzawan rituals that mention fork in roads reflect the aspect of the Luwian religion.

32 In this case, the landscape of Nenašša appears to be parallel to that of the site of Büklükale, which belonged to the central Hittite area and from where a difficult but important passage stretches far to the west.

Conclusion

Crossroads rituals may have originated from the Luwian religious culture and were particularly well-represented in Arzawan ritual practices and also in Ḫattuša, apparently even during the early days of the kingdom. Crossroads were places where specific deities were evoked and lured by through offerings for atonement or purification.

Although we cannot reconstruct the entire content of the fragment KUB 26.87, there were probably important paths around Nenašša from and to the outside lands, or the city reminded the Hittites of the lands in the west and/or the south from which the kingdom imported the cultic elements of crossroads rituals. This might place Nenašša in a northerly position owing to its cultural connection with the western Arzawan lands and possible Kaškaean invasion. Although this does not conclude the identification of the site of Büklükale with Nenašša, the research on the cultural aspects of the Hittite cities demonstrated in this paper would provide important evidence for the further analysis on the identification. With this knowledge, the author intends to further study the geography and cultural landscapes of other possible ancient cities associated with the site.

Acknowledgements

This work was supported by JSPS KAKENHI Grant Numbers JP19H01351 and JP18J00124. I am grateful to Dr. Sachihiro Omura as well as Dr. Masako Omura and Dr. Kimiyoshi Matsumura for their continuing support for my research in Turkey, and I am pleased to dedicate this article in the commemoration of the 77th birthday of Dr. Sachihiro Omura.

Bibliography

Barjamovic G.
- 2011 *A Historical Geography of Anatolia in the Old Assyrian Colony Period*, CNIP 38, Copenhagen.

Beckman G. M.
- 1983 *Hittite Birth Rituals. Second Revised Edition*, StBoT 29, Wiesbaden.

Bryce T.
- 2005 *The Kingdom of the Hittites*, Oxford.
- 2009 *The Routledge Handbook of the Peoples and Places of Ancient Western Asia. The Near East from the Early Bronze Age to the Fall of the Persian Empire*, London and New York.

Collins B. J.
- 2006 "Pigs at the Gate: Hittite Pig Sacrifice in Its Eastern Mediterranean Context," *Journal of Ancient Near Eastern Religions* 6, pp. 155–188.

Corti C.
- 2017 "The North: Hanhana, Hattena, Ištahara, Hakpiš, Nerik, Zalpuwa, Tummana, Pala and the Hulana River Land," in M. Weeden and Z. Ullmann (eds.), *Hittite Landscape and Geography*, HdO 121, Leiden and Boston, pp. 219–238.

Dardano P.
- 1997 *L'aneddoto e il racconto in età antico-hittita: la cosiddetta "Cronaca di Palazzo,"* Rome.

Forlanini M.
- 2010 "An Attempt at Reconstructing the Branches of the Hittite Royal Family of the Early Kingdom Period," in Y. Cohen, A. Gilan and J. L. Miller (eds.), *Pax Hethitica –Studies on the Hittites and their Neighbours in Honour of Itamar Singer*, StBoT 51, Wiesbaden, pp. 115–135.
- 2012 review of: Barjamovic, *A Historical Geography of Anatolia in the Old Assyrian Colony Period* (CNIP 38, Copenhagen 2011), *Bibliotheca Orientalis* 69/3–4, col. 290–299.

Fuscagni F.
- 2010 "KUB 10.72 (CTH 669.4): una proposta di catalogazione," *Studi micenei ed egeo-anatolici* 52, pp. 137–147.
- 2016 "Das Ritual des Auguren Dandanku (CTH 425.2), hethiter.net/: CTH 425.2 (INTR 2016-08-01)," https://www.hethport.uni-wuerzburg.de/txhet_besrit/intro.php?xst=CTH %20 425.2&prgr=&lg=DE&ed=F. %20Fuscagni (2020/12/24).

Görke, S.
- 2015 "Das Ritual der Bappi (CTH 431), hethiter.net/: CTH 431 (INTR 2015-05-27)," https://www.hethport.uni-wuerzburg.de/txhet_besrit/intro.php?xst=CTH %20431&prgr=&lg=DE&ed=S.%20G%C3%B6rke (2020/12/25).

Hout, T. P. J. van den.
- 1998 *The Purity of Kingship. An Edition of CTH 569 and Related Hittite Oracle Inquiries of Tuthaliya IV*, Leiden, Boston and Köln.
- 2003 "The Proclamation of Telipinu," in W. W. Hallo (ed.), *The Context of Scripture*, Vol. 1, Leiden, New York and Köln, pp. 199–203.

Hutter, M.
- 2003 "Aspects of Luwian Religion," in Melchert H. C. (ed.), *The Luwians*, HdO I/68, Leiden and Boston, pp. 211–280.
- 2004 "Der Gott Tunapi und das Ritual der "Bappi im Ḫuwaššanna-Kult," in M. Hutter and S. Hutter-Braunsar (eds.), *Offizielle Religion, lokale Kulte und individuelle Religiosität. Akten des religionsgeschichtlichen Symposiums „Kleinasiens und angrenzende Gebiete vom Beginn des 2. bis zur Mitte des 1. Jahrhunderts v. Chr." (Bonn, 20.–22. Februar 2003)*, AOAT 318, Münster, pp. 249–257.

Kloekhorst A.
- 2014 *Accent in Hittite: A Study in Plene Spelling, Consonant Gradation, Clitics, and Metrics*, StBoT 56, Wiesbaden.

Kryszeń, A.
- 2016 *A Historical Geography of the Hittite Heartland*, AOAT 437, Münster.

Matsumura, K.
- 2018 "The Glass Bottle and Pendant from Büklükale and their Dating," in J. Henderson and K. Matsumura (eds.), *Aspects of Late Bronze Age Glass in the Mediterranean. Anatolian Archaeological Studies 21. Japanese Institute of Anatolian Archaeology, Tokyo*, pp. 11–29.
- 2020 "New Evidence on Central Anatolia during the Second Millennium B.C.E: Excavations at Büklükale," *Near Eastern Archaeology* vol. 83, no. 4, pp. 234–247.

Matsumura, K. and M. Weeden
- 2019 "Büklükale in the Hittite Period," in A. Süel (ed.), *Acts of the IXth International Congress of Hittitology, Çorum September 08–14, 2014*, vol. I–II, pp. 533–566.

Mouton, A.
- 2007 *Rêves hittites. Contribution à une histoire et une anthropologie du rêve en Anatolie ancienne*, CHANE 28, Paris.
- 2008 *Les rituels de naissance kizzuwatniens. Un example de rites de passage en Anatolie Hittite*, Paris.
- 2012 "Le concept de pureté/impureté en Anatolie Hittite," in Rösch, P. and U. Simon (eds.), *How Purity Is Made*, Wiesbaden.
- 2016 *Rituels, mythes et prières hittites*, Paris.

Sir Gavaz Ö.
- 2019 "Büklükale'nin Hititler Dönemindeki Adi Üzerine Yeni Bir Değerlendirme," *Türkiye Bilimler Akademisi Arkeoloji Dergisi* 25, pp. 85–94.

Ünal A.
- 2018 *Eski Anadolu Siyasi Tarihi, Kitap 1: Eski Taş Devri'nden Hitit Devleti'nin Yıkılışına Kadar (M. Ö. 60.000–1180)*, Ankara.

Weeden, M.
- 2013 "A Hittite Tablet from Büklükale," *Anatolian Archaeological Studies* XVIII, pp. 19–35.
- 2016 "Hittite Epigraphic Finds from Büklükale 2010–14," *Anatolian Archaeological Studies* XIX, pp. 81–104.
- 2017 "A Cuneiform Fragment from the 2016 Season at Büklükale, BTK 3: Part of a Diplomatic Text?," *Anatolian Archaeological Studies* XX, pp. 17–21.

Yakubovich, I.
- 2010 *Sociolinguistics of the Luvian Language*, BSIEL 2, Leiden and Boston.

A Bronze Plaque from Dūr-Katlimmu – An Assyrian-Urartian Hybrid

Hartmut Kühne *

Abstract

A sheet bronze plaque with a diameter of 9 cm from the excavation of Tall Šēḫ Ḥamad / Dūr-Katlimmu (Syria) with an incised depiction of a male god emerging from a winged sun disc hovering over a tree supported by two atlantid figures is interpreted as a mirror. Albeit unstratified, the findspot within the Building F/W reflects an upper-class environment. In the discussion of the stylistic peculiarities of the depiction it is argued that the Dūr-Katlimmu plaque/ mirror is an Assyrian-Urartian hybrid reflecting mutual interaction rather than Assyrian domination or Urartian emulation. Due to the iconographic comparisons a more precise date of the artefact at the end of the eighth century B.C. is suggested but remains arguable.

Öz

Tall Šēḫ Ḥamad / Dūr-Katlimmu (Suriye) kazısında tabakalanmamış bir Yeni Asur bağlamından çıkarılan 9 cm çapındaki levha bronz plaka, iki atlantid figür tarafından desteklenen bir ağacın üzerinde gezinen kanatlı bir güneş diskinden çıkan bir erkek tanrının kazıma tasviriyle ayna olarak yorumlanmaktadır. Tabakalandırılmamış olsa da F/W Binası içindeki buluntu yeri üst sınıf bir çevreyi yansıtmaktadır. Tasvirin biçimsel özelliklerinin tartışılmasında, Dūr-Katlimmu levhasının/aynasının Asur egemenliği ya da Urartu taklitçiliğinden ziyade karşılıklı etkileşimi yansıtan bir Asur-Urartu karışımı olduğu savunulmaktadır. Karşılaştırmalar nedeniyle eserin Yeni Asur dönemi içinde daha kesin bir tarihe sahip olup olmadığı tartışmalıdır.

It is a pleasure to dedicate this paper to Dr. Sachihiro Omura with reverence for his great achievements in Anatolian Archaeology surveying a formerly unexplored region of Central Anatolia, directing his interdisciplinary excavation in Kaman-Kalehöyük, and founding the Japanese Institute of Anatolian Archaeology Çağırkan, Kaman.

Find Circumstances

During the excavation season of 1989 in Tall Šēḫ Ḥamad / Dūr-Katlimmu on the Lower Habur in NE-Syria (Kühne 2020) a tanged circular plaque of sheet bronze (Figs. 2–5) was discovered in the second aisle from the east of room K1 of Building F/W, the palatial residence in the Northeast Corner of the Lower Town II (Fig. 1a–b) that covers an area of 3800 m^2.

> Site: Tall Šēḫ Ḥamad / Dūr-Katlimmu (Arab Republic of Syria)
> Excavation registration number: SH 89/ 8779/0201
> Day of discovery: 1989–09–23
> Location of discovery: Excavation unit: Northeast Corner of Lower Town II; excavation section: Building F/W, Room K 1; find unit ("Fundstelle") Fs 109 (reddish earth layer of decayed mudbrick), 40 cm above floor level
> Stratigraphy: unstratified

The main entrance to Building F/W (Fig. 1a) is situated in the west giving access to part W of Building F/W via Room XX. Part W consists of a double row of rectangular rooms which form a square around a large courtyard EZ

* Prof. em. Dr. Hartmut Kühne, Freie Universität Berlin, Institut für Vorderasiatische Archäologie

($500\,m^2$) that had to be crossed to get to Part F of the Building. Part W almost certainly represents the commercial wing of the compound Building F/W.

Entering Room XX from outside one had to continue in a zigzag fashion via Rooms ZZ and NZ to get to the courtyard EZ. South of Rooms ZZ and NZ lies Room K1, the western-most of the three K-Rooms. It was accessible from Room NZ via a preserved vaulted entrance. The architectural features of Room K1 are rather peculiar consisting of five aisles, each vaulted (Fig. 1b). These vaulted aisles were then surmounted by another vault covering the whole room. Obviously, the room functioned as a cooling chamber and the aisles as walk-in shelves; because of its position near the main entrance it has been interpreted as a facility for the storage of perishable goods (Kühne 1993–1994: 269). Similar constructions have been excavated in the "Red House" (Kreppner and Schmid 2013: 289–299).

The biography of Building F/W extends over the whole Neo-Assyrian Period and beyond to Post-Assyrian times (Kühne 2021). Since there is no indication of an upper storey in Part W, the decayed mud brick debris in which the plaque was embedded may stem from the destruction or from the final deterioration of it. A *terminus post quem* for the destruction would be the middle of the 6th century B.C. when the Red House in the Central Lower Town II was destroyed by fire. This incident indicates a shift from full to patchwork occupation in the Lower Town II. The latter continued until the first quarter of the 5th century B.C. (Kreppner / Schmid 2013: 360 Abb. 388; Kühne 2006–2008, 550; Kühne 2021: 363, Tabelle 17.01). Thereafter the Lower Town II was abandoned and the ruins were deteriorating over a longer period of time before the whole area was converted to a burial ground of the city of Magdala, as the site was called then, at some time during the third century B.C. Thus, the find spot of the sheet plaque is of no chrono-stratigraphic or functional value.

The Object (Figs. 2–5)

Object: tanged circular plaque
Material: Sheet Bronze
Measurements: diameter of plaque 8.5–9.0 cm; length including the tang: 10.5 cm; averaging thickness 0.4 cm as corroded (Fig. 5b), the original sheet was probably thinner.
Safekeeping: National Museum Deir ez-Zor, Syria, registration number: DeZ 11889
Publication: Sperlich 1996:75; Bonatz/ Kühne/Mahmoud 1998: 122 no. 112; Rehm 2018: 282 Abb. 2.

The plaque was not complete when discovered (Fig. 2), an upper right section of it was missing. The next day a fragment of the missing part was found in the same debris, joining to the upper edge (Fig. 5a). The remaining missing part has never shown up; the restorer replaced it (Fig. 4). One side of the plaque was well preserved (Figs. 2, 4) while the other side was heavily corroded (Fig. 3). Fortunately, the well-preserved side carried a figurative rendering (Fig. 4, 5a).

At the time of the first publication of the object the preliminary interpretation of the archaeological context of the excavation area suggested a date of the second half of the 7th century B.C. for the object (Bonatz/Kühne/Mahmoud 1998: 122 no. 112). More recently, Rehm (2018) has argued that the Dūr-Katlimmu plaque should have functioned as a votive offering to the god Šamaš because of the depiction of the winged sun disc (Rehm 2018: 285–286). Both, the date and the depiction, will be debated in this paper.

Function

The lower end of the tang is broken off (Fig. 2). Originally extending further the tang indicates that the plaque has had a handle that was attached to the tang. The handle is situated exactly below the baseline of the depiction (Fig. 4, 5a). To look at the depiction the person had to hold up the plaque. This suggests that the plaque functioned as a mirror; according to Albenda 1985 the diameter of mirrors varies between 9 and 19, exceptionally 27 cm. At the same time, the tang excludes an interpretation of the Dūr-Katlimmu plaque as a medallion (Seidl 2001) or as a votive sheet as known from Urartian sites (Rehm 2000; Seidl 2004, 169ff.).

Mirrors are well known in the material repertoire from ancient Near Eastern settlements since the Ceramic Neolithic of Catal Höyük (Albenda 1985; Pappi 2009–2011). In Middle Assyrian glyptic art Assyrian queens hold a mirror (Lassen 2020: 34–35Fig. 3.21; Matthews 1990: 95, 107 nos. 509, 511–513). In the Early Iron Age, the mirror became the standard religious symbol of the Hittite/Late Hittite goddess Kubaba as identified by inscriptions on stelae from Carchemish and Malatya (Hawkins 1981; Hawkins 1980–1983; Bittel 1980–1983). The archaeological context in Neo-Assyrian graves from Assur suggests that mirrors were used as a commodity of high society. Two Neo-Assyrian queens, Naqi'a/Zakutu, wife of king Sennacherib (705–681 B.C.), and Libbâli-sharrat, wife of king Assurbanipal (669–630 B.C.), are depicted holding a mirror in their left hands (Börker-Klähn 1982: 214, 216 nos. 220, 227). A physical mirror of electron from tomb II in Nimrud bears an inscription allocating it to queen Ataliya, wife of king Sargon II (722–705 B.C.) (Al-Rawi 2008: 138 Fig. 15-cc).

So far only three plaques are known bearing incisions of figurative scenes (Rehm 2018), one of them being the Dūr-Katlimmu plaque. On the latter, small bulges along the edge of the plaque and perhaps also the larger bulge in its centre (Fig. 5b) indicate that the bronze sheet may have been mounted to some other material like for instance precious wood or ivory of which nothing remained. In that case, the incision would have decorated the mirror side (Fig. 2, 4) which would have interfered with its function while the corroded side (Fig. 3) would not have been visible.

Alternatively, it may be assumed that the plaques were framed by some other material so that the undecorated side functioned as mirror and the reverse was decorated. In comparison to Etruscan mirrors of the 5th century B.C. (Pfister-Roesgen 1975) it is also conceivable that a second separate disc was produced serving as the mirror that was soldered to the decorated one and framed together.

The Depiction (Figs. 405a)

A chevron (or feather) pattern and the above-mentioned little bulges frame the figurative scene. In the center there is a triangular shaped winged disc hovering above a tree. Situated in the lower center of the wings the larger bulge is styled as a rosette. Emerging from the wings and extending to the upper edge of the plaque an anthropomorphic figure is incised. While the body is inscribed in the wings, the shoulders and the head are raised clearly above them; no feet are rendered. In comparison to half figures and full figures discussed below this anthropomorphic representation may be called a two third figure.

The figure is turned to the right. The head is given in profile. The face is marked by a prominent nose and an eye. Rising above the head is a cylindrical headgear styled by two compartments of which the upper one is decorated by vertical lines; the lower one incorporates a protruding horn. A chignon emerges from below the headgear curling in above the right shoulder. The neck of the figure is obscured but the lower part of a long beard is extending to the left shoulder and the upper chest. The horn and the beard identify the anthropomorphic figure as a male god.

The body seems to be rendered *en face*. Both arms are turned to the right. Stretched diagonally down the right wing, the left arm is overlapped by the right one, that, extending straight forward, is holding a bent object in the hand that looks like a sickle.

In the upper left section of the plaque, eight tiny circles are engraved. On the opposite side two fragmentary lines seem to indicate a depiction of a moon sickle.

A double line frames the winged disc. Arranged in diagonal stripes the wings are decorated by the same chevron/feather pattern as the edge of the plaque; similarly, the tail is rendered. On each side of the tail streamers are emerging from the wings ending in a loop. The tail feathers are overlapping the upper limit of the tree. Framed by a double line the tree consists of a thick trunk with festoon-like arranged undecorated branches.

The sections left and right of the tree below the wings are engraved by kneeling atlantid figures supporting the wings with their raised arms and hands. The left figure is completely preserved while most of the right one is gone; from the remaining traces it may be assumed with some certainty that it corresponded to the left one. The left figure wears a spherical cap with a chignon escaping below it. A beard extends to the breast. A T-shirt and a short skirt are dressing the body. The S-curved rendering of the body in conjunction with the kneeling attitude gives the figure a dynamic that is reminiscent of dancing.

A large empty space behind and in front the god emerges above the wings. The eight little circles must be considered a negligence because they ought to have represented the seven circles of the symbol of Sibittu (Pleiades). They and the moon sickle are completely marginalized, thereby highlighting the god's image. The god is incorporated in the sun disc, he and the sun disc are one body, or – one might say – this composition anthropomorphizes the sun disc. Both fill two thirds of the space available for imagery. Consequently, the tree below is compressed and because of the missing inner decoration marginalized. By contrast, the two 'dancing' atlantid men are a most prominent feature of the composition.

The depiction is fairly carefully chiseled, the figures are engraved distinctly; but the chevron pattern seems to have been executed somewhat hastily. Clearly, the artist was in conflict with the traditional rendering of a person's body fully *en face*.

Discussion

On first glance, the depiction on the Dūr-Katlimmu plaque appears to reflect pure Neo-Assyrian iconography. However, there are a number of iconographic peculiarities that do not correspond easily to this assessment.

The center of the winged disc is usually marked by a larger circle or a ring in which the anthropomorphic god is inscribed (Fig. 6–07); here it is replaced by the small protruding rosette that resembles an omphalos (Seidl 2003). The feathers of the wings are usually arranged horizontally, here they are set up diagonally; furthermore, they are decorated by chevrons which is uncommon. The double boundary line of the winged disc does not occur elsewhere (Collon 2001: 80–82). The tail of the winged sun disc is normally placed outside the circle, the lines of the circle separating it from the body inside (Fig. 6; Collon 2001: no. 152). However, on some early Neo-Assyrian reliefs the circle covers the "tail" (Fig. 7); thus, it appears that the "tail" is becoming a functional part of the dress of the anthropomorphic god inside (Budge 1914: Pl. XVII-1, Pl. XXIII-1) so that for the completion of the anthropomorphic figure only the feet are missing. On the Dūr-Katlimmu plaque (Figs. 4–05a) the double line of the wings separates the tail from the body inside the wings.

As known from the reliefed orthostats B 13 and B 23 from the throne room of the Northwest Palace of Ashurnasirpal II in Nimrud (Meuszynski 1981: Tf. 1 B-23, Tf. 2 B-13; Orthmann 1975: Abb. 198) or – very similar – from a cylinder seal from Sherif Khan (Fig. 6 = Collon 2001: no. 151) the upper body of the god fills the circle with the head slightly overlapping and sticking out; he can face to either side, wears a horned cap or a (feather-) polos, raises one hand and holds an object in the other. "As a general rule, the earlier the piece, the more of the god's body is shown." (Collon 2001: 80). On the Dūr-Katlimmu plaque, the god stands out much higher than usual above the wings and holds an indefinable object. This compositional feature and the stylization of the headgear of the god with the protruding horn seem to resemble Neo-Hittite/Aramaic emulations of Assyrian representations (Börker-Klähn 1982: 226–227 nos. 252, 255 being a very close comparison to the headgear of the Dūr-Katlimmu plaque).

The boundary lines of the tree may be compared to Neo-Assyrian glyptic evidence, particularly to Collon 2001: no. 158; the stylization of the branches seems to be unique (Collon 2001: 83–85 sketches).

Atlantid figures supporting the winged sun disc are known from Middle Assyrian glyptic (Matthews 1990: 108–110). They appear as antithetical bull men, gods, winged monsters, lahmu, and unspecified heroes in standing and kneeling positions (Matthews 1990: nos. 472, 477, 476 [Eriba-Adad], 474, 499, 501). In Neo-Assyrian glyptic standing antithetical bull men and scorpion men (Collon 2001: no. 210, 211) as well as single standing heroes and bull men occur (Collon 2001: nos. 200, 208); more frequent are single kneeling heroes (Collon 2001: 204, 207), rare are four-winged genii (Collon 2001: 203) and a levitating kneeling figure (Fig. 8 = Collon 2001: no. 202). Standing supporting figures also occur on stamp seals (Herbordt 1992: Tf. 13, 2.3.8.13; Fügert 2015: no. 254, 255). The styling of all of these examples does not have anything in common with the kneeling men supporting the winged sun disc on the Dūr-Katlimmu plaque!

The most striking comparisons with them come from Urartu, unfortunately from unrecorded provenience. The full figure of a god in a winged ring occurs on two discs (Figs. 9–10) probably belonging to the time of the kings Išpuini/Menua of the end of the ninth/early eighth century B.C. (Seidl 2004: Abb. 74=Taf. 24c, Taf. 36a; Calmeyer/Seidl 1983: Fig. 1–2) (Figs. 9–10). It should be noted that the full disc (Fig. 9) has a diameter of 28 cm; however, the inner circle with the depiction of the god has a diameter of only about 7 cm; the height of the god on Fig. 10 is about 7 cm. Thus, the depiction is smaller than the one on the Dūr-Katlimmu mirror!

The headgear of the god with the protruding horn on Fig. 9 is very similar to the one on the Dūr-Katlimmu plaque. More conspicuous are the two kneeling figures in a very similar atlantid attitude to the Dūr-Katlimmu plaque supporting the wings of the sun disc. They vary in the stronger bending of the knees positioned on the peak of mountains and in their dresses and headgears, the latter clearly designating them as gods, but the posture of their raised arms is strikingly similar and differs equally strikingly from Assyrian atlantid scenes on cylinder seals as described above. Furthermore, the arrangement of the atlantid figures within the composition of the image is very similar. Except for another scene with a single atlantid figure supporting a winged sun disc on a fragmentary bronze sheet from Karmir Blur (Meyer 1957: Abb. 30) atlantid figures do not seem to be very common in Urartian art.

Iconological Thoughts

The god in the winged circle depicted on the Urartian discs is the sun god Šiuini. He is third in the hierarchy of the Urartian pantheon (Seidl 2004: 201; Hazenbos 2009–2011; Seidl 2009–2011), the first being Ḫaldi (Seidl 2004: 200, Abb. 48), and his cultic center is Tušpa. This corresponds to the Assyrian representations of the winged sun disc with or without inscribed anthropomorphic god interpreted as the symbol of Šamaš (Calmeyer 1984; Seidl 2020) as opposed to the long intensive debate whether or not it should represent the god Aššur; in my opinion, this is not a contradiction because in their mission to bring order and justice to all people the Assyrians had syncretized Šamaš with Aššur. In any case, the theme of a winged disc with an inscribed anthropomorphic god as half figure hovering over a tree dominates the Assyrian iconography of the ninth to the middle of the eighth century B.C. (Figs. 6, 7) (Seidl/Sallaberger 2005–2006). It represents the central expression of Assyrian imperial ideology. After about the middle of the eighth century B.C. the theme gets out of focus but shows up again under Sargon II (Fig. 8) (Börker-Klähn 1982: 203 Abb. 176 =

Collon 2001: no. 173). In Urartu the rendering of the god as half figure in the winged sun disc is common in the early period to about the reign of Menua while the full standing figure in the circle or ring dominates later representations (Seidl 2004: 201, Abb. 91, Tf. 32).

However, the inspiration of Assyrian iconography on Urartian art seems to have been continued if we consider the seventh century lid of a pyxis from Karmir Blur with a diameter of eight cm (Fig. 11), which shows a tree over which a winged disc hovers without anthropomorphic figure but flanked by bird *apkallus*, reminiscent of the ninth century decoration in the Northwest palace of Nimrud. Yet, the depiction is styled in an Urartian fashion, thus representing a hybrid (van Loon 1975: 465 Abb. 394a; Wartke 1993: 137 Abb. 70; Meyer 1957: 840 Abb. 8–9).

Synthesis

The relationship between Assyria and Urartu has been perceived rather unilaterally in favor of Assyria. Scholars have highlighted the fact that the founder of the dynasty, Sarduri I (prior to 830 B.C.), had introduced Assyrian language and cuneiform writing. His son, Išpuini, applied cuneiform writing to the Urartian language. Similarly, Assyrian visual arts were "imported" (Seidl 2004:2). However, after an in-depth evaluation John Curtis concluded: "*On the whole, therefore, we should perhaps regard Assyrian and Urartian metalwork as parallel traditions, with evidence of influence from one culture or the other at particular times, but with both industries mostly operating independently from one another.*" (Curtis 2012: 443; Herrmann 2012).

I consider the Dūr-Katlimmu plaque/mirror a hybrid reflecting mutual Assyrian and Urartian interaction stylizing objects in their own right and fashion. Being an object of prestige of the upper class the mirror was found *out of situ* but still associated with the architecture of the palace-like residence Building F/W that meets the standards of the upper class.

The late date of the Karmir Blur pyxis lid does not outweigh the iconographic similarities between the Dūr-Katlimmu plaque/mirror and the earlier dated Urartian bronze discs Figs. 9–10. Therefore, as opposed to my earlier chronological setting, I suggest a late eighth century B.C. date for the Dūr-Katlimmu plaque/mirror, the time when Sargon II had finally settled the centuries-long military skirmish between Assyria and Urartu in favor of Assyria. Would it be too far-fetched to imagine that a lady of Urartian origin was living in the Building F/W of Dūr-Katlimmu, married to an Assyrian landlord of Aramaean origin (because of the bit hilani type building within Gebäude F)?

Acknowledgement

The information on the Neo-Assyrian graves from Assur was kindly provided by Friedhelm Pedde who is preparing the volume: Die Gräber und Grüfte in Assur III. Die neu- und nachassyrische Zeit, WVDOG.

Abbreviations

BATSH: Berichte der Ausgrabung Tall Šēḫ Ḥamad/Dūr-Katlimmu

RlAVA: Reallexikon der Assyriologie und Vorderasiatischen Archäologie

SAAS: State Archives of Assyria Studies

Bibliography

Albenda, P.
- 1985 "Mirrors in the Ancient Near East," *SOURCE* Vol. IV-2 (3), pp. 2–9.

Al-Rawi, F. N. H.
- 2008 "Inscriptions from the Tombs of the Queens of Assyria," in J. E. Curtis, H. McCall, D. Collon and L. al-Gailani Werr (eds.) *New Light on Nimrud*, London, pp. 119–138.

Bittel, K.
- 1980–1983 "Kubaba. B. Ikonographie," RlAVA 6, pp. 261–264.

Biainili-Urartu
- 2012 S. Kroll *et al.* (eds.), *The Proceedings of the Symposium in Munich 12–14 October 2007.* Acta Iranica 51. Leuven.

Börker-Klähn, J.
- 1982 *Altvorderasiatische Bildstelen und vergleichbare Felsreliefs*, Baghdader Forschungen 4, Mainz.

Bonatz, D., H. Kühne and A. Mahmoud,
- 1998 *Rivers and Steppes*. Cultural Heritage and Environment of the Syrian Jezireh, Catalogue to the Museum of Deir ez-Zor, Ministry of Culture, Damascus.

Budge, E. A. Wallis
- 1914 *Assyrian Sculptures in the British Museum*, London.

Calmeyer, P.
- 1984 "Das Zeichen der Herrschaft ... ohne Šamaš wird es nicht gegeben," *Archäologische Mitteilungen aus Iran* 17, pp. 135–153.

Calmeyer, P. and U. Seidl
- 1983 "Eine Frühurartäische Siegesdarstellung," *Anatolian Studies* 33, pp. 103–114.

Collon, D.
- 2001 *Cylinder Seals V. Catalogue of the Western Asiatic Seals in the British Museum*, London.

Curtis, J.
- 2012 "Assyrian and Urartian Metalwork: Independence or Interdependence?," in *Biainili-Urartu*, pp. 427–443.

Fügert, A.
- 2015 *Die neuassyrische und spätbabylonische Glyptik aus Tall Šēḫ Ḥamad*, BATSH 16, Wiesbaden.

Hawkins, J. D.
- 1981 "Kubaba at Karkamiš and Elsewhere," Anatolian Studies 31, pp. 147–176.
- 1980–1983 "Kubaba. A. Philologisch," *RlAVA* 6: 257–261.

Hazenbos, J.
- 2009–2011 „Sonnengott. A III. A. Urartäisch. Philologisch," *RlAVA* 12: 613–614.

Herbordt, S.
- 1992 *Neuassyrische Glyptik des 8.–7. Jh. v. Chr.*, SAAS 1, Helsinki.

Herrmann, G.
- 2012 "Some Assyrianizing Ivories found at Nimrud: Could they be Urartian?," in *Biainili-Urartu*, pp. 339–350.

Kreppner, F. J. and J. Schmid
- 2013 *Stratigraphie und Architektur des ‚Roten Hauses' von Tall Šēḫ Ḥamad/Dūr-Katlimmu.* BATSH 11, Wiesbaden.

Kühne, H.
- 1993/1994 "Tall Šēḫ Ḥamad/Dūr-katlimmu 1988–1990," *Archiv für Orientforschung* XL/XLI, pp. 267–272.
- 2006–2008 "Šaiḫ Ḥamad, Tall. B. Archäologisch." *RlAVA* 11, pp. 543–551.
- 2020 "Dur-Katlimmu." Wissenschaftliches Bibel Lexikon. http://www.bibelwissenschaft.de/stichwort/45507/
- 2021 "Dūr-Katlimmu in neuassyrischer Zeit," in H. Kühne (ed.), *Die Zitadelle von Dūr-Katlimmu in mittel- und neuassyrischer Zeit*, BATSH 12.1, Wiesbaden, pp. 361–390.

Lassen, A. W.
- 2020 "Women and Seals in the Ancient Near East," in A. W. Lassen and K. Wagensonner (eds.), *Women at the Dawn of History*, New Haven, pp. 24–37.

Matthews, D. M.
- 1990 *Principles of Composition in Near Eastern Glyptic of the Later Second Millennium B.C.*, Freiburg Schweiz, Göttingen.

Meuszynski, J.
- 1981 *Die Rekonstruktion der Reliefdarstellungen und Ihrer Anordnung im Nordwestpalast von Kalḫu (Nimrud)*, Baghdader Forschungen 2, Mainz.

Meyer, G. R.
- 1957 „Die Sowjetischen Ausgrabungen in Teschebaini und Ir(e)pûni," in *Wissenschaftliche Annalen (Berlin)* VI/12, pp. 837–851.

Orthmann, W.
- 1975 *Der Alte Orienti* Propyläen Kunstgeschichte Band 14, Berlin.

Pappi, C.
- 2009–2011 „Spiegel," RlAVA 12, pp. 645–646.

Pfister-Roesgen, G.
- 1975 *Die etruskischen Spiegel des 5. Jhs. v. Chr.*, Bern.

Rehm, E.
- 2000 „Votivbleche im 1. Jt. v.Chr.," in R. Dittmann *et al.* (eds.), *Variatio Delectat. Iran und der Westen, Gedenkschrift für P. Calmeyer*, Alter Orient und Altes Testament Bd. 272, Münster, pp. 627–649.
- 2018 „Die glänzende Sonne – Spiegel als Weihgaben für Schamasch?," in Kaniuth, K., D. Lau und D. Wicke (eds.), *Übergangszeiten. Altorientalische Studien für Reinhard Dittmann*

anlässlich seines 65. Geburtstags, Marru 1, pp. 279–288.

Seidl, U.
- 2001 „Der Mond, der vom Himmel fällt," *Damaszener Mitteilungen* 13, pp. 105–111.
- 2003 „Omphalosschale," *RlAVA* 10, p. 90.
- 2004 *Bronzekunst Urartus*, Mainz.
- 2009–2011 „Sonnengott. B. III. a. Urartäisch. Archäologisch," *RlAVA* 12, pp. 623–624.
- 2020 "The Winged Disc in Mesopotamia," in Otto, A., M. Herles and K. Kaniuth (eds.) Proceedings of the 11th International Congress on the Archaeology of the Ancient Near East, Wiesbaden, Vol. 1, pp. 119–150.

Seidl, U. und W. Sallaberger
- 2005–2006 „Der „Heilige Baum"", *Archiv für Orientforschung* 51, pp. 54–74.

Sperlich, W.
- 1996 „Wie Gott in Assyrien," *Bild der Wissenschaft* 3, pp. 70–79.

Van Loon, M.
- 1975 „Die Kunst von Urartu," in Orthmann 1975, pp. 453–466. Wartke, Ralf-Bernhard
- 1993 *Urartu – Das Reich am Ararat*, Mainz.

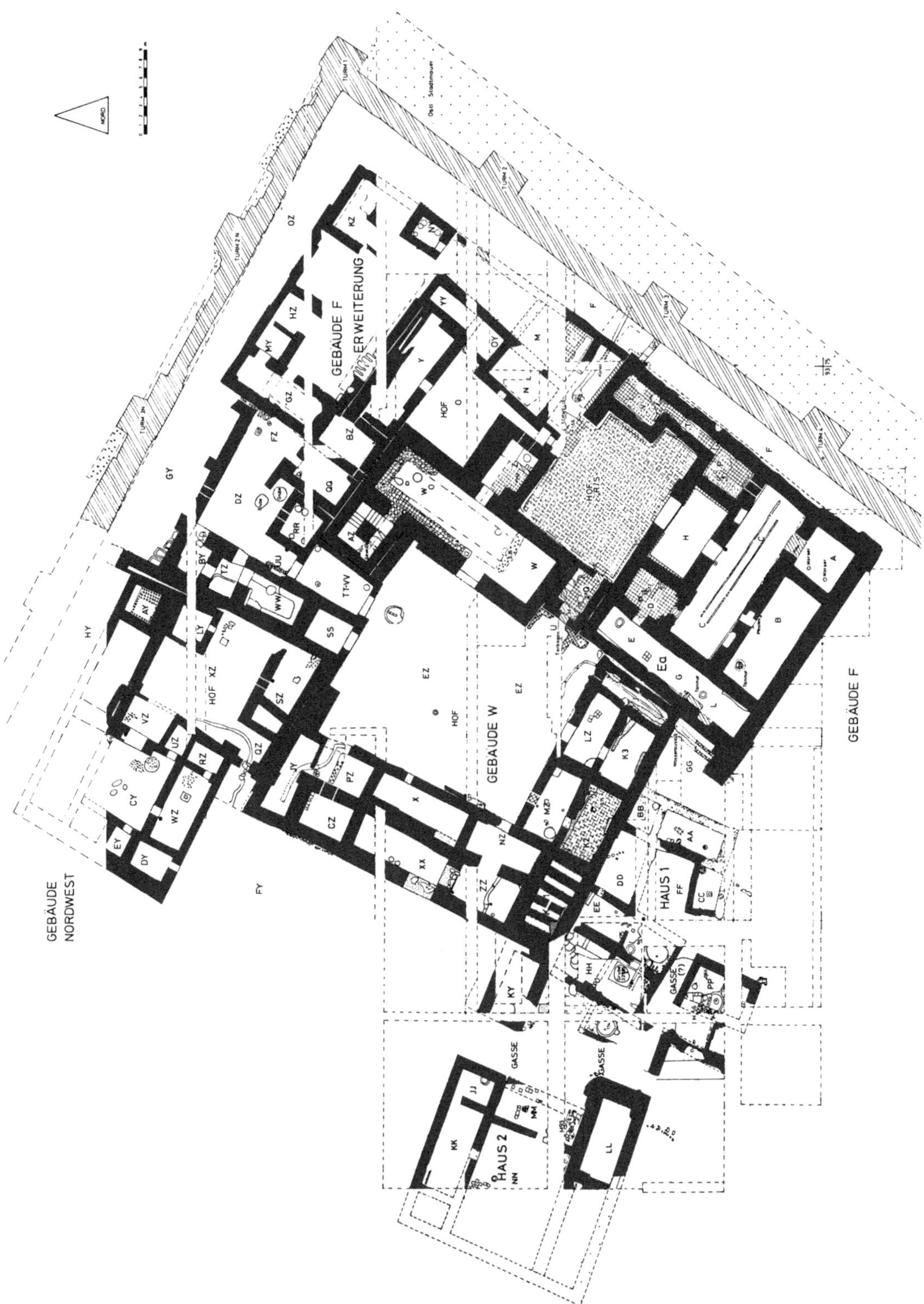

Fig. 1a. Tall Šēḫ Ḥamad / Dūr-Katlimmu, schematic plan of excavation section NE-corner, Building F/W. © Tall Šēḫ Ḥamad archive, Berlin.

Fig. 1b. Tall Šēḫ Ḥamad / Dūr-Katlimmu, schematic plan of excavation unit NE-corner, Lower Town II, including Building F/W. © Tall Šēḫ Ḥamad archive, Berlin.

Fig. 2. Tall Šēḫ Ḥamad / Dūr-Katlimmu, Bronze plaque SH 89/8779/0201 in the condition as excavated; Foto no.: SH-K 16760–05, © Tall Šēḫ Ḥamad archive, Berlin.

Fig. 3. Tall Šēḫ Ḥamad / Dūr-Katlimmu, corroded reverse of Bronze plaque SH 89/8779/0201; Foto no.: SH-K 18508, © Tall Šēḫ Ḥamad archive, Berlin.

Fig. 4. Tall Šēḫ Ḥamad / Dūr-Katlimmu, Bronze plaque SH 89/8779/0201 as cleaned and restored; Foto no.: SH-K 18507, © Tall Šēḫ Ḥamad archive, Berlin.

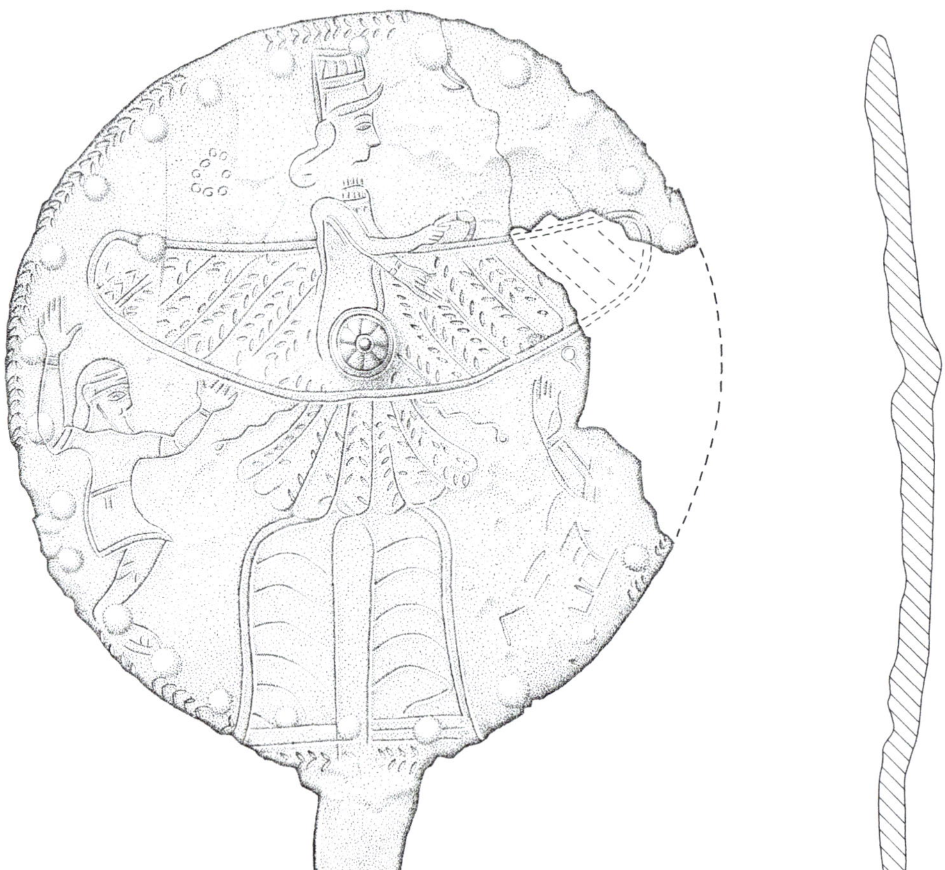

Fig. 5a. Tall Šēḫ Ḥamad / Dūr-Katlimmu, drawing of depiction of Bronze plaque SH 89/8779/0201; illustrator: M. Leicht. © Tall Šēḫ Ḥamad archive, Berlin

Fig. 5b. Tall Šēḫ Ḥamad / Dūr-Katlimmu, section of Bronze plaque SH 89/8779/0201; illustrator: M. Leicht. © Tall Šēḫ Ḥamad archive, Berlin.

Fig. 6. Sherif-Khan, impression of the cylinder seal of Mušezib-Ninurta, British Museum WA 89135, Collon 2001: no. 151.

Fig. 6. Nimrud, Northwest Palace of Ashurnasirpal II, Budge 1914: Pl. XVIII,1 section.

Fig. 8. Impression of a cylinder seal, British Museum WA 89082, Collon 2001: no. 202.

Fig. 9. Urartian Bronze disc, Calmeyer / Seidl 1983: 105 Fig. 1.

Fig. 10. Fragment of Urartian Bronze disc, Calmeyer / Seidl 198:. 109 Fig. 2 (section).

Fig. 11. Karmir Blur. Decorated lid of pyxis of steatite, Wartke 1993: 138 Abb. 70.

Horse-, Donkey-, and Ox-Shoes from the Ottoman Period at Kaman-Kalehöyük

Hidetoshi Tsumoto *

Abstract

Nearly 140 pieces of animal shoes have been found at the settlement of Kaman-Kalehöyük Stratum I, which belong to the Ottoman period (16th–17th century). They are divided into three categories: horseshoe, donkey shoe, and ox shoes, and donkey shoes make up more than half of the total of animal shoes. This article will give an overview of these objects.

Öz

Kaman-Kalehöyük Stratum I tabakasında Osmanlı Dönemine tarihlenen (16–17. yy) 140'a yakın hayvan nalı keşfedilmiştir. Bunlar üç kategoriye ayrılmaktadır: at nalı, eşek nalı ve öküz nalı. Eşek nalları bu nal grubunun yarısını teşkil etmektedir. Makalede nal grubu hakkında genel özet verilecektir.

Introduction

Since 2018, the author has been engaged in studying iron artifacts excavated from Kaman-Kalehöyük in order to analyze them typologically. A large number of iron artefacts have been excavated at the site over the past 30 seasons since 1986, and it is hoped that a stratified study of these finds will provide a more detailed picture of the changes and realities of iron use at the site over thousands of years. In the database of the excavation team, more than 3,000 iron objects ranging from the Ottoman period (Stratum I) to the Early Bronze Age (Stratum IV) have been registered.

In the 2018 season, the author started to study the artifacts excavated in 1986, in order from the first season of the excavations, in the storeroom of the Japanese Institute of Anatolian Archaeology located at Çağırkan-Kaman, and noticed that there was a considerable amount of horseshoes, animal shoes and nails excavated in Stratum I. By the time of the 2019 study survey, the author had checked and measured most of the complete horseshoes excavated, and the author furthermore intends to add stratigraphic analysis. It should be noted that this brief paper is a tentative result of work in progress.

Date and Distribution on the Site

There are some theories about the origin of animal (horse, donkey, or ox) shoes in metal, which enabled horses and animals to travel long distances and carry heavy loads, but it is appropriate to assume that their usage began after the medieval periods, at least in West Asia[1]. Such finds from Kaman-Kalehöyük are naturally limited to Stratum I or the topsoil, and almost all of them can be dated to Stratum I-1, i.e. to the Ottoman period or after.

Stratum I of Kaman-Kalehöyük can be divided into several periods (Omura 1993), but the animal shoes are most likely from the last level, I-1, which is dated to the 16th–17th centuries based on the Ming Dynasty porcelain and Polish coins found from this level (Mikami and Omura 1987; Mori and Omura 1995; Fenwick 2017). It is possible, but unlikely, that some of the horseshoes may have fallen off during cul-

* The Ancient Orient Museum, Tokyo. tsumoto@orientmuseum.com.

1 Horseshoes were first introduced to Japan from Europe in the late 19th century during the *Meiji* period. Prior to this, metal horseshoes or any animal shoe did not exist at all, and shoes made of woven plant fibers were used.

tivation, after the hilltop settlement at Kaman-Kalehöyük was abandoned sometime in the 17th century and the land used for cultivation until the start of the archaeological investigations in 1985.

As far as the author has researched, 138 animal shoes in total have been excavated from Kaman-Kalehöyük, including fragments, some of which are listed in the database but the author has not yet checked them. These animal shoes were divided into three categories typologically according to their usage: for horses, donkeys/mules and ox.

Figs. 1 and 2 show the number of animal shoes found in each grid without classification of types. Although the find spots are spread over a relatively large area of the hilltop, they are particularly numerous in the central part of the hilltop and slightly to the west of the central part of the hilltop (especially in the northwestern part of the South sector). South LVI sector and South LV sector both have a particularly large number of finds (13 pieces).

Hoof Shoes in the Ottoman Period at Kaman-Kalehöyük

The practice of shoeing for livestock has basically been practiced since the medieval period, thus it is limited to Stratum I at Kaman-Kalehöyük. Horses (or mules), donkeys and cattle need to be shod. Studies on the faunal remains from Stratum I (Hongo 1992) show that remains of all these animals were found, and it is clear that they were kept here. None of the animal remains were found with shoes attached.

The shape of the hoof shoes varies according to the type of animal to which it is attached, with the shoe of the odd-toed ungulates such as horses and donkeys being a single piece, U (or O) -shaped. It is difficult to distinguish between shoes for horses, ponies and donkeys (see below), but in Kaman-Kalehöyük there are two groups of U-shaped horseshoes, one converging at around 8cm and the other over 11cm, and according to the size of the hoof we can assume that the former belonged to donkeys and the latter to horses. In addition to size, horses and donkeys seem to wear their shoes differently, as we shall see below.

Because the hoof of the even-toed ungulates is split in the middle, ox-shoes are completely different in shape to that of the horse or donkey, and consist of two semi-circular plates.

Horseshoes (Fig. 3)

They are more than 11 cm in width (Mikami and Omura 1988: Fig. 6–17, 18; Fig. 17–27, 28). There are only two horseshoes that can be classed as such, both of which have closed heels, forming an O-shape and covering the entire hoof. There are several round holes (nail-holes) near the rim, and they were attached to hooves by nails. They are relatively thick. A number of small nails with a rectangular cross-section were found in Stratum I. These may have been used for horseshoes or ox-shoes (see below). Considering the overall number of animal shoes found, the small number of horseshoes is astonishing.

Domestic horses have weaker hooves than wild horses, and the use of horseshoes to protect their hooves has been practiced since ancient times. The use of horseshoes (fastened with nails; Hipposandal is not included) is thought to have started in northern Europe around the Roman period (Sparkes 1976: 3) and spread throughout Europe around the 8th century (Sparkes 1976: 4; Rosen 2000: 204), and then the world. But the origin and time of this practice is still not clear. The date of its introduction to West Asia is also unclear[1], but there are examples of excavations

1 Ghirshman (Ghirshman 1954: 187; 285) states that bronze horseshoes began to be used in the Achaemenid Persian period and iron horseshoes in the Parthian period, but this is not supported by archaeological evidence. On the other hand, semi-circular bronze objects with nail holes found at an Etruscan tomb at Corneto, Italy, are said to be one of the earliest examples of horseshoe (Bates 1902). Interestingly, a bronze semi-circular and plate with three nail holes was found at Arsameia on the Nymphaios, Turkey (Stronach 1963: 278; Pl. 74: 23; Pl. 75: 23). It was reported as an "ornament", but Redford considered it as "equid shoe" (Redford 1998: 162). This is dated probably to the Hellenistic period.

at sites throughout Western Asia from the 9th to 13th centuries (Ploug *et al.* 1969: 58; Fig. 22 no. 2; Fig. 23 no. 1; Ben-Dov 1975: 106; Kroll 1979: Abb. 6.12; 8.6; 14.9–10; 14.17; Whitcomb 1985: Fig. 60q; Redford 1998: Fig. 4.3 B; Boas 1999: Fig. 6.2.10; Takeuchi 2005: 147).

The horseshoes of West Asia between the 14th and 19th centuries have the distinctive feature of being of closed shape (branches of horseshoes are closed at the heel, or O-shaped), as opposed to the open shape of the traditional European horseshoe (Kleiss 1992; Ünal 1993: 404, res. 41 right; Takeuchi 2005: 147; Arbel 2020: 367, Fig. 2). This feature is also depicted in West Asian paintings from the 14th to 16th centuries[2]. The fact that the horseshoes used in pre-modern West Asia differed in shape from those used in Europe was noted early on, and in the late 19th century William Tweedie, the British consul-general in Baghdad, reported that the local horseshoe was "the only horseshoe which the Arabs use" (Tweedie 1970: 180). This horseshoe was similar to these found in Kaman-Kalehöyük.

The archaeological study of horseshoes in West Asia in general is not very advanced, with the exception of some reported cases and studies in Israel. This is due to the fact that European-style horseshoes have been found in Crusader period sites in Israel/ Palestine. The Crusaders brought large numbers of horseshoes from Europe to "the Holy Land" and were accompanied there by European farriers (Rosen 2000: 204).

Donkey Shoes (Fig. 4)

They are around 6–8cm in width. At least 72 pieces belong to this group, the most common of all animal shoes species found. They have a U-shape, almost a semicircular shape.

As opposed to the horses, the donkey's hoof is longer in relation to its width, which is why European donkey shoes are smaller and longitudinally longer than horseshoes (Sparkes 1976: 29; Redford 1998: 162; Fig. 4.3C; Plate 4:6; Baker 2013: Fig. 46.10–371). But donkey shoes from Kaman-Kalehöyük are clearly different in that they cover only the front half of the donkey's hoof, judging from its shape. They were attached from the insides of the hoof with three to five hooks which are bent over, and no nails seem to have been used. This is not the case with horses, but may be due to the fact that donkeys are adapted to arid climates and have a higher moisture retention in their hooves than horses. As far as the author is aware, just one parallel has been yet reported from excavations at İncir Han in Bucak (Burdur), a caravansaray used between the 13th and 19th centuries (Ünal 1993: res. 41 top right). . The shape of the donkey shoes from Kaman-Kalehöyük resembles that of the "grass tip", pony shoes which covered only the front half of the hoof to prevent it from breaking, but these are no longer in use (Webber 1990: 10).

Because donkeys have sturdier hooves than horses, so the use of horseshoes is not generally considered necessary, but donkeys used as draft animals were often shoed in many parts of the world. There is little previous research on donkey shoes in West Asia[3], as far as the shoes are concerned, we can conclude that in Kaman-Kalehöyük Stratum I, i.e. in Central Anatolia in the 16th and 17th centuries, a large number of donkeys were used for transport and were also shoed.

Ox Shoes (Fig. 5)

Thirty pieces belong to this category. They are semi-circular shaped, because the ox's hoof is separated in the middle, and were used in pairs (Sparkes 1976: 28). They were nailed together using three or four holes in each side.

Oxen run slower than horses and do not put as much stress on the hoof, so shoeing is not

2 For example, 14th or 15th century illustrations of nomad Turkmen of Persia or Anatolia, manuscript f84a, Hazine 2153 (Fatih Album) of the Saray Albums, Topkapı Palace Museum, Istanbul, or 15th century Iranian? illustration "Groom and horse", Ya'qub Beg Album, Topkapı Palace Museum, Istanbul, H. 2160.

3 Kleiss (Kleiss 1992) reported on "horseshoes" collected in Iran without separating those for horses from those for donkeys/mules.

usually necessary, but oxen used for drafting and pulling heavy loads were often also shoed. As for ox shoes, there is little previous research, but it is assumed from written sources that ox shoeing was practiced in England around the 11th century (Sparkes 1976: 29). Ox shoes have also been found at La Grava, an English monastic site dating from the 12th to 15th centuries, along with horseshoes and donkey shoes (Baker 2013: Fig. 46.10–372). In some areas of Anatolia, such as Artvin, ox shoes are still used for bullfighting.

These are the hoof shoes for three different animals excavated from Stratum I of Kaman-Kalehöyük. Previous excavations in and around Anatolia have yielded horseshoes in a small numbers, but never has such a large quantity been reported from a single site. This is probably because the Ottoman settlement of Kaman-Kalehöyük was excavated over a large area and all the excavated soil was sieved to pick up as many artefacts as possible.

Because it is difficult to distinguish between horseshoes and donkey shoes, previous reports have referred to them simply as "horseshoes" or "equid shoes". However, the finds from Kaman-Kalehöyük suggest that donkey shoes may have existed in the Ottoman period. Similarly, this is probably the first example of the use of ox shoes reported in archaeological excavations in Anatolia.

Conclusion

In Anatolian archaeology, except for the recent redevelopment of the urban areas, the medieval and early modern period has not been the subject of much archaeological research[4], and as far as the author is concerned, there is no previous research on horse- or animal shoes. In West Asia as a whole, there are a few reports of horseshoes from Iranian Caravansaray (trading posts) or from Israel/ Palestine in the medieval and early modern period, but these are very exceptional. However, the study of the use of horses and livestock is important because it provides an insight into the lifestyle, technology and economy of the time. It is also considered important for the character of the settlement of Kaman-Kalehöyük Stratum I, which is located on the old caravan route connecting east and west Anatolia.

Compared to the military importance of horses, the role of donkeys and oxen has received less attention as draft animals. Judging from the number of objects found at Kaman-Kalehöyük, the role of donkeys (mules) and oxen in pre-modern transport by animals should be appreciated more than ever.

Horseshoes are an artifact-type that has received little attention so far, but it is hoped that the excavations of the Kaman-Kalehöyük, which have been carried out with great care and attention to the stratigraphy of all the layers from the topsoil to the bottom, can be expected to produce results. The author hopes that further research on these artifacts, and collaboration with related disciplines, such as zooarchaeology, Ottoman history (regional, economic and transport history) and Anatolian ethnography, will lead to a better understanding of the reality of the last period of Kaman-Kalehöyük's long history.

4 There are, of course, many reports of excavations of medieval sites, particularly in the context of emergency work in the submerged dam areas of southeastern Anatolia. Among them, however, the study by Redford (Redford 1998) is a valuable achievement in providing an in-depth study of medieval village sites in Anatolia using archaeological data.

Bibliography

Arbel, Y.
- 2020 "Miscellaneous finds from the Magen Avrahm Compound," Yafo (Jaffa), *'Atiqot* 100, pp. 363–372.

Baker, E.
- 2013 *La Grava. The Archaeology and History of a Royal Manor and Alien Priory of Fontevrault*. Council for British Archaeology Research Report: York.

Bates, W. N.
- 1902 "Etruscan Horseshoes from Corneto," *American Journal of Archaeology* 6(4), pp. 398–404.

Ben-Dov, M.
- 1975 "Crusader Fortresses in Eretz-Israel," *Qadmoniot* 8/4, 102-12 (in Hebrew).

Boas, A. J.
- 1999 *Crusader Archaeology*. London/ New York, Routledge.

Fenwick, R. S. H.
- 2017 "The Inscription on a Ming Dynasty Porcelain Sherd from Ottoman Kaman-Kalehöyük," *Anatolian Archaeological Studies* vol. XX, pp. 37–42.

Ghirshman, R.
- 1954 *Iran*. Penguin Books. London.

Hongo, H.
- 1992 "Animal Remains from Kaman-Kalehöyük," *Anatolian Archaeological Studies* I *Kaman-Kalehöyük 1*, pp. 101–164 (in Japanese).

Kleiss, W.
- 1992 "Hufeisen aus Iran", *Archäologische Mitteilungen aus Iran 23*, pp. 299–310.

Kroll, S.
- 1979 "Die Kleinfunde," in W. Kleiss (ed.), *Bastam I*, Berlin, pp. 151–82.

Mikami, T. and S. Omura
- 1988 "The First Preliminary Report of Excavation at Kaman-Kalehöyük in Turkey, 1986," *Kokogaku Zasshi* 73-4, pp. 36–65 (in Japanese).

Mori, M. and S. Omura
- 1995 "A Preliminary Report on the Excavations at Kaman-Kalehöyük in Turkey (1989–1993)," in H. I. H. Prince Takahito Mikasa (ed.), *Essays on Ancient Anatolia and its Surrounding Civilizations*, Wiesbaden, pp. 1–42.

Omura, S.
- 1993 "The Buildings and Stratigraphy of Kaman-Kalehöyük Stratum I," *Anatolian Archaeological Studies* II, pp. 103–112 (in Japanese).
- 2007 "Preliminary Report on the 21st Excavation Season at Kaman-Kalehöyük (2006)," *Anatolian Archaeological Studies* XVI, pp. 1–44.

Ploug, G., E. Oldenburg, E. Hammershaimb, R. Thomsen, and F. Løkkegaard
- 1969 *Hama. Fouilles et recherches de la foundation Carlsberg 1931–1938. Les petit objets médiévaux sauf les verreries et poteries*. Nationalmuseet, København.

Redford, S.
- 1998 *The Archaeology of the Frontier in the Medieval Near East. Excavations at Gritille, Turkey*. University of Pennsylvania, Philadelphia.

Rosen, J.
- 2000 "Crusader-Period Horseshoes from Ḥorvat Bet Zeneta," *'Atiqot* 39, pp. 107*–108* (Hebrew; English summary, p. 204).

Sparkes, I. G.
- 1976 *Old Horseshoes*. Shire Album 19. Shire Publications. Aylesbury.

Stronach, D.
- 1963 "Metallfunde in Arsameia am Nymphaios," in Dörner, F. K. and Th. Goell (eds.), *Arsameia am Nymphaios. Die Ausgrabungen in Hierothesion des Mithradates Kallinikos von 1953–1956*, Berlin, pp. 275–281.

Takeuchi, R.
- 2005 "Notes on the Horseshoes from Wadi Burma, Southern Jordan," *Journal of West Asian Archaeology* 6, pp. 143–150 (in Japanese).

Tweedie, W.
- 1970 *The Arabian Horse*. Reprint of 1894. Libraire du Liban, Beirut.

Ünal, R. H.
- 1993 Burdur/Bucak İncir Hanı'nda temel araştırmaları ve temizlik çalışmaları (Eylül 1992) X. *Vakıflar Haftası Kitabı*, pp. 399–422.

Webber, T.
- 1990 *Feet and Shoes*, Buckingham.

Whitcomb, D. S.
- 1985 *Before the Roses and Nightingales. Excavations at Qasr-Abu Nasr, Old Shiraz*. New York.

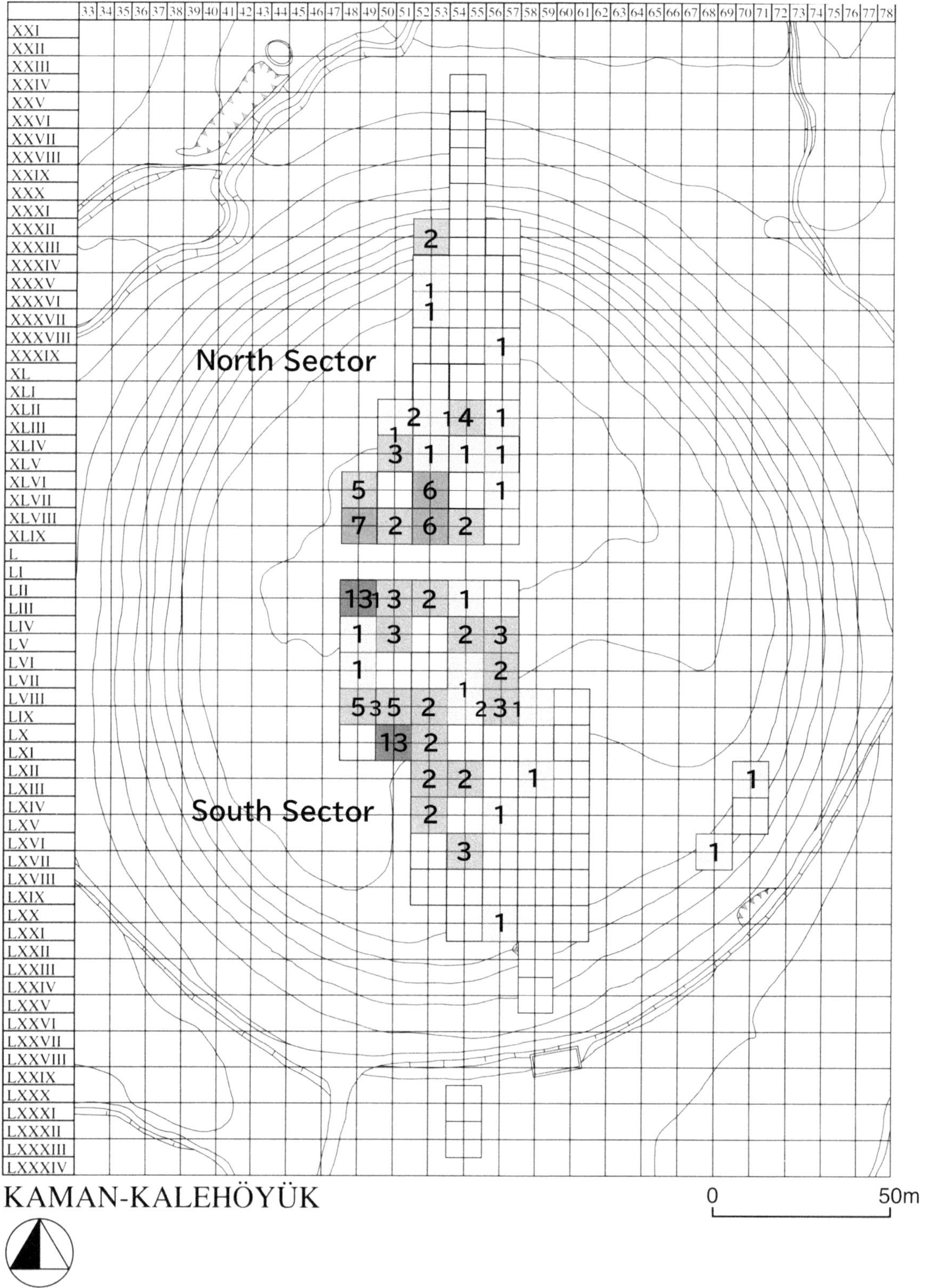

Fig. 1. Distribution of the number of animal shoes excavated per Sector (adapted from Omura 2007: Fig.5)
Note: Smaller numbers indicate the number of animal shoes excavated from the baulks (between sectors).

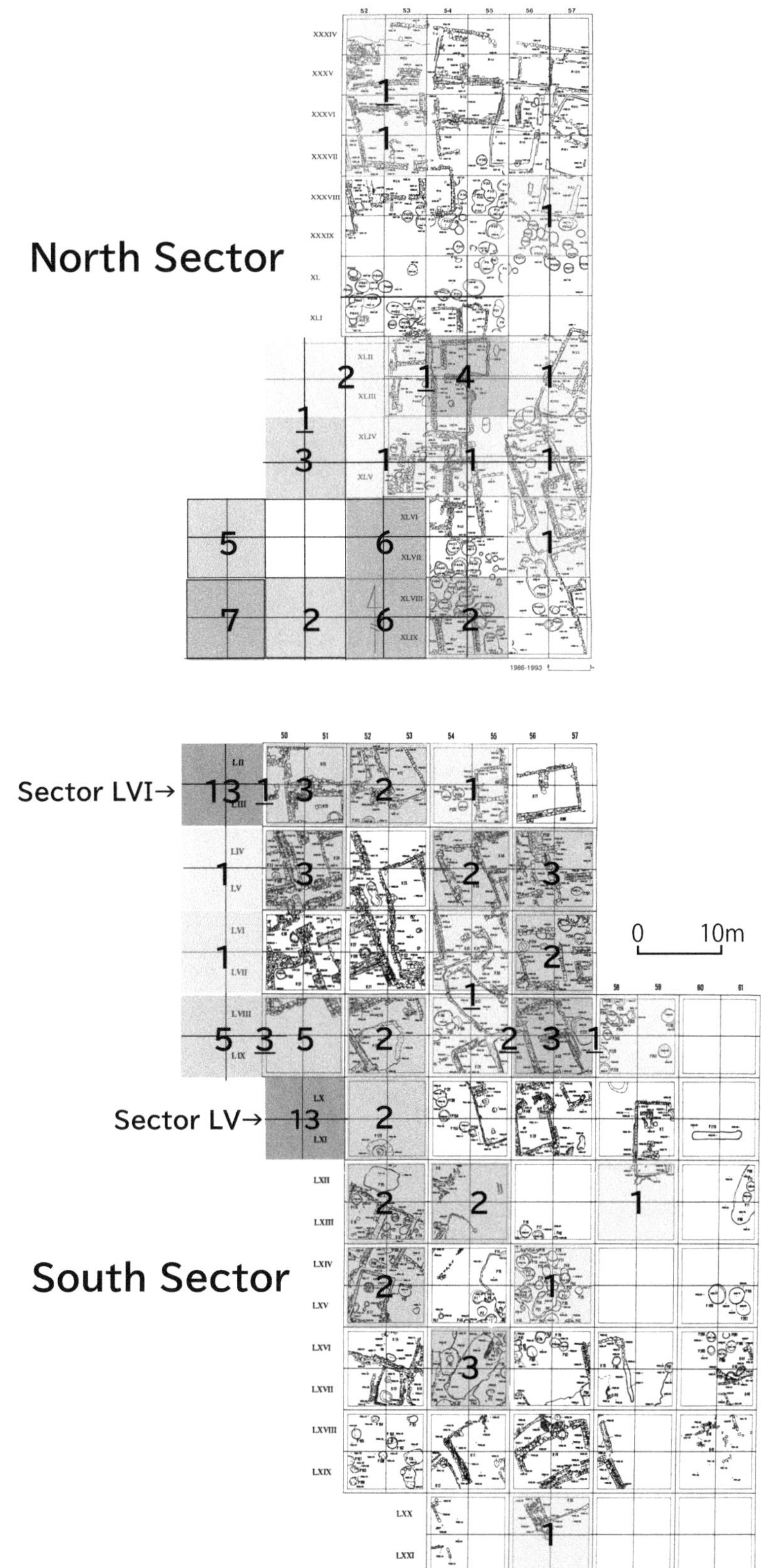

Fig. 2. Relationship between the number of animal shoes excavated per grid and the architectural remains of Stratum I at Kaman-Kalehöyük (adapted from Omura 1995: Figs. 2 and 3).

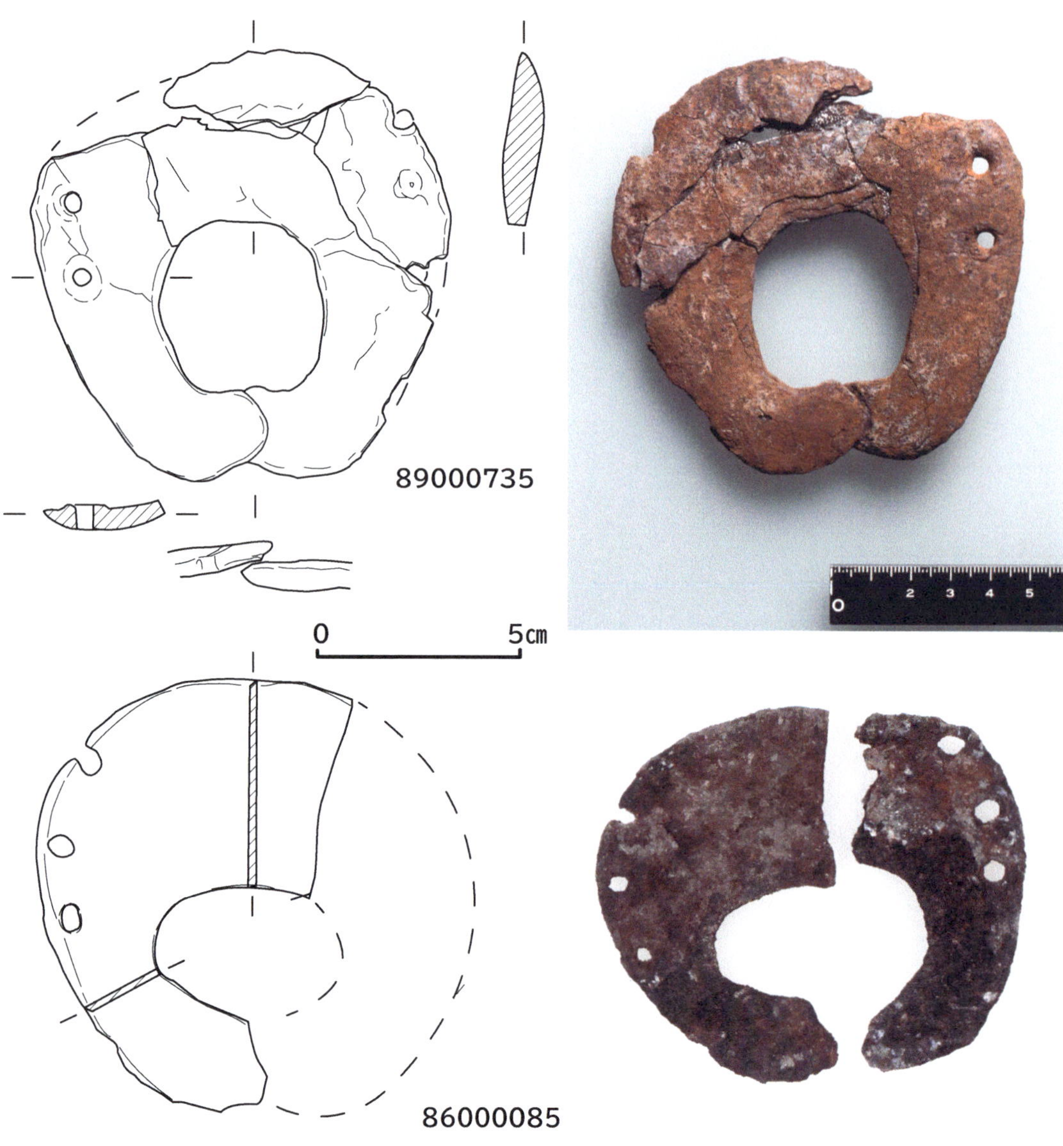

Fig. 3. Horseshoes from Kaman-Kalehöyük.

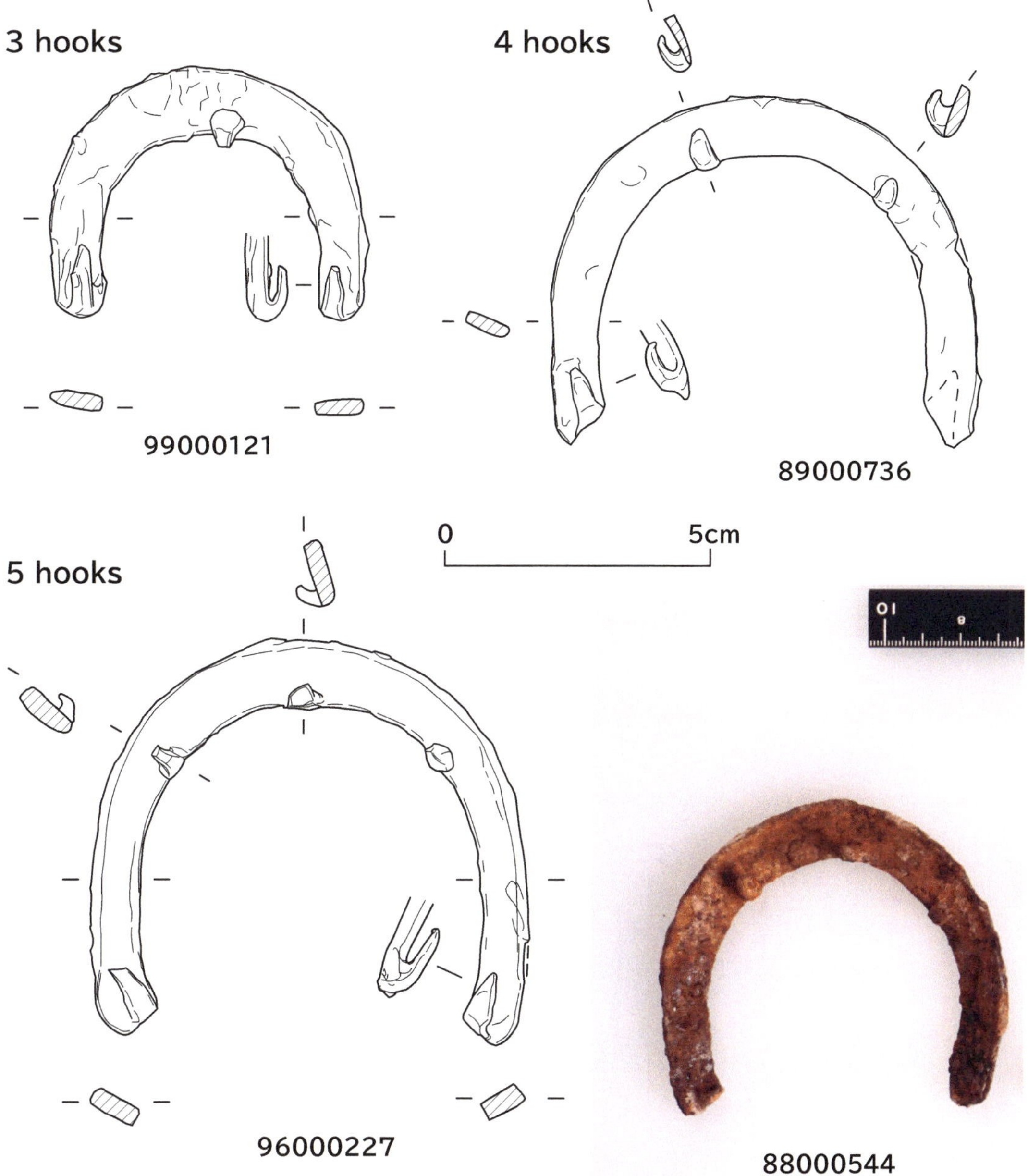

Fig. 4. Donkey (mule) shoes from Kaman-Kalehöyük.

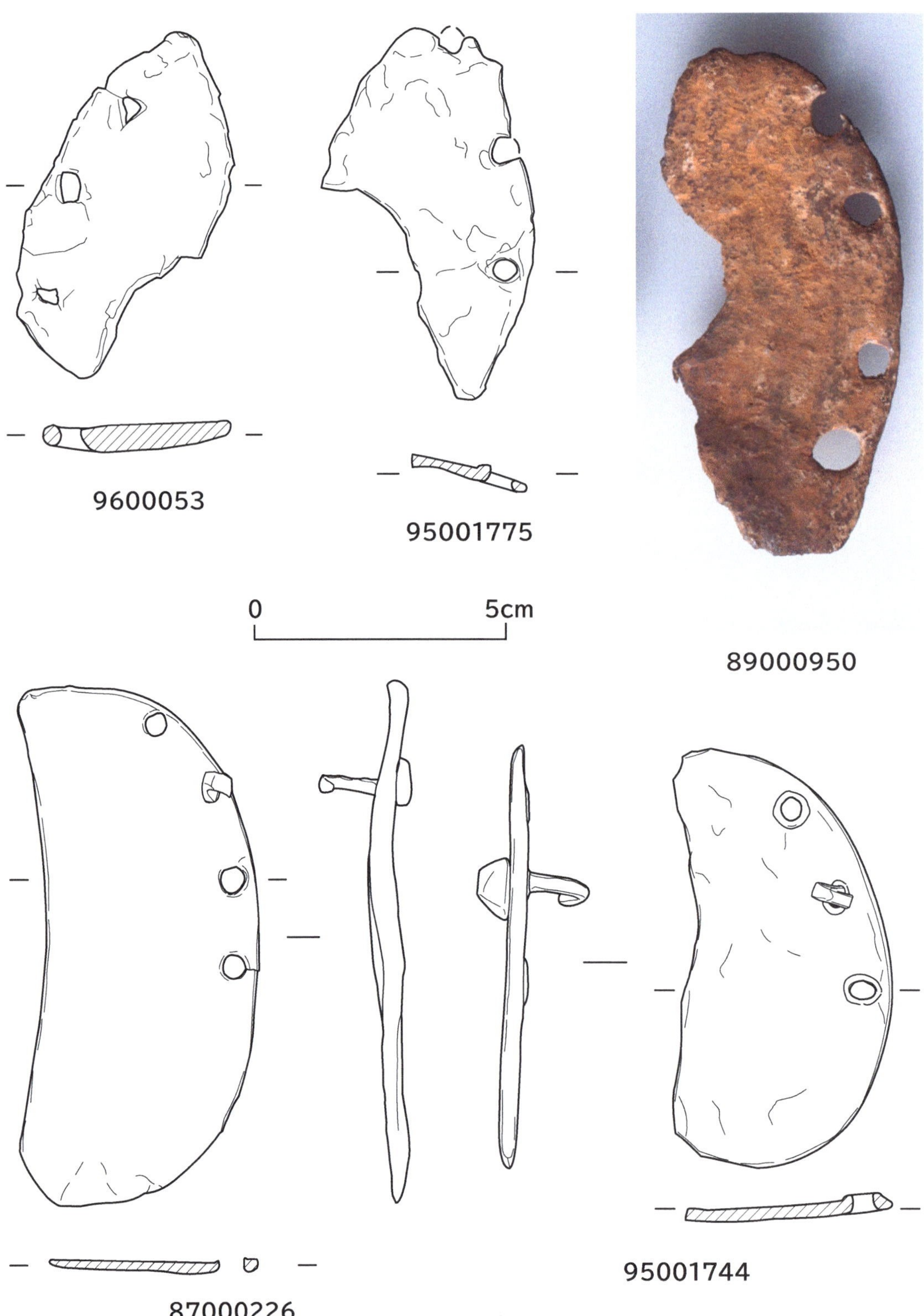

Fig. 5. Ox shoes from Kaman-Kalehöyük.

Examination of the Painted Ware of the Early Phases of the Early Bronze Age in Central Anatolia, Collected by the *Kayseri Arkeolojik Yüzey Araştırması Projesi*

Hiroshi Sudo *

Abstract

In 2008–2013, several campaigns of the Archaeological Survey Project in Kayseri (*Kayseri Arkeolojik Yüzey Araştırması Projesi*) collected characteristic painted potsherds from several sites in Kayseri Province, Turkey. The potsherds are decorated with curved lines of reddish-brown pigment on a thick slip of light-yellow or light-orange color. A comparison with similar examples from other studies suggests that the curved lines are part of a multiple swirl pattern. The painted pottery of the swirl pattern is distinguished as a particular group of painted wares dating back to the early phase of the Early Bronze Age in Central Anatolia. Further research on this painted ware will enhance the current understanding of the prehistoric material culture of Central Anatolia.

Öz

2008–2013 yılları arasında, Kayseri *Arkeolojik Yüzey Araştırması Projesi*'nin çeşitli dönemlerinde, Türkiye'nin Kayseri ilindeki çeşitli yerleşimlerden karakteristik boyalı çanak çömlek parçaları toplanmıştır. Çanak çömlek parçaları, açık sarı veya açık turuncu renkli kalın bir astar üzerine kırmızımsı kahverengi pigmentten kıvrımlı çizgilerle bezenmiştir. Diğer çalışmalardan elde edilen benzer örneklerle karşılaştırıldığında, kıvrımlı çizgilerin çoklu burgu deseninin bir parçası olduğu anlaşılmaktadır. Burgu desenli boyalı çanak çömlek, Orta Anadolu'da Erken Tunç Çağı'nın erken evresine tarihlenen özel bir boyalı çanak çömlek grubu olarak ayırt edilmektedir. Bu boyalı mallar üzerine yapılacak daha fazla araştırma, Orta Anadolu'nun tarih öncesi maddi kültürüne dair mevcut anlayışı geliştirecektir.

Introduction

The Archaeological Survey Project in Kayseri (KAYAP) was initiated in 2008 under the direction of Professor Fikri Kulakoğlu of Ankara University, Turkey, and Professor Ryoichi Kontani of Notre Dame Seishin University, Okayama, Japan. The acronym KAYAP comes from the Turkish name of the project, *Kayseri Arkeolojik Yüzey Araştırması Projesi*. The objectives of the research project were to 1) increase the available archaeological data on sites in Kayseri Province, Turkey; 2) discuss the historical development of human settlements around Kayseri; and 3) discuss the prehistoric origins of the enormous city of Kültepe, which became the trading capital of Central Anatolia during the Early and Middle Bronze Age.

To realize these objectives, the project team surveyed the research area and registered 124 sites through six campaigns until 2013 (Fig. 1). Their efforts included recording precise geographical coordinates for every site, making topographical and ground-penetrating radar surveys at some sites, and collecting archaeological material from the surface of these sites to understand the settlement pattern in Kayseri.

To obtain preliminary survey results, first, 124 sites were dated according to the classification of their archaeological materials, then the team observed diachronic trends in the number of settlement sites in Kayseri. As a result, the number of sites increased abruptly from the

* Curator, Okayama Orient Museum, Japan.

Chalcolithic period to the Early Bronze Age (EBA) III. However, in the Middle Bronze Age (MBA), when the region's economy was probably flourishing as a result of the international trading activities of Assyrian merchants, the number of sites decreased. Subsequently, in the Iron Age or a later period, the number of sites increased again. Second, the distribution of sites and size of mounds indicated it unlikely that the decrease in the number of sites during the MBA, including the Assyrian Colony Period, was caused by a demographic decline. Rather, it was caused by a concentration of population in the principal settlements (Kontani *et al.* 2014). Third, a typological investigation of potsherds from the surface collection revealed the presence of Chalcolithic sites, which had hitherto not been recognized in Kayseri Province clearly. Further, the team applied radiocarbon dating to confirm the date of the Chalcolithic potsherds. A comparison of the Chalcolithic pottery of KAYAP sites and that of surrounding regions suggests a chronological change in regional interactions between Central and Southeastern Anatolia (Sudo *et al.* 2017). Finally, Canaanean blades were found among the materials excavated from Kültepe and the surface collection of KAYAP sites. The Canaanean blade is one of the characteristic archaeological materials dating back to the 4th and 3rd millennia B.C. found in the Near East. This type of blade is widely found in Southeast Anatolia, Northern Mesopotamia, and the Southern Levant. It is found in Iran and, possibly, Egypt, as well. The Canaanean blades found in the Kültepe excavations and at KAYAP sites have particular significance because the presence of such blades has not been reported to the north of Southeast Anatolia. The discovery of Canaanean blades at the Kültepe and KAYAP sites initiates discussions on the distribution system of Canaanean blades and relevant regional interactions (Sudo 2021).

In this paper, we examine a group of painted wares, which probably date back to the earlier phases of the EBA or Chalcolithic period, found in Central Anatolia. This painted ware is decorated with curved lines (part of a multiple swirl pattern, as explained later) in a reddish-brown pigment on a thick slip of light color. Prehistoric pottery in Anatolia is compiled in the works by Orthman (1963), and recently by Schoop (2005). However, pottery with multiple swirl patterns is not dealt with sufficiently in previous literature. This paper discusses that the painted ware with curved lines can be recognized as a particular group of painted wares in the early phase of the EBA or Chalcolithic period in Central Anatolia. The evaluation of the early phases of Central Anatolia is still controversial because the archaeological information is insufficient due to the number of excavations and the quality of information of the early research (Steadman 2011). The recognition of the group of painted wares with multiple swirl patterns can enhance the current understanding of the prehistoric material culture of Central Anatolia.

Painted Ware of Curved Lines in KAYAP Collection

The KAYAP campaigns collected archaeological materials, mainly potsherds, from sites. The pottery was roughly classified into different cultural phases, such as the phase predating the EBA III (the EBA II or I or Chalcolithic period), EBA III, MBA, Late Bronze Age, and later than the Iron Age. An earlier study examined pottery that was dated earlier than the EBA III (Sudo *et al.* 2017). Subsequently, radiocarbon dating was conducted on a small carbon sample collected from a few potsherds of the earlier pottery of the red-black, incised, and black-burnished wares. The results suggest that these types of pottery can be attributed to the Chalcolithic period or earlier (Sudo *et al.* 2017). The painted ware, which is another group of pottery, was attributed to the earlier phases, as well, despite not being subjected to radiocarbon dating.

The KAYAP campaigns collected one to three potsherds distinguished as early painted ware from four Kayseri sites (Fig. 1); these potsherds have similar characteristics: The clay is tempered with fine (<0.5 mm) mineral grains and plant chaff. The surface was decorated with several curved lines in a reddish-brown pigment on a thick slip of light-yellow or orange color; however, the complete form of the pottery and its motifs are not reconstructed from small sherds (Fig. 2). Even though the wares collected from Kayseri sites were largely fragments, the motifs of curved lines on whitish slip on the potsherds were clearly differentiated from the motifs of painted pottery of later periods, such as the Intermediate ware and Alişar III ware attributed to EBA III or later, which contain geometric designs of straight lines in purple or black colors.

The KAYAP campaigns discovered this type of painted ware in following four sites: Küçük Höyük (KAYAP reg. no. 09–08), Soğulca Höyük (10–16), Kara Höyük (09–14), and Sarca Deve Tepesi (11–19). It is noted that KAYAP registered archaeological sites in all areas of Kayseri province. However, the painted ware of curved lines was discovered only in the western half of Kayseri province. Currently, the meaning of this tendency of the distribution of the painted ware remains unclear. Now, we examine comparable examples of painted ware collected from other sites to further clarify the characteristics of the group of painted wares in the KAYAP collection.

Examples of the Painted Ware of Curved Lines

Yeniyapan

The General Survey of the Japanese Institute of Anatolian Archaeology (JIAA), Kaman, Turkey, collected painted potsherds similar to the ones discovered by KAYAP from Yeniyapan along Delice River in Kırıkkale, near the border between Kırşehir and Yozgat. The potsherds collected from Yeniyapan were divided into four groups: cream polished ware, dark-faced polished ware, orange polished ware, and painted ware. Among them, nine potsherds were published as painted ware (Miyake 1992: Fig. 6). The jar is the dominant vessel form of the painted ware discovered at Yeniyapan, and the ware includes necked and no-neck jars. In this ware, brown or blackish paint is applied on a light orange slip. The multiple swirl pattern seems to be the main motif of the painted ware found at Yeniyapan. The swirl pattern is drawn both on the neck and body of the jars. When the swirl pattern is drawn on the neck, parallel straight lines are arranged around the swirl pattern, and a horizontal line divides the motifs on the neck and body (Miyake 1992: Figs. 6–2, 6–3, and 6–6). The latter feature can be seen also in the examples from Söğütçük Pınarı West mentioned later. The curved parallel lines visible on some potsherds of the KAYAP collection are similar to the multiple swirl pattern present on Yeniyapan samples. The painted ware discovered at Yeniyapan is considered a Chalcolithic material (Miyake 1992; Omura 1992).

Cevizlibağı

The JIAA collected painted pottery similar to that found at Yaniyapan at Cevizlibağı, North of Kırşehir City, in the 1988 survey (Mori and Omura 1990). The Cevizlibağı collection comprises a large fragment of painted pottery, some plain jars, and a deep bowl decorated with a line of irregularly shaped holes. The deep bowl seems to date back to the earlier phases of the EBA; however, the survey report attributes the site to the latter part of the EBA, or around 2000 B.C. (Mori and Omura 1990). The painted pottery fragment is a part of the shoulder of a necked jar that probably had a globular body (Fig. 3). The surface of the pottery is decorated with curved lines of reddish-brown pigment on a thick slip of light orange color. The curved lines seem to be a part of multiple swirl motifs similar to the Yeniyapan collection mentioned earlier; however, the center of the swirl is missing in the piece found in Cevizlibağı. A part of another unit of the motif is visible on both sides of the central motif. This suggests that the original vessel had several swirl patterns arranged around it.

Söğütçük Pınarı West

The archaeological investigations in the western part of Yozgat Province, which was launched by Karl Strobel in 1997, collected potsherds of comparable painted ware from a site, Söğütçük Pınarı West, along Delice River, near the border between Kırşehir and Kırıkkale (Gerber 2008; Strobel and Gerber 2007, 2010). The potsherds of Söğütçük Pınarı West are very similar to the examples mentioned above, especially to those of Yeniyapan. The shapes of the vessels are reconstructed as hole-mouth jar, which is similar to the several examples from Yeniyapan. Curved lines are drawn with dark brown pigment on cream slip applied on the surface of pottery. In some samples, a horizontal line is drawn below the motif arranged on the rim (Gerber 2008: Figs. 2–1, 2–2, 2–3, and 2–4). This feature can be seen in the examples of Yeniyapan as mentioned above. The similarity of the painted ware between Söğütçük Pınarı West and Yeniyapan might be related to the regionally close distance between the settlements. The painted ware of Söğütçük Pınarı West is attributed to the early phase of Chalcolithic period from the typological consideration (Gerber 2008: 194).

Kültepe

The final example of the painted ware was discovered at Kültepe, Kayseri. In 2015, new excavation squares were opened at the northern edge of the large mound of Kültepe. The excavations' objectives are to confirm the settlement area's limit and reveal layers of EBA II or earlier periods, which are not yet well exposed at Kültepe (Kulakoğlu *et al.* 2020). The deep sounding at Trench 1 reached a depth of five meters, and the stratigraphy is divided into fifteen levels. The application of accelerator mass spectrometry ^{14}C dating indicates the early to middle 3rd millennium B.C. for Levels XII–VIII.

A painted ware potsherd was found at Level XI of the Excavation Trench 1 of the Northern Sector in Kültepe (Kulakoğlu *et al.* 2020: Figs. 2.63.191 and 2.86.15). In this potsherd, reddish-brown curved lines are visible on the light orange slip of probably the body part of a jar. This painted potsherd is quite similar to the potsherds in the KAYAP collection and the other potsherd examples mentioned earlier. However, it is unknown whether the lines are part of a swirl or a concentric circle because the center of the motif is missing.

Discussion

The KAYAP campaigns found characteristic painted potsherds of curved lines but failed to provide clarifications on the overall motifs and regional and chronological positions of these materials due to the scarcity of comparable examples and the nature of surface collection. However, this paper examined the examples provided by other field research, as well. Now, this section discusses the motif of curved lines depicted in the painted ware and the regional and chronological positioning of the painted pottery with curved lines.

Reconstruction of the motif of curved lines on potsherds in the KAYAP collection

The General Survey of the JIAA collected similarly painted pottery from two sites in the area between the Delice River and Kızılırmak in 1988 and 1990 (Mori and Omura 1990; Miyake 1992; Omura 1992). The examples of pottery found in Yeniyapan, East end of Kırıkkale, suggest that the curved lines are part of a multiple swirl pattern (Miyake 1992; Omura 1992). A large sherd found at Cevizlibağı, North of Kırşehir City, depicts several units of a motif comprising curved lines (which is probably part of a multiple swirl pattern) arranged around the vessel's body. The presence of brown or reddish paint on thick slips of light orange or cream also is a common characteristic of the KAYAP examples, as well. Further, the curved lines on small sherds of the KAYAP collection were probably part of a multiple swirl pattern.

Uniqueness of the Multiple Swirl Pattern Pottery in the Central Anatolia

The JIAA General Survey discovered a group of painted wares designated as the Delice ware at nine sites along the Delice River (Omura 1991). The Delice ware is also applied with light-colored slip, on which the motif is painted in a dark color. The technique of pottery decoration is the same as that used in the painted ware of curved lines mentioned earlier in this paper. However, the principal motifs of diagonally arranged thin straight lines found in the Delice ware differ from the motif found in the painted ware of curved lines. Further, the Delice ware is dated to the middle of the 3rd millennium B.C. (Omura 1991).

The reddish-brown paintings on the light orange slip were well known at Hacılar in Burdur, Turkey, during the late 7th to early 6th millennia B.C. The painted motifs of Hacılar pottery are generally composed of straight diagonal lines. Several examples of swirl patterns exist; in some cases, they generally comprise a single swirl and form part of a larger design (Schoop 2005: Taf. 63–84). On the other hand, several units of multiple swirls were probably applied to the entire surface of the pottery from the KAYAP and JIAA collection, Söğütçük Pınarı West, and the recent deep sounding at the Northern Sector of Kültepe.

Hence, the swirl pattern pottery mentioned in this paper can be considered a particular group of painted wares.

Area of Distribution

The KAYAP campaigns collected painted wares of curved lines (which are probably part of multiple swirl patterns) from sites in the western half of Kayseri province alone. Examples from the JIAA's collection and Söğütçük Pınarı West extend the area of this painted ware to the crossing point of the border between Kırıkkale, Kırşehir and Yozgat. The estimation of the area of distribution is temporal and further investigation of the literature is necessary to identify the area precisely, although the broad area of the distribution and the tendency of the distribution in Kayseri seems meaningful. The interpretation of the distribution tendency is one of the problems to be addressed by future studies.

Chronological Examination

The painted pottery of swirl patterns found in Yeniyapan and Söğütçük Pınarı West is tentatively attributed to the Chalcolithic period following typological examination (Gerber 2008; Miyake 1992: table 1). Further, the Cevizlibağı collection, which includes a large piece of painted pottery of curved lines (probably a multiple swirl pattern), is attributed to the end of the EBA or approximately two thousand B.C. (Mori and Omura 1990). However, a potsherd of a deep bowl adorned with a line of holes from the same site is attributed to what is likely the earlier phases of the EBA.

The examples from the KAYAP and JIAA's General Survey are surface collections without stratigraphic information; hence, further chronological examination of these examples is difficult. In this scenario, the small potsherd with curved lines collected from Kültepe is significant because it was stratigraphically excavated recently by careful deep sounding (Kulakoğlu *et al.* 2020: Figs. 2.63.191 and 2.86.15). The sherd was found in Level XI at the Northern Sector of the mound of Kültepe, which is attributed to the early to middle third millennium B.C., or EBA I, in Central Anatolia.

Considering the latter example, the painted wares of curved lines collected by KAYAP campaigns are plausibly attributed to the early phases of the EBA in Central Anatolia.

The previous literature has ignored painted ware with multiple swirl patterns. The recognition of this painted ware in a wide area and its chronological positioning can enhance the current understanding of the prehistoric material culture of Central Anatolia.

Conclusions

This paper examines how KAYAP's collection of six potsherds with curved lines painted on them are distinguished as a group of a particular painted ware. This paper revealed that the curved lines are part of multiple swirl motifs painted around the surface of the vessels. This type of painted ware was discovered in the area between the western half of Kayseri and the crossing point of border between present-day Kırıkkale, Kırşehir and Yozgat. This painted ware dates back to the early to middle 3rd millennium B.C., or EBA I, in Central Anatolia.

To date, research has not obtained comparable data from other sites sufficiently. However, further research on this painted ware is expected to enhance the current understanding of the prehistoric material culture of Central Anatolia. A more precise evaluation of the distribution area and chronological position of this painted ware with multiple swirl patterns will be necessary to examine its typological, regional, and chronological relationships with the other kinds of painted ware in Central Anatolia.

Acknowledgments

I am grateful to Dr. Sachihiro Omura, director of the Japanese Institute of Anatolian Archaeology, for offering me the opportunity to study archaeological materials stored in the institute. Further, I thank Dr. Ryoichi Kontani, who is a professor of Notre Dame Seishin University and the founder of KAYAP, for providing me with an opportunity to participate in the project. I acknowledge the efforts of Prof. Dr. Fikri Kulakoğlu, Professor at Ankara University and the director of Kültepe-Kaniş Excavations, for supporting KAYAP members both academically and non-academically, such as in performing administrative tasks and ensuring accommodations.

This work was supported by the Japan Society for the Promotion of Science KAKENHI (Grant Number JP20H00690).

I also would like to thank Editage (www.editage.com) for English language editing.

Bibliography

Gerber, C.

– 2008 "New Insights into the Settlement History of the Tavium Region (NW Part of the Yozgat Province)," in K. Strobel (ed.), *New Perspectives on the Historical Geography and Topography of Anatolia in the II and I Millenium B.C.*, Firenze, pp. 189–234.

Kontani, R., H. Sudo, Y. Yamaguchi, Y. S. Hayakawa and T. Odaka

– 2014 "An Archaeological Survey in the Vicinity of Kültepe, Kayseri Province, Turkey," in L. Atici and F. Kulakoğlu, G. Barjamovic and A. Fairbairn (eds.), *Current Research at Kültepe-Kanesh: An Interdisciplinary and Integrative Approach to Trade Networks, Internationalism, and Identity*, The Journal of Cuneiform Studies Supplemental Series 4, Atlanta, pp. 95–106.

Kulakoğlu, F., R. Kontani, A. Uesugi, Y. Yamaguchi, K. Shimogama, and M. Semmoto

– 2020 "Preliminary Report of Excavations in the Northern Sector of Kültepe 2015–2017," in F. Kulakoğlu and C. Michel (eds.), *Integrative Approaches to the Archaeology and History of Kültepe-Kaneš*, Subartu 45, Turnhout, pp. 9–88.

Miyake, Y.

– 1992 "The Chalcolithic Period in Central Anatolia: Questions in Chronology Looking from the General Surveys (in Japanese)," AAS 1, pp. 196–223.

Mori, M. and S. Omura

– 1990 "1988 Kırşehir, Yozgat ve Nevşehir İlleri Yüzey Araştırmaları," *VII Araştırma Sonuçları Toplantısı*, Ankara Üniversitesi Basımevi, pp. 295–310.

Omura, S.

– 1991 "Painted Pottery Collected from the Basin of the Delice River in Central Anatolia," *Bulletin of the Middle Eastern Culture Center in Japan 5*, pp. 279–292.

– 1992 "1990 Yılı Orta Anadolu'da Yürütülen Yüzey Araştırmaları," in *IX Araştırma Sonuçları Toplantısı*, pp. 541–560.

Orthmann, W.

– 1963 *Die Keramik der Frühen Bronzezeit aus Inneranatolien*, Berlin.

Schoop, U.-D.

– 2005 *Das anatolische Chalkolithikum: Eine chronologische Untersuchung zur vorbronzezeitlichen Kultursequenz im nördlichen Zentral-*

anatolien und den angrenzenden Gebieten, Urgeschichtliche Studien I, Greiner.

Steadman, S. R.

- 2011 "The Early Bronze Age on the Plateau," in S. R. Steadman and G. McMahon (eds.), *The Oxford Handbook of Ancient Anatolia: 10,000–323 B.C.E.*, Oxford, Oxford University Press, pp. 229–259.

Strobel, K. and C. Gerber

- 2007 "Tavium (Büyüknefes, Provinz Yozgat) – Bericht über die Kampagnen 2003–2005," *Istanbuler Mitteilungen* 57, pp. 547–621.
- 2010 "Tavium (Büyüknefes, Provinz Yozgat) und seine Region. Bericht über die Kampagnen 2006–2009," *Istanbuler Mitteilungen* 60, pp. 291–338.

Sudo, H.

- 2021 "Canaanean Blades from Kültepe (Central Anatolia)," in F. Kulakoğlu, G. Kryszat and C. Michel (eds.), *Cultural Exchanges and Current Researches at Kültepe and Surroundings. Kültepe, August 1–4, 2019, Kültepe International Meetings 4*, Subartu 46, Turnhout, pp. 51–63.

Sudo, H., Y. Yamaguchi and R. Kontani

- 2017 "An Archaeological Assessment of the Kayseri Province during the Chalcolithic Period: New Evidence from the Archaeological Survey Project in Kayseri, Turkey (KAYAP)," in F. Kulakoğlu and G. Barjamovic (eds.), *Movement, Resources, Interaction. Proceedings of the 2nd Kültepe International Meeting, Kültepe, 26–30 July 2015*, Subartu 39, Turnhout, pp. 227–242.

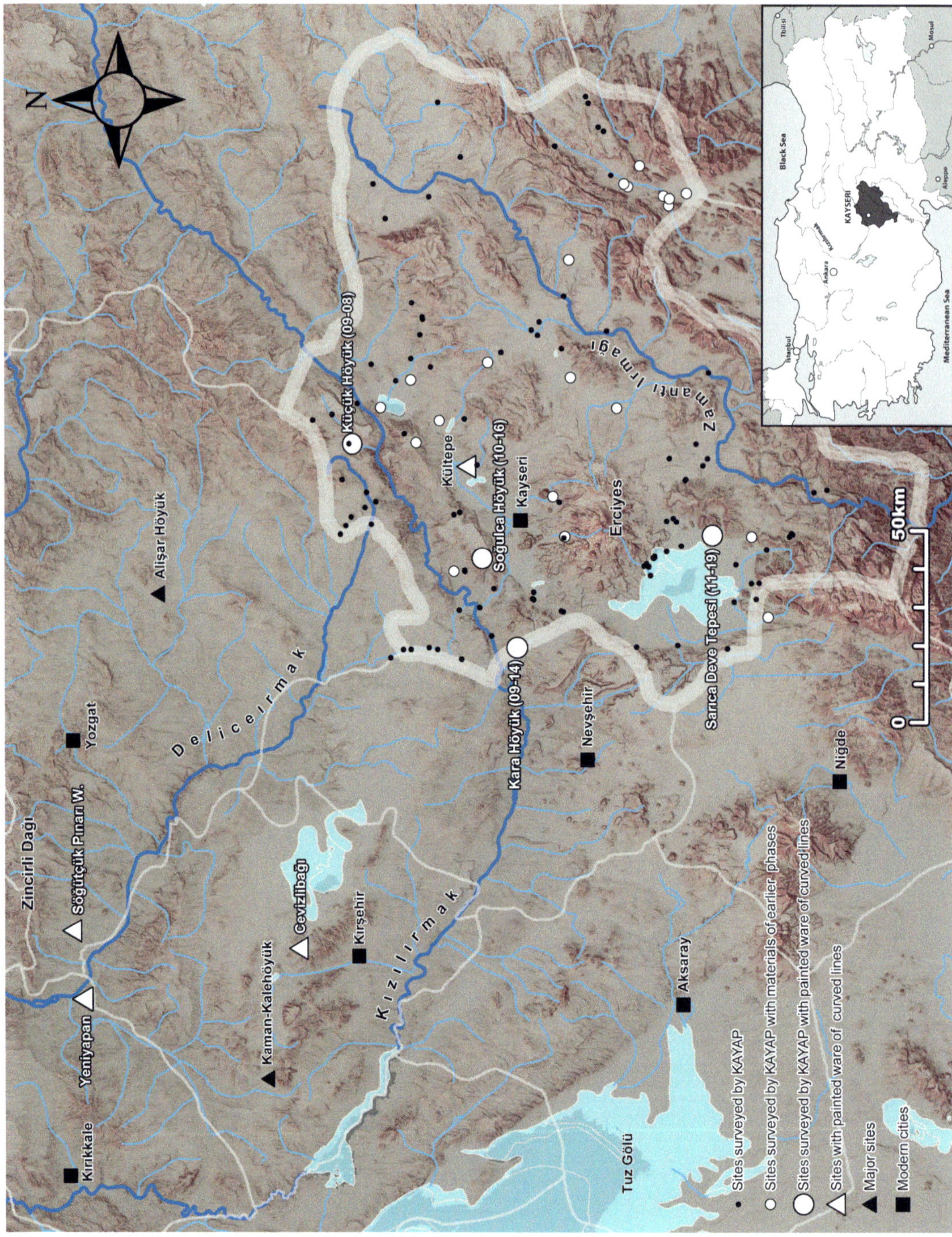

Fig. 1. Sites surveyed by the Archaeological Survey Project in Kayseri campaigns and the related sites examined in this paper.

Fig. 2. Painted ware of curved lines from the Archaeological Survey Project in Kayseri collection.

Fig. 3. Painted ware of Cevizlibağı collected by the Japanese Institute of Anatolian Archaeology's General Survey in 1988.

The Positive Impacts of an Archaeological Excavation on Local Cultural Development

İlkay İvgin *

Abstract

In summer 2017 I had joined the Kaman-Kalehöyük excavation mission as the ministry representative. This short conversation is about the life and academic achievements, beginning of the journey in the field of archaeology, education of the local population and workmen, the idea behind the establishment of the museum and institute of Dr. Sachihiro Omura and how he turned the central Anatolian steppe into paradise.

Öz

2017 kazı sezonunda Bakanlık temsilcisi olarak katıldığım Kaman-Kalehöyük arkeolojik kazılarında Japon arkeolog Dr. Sachihiro Omura'nın arkeoloji dünyasına kazandırdığı bilimsel verilerin içeriği ile hocanın hayat hikâyesi bu söyleşiye konu olmuştur. Omura hocanın arkeolojiye başlama serüveni, yerel halkın ve işçilerin eğitilmesi, enstitü ve müzenin kurulma fikri ile kısaca Orta Anadolu bozkırının nasıl cennete dönüştürüldüğü üzerine mini bir sohbet gerçekleştirilmiştir.

There are many interdisciplinary studies from various fields concerning preventive measures aimed at prohibiting the destruction of cultural heritage. These preventive measures are occasionally specific, but all aim at minimizing or fully eliminating the potential for damage and destruction.[1]

Preventive measures against natural factors such as weather, climate events and earthquakes, differ from measures used against biological factors such as animals. However, the most dangereous and most destructive factor is human activity. Without doubt, the best preventive measure against the damage caused by people is education. The importance of education, starting from the preschool level, has been emphasised in the past (Külcü 2015: 30).

In the early years of the Turkish Republic, Mustafa Kemal Atatürk was a key proponent in emphasising the importance of education in the protection of cultural heritage. The first step towards raising the public's awareness of the issue was the 1935 drafting of ten instructions to Hasan Cemil Çambel, then head of the Turkish Historical Society (Türk Tarih Kurumu), and Afet İnan. The third of these instructions was especially significant for the public's awareness: "under close interest and responsibility of the government authorities and municipalities, the Republican People's Party will make the community centers and party bodies provide a continuous propaganda, and under the close interest of General Directorate of Press and Publications, the daily newspapers and magazines will provide continuous, popular and effective publications to allow cultural heritage to be protected by its real owners, the Turkish people" (Ünar 2020: 135).

Despite the Republic's early recognition of education as a critical factor in the protection and preservation of cultural heritage, it is clear that university departments, institutes, associations, and foundations concerned with archaeology and art history have been insufficient in both raising public awareness, and creating a culture of protection. Although the efforts to

* Dr. İlkay İvgin, T.C. Kültür ve Turizm Bakanlığı, Kültür Varlıkları ve Müzeler Genel Müdürlüğü, Proje Koordinatörlüğü, ivginilkay@gmail.com

create a culture of protection are increasing, they are hindered by the limited and sporadic nature of public education (Akurgal 1998: 21).

The question becomes, had the excavation directors and foreign archaeological institutions tasked with the study of Anatolia and Thrace during those early years of the Republic played a more active role in the efforts towards public education and awareness, would we see an effect on the current state of cultural heritage destruction? Similarly, if foreign instutions of archaeology were to consider local public campaigns where they were excavating, would this result in discouraging illegal excavations? We posed these questions to an excavation director from a foreign institute of archaeology in the following interview.

This interview was conducted with Dr. Sachihiro Omura in August 2017 by İlkay İvgin[1] and Çiğdem Maner (Fig. 1). The original language of the interview is Turkish, an English translation is provided here as well. We thank Ms. Nuray Nisan Köknar, M.A., for typing the recording of the Turkish interview for us.

İL İlkay İvgin
ÇM Çiğdem Maner
O Dr. Sachihiro Omura

İL: **Hocam, ilk sorudan başlayalım.**
O: Ne kadar soru var?
İL: **Professor Omura, let's start with the first question.**
O: How many questions do you have?
İL-Ç.M: **Baya var, bitmez bugün.**
İL-Ç.M: **There are a lot, it won't finish today.**
İL: **İlk önce temel sorulardan başlıyorum. Arkeolojiye merakınız nasıl ve ne zaman başladı?**
O: Arkeolojiye merakım 8 yaşında başladı. 8 yaşındayken diğer arkadaşlarımın yaptığı rutin işleri yapmıyordum. Çok farklı şeyler yapıyordum, o yaştayken okula da pek fazla gitmezdim açıkçası.
İL: **I'll start with the basic questions first. How and when did your interest in archaeology begin?**
O: My interest in archaeology started at the age of 8.
When I was 8 years old, I didn't follow the same routine works as my friends. I did different things, and honestly, I didn't go to school much at that age.
Ç.M: Yaramaz bir öğrenci miydiniz?
O: Yok, yaramaz değildim, kazı yapıyordum.
Ç.M: **Were you a naughty pupil?**
O: No, I wasn't naughty, I would excavate.
Ç.M: **Nasıl yani?**
O: Bir gün ilkokulun müdürü tarla sahibiyle babamın yanına geldi: "sizin çocuğunuz tarlamıza geliyor, sabahtan akşama kadar kazı yapıyor, çanak çömlek parçaları topluyor, ne yapacak onları bilemiyorum, ekinlerime zarar veriyor." dedi.
Sonra bir gün okul müdürü beni odasına, yanına çağırdı, bana hiç kızmadı. Sadece, "Kazı yapmak istiyorsan izin alırsın, ondan sonra kazı yaparsın" dedi.
Bende hakikaten gittim tarla sahiplerinden izin aldım, kazdıkça ve çanak çömlek parçaları çıktıkça mutlu oluyordum. 8–9 yaşındayken ne kadar toprak kazılabilir ki, çok fazla kazamazsın. Bu şekilde 4–5 sene uğraştım, ortaokul zamanlarımda da uğraştım. O zamanlar karar vermiştim, arkeolog olacaktım. Bazen babam da geliyordu yanıma, o da çok seviyordu arkeolojiyi.
Ç.M: **How?**
O: One day, the director of the primary school came to my father with the owner of a field, who was saying : "Your child comes to our field, he digs from morning to night, and collects pottery pieces. I don't know what he is going to do with them, but he is harming my crops."
Then one day, the director of my school invited me to his office, but he didn't get angry at me at all. He just said; "If you want to dig, you have to get permission, then you can dig."

1 İvgin was the ministry representative of the 2017 excavation season.

After that, I actually went and got permission from the field owners. I was happy finding pottery pieces as I dug. How much soil can be dug when you are 8–9 years old? You can't dig too much. I struggled in this way for 4–5 years, and the struggle continued into my secondary school years as well. It was at that time I decided to become an archaeologist. Sometimes my father also came along with me, he also loved archaeology very much.

Ç.M: Define mi arıyordunuz?

O: Yok yok, altın değil, seramik topluyordum. Topladığım seramiklerle okulda sergi bile yaptım. Topladığım seramikleri tasnifledim, kitaplardan bakarak tarihlendirdim, şu Neolitiktir bu Demir Çağı'dır diye her şeyi yazdım. Hocam da çok beğendi ve sergi açtık.

Hocam bir gün bana; "Matematik, fen gibi dersler yerine arkeolojiyi çok seviyorsun sen. Başka hiçbir şey yapma." diyordu. Liseye giderken de çok zorluk çekiyordum. Sınava giriyor kazanamıyordum, çünkü normal derslerle ilgim çok fazla yoktu. Üniversiteye girerken de benzer nedenlerden ötürü çok zorluk çektim. Kazıya ve arkeolojiye merak sarmamak lazım, bir kere bulaştın mı kopmak çok zor.

Babam arkeoloji konusunda benim yol göstericim olmuştu. Bana, eskiden insanların yerleşebileceği yerleri tarif ediyor; "şurada nehir var, çay var; bu taraftan çay geliyor, ortasında bir tepe var, tam ortada yer alan tepede eskiden insanlar otururmuş" gibi tariflerde bulunuyordu. Okuldan gelir gelmez babamın tarif ettiği yerlere gidiyor, kazıyor kazıyor bir şey bulamıyordum. Baba "bir şey çıkmıyor" diyordum, o da bana "sen biraz daha ciddi kaz" diyordu. Yine tarif ettiği yerlere gidiyordum. Kazıyor, kazıyor taşlardan başka bir şey bulamıyordum. Ben liseden mezun olduktan sonra Tokyo'dan babamın bir arkadaşı geldi. O da çok seviyordu kazı işlerini. Okuldan geldiğimde beni bir yerlere götürüyordu hep "hadi kazalım" diye. Öyle öyle başladım ben bu işe.

Ç.M: Were you looking for a treasure?

O: No, not gold, I was collecting ceramics. I even held an exhibition at school with the ceramics I had collected. I classified the collected ceramics, dated them by looking at the books, and I wrote down everything such as "this is the Neolithic, this is the Iron Age". My teacher liked it immensely and we held an exhibition.

My teacher told me one day; "You love archaeology more than math and science courses. Don't do anything else."

I had difficulties in high school. I could not pass my exams because I was not very interested in the ordinary lessons. For similar reasons, I had a lot of difficulties when I studied in university. It's dangerous to be interested in excavation and archaeology, once you get involved, it is impossible to break away.

My father was my mentor in archaeology. He described to me the places where people used to settle; "there is a river, there is creek; the creek flows from this direction, and there is a hill in the middle. People used to live on that hill right in the middle". As soon as I came back from school, I went to the places that my father had described, I excavated again and again, but couldn't find anything. I said to my dad "nothing is coming out", and he replied "you should dig more seriously". I kept going back to the places he described. I was excavating, excavating and finding nothing except stones. After I graduated from high school, a friend of my father's came from Tokyo. He also loved excavations. When I would come home from school, he always took me places, saying "let's dig". That's how I started this job.

İL: Üniversiteyi Japonya'da mı okudunuz?

O: Evet, Japonya'da okudum.

İL: Did you study in university in Japan?

O: Yes, I studied in Japan.

İL: Arkeoloji bölümünde mi okudunuz?

O: Tarih bölümünde okudum. Arkeoloji bölümü olarak özel bir bölüm yoktu. Arkeoloji, tarih bölümü içindeydi ve tarih bölümü içinde Mısır, Irak arkeolojisi gibi kürsüler vardı. Hocalar da çok iyiydi. Ben kendimi yaktım aslında. Arkeolojiyi daha çok kitaplardan okudum, kütüphanede çok kitap karıştırdım bu konuda. Sonra Anadolu'yu okudum... Çatalhöyük'ü henüz bilmiyordum o zamanlar. Fakat siz bilirsiniz hani, Bossert'in kitabı var ya, "Karatepe Üzerine Yazılar[2]." O kadar ilgi çekici bir kitaptı ki, kitabın sonunda Tahsin Hoca'nın ismi geçiyordu. Tahsin Özgüç, Sedat Alp ve Nimet Özgüç'ün adları geçiyordu bu kitapta. İşte bu kitaptan sonra benim de hayatım değişti. Türkiye'ye geldim, kitapta ismi geçen insanlar yaşıyor mu yaşamıyor mu, gitmiş mi bilmiyordum. Fakat Ankara Üniversitesi Dil ve Tarih Coğrafya Fakültesi'nin koridorlarında gezerken, kapılarda Sedat Alp yazıyordu, Tahsin Özgüç yazıyordu, mutlu olmuştum.

İL: Did you study archaeology?

O: I studied history. There was no special department for archaeology. Archaeology was part of the history department, and within the history department there were strands such as the archaeology of Egypt and Iraq. The teachers were very good. But I actually ended up getting burned. I read archaeology mostly from books, searching the library for texts on the subject. Then I read about Anatolia... I was not aware of Çatalhöyük at that time. But you know, Bossert's book, " Karatepe Excavations" it was such an interesting book. Tahsin Hoca's name was mentioned at the end of the book, as well as the names of Tahsin Özgüç, Sedat Alp and Nimet Özgüç throughout. My life changed after this book actually. I came to Türkiye, but I didn't know if these people mentioned in the book were alive or not. But whilst I was walking the corridors of Ankara University's Faculty of Language, History and Geography, I saw that Sedat Alp's name was written on one of the doors, and Tahsin Özgüç was written on another. I was so happy.

İL: Sene kaçtı Hocam?

O: 1972. Sözünü ettiğim hocaların yaşını 80–90 olarak düşünürken, genç olduklarını gördüm. Tahsin Hoca daha 60 yaşına gelmemişti bile.

İL: What was the year?

O: 1972. When I was imagining the age of the teachers, I pictured them as 80 or 90 years old, but I saw that they were young. Tahsin Hoca was not even 60.

İL: Türkiye'ye gelmeden önce kazılara katıldınız mı? Yoksa ilk Anadolu'da mı kazılara katıldınız?

O: Kazılara katılmak için Türkiye'ye geldim, ama ilk kazılara Japonya'da katıldım. Üniversite zamanlarımda Tokyo'da, kurtarma kazıları olduğu zaman hocalarım da gidiyordu, bende onlarla kazılara katılıyordum. Kazılardan kemikler, çanak-çömlerler çıkardı, çıkanları araştırır hocalara sorardım. Bu çıkan eserlerle ilgili hangi kitapları okumak lazım gibi sorular sorardım hocalarıma. Şu kesin bir durum ki; arazide pratik sağlamak için iyi hoca ile sahada çalışmak lazım. Boş hocanın yanında 10 sene çalışsan da hiçbir şey olmuyor maalesef.

Mesela Türkiye'de Halet Hanım[3] var, Mehmet Özdoğan Bey var. Tahsin Hoca[4] var. Tahsin Hocayı baba olarak görürdüm, benim için çok çok büyük insandı. Tahsin Hoca gibi adam çıkmaz, çok sağlam adamdı. Ama maalesef artık bizim dönemde öyle olmuyor, iyi işler bırakmak lazım arkada.

2 Bossert 1950.

3 Halet Çambel

4 Tahsin Özgüç

İL: Did you participate in any excavations before you came to Türkiye? Or did you participate in your first excavations in Anatolia?

O: I came to Türkiye in order to participate in excavations, but I participated in my first excavations back in Japan. During my university years in Tokyo, when there were rescue excavations, my teachers would attend and I would attend the excavations with them. I would find bones and pottery during these excavations, and ask the teachers about them. I used to ask my teachers which books should I read about the various artifacts. The reality of the matter is that in order to practice in this field, it is necessary to work with a good teacher. Unfortunately, nothing happens if you work with an inexperienced teacher, even if you do so for 10 years.
For example, there is Halet Hanım (Halet Çambel) and Mehmet Özdoğan Bey in Türkiye. There is Tahsin Hoca (Tahsin Özgüç). I used to see Tahsin hoca as a father, he was an incredibly important person for me. There is no man like Tahsin Hoca, he was a very great man. But unfortunately, this is not the case in our era, you must leave behind good work to the next generations.

İL: Lisans eğitimindeyken de geldiniz mi Türkiye'ye?

O: Yok, Türkiye'ye yüksek lisans eğitimi için geldim.

İL: Did you come to Türkiye while you were studying in undergraduate education?

O: No, I came to Türkiye for graduate study.

İL: Peki, araştırmaya başladığınız ilk andan itibaren Kalehöyük'ün Anadolu arkeolojisi için önemli bir yer olduğunu düşündünüz mü?

O: Yok.

İL: Well, from the first time you started your research, did you think that Kalehöyük was an important place for Anatolian archaeology?

O: No.

İL: Düşünmediniz... Ama şu an için önemli bir yer.

O: Tahsin Hoca önce ne dedi biliyor musunuz? Kalehöyük'ü kazarken amacımız yok dedi. "Burayı kazarken amacımız şöyledir, böyledir diye fazla konuşma" dedi. "Kazıya başladıktan sonra amaç da çıkar, her şey çıkar ortaya, ona göre devam edersin" dedi. "Kendi amacın varsa da onu ortaya koyma" dedi. "Kazıya başla sonra düşünürsün" derdi. Fakat ben stratigrafi üzerine konuşmaya başladıkça "o olur tamam, takip edersin stratigrafiyi" dedi. "Ama ulaştığın hedef çıkınca da sağa sola işi büyütme" dedi.

İL: You didn't think about it... but it has now become an important settlement.

O: Do you know what Tahsin Hoca said first? He said that we have no purpose while excavating Kalehöyük. "Don't talk too much about our purpose while digging this place". He would say, "After you start excavating, the purpose is revealed, everything is revealed, and you continue accordingly. Even if you have a purpose of your own, don't act on it". He told me, "Start excavating, then you'll think." But as I started to talk about stratigraphy, he said that, "It's okay, you follow the stratigraphy". "But when you reach the goal, do not expand the excavation," he said.

İL: Step trench şeklinde mi kazıya başladınız?

O: Step trench değil bizimki, höyüğün üst noktasından olduğu gibi aşağıya iniyoruz.

İL: Did you start excavating in the form of a step trench?

O: Our excavation is not a step trench, we go down from the top of the mound as it is.

İL: Peki, Kaman-Kalehöyük'ün şu an Anadolu arkeolojisi için önemi nedir?

O: Buranın önemi İç Anadolu'nun stratigrafisini ortaya koymak. Bu stratigrafiyi ortaya koymak için çok da acelemiz yok, ne kadar geç olursa olsun, önemli olan en sağlam stratigrafiyi oturtmak lazım. Demir çağını, 2. veya 3. Bini, herkes çok çabuk kazıyor, öyle iki senede üç senede kazılmaz ki. Kalehöyük sonuçları çok iyi gidiyor aslında; 2–3 sene içinde burayı Alişar 3, Intermediate ve Çıradere ile yüzde yüz oturtturabileceğim. Harris matrix içine koyabileceğim. Ondan sonra da buradan Alişar 3 başlıyor, sonra Intermediate şurada tespit edildi, Çıradere buradan çıkıyor diye söyleyebileceğim. Ama yine de sonuç olarak, bu stratigrafi Kalehöyük'e göre diyeceğim.

İL: **What is the importance of Kaman-Kalehöyük for Anatolian archaeology right now?**

O: The importance of this site is that it reveals the stratigraphy of Central Anatolia. We are not in a hurry to present this stratigraphy, no matter how late it is, the most important thing is to establish that the stratigraphy is reliable. Everyone excavates too quickly, to the Iron Age or the 2nd or 3rd millennium, it is not excavated in two or three years. Kalehöyük results are actually going very well. In 2–3 years, I will be able to overlay this place with Alişar 3, Intermediate and Çıradere one hundred percent. I'll be able to put it in the Harris matrix. After that, I can say that Alişar 3 begins here, then Intermediate is detected there, and Çıradere is exposed here. But still, in conclusion, I will say this stratigraphy is according to Kalehöyük.

İL: **Evet, önemli olan nokta da o. Bazı eksik noktaların bu kazıyla değişebileceğini de görüyoruz.**

O: Biz bunu sonuç olarak ortaya koyacağız. Sizinkiler yanlış oldu da demek olmaz açıkçası. Çünkü Tahsin Hoca'nın yaptıklarına saygı göstereceğim. Mesela Genz[5] Bey'in yaptıklarına saygı göstereceğim. Ama Kalehöyük'e göre diğer yerleşmeler arasındaki stratigrafi bu şekilde ortaya çıkıyor demek lazım.

İL: **Yes, that is the important point. We also see that some missing points may change with this excavation.**

O: We will put it as a conclusion. Frankly, it doesn't mean that yours was wrong. Because I will respect what Tahsin Hoca does. For example, I will respect what Mr. Genz (Hermann Genz) did. But according to Kalehöyük, this is how the stratigraphy among other settlements emerges.

İL: **İç Anadolu bölgesinde, diğer kazısı yapılmış merkezler buraya göre kendilerini konumlayabilecek.**

O: Evet, konumlayabilecek ama onu da bizim söylememiz olmaz. Biz sonucu ortaya bırakacağız, ondan sonrasında kim kullanmak istiyorsa kullansın, istemiyorsa da kullanmasın.

İL: **In the Central Anatolia region, other excavated cites will be able to reevaluate their stratigraphy.**

O: Yes, they will be able to reevaluate it, but we cannot say that. We will reveal our results, and after that, whoever wants to use it, can use it or not.

İL: **Kalehöyük'te kazılara başladığınız zamanda işçileri hangi kriterlere göre seçtiniz?**

O: İlk kazıya başladığım zamanlar işçileri belediye başkanı seçmişti. Ben bilmiyordum o zamanlar kimlerle çalışabileceğimi. Kimseyi tanımıyordum, belediye başkanı kendi adamlarını göndermişti. Kötü de değillerdi aslında ama daha iyi olabilirlerdi. Birinci ve ikinci sezon bu şekilde geçti, sonrasında yavaş yavaş ben çalışmak istediğim adamlara karar verdim, şartlar koydum. Şartlar derken, yevmiye ne kadar olmalı, maaş nasıl verilmeli diye. Çünkü Konya'da Karahöyük'te bunun dersini almıştım. Konya'dayken işçiler bir iki hafta çalışıyor, sonra yevmiye ne kadar diye kendi

5 Herman Genz

aralarında konuşuyorlar, sonra da parayı az bulup gidiyorlardı. Hoca da bu duruma çok kızıyordu. O yüzden şartları en başından belirtmek, söylemek lazım.

İL: **When you started the excavations in Kalehöyük, according to what criteria did you choose the workers?**

O: When I first started excavating, the mayor had chosen the workers. I didn't know who I could work with. The mayor had chosen his own workers, so I didn't know anyone,. They weren't bad, but they could have been better. The first and second excavation seasons went on like this, then gradually I decided on the workers I wanted to work with, and I began to set conditions. I had learned to pay attention to the working conditions when I was working in Konya Karahöyük; conditions such as how much a daily wage should be, or much salary should be given. While we were working in Konya, the workers would work for a week or two, then they would talk among themselves about how much the daily wage was, and then they would find the money not enough and leave. The excavation director was very angry about this situation. Therefore, it is necessary to state the conditions from the very beginning.

İL: **Yani siz, kendiniz seçtiniz işçileri. Peki, ondan sonra, her sene bu işçilerin geri gelmesini nasıl sağladınız? Nasıl elinizde tuttunuz?**

O: İşçilere, iki, üç ay çalıştıktan sonra hadi gidin diyemeyiz. Arazi çalışmalarından sonra da çıkan malzemeler üzerinde çalışmak zorundayız. İşçilerin içinde sağlam adamlar var mı yok mu, işi yapabilecek yetenekli insanlar var mı yok mu tespit etmek zorundaydım.

İL: **So, you chose the workers yourself. How did you get these workers to come back year after year? How did you hold them?**

O: We cannot tell the workers to go on after two or three months of work. After the field work, we have to work on the materials that come out. I had to determine if there were good men among the workers, and whether there were talented people who I could trust to do the job.

İL: **Yetenekli adamları da bırakmak istemediniz.**

O: Hiç istemedim.

IL: **You didn't want to leave the talented guys either.**

O: I never wanted to.

İL: **Aynı zamanda işçilere dersler de veriyorsunuz. Daha önce başka kazılarda böyle bir örnek görmemiştim açıkçası.** (Fig. 2)

O: Neden derseniz, bilerek kazı yapmakla bilmeyerek yapmak başka bir şey. Ne biliyorsak işçilere hepsini göstermek lazım. Gösterdikten sonra onlar alır mı almaz mı bilemiyorum ama bunu yapmak zorundayız.

İL: **You also give lessons to the workers. Frankly, I have never seen such an example in other excavations before.**

O: Knowledgable excavation is one thing, excavating with a lack of knowledge is completely different. We need to show all of the workers what we know. Wether or not they understand and apply it afterwards is something I can't know, but we have to try.

İL: **İlk ne zaman başladınız işçilere eğitim vermeye?**

O: İlk 1988'de başladık derslere.

İL: **When did you first start providing training to workers?**

O: We first started classes in 1988.

İL: **Kazının ilk yıllarından beri vardı bu eğitimler.**

O: Evet, kazının ilk yıllarında başladık eğitimlere. Sonra 1992–93'te tam olarak sistemli bir hale getirdik. Çünkü öğrenci gibi aralarından çıkıyordu meraklı insanlar, sonra da kendileri istiyorlar eğitimleri. İşçi olarak değil de severek çalışırlarsa iş yürüyor zaten. Yoksa sevilmeden, anlamadan yürümez bu iş. Sevdirmek lazım, kazılardan ne çıktığını bilmezse nasıl sevecek. Kazılardan çıkanların önemini, çıkanın ne olduğunu anlatmazsan, hiçbir işe yaramaz yapılan iş. Mesela, tabletler şöyledir böyledir, detaylı anlatıyorum, sonra onun önemini anlıyor. İşçi işçidir diye düşünüp, kaz dersin, kazar ama yapılan iş verimsiz oluyor.

İL: These training sessions have existed since the first years of the excavation.

O: Yes, we started training sessions in the first years of the excavation. Then in 1992–93 we made it fully systematized. Curious people were coming out of their midst like students, and they wanted the education themselves. If they work with passion, not as workers, the business is already running itself. The work won't run effectively without love and understanding shown by the team. It has to be loved, and so how will they love it if they don't know the results of their excavations . If you don't explain the importance of the excavations and what we've achieved, the work is useless. For example, after I have explained in detail how tablets are of a certain significance, he understands the importance of the artefact. Thinking that the worker is a "worker," and that when you say "dig," he digs, is inefficient for the work.

İL: Yani işçilere, kazı nasıl yapılır, tabaka nasıl takip edilir hepsini anlattınız. Ayrıca bir de arkeolojik bilgiler verdiniz. Mesela, İlk Tunç Çağı ne zaman başlıyor, Paleolitik dönem ne zaman bitiyor, Hitit dönemi seramik özellikleri nedir gibi bilgiler verip, sorular da sordunuz.

O: Tabi. Ancak o zaman bu şekilde güzel, yavaş ve detaylı iş yapıyorlar. Temel çok önemli. İlk iki sezon bir şekilde kazarsınız, eser çıksa da olur çıkmasa da ama önemli olan onuncu sezonda bile olsa sağlam iş çıkarabilmek. Fotoğraf, çizim, seviye ne olursa olsun her şeyi öğretmek lazım.

İL: So, you told the workers how the excavation is done and how the layers are tracked. You also gave archaeological information. For example, you gave information such as when the Early Bronze Age begins, when the Paleolithic period ends, what the ceramic characteristics of the Hittite period are, and you asked questions.

O: Sure. Only then can they do good, slow and detailed work . The baseline is very important. In the first two seasons, you will excavate somehow, whether the artefacts come out or not, but the important thing is to do a perfect job even in the tenth season. Photography, drawing, whatever the level, everything should be taught.

İL: İlgililer ama değil mi? Öyle mi öğreniyorlar?

O: Mesele bizde aslında, biz iyi anlatmazsak kimse ilgili olmaz, iyiyi, doğruyu en güzel şekilde göstermek lazım. Gizlememek lazım.

IL: They're interested, aren't they? Is that how they learn?

O: Actually, it's our business. If we don't explain it well, no one will be interested. It is necessary to show the good and the truth in the best possible way. You must not hide.

İL: Geçen sene eğitimlerde anlatılanları hatırlıyorlar mı?

O: Geçen sene anlattıklarımı bu sene yine anlatıyorum, pekiştirme yapıyoruz, kazı esnasında da hatırlatmak için sorular soruyoruz. Tabakaları takip ediyorlar mı diye, neyi neden yaptıklarını soruyorum. Bazen de soru sorarım diye korkuyorlar. Ama ben yine de soruyorum bunu niye yapıyorsun diye. Sorularıma cevap verebilecek çocuk lazım bana. Mesela Çetin (Helvacı), bana çok şey söylüyor. Ben bir şey anlattığım zaman, şöyledir böyledir diye tartışıyoruz, tartışmanın olması lazım. Onları serbest bırakıp konuşabilecek insanlar haline getirmemiz lazım. (Fig. 2)

İL: Do they remember what was told in the trainings last year?

O: I repeat what I said last year, we reinforce it, and we ask questions to remind them throughout the excavation. I ask if they are following the layers, what they are doing and why they are doing it. Sometimes they are afraid that I will ask questions. But I still ask; "why are you doing this?" I need a person who can answer my questions. For example, Çetin (Helvacı) explains a lot to me. When I say something, we argue and such and such, but the key is there has to be a discussion. We need to free them and ensure that they are people who can speak (Fig. 2).

İL: Bu verdiğiniz dersler sayesinde kültürel mirası koruma farkındalığı oluştu mu? Mesela bölgedeki defineciliği önledi mi?

O: Kültürel mirası koruma farkındalığı oluştu demek zor, ama bu insanlar kaçak kazı yapmazlar, ne olduğunu anladılar. Mesela müzeye geliyorlar, ne kadar küçük parça olursa olsun önemini anlatıyoruz, anlıyorlar. Önemli olan altın bulmak değil diyorum. Zaten çıkmayacağını da biliyorlar…

İL: Did you raise awareness of cultural heritage preservation after these lessons? For example, did it prevent treasure hunting in the region?

O: It's hard to say that there has been an increased awareness of protecting cultural heritage, but these people don't excavate illegally, they understand the consequences of doing so. For example, they come to the museum, we explain the importance of all the artefacts no matter how small it is, and they understand. I say the important thing is not to find gold. They already know that gold won't be discovered.

İL: Yani höyüğün ne olduğunu anladılar?

O: O seviyeye kadar konuşmak lazım. Mesela, dersleri ikinci kalite vermemek lazım. Çocuğa anlatır gibi değil de üniversitede ders verir gibi anlatmak lazım. Eğitmenlerimize, üniversitedeki derslerden daha ciddi şekilde anlatacaksınız diyorum. Ne kadar zor olursa olsun, sen anlatmayı biliyorsan, anlayacaklardır, yoksa olmaz.

İL: So, they figured out what the mound was?

O: It is necessary to speak up to that level. For example, we should not give second quality lessons. It should be explained as if you were teaching at a university, not lecturing a child. I advise our instructors to communicate with more seriousness then a university lecturer. No matter how hard it is, if you know how to explain, they will understand, otherwise they won't.

İL: Bu kazılar sayesinde bölgenin sosyal, kültürel özellikleri değişti mi? Bunu gözlemlediniz mi?

O: Epey değişti. Bu bölge tamamen değişti.

İL: Have the social and cultural characteristics of the region changed after these excavations? Did you observe this?

O: It has changed a lot. This region has completely changed.

İL: Mesela göç azaldı mı?

O: Evet, bölgede kalmak istiyorlar artık. Müze var, enstitü var, hiçbir şey yoktu buralarda. Yemyeşil oldu buralar.
Mesela ağaçlandırma çalışmaları başlattık. Bu çalışmalar için de niye biz böyle bir iş yapıyoruz demiyorum. Dememek lazım, bölgeyi kalkındırmak lazım. Her sene özel kalem 10–20 bin tane ağaç veriyorlar bana, biz de köye getiriyor dikiyoruz. Böylece bu bölge de yavaş yavaş değişiyor.

İL: For example, has emigration decreased?

O: Yes, they want to stay in the region now. There is a museum, and an institute where there was nothing here before. It has become as green as grass now.
For example, we have begun an afforestation project. I don't need to explain why we initiate such activities. Needless to

say, it is necessary to develop the region. Every year, they give me 10–20 thousand trees, and we bring them to the village and plant them. Thus, this region is also slowly changing.

İL: **Enstitünün karşısında bir yapı gördüm mesela, Japon evlerine benziyor.**

O: Benzettiler evet.

İL: **For example, I saw a building opposite the institute, it looks like a Japanese house.**

O: They made it look like that, yes.

İL: **Yapısal olarak da değişiklikler olmuş, insanlar evlerini bile değiştirmişler, çok farklı bir köy burası aslında.**

O: Evet, baya değişti. Ama en büyük değişiklik; bölge çocuklarının üniversiteye gitme isteği arttı. Herhalde bizden etkilenmiş olabilirler. Bu öğrenciler yazları kazıda çalışıyorlar. Yabancı dil öğrenmek lazım diyorum, yabancı dil öğrenmek istiyorlar. Yabancılarla konuşun öğrenmek istiyorsanız diyorum, çabalıyorlar, sonra da yavaş yavaş konuşuyorlar. Mesela Kader'in (Sevindir) oğlu hukuk kazanmış. Hukuk okuyabilecek bir çocuk değildi önceden. Ama kazanayım diye çok uğraşmış, hukuk kazanmış. Buradaki ortamdan etkilenmiş olabilir mesela.

İL: **There have been structural changes, people have even changed their houses. This is a very different village, actually.**

O: Yes, it has changed a lot. But this is the biggest change; The desire of the children of the region to go to university has increased. They may have been influenced by us. These students work in excavations in the summer. I tell them that they need to learn a foreign language. They want to learn a foreign language. I encourage them to talk to foreigners if they want to learn a foreign language, and then they will begin to gradually learn to speak it. For example, Kader's (Sevindir) son gained a position in law. He wasn't a kid who could study law before. But he tried so hard to win, he won a position in law. For example, he may have been affected by the environment from here.

İL: **Bildiğim kadar bu öğrencilere burs da veriyorsunuz değil mi?**

O: Evet, veriyoruz.

İL: **As far as I know, you also give scholarships to these students, right?**

O: Yes, we do.

İL: **Peki kazı bütçesinden mi kişisel mi?**

O: Kişisel bütçemizden karşılıyoruz. Fazla değilse de 60–70 kadar öğrenci bizlerden burs alıp mezun oldu. Biri doktor oldu örneğin, İstanbul'da hastanede çalışıyor şimdi. Bizlerle de çok çalıştı önceden. Kayseri Erciyes Üniversitesi Tıp Fakültesini kazandı, 6–7 sene destekledim. Artık kazıya gelme dedim yine de geliyor yardım etmeye sağ olsun.
Geçen gün o kadar komik bir anısını anlattı ki. Çok hasta geliyor mu sana dedim. "Çok geliyorlar" diyor. Nasıl memnunlar mı senden diyorum. "Çok memnunlar" deyince, neden dedim, "ben kazıyı anlatıyorum" diyor. Hastalar hastalıklarını unutuyor, merak edip soruyorlarmış; hocam neler çıkıyor diye. "Anlatıyorum, seviniyorlar, sonra sen hasta değilsin diye gönderiyorum" diye anlatıyor. Çok iyi bir adam oldu, çok.

İL: **So, is it from the excavation budget or is it personal?**

O: We finance it from our personal budget. If not more, about 60–70 students received scholarships from us and graduated. For example, one of them became a doctor, now he works at the hospital in Istanbul. He has worked with us a lot before. He won a position at Kayseri Erciyes University Faculty of Medicine, and I supported him for 6–7 years. I said "don't come to the excavation anymore," but he's still coming, thanks to the help. He told such a funny memory the other day. I asked to him, "Do you look for too many patients"" "Too many patients come," he said. I asked "Are they satisfied with you?" When he said "They are very pleased", I asked why. "I tell them about the excavation", he said. The patients forget their diseases, they wonder and ask; "what's going on?" I tell them and they become happy, then I send them away saying that they are not sick," he said. He is a very good man.

İL: Sayenizde birçok çocuk yetişmiş burada, ne güzel.

O: Eskiden benimle çalışmış gençler ara sıra çocuklarıyla beraber geliyor. "Hocam araba aldım, göstermeye geldim" diyorlar. Omura Bey görsün diye çocuklarını getiriyorlar. Çocukları hakkında bilgiler veriyorlar, okula gidiyor, okula başladı diye anlatıyorlar. Bu mutluluk yetiyor bana. Zaten ben dedeleri gibiyim. İyi yapmışsın, aferin diyorum. Eskiden benimle birlikte çalışan çocuklar geldiği zaman çok mutlu oluyorum.
Ama aralarında beni mahkemeye verenler de çıkıyor, üzülüyorum aslında.

İL: Thanks to you, many children have grown up here, it's nice.

O: Young people who used to work with me sometimes come with their children. They'll say, "Hoca, I bought a car, I came to show you". They bring their children for "Mr. Omura" to see. They give information about their children, that they go to school, that they started school. This happiness is enough for me. I'm just like their grandparents. You did well, I say well done. I am very happy to see them, the children who used to work with me.
But there are also those who took me to court among them, and I actually feel sad.

İL: Neden veriyorlar mahkemeye?

O: Kızmış bana, eksik para verdi diye veya sigortası 1 hafta gecikti diye veriyor. Buradan emekli olanların bile eksik ödemeleri varsa bir sene ben ödüyorum, hiç çalıştırmadan. 1 hafta 10 gün için neden kızıyorsun bana diyorum. Mesela ilerde emekli olurken, ben olmasam bile Matsumura Bey'e söylerim, mutlaka emekli ederiz seni diyorum. Hiç kimseyi yarı yolda bırakmadım ben. Hüseyin (Çam) mesela, emekli olacakmış 11. ayda. O zamana kadar ben bakarım, emekli ol, gerekirse ben sana yine iş veririm, merak etme dedim.
Fakat yine de memnunum ben. Kızmıyorum, hiç kızmıyorum.

İL: Why are they taking you to court?

O: If someone is angry with me, he'll take me to court. It could be because he believes the money was lacking, or because the insurance was a week late. If even those who retire from here have missing payments, I'll pay for a year, without any employment. I'd say, "why are you angry at me for 1 week and 10 days?" For example, when they retire in the future, I will tell Mr. Matsumura that even if I am not here, that we will definitely retire you. I've never let anyone down. For example, Hüseyin (Çam), he will retire in 11 months. I said that I would take care of him until then, and he could retire, but, if necessary, I would give him a job again, saying to him "don't worry".
But still, I am satisfied. I'm not angry, I'm not angry at all.

İL: Enstitüyü kaç yılında kurdunuz ve enstitünün gelişmesi ve sürdürülmesi için nasıl fon buluyorsunuz?

O: 1991 yılı Ekim ayında Tokyo'daki saraya çıkmıştım. Prensle konuşurken enstitüye ihtiyaç olduğunu ve çok ihtiyaç olduğunu söylemiştim. Bir sene sonra, 1992'nin Ocak ayında, Prens, Kyoto Kültür Merkezi'nde toplantı yaptı, o toplantıda herkesin önünde Anadolu arkeolojisine enstitünün lazım olduğunu anlattı. O tarihten sonra çalışmalar başladı, fikri ben vermiştim. 1990'da bir tablet çıkmıştı, prensin bu tabletten haberi vardı. Gelen araştırmacı arkadaşlara malzemeleri nasıl verip çalıştıracağız diye uğraşıyorduk, sonra depo lazım derken, bizim için esas önemli olan yani çıkan eserleri nasıl sergileyeceğiz sorunsalı oldu. İşte o zaman müze lazım dedik.

Müzeydi, enstitüydü, lojmandı derken iş baya büyüdü.

İL: In what year did you establish the institute and how do you find funds for the development and maintenance of the institute?

O: In October 1991, I went to the palace in Tokyo. Talking to the prince, I said that the institute was needed and very much needed. A year later, in January 1992, the Prince held a meeting at the Kyoto Cultural Center, where he explained in front of everyone that the institute was needed for Anatolian archaeology. After that date, the work started. I gave the idea. A tablet was a tablet was unearthed in 1990, and the prince knew about it. We were dealing with how we could give the materials to the incoming researchers, then when we said we needed a warehouse, the most important question for us was how we would exhibit the artefacts. That's when we said that we need a museum. When we say that it was a museum, an institute, and a residence, the activities grew a lot.

İL: Müzeyle enstitü fikri birlikte miydi?

O: Evet, aynı fikirdi önce. Ama Türkiye Cumhuriyeti bu projeyi kabul etmedi. Çünkü çıkan eserler tabiki Türkiye'ye ait, Japonlara veremeyiz dediler, bu da doğru bir yaklaşım. Bu nedenle 2001'de projeye başlarken müze ve enstitü arasına çizgi koyalım demiştik. Fakat 1992'den itibaren 1997'ye kadar hiç hareket olmadı enstitü için. O tarihe kadar çok büyük vakıflara gittim. Sonra 1997'de çok büyük bir vâkıfın genel müdürü Türkiye'ye gelmişti, ona refakat etmiştim. Sonrasında o vakfa müracaat ettim. Enstitünün bir kısmına depo lazım dedim ve 20–30 sayfalık yazıyla müracaat ettim. Depo projesine olumlu baktılar. "Tamam, bir milyon dolar gelecek" dediler. Nereye depo yapacağımızın hesabını yapıyorduk ki sonra bir gün oradaki genel müdür beni yanına davet etti. Proje izni çıktı artık diye yanına gittik ki birdenbire "bu iş olmuyor, bizim vakfa uymaz" dedi. Çok üzüldüm, 2–3 senedir uğraşıyordum. Ama karar karardır dedim, ayrıldım oradan.

1990'da prens iki adamıyla yanıma gelmişti, o adamlardan biri 1997'de, bu iş olmaz dediği o gün, bana telefon açtı. "Gelir misiniz" dediler. Bende sebep nedir diye sordum, çünkü 8 sene geçmiş aradan, hiçbir şey anlayamadım. "Gelin, yemek yiyelim" dediler.

İL: Was the idea to have the museum and the institute together?

O: Yes, it was the same idea before. But the Republic of Türkiye did not accept this project. They argued that, of course, the artefacts that come out belong to Türkiye, and that they could not give them to the Japanese, which is the right approach. For this reason, when we started the project in 2001, we said that we should draw a line between the museum and the institute. But from 1992 to 1997, there was no movement for the institute. During that time , I went to very large foundations. Then, in 1997, the general manager of one such foundation came to Türkiye, and I accompanied him. I applied to that foundation. I said that one part of the institute needed a warehouse, and applied with a 20–30 page article. They approached the warehouse project positively, telling me "a million dollars will come." We began to plan where to build a warehouse, one day soon after the general manager invited me to join him. We went to him thinking that the project permission has been obtained; however, he suddenly said, "This is not working, as it does not fit our foundation." I was devastated, I'd been planning it for 2–3 years. But I said the decision is the decision, so I left it there.

In 1990, the prince approached me accompanied by two of his men. One of those men called me on the phone in 1997, when I'd been informed that the institute project would no longer work. "Will you come?" he said. I asked for the reason. 8 years had passed, and I could no longer understand anything. They said, "Come, let's have some food"

İL: **Nereye çağırdılar?**

O: Saraya. Saraya gittim, prens yoktu o gün, ama prensese "Omura bugün gelecek, yemeğe götür" demiş. Beni görünce çok şaşırdı prenses. Bir şey mi oldu dedi. Ben zaten bir milyonu kaçırmışım, çok üzülüyordum. O zaman anlamışlar adamlar herhalde bir şey oldu diye. Bende anlattım, böyle böyle para çıkmadı, ne yapacağımı bilmiyorum dedim. Bir sene ya da sekiz ay sonra prensle görüştüm. 1998'de Türkiye'ye tekrar geldi, buraya Kaman'a. Kapıda tabela var ya, onu taktı prefabrik binaya. "Burayı artık enstitü olarak kabul ediyorum..." dedi. Fig. 3)

İL: **Where did they call you?**

O: To the palace. I went to the palace, and whilst there was no prince that day, he said to the princess, "Omura will come today, take him to dinner." The princess was very surprised to see me. She asked if something had happened. I had already missed out on a million, so I was very upset. That's when the guys realized that something must have happened. I told her, I'd tried everything but hadn't obtained the money, saying that I didn't know what else to do. A year or eight months later, I met the prince. He came back to Türkiye in 1998, here to Kaman. There's a sign on the door, he put it on the prefabricated building. He said that "I accept this place as an institute now." (Fig. 3).

İL: **Türkiye Cumhuriyeti de kabul etti.**

O: Ne yapacaksınız dedi önce, başta tam kabul etmedi, sonra kabul etti. 1998'de prens Kaman'a geldikten sonra, babası (Takahito Mikasa) ile görüştü. Ben önce babası ile geziyordum bana yardımcı oluyordu ama fazla para toplayamadım enstitü kurulumu için. O arada imparatorun hanımı vefat etti. Sonra Prens Tomohito Mikasa babasına gitmiş. O arada söylemiş, Omura böyle böyle istiyor, pek fazla para toplayamadık, sende yardımcı olur musun diye. Ben buradaydım o sırada, Kaman'da. Ağustos ayıydı, hemen Japonya'ya gittim yanına. "Sen ciddi yapacak mısın bu işi, istiyor musun, sonuna kadar yapacaksan yardım edeyim" dedi. "Yapamam dersen, hemen bırak bu işi yapma, en az 5–6 sene seninle gezeceğim, fakat hiç bırakmadan yaparsan bende yardım ederim" dedi. 2000'de bakanları, başbakanı çağırdı saraya. "Böyle bir konu var, yardımcı olur musunuz" dediği anda hepsi yardımcı olacağız dedi. Ertesi sene 2001 yılında, Nisan ayından itibaren 320 kere konferans yaptı. Ben de 100'den fazla kez gittim yanına. Öyle öyle topladı enstitü kurulumu için gereken parayı. "Üç milyon dolar topladık, başlayabilirsiniz" diye haber geldi bana da, ama yetmez aslında. Sonra Prens, babasına gitmiş, "üç milyon dolar topladık Japonya'nın her yerinden" demiş, o da "çok güzel yapmışsınız" diye yanıtlamış. İstiyorsanız hemen başlayın artık demek bu. Sonra tekrar gezdim, yedi milyon dolar daha topladım, ancak o zaman başlayabildik inşaata. Fakat inşaat zamanı Irak savaşı başladı. Demir olsun, beton olsun, çimento olsun, benzin olsun hepsi yüksekti, inşaat yavaş ilerliyordu. Tekrar 300'den fazla konferans yaptık. Büyük firmaların hepsi vardı gezimizin içinde.

İL: **The Republic of Türkiye also accepted it.**

O: They said What are you going to do? At first, they did not fully accept it, but after a while they accepted . After the prince visited Kaman in 1998, he met with his father (Takahito Mikasa). I had been with his father before, he helped me, but I couldn't raise enough money for the establishment of the institute. Meanwhile, the emperor's wife had passed away.

Then Prince Tomohito Mikasa went to his father Takahito Mikasa. His father said by the way, "Omura wants it like this, but we couldn't raise enough money; can you help me?" I was here at that time, in Kaman. It was August and I left for Japan immediately. He asked me, "Are you going to do this seriously, do you want it? And if you're committed until the end, I will help you". He continued, "If you decide you can't do it, stop doing this job right away, because I will travel with you for at least 5–6 years, but if you do it without quitting, I will help you." Then in 2000, he summoned the ministers and the prime minister to the palace. As soon as he said, "There is something you can help me with, if you would", they agreed unanimously to help. The following year, in 2001, he had given 320 lectures by April. I'd been to him more than 100 times and just like that, he collected the money needed for the establishment of the institute. I was also told, "We have collected three million dollars, you can start", but it was still not enough.

Then the Prince went to his father, saying "We collected three million dollars from all over Japan", and his father replied, "You did very well". If you want, start now, that's what this means. I toured again, collecting another seven million dollars, and after that we were finally able to start construction. But unfortunately, at the time of construction, the Iraq war began. The prices of iron, concrete, cement, gasoline; those were all high and the construction progressed slowly. Again, we held more than 300 lectures. All of the big companies were on our tour-route.

İL: **Açılış tarihi ne oldu?**

O: Açılış 2005'te oldu.

İL: **What was the opening date?**

O: The opening was in 2005.

İL: **Zorlu bir süreç olmuş.**

O: O zamanlar para toplarken prens, "Türkiye güzeldir, arkeolojisi güzeldir, Anadolu'nun havası güzeldir, yemekleri güzeldir dersen anlamaz o firma sahipleri" derdi. "Hepsini Türkiye'ye getirelim, gezdirelim" dedi ve parça parça iş insanlarını getirmeye başladı. Bir nevi turizm kondüktörlüğü yaptı kendisi. Bir seferinde en fazla 350 kişi getirmişti. Jumbo kiralayarak getirdi. Öyle adamdı. Esenboğa Havalimanı'na jumbo zor indi.

İL: **It has been a difficult process.**

O: At that time, while collecting money, the prince used to say, "If you say that Türkiye is beautiful, its archaeology is beautiful, the weather in Anatolia is good, the food is good, those company owners will not understand." He said to me, "Let's bring them all to Türkiye, let's show them around" and began to bring business people bit by bit. He was a kind of tour operator himself. At one time, he brought as many as 350 people. He hired a jumbo-jet. He was that kind of man. The jumbo-jet landed at Esenboğa Airport with difficulty.

İL-Ç.M: Çok güzel bir sohbet oldu değerli Omura hocam verdiğiniz bu kıymetli bilgiler için çok teşekkür ederiz.

İL-Ç.M: It was a very nice conversation, dear Omura San, thank you very much for the valuable information you provided.

Bibliography

Akurgal, E.
- 1998 *Türkiye'nin Kültür Sorunları*, Ankara.

Bossert, H. Th.
- 1950 Karatepe Kazıları: Birinci Ön Rapor, Türk Tarih Kurumu, Ankara.

Külcü, Ö. T.
- 2015 "The Importance of the Concept of Cultural Heritage in Education," *Journal of Interdisciplinary Scientific Research* 1 (1), pp. 27–32.

Ünar, Ş.
- 2020 "Turkish Archaeology in Atatürk Period," ANASAY 11, pp. 129–148.

Fig. 1.
Söyleşi sırasında Dr. Sachihiro Omura ile Kaman Kalehöyük kazı evi yemekhanesinde (sol: S. Omura, orta: Ç. Maner, sağ: İ. İvgin).

During the interview with Dr. Sachihiro Omura in the dining hall at the excavation house in Kaman Kalehöyük (left: S. Omura, center: Ç. Maner, right: İ. İvgin).

Fig. 2.
Dr. Sachihiro Omura kazıda ders esnasında.

Dr. Sachihiro Omura during a lesson on the site.

Fig. 3.
Enstitü kapısında bulunan ahşap pano.

The wooden panel at the entrance of the Institute.

90 Years after Alişar: The Stratigraphy and Chronology of the Late 4th/Early 3rd Millennium B.C. in Central Anatolia

Jan-Krzysztof Bertram and Gülçin İlgezdi Bertram *

Abstract

The highlighting and structuring of the Late Chalcolithic and the older Early Bronze Age (EBA I) in Central Anatolia are closely connected with the excavations at Alişar Höyük (1927–1932). With the work on this site and the final publication of H. H. von der Osten in 1937, a controversial discussion, which lasted until the 1990s and is still relevant today, arose on the dating of the "Chalcolithic" layers of Alişar. Among other things, it dealt with the question of how old the Central Anatolian "Chalcolithic" actually is, and how the Early Bronze Age can be meaningfully divided. More recently, it has been possible to examine Late Chalcolithic and older Early Bronze Age (4th and early 3rd millennium B.C.) strata at a number of settlements, including Çadır Höyük, Çayyolu Höyük, Çamlıbel Tarlası, and others. Consequently, 14C-data and new stratigraphies have provided a good opportunity to shed light on this issue from a contemporary perspective. With this paper, we want to give a short overview of the state of the research on the 4th and early 3rd millennium B.C. in Central Anatolia.

Öz

Orta Anadolu'da Geç Kalkolitik ve Erken Tunç Çağı'nın (İTÇ I) tanımlanması ve bölümlendirilmesi Alişar Höyük (1927–1932) kazılarıyla yakından bağlantılıdır. Bu buluntu yerindeki çalışmalar ve ardından H. H. von der Osten'nin 1937'de yapmış olduğu son yayınla birlikte, Alişar'ın „Kalkolitik" tabakalarının tarihlendirilmesi hakkında 1990'lara dek süren hararetli bir tartışma başladı. Bu tartışma günümüzde de halen geçerliliğini korumaktadır. Sorulardan bir tanesi, Orta Anadolu Kalkolitiğinin gerçekte ne kadar eski olduğu ve İlk Tunç Çağı'nın anlamla bir şekilde nasıl bölümlendirilebileceğiydi. Yakın geçmişte Geç Kalkolitik ve İlk Tunç Çağı'nın erken katmanları, bir dizi yerleşimde (MÖ 4. ve 3. binyıl; Çadır Höyük, Çayyolu Höyük, Çamlıbel Tarlası ve diğerleri) incelenebilmiştir. Bu kazılardan elde edilen C14 verileri ve yeni stratigrafiler, bu soruna günümüz perspektifinden ışık tutmak için bize iyi bir fırsat vermektedir. Okumakta olduğunuz makale ile İç Anadolu'da MÖ 4. ve 3. binyılın başlarına tarihlenen araştırmaların durumuna kısa bir bakış sunmak istiyoruz.

Introduction [1]

For many decades, the stratigraphy of Alişar Höyük (Fig. 1), excavated in the 1920s and 1930s, formed the backbone of later Central Anatolian prehistory. Here, an exceptionally extensive sequence of 3rd millennium B.C.

* Ahi Evran Üniversitesi, Bağbaşı Yerleşkesi, Fen-Edebiyat Fakültesi, Arkeoloji Bölümü, TR-40100 Kırşehir.

1 For the support of our work, we wish to thank the T. C. Kültür ve Turizm Bakanlığı, Kültür Varlıkları ve Müzeler Genel Müdürlüğü (Republic of Türkiye, Ministry of Culture and Tourism, General Directorate of Cultural Heritage and Museums).

The fieldwork and material studies we have conducted over the last 15 years have always had the support of Dr. S. Omura und Dr. M. Omura (both of the Japanese Institute of Anatolian Archaeology, Kaman). We are grateful for the many discussions and inspiring conversations. Special thanks also go to G. Ensarı (Ankara) for his support of our work over the years. Our thanks also go to our colleagues at the Ankara Anadolu Medeniyetleri Müzesi, Kırşehir Müzesi, Yozgat Müzesi, Çorum Müzesi, and Konya Müzesi. We would also like to thank Prof. Dr. H. Çambel and Prof. Dr. M. Özdoğan (İstanbul) for providing the Hashöyük finds for processing. This study includes results from BAP-projects funded by Kırşehir Ahi Evran University (Project-Codes PYO-FEN.4001.12.037, PYO-FEN.4001.13.010,

strata could be studied (von der Osten 1937). Later, a controversy arose as to the extent of the Alişar sequence, and it was debated whether it ranged to the 4th millennium B.C. or was even much older still. In the absence of 14C-dating, arguments were based primarily on typological comparisons and in some cases over very long distances, reaching as far as southeastern Europe. Thus, dating schemes varying by as much as several millennia apart have been proposed (Fig. 2; see Bittel 1934: 15; Orthmann 1963: 10; Oğuz 1933: 39; Miyake 三宅裕 1992: Table 1; Thissen 1993). In addition, the pottery from the period of interest to us was not considered separately according to strata. This led to uncertainties in the assessment of the stratigraphy and from this, to the consideration of the Late Chalcolithic in Central Anatolia as a whole. In the decades following the end of the excavations in Alişar, systematic investigations of the Late Chalcolithic and the older Early Bronze Age took place in only a few more sites (Bertram and İlgezdi Bertram 2021, chapter 4). For several decades, the period between ca. 4000 and 2800/2700 B.C. remained a *terra incognita*. It is only in the last 20–25 years that excavations at various sites in Central Anatolia (e. g., at Çadır Höyük, Çayyolu Höyük, Küllüoba, and Çamlıbel Tarlası) have made it possible to examine layers of the (late) 4th and early 3rd millennia B.C. (Fig. 3), thus providing a view of the Late Chalcolithic and the older Early Bronze Age independent of Alişar (Steadman *et al.* 2008; Arslan, İlgezdi Bertram and Bertram 2013; Efe and Ay 2000; Schoop 2011). The new excavations are slowly closing a long-standing research gap. On the one hand, it is now possible, based on 14C-data, to clarify the dating of the "Chalcolithic" highlighted by Hans Henning von der Osten in Alişar (von der Osten 1937: 28–109). Furthermore, it will now be equally possible to better understand the material culture, especially the characteristics of the pottery and its development. With these excavations, the Gordian knot of recent Central Anatolian prehistory is slowly unravelling, and in the following sections, we will give a concise overview of the situation in Central Anatolia from ca. 3600/3500 B.C. to ca. 2800/2700 B.C. from a current perspective – almost 90 years after the completion of the excavations in Alişar.

and PYO-FEN.4001.15.003) and Orta Doğu Teknik Üniversitesi (Project-Code BAP-07.03.2009.03, 2763). The drawings were executed by T. Tekin (Ankara) and M. Ülker (Ankara). B. Zafer (Ankara) helped with the statistical analysis of the ceramic finds from Çayyolu Höyük. The linguistic correction of this article was kindly undertaken by N. Umm-Süleyman Peaci (Düzce). We would like to thank all the people involved in the project for their support over the years.

The Tripartition at Alişar: A Confusing Terminology

In the final publication on the Alişar excavations, von der Osten summarised the oldest layers on the Höyük (19M to 12M) as "Chalcolithic" (Table 1). The following layers on the Höyük (11M to 7M) and on the adjacent terrace (14T to 13T) were called "Copper Age", and 5M to 6M on the Höyük and 12T on the terrace "Early Bronze Age" (von der Osten 1937).[2] As explained in more detail elsewhere (Bertram and İlgezdi Bertram 2021, chapter 4), this terminology is confusing from today's point of view. However, von der Osten could hardly fall back on comparative finds or stratigraphies during his time. In the find material, there were simply too few vessel remains or small finds to allow a reliable connection with the Near Eastern chronology or sites further west (e.g., Troia). From today's point of view, the "Copper Age" is part of the Early Bronze Age (Bertram and İlgezdi Bertram 2020). Von der Osten's "Early Bronze Age" designates only a late section of the Early Bronze Age and the transition to the Middle Bronze Age (and perhaps includes at least part of the Middle Bronze Age). The subsequent dating of the "Chalcolithic" has raised a controversy. Winfried Orthmann considered the "Chalcolithic" of Alişar as be-

2 We use in this article the tripartite structure of the Early Bronze Age based on Alişar as given in Table 1.

ginning only after 3000 B.C. (Orthmann 1963: 10). This would assign it to the Early Bronze Age (not the Late Chalcolithic) from today's perspective. Other authors dated it much older and placed it up to nearly 2000 years earlier (Fig. 2; see below). From the 1960s on, this classification was replaced by the three stages of the Early Bronze Age (I, II, and III). The "Copper Age" corresponds to Early Bronze Age II/III, whereas the "Early Bronze Age" in the sense of von der Osten represents, from today's point of view, a very late stage of the Early Bronze Age (EBA III) and the transition to the Middle Bronze Age (Table 1; Bertram and İlgezdi Bertram 2021, chapter 4). Regardless of how the three phases highlighted by von der Osten are designated, we would like to emphasize at this point that this threefold division certainly stands up to critical scrutiny from today's perspective. With our fieldwork as well as with the material studies we have carried out, we can confirm and also comprehend the three-phase division made by von der Osten. To transfer the three-stage model of the Early Bronze Age (I, II and III) to Central Anatolian find complexes is already more difficult. The development of the material culture was probably not synchronous with other regions. Moreover, "Chalcolithic" and "Copper Age" finds (vessel forms, small finds, etc.), which would allow a reliable supraregional comparison, are largely missing. Not enough 14C-data are currently available to establish a typology-independent, absolute chronology (Bertram and İlgezdi Bertram 2021, chapter 4.3).

The Dating of Chalcolithic Alişar

A compilation of dating proposals and comparable inventories for the "Chalcolithic" in Alişar is shown in Fig. 2. The proposals cover a rather large period, ranging from the early 5th to the early 3rd millennium B.C. The background and arguments for these datings will not be discussed again here (cf. in detail Bertram and İlgezdi Bertram 2021, chapter 4). Rather, we refer to a series of findings that point to a dating of the Central Anatolian "Chalcolithic" in the sense of von der Osten, i. e., into the 4th and early 3rd millennium B.C. It has been known for quite a long time that Central Anatolian influences appear in pottery at Tepecik in the Keban area in a late Uruk context. Among other things found here were fruit stands, which have their counterparts in the Central Anatolian Chalcolithic (Esin 1979: 112, Pl. 57.6; 1982: 117, Pl. 72–73). Fruit stands were also known from Arslantepe VI A. Their appearance has been attributed to contacts with Central Anatolia (Frangipane 2004: 182–183, cat. no. 31, 33; 2017: 189, Figs. 13.2a, d; 2000: 447, Figs. 6a–b). So far, some 14C-data from various sites (Çadır Höyük, Çayyolu Höyük, and Çamlıbel Tarlası) have enabled us to narrow down the "Chalcolithic" to the period from *ca.* mid 4th millennium B.C. to *ca.* 2800/2700 B.C. (Bertram and İlgezdi Bertram 2021, chapter 4.3 and appendices 1–2). The most extensive 14C-data is available from Çadır Höyük. A sequence covering the second half of the 4th millennium B.C. has certainly been recorded here. Presumably, the strata extend further back into the 4th millennium B.C., but numerous 14C-dates have been published without BP dates, making calibration impossible for us (cf. overview in Bertram and İlgezdi Bertram 2021, chapter 4.3 and appendices 1–2). The oldest 4th millennium B.C. 14C-data we are aware of are those from Çamlıbel Tarlası from the middle of the millennium or just before (Schoop *et al.* 2009). Thus, what inventories dating to the early 4th millennium B.C. look like is unclear. There is much to suggest that inventories such as those assigned to the "Chalcolithic" in Alişar can be dated to the 4th and early 3rd millennia B.C. Admittedly, this does not provide any information as to how far the layers in Alişar themselves extend into the 4th millennium B.C. (and beyond ?). However, it is very likely that a part of the "Chalcolithic" layers of Alişar can be assigned to this period. Only new work at the site can provide a reliable clarification. This appears to close the earlier formulated gap in the tradition for the Early Bronze Age I (Gerber 2008: 199).

New Excavations and Stratigraphies on the Late Chalcolithic and the Older Early Bronze Age in Central Anatolia

Fig. 3 gives a compilation of Central Anatolian sites where layers of the 4th and early 3rd millennium B.C. have been excavated and which have been dated in the past to the "Chalcolithic" or to the "Early Bronze Age I". However, the map also clearly shows these sites to be unevenly distributed. Although there are numerous sites from northern Central Anatolia (approximately north of the Tuz Gölü), there are no investigations for this period in the south. A number of sites have been known for a long time, such as Alaca Höyük, Hashöyük, Çengeltepe, and Kuşsaray (Schoop 2005a: 38–43; Delaporte 1932; Ünal 1968; Koşay 1968). Excavations that are more recent and having detailed layer observations include Küllüoba, Çadır Höyük, Çayyolu Höyük, Devret Höyük, and Çamlıbel Tarlası (Efe and Ay 2000; Steadman *et al.* 2008; Arslan, Ilgezdi Bertram and Bertram 2013; Türker 2014; Schoop 2011). Çadır Höyük, only about 13 km northeast of Alişar, is of particular importance. Excavations here yielded a very detailed documented, and extensive 4th millennium B.C. sequence that was also 14C-dated (cf. overview in Bertram and İlgezdi Bertram 2021, chapter 4.3 and appendices 1–2). Further west, in Ankara, at Çayyolu Höyük in trench H9, an extensive stratigraphy could be worked out covering the "Chalcolithic" and the "Copper Age". A total of 43 layers are present here, and these allow a detailed insight into the ceramic development. Similar early layers (older than "Copper Age") could be documented in the nearby vicinity at Karaoğlan Höyük and at Sincan Höyük II (Bertram and Ilgezdi Bertram 2018). In Çamlıbel Tarlası, between 2007 and 2009, a small, multi-layered settlement was investigated and 14C-dated. Copper was apparently intensively worked here, *ca.* in the mid-4th millennium B.C. (Schoop 2011). Farther west, Küllüoba (Efe and Ay 2000) and Kaklık Mevkii settlements (Efe, İlaslı and Topbaş 1996) are worth mentioning. At Küllüoba, several settlement layers were investigated in the Western sector, covering the period from the Late Chalcolithic to the early Early Bronze Age II (summarised into eight phases). A larger building complex of about 42-m long and 41-m wide is dated from the Transitional period to the Early Bronze Age (Fidan 2012: 7–9). Roughly contemporaneous is the flat settlement of Kaklık Mevkii, which was investigated in 1983 and 1984 (Efe, İlaslı and Topbaş 1996; Topbaş, Efe and İlaslı 1998). It too is dated to the transition to the Early Bronze Age.

On the Settlement Dynamics in Central Anatolia in the 4th and Early 3rd Millennium B.C.

It is striking that many settlements of the 4th and early 3rd millennium B.C. do not show on-site continuity, i. e., settlements of this period often have no immediately preceding, earlier settlements. Rather, it appears that many settlements may have been newly founded in the 4th and early 3rd millennia B.C. At many sites, the excavations reached virgin soil beneath the oldest settlement layers of this period (Fig. 4; Bertram and İlgezdi Bertram 2021, chapter 8). At the least, it must be considered that older settlement remains were not encountered during the excavations because they could be located elsewhere in the settlement. On the other hand, the number of such observations is not small, which could merely indicate that in the 4th and early 3rd millennium B.C., a rather intensive occupation of (northern) Central Anatolia began and that numerous settlements were actually newly founded. These settlements then often continued into the "Copper Age". Areas preferred for settlement in the 4th and early 3rd millennium B.C. included small hills with access to water, from which the surrounding area could be seen, and which also offered a certain amount of protection by their altitude, but which at the same time, also had more or less fertile soil in the immediate vicinity. Likewise, valley and hillside locations were readily used if they offered a certain natural protection and demarcation from the surrounding landscape. Here again, we can see the relation to water and agriculturally usable soil. Höyüks could then develop from these latter settlements, which were intensively used in later times (e.g., Hashöyük, Karaoğlan Höyük). Only a relatively few sites can be mentioned for the preceding period from the late 6th to the end of the 5th millennium B.C. Perhaps the region as a whole was only very sporadically populated at this time. Such settlement finds still represent an exception. Only a handful of sites provide insights into the chronology, architecture, and settlement structures. Of particular note is Güvercinkayasi (Gülçur 2012)[3], which has been intensively studied through the work of Sevil Gülçur. New evidence for this period has recently been found at Derekutuğun (Yalçın and Yalçın 2019). Presumably, the strata at Çadır Höyük also dates back much further. From a deep sounding, layers dating to the 5th millennium B.C. are mentioned (Steadman *et al.* 2008: 53 and Table 1). A look at the settlement pottery of this period shows that its appearance can be quite unremarkable (cf. Yalçın and Yalçın 2019). Since the find material of the 5th millennium B.C. seems in part quite unspecific, it can easily be confused with Early Bronze Age or Late Chalcolithic material. The presence of other sites cannot be excluded, but their find material could not be identified as being so old. During surveys, such finds picked up from the surface can easily be addressed as Late Chalcolithic or Early Bronze Age. Perhaps, therefore, the gap here is not so great. However, in the intensive material studies that we have been able to carry out in recent years in numerous museums and on excavations between Afyon, Konya, Sivas, and Tokat, we have not been able to identify any new material that indisputably dates to this early period. At the moment, the few settlements of this period indicate that large parts of Central Anatolia were rather sparsely populated in the 5th millennium B.C., and that these settlement sites were not continuously used over a long period of time.

3 See also the comments by A. Hacar 2020 on the Niğde region.

The Period from ca. 3600/3500 to ca. 2800/2700 B.C. and the Beginning of the "Copper Age"

Currently, two sites can help to determine the duration of the Central Anatolian "Chalcolithic" in absolute chronological terms. First, Çamlıbel Tarlası provides the earliest dates. They are calibrated to be around the middle of the 4th millennium B.C. or slightly earlier[4]. No clear picture of the pottery can yet be drawn from the preliminary reports. What is important, however, is the occurrence of incised decoration (Schoop 2011: Fig. 21), as found in varying degrees in numerous other sites such as Alişar (von der Osten 1937: Figs. 65–66), Hashöyük (Delaporte 1932: Fig. 1), and Kuşsaray (Fig. 5). The occurrence of such pottery at Çadır Höyük thus indicates a rather long duration of such decoration (Steadman *et al.* 2008: Figs. 17.a–d – "Latest Late Chalcolithic", 18.n – "Transitional period", and 20.g – "Early Bronze I period"). The upper chronological limit for the "Chalcolithic" coincides with the beginning of the "Copper Age" and corresponding inventories (see Table 1). At Çayyolu Höyük, a stratigraphic sequence that records this transition could be worked out in trench H9. According to a 14C-date from layer 13, the beginning of the "Copper Age" could already be expected around 2900/2740 B.C. cal. (Fig. 6). This also indicates that the origins of inventories such as those from Ahlatlıbel and Koçumbeli extend quite far into the 3rd millennium B.C.[5]. Fruit stands, among other items, are found in the immediately preceding strata at Çayyolu Höyük. The dating of these vessel forms would consequently fall into the period around and shortly after 3000 B.C. At Çadır

4 Also, from Çadır Höyük come a number of other apparently older data. However, for the most part, no BP data are available as a basis for calibration. Therefore, we cannot consider these data here. For this problem, see Bertram and İlgezdi Bertram (2021), chapter 4.3 and appendices 1–2.

5 We previously made such an assumption a few years ago (see Bertram 2008).

Höyük, they occur in the Transitional period and in the Early Bronze I period (fruit stands/footed vessels: Steadman *et al.* 2008: Figs. 18.d, r, s and 20.f). Such dating would chronologically overlap with the observations at Arslantepe and Tepecik (Palumbi 2008: 74, 223, and 236).

The stratigraphy of Çayyolu/trench H9 (layers 43 to 14) indicates a notably continuous ceramic development. Some vessel forms, such as bowls and pots, occur over a long period of time and show few changes (Figs. 7–8). This makes it very difficult to subdivide the period based on the material culture. Consequently, it is also very difficult to draw a clear dividing line between the Late Chalcolithic and the Early Bronze Age. Significant changes in the pottery only become noticeable with the "Copper Age" (see Table 1). We therefore assume that in the early 3rd millennium B.C., Late Chalcolithic traditions still persisted. The transition from the 4th to the 3rd millennium B.C. is therefore likely to have been, overall, fluid and continuous. At the same time, regional differences in pottery may also have existed, as even a cursory comparison of the pottery from Çayyolu (Figs. 7–8) with that of Çadır Höyük (Steadman *et al.* 2008) and Alişar (von der Osten 1937: Figs. 62–84) demonstrates. It seems that deep black, polished pottery of very good quality occurred in the Kızılırmak arc, while further west in the Ankara region, the pottery was much more poorly formed. The surfaces for the most part are only slightly polished and the colours pale (Fig. 9). Vessel forms are mainly simple bowls and large pots with knobs. White painting, as occurs at Çadır Höyük, is not seen here (Steadman *et al.* 2008: Figs. 13.q – "Middle Chalcolithic and earlier Late Chalcolithic", and 17, f–g – "Latest Late Chalcolithic"). With the "Copper Age", changes in the pottery become noticeable. These changes affect the shape as well as the surface treatment and the firing of the vessels. At this time, bright red polished pottery and black polished vessels with grooved decoration are widespread in Central Anatolia (Bertram and İlgezdi Bertram 2020). Metal finds of various kinds (weapons, jewellery, and vessels) are quite common. In addition, white painting now appears on pottery quite frequently in the Ankara region[6].

Difficult Datable Find Complexes

At this point, we would like to discuss briefly two sites in which painted pottery was found. Since both are survey finds, it is not clear from which context the pottery originates and with which vessel forms and wares it is associated. Yeniyapan is located about 52 km east of Kırıkkale and about 17 km south-southeast of Delice. It is a flat settlement of about 100 m in diameter. Several painted pieces were found among the numerous vessel remains (Miyake 1992: 195–197 and Pl. 6.1–9). Rim sherds indicate vessels with narrow mouths. The painting clearly shows smaller spiral motifs, which appear on the rim or belly area of the vessels. They are combined with groups of lines. Other motifs are cross-hatching and angular bands (Miyake 1992: Pl. 6.1–9). The second site, Zencir (Söğütcük Pınarı-West), is also a flat settlement and is located about 45 km west of Yozgat on a terrace (Strobel and Gerber 2007: 584–587; 2010: 304–305). The painted pottery shows similarities to that of Yeniyapan. Among others, narrow-mouthed and slightly biconical vessels appear. The motifs, painted in dark colour on a light ground, consist, as far as recognizable, of straight and arched line groups, hatching, and spirals (Strobel and Gerber 2007: Figs. 34–35; 2010: Fig. 9a.1–12; Gerber 2008: 193–194). Christoph Gerber has assumed an Early Chalcolithic date in the 6th millennium B.C. for Zencir (Strobel and Gerber 2007: 584–587; 2010: 304; Gerber 2008: 193–194). Finds from Yeniyapan have also been assigned a similarly early date (Miyake 1992: Table 1). However, convincing parallels are lacking for these find complexes. There are recognisable differences in the painting and the vessel forms from those of Büyükkaya (Schoop 2005b). There are also no secure or convinc-

6 For more detail on the "Copper Age", see Bertram and İlgezdi Bertram 2020.

ing parallels from the Central Anatolian Late Chalcolithic. However, there are several indications of painted pottery in this period. In Alişar, painting occurs in layers 12M–13M and 17M and even bears some resemblance to that of Yeniyapan and Zencir (e.g., lines, groups of lines and angular motifs formed from several lines, spiral decoration ?; von der Osten 1937: 54–57, Figs. 63–64). Painting was also found at Çadır Höyük dating back to the latest Late Chalcolithic (Steadman *et al.* 2008: Fig. 17.k – "Latest Late Chalcolithic"). However, some of the vessel forms with painting from Yeniyapan and Zencir are quite different from the (Late) Chalcolithic and older Early Bronze Age forms known to us from Central Anatolia, such as the strongly pronounced biconical design of vessels (Miyake 1992: Fig. 6.2–3; Strobel and Gerber 2007: Fig. 35.2; 2010: Fig. 9a.4). Even if convincing parallels are ultimately lacking, the finds from Yeniyapan and Zençir represent an exceptional ensemble for North-Central Anatolia.

Supraregional Integration

A supraregional integration and consideration of the pottery is quite difficult. On the one hand, incomparably much less is known about the 4th millennium B.C. than about the Early Bronze Age. On the other hand, important reference sites are quite far away (e.g., Beycesultan *etc.*). For us, the most likely reference is to the west. Küllüoba is already close to the border of Central Anatolia. Several layers were investigated in the Western sector and have been assigned to the latest Late Chalcolithic, the Transitional period, and the older Early Bronze Age (phases 1 to 6; Efe and Ay 2000). A comparison with pottery from these phases shows that the similarities are limited and manageable. Here, as in the case there, simple bowls, simple cups, and baking platters were found (e.g., Efe and Ay 2000: Pls. 1.1–3, 5–7, 3.2–4, 6.4–5, 10.2–14, and 14.4–7). However, in general, these vessels are chronologically unspecific and cover a longer period. White-painted decoration also occurs at Küllüoba, linking this site to those in the Kızılırmak arc (Kuşsaray and others; Efe and Ay 2000: Fig. 17). However, we could not detect this decoration at Çayyolu in such early layers. Moreover, footed vessels reminiscent of fruit stands may indicate connections with Central Anatolia (Efe and Ay 2000: Pls. 1.13–14 and 14.18). From Küllüoba there are also bowls with pointed rims, which are also known from Çayyolu (Efe and Ay 2000: Pl. 15.1). Even if the comparisons are rather weak, a rough contemporaneity of the Küllüoba/Western sector (phase 6 to 2) with Çayyolu H9/layers 14–43 seems possible.

The view to the east and southeast is still quite problematic as well. Reference sites for the 4th millennium B.C. and the older Early Bronze Age are quite far away. Similarities of Central Anatolian finds to Karaz pottery already have been pointed out several times. Red-Black Burnished Ware is not uncommon in Central Anatolia and is also found at Çayyolu Höyük[7]. In Arslantepe, the Central Anatolian influence is emphasized in Phase VI A (Palumbi 2008: 74–93), and the references are easily visible in the pottery. In addition to black burnished ware, Red-Black Burnished Ware also occurs. Vessel forms include simple bowls and cups (Palumbi 2008: Fig. 3.18), fruit stands, pointed rim bowls (Palumbi 2008: Fig. 3.19), and S-profile vessels (Palumbi 2008: Fig. 3.20, nos. 4–5, 8–9). With Arslantepe VI B1 (Palumbi 2008: 223–235), a clear cultural change becomes visible with the appearance of Karaz pottery. However, the find material from VI B still indicates connections to Central Anatolia. These include bowls (Palumbi 2008: Fig. 6.9), footed cups (but these are handmade in Central Anatolia; Palumbi 2008: Fig. 6.17, no. 10), simple bowls and bowls with knobs on the rim (Palumbi 2008: Figs. 6.19, nos. 10–11 and 6.20, nos. 10–14), and S-shaped vessels (Palumbi 2008: Fig. 6.20, nos. 1–3)[8]. With the

7 A more detailed consideration of this ceramic genre will be dealt with at a later date.

8 In general, there seem to be many connections to the Karaz pottery in the Central Anatolian "Chalcolithic"

finds of the Late Chalcolithic and the older Early Bronze Age, a bridge can be built from Western Anatolia (Küllüoba) over Central Anatolia to Southeastern Anatolia. What we have briefly sketched here, however, requires further, detailed explanation that cannot be given here. In particular, the chronological position of old excavations like Hashöyük, Çengeltepe, Kuşsaray and others within the long period outlined here is difficult to evaluate, as well as the stratigraphy of Alaca Höyük with the Chalcolithic layers 9 to 14[9].

Summary

In the meantime, there are numerous sites from Central Anatolia where layers of the Late Chalcolithic and the older Early Bronze Age have been investigated, or from which exceptional and extensive ceramic ensembles originate (Fig. 3). These sites are mainly concentrated in the north, whereas excavations of such layers are largely absent from the south of Central Anatolia. The work at Çamlıbel Tarlası, Çadır Höyük, and Çayyolu Höyük, which has also been 14C-dated, stratigraphically covers a long period of the 4th and early 3rd millennium B.C. It seems likely that an intensive occupation of Central Anatolia took place during this period and numerous settlements were newly founded there. Overall, there is evidence of a continuous development that extends into the early 3rd millennium B.C. Thus, it is very difficult to draw a clear boundary between Late Chalcolithic and Early Bronze Age. This exposes the problem created by archaeologists with periodisation, and consequently, artificially created time boundaries cannot always be easily reconciled with cultural developments, especially ceramic development. With the transition to the "Copper Age", striking changes become noticeable in the material culture. There are regional differences in pottery, which is not surprising given the size of Central Anatolia. These differences concern the composition of vessel forms at different sites (*cf.* Çayyolu, Çadır Höyük, Alişar), the occurrence of decoration (white painting, incised decoration) as well as the quality of pottery production (polishing, firing). In the case of a supra-regional integration, comparisons can be found in the west (Küllüoba) and southeast (Arslantepe, Tepecik), thus enabling a rough connection. Consequently, Central Anatolia can also be seen as a "bridge" for the period treated here – spanning the West and the Southeast. Moreover, at the same time, Karaz culture (echoes of Karaz pottery, Red-Black Burnished Ware, and others) seems to represent a periphery of the eastern cultural development in the late 4th and early 3rd millennium B.C.

and "Copper Age". However, it is not possible to present these in detail here. They will be discussed elsewhere. *Cf.* Yalçın 2011: map 1.

9 Here, too, the pottery has not been evaluated separately according to strata. For interpretation problems, see Schoop 2005a: 38–43.

Bibliography

Arslan, M., G. Ilgezdi Bertram and J.-K. Bertram

– 2013 "Çayyolu Höyük – Ankara'da Bir Geç Kalkolitik/İlk Tunç Çağ Yerleşmesi," *Anadolu/Anatolia* 39, pp. 139–164.

Bertram, J.-K.

– 2008 "Ahlatlıbel, Etiyokuşu, Koçumbeli – Zur Neubewertung der Ankara-Gruppe. Ahlatlıbel, Etiyokuşu, Koçumbeli – Ankara Çevresine Ait Bazı Buluntu Topluluklarının Yeniden Değerlendirilmesi," *TÜBA-AR* XI, pp. 73–84.

Bertram, J.-K. and G. İlgezdi Bertram

– 2018 "The Later Prehistory of the Ankara Region," In A. Batmaz, G. Bedianashvili, A. Michalewicz and A. Robinson (eds.), *Context and Connection. Studies on the Archaeology of the Ancient Near East in Honour of Antonio Sagona*, Orientalia Lovaniensia Analecta 268, Leuven/Paris/Bristol, pp. 847–865.

– 2020 "The Alişar 7M–11M/Ahlatlıbel/Çayyolu III-Horizon in Central Anatolia. A Reminiscence to H. H. von der Osten's "Copper Age"," In H. Gönül Yalçın and O. Stegemeier (eds.), *Metallurgica Anatolica. Festschrift für Ünsal Yalçın anlässlich seines 65. Geburtstags. Ünsal Yalçın 65. Yaşgünü Armağan Kitabı*, Bochum, pp. 99–110.

– 2021 *The Late Chalcolithic and Early Bronze Age in Central Anatolia. Introduction – Research*

History – Chronological Concepts – Sites, their Characteristics and Stratigraphies, İstanbul.

Bittel, K.
- 1934 *Prähistorische Forschung in Kleinasien*, Istanbul.

Delaporte, L.
- 1932 "Grabung am Hashüyük 1931," *Archäologischer Anzeiger 47*, pp. 230–233.

Efe, T., A. İlaslı and A. Topbaş
- 1996 "Salvage Excavations of the Afyon Archaeological Museum, Part 1: Kaklık Mevkii, a Site Transitional to the Early Bronze Age," *Studia Troica 5*, pp. 357–399.

Efe, T. and D. Ş. M. Ay
- 2000 "Early Bronze Age I Pottery from Küllüoba near Seyitgazi, Eskişehir," *Anatolia Antiqua* VIII, pp. 1–87.

Esin, U.
- 1979 "Tepecik Excavations, 1973," In *Keban Projesi 1973 Çalışmaları. Keban Project 1973 Activities. Orta Doğu Teknik Üniversitesi Keban Projesi Yayınları, Seri I. No. 6. Middle East Technical University Keban Project Publications, Series, I, No. 6*, Ankara, pp. 97–112.
- 1982 "Tepecik Excavations, 1974," In *Keban Projesi 1974–1975 Çalışmaları. Keban Project 1974–1975 Activities. Orta Doğu Teknik Üniversitesi Keban Projesi Yayınları, Seri I. No. 7. Middle East Technical University Keban Project Publications, Series, I, No. 7*, Ankara, pp. 95–118.

Fidan, E.
- 2012 "Küllüoba İlk Tunç Çağı Mimarisi," *Masrop E-Dergi 7*, pp. 1–44.

Frangipane, M.
- 2000 "The Late Chalcolithic / EB I Sequence at Arslantepe. Chronological and Cultural Remarks from a Frontier Site," In C. Marro and H. Hauptmann (eds.), *Chronologies des Pays du Caucase et de l'Euphrate aux IVe–IIIe Millénaires. From the Euphrates to the Caucasus: Chronologies for the 4th–3rd Millennium B.C. Vom Euphrat in den Kaukasus: Vergleichende Chronologie des 4. und 3. Jahrtausends v. Chr. Actes du Colloque d'Istanbul, 16–19 Décembre 1998. Varia Anatolica* XI, Istanbul, pp. 439–471.
- 2004 *Alle Origini del Potere. Arslantepe, la Collina dei Leoni*, Milano.
- 2017 "The Role of Metal Procurement in the Wide Interregional Connections of Arslantepe during the Late 4th–Early 3rd Millennia B.C.," In Ç. Maner, M. T. Horowitz and A. S. Gilbert (eds.), *Overturning Certainties in Near Eastern Archaeology. A Festschrift in Honor of K. Aslıhan Yener*, Leiden/Boston, pp. 186–210.

Gerber, C.
- 2008 "New Insights into the Settlement History of the Tavium Region (NW Part of the Yozgat Province)," In K. Strobel (ed.), *New Perspectives on the Historical Geography and Topography of Anatolia in the II and I Millenium B.C.*, Firenze, pp. 189–234.

Gülçur, S.
- 2012 "The Chalcolithic Period in Central Anatolia Aksaray-Niğde Region," *Origini* XXIV, *Nuova Serie* V, X–XX, pp. 213–227.

Hacar, A.
- 2020 "Orta Torosların Kuzey Sınırında Orta-Geç Kalkolitik Geçiş Süreci: Ubaid-İlişkili (?) Etkiler. Middle-Late Chalcolithic Transitional Period in the Northern Margin of the Central Taurus: Ubaid-Related (?) Effects," *TÜBA-AR* 26, pp. 27–43.

Koşay, H. Z.
- 1968 "Kuşsaray (Çorum) Sondajı," *Türk Arkeoloji Dergisi* XV/I, pp. 89–97.

Miyake, Y.
- 1992 "The Chalcolithic Period in Central Anatolia: Questions in Chronology Looking from the General Surveys (in Japanese)," *AAS* I, pp. 195–223.

Oğuz, R.
- 1933 "Anadolu Arkeologya Tarihinde Alişar Hafriyatı," *Türk Tarih, Arkeologya ve Etnografya Dergisi. Sayı 1*, Temmuz 1933, pp. 22–63.

Orthmann, W.
- 1963 *Die Keramik der Frühen Bronzezeit aus Inneranatolien*, Berlin.

Palumbi, G.
- 2008 *The Red and Black. Social and Cultural Interaction between the Upper Euphrates and the Southern Caucasus Communities in the Fourth and Third Millennium B.C.*, Roma.

Schoop, U.-D.
- 2005a *Das anatolische Chalkolithikum. Eine chronologische Untersuchung zur vorbronzezeitlichen Kultursequenz im nördlichen Zentralanatolien und den angrenzenden Gebieten*, Remshalden.
- 2005b "Early Chalcolithic in North-Central Anatolia: The Evidence from Boğazköy-

Büyükkaya. Kuzey-Orta Anadolu'da İlk Kalkolitik Çağ: Boğazköy-Büyükkaya Verileri," *TÜBA-AR* 8, pp. 15–37.
– 2011 "Çamlıbel Tarlası, ein metallverararbeitender Fundplatz des vierten Jahrtausends v. Chr. im nördlichen Zentralanatolien," In Ü. Yalçın (ed.), *Anatolian Metal* V, Bochum, pp. 53–68.
Schoop, U.-D., P. Grave, L. Kealhofer and G. Jacobsen
– 2009 "Radiocarbon Dates from Chalcolithic Çamlıbel Tarlası," *Archäologischer Anzeiger* 2009/1, pp. 66–67.
Steadman, S.R., J.C. Ross, G. McMahon and R.L. Gorny
– 2008 "Excavations on the North-Central Plateau: The Chalcolithic and Early Bronze Age Occupation at Çadır Höyük," *Anatolian Studies* 58, pp. 47–86.
Strobel, K. and C. Gerber
– 2007 "Tavium (Büyüknefes, Provinz Yozgat) – Bericht über die Kampagnen 2003–2005," *Istanbuler Mitteilungen* 57, pp. 547–621.
– 2010 "Tavium (Büyüknefes, Provinz Yozgat) und seine Region. Bericht über die Kampagnen 2006–2009," *Istanbuler Mitteilungen* 60, pp. 291–338.
Thissen, L.
– 1993 "New Insights in Balkan-Anatolian Connections in the Late Chalcolithic: Old Evidence from the Turkish Black Sea Littoral," *Anatolian Studies* 43, pp. 207–237.
Topbaş, A., T. Efe and A. İlaslı
– 1998 "Salvage Excavations of the Afyon Archaeological Museum, Part 2: The Settlement of Karaoğlan Mevkii and the Early Bronze Age Cemetery of Kaklık Mevkii," *Anatolia Antiqua. Eski Anadolu* VI, pp. 21–94.
Türker, A.
– 2014 "Devret Höyük 2013 Yılı Kazısı ve İlk Sonuçlar," *36. Kazı Sonuçları Toplantısı 1. Cilt*, pp. 363–382.
Ünal, A.
– 1968 "1966 Çengeltepe (Yozgat) Sondajı Önraporu," *Türk Arkeoloji Dergisi* XV/1, pp. 119–142.
von der Osten, H.H.
– 1937 *The Alishar Hüyük Seasons of 1930–32. Part I*, OIP 28, Chicago.
Yalçın, H.G.
– 2011 "Die Karaz-Kultur in Ostanatolien," in Ü. Yalçın (ed.), *Anatolian Metal* V, Bochum, pp. 31–51.
Yalçın, H.G. and Ü. Yalçın
– 2019 "Derekutuğun Madenci Yerleşmesi Kalkolitik Çağ Çanak Çömleği," in P. Çaylı, I. Demirtaş and B. Eser (eds.), *Arkeolojiyle Geçen Yarım Asır: Sevil Gülçur Armağanı. Half a Century Dedicated to Archaeology: A Festschrift in Honor of Sevil Gülçur*, Ankara, pp. 263–280.

<table>
<tr><th colspan="2">Alişar Stratigraphy</th><th rowspan="2">von der Osten 1937</th><th colspan="3">Orthmann 1963</th></tr>
<tr><th>Mound</th><th>Terrace</th><th colspan="2">Periodisation</th><th>Characteristics</th></tr>
<tr><td>5 M</td><td>12 T</td><td rowspan="2">Early Bronze Age</td><td colspan="2">Übergangszeit</td><td></td></tr>
<tr><td>6 M</td><td>---</td><td>b</td><td>FBZ 3</td><td>Beginning of Cappadocian ware</td></tr>
<tr><td>7 M</td><td>---</td><td rowspan="5">Copper Age</td><td>a</td><td>FBZ 3</td><td>Intermediate ware, depas-like vessels</td></tr>
<tr><td>8 M</td><td rowspan="4">13 T
14 T</td><td colspan="2" rowspan="4">FBZ 2</td><td rowspan="4">Red Alişar Ib-ware, painted pottery</td></tr>
<tr><td>9 M</td></tr>
<tr><td>10 M</td></tr>
<tr><td>11 M</td></tr>
<tr><td>12 M</td><td>---</td><td rowspan="8">Chalcolithic</td><td rowspan="3">b</td><td rowspan="8">FBZ 1</td><td rowspan="8">Fruit stands and others</td></tr>
<tr><td>13 M</td><td>---</td></tr>
<tr><td>14 M</td><td>---</td></tr>
<tr><td>15 M</td><td>---</td><td rowspan="5">a</td></tr>
<tr><td>16 M</td><td>---</td></tr>
<tr><td>17 M</td><td>---</td></tr>
<tr><td>18 M</td><td>---</td></tr>
<tr><td>19 M</td><td>---</td></tr>
</table>

Table 1. Characterisation of the Alişar stratigraphy (von der Osten 1937; Orthmann 1963: 14–21, 68–69). FBZ = Early Bronze Age; Übergangszeit = Transitional period.

Fig. 1. Alişar Höyük: Present-day view to the north with the "terrace" in the foreground.

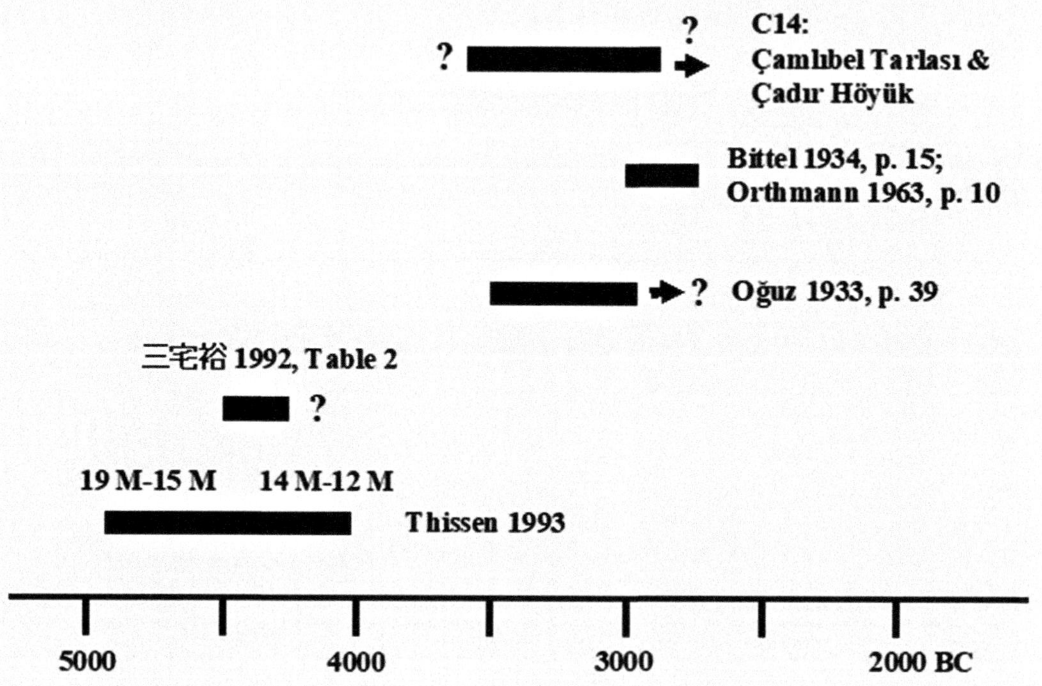

Fig. 2. Dating proposals for the "Chalcolithic" of H. H. von der Osten (1937).

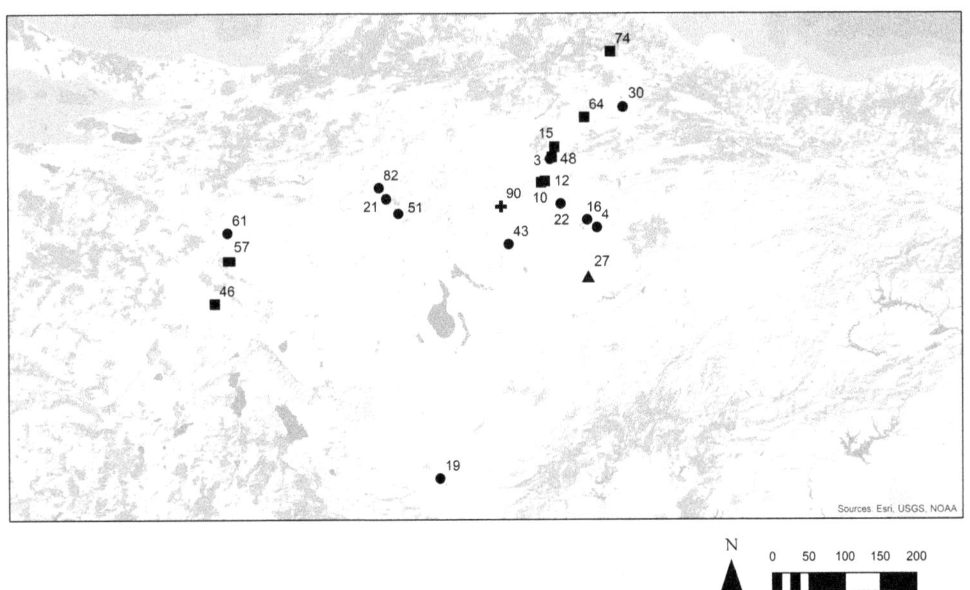

Fig. 3. Important sites (excavations and important suface material) of the Late Chalcolithic and Early Bronze Age I. Numbers correspond to Table 9 in Bertram and İlgezdi Bertram 2021. Höyüks excavated (circles): (3) Alaca Höyük, (4) Alişar, (16) Çadır Höyük, (19) Canhasan, (21) Çayyolu, (22) Çengeltepe, (30) Devret Höyük, (43) Hashöyük, (51) Karaoğlan Höyük, (61) Küllüoba, and (82) Sincan Höyük II; Höyük surveyed (triangle): (27) Çokumağıl (Esentepe); Flat/hilltop settlements excavated (squares): (10) Boğazköy/Çamlıbel Tarlası, (12) Boğazköy/Yarıkkaya, (15) Büyük Güllücek ?, (46) Kaklık Mevkii, (48) Kalınkaya-Toptaştepe, (64) Kuşsaray, and (74) Oymaağaç; Flat/hilltop settlement surveyed (cross): (90) Yeniyapan; Burials (rectangle): (57) Keçiçayırı (Terrace).

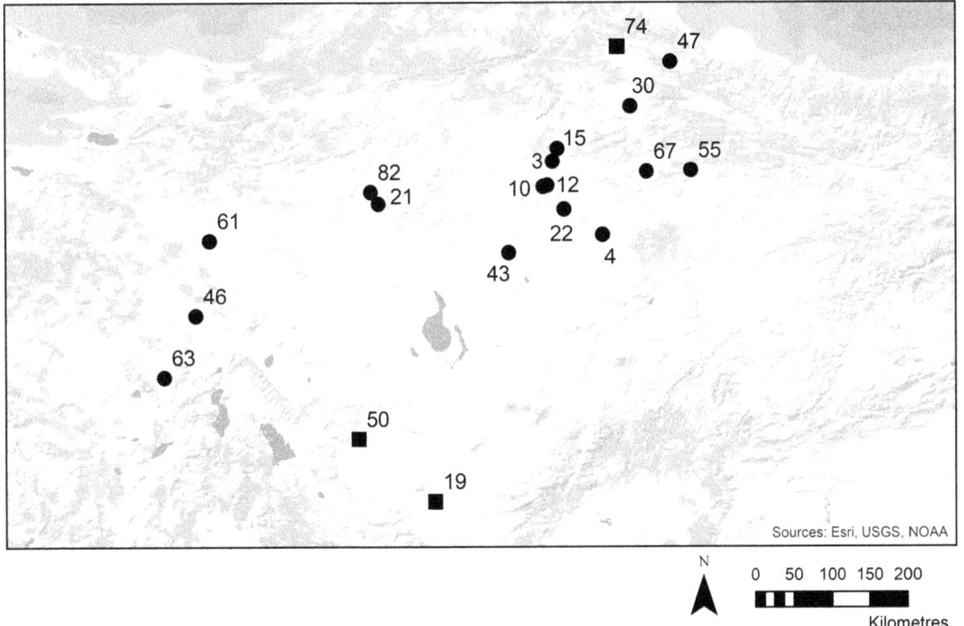

Fig. 4. Sites with Chalcolithic/Early Bronze Age I occupation on virgin soil and after an occupation hiatus. On virgin soil (circles): (3) Alaca Höyük, (4) Alişar, (10) Çamlıbel Tarlası, (12) Yarıkkaya, (15) Büyük Güllücek, (21) Çayyolu, (22) Çengeltepe, (30) Devret Höyük, (43) Hashöyük, (46) Kaklık Mevkii, (47) Kaledoruğu/Kavak, (55) Kayapınar, (61) Küllüoba, (63) Kusura, (67) Maşat Höyük, and (82) Sincan Höyük II; After hiatus (squares): (19) Canhasan, (50) Karahöyük (Konya), and (74) Oymaağaç.

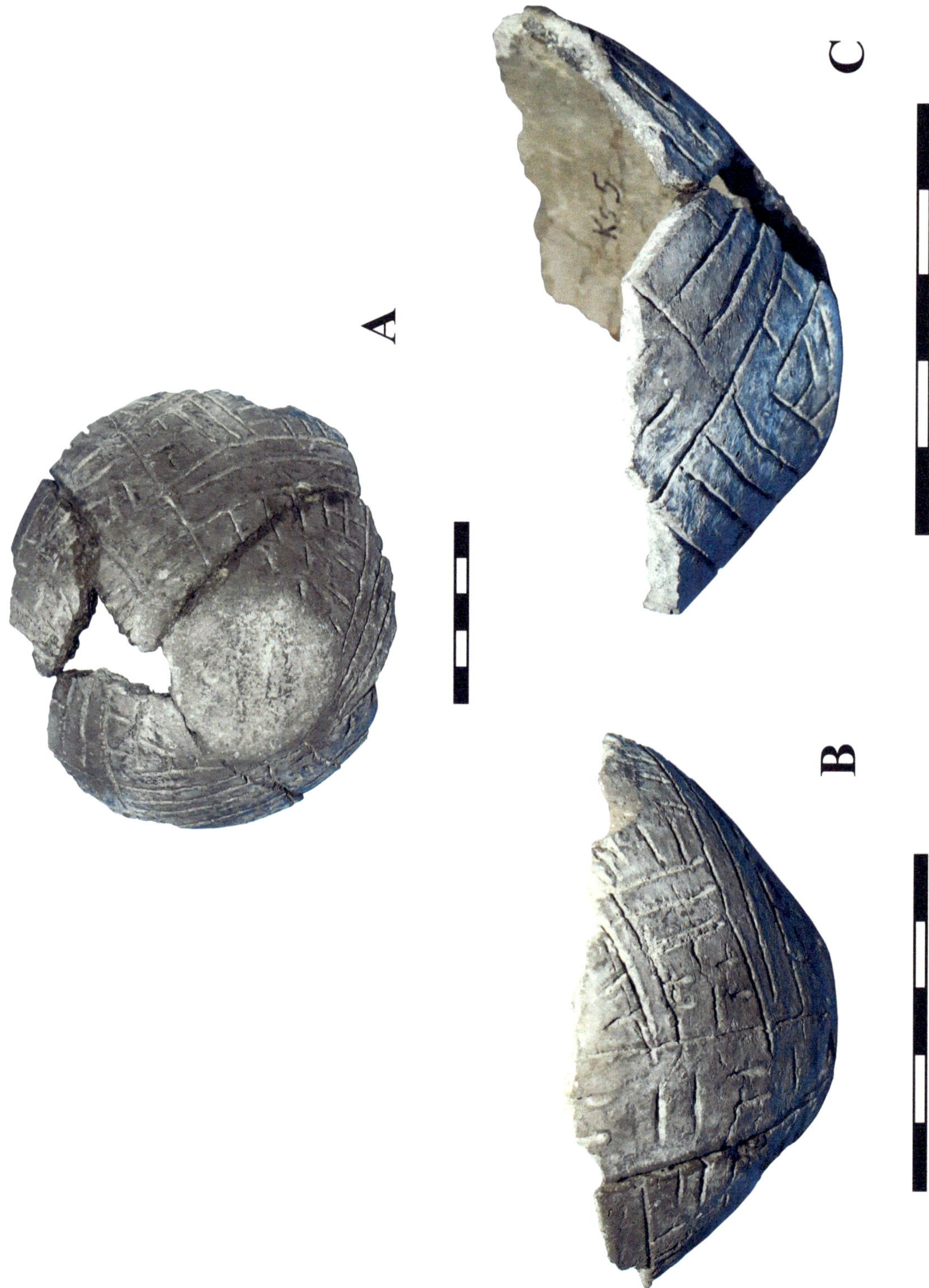

Fig. 5. Kuşsaray: Incised vessel fragment (Çorum Museum, inv. no. 5-450-68 448).

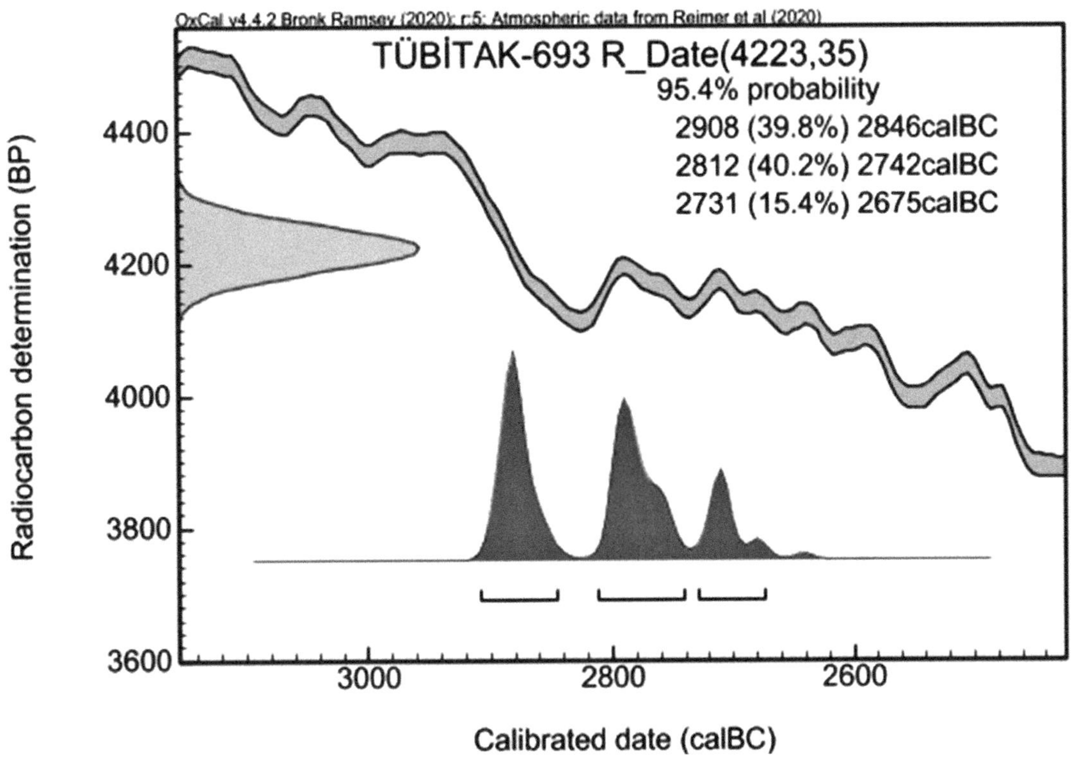

Fig. 6. Çayyolu Höyük: 14C-date for layer 13 (TÜBİTAK-693). Sample material: animal bone. Calibration with OxCal 4.4.2.

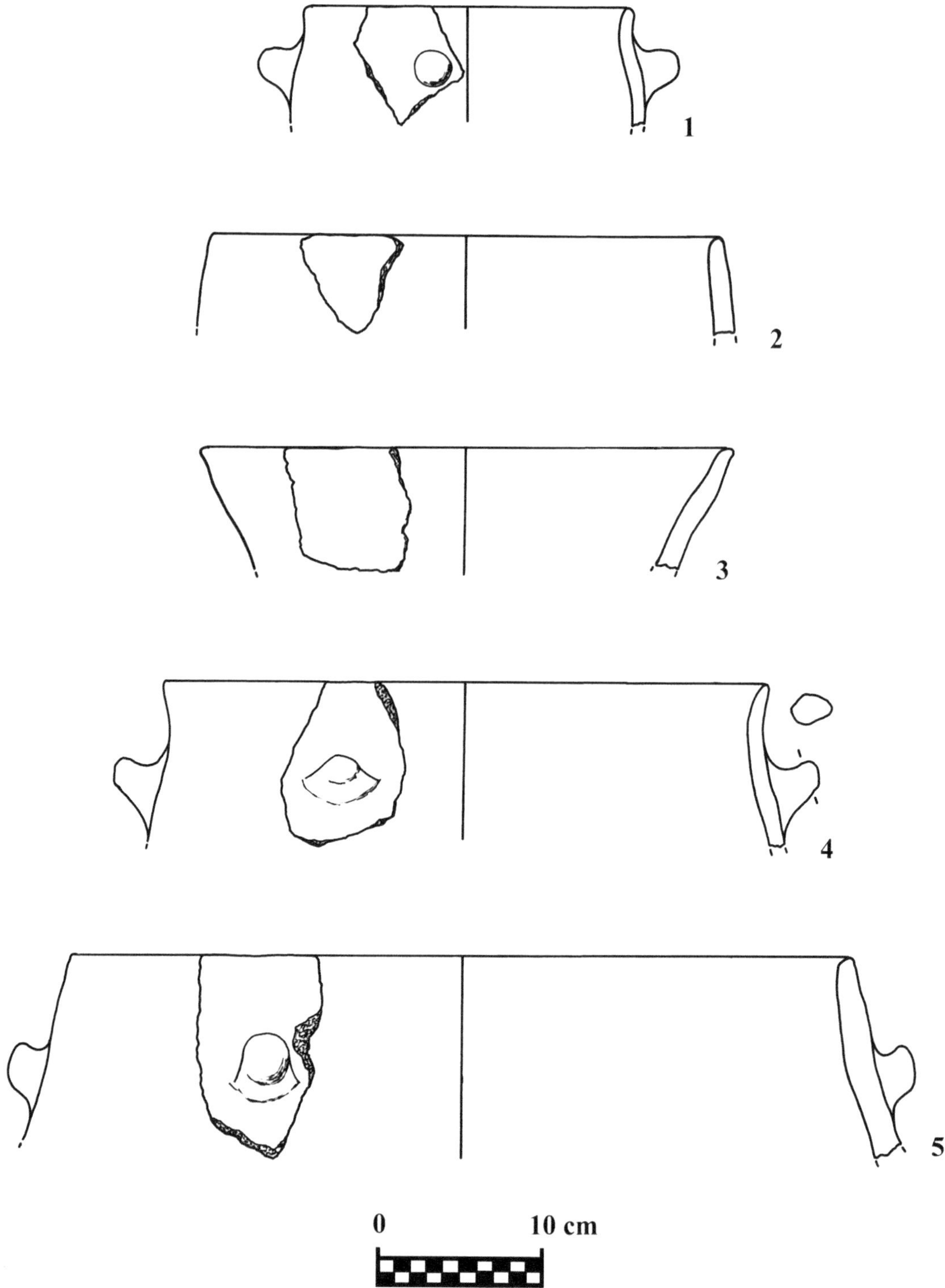

Fig. 7. Çayyolu Höyük: Pottery from trench H9, layer 40.

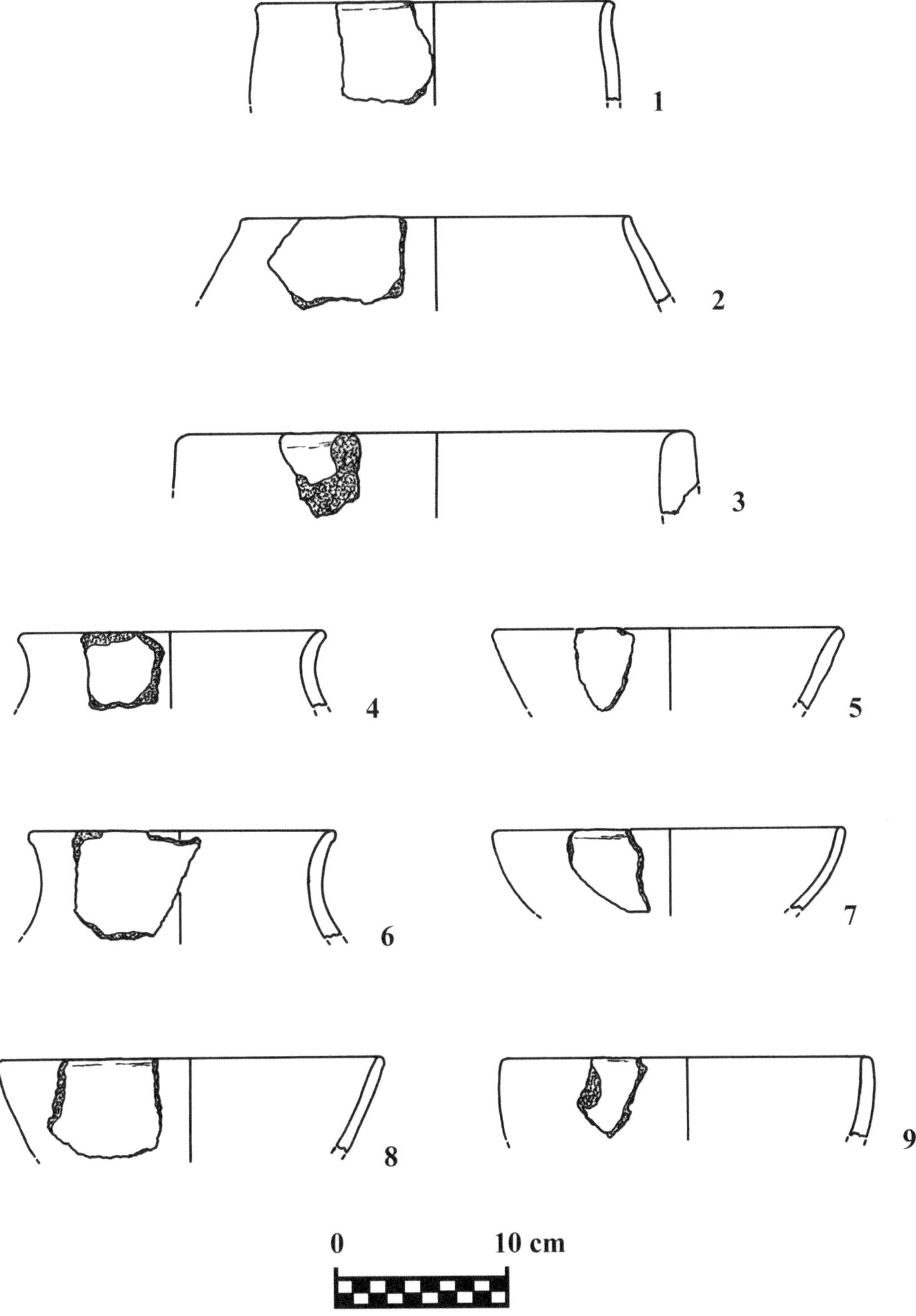

Fig. 8. Çayyolu Höyük: Pottery from trench H9, layer 19.

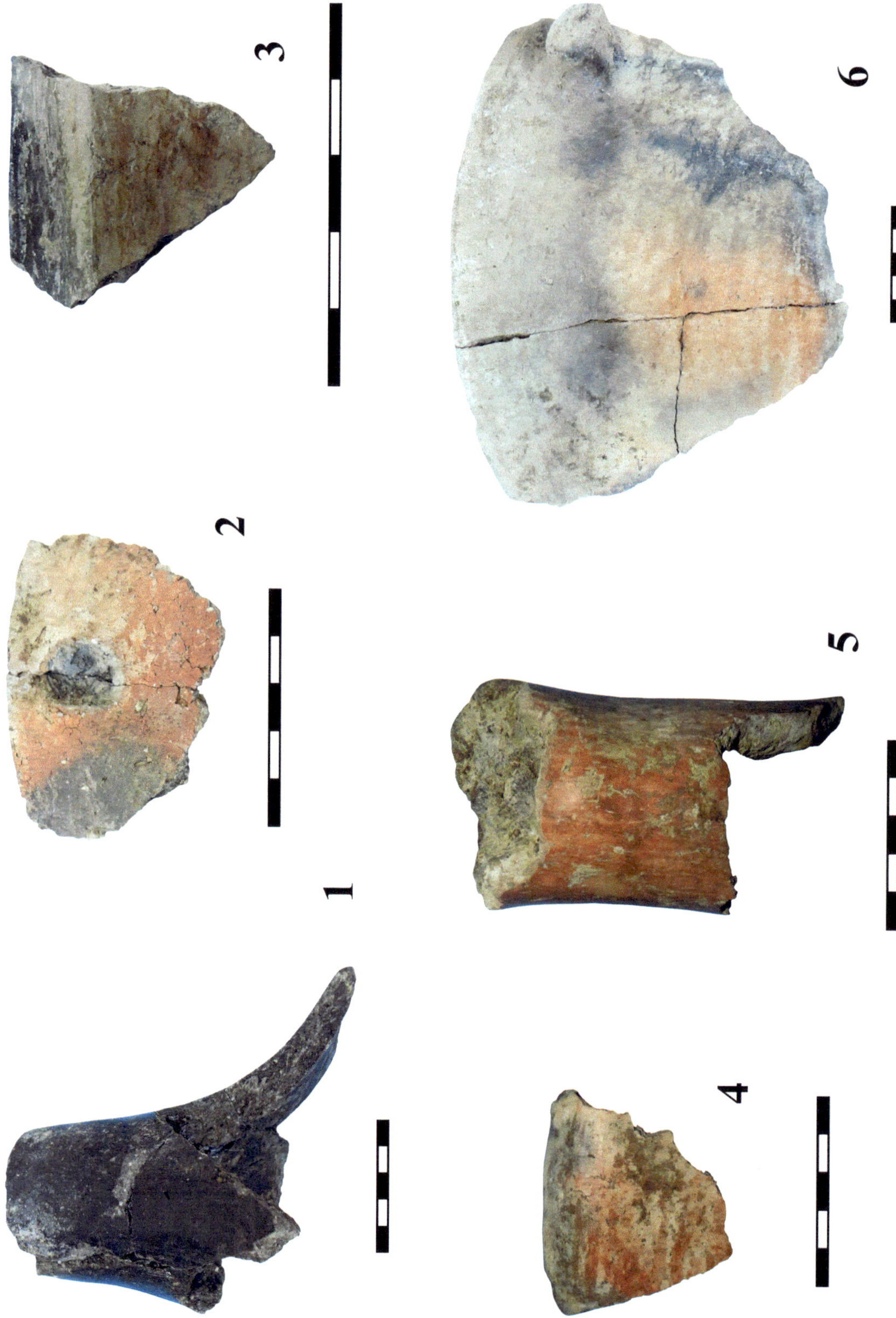

Fig. 9. Çayyolu Höyük. Pottery from trench H9: 1 – Layer 26 (foot of a fruit stand); 2 – Layer 26 (rim sherd); 3 – Layer 24 (rim sherd of a fruit stand ?); 4 – Layer 30 (rim sherd of a fruit stand ?); 5 – Layer 30 (part of foot of a fruit stand); 6 – Layer 28 (rim sherd).

Social and Technological Transitions and Black Iron Age Glass Beads from Kaman- Kalehöyük, Central Anatolia

*Julian Henderson, Simon Chenery and Kimiyoshi Matsumura**

Abstract

The clear socio-economic changes that occurred as a result of the collapse of the Late Bronze Age palatial economies across Mesopotamia, Egypt, Anatolia and Greece saw the emergence of smaller socio-economic units with the associated disruption of connections across these areas including trade networks. The scientific analysis of 19 mainly 9th–4th century B.C. 'black' (mainly deep translucent brown) glass beads from Kaman has revealed a wide range of different glasses were used: wood ash, plant ash, natron and soda-rich borate types. We suggest that production of these glasses (and beads) occurred in several different places. There is evidence for technological continuity and innovation with new raw materials at this time of socio-economic change. The use of lead-tin oxide as an opacifier – to produce yellow decorative glass – is amongst the earliest in the world. We discuss possible links between iron technology and the use of iron as a glass colorant.

Öz

Geç Tunç Çağı'nda Mezopotamya, Mısır, Anadolu ve Yunanistan'da saray ekonomilerinin çöküşünün bir sonucu olarak meydana gelen belirgin sosyo-ekonomik değişiklikler, daha küçük sosyo-ekonomik birimlerin ortaya çıkmasına ve buna bağlı olarak ticaret ağları da dahil olmak üzere bu alanlar arasındaki bağlantıların bozulmasına yol açmıştır. Kaman-Kalehöyük'te bulunan, çoğunlukla MÖ 9.–4. yüzyıllara tarihlenen siyah (çoğunlukla koyu yarı saydam kahverengi) 19 cam boncuğun bilimsel analizi, çok çeşitli camların kullanıldığını ortaya çıkarmıştır: odun külü, natron ve soda bakımından zengin borat türleri. Bu camların (ve boncukların) üretiminin birkaç farklı yerde gerçekleştiğini öne sürmekteyiz. Sosyo-ekonomik değişimin yaşandığı bu dönemde teknolojik süreklilik ve yeni hammaddelerle yenilik yapıldığına dair kanıtlar mevcuttur. Sarı dekoratif cam üretmek için kurşun-kalay oksidin opaklaştırıcı olarak kullanılması dünyadaki en eski uygulamalar arasındadır. Bu makalede demir teknolojisi ile demirin cam renklendirici olarak kullanımı arasındaki olası bağlantıları tartışmaktadır.

Introduction

The early Iron Age in Anatolia was a period that saw substantial socio-economic changes following the collapse of the Hittite empire. It is apparent that there was increasing decentralisation with the emergence of smaller social units following a period of socio-economic crisis (Silberman and Bauer 2012: 467) brought about by drought and crop failures starting at the end of the Late Bronze Age, beginning c. end of the 13th century B.C. (Kaniewski *et al.* 2019). Such radical changes in society could potentially disrupt the supply of raw materials for the production of material culture, such as for pottery, glass and metal objects. At the same time the social changes may have generated the possibility of accessing new raw material sources with associated experimentation and innovation while there may have been a level of continuity. Technological continuity might partly depend on the continued presence of specialist craftsmen with the right technical knowledge

* Professor of Archaeological Science, Department of Classics and Archaeology, University of Nottingham, julian.henderson@nottingham.ac.uk

who may even have been in a 'guild' as apparently was the case at Late Bronze Age Ugarit (Van Soldt 1995: 1260). Another aspect is the changing social and ritual values and meanings of material culture moving from the Late Bronze Age to the Early Iron Age. Centralised Mesopotamian glass production was heavily controlled by ritual, as described extensively and in great detail in cuneiform texts, some of which date to the Iron Age (Oppenheim *et al.* 1970; Schmidt 2019: 118–135).

A means of investigating the impact of such social changes in the Iron Age is by considering whether Late Bronze Age glass technology evolved or underwent radical changes. Such an investigation should be able to provide evidence of technological continuity and/or whether this was a time of flux with the introduction of new glass technologies and raw materials. A period of transition when the social and ritual value of material culture would have changed is certainly what might be anticipated, leading to 'new' technologies involving a period of experimentation.

However, there is clear scientific evidence that during the Late Bronze Age plant ashes were fused with crushed quartz or sand in Mesopotamia and Egypt respectively (Sayre and Smith 1961, Shortland *et al.* 2007, Walton *et al.* 2009, Henderson *et al.* 2010, Henderson 2013: 160). There is also possible archaeological evidence for glass making in Anatolia (Dardeniz 2018). Once fused, this plant ash glass was used by the Mesopotamians, Egyptians, Mycenaeans and Hittites for the manufacture of an impressive range of glass objects which were used in ritual, social and economic contexts (e.g. Hodgkinson 2018). Some glass was traded widely in ingot form (Pulak 2001). Generally, once Late Bronze Age glass technologists had established the techniques for fusing ashed plants with crushed quartz or sand, including using a wide range of mineral-based colorants, their energies became focused on the manufacture of often highly decorated objects. Nevertheless, although early glass objects of c. 16th–15th century B.C. date have been studied in detail (Jackson and Nicholson 2013, Kemp *et al.* 2020) we lack clear evidence of experimentation with raw materials, including colorants, which must have occurred during the early phases of glass production (Henderson 2013: 11–12). Moorey (2001) was of the opinion that the most important early phase of glass making was in the 1st quarter of the 2nd millennium B.C.E. However there is minimal evidence for glass at this time. By the 15th century B.C.E plant ash glass technology was 'fully-formed'.

Although plant ash glass continued to be used in the early 1st millennium B.C.E (Reade *et al.* 2005, Reade *et al.* 2009, Stapleton 2003, Brill 1999a: 18–24; Brill 1999b, 18–24, Gratuze 2009, Braun 1983, Conte *et al.* 2016a, Henderson *et al.* 2018, Conte *et al.* 2019), there is evidence in the Early Iron Age for the introduction of a different glass technology using a new mineral flux – natron. Therefore, it is likely that the radical changes in society had a knock-one effect and may have led to changes in glass technology, although this deserves careful consideration. There are several reasons for saying this, including the following. This is a fascinating time when Late Bronze Age palatial societies and their luxury good economy under elite control broke apart and smaller social units were formed with decentralised production (Sherratt and Sherratt 2001). Secondly we may be able to observe how changes in different technologies were modified and/or evolved over time.

By focussing on a single technology- glass- it becomes possible to examine such technological changes by using scientific analysis. One glass colour that was used in the Iron Age but was considerably less common in the Late Bronze Age, and which could potentially have involved the use of 'new' raw materials to make it, was 'black' glass. Although it appears 'black' a very thin sample of such glass shows that it is usually either a very dark translucent brown (or green) colour: no true ancient black glass exists. Significant scholarly attention has been paid to such glass when found in Roman contexts (e.g. Van der Linden *et al.* 2009; Cosyns 2011; Cagno *et al.* 2014; Ceglia *et al.* 2014), and with an increasing number of publications on earlier 'black' glass including Iron Age examples (Gratuze and Picon 2006; Reade *et al.* 2009; Conte *et al.* 2016a; Conte *et al.* 2016b; Conte *et al.* 2019).

These publications have provided evidence for the possible existence of the earliest use of wood ash to make the black glass beads, found at Chotin, Slovakia (Conte *et al.* 2016a). They have also shown that some of the earliest natron glass was also used to make black glass too (Gratuze and Picon 2006, Gratuze 2009, Reade *et al.* 2009 , Conte *et al.* 2016a). These early natron black beads have been found in France, Switzerland, Italy and Jordan. It has been suggested that they were made with an impure sand that contained heavy minerals, some iron-bearing, that imparted the dark colour to the glass. Undissolved minerals such as iron oxide/ iron spinels and feldspar have been observed using a scanning electron microscope by Conte *et al.* (2019). The presence of elevated concentrations of chromium, zirconium and thorium indicate the presence of chromites, zicons and monazites in the sand used to make the black glasses. Analysis of black glasses dating to the 7th–6th centuries B.C.E (Archaic period) from Torre Galli, Italy (Conte *et al.* 2019) showed that the manufacturers of these later glasses used purer raw materials, presumably as the glassmakers started to master their art.

This chapter focuses on one specific type of Iron Age 'black' glass object – a bead type decorated with trailed-on annulets ('eyes') in contrasting opaque white or yellow colours. Nineteen examples of black beads found in Iron Age contexts at Kaman-Kalehöyük have been chemically analysed so as to investigate the technologies used to make them. Here we will reflect on the extent to which their chemical compositions provide evidence for a technological transition and/ or experimentation at a time of social change. We will also consider where the glass used for making the beads was manufactured (primary production)- which may not be the same place as where the beads themselves were made in secondary workshops.

Black Glass Beads

Globular or sub-triangular 'black' glass beads with trailed-on opaque white or yellow (annular) 'eye' decorations are quite widely distributed across Europe with other examples also having been discovered in the Middle East. An important place to start when searching for *comporanda* is the volume by Spaer (2001: 79–81), which will be difficult to supersede. Spaer dates the appearance of these beads to the second half of the 9th century to the 7th century B.C.E. She observes that while almost all are of a very dark brown translucent hue, very dark blue (broken) examples have also been found. Spaer also notes that these beads are the most common glass find of Iron Age date (in the Middle East) and are therefore important. They have been found in Sinai, the Syro-Palestinian area, Cyprus, the Aegean (where at Lindos alone, 133 black examples with 'eyes' were found) and Turkey ('Asia Minor'). There is limited information about finds from Mesopotamia and they have not been found in Egypt. Haevernick (1953: Taf. 1) described examples from Hallstatt B (c. 1300–750B.C.E) contexts at Allendorf, Germany. Purowski *et al.* (2012) report a single 'black' glass with high iron from a Hallstatt D (600–400 B.C.E) context with a natron composition. Spaer (2001) noted that Europe could be a possible production area for black eye beads.

No examples of this bead type are noted by Venclová (1990) in her detailed discussion of beads found in Bohemia or by Guido (1978) in her book on glass beads found in Britain and Ireland. Nevertheless, Gratuze (2009) notes that annular and globular black beads with linear and eye decoration have been found on several mainly Iron Age sites in France and Switzerland. Large numbers of examples of black eye beads have been found in southern Europe, especially, it seems in Italy at Bologna and Cumae. Others have been found in the Slovakia (Conte *et al.* 2016a). Some have been found in contexts as late as the 5th century.

The 19 Kaman-Kalehöyük examples of black glass almost all date to the Iron Age. The samples are mainly the eye beads described above. However, 4 other decorated black bead types have been included for comparison: wave decorated, zig-zag decorated, band decorated and a ribbed bead (Table 1). A bead decorated with opaque white bands (KAM 145) may date to the Hittite period (phase IIIa).

Three were found in phase IIc (9th–8th centuries), the start of IIc has been dated to 890–860 B.C.E (Omori and Nakamura 2007) and 13 in phase IIa (7th–4th centuries). A single sample appears to date to 1600–1400 B.C.E, the Hittite period though it is possible it fell out of the baulk. A surface find, derives from the Yüzey part of the site. KAM121 was redeposited in an Ottoman context, Ia (see Table 1). An example of one of the beads found at Kaman-Kalehöyük is shown in Figure 1.

Scientific Analysis

Two scientific techniques were used to investigate 19 black glass beads from Kaman: electron probe microanalysis (EPMA) to determine major and minor oxides and laser ablation inductively coupled plasma mass spectrometry (LA-ICP-MS) to determine trace elements. Microsamples (1–2mm) were removed from the beads by percussion. The samples were mounted in epoxy resin blocks and polished to a 0.25 µm diamond paste finish so as to reveal unweathered glass.

Electron probe microanalysis (EPMA)

The blocks were carbon coated so as to prevent surface charging and the distortion of the electron beam during analysis. A JEOL JXA-8200 electron microprobe in the Nano and Microscale Research Centre in Nottingham University was used to analyse the glass samples. The system is equipped with four wavelength-dispersive spectrometers, a single energy-dispersive spectrometer and both secondary- and back-scattered detectors. A defocused electron beam with a diameter of 50µm was used so as to prevent volatilisation of light elements such as sodium. The probe was run at an accelerating voltage of 20 kV and a beam current of 40nA. Emitted X-rays were counted for 20 seconds for peaks (100s for magnesium) and 10 seconds for background (20s for magnesium). The system was calibrated with a mixture of mineral and metal standards. Accuracy and precision of both sets of analyses have been checked by comparing them with Corning B standard analyses, which was analysed at the start and at the end of each analytical session, for a total of ten for the first set of analyses, and twenty-two for the second set. Averaged values for Corning B and our measured values plus accuracy and standard deviations are reported in Appendix C for both sets of analyses, together with the standard deviation for each element. The precisions of SiO_2, Al_2O_3, Na_2O, K_2O, CaO, MgO, FeO, MnO and CuO are ideal (RSD<5 %). For minor elements, the RSD is above 5 % but below 20 % aside from V_2O_5 in the first set. In the second set, the precision of all fore-mentioned major oxides is ideal (RSD<5 %), except TiO_2. For minor elements, the RSDs are above 5 % but below 20 %, apart from SnO_2, BaO, NiO, CoO, and V_2O_5. For the majority of oxides, the measured value was within 20 % of the quoted value for both the first and second sets of analyses, and most are much lower, and therefore the values can be considered acceptable. Overall, for four oxides (PbO, BaO, V_2O_5, and SO_3) the error is in excess of this level and these results have to be considered as a semi-quantitative; BaO and V_2O_5 were close to minimum levels of detection or not detected. The following elements were sought but not detected in the first set: SnO_2 and As_2O_5.

Laser-ablation inductively coupled plasma mass spectrometry (LA-ICP-MS)

The same blocks of glass samples prepared for EMPA were used for LA-ICP-MS analysis. Prior to LA-ICP-MS analysis the samples were cleaned by rubbing a tissue soaked in dilute acid over the surface for a few seconds. The laser ablation unit was a NewWave (Electro Scientific Industries, Inc.) UP193 nm excimer system at the British Geological Survey, Keyworth, UK. The sample block was placed in a simple single

Table 1: Samples of black glass analysed with excavation details and dated phase in the last column; IIIa =1600–1400 CE; IIc=900–700 CE; IIa=700–400 CE; 1a=17th–16th centuries CE

Sıra No		Sector No	Date	Grid No	PL	Remarks	Year Number	Dating
1	Kam 36	Kuzey XXV	95 06 27	XLII-53 (58)	(PL 3) R94 Kaldırma	triangular	95001863	IIa
2	Kam 41	Kuzey XV	05 08 15	XXXVI-52(5)	PL 74	half	05000740	IIc
3	Kam 43	Kuzey XXV	03 06 25	XLIII-52(59)	PL12 (P2223-P1881)	wave dec	03001356	IIa
4	Kam 46	Güney LV	97 07 01	LXI-51(84)	PL10 -PL12	eye fallen out	97000381	IIa
5	Kam 48	Kuzey XV	03 06 27	XXXVI-52(5)	PL 51	half	03001357	IIa
6	Kam 53	Kuzey IV	87 08 12	XXXIX-54(G)	PL 16	half	87000647 (KL87–183)	IIa
7	Kam 54	Kuzey III	87 06 29	XLI-55(D)	PL 22	broken	87000532 (KL87–68)	IIa
8	Kam 62	Kuzey XXV	99 08 02	XLII-52(57)	PL 31		99000457 (KL99–109)	IIc
9	Kam 64	Kuzey XVIII	99 09 17	XXXVIII-57(18)	PL 24		99001724	IIa
10	Kam 65	Kuzey XIX	99 08 09	XXXVII-57(24)	PL 10		99001725	IIa
11	Kam 66	Kuzey XXVI	99 07 05	XLV-52(63)	PL 15 (P1859)		9900449	IIc
12	Kam 121						89002244	1a
13	Kam 131	Kuzey XV	94 06 27	XXXVII-52(7)	PL 15a		94000043	IIa
14	Kam 133	Surface find	90 08 27				90000818	(Surface)
15	Kam 141	Kuzey XIV	92 07 15	XXXIX-53(4)	5a	half	92001059	IIa
16	Kam 142	Kuzey XV	99 08 19	XXXVII-52(7)	26 (P2192)	bicone oy zig zag dec	99000493	IIa
17	Kam 145	Kuzey IV	89 06 29	XXXIX-55(H)	35	half ow bands	89001443	IIIa
18	Kam 164	Kuzey XXV	95 06 28	XLII-53 (58)	4	eyes round horn	95000552	IIa
19	Kam 165	Kuzey XIV	97 07 17	XXXIX-53(4)	8	ribbed op yellow trails	97003602	IIa

volume ablation cell with a 0.8 L min–1 He flow. In addition to the sample block, NIST glass standards SRM610 and 612 were placed in the chamber. The laser was normally fired at 10 Hz for 40 s using a beam diameter of 70 μm. Fluence and irradiance as measured by the internal monitor were typically 3 J/cm2 and 0.85 GW/cm2 respectively. Prior to introduction into the ICP-MS the He flow was mixed, via a Y-junction, with a 0.85 L min^{-1} Ar and 0.004 L min^{-1} N_2 gas flows supplied by a Cetac Aridus desolvating nebuliser. The Aridus allowed introduction of ICPMS tuning solutions and optimisation of the Aridus sweep gas (nominal 4 L min^{-1} Ar). During solid analysis by the laser, the Aridus only aspirated air. The ICP-MS used in this study was an Agilent 7500cs series instrument. The instrument was set for the 47 isotopes of interest, the dwell time for each isotope was 10 ms giving an integration time of 0.5s per time slice. Data were collected in a continuous time resolved analysis (TRA) fashion. Prior to laser firing a period of at least 120 s of 'gas blank' was collected, then 3 ablations being made on the SRM610; 3 ablations on the SRM612; 3 ablations on up to 8 samples and finally 3 ablations on the SRM610. The SRM610 was used to calibrate the system whilst the SRM612 was used as a quality control (QC) material. All calculations and data reduction were performed manually in Excel spreadsheets. The precision of most elements was typically good for both sessions (<5 RSD %), while the accuracies for most the elements ranged between -2 and +1 %, which are considered within the range of quantitative results notable exceptions were P, K and Ti with poorer accuracy and precision (>10 %).

The Variety of Glass Types Used to Make Kaman-Kalehöyük Black Glasses

As noted elsewhere, these black glasses can have quite a wide range of chemical compositions (Conte *et al.* 2016a). These examples from Kaman-Kalehöyük are no exception. A simple plot of weight % magnesium oxide versus potassium oxide provides evidence of this. The plotted points for Kaman-Kalehöyük black glasses in Fig. 2 have, for the sake of simplicity, been assigned to four groups according the relative levels of these two oxides (and others -see below). The first with the lowest magnesium oxide concentrations of below 1.33 % are mainly 'natron' glasses.

However even here there are examples of 'natron' glass that contain 1.14, 1.52 and 2.5 % potassium oxide. One explanation for this is that a potassium feldspar impurity in the sand has caused the potassium oxide level to increase. The natron glasses contain variable sodium oxide levels of between 14.7 and 21.6 %, low levels of phosphorus pentoxide (<0.2 %) and all contain low levels of calcium oxide (1.8–3.9 %). The use of sands with heavy mineral impurities to make these black glasses has introduced high levels of titanium oxide (<0.5 %), iron oxide (6.9–12.6 %) and highly variable alumina (1.0–10.1 %). Although the deep translucent coloration is mainly due to high iron levels a single example contains 1.4 % manganese oxide which may therefore have rendered the glass a deep purple colour. KAM142, a bead decorated with opaque yellow zig-zags contains 2.5 % potassium oxide and a high manganese oxide (1.395 %) concentration. It also contains a much lower level of iron oxide than the other natron glasses. The opaque yellow glass is opacified with lead-tin oxide (see below). The bead with a natron composition from a possible Hittite context (KAM145) has a decorative band rather than an eye.

The second group (labelled 'borate glass' in Fig. 2) contains between 1.63 % and 3.04 % magnesium oxide and between 1.0 % and 1.9 % K_2O. These glasses contain sufficient magnesium oxide to be classified as a plant ash glass but their potassium oxide levels, mainly between 1 % and 1.54 %, suggest that they are not typical plant ash glasses. Normally, plant ash glasses contain significantly higher concentrations of between about 1.5 and 5 % potassium oxide (Conte *et al.* 2016a; Henderson *et al.* 2018). Indeed, a recent study of 9th–8th century glasses from Must Farm, UK (Henderson *et al.* 2024) has revealed that glasses with elevated magnesium but relatively low potassium contain 'high' concentrations of boron; all these glasses from Kaman-Kalehöyük contain high levels of boron and are best classified as borate glasses. As suggested by Van Ham-Meet *et al.* (2019), the elevated magnesium oxide and slightly elevated potassium oxide levels could have been introduced in the glass due to magnesium and potassium occuring in borate deposits formed in hot springs. However, there are three 'natron' glasses and one plant ash glass which contain high boron levels. The situation is therefore complex and these high boron glasses will be considered in more detail in a forthcoming paper.

Plant ash glasses in Fig. 2 are defined according to their relative levels of magnesium oxide and potassium oxide, as originally defined by Sayre and Smith (1961). All four have relatively high soda levels for a plant ash glass of up to 18.3 %. As already noted one has an elevated boron content which probably results from the plant growing on a borate deposit (Brill and Stapleton 2012). All but one of these glasses contain positively correlated magnesium and calcium oxide (3.1–5.3 %) concentrations as discussed in more detail below suggesting that dolomitic limestone was added as a third ingredient to the sand and plant ash. The relatively impure sands used would have introduced 1.9–3.7 % aluminium oxide and 0.9–3.1 % iron oxide to the glass; the glasses contain between 0.1 and 0.3 weight % copper oxide and very low manganese oxide close to the lowest level of detection (c. 0.1 % weight) or not detected. KAM43, of a plant ash composition, is wave decorated.

The 'wood ash' glasses contain high potassium oxide levels, three with between 6 % and 8 % weight. These three also contain quite high sodium oxide levels of between 15.4 and 17.7 weight %. These glasses although labelled as 'wood ash' glass (which they may well be) can therefore be defined as mixed-alkali. They could have been made as a result of (1) mixing soda-rich and potassium-rich raw materials, (2) the use of plant or more likely wood ashes containing mixed sodium and potassium or (3) the addition of potassium and iron-rich slags (Gratuze 2009) which would also introduce a range of other elements. All contain moderate levels of calcium oxide (5.1–6.6 weight %) and along with the plant ash glasses contain higher phosphorus pentoxide than detected in the 'natron' and borate glasses. The matrices of the beads contain quite high iron oxide of between 1.6 % and 2.9 % causing a dark translucent colour; one glass bead (KAM46) which contains 2.9 % iron oxide also contains 3.1 % manganese oxide. It is therefore possibly a deep translucent purple colour. KAM165 of this 'wood ash' composition is ribbed and decorated with opaque yellow trails. The other beads of this composition are eye beads.

KAM165 contains high lead and tin oxides and is therefore a rare example of the early use of lead-tin oxide as an opacifier. It is especially intriguing because the glass itself has a mixed-alkali composition. It appears to be the first example of such a glass. Other rare early examples have been found in Poland (Purowski *et al.* 2012) and Turkey (Van Ham-Meert *et al.* 2019) with 6th-4th century B.C.E examples decorating high potassium glass beads from the Kizil cemetery, Xinjiang (Li *et al.* 2014, table 1, Fig. 7, Henderson *et al.* 2018b). Tin opacified glasses become increasingly more common from around the 2nd century B.C.E in Europe (Henderson 1985; Matin 2018).

Although in Fig. 3 plant ash and borate glasses occupy overlapping spaces there are some key compositional characteristics that provide distinctions between the other glasses plotted. Most 'natron' glasses contain low calcium oxide levels (>3 %). The plot of borate glasses provides a strong positive correlation between the magnesium and calcium oxides (indicated by a line) suggesting that dolomitic limestone was used as the calcium source to make the glasses, as noted elsewhere (Henderson *et al.* 2024). This means that 3 primary raw materials were used to make the Kaman borate glasses: sand, a sodium-rich borate deposit and dolomitic limestone. Nevertheless, like the Kaman natron glasses, the borate glasses from the site contain low calcium oxide levels of between 0.9 and 4.6 weight %. The plant ash glasses contain variable calcium oxide levels which are low compared to some Late Bronze Age plant ash glasses of other colours as noted elsewhere (Reade *et al.* 2009, Henderson *et al.* 2018). Black glasses with such low calcium oxide levels generally lead to poor durability. In this case high iron combined with aluminium oxide increases the durability (Conte *et al.* 2016a).

It is important to discuss the relationship between context date and glass technology for the Kaman black glasses. One black glass bead decorated with opaque white bands of a natron composition may derive from phase IIIa (1600–1400B.C.E). This natron glass is very unusual for the date and deserves further detailed consideration though it is possible that it fell out of the excavation section. The glasses dating to phase IIc (9th–7th centuries B.C.) are plant ash and borate compositions. Those dating to phase IIa (7th–4th centuries B.C.) involve four different production technologies: natron, plant ash, borate and 'wood ash'. Therefore, borate glasses first appear at Kaman in the 9th century B.C. at the earliest, plant ash glasses continue to be used between the 9th and 4th centuries B.C. and black 'wood ash' glasses first appear at Kaman after the 7th century B.C. The single black glass bead redeposited in an Ottoman context is of a borate composition. Apart from one, all natron glasses have been found in 7th–4th century contexts.

Discussion

These decorated black beads from Kaman therefore have an unexpectedly wide range of chemical compositions. In order to place them in a wider geographical context the analytical results will be compared with some for globular black beads decorated with white annulets from Italy and the Czech republic (Conte *et al.* 2016a).

The data plotted in Fig. 4 shows that that Kaman plant ash glasses and 'wood ash' glasses are compositionally distinct from the Bologna, Pozzuoli, Cumae and Chotin glasses. This plot also raises the possibility that Bologna and Pozzuoli glasses originally classified as being made from plant ash, with high and variable magnesium oxide concentrations and relatively low potassium oxide, are borate glasses. However, until boron data are available for these glasses, this remains speculative.

As noted above, magnesium and calcium concentrations in Kaman borate glasses form a positive correlation (Figs. 3 and 5) indicating that the source of lime used was dolomite. There is an indication that the relative concentrations of calcium and magnesium oxide in these Kaman plant ash glasses are also positively correlated. It is also clear from Fig. 5 that Pozzuoli high magnesium glasses form a positively correlated dispersion which not only plots with Kaman borate glasses but extends the correlated group to include Pozzuoli glasses with magnesium oxide concentrations as low as 1.23 %. This is a further indication that Pozzuoli 'high magnesium oxide' glasses could instead be borate glasses. It is also notable that some Chotin glass are characterised by this correlation suggesting that dolomite was the source of calcium used in those glasses too. It notable that Kaman 'wood ash' and Chotin 'wood ash' glasses contain the highest calcium oxide concentrations with up to 10.23 % in a bead from Chotin. Furthermore, the higher calcium oxide concentrations in Kaman 'natron' glasses make them quite distinctive from natron glasses from Bologna, Pozzuoli and most from Cumae.

Turning to phosphorus concentrations in the glasses, it is clear that the highest levels of phosphorus pentoxide are to be found in the 'wood ash' glasses from Chotin (Fig. 6); Kaman wood ash glasses also contain high phosphorus pentoxide levels. As already noted, elevated levels have been found in Kaman plant ash glass. High levels of phosphorus pentoxide are generally considered to characterise fluxes of organic origin such as wood and plant ashes, as these glasses exemplify. Again the 'plant ash glasses' (high magnesium oxide) from Pozzuoli, Cumae and Bologna contain low phosphorus pentoxide providing more evidence that they may have been made using inorganic mineral sodium-rich borate deposits. As is to be expected, the other mineral flux used to make these black glasses, natron, also contains low or very low concentrations of phosphorus pentoxide.

Two plots of selected trace elements found in black glass beads from Kaman, Chotin, Bologna and Pozzuoli are given in Figs 7 and 8 (no trace elements have been published for Cumae). Fig 7, a plot of zirconium (Zr) ppm vs chromium (Cr) ppm, provides a further insight into the purity of the sands used to make the glasses. Zirconium is an element that characterises zircons, and chromium is found in chromite: both are found in sands. Figure 7 again shows how some Kaman glass is compositionally distinct from the rest: Kaman wood ash, plant ash, borate and even 2 'natron' glasses contain higher zircon levels than found in the wood ash glasses from Chotin as well as other glasses from Bologna and some from Pozzuoli. All the latter are focused in a tight low chromium group with concentrations of zirconium of up to 100 ppm. This figure also provides evidence for the use of sands containing relatively high chromium levels in high magnesium (possible borate) Pozzuoli glasses. The highest chromium concentration is in a single Kaman borate glass.

Strontium and neodymium are elements that are generally geologically associated with calcium and silica sources respectively and also provide a means of characterising ancient glasses by using neodymium and strontium isotopes (Degryse *et al.* 2010, Henderson *et al.* 2010, Ganio *et al.* 2013). Therefore, they are geologically expected to be independent of each other. Concentrations of neodymium, along with, for example, chromium, zirconium, aluminium and iron can be used as a means to estimate how pure the sands used were. When quartz from veins or pebbles is used to make glass, the concentrations of neodymium can be as low as 2–3 ppm (Henderson *et al.* 2010). Therefore, the concentrations of neodymium of up to 21 ppm in Kaman black glasses are very high and reflect the impure sands that were used to make the black beads. Most of the other glasses plotted in Fig 8 contain between c. 5 ppm and 15 ppm neodymium. A single Kaman wood ash glass bead (KAM43 a plant ash glass) contains 2.6 ppm neodymium which suggests that crushed quartz was used to make the glass, reflecting this period of transition during which a range of raw materials were used.

Figure 8 shows that the Kaman 'wood ash' glasses contain the highest strontium concentrations of upto 596 ppm. A single Chotin wood ash glass and 2 Kaman plant glasses also contain high concentrations above 240 ppm. As noted elsewhere (Henderson *et al.* 2010), high concentrations of strontium, of typically between 300 ppm and 1300 ppm are found in Late Bronze Age plant ash glasses. Here the black Kaman plant ash glasses contain between 153 ppm and 341 ppm which can be considered to be quite low for a plant ash glass.

Interestingly a group of 6 out of 8 Chotin 'wood ash' black glasses form a very tight group as we saw for zirconium and chromium concentrations in Fig. 7 above, so this suggests that these 6 glasses, which also plot close together in other Figures, were made in the same batch or at least using very similar raw material sources at different times. Two other Chotin samples fall away from this group in Fig 8.

We have suggested above that dolomite was the main source of calcium used in wood ash glass from Chotin, as well as plant ash and borate glasses from Kaman, possibly 'wood ash' glass from Kaman and, tentatively in high magnesium glass from Pozzuoli. The source of calcium used in many natron glasses is sea shells containing the mineral aragonite or calcite (Freestone *et al.* 2003): eastern Mediterranean coastal beaches containing shell fragments provide levels of calcium oxide (5–10 %) which produce a durable glass (Freestone *et al.* 2000; Salviulo *et al.* 2004). The use of this source of calcium can be proven using strontium isotope analysis (Freestone *et al.* 2003, Henderson *et al.* 2020), the strontium having a 'Holocene' signature. Calcium (limestone) formed during older geological epochs have a different strontium isotope signature (Freestone *et al.* 2003).

A further potential source of calcium in glass making is bone ash. There are a restricted number of examples where this has been found in ancient glasses (Silvestri *et al.* 2016, Wang *et al.* 2020, Wang *et al.* 2021, Henderson 2013, 65). Fig 9, a plot of weight% calcium oxide versus phosphorus pentoxide, shows that the oxides are correlated in some of the wood ash glasses from Kaman and Chotin but not is the other glass types. These 'wood ash' glasses also contain the highest concentrations of calcium oxide. This does suggest that the glasses were made from three ingredients: bone ash, wood ash and sand with the calcium being present as calcium phosphate. Perhaps the wood ash used did not provide enough lime to create a durable glass so the glassmakers used an additional source.

The neodymium and strontium concentrations in Kaman natron glasses are clearly positively correlated (Fig. 8). Such a correlation has been found in Late Bronze Age plant ash glasses before (Henderson *et al.* 2010) and recently in natron glasses from 6th–4th century Pydna (Greece), 6th–4th century Den Delyan (Bulgaria), 4th–3rd century Satricum (Italy) and 4th–3rd century Son Mas (Spain) (Lü *et al.* 2021). Moreover this correlation is a way of uniting the Kaman natron glasses in Fig. 8. Relative levels of sodium oxide and aluminium oxide in the 6 natron glasses for which there is probe data show that there is also a compositional similarity with the natron glasses from Pydna and Satricum, but also 7th century Rhodes. Nevertheless, the maximum calcium oxide concentration in Kaman black natron glasses is 3.9%, lower than any of the many considered by Lü *et al.* (2021) so this appears to make them distinctive even when taking elevated iron concentrations into account. These calcium oxide levels in Kaman black glasses are also higher than found in glasses from Bologna, Pozzuoli and Cumae (Conte *et al.* 2016).

Aluminium oxide concentrations in Kaman glasses vary according to glass type. The aluminium oxide concentrations in the black plant ash glasses have a range of between 1.89 and 3.67 weight% and in borate glasses between 0.97 and 2.42 weight%. The other two glass types contain widely variable aluminium oxide concentrations of between 1.05 and 10.18 weight% in 'natron' glasses and 3.06 and 9.24 weight% in 'wood ash' glasses. These concentrations of aluminium in borate glasses suggest that they did not derive from Turkish borate deposits (Van Ham-Meert *et al.* 2019) but that they are more likely to have derived from Iran (Henderson *et al.* 2024).

Moreover, such high aluminium concentrations adds to the evidence for the use of impure sands with widely varying levels of impuritities, especially for the production of Kaman wood ash and natron glasses. The aluminium oxide is likely to have been introduced in 'natron' and 'wood ash' glasses in the form of feldpars; the introduction of significant quantities of other elements such as strontium supports this interpretation. The other possible source of elevated aluminium is metal slag, if introduced. Two Kaman 'wood ash' glasses contain very high alumina levels, but the rest do not.

Concluding Comments: A Time of Transition and Technologies in Flux

These results for black glass beads provide a window into a complex series of socio-economic changes that occurred following the collapse of the Hittite empire. Based on variations in bead typology, Spaer strongly suggested that several separate production centres existed for these black beads decorated with eyes (2001, 80). The question of whether any of the beads were made in central Anatolia is difficult to establish but is not out of the question. The wood ash glasses from Kaman have quite distinctive chemical compositions so they may be local products, though (Nd/Sr) isotope analysis would help to confirm this. A wide variety of glass technologies were used to make the black beads found at Kaman (wood ash, plant ash, natron and borate) involving a wide range of raw materials-plant ash, wood ash, soda-rich borate minerals, soda-rich natron, dolomitic limestone, impure sands and possibly bone ash and metal slag.

It is very unlikely indeed that the manufacture of these glasses occurred in the same place so the wide range of glass types supports Spaer's suggestion that several production centres existed, as already indicated for Italian and Czech black beads (Conte *et al.* 2016a). Nevertheless, the raw unworked glass of each compositional type could have been exported from primary production sites to a small number of secondary bead making centres. Moreover, the analysis of the Kaman black glass beads provides evidence for the presence of plant ash glass at Kaman in both Late Bronze Age and 9th–7th century B.C.E contexts. However, concentrations of chromium and lanthanum in the black glasses distinguish many of them from both Egyptian and Mesopotamian non-black glasses. There is also evidence for the introduction of some of the earliest 'wood ash' in the 7th century, borate glass with a single possible natron glass bead from the Hittite period at Kaman. The decoration of two black beads from phase IIa are opacified with lead-tin oxide. This adds to the rare evidence for the early use of this opacifier- in Anatolia. The opacifier used in the opaque white eyes is calcium antimonate.

The early iron age and later, in central Anatolia, may therefore have been a time when innovation (and experimentation) with glass raw materials occurred. Research on iron and pottery from Kaman supports this notion. Masubuchi (2017) used LA-ICP-MS to analyse 49 iron objects found in Late Bronze Age and Early-Middle Iron Age contexts at Kaman. As seen with the glass results there is evidence for the introduction of a new raw material, an iron-rich pyrite source characterised by a positively correlated array of cobalt and nickel ratios. Masubuchi (2017, 60) refers to a 'diversity of materials' used in central Anatolian iron production from the early iron age – precisely what we have found in the early and middle iron age black glasses. Masubuchi (2016) also noted a large peak in iron and hard steel production just after c. 900 B.C.E supported by other studies in western Asia and she suggests that this was the adoption of a new technology rather than the invasion of a new population. The evidence from iron work suggests that there was no continuity from the Hittite period into later periods. However there may have been continuity for the (plant ash) glass used.

Matsumura's work on the Iron Age ceramics from Kaman and central Anatolia (2005, 2008) has indicated contrasts not only in the pottery produced between the Late Bronze Age and the Early Iron Age, but also among regions in the Early Iron Age. There were at least three different pottery cultures in the Early Iron Age of Central Anatolia. At Kaman and further south wheel-made bichrome painted pottery is found, for example at Porsuk (Dupré 1983). This pottery technology probably came from the south, around the Mediterranean coastal region. Furthermore, its typical wavy motive shows a relationship with the Mycenaean culture. This has been demonstrated clearly during Iron Age I further south, in the Amuq valley (Pucci 2019). So, the ceramic types show changes and also influences from the south and this is also suggested by Masubuchi (2016) for iron. Secondly, there is also handmade pottery with incised decoration from Early Iron Age Kaman that is possibly comparable with the handmade pottery from the Troy VIIb (Blegen *et al.* 1958) and from YHSS 7b in Gordion (Voigt and Henrickson 2000). Such pottery is regarded as having been brought to Anatolia from the Balkans. Thirdly, in north central Anatolia there was a red painted pottery culture in the Early Iron Age, for example at Büyükkaya in Boğazköy (Genz 2004; Seeher 2018) that could have been introduced by the Kaška people from the Black Sea region (see Mielke 2016).

Unlike glass and metal it is likely that a higher proportion of pottery was made locally and therefore somewhat more specific implications can be drawn from its study about the organisation of production than for glass. Based on the evidence for mass production in the Late Bronze Age, Matsumura (2008) pointed out that the Hittite centralised pottery production broke down when the Hittite palatial society collapsed and that the mode of pottery production during the Early Iron Age in central Anatolia became a decentralised one. Even if any of compositional types of black glass from

Kaman were manufactured in central Anatolia, the very wide range of compositional types discussed here clearly shows that the established centralised Late Bronze Age production of plant ash glasses no longer existed. This therefore supports the existence of decentralised glass production in the Iron Age with several possible production centres for black glass. One of the production centres may have been in the southern and eastern areas of the Mediterranean (based on high concentrations of black glass found there, some found to have distinctive chemical compositions) with influences from this area being suggested for both pottery and iron. Given the variety of glass compositions and geographical concentrations of black beads, other possible production zones could have been central Europe- and perhaps Anatolia. The high iron contents in the black glass could indicate a link to the iron industry: this deserves to be examined further. Nevertheless, plant ash glass was used in both the Late Bronze Age and in the Iron Age. It is difficult to be sure if this represents technological continuity, as such, because plant ash glass may possibly have been introduced from the Black Sea region by immigrants in the Iron Age. Seeher (2018) is of the opinion that such people moved into central Anatolia once the Hittite people had left; in that sense plant ash glass technology was 'new'.

Bibliography

Braun, Ch.
- 1983 Analysen von Gläsern aus der Hallstattzeit mit einem Exkurs über römische Fenstergläser," in O.-H. Frey, *Glasperlen der Vorrömischen eisenzeit, Marburger Studien zur Vor- und Frühgeschichte*, Band 5, Mainz am Rhein, pp. 129–15.

Blegen, C.W., C.G. Boulter, J.L. Caskey and M. Rawson
- 1958, *Troy IV: Settlements VIIa, VIIb and VIII*, Princeton.

Brill, R.H.
- 1999a *Chemical Analyses of Early Glasses, Volume 1, The Catalogue*, Corning, New York.
- 1999b *Chemical Analyses of Early Glasses, Volume 2, Table of Analyses*, Corning, New York.

Brill, R.H. and C.P. Stapleton
- 2012 *Chemical Analyses of Early Glasses, Volume 3, The Years 2000–2011, Reports and Essays*, Corning Museum of Glass, Corning, New York.

Cagno, S., P. Cosyns, A. Izmer, F. Vanhaecke, K. Nys and K. Janssens
- 2014 "Deeply Colored and Black-Appearing Roman Glass: A Continued Research, *Journal of Archaeological Science*" 42, pp. 128–139.

Ceglia, A., G. Nuyts, S. Cagno, W. Meulebroeck, K. Baert, P. Cosyns, K. Nys, H.K. Thienpont, K. Janssens and H. Terryn
- 2014 "A XANES Study of Chromophores: The Case of Black Glass· Analytical Methods, 2014," 6, pp. 2662–2671, DOI: 10.1039C3AY42029A

Conte, S., R. Arletti, and J. Henderson *et al.*
- 2016a "Different Glassmaking Technologies in the Production of Iron Age Black Glass from Italy and Slovakia," *Archaeological and Anthropological Sciences* 10, pp. 503–521. https://doi.org/10.1007/s12520-016-0366-4

Conte, S., R. Arletti, F. Mermati and B. Gratuze
- 2016b "Unravelling the Iron Age Glass Trade in Southern Italy: The First Trace Element Analyses," *European Journal of Mineralogy* 28, pp. 409–433.

Conte, S., Matarese, I., Vezzalini, G., Pacciarelli, M., Scarano, T., Vanzetti, A., Gratuze, B., Arletti, R.
- 2019 "How much is known about glassy materials in Bronze and Iron Age Italy? New Data and General Overview," *Archaeological and Anthropological Sciences* 11, pp. 1813–1841.

Cosyns, P.
- 2011 *The Production, Distribution and Consumption of Black Glass in the Roman Empire During the 1st–5th century AD. An Archaeological, Archaeometric and Historical Approach*, PhD thesis, Vrije Universiteit Brussel.

Czichon, R.M. *et al.*
- 2016 "Archäologische Forschungen am Oymağaç Höyük/Nerik 2011–2015," *Mitteilungen der Deutschen Orient-Gesellschaft* 148, pp. 5–141.

Dardeniz, G.
- 2018 "Preliminary Archaeological and Scientific evidence for Glass Making at Tell Atchana/Alalakh, Hatay (Turkey)," *Anatolian Archaeological Studies* 21, pp. 95–110.

Degryse P., I. Freestone, J. Schneider, and J. Jennings
- 2010 "Technology and Provenance Study of Levantine Plant Ash Glass Using Sr-Nd Isotope Analysis," in Drauke J. and D. Keller (eds.) *Glass in Byzantium – Production, Usage, Analyses.* Mainz: Romisch-Germanischen Zentralmuseums, pp. 83–91.

Dupré, S.
- 1983 *Porsuk I: La Céramique de l'Age du Bronze et de l'Age du Fer.* Editions Recherche sur les Civilisations, 'Memoire' 20, Paris.

Freestone, I. C., K. A. Leslie, M. Thirlwell and Y. Gorin-Rosen
- 2003 "Strontium Isotopes in the Investigation of Early Glass Production: Byzantine and Early Islamic Glass from the Near East," *Archaeometry 45*, pp. 19–32.

Freestone, I. C., Y. Gorin-Rosen and M. J. Hughes
- 2000 "Primary Glass from Israel and the Production of Glass in Late Antiquity and the Early Islamic period," in M.-D. Nenna (ed.), *La Route du verre: Ateliers primaires et secondaires du second millénaire av. J.-C. au Moyen Age*, Lyon: Maison de l'Orient Méditerraneéan-Jean Pouilloux, pp. 65–84.

Ganio, M., M. Gulmini, K. Latruwe, F. Vanhaecke and P. Degryse
- 2013 "Sasanian Glass from Veh Ardašīr Investigated by Strontium and Neodymium Isotopic Analysis, *Journal of Archaeological Science*," *40*, pp. 4264–4270.

Genz, H.
- 2004 Büyükkaya 1. *Die Keramik der Eisenzeit. Funde aus den Grabungskampagnen 1993–1998.* Boğazköy-Hattusa XXI, Mainz.

Gratuze, B.
- 2009 "Les premiers verres au natron retrouvés en Europe occidentale: composition chimique et chronotypologie," in K. Janssens, P. Degryse, P. Cosyns, J. Caen and L. Van'tdack (eds.), *Proceedings of the Congress of the International Association for the History of Glass*, Antwerp: AIHV, pp. 8–14.

Gratuze B. and J. Picon
- 2006 "Utilisation par l'industrie verrière des sels d'aluns des oasis égyptiennes au début du premier millénaire avant notre ère'," in J.-P. Brun (ed.), *L'Alun de Méditerranée*, Institut Français de Naples, pp. 269–276.

Haevernick, T. E.
- 1953 "Der Hortfund von Allendorf. Hals- und Haarschmuck," *Prähistorische Zeitschrift* 34/35, pp. 213–217.

Henderson, J.
- 1985 "The Raw Materials of Early Glass Production," *Oxford Journal of Archaeology* 1985, 4, pp. 267–291.
- 2013 *Ancient Glass, An Interdisciplinary Exploration*, New York and Cambridge.

Henderson, J., Evans, J. and J. Nikita
- 2010 "Isotopic Evidence for the Primary Production, Provenance and Trade of Late Bronze Age Glass in the Mediterranean," *Journal of Mediterranean Archaeology and Archaeometry* 10, 1, pp. 1–24

Henderson, J., Chenery, S., Omura, K., Matsumura, K., and E. Faber
- 2018a "Hittite and Early Iron Age Glass from Kaman-Kalehöyük and Büklükale, Turkey: Evidence for Local Production and Continuity?" *Journal of Anatolian Archaeology* 21, pp. 1–15

Henderson, J., An, J and H. Ma
- 2018b "The Archaeology and Archaeometry of Chinese Glass: A Review," *Archaeometry* 60, pp. 88–104.

Henderson, J., Ma, H., Evans, J.
- 2020 "Glass production for the Silk Road? Provenance and Trade of Islamic Glasses Using Isotopic and Chemical Analyses in a Geological Context," *Journal of Archaeological Science* 119, pp. 105–164

Henderson, J., Sheridan, A., Chenery, S., Timberlake, S., Towle, A., Knight, M., Wiseman, R., and L. Troalen
- 2024 Necklace and beads, in *The Must Farm Pile Dwelling Settlement, Volume 2, Specialist Contributions*, McDonald Institute, University of Cambridge.

Hodgkinson, A.K
- 2018 *Technology and urbanism in Late Bronze Age Egypt.* Oxford Studies in Egyptian Archaeology, Oxford.

Kaniewski, D., N. Marriner, J. Bretschneider, G. Jans, C. Morhange, R. Cheddadi, T.Otto, F. Luce and E. Van Campo, E.
- 2018 "300-year Drought Frames Late Bronze Age to Early Iron Age Transition in the Near East: New Palaeoecological Data from Cyprus and Syria," 1,2 *Regional Environmental Change* 19, pp. 2287–2297

Kemp, V., A. McDonald, F. Brock and A.J. Shortl
- 2020 "LA-ICP-MS Analysis of Late Bronze Age Blue Glass Beads from Gurob, Egypt," *Archaeometry* 62, pp. 42–53.

Li, Q.I., S. Liu, H.X. Zhao and F.X. Gan
- 2014 "Characterization of Some Ancient Glass Beads Unearthed from the Kizil Reservoir and Wanquan Cemeteries in Xinjiang, China," *Archaeometry*, 56, pp. 601–624.

Masubuchi, M.
- 2008 "Metallographic Study on Iron and Steel Arrowheads from Kaman-Kalehöyük," *Anatolian Archaeological Studies* 17, pp. 183–194.
- 2016 "A Study on the Beginning of the Iron Age at Kaman- Kalehöyük," *Anatolian Archaeological Studies* 19, pp. 111–122.
- 2017 "The Chemical Characterisation of Iron and Steel Objects from Kaman-Kalehöyük," *Anatolian Archaeological Studies*, pp. 51–62.

Matin M.
- 2018 Tin-Based Opacifiers in Archaeological Glass and Ceramic Glazes: A Review and New Perspectives. *Archaeological and Anthropological Sciences*, 11, pp. 1155–1167.

Matsumura, K.
- 2005 *Die Eisenzeitliche Keramik in Zentralanatolien Aufgrund der Keramik in Kaman-Kalehöyük*, PhD Dissertation, Freie Universität Berlin, MIK-Center GmbH, Berlin.
- 2008 "The Early Iron Age in Kaman-Kalehöyük – The Search for its Roots," in *Fundstellen: Gesammelte Schriften zur Ärchäologie und Geschichte; ad honorem Hartmut Kühne*, Berlin, pp. 41–50.

Mielke, P.D.
- 2016. "Spätbronzeitliche Keramik," in Czichon *et al.* 2016, pp. 42–52.

Moorey, P.R.S.
- 1994. *Ancient Mesopotamian Materials and Industries. The Archaeological Evidence*, Oxford.
- 2001 "The Mobility of Artisans and Opportunities for Technology Transfer Between Western Asia and Egypt in the Late Bronze Age," in A.J. Shortland (ed.), *The Social Context of Technological Change: Egypt and the Near East, 1650–1550 B.C.*, Oxford, pp. 1–14.

Nicholson, P.T. and Jackson, C.
- 2013 "Glass of Amenhotep II from Tomb KV55 in the Valley of the Kings," *Journal of Egyptian Archaeology* 99, 85–99.

Omori, T. and T. Nakamura
- 2007 "Radiocarbon Dating of Archaeological Materials Excavated at Kaman-Kalehöyük: Second Report," *Anatolian Archaeological Studies*, 16, 111–123.

Oppenheim A.L., R.H. Brill, D. Barag and A. Von Saldern
- 1970. *Glass and Glassmaking in Ancient Mesopotamia*, The Corning Museum of Glass, Corning, New York.

Pucci, M.
- 2019 "Cultural Encounters During the LBII and IAI: Hittites and 'Pelesets' in the Amuq (Hatay) Turkey," *Asia Anteriore Antica, Journal of Ancient Near Eastern Cultures*, 1, pp. 169–194.

Pulak, C.
- 2001 "The Cargo of the Uluburun Ship and Evidence for Trade with the Aegean and Beyond, in Italy and Cyprus in Antiquity, 1500–450 B.C." in L. Bonfante and V. Karageorghis, *Proceedings of an International Symposium held at the Italian academy for Advanced Studies in America at Columbia University*, November 16th–18th, 2000, Nikosia, pp. 13– 60.

Purowski, T., P. Dzierżanowski, E. Bulska, B. Wagner and A. Nowak
- 2012 "Study of the Glass Beads from Hallstatt C-D from Southwest Poland: Implications for Glass Technology and Provenance," *Archaeometry* 54, pp. 144–66.

Reade, W., I.C. Freestone and St.J. Simpson
- 2005 "Innovation or Continuity? Early First Millennium B.C.E Glass in the Near East: The Cobalt Blue Glasses from Assyrian Nimrud," *Annales of the 16e Congrès de l'Association Internationale pour l'Histoire du Verre*, London 2003, Nottingham, pp. 23–27.

Reade, W., I.C. Freestone and S. Bourke
- 2009 "Innovation and Continuity in Bronze and Iron Age Glass from Pella Jordan," *Annales of the 17e Congrès de l'Association Internationale pour l'Histoire du Verre*, 4–8 September 2006, Antwerp, pp. 48–54.

Silvestria, A., Nestola, F. and L. Peruzzo
- 2016 "Multi-Methodological Characterisation of Calcium Phosphate in Late-Antique Glass Mosaic Tesserae," *Microchemical Journal*, 124, pp. 811–818

Sayre, E.V. and R.W. Smith
- 1961 "Compositional Categories of Ancient Glass," *Science* 133, pp. 1824-1826.

Schmidt, K.
- 2019 *Glass and Glass Production in the Near East during the Iron Age Period: Evidence from Objects, Texts and Chemical Analysis*. Oxford.

Seeher, J.
- 2018 *Büyükkaya II. Bauwerke und Befunde der Grabungskampagnen 1952–1955 und 1993–1998*, Boğazköy-Hattuša 27, Berlin/Boston.

Sherratt, A. and Sherratt, S.
- 2001 "Technological Change in the East Mediterranean Bronze Age: Capital, Resources and Marketing," in A.J. Shortland (ed.), *The Social Context of Technological Change: Egypt and the Near East, 1650–1550* B.C., Oxford, pp. 16–38.

Shortland, A., Rogers, N. and K. Eremin
- 2007 "Trace Element Discriminants Between Egyptian and Mesopotamian Late Bronze Age Glasses," *Journal of Archaeological Sciences* 34, pp. 781-789.

Silberman, N.A. and A.A. Bauer (eds.)
- 2012 Near East: Iron Age Civilisations in the Southern Levant, *The Oxford Companion to Archaeology*, Volume 2, Oxford.

Stapleton, C.P.
- 2003 *The Manufacture of Glasses and Glazes Excavated from Period IVB level (11th–9th century B.C.) at Hasanlu, Iran in Geochemical Analysis of Glass and Glaze from Hasanlu. Northwestern Iran: Constraints on Manufacturing Technology*, The University of Georgia PhD Dissertation, pp. 100–149.

Van der Linden, V., Cosyns, I.P., Schalm, O., Cagno, I.S., Nys, I.K., Janssens, K., Nowak, I.A., Wagner, B., and Bulska, E.
- 2009 "Deeply Coloured and Black Glass in the Northern Provinces of the Roman Empire: Differences and Similarities in Chemical Composition Before and After ad 150," *Archaeometry* 51, pp. 822–844.

Van Ham-Meert, A., S. Dillisa, A. Blomme, N. Cahill, P. Claeys, J. Elsena, K. Eremin, A. Gerdese, S. Steuwef, M. Roeffaers, A. Shortland and P. Degryse
- 2019 "A Unique Recipe for Glass Beads at Iron Age Sardis," *Journal of Archaeological Science* 108, pp. 1–9.

Van Soldt, W.H.
- 1995 "Ugarit, A Second Millennium Kingdom on the Mediterranean Coast," in M. Sasson (ed.), *Civilizations of the Near East*, Peabody, MA, pp. 1255–1266.

Voigt, M.M. and R.C. Henrickson
- 2000 "Formation of the Phrygian State: The Early Iron Age at Gordion," *Anatolian Studies* 50, pp. 37–54.

Walton, M.S., A. Shortland, S. Kirk and P. Degryse
- 2009 "Evidence for the Trade of Mesopotamian and Egyptian Glass to Mycenaean Greece," *Journal of Archaeological Science* 36, pp. 1496–1503.

Wang, D., R. Wen and J. Henderson *et al.*
- 2020 "The Chemical Composition and Manufacturing Technology of Glass Beads Excavated from the Hetian Bizili site, Xinjiang," *Heritage Science* 8, 127.

Wang, K-W., K-T., Li, Y. Kilizuka Y-K. Hsieh and C. Jackson
- 2021 "Glass beads from Guishan in Iron Age Taiwan: Inter-regional Bead Exchange Between Taiwan, Southeast Asia and Beyond," *Journal of Archaeological Science: Reports* 35. 102737.

Qin-Qin, L., J. Henderson, Y. Wang, and B. Wang
- 2021 "Natron Glass Beads Reveal Early Silk Road Between the Mediterranean and China in the 1st Millennium B.C.E.," *Scientific Reports* 11, 3537.

Fig. 1. An example of an Iron Age 'black' glass bead excavated at Kaman-Kalehöyük.

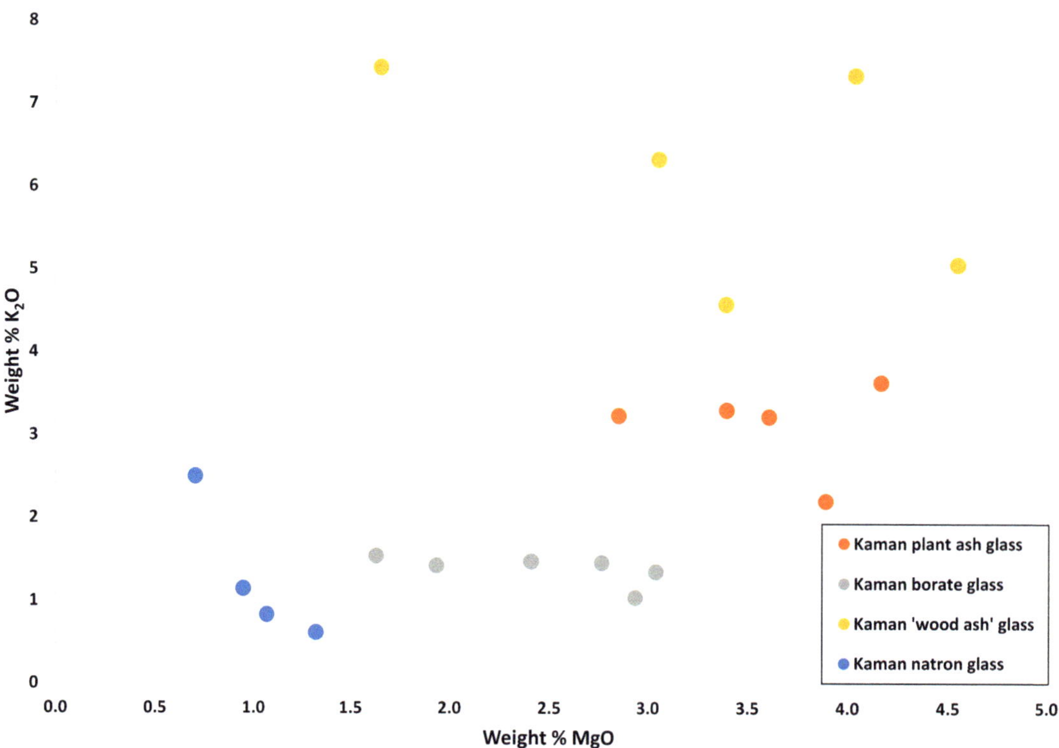

Fig. 2. Weight percent magnesium oxide versus potassium oxide in black glass beads from Kaman-Kalehöyük.

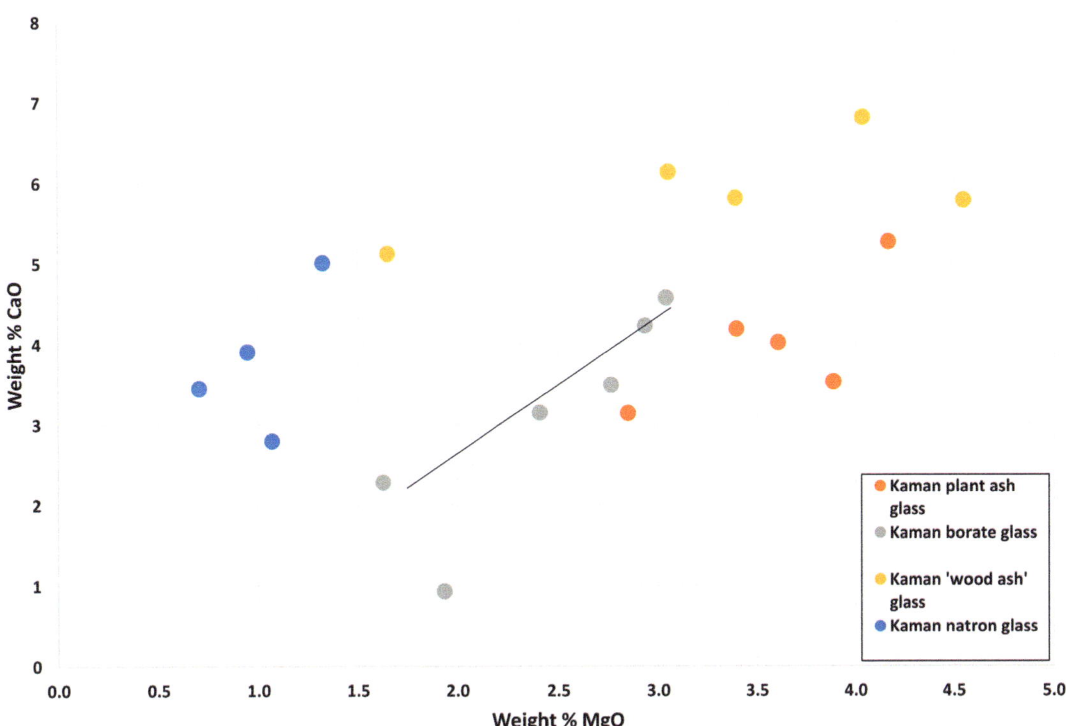

Fig. 3. Weight percent magnesium oxide versus calcium oxide in black glass beads from Kaman-Kalehöyük.

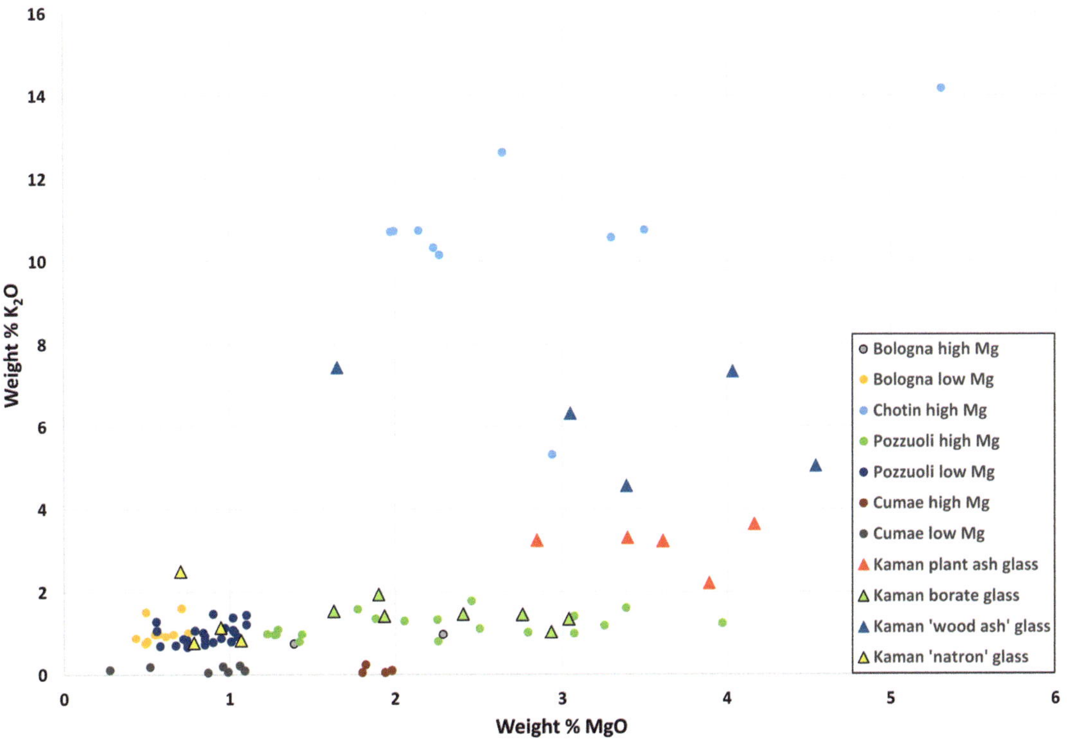

Fig. 4. Weight percent magnesium oxide versus potassium oxide in black glass beads from Kaman-Kalehöyük, Bologna, Chotin, Pozzuoli and Cumae.

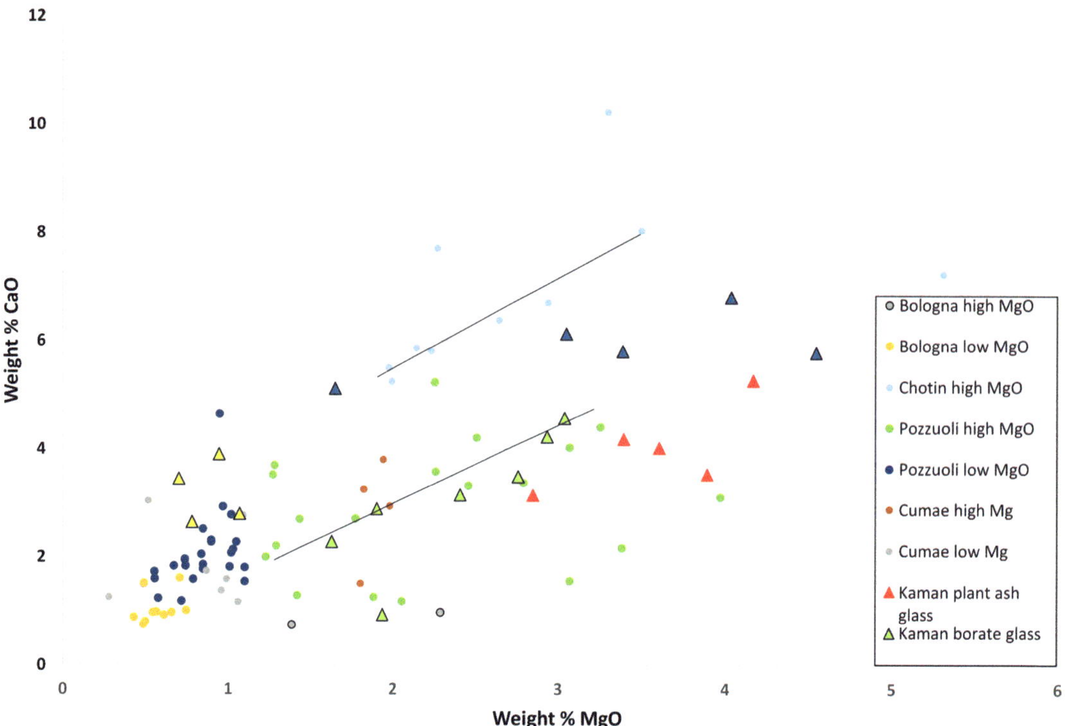

Fig. 5. Weight percent magnesium oxide versus calcium oxide in black glass beads from Kaman-Kalehöyük, Bologna, Chotin, Pozzuoli and Cumae.

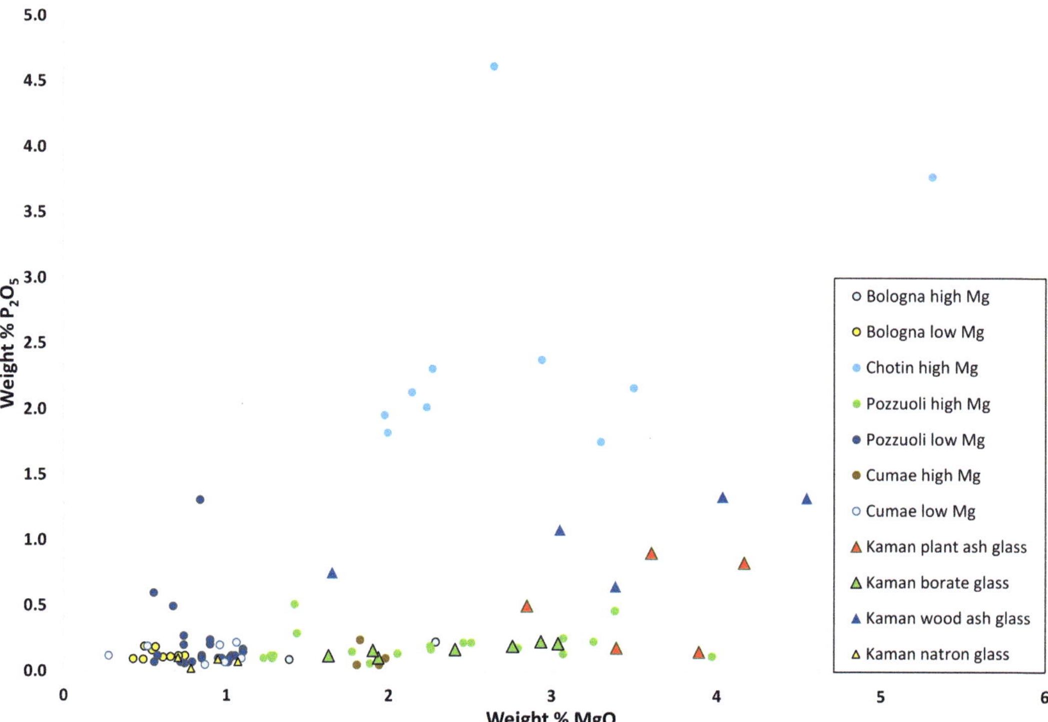

Fig. 6. Weight percent magnesium oxide versus phosphorus pentoxide in black glass beads from Kaman-Kalehöyük, Cumae, Bologna, Pozzuoli and Chotin.

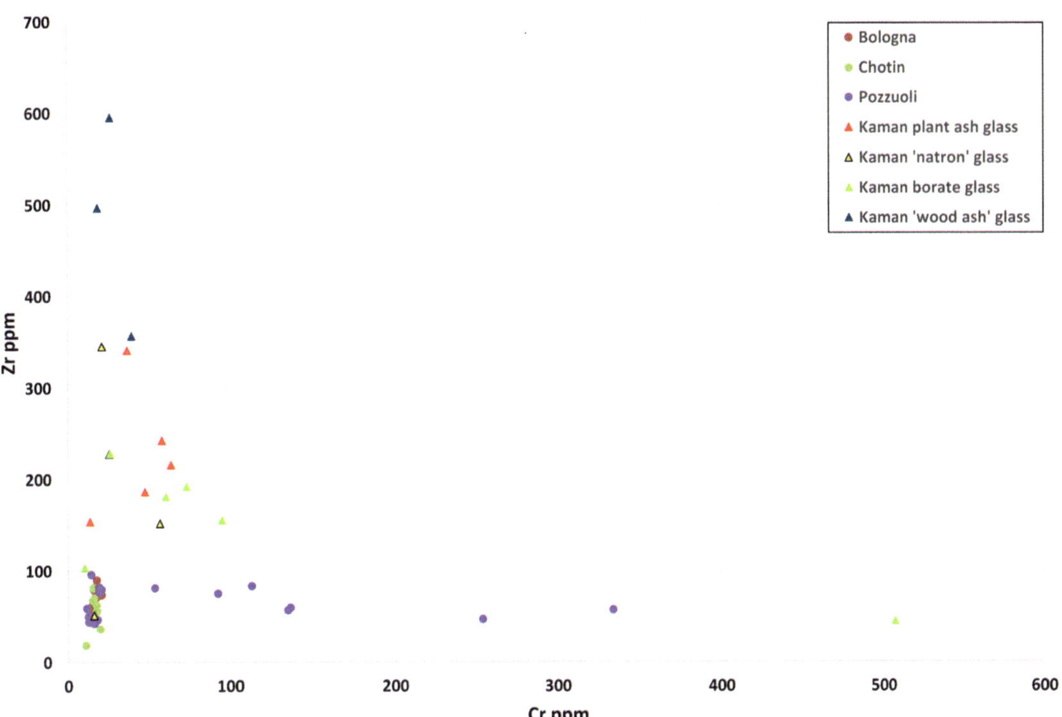

Fig. 7. Relative concentrations of chromium (Cr) and zirconium (Zr) (ppm) in black glass beads from Kaman-Kalehöyük, Bologna, Chotin and Pozzuoli.

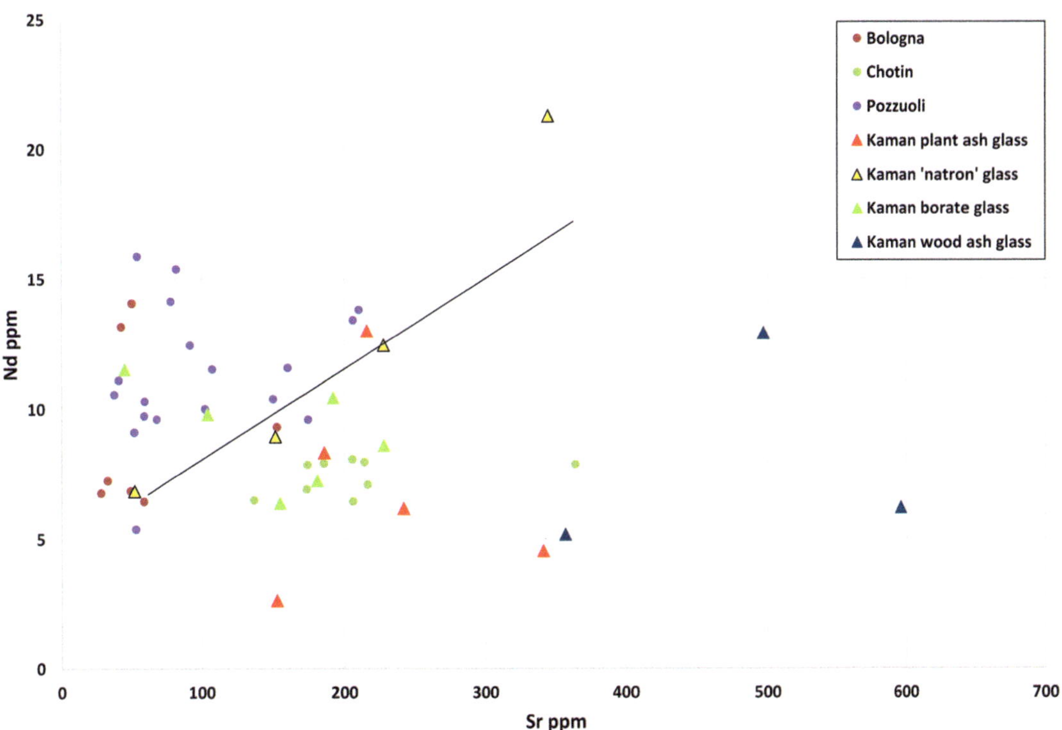

Fig. 8. Relative concentrations of strontium (Sr) and neodymium (Nd) (ppm) in black glass beads from Kaman-Kalehöyük, Bologna, Chotin and Pozzuoli.

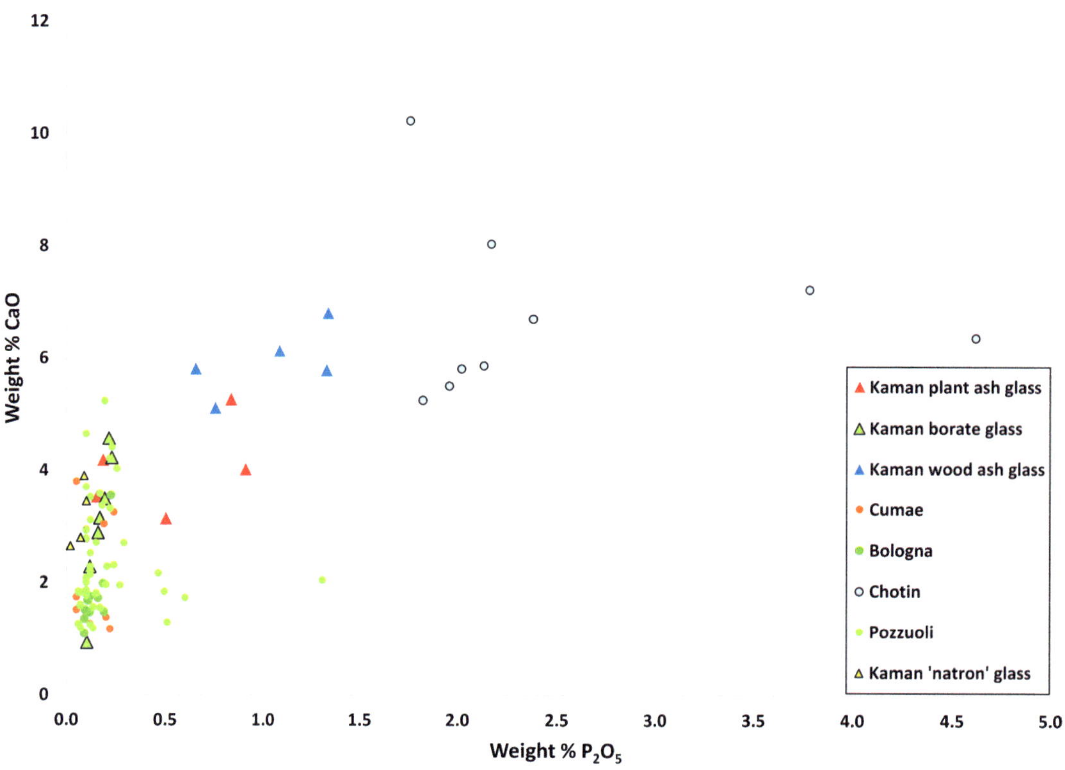

Fig. 9. Relative concentrations of phosphorus pentoxide (P_2O_5) and calcium oxide (CaO) in black glass beads from Kaman-Kalehöyük, Bologna, Chotin and Pozzuoli.

Part of an 'Early Iron Age Package': The Revival of Beak Spouted Jugs in the Hittite Heartland after the Collapse of the Empire

*Jürgen Seeher**

Abstract

Beak spouted jugs are found in Anatolia since the Early Bronze Age. They are still popular in the Middle Bronze Age/Karum period and the Old Hittite period, but in the Empire period this type of vessel almost completely disappears. In the repertoire of the Early Iron Age after the collapse of the Hittite Empire, on the other hand, beak spouted jugs are present again, decorated with red painting. But these vessels are not based on Hittite forms. Their predecessors can be located in the Pontus area where they were part of a red-painted Late Bronze Age pottery complex. During their immigration in the course of the 12th century B.C., people from this area assimilated still existing remains of the Hittite population and brought with them not only their material and technical culture, but also economic and settlement practices and political and social order: the 'Early Iron Age package'.

Öz

Gaga ağızlı testiler Anadolu'da İlk Tunç Çağı'ndan itibaren mevcuttur. Orta Tunç Çağı/Karum ve Eski Hitit Krallığı dönemlerinde de bu kap biçimi sevilerek kullanılmış, ancak Hitit İmparatorluk döneminde neredeyse tamamen ortadan kalkmıştır. Hitit İmparatorluğu'nun çöküşünden sonra Erken Demir Çağı'nda gaga ağızlı testiler, kırmızı boya bezemeli olarak keramik repertuvarına yeniden girmiştir. Ancak bu testilerin öncülleri Hitit formları arasında değil, Pontus bölgesindeki Geç Tunç Çağı'na özgü kırmızı boya bezemeli keramik kompleksindedir. MÖ 12. yüzyıl boyunca bu bölgeden göç eden gruplar Hitit nüfusundan geriye kalanları asimile etmiş, yalnızca kültürlerinin maddi ve teknik özelliklerini değil, ekonomi ve yerleşim tarzlarını, politik ve sosyal düzenlerini de beraberlerinde getirmişlerdir. Bu yeni oluşuma 'Erken Demir Çağı Paketi' adını vermek mümkündür.

Almost thirty years ago, remains from the 'Dark Age' after the fall of the Hittite Empire were excavated for the first time in Boğazköy/Ḫattuša. The difference between these and the Hittite remains is so fundamental that one can speak of a new beginning – obviously people of a different culture have settled here. But can we also speak of an 'Early Iron Age package', analogous to the 'Neolithic package' that the colonists brought with them? In the last part of the paper I will return to this question.

A hallmark of this Early Iron Age is pottery with red painted decoration. Based on survey finds, it had long been suspected that these immigrants had come to the Hittite heartland from the north. Convincing support for this assumption is now provided by pottery finds from the excavations at Oymaağaç near the Black Sea coast. With their help, new observations on cultural contexts and the genesis of Iron Age pottery are possible. In this paper, beak spouted jugs will serve as a case study. With this contribution I would like to express my best wishes for Dr. Sachihiro Omura, who was already interested in this type of vessel many years ago (Omura 1984).

* German Archaeological Institute, retired researcher, seeherj@gmail.com

Hittite Beak Spouted Jugs

Let us first have a short look at Hittite beak spouted jugs. More than sixty years ago, Franz Fischer, in his treatment of the pottery from Boğazköy/Ḫattuša, stated: "The beak spouted jug is one of the most characteristic forms of Hittite pottery" (Fischer 1963: 36). At that time, this statement was based almost exclusively on publications from early excavations at Boğazköy, Kültepe, Alişar Höyük, and Alaca Höyük. In the meantime, however, various studies of large ceramic complexes from Hittite settlements have shown that Fischer's statement is only valid for the Old Hittite period. By the time of the Empire period, such vessels had almost completely disappeared from the ceramic repertoire (Mielke 2017: 134), as shown in the following list:

Over 26,000 diagnostic sherds of pottery from the Upper City of Ḫattuša, essentially finds from settlement and workshop contexts of the Empire period as well as from Temple 6, yielded only two spout fragments of beak spouted jugs, one of which was from Temple 6 (Müller-Karpe 1988: 25). In a second study of mainly Empire period pottery from the Upper city of Ḫattuša, both from dwellings and workshops and from various temples, 6,927 diagnostic pieces were analyzed. In this case there were seven spout fragments of beak spouted jugs, six of them from temple 7 and one from temple 8 (Parzinger – Sanz 1992: 117–155, Pl. 4,23–24). The third complex from Ḫattuša is the pottery from the GAL *MEŠEDI* house, dating to the late 15th to first half of the 14th century B.C. Here, among 3,700 diagnostic pieces, there was not a single fragment of a beak spouted jug (Gruber 2017: 64). Then, two studies from other sites can be cited: The analysis of Empire period pottery from the western slope in Kuşaklı/Sarissa, essentially settlement pottery, yielded only two fragments of beak spouted jugs among 14,650 diagnostic pieces (Mielke 2006: 46). And the examination of pottery from Building B at Kayalıpınar, presumably part of a palace complex destroyed in the early 14th century B.C.E, yielded only one tiny spout fragment of a beak spouted jug among over 4,180 diagnostic pieces (Mühlenbruch 2014: 26).

In other words, tons of sherds from different find contexts of the Middle Hittite and Empire period have yielded only a handful of sherds of beak spouted jugs. At Ḫattuša, most of the specimens are from temples. This indicates that this type of vessel still played a role in libations during the Empire period. Pictorial representations, for example on the stag rhyton in the Metropolitan Museum and probably also on the rock relief at Fraktin, also attest to the existence of beak spouted jugs in this period. However, these vessels may have been made of metal (Müller-Karpe 1988: 24). But also some ceramic specimens still existed, as shown by the find of four unusually slender specimens from Building C at Büyükkale (Fischer 1963: Pl. 23, 260–264). In any case, it may be stated that the beak spouted jug was presumably only a relic in the Empire period: A device bound to traditions, which no longer played a role in everyday life. The function of containers for liquids and of pouring vessels had long since been taken over by the single-handled jugs with straight rims, which were found in large quantities in the settlements: For example, a quarter of all vessels in the study by Müller-Karpe mentioned above were such jugs (Müller-Karpe 1988: 31).

Vessels of a Different Kind: Late Bronze Age Red Painted Beak Spouted Jugs

However, beak spouted jugs continued to exist in some areas on the periphery or outside the Hittite empire. Of particular interest for our topic are the new finds from Oymaağaç near Vezirköprü: Here a previously unknown kind of Late Bronze Age pottery has been identified in layers of the 15th –13th centuries B.C. (Mielke 2016: 50–52; Mielke 2019: 75–82; Mielke 2022a: 96–104; Mielke 2022b). This pottery is made on the wheel and is characterized by forms and decorations that are absent in Empire period Hittite pottery. A special characteristic is a geometric painting with red lines on the vessels body, in addition to transverse lines applied on the thickened and often faceted rims. The closest parallels are found in the handmade red-painted pottery of the Early Iron Age, which is now known from Boğazköy as well as from a larger area in north-central Anatolia and the Pontus region (Genz 2003; 2004; Özsait 2003; Seeher 2010; up-to-date mapping of sites in Mielke 2022b: Fig. 16). Obviously, the red-painted Late Bronze Age pottery from Oymaağaç belongs to their precursors. Dirk Paul Mielke is most probably right in assuming that it is a product of the Kaška people living in this area – for the first time, an element of material culture can thus be attributed to this population group, which was previously known only from texts.

At Oymaağaç, 371 sherds of this Late Bronze Age red-painted pottery have been identified so far. Fragments of jugs and jars, mostly body sherds, are predominant, and among these there are at least two examples of beak spouts. One of the two (Fig. 1.1, after Mielke 2022b: Fig. 8,2; 9,2) is a piece of a jug with a short squat neck and a flaring shoulder. On the base of the neck there is a broad horizontal painted line; above and below it are bundles of narrower lines arranged into zigzag patterns. On top of the stout handle are painted transverse lines. The flattened rim of the beak spout is noteworthy. As a comparative find for the pieces from Oymaağaç, Mielke cites a beak spouted jug from Maşat Höyük (Fig. 1.2). It comes from the Empire period layer I (Özgüç 1978: 124, Pl. 48,3; Özgüç 1982: 102, Fig. 34; for a color photograph see Mielke 2022b: Fig. 13, 4a–b). The vessel is made on the wheel and bears a geometric painting of broad red lines on the shoulder. For the shape of this vessel there are pre-Empire period Hittite parallels, but the painting is singular. It seems that we are dealing here with a synthesis of Hittite form and North Anatolian decoration.

Based on these finds, I come to a piece from Ḫattuša, which was already found in 1995 in the excavation on the ridge of Büyükkaya (Fig. 1.3). This neck of a beak spouted jug is decorated with red paint and consequently it was classified as Early Iron Age. However, Hermann Genz, who worked on the Iron Age pottery of Büyükkaya a few years later, considered it to be of Bronze Age date and did not take it into account. After that, the piece was forgotten for the time being, until the time when Mielke sent me his manuscript on the Late Bronze Age painted pottery from Oymaağaç.

The piece comes from a jug which is probably handmade. It shows a short squat neck and a flaring shoulder and a distinctly flattened rim. The spout is relatively steep, even steeper than that of the jug from Maşat Höyük. The beak was either once equally elongated, or the spout was cut off at the front. The piece bears a dull red painting with carelessly applied broad lines: A horizontal line at the bottom of the neck and zigzag lines extending to the shoulder below. Additional lines are applied around the spout, and the flattened rim bears transversely applied lines at short intervals.

This piece exhibits characteristics of both the jug from Maşat Höyük and the neck fragment of the jug from Oymaağaç. It thus confirms this connection postulated by Mielke: the latter has a similar squat neck and flattened rim, and the former shows a more exact match in the painting and the shape of the beak. However, it is not clear what the beak of the Oymaağaç piece actually looked like. Possibly it was significantly higher, which is why the reconstruction here is provided with a question mark.

The neck fragment from Ḫattuša was found in a backfill on the floor of a Phase 8 building, the last Hittite settlement phase on the ridge of Büyükkaya (Seeher 2018: 80–81). Ulf Dietrich Schoop compares the pottery from this area with material from the latest occupation in the Upper City of Ḫattuša (Schoop 2006: 224: Complex K13b). A radiocarbon sample indicates a dating to the second third of the 13th century B.C. (Schoop – Seeher 2006: Fig. 12,13). Since no Iron Age sherds have been found in this horizon and any other evidence of disturbance is missing, the pre-Iron Age dating of this fragment of a red painted jug seems certain. In view of the parallels mentioned above, it must be regarded as a probable import from the north.

After knowing the evidence from Oymaağaç it becomes obvious that there are more such Late Bronze Age imports from the north in the Hittite heartland. Mielke has compiled examples of red-painted and wheelmade pottery from Ḫattuša and other sites that resemble the red-painted Late Bronze Age pottery from Oymaağaç (Mielke 2022b: Figs. 13–14). Pieces of this kind can now be taken as evidence for relations of the Hittites to the "Kaška country". Hittites and Kaška were not always enemies, as many of the one-sided Hittite accounts suggest. There were also peaceful times, when exchange of goods must have taken place again and again (summary of the relations in Glatz – Matthews 2005: 52–55). Furthermore, the area north of the Hittite empire was inhabited by various tribes. Warlike conflicts in one area did not exclude simultaneous exchange and trade with another area. This would also explain why the jug fragment from Büyükkaya is probably not wheelmade. The potter's wheel was perhaps not – or no longer – in use everywhere in the same way.

Continuing the Tradition: Early Iron Age Beak Spouted Jugs

The Early Iron Age pottery from Boğazköy yields comparative material for the Büyükkaya spout. The geometric red paint as well as flattened or faceted rims, often with transversely painted short strokes, are typical features of various kinds of vessels. Well comparable to our jug neck are beak spouts attached to the sides of pots, which have a flattened, often even widened rim, which in some cases is also painted with transverse strokes (Figs. 1,4–6, after Genz 2004: Pl. 19,8; 36,3; 26,6; similarly Bayburtluoğlu 1979: res. 6a). But there are also various examples of genuine beak spouted jugs of this period. They are – with one exception – all handmade, and all of them bear red painting. Among the unpainted pottery of this period, at least in Boğazköy, beak spouted jugs are missing. Only jugs with horizontal rim are found here (e.g. Genz 2004: Pl. 16; 30,1–5).

The neck fragment Fig. 2.1 (Seeher 2004: Fig. 24) comes from unstratified alluvial sediments in the Sarıkale valley. The painting is reminiscent of finds from Büyükkale, which Genz dates to the later part of the Early Iron Age (Genz 2003: 118). The flattened rim painted with short tranverse lines is noteworthy, a good analogy to the piece from Büyükkaya described above (Fig. 1.3). A knob is placed near the handle and surrounded by a circular painted line.

Fig. 2.2 shows a fragment of a particularly large beak spouted jug (neck diameter 13 cm), found in "Phrygian strata" at Büyükkale in Boğazköy (Genz 2003: Fig.1,3). It is handmade and bears irregular lattice patterns applied with dull red paint. A large knob is attached to the side of the neck.

Fig. 2.3 shows the neck of a beak spouted jug from the "rubble" of the latest Hittite stratum of Büyükkale (Fischer 1963: 118 Pl. 30, 255), This piece too shows a flattened rim which merges into a strongly faceted handle. Red painting starts at the neck below a horizontal line, and also the handle facets as well as the knobs attached to the side of the handle were once painted red (only faintly visible on one side). According to Fischer, some other sherds with red painting (Fig. 2.3) may also belong to this piece.

Fig. 2.4 shows a complete handmade jug with cutaway spout from Eskiyapar (Bayburtluoğlu 1979: res. 1a–1b). Unfortunately, some details of the painting are not visible in the photos in the publication. On the neck at the front there is a twig-like pattern, on the neck at the bottom there is a band with vertical lines and on the shoulder of the vessel there are lozenges formed from zigzag lines with dot filling. The handle has multiple facets and the rim also appears to be flattened. According to Bayburtluoğlu 1979: 298, the rim and handle are painted: The rim obviously bears transverse lines and on the handle a painted line seems to run along the faceting as here on Fig. 2.3.

Another piece, which unfortunately is lost, can be added here: The neck fragment of a small handmade beak spouted jug with red painting "in geometric manner" and a knob near the rim (Fischer 1963: Pl. 19,188). It was found at Büyükkale "under a disturbance in the pavement of layer IVb," but the painting and knob strongly suggest that this find context was disturbed.

Finally, there is another neck of a beak spouted jug with red paint and knobs on the side of the spout (Fig. 2.5, Genz 2004: Pl. 35,10). The pattern at the front of the neck is reminiscent of the twig motif on the jug from Eskiyapar. The piece was found in Boğazköy on the Middle Plateau of Büyükkaya near the surface, i.e., it is without a definite stratification (in the northern part of Zone 116, cf. Seeher 2018: Fig. 44). This fragment comes from a vessel made on the wheel, and also the shape of the handle does not fit well with the examples mentioned so far. This could argue for a date in the Late Bronze Age (Mielke 2022b: Fig. 14). But I do not want to exclude a dating to the early Iron Age. It could be an import from an area where the potters wheel was still in use during this period.

To sum up, we are dealing with a complex situation. The examples of Early Iron Age beak spouted jugs described above are quite diverse. However, various elements connect individual pieces: the flattened rims and faceted handles, the knobs placed on the sides of the rim, and the type of painting. This red painting is the unifying element common to all pieces. It is the main reason why these pieces, all of which are not well stratified, can be grouped together. In Boğazköy, painting vessels with red color was en vogue for more than two centuries in the Early Iron Age after the end of the Hittite Empire. After that, in the Middle Iron Age, it was replaced by dark brown to black-brown painting, which also had many new decorative elements. Red color was then only used on bichrome painted vessels (Bossert 2000: 23–25).

Beak spouted jugs, however, remained popular. Specimens of the Middle Iron Age (= Büyükkaya 4–3/Büyükkale II/Alişar IV) still show various elements that seem like echoes of the early jugs, like narrow spouts and slender necks, flattened rims painted with transverse lines, or zigzag painting with bundles of lines (e.g., von der Osten 1937: Pl. 411; Bossert 2000: 76 Pl. 35; Genz 2004: Pls. 61–62). And in the further course of the Iron Age the well-known showpieces were created, which served representative and presumably also cultic purposes.

The 'Early Iron Age Package'

Let us now return to the question raised at the beginning. The term 'Neolithic package' refers to a whole series of technical and social changes that took place in parallel with the domestication of plants and animals (Çilingiroğlu 2005). Among various changes in material culture, the introduction of ground stone and pottery is probably the most significant, and in the social sphere it is the sedentism that leads to new forms of coexistence. But the term package here refers not only to the combination of different elements, but it also implies movement – the package moves with people from one area to another, leading to a spread of the elements it contains. The benefits of the new subsistence model then also led to assimilation or complete displacement of existing local elements. In this sense, I think it is quite reasonable to speak of an 'Early Iron Age package', because the changes in Central Anatolia were fundamental:

Shortly before or around 1200/1180 B.C., a large part of the Hittite population apparently disappeared from the heartland in the area of the Halys River bend, and thus the Bronze Age ended here. In this region pasture and farmland abounded and soon attracted Early Iron Age immigrants. In the northern to central part of the river bend, immigration from the Pontus region is now attested thanks to the identification of the red-painted Late Bronze Age pottery from Oymaağaç. It represents one of the precursors of the red-painted Early Iron Age pottery in north-central Anatolia. The southernmost sites to date of the latter are Çadır Höyük (Genz 2001: 159–160; Steadman e.a. 2015: 98–105) and Uşaklı Höyük (Orsi 2020), both east of Yozgat.

However, immigration from the north did not take place immediately and on a large scale. Rather, phases of transition can be recognized in the ceramic development at the sites known so far. Only then a more uniform Early Iron Age culture becomes apparent: At Boğazköy, in the earliest Iron Age phase Büyükkaya 7, various sorts of references to the pottery of the Hittite Empire period are visible (Genz 2004: 26). Only after that a more uniform spectrum of shapes is formed, which is typical for the middle and late phase of the Early Iron Age (= Büyükkaya 6–5). Exactly this spectrum has also been found at Uşaklı Höyük, but here, too, there are indications that the first phase of the Early Iron Age also contains forms that point to a local development at the end of the Hittite Empire period (Orsi 2020: 290–291). At Çadır Höyük the situation is somewhat different. In the stratified Early Iron Age pottery from trench USS 4, continuities of Late Bronze Age wares and forms can be discerned, but only general similarities with the Early Iron Age pottery from Boğazköy or Uşaklı Höyük (Ross *et al.* 2019: 29–31). This is in stark contrast to the finds published by Genz (Genz 2001), which are mostly from surface contexts. The excavator's interpretation is that this portion of the site was industrial in function. "The ceramics would therefore not be expected to match diagnostic forms from other residential sites, or even the as-yet-unexcavated residential area at Çadır Höyük" (Ross *et al.* 2019: 29). This may be true, because it is highly unlikely that a significantly different ceramic spectrum existed here than in Uşaklı Höyük, which is only 17 km away as the crow flies. But it seems to me even more likely that the strata recorded in this section represent only the early part of the Early Iron Age, and that the later strata have not yet been discovered.

This means that after a phase of resilience, which in some places began as early as the late 13th century B.C. and probably covered a larger part of the 12th century B.C., reorganization and, above all, transformation was the consequence of the collapse of the Hittite Empire in the northern area of the Halys bend (d'Alfonso 2020). A change in social, political, and economic conditions was brought about by population exchange. This is recognizable, on the one hand, in the material culture. The familiar Hittite implements and weapons disappear and are replaced by a different set of tools and implements for craft work, along with the completely new ceramics (Seeher 2018: 102–105 and 159–160; Seeher-Baykal and Seeher, in preparation). Architecture (light structures, semi-subterranean rooms) and certainly settlement organization change (Steadman 2015: 100–102; Seeher 2018: 101–102; Orsi 2020: 295). And the mode of animal exploitation is also different, as the composition and use of livestock changes significantly with the onset of the Iron Age (von den Driesch and Pöllath 2004: 49; Arbuckle 2009: 204–205). The new settlers bring their subsistence model and, in addition to their material culture, of course their own political and social order (household-scale economy vs. state-controlled economy). Perhaps it is more accurate to speak of a 'Pontic Early Iron Age package' instead of 'Early Iron Age package', because the results of the excavations at Kaman-Kalehöyük (Matsumura 2008) and Gordion (Voigt and Henrickson 2000; Kealhofer, Grave and Voigt 2019) show that other developments took place further to the southwest and west. The homogeneous Hittite culture was not simply replaced by an equally homogeneous Iron Age culture, for such a culture did not exist.

The shape of the beak spouted jug is obviously part of this 'Pontic Early Iron Age package': The finds from Oymaağaç prove that this type of vessel outlasted the Late Bronze Age in the Pontus region. Together with the colonists, it 'immigrated' again to the former Hittite heartland after the fall of the empire. The varying design of the specimens presented here could be explained chronologically in view of the period of more than 200 years from which these pieces must originate. But it could also be partly due to different form traditions existing in parallel, which developed in individual areas (= ceramic regionalization). Movements of people and goods in these newly occupied regions, where the boundaries between different areas of interest were not yet fixed, may have brought together elements of quite different origins.

In the past, we have pointed out elements in the Early Iron Age pottery spectrum in Boğazköy that can be traced back to the Early and Middle Bronze Age in the west and south of Anatolia. Among those are various types of jugs, sieve lids, and diverse forms of handles and spouts, as well as the tradition of vessel painting (Genz 2004: 37–44; 2005; Seeher 2010: 226–227). To these we must also include the knobs attached to the sides of the neck of jugs shown here in Figs. 1,4.5 and 2,1–3.5. They are a very typical element of Early Bronze Age and Middle Bronze Age beak spouted jugs especially in the western part of the country. Occasionally they have been interpreted as representing eyes (e.g. Fischer 1963: 41). However, there are examples from the Early Bronze Age where metal rings or small nail-like pins made of clay are sitting in these knobs (Kâmil 1982: Fig. 51; Seeher 1987: 131). Thus it is clear that the knobs were meant to represent ears. The combination beak spouted jug plus ear knob is actually unspectacular, but is all the more significant for that very reason. Hittite jugs do not have ear knobs, and so we are dealing here with a clear connection of the Early Iron Age with an old, pre-Hittite form tradition. So far it is not clear whether this combination already existed in the Pontus area in the Late Bronze Age and reached the south from there, or whether it perhaps migrated from another area only in the Early Iron Age. Knobs next to the spout occur, of course, also in more distant areas such as the Aegean or Cyprus, there actually thought to be eyes. But given the other typical pre-Hittite form elements in both Early Iron Age pottery and other find categories, I do not see a connection here. One example is the clay spindle whorls, which are rather rare in Hittite strata. Almost all of them are flattened conical or hemisherical and typically have a trough-like depression on one side. From the Early Iron Age onwards, instead, spindle whorls appear in large quantities. Now they are mostly biconical to globular, which is also the typical shape variation of the Early Bronze Age in Anatolia, where spindle whorls were used in similar numbers.

As far as our knowledge of the interrelationships in the early 12th century B.C. is concerned, we are still at the very beginning. Not enough material is available so far from the few excavations that yielded Early Iron Age strata in north-central Anatolia. Oymaağaç is up to now the only site which yielded substantial evidence to trace this cultural complex back to the Late Bronze Age. Another promising site is Oluz Höyük near Amasya, where Late Bronze Age wheel made ware was found in layer 7B and Early Iron Age handmade ware in layer 7A, both decorated with red painting typical of the respective period (Dönmez – Abazoğlu 2019). But we are still far from understanding this cultural development and its spread southward. How and where did the transition from the red painted wheelmade Late Bronze Age pottery to the handmade Early Iron Age pottery take place? Was this really a chronological sequence, or was there a parallel development in different areas that led to the potter's wheel losing its importance? And it may turn out that the 'Early Iron Age package' did not reach everywhere in the same way, but in some places only components of it[1].

1 I would like to thank Dirk Paul Mielke, Kimiyoshi Matsumura and Hermann Genz for their comments on this paper and Andreas Schachner for photographs and drawings of several pieces from Ḫattuša/Boğazköy.

Bibliography

Arbuckle, B. S.
- 2009 "Chalcolithic caprines, Dark Age Dairy, and Byzantine Beef: A first look at Animal Exploitation at Middle and Late Holocene Çadır Höyük, North Central Turkey," *Anatolica* 35, 2009, pp. 179–224.

Bayburtluoğlu, İ.
- 1979 "Eskiyapar 'Phryg Çağı," *VIII. Türk Tarih Kongresi*, Ankara, pp. 293–303.

Bossert, E.-M.
- 2000 *Die Keramik phrygischer Zeit von Boğazköy. Funde aus den Grabungskampagnen 1906, 1907, 1911, 1912, 1931–1939 und 1952–1960*, Boğazköy-Hattuša 18, Mainz.

Czichon, R. M. *et al.*
- 2016 "Archäologische Forschungen am Oymaağaç Höyük/Nerik 2011–2015," *Mitteilungen der Deutschen Orient-Gesellschaft* 148, pp. 5–141.
- 2019 "Archäologische Forschungen am Oymaağaç Höyük/Nerik 2016–2018," *Mitteilungen der Deutschen Orient-Gesellschaft* 151, pp. 37–200.

Çilingiroğlu, Ç.
- 2005 "The Concept of "Neolithic Package": Considering its Meaning and Applicability," *Documenta Praehistorica* 32, 1–13.

d'Alfonso, L.
- 2020 "An Age of Experimentation: New Thoughts on the Multiple Outcomes Following the Fall of the Hittite Empire After the Results of the Excavations at Niğde-Kınık Höyük (South Cappadocia)," in S. De Martino and E. Devecchi (eds.), *Anatolia between the 13th and the 12th century B.C.E.*, Eothen 23, Torino, pp. 95–116.

Dönmez, Ş. and F. Abazoğlu
- 2019 "Hitit Sonrası Kuzey-Orta Anadolu: Oluz Höyük'te Karanlık Çağ ile İlgili Yeni Bulgular," in A. Süel (ed.), *IX. Uluslararası Hititoloji Kongresi Bildirileri / Acts of the IXth International Congress of Hittitology*, Vol. I, Çorum, pp. 237–260.

Fischer, F.
- 1963 *Die hethitische Keramik von Boğazköy*, Boğazköy-Hattuša 4, Berlin.

Genz, H.
- 2001 "Iron Age Pottery from Çadır Höyük," *Anatolica* 27, pp. 159–170.
- 2003 "Früheisenzeitliche Keramik von Büyükkale in Boğazköy/Hattuša," *Istanbuler Mitteilungen* 53, pp. 113–129.
- 2004 *Büyükkaya I. Die Keramik der Eisenzeit. Funde aus den Grabungskampagnen 1993 bis 1998*, Boğazköy-Hattuša 21, Mainz.
- 2005 "Thoughts on the Origin of the Iron Age Pottery Traditions in Central Anatolia," in: A. Çilingiroğlu and G. Darbyshire (eds.), *Anatolian Iron Ages 5. Proceedings of the Fifth Anatolian Iron Ages Colloquium Held at Van, 6–10 August 2001, BIAA Monograph 31*, Ankara, pp. 75–84.

Glatz, C. and R. Matthews
- 2005 "Anthropology of a Frontier Zone: Hittite-Kaska Relations in Late Bronze Age North-Central Anatolia," *BASOR* 339, pp. 47–65.

Gruber, M.
- 2017 "Hethitische Keramik vom Mittleren Plateau," in A. Schachner (ed.), *Ausgrabungen und Forschungen in der westlichen Oberstadt von Hattuša II*, Boğazköy-Hattuša 25, Berlin/Boston, pp. 63–216.

Kâmil, T.
- 1982 *Yortan Cemetery in the Early Bronze Age of Western Anatolia*, BAR International Series 145, Oxford.

Kealhofer, L., P. Grave and M. M. Voigt
- 2019 "Dating Gordion: The Timing and Tempo of Late Bronze and Early Iron Age Political Transformation," *Radiocarbon*, 61(2), pp. 495–514.

Matsumura, K.
- 2008 "The Early Iron Age in Kaman-Kalehöyük. The Search for its Roots," in Bonatz, D., R. M. Czichon and F. J. Kreppner (eds.), *Fundstellen. Gesammelte Schriften zur Archäologie und Geschichte Altvorderasiens. Ad honorem Hartmut Kühne*, Wiesbaden, pp. 41–50.

Mielke, D. P.
- 2006 *Die Keramik vom Westhang*, Kuşaklı-Sarissa 2, Rahden/Westfalen.
- 2016 "Spätbronzezeitliche Keramik", in Czichon *et al.* 2016, pp. 42–52.
- 2017 "From "Anatolian" to "Hittite". The Development of Pottery in Central Anatolia in the 2nd Millennium B.C.," in A. Schachner (ed.), *Innovation versus Beharrung: Was macht den Unterschied des hethitischen Reiches im Anatolien des 2. Jahrtausends v. Chr.?*, Byzas 23, Istanbul, pp. 121–144.
- 2019 "Keramikbearbeitung," in Czichon *et al.* 2019, pp. 69–83.
- 2022a "Die Kaškäer: eine archäologische Spurensuche," Istanbuler Mitteilungen 72, pp. 72–115.

– 2022b "Geometric Painted Pottery of the Second Millennium B.C. in the Central Black Sea Region. A Contribution to the Archaeology of the Kaška," in F. Manuelli and D. P. Mielke (eds.), *Late Bronze Age Painted Pottery Traditions at the Margins of the Hittite State*, Oxford, pp. 21–58.

Mühlenbruch, T.
– 2014 *Hethitische Keramik im Kontext: das Gebäude B von Kayalıpınar und die Nutzung institutioneller Gebäude des 2. Jt.s v. Chr. im ostmediterranen Raum*, Kayalıpınar 1, Rahden/Westfalen.

Müller-Karpe, A.
– 1988 *Die hethitische Töpferei der Oberstadt von Ḫattuša*, Marburg/Lahn.

Özgüç, T.
– 1978 *Maşat Höyük kazıları ve çevresindeki araştırmaları / Excavations at Maşat Höyük and Investigations in its Vicinity*, Ankara.
– 1982 *Maşat Höyük II. Boğazköy'ün Kuzeydoğusunda Bir Hitit Merkezi / A Hittite Center Northeast of Boğazköy*, Ankara

Özsait, M.
– 2003 "Les Céramiques du Fer Ancien dans les Régions d'Amasya et de Samsun," in. B. Fischer *et al.* (ed.), *Identifying Changes. The Transition from Bronze to Iron Ages in Anatolia and its Neighbouring Regions. Proceedings of the International Workshop Istanbul, November 8–9, 2002*, Istanbul, pp. 199–212.

Omura, S.
– 1984 "Beak-spouted Jug in the Central Anatolia," *Bulletin of the Society for Near Eastern Studies in Japan* 27/1, 1984, pp. 1–27 (in Japanese with English abstract).

Orsi, V.
– 2020 "The Transition from the Bronze to the Iron Age at Uşaklı Höyük: The Ceramic Sequence," in S. De Martino and E. Devecchi, *Anatolia between the 13th and the 12th century B.C.E.*, Eothen 23, Torino, pp. 271–316.

Parzinger, H. and R. Sanz
– 1992 *Die Oberstadt von Hattuša. Hethitische Keramik aus dem zentralen Tempelviertel. Funde aus den Grabungen 1982–1987*, Boğazköy-Hattuša 15, Berlin.

Ross, J. C. *et al.*
– 2019 "When the Giant Falls: Endurance and Adaptation at Çadır Höyük in the Context of the Hittite Empire and Its Collapse," *Journal of Field Archaeology*, 44:1, pp. 19–39

Schoop, U.-D.
– 2006 "Dating the Hittites with Statistics. Ten Pottery Assemblages from Boğazköy-Hattuša," in D. P. Mielke, U.-D. Schoop and J. Seeher (eds.), *Strukturierung und Datierung in der hethitischen Archäologie*, Byzas 4, Istanbul, pp. 215–239.

Schoop, U.-D. and J. Seeher
– 2006 „Absolute Chronologie in Boğazköy-Hattuša: Das Potential der Radiokarbondaten," in D. P. Mielke, U.-D. Schoop and J. Seeher, *Strukturierung und Datierung in der hethitischen Archäologie*, Byzas 4, Istanbul, pp. 53–75.

Seeher, J.
– 1987 *Demircihüyük III,1, Die Keramik 1*, Mainz.
– 2002 "Die Ausgrabungen in Boğazköy-Hattuša 2001," *Archäologischer Anzeiger* 2002/1, pp. 59–78.
– 2004 "Die Ausgrabungen in Boğazköy-Hattuša 2003," *Archäologischer Anzeiger* 2004/1, pp. 59–76.
– 2010 "After the Empire. Observations on the Early Iron Age in Central Anatolia," in I. Singer (ed.), *ipamati kistamati pari tumatimis. Luwian and Hittite Studies Presented to J. David Hawkins on the Occasion of his 70th Birthday*, Tel Aviv, pp. 220–229.
– 2018 *Büyükkaya II. Bauwerke und Befunde der Grabungskampagnen 1952–1955 und 1993–1998*, Boğazköy-Hattuša 27, Berlin/Boston.

Seeher-Baykal, A and J. Seeher
– in preparation *Büyükkaya III. Die Kleinfunde der Grabungskampagnen 1994–1998.*

Steadman, S. R. *et al.*
– 2015 "The 2013 and 2014 Excavation Seasons at Çadır Höyük on the Anatolian North Central Plateau," *Anatolica* 41, pp. 87–124.

von den Driesch, A. and N. Pöllath
– 2004 *Vor- und frühgeschichtliche Nutztierhaltung und Jagd auf Büyükkaya in Boğazköy-Ḫattuša, Zentralanatolien*, Boğazköy-Berichte 7, Mainz.

Voigt, M. M. and R. C. Henrickson
– 2000 "The Early Iron Age at Gordion. The Evidence from the Yassıhöyük Stratigraphic Sequence," in E. D. Oren (ed.), *The Sea Peoples and their World. A Reassessment*, Philadelphia, pp. 327–360.

Von der Osten, H. H.
– 1937 *The Alishar Hüyük. Seasons of 1930–32, Part II*, Oriental Institute Publications Vol. 29, Chicago.

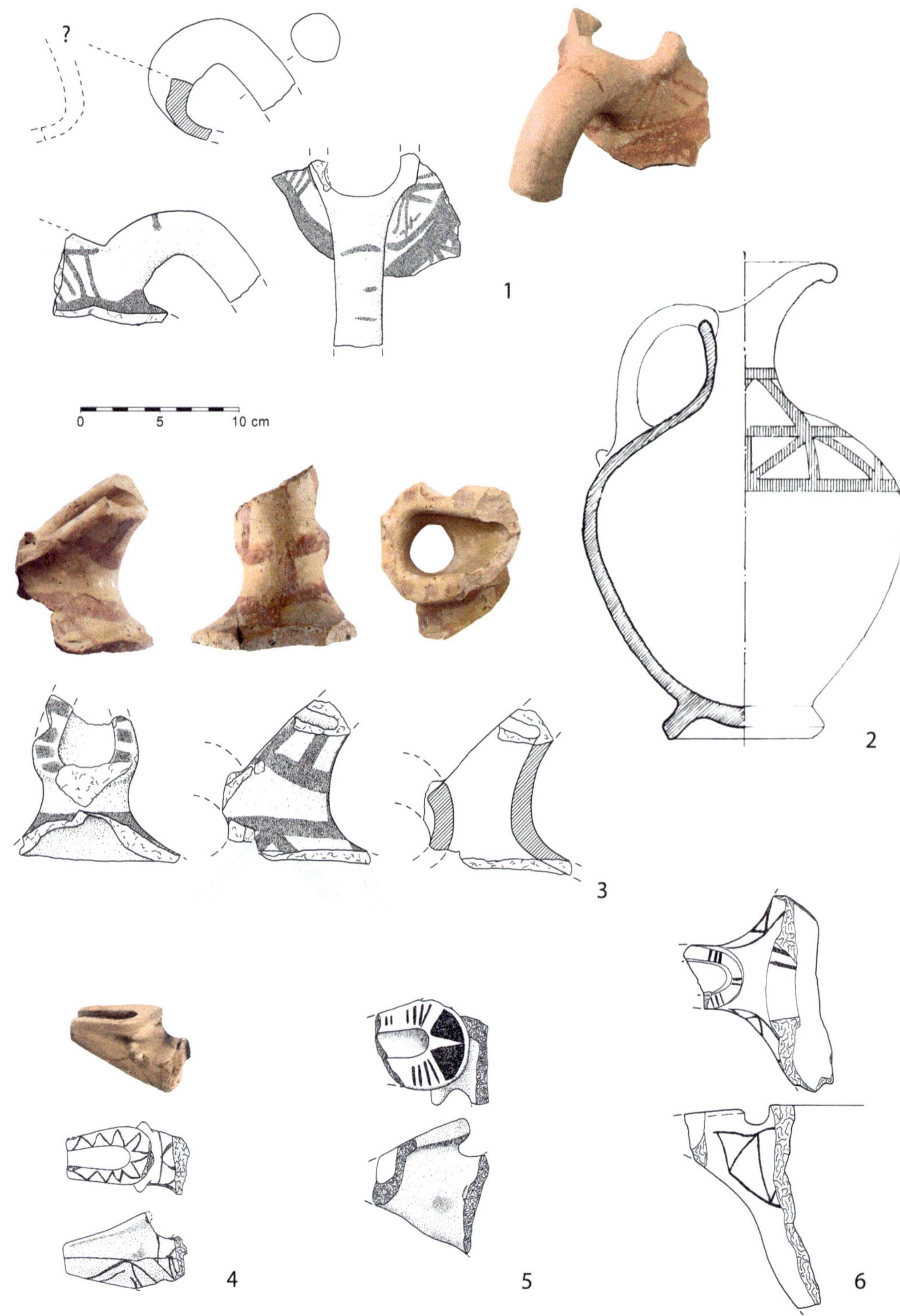

Fig. 1. 1–3 Late Bronze Age beak spouted jugs; 4–6 Early Iron Age side spouts: 1 Oymaağaç; 2 Maşat Höyük; 3–6 Büyükkaya at Ḫattuša/Boğazköy
[1 Mielke 2022b: Figs. 8,2 and 9,2; 2 Özgüç 1982: 102, Fig. 34; 3 Find No Boğazköy 1995 355/427.105, drawing J. Seeher, photographs A. Kurz/M. Piepenburg; 4 Genz 2004: Pl. 19,8 and 77,b; 5 Genz 2004: Pl. 36,3; 6 Genz 2004: Pl. 26,6]

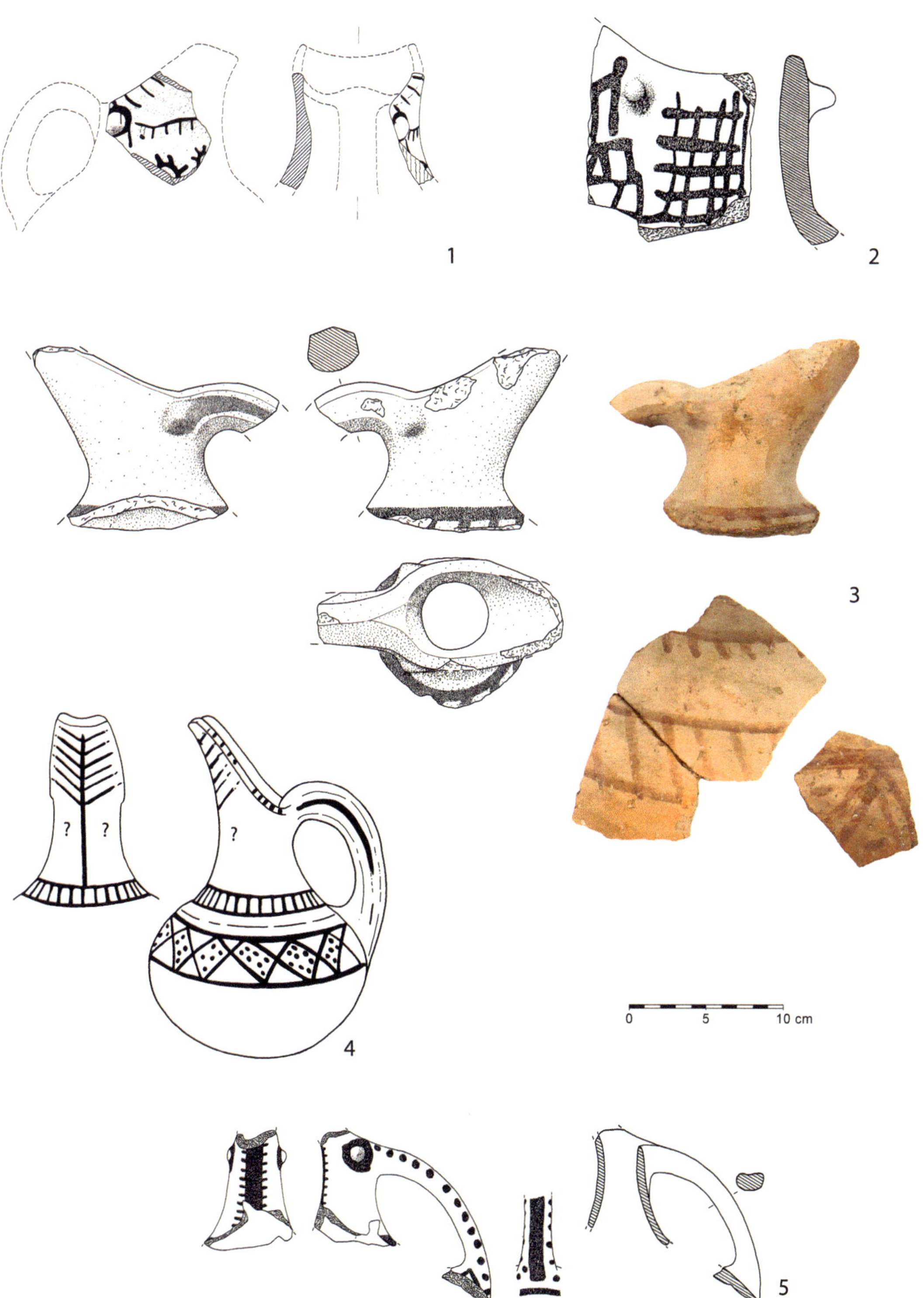

Fig. 2. Early Iron Age beak spouted jugs: 1–3. 5 Ḫattuša/Boğazköy; 4 Eskiyapar [1 Seeher 2004: Fig. 24; 2 Genz 2003: Fig.1,3; 3 Fischer 1963: Pl. 30, 255, drawing E. Arnold, photographs A. Kurz/M. Piepenburg; 4 Genz 2004: Fig. 18,c, with additions; 5 Genz 2004: Pl. 35,10]

A Cimmerian Citadel at Büklükale?

Kimiyoshi Matsumura *

Abstract

The Late Iron Age is one of the periods in Central Anatolian history which have been left unresolved. In this period, nomadic peoples from the Caucasus region were said to have invaded Anatolia, as described in historical texts. However, they are not yet clearly identified archaeologically except for some sporadic finds. The excavations at Büklükale revealed a settlement with a large citadel wall and a bone object which was decorated in the so-called Scythian animal style. This article tries to evaluate these findings from two perspectives: from the written textual evidence, and from the archaeological and stratigraphical point of view. The results of analysis on buildings and artifacts are suitable to propose that there might have been a Cimmerian settlement at Büklükale.

Öz

İç Anadolu tarihide çözülmemiş olan dönemlerden biri ise Geç Demir Çağı'dır. Bu dönemde Kafkasya bölgesinden gelen ata binen göçebelerin Anadolu'ya akın edildiği tarih kaynaklarda belirtilmiştir. Fakat, onların izleri birkaç eser hariç arkeolojik açıdan tam olarak izlenememiştir. Büklükale kazılarında büyük bir kale yerleşim ve sözde İskit hayvan motif ile süslenen kemik obje ile çeşitli eserler bulundu. Bu makalede söz konusu bulgular hem yazılı kaynakların bilgileriyle hem de arkeolojik ve stratigrafik açıdan incelendi. Bu mimari ve eserlerin inceleme sonucu Büklükale'de Kimmerler'e ait yerleşme olabileceğini göstermektedir.

Introduction

Since 1986, the excavations at Kaman-Kalehöyük have been carried out under the directorship of Dr. Sachihiro Omura with the greatest priority given to establishing the cultural chronology in Central Anatolia. A stratigraphical excavation method has been pursued in the project and is one of the most fundamental tasks for archaeological excavation. Additionally, we are aware that this is one of the most critically viewed issues in archaeological excavations. The present study was undertaken in order to demonstrate the importance of stratigraphical excavation by taking the case study on the Late Iron Age in Büklükale as an example (Fig. 1).

Herodotus writes on the "Battle of Halys" between the Lydians and Medians in Histories 1.73–74.

> *After this, seeing that Alyattes would not give up the Scythians to Cyaxares at his demand, there was war between the Lydians and the Medes for five years; each won many victories over the other, and once they fought a battle by night. They were still warring with equal success, when it chanced, at an encounter which happened in the sixth year, that during the battle the day was suddenly turned to night... So when the Lydians and Medes saw the day turned to night they ceased from fighting, and both were the more zealous to make peace.* (Herodotus, The Histories, 1.74.2)[1]

* Japanese Institute of Anatolian Archaeology/Ahi Evran Üniversitesi, Kırşehir, Department of Archaeology, k.matsumura@jiaa-kaman.org.

1 Godley 1975: 91–93.

The "Battle of Halys", which came to an end by the eclipse in 585 B.C. (cf. Tuplin 2004: 238), was the fight at the periphery of the Kızılırmak river. However, the place where the battle occurred is still under discussion. After the battle, the Kızılırmak was defined as a boundary by treaty. The border between countries adjacent to each other east and west must have been located in a region where the Kızılırmak flows south to north. On the west bank of the Kızılırmak river which runs from south to north, the ancient city of Büklükale was situated (Fig. 2).

Büklükale was firstly surveyed in 1991 by the General Survey Project in Central Anatolia of the Japanese Institute of Anatolian Archaeology (JIAA) directed by Dr. Sachihiro Omura, thereafter in 2006 and 2008 (Omura 1993: 368; 2007: 50). Since 2009, the excavations continued up to the present under my directorship. During the 2018 excavation season, a button-shaped bone object was unearthed, on which a so-called "Scythian Animal Style" motif was engraved. In this article, with the Scythian Animal Styled find as a springboard, the question of Scythian or Cimmerian associations in Büklükale is approached by way of stratigraphic analyses.

Scythian and Cimmerian History in Anatolia According to the Written Sources

The history of the horse-riding peoples was reported by Assyrian cuneiform texts from the 8th and 7th century B.C. Assyrian texts distinguish two different groups of mounted nomads: Gimirrāya (the Cimmerians) and Iškuzāya (the Scythians) (see Adalı 2017a: 62). There have been a lot of studies over many years which were focused on the classification of the two groups according to certain finds. But such continual studies and discussion have reached no common ground yet.

According to Herodotus, the Scythians were forced out of Central Asia and they in turn forced the Cimmerians out of their homeland. As a result, the Cimmerians migrated into Anatolia and the Scythians chased them into Media. However, both people used different passes of the Caucasus.

> *The nomad Scythians inhabiting Asia, being hard pressed in war by the Massagetae, fled away across the river Araxes to the Cimmerian country (for the country which the Scythians now inhabit is said to have belonged of old to the Cimmerians)* (Herodotus, The Histories, 4.11.1)[2]
>
> *He defeated the Assyrians in battle; but while he was besieging their city there came down upon him a great army of Scythians, led by their king Madyes son of Protothyes. These had invaded Asia after they had driven the Cimmerians out of Europe: pursuing them in their flight the Scythians came to the Median country.* (Herodotus, The Histories, 1.103.3)[3].

There is no reference in ancient Near Eastern texts according to which the Scythians chased the Cimmerians (Adalı 2017a: 60). Regarding the matter of Scythian movement southward, Assyrian records give us a clue. The Scythians appeared for the first time in Assyrian reports during the 7th century B.C. By 676 B.C. at the latest, royal inscriptions claim Esarhaddon's (681–669 B.C.) victory against a Mannaean-Scythian alliance led by a Scythian named Išpakāya (Adalı 2017b: 317; Leichty 2011: 29–30). The Scythians were also reported to have defeated Media, and after that are mentioned in relation with the Iranian frontier of Assyria and Urartu (Starr 1990: lxi–lxii).

The extispicy reports mentioning the Scythians (edited in Starr 1990) refer either to the Scythians militarily active in certain parts of western Iran close to Mannaea, or to the diplomatic initiative by a certain Bartatua, named "king of Scythia" in the reports. Bartatua is known by Herodotus as Protothyes (Histories 1.103). He requested an Assyrian princess in marriage, but no inscribed date is preserved on any of these existing reports (Adalı 2018: 215).

2 Godley 1928:211.
3 Godley 1975: 135.

Consequently, the Scythians seem to have no direct relevance for Anatolian history[4].

It was the Cimmerians who are more deeply related to Central Anatolian history. The Cimmerians appeared for the first time in Assyrian sources during the reign of Sargon II (ca. 722–705 B.C.), according to which Sargon II was informed that they came from a land Gamir and the Urartians had been defeated by them (Lanfranchi and Parpola 1990: 92: 5–6), during the reign of either Rusa I in a battle before 714 B.C., or his son Argishti II with a battle in 707 B.C. (Adalı 2017a: 62; Berndt-Ersöz 2008: 22). Central Anatolia had been opened for the Cimmerians when Urartu was unable to stop them in the late 8th century B.C. (Adalı 2017a: 67).

Accordingly, it was the end of the 8th century B.C. when the Cimmerians entered the Near East, and the southward movement by Cimmerians and Scythians, as described by Herodotus, began at least from the late 8th to the early 7th century B.C. The Cimmerians are reported from two areas: around Urartu in the east, and along Assyria's north-western borders towards Cilicia, Tabal and Melid (Malatya).

Tabal, the Cimmerian and Midas

The Central Anatolian land of Tabal appears in Assyrian texts during the 9th century B.C. Under the reign of Shalmaneser III, Tuwati I, the king of Tabal, gave tribute together with 24 kings in Anatolia (Grayson 1996: 67; Adalı 2018: 277). By the period of the Assyrian King Tiglat-Pileser III (744–728 B.C.), 5 kings including the king Wasusarmas, the son of Tuwati II, in Tabal provided tribute to Assyria (Bryce 2009: 682). We know that Wasusarmas was tributary two times, in 738 B.C. and in 732 B.C. (Weeden 2010: 41; Hawkins 2000: 427).

However, it is likely some time after (between 732 and 729 B.C.), Wassurme stopped giving tribute to Tiglath-Pileser III and had to be replaced (Weeden 2010: 42). In 718 B.C., Kiakki of Šinuḫtu and in 717 B.C., Pisiri of Karkemish had been removed by Sargon and Ambaris, the king of Tabal rebelled in 713 B.C. Both Pisiri and Ambaris and possibly Kiakki were accused of conspiring with Mita of Muški (Weeden 2010: 42; Hawkins 2000: 427, n.44). Mita of Muški (Midas of Phrygia) was against the Assyrians at this point. Sargon II possibly pursued a policy of direct intervention in Tabal, where he encountered the power of Mita of Muški.

However, the situation changed thereafter, as Sargon reports in a reply which he intended to send from Nimrud to Ashur-sharru-usur, the Assyrian governor of Que in Cilicia (Parpola 1987: 4–7, no. 1). It is stated that Urik (Awariku of Hiyawa/Adanawa) attempted to break his ties with Assyria. Urik/Awariku had secretly sent a fourteen-men delegation to the Urartian king, possibly Argishti II, but they were seized by the agents of Mita of Muški and he handed over them to Ashur-sharru-usur (cf. Bryce 2012: 158; Weeden 2010: 42).

Sargon II's continuing interest in the Tabal region is shown by his campaign there in 705 B.C., possibly undertaken in collaboration with Mita of Muški. Bryce supposes that the Cimmerians were the chief target of the campaign (Bryce 2012: 288). However, Sargon II was killed by Gurdi in 705 B.C. in battle almost certainly in Anatolia and probably in Tabal. Gurdi is described in Assyrian eponym lists as a Kulummean (Kulummāya). Gurdi was probably one of the local Tabalian rulers, not a Cimmerian (DeVries 2011: 53).

A group of the Cimmerians was supposed to migrate to Anatolia around this time. By 679 B.C., Cimmerians were certainly in Central Anatolia, where the Assyrian king Esarhaddon (680–669 B.C.) defeated 'Teušpa the Cimmerian' around 679 B.C. in Cybistra (Hupisna in Hittite), which is in the Konya-Ereğli region in Central Anatolia (DeVries 2011:

4 There is only one mention of Scythians under Madyes, son of Protothyes, campaigning and controlling Anatolia, "Asia", during the third quarter of the 7th century B.C. by Herodotus (Histories 1, 104) (Millard 1968: 120; Adalı 2018: 217).

53). Hereafter in 679 B.C. the Cimmerians held power in the region of Ereğli, Konya.

During the 670s B.C., Cilicia, Tabal, Phrygia (Muški) and the Cimmerians are described in Assyrian sources mostly as being anti-Assyrian (Starr 1990: nos. 1, 17). In one such oracle query, dated to 678–676 B.C., Esarhaddon asks whether Mugallu or the king of the Muški (Phrygia) allied with the Cimmerians will attack Melid (Malatya) or not (Starr 1990: 4, no. 1). This indicates an alliance between the Phrygians and the Cimmerians, and demonstrates that the Cimmerians were interested in the area east, not west, of Tabal. Thus, Berndt-Ersöz claims that there is no evidence that the Cimmerians were threatening western Anatolia, including Phrygia, before the 660s B.C. (Berndt-Ersöz 2008: 23).

Here arises the question as to the attack by the Cimmerians in Gordion and king Midas's death in relation to it. Strabo linked both events and the traditional date of 695 B.C. for Midas's death and this was adopted by Eusebius from the 3rd–4th century AD (Mellink 1991: 614; Wittke 2004: 221–2 and see also Strabo 1.3.21). Berndt-Ersöz proposes three different Midas figures in Iron Age Anatolia. The first Midas is famous for committing suicide by drinking bull's blood, and the second Midas is the Midas (II) who is mentioned in an Assyrian source of the 670s B.C. The third one is the one who died in connection with the Cimmerian invasion during the reign of Ardys, the son of the king Gyges of Lydia. So, the Midas referred to by Strabo should therefore be both Midas III, who died during the period of Ardys, shortly after 645/4 B.C. and the death of Midas I (r. c. 723–c. 677 B.C.) (Berndt-Ersöz 2008: 30).

There may in fact be some evidence for a Cimmerian attack on Gordion and it is to be found in an extramural Middle Phrygian settlement northeast of the citadel. Houses in this area have been destroyed by an attack ca. 700 B.C. but the citadel was not seriously damaged (Ross 2012: 15).

Although the Phrygians were not terminally wounded by the Cimmerians as recent research shows, it seems that king Tugdamme of the Cimmerians was active from the Aegean Sea to the Cilician region. It may show at least the weakness of the Phrygians during this time if the Phrygians were not terminally damaged by the Cimmerians.

Lydia and the Cimmerians

Around 665 B.C., Gyges and probably also the kings of Cilicia and Tabal asked for help from Ashurbanipal against Cimmerian attack (cf. Hawkins 1982: 431–432). None of the kings of western Anatolia had asked for Assyrian assistance before. The Cimmerians appear not to have threatened western Anatolia including Phrygia until then (Berndt-Ersöz 2008: 24). However, embassies were sent by Sandasarme of Hilakku (Cilicia) and Mugallu of Tabal to Ashurbanipal around the same time, probably with the intention of asking for help against the Cimmerians (Berndt-Ersöz 2008: 24).

Texts from the time of Ashurbanipal (r. 668–c. 627 B.C.) refer to Cimmerian city-lords (EN URU.MEŠ) bordering the eastern frontiers of Lydia. (Borger 1996: 31; Adalı 2017a: 64). This Cimmerian threat was obviously overcome by Gyges at this point, since he presented the Assyrian king with Cimmerian captives (Cogan and Tadmor 1977: 77). The previously mentioned alliance between the Phrygians and the Cimmerians may explain why the Phrygians did not turn to the Assyrians for help against the Cimmerians, as supposed by Berndt-Ersöz (2008: 24).

Around 657 B.C., the Cimmerians probably annexed Assyrian territory in Asia Minor. Then, Gyges allied himself with Psammetichus I of Egypt in the mid-650s B.C. Berndt-Ersöz supposes that Gyges must have allied with Psammetichus since a peace treaty between the Cimmerian ruler Tugdamme and Ashurbanipal was established, and he could no longer count on Assyria for help against the Cimmerians (Cogan and Tadmor 1977: 84; Berndt-Ersöz 2008: 24).

In about 645 B.C., the Cimmerians again threatened Lydian territory and Gyges was killed by them, possibly in 644 B.C., as is reported in Assyrian sources dated to 643 B.C. (Prism A/ Rassam Cylinder) (Berndt-Ersöz 2008: 24). In those days, Lydia seems to have continued to be troubled by the Cimmerians after the death of Gyges, as the Prism A /Rassam Cylinder also reports that Ardys, the son of Gyges, had turned to the Assyrians for help (Cogan and Tadmor, 1977: 78–80, 84; Berndt-Ersöz 2008: 24).

Between Gyges's first plea to Assyria (c. 665 B.C.) for help against the Cimmerians in the middle of 7th century B.C. and the time of Tugdamme's death at around 640 B.C. (Grayson 1980: 232), the Cimmerians under King Tugdamme dominated Anatolia and controlled territories from Lydia through Phrygia up to Cilicia and to the border of Urartian state (Adalı 2017a: 63).

At the time of Gyges's first plea, the Cimmerians possibly marched already to the west of Gordion. Therefore, it was reported in the royal inscriptions from the period of Ashurbanipal's reign (r. 668–c. 627 B.C.) that Cimmerian city-lords had a border with Lydia (Borger 1996: 31). It seems to be appropriate that the Phrygians had already lost their power by the beginning of the 7th century B.C. or ca. 670 B.C.

The Assyrians recognized Cimmerian city-rulers in Central and West Anatolia. The territories controlled by the Cimmerians in Anatolia fluctuated according to their political and military fortunes. Tugdamme is reputed to have a capital city called Harzalle (Borger 1996: 196; Adalı 2017a: 64).

Moreover, Assyrian texts suggest that Tugdamme had probably joined forces with a king of Tabal against Assyria shortly before his death (Spalinger 1978: 407; Kuhrt 1990: 188). In 652 B.C., Cimmerian leader Tugdamme was defeated by Ashurbanipal. The Cimmerian leader Tugdamme died through sickness as reported in the Assyrian texts of 639 B.C. (Prism H/ Ishtar Tablet) (Millard 1968: 109–110). According to Strabo (1.3.21), Lygdamis was killed in Cilicia after returning from an expedition to Lydia and Ionia.

After the death of Tugdamme in c. 640 B.C., the Cimmerians dispersed. The Cimmerians became debilitated possibly after the reseizure of Sardis by the Lydians in 619 B.C., and were expelled almost entirely from Anatolia by the conquest of Lydia by the Achaemenids in 547 B.C.

According to the history constructed by the above mentioned written resources, it seems reasonable that the arrival of the Cimmerians at Büklükale was almost at the same time or before the "Cimmerian destruction" of Gordion. That is, the Cimmerians passed through the region before the death of Midas (695 B.C.). This brings me to the point that the Cimmerian settlement was probably established at the end of 7th century B.C., whether or not they did settle at Büklükale. An earlier Cimmerian settlement at Büklükale seems to be difficult to suppose.

Considering such history, the Middle and Late Iron Age in Central Anatolia can be divided into the following four sub-periods:

1. Tabalian and Phrygian period (ca. 900–700 B.C.)
2. Cimmerian period (ca. 700–620 B.C.)
3. Lydian period (ca. 619–547 B.C.)
4. Achaemenid period (ca. 547–333 B.C.)

After the overview of the Iron Age history of Anatolia, it seems that the Scythians did not play any important role, but the Cimmerians had a key role in the Middle to Late Iron Age of Central Anatolia.

A Bone Object with the Scythian Animal Motif from Büklükale

During the Büklükale Excavations in 2018, a button shaped bone object, which bears a so-called Scythian animal motif, was found from layers dated to the Late Iron Age (BK180085; Fig. 3). It was unearthed directly on the floor of the room R181 from the provisional layer PL 119 in the grid N5W4 of Area A on 25th June 2018. The find spot clearly shows that it belongs to the room R181.

It is 2.3 cm in diameter and 0.8 cm in height, and is shaped like a round button. Its weight is 1.56 g. On its back, there is a round stem of

5mm in diameter and 0.7 cm long. On the stem, there is no hole or trace of breakage which verifies the existence of a hole. Probably it might have been inserted into a conformable socket. In previous studies, such types of artifacts have been proposed to be a chape or the ornament of a scabbard (see e.g., Goldman 1957: Fig. 2-f; Greenewalt *et al.* 1973: 33, Fig. 11).

On the obverse, there is an incised ornament with the image of an animal curled into a ring, inside which the paws and tail are located, and there is an empty field in the center. The front side has a lustrous surface, although the back shows scratches, possibly processing marks. This indicates that this object was made in order to display its obverse.

The depicted animal seems to be a feline. Its head, a nose, an eye, and an ear protrude beyond the outer contour of the head. An elongated sub-rectangular muzzle and a closed mouth without teeth are expressed. The eye and nostril are displayed as a small hole, although the nose, ear and earhole are expressed quite large. The ear is represented by a semicircle. The front paw raised upwards is tightly pressed to the neck. Its end is in contact with the base of the lower jaw, the tail adjoins the front paw and the hind leg adjoins the knee of the front leg. Paws and tail endings are formed in a circle. The femur and scapula of the animal are poorly defined, and look rather amorphous. As a result, the Büklükale sample resembles more closely the image of a feline predator than a dog or a wolf.

A quick overview of the origin and spread of Scythian animal motifs shows that they are attested over a broad area from Tuva to the northern Caucasus. Characteristics for this motif are as described above; the image of an animal curled into a ring with head and hip coming into contact, inside which the paws and tail are located. In many cases, predators open their mouth and show their teeth in anger.

The oldest example of this type is a bronze plaque from Aržan I which is possibly a breastplate (810 B.C., Zaitseva *et al.* 1997: 579). Such a motif, dating back to the end of the 8th or early 7th century B.C., was confirmed in the basin of Ural river, North Caucasus, and Ukraine, and it reveals the Scythian movement westward from the eastern steppe (Yukishima 2008: 85).

Recent studies on the Scythian animal motif address the stylization of the motif (eg. Makhortykh 2020). On the oldest example from Aržan I, stylization is already recognizable, although the hooves are depicted realistically. According to Makhortykh's studies, the main period for the existence of images of coiled predators in the Near East covers the second half of the 7th–early 6th century B.C., having undergone certain changes specifically and stylistically. It continues to exist in the territory of Iran and adjacent regions in the 6th–5th centuries B.C., and becomes one of the components of Achaemenid imagery (Makhortykh 2020: 362).

There are several examples found in Anatolia. One of them is a bone scabbard in the Urartian fortress Ayanis (Fig. 4-a; Çilingiroğlu 2018: 22, Fig. 12). The scabbard from Ayanis is one of the reliable ancient Eastern finds with the image of a curled predator, in which their nostril, tail and ends of the paws are decorated with concentric circles. Such renderings of the ends of the predator's paws in concentric circles, and additionally a large, tear-shaped ear turned with a sharp end downward, are known from an example from Ephesus (Hogarth 1908, Pl. 26, 3a). The destruction of the Ayanis fortress dates to around or most likely a little later than 650 B.C. (Çilingiroğlu 2018: 24).

On the other hand, examples found in the Western Anatolian site Sardis, the capital of Lydia, show much more stylization. Quite original is also a bone plate decorated with the image of a coiled beast which serves as the tip of an *akinakes* scabbard (Fig. 4-b; Greenewalt *et al.* 1990: 166, Fig. 34). One eye is depicted by a concentric circle with a point in the middle, and one ear is formed of the sole of a horse's hoof. The lower part of the muzzle and the mouth of the animal are rendered in the form of semi-ovals. The boundaries are outlined by two lines filled with a notch. The image on the Sardis plate is, compared to the one from Ayanis, more schematic and stylized, and was carried out as well as the loss of components like nostril and thigh. Therefore, it can be regarded as of a later date compared to the one from Ayanis (Makhortykh 2020: 356). The date of the Sardis sample in question should be determined within the second half of the 7th–early 6th century B.C. (Makhortykh 2020: 357)[5].

After an overview of the stylization of the Scythian animal motif, it seems that the example from Büklükale bears a resemblance to the one from Sardis, but is more schematic than the one from Ayanis. Therefore, it might be dated to the second half of the 7th to early 6th century B.C. according to stylistic analysis.

Late Iron Age Stratigraphy in Büklükale

In this section, the Late Iron Age stratigraphy in Büklükale will be outlined. Up to now, in total 15 building levels were recognized between the Hellenistic period and the period of the 2nd Millennium B.C. on the northern part of the citadel area (Fig. 5, enclosed by a heavy line). They are numbered from younger to older as Iron Age (IA) 1 to 15 tentatively. Through previous studies it has already been confirmed that the first three building levels under the Ottoman period are dated to the Hellenistic period, under which there is a building level belonging to the Achaemenid period (Matsumura 2017). According to changes in architectural features that have been recognized, the Iron Age building levels are divided into 5 main building periods and between each building period there are some building layers which are too fragmentary to evaluate under the existing conditions.

Building Period 1 (BP 1): Achaemenid period: Iron Age Building Level 1 (IA 1)

There is a stone paved foundation of a large architectural structure with that is 20 m long. However, its width is unknown because its southwest side is destroyed by later construction activities. Because of the finds from layers of this BP 1, it is dated to the Achaemenid period (Fig. 6; see Matsumura 2017).

Under the Achaemenid Period, two building layers (IA 2 and 3) are found. Their architectural structures are very fragmentary and are recognized in a very small area. Typical architectural feature for this period is a bi-faced wall which indicates the building was ground-level house.

Building Period 2 (BP 2): IA 4 and 5

There are two building levels and both have almost the same structures, and they must be interpreted as one building period with two building phases. Additionally, both phases were built with almost the same plan with some modifications, and they are burnt as well. Both architectural structures were cut by the Achaemenid stone-paved architectural structures of BP 1 (Fig. 7).

Under BP 2 appeared probably two different building levels (IA 6, 7), although they were found separately in different small areas and their orientations differ from each other. Differently from BP 2, all buildings are constructed with one-faced walls which indicate half-subterranean houses. At least R162 and R163 are located above the pits which belong to BP 3.

Building Period 3 (BP3), Period with Large Storage Pits: IA 8

Two large storage pits (P292 and PP359) without any coeval building remains were found (Fig. 8). Both pits are square with round edges and one is 7m wide, the other is 5m wide and 2m deep. Both have a white layer at the bottom which is fibrous material originating from plants (see Kimura *et al.* 1998). Such large storage pits were also found in the southern part of the Citadel area. They are supposed to have been built together with a kind of buildings which required such large pits for preserving a large quantity of grain. The southeast wall of the pit P292 was constructed with stone, probably this part was appended or repaired later, since there is a fragile burnt layer behind the stone wall.

Under BP 3, there are three building layers (IA 9 to 11) which are identified respectively in a limited area.

5 In Sardis, a bone object with bird motif was also found (Greenewalt *et al.* 1973: Fig. 11, left). An almost identical one was reported in Kaman-Kalehöyük (Takahama 1999, 178, Photo 1a–b, 2).

Building Period 4 (BP 4), 'Cimmerian Citadel': IA 12 to 14

There is one building level containing four building phases in BP 4. During this period the citadel wall (W11) was built (Fig. 9). It was reused continuously thereafter until the Ottoman period.

The building R182 was built together with the citadel wall at first (Fig. 9). Only one building (R182) was found thus far, and its western part was cut by the pit P359 and the southern part was cut by pits P344 and P292. All three pits belong to BP 3. A small part of its south wall (W 474) was found at the southwest corner of the grid.

Room R182 is almost rectangular with dimensions of 10x11m. A floor was found. Walls except the south wall are quite wide with ca. 1.5m and only the inner surface of the wall is arranged by using rectangular stones, and behind them irregular stones were filled in. The outer surface of each wall seems to have not been arranged in a straight line. Accordingly, this building was a half-subterranean architectural structure. Only the south wall is bi-faced and therefore the outer and inner floor of this part seems to be built on the same level. Thence, this building was built on an inclined plane which sloped down to the southwest.

In front of northwest and northeast corners, two pit-shaped hearths (H63 and H62) were constructed surrounded with stones. Their diameter is ca. 75 cm and ca. 50 cm deep respectively and the fire-holes are facing the center of the room. Each was connected to a pit, probably ashes were raked out from the fire-place to the pit. This kind of fire-place is unknown in the Iron Age of this region, for example at Kaman-Kalehöyük. There is an installation paved with small pebbles at the northeast of the pit-shaped hearth H63.

Some of the most important finds from this building are terracotta figures of two horses with riders, which were found on the floor at the south of the hearth H62 and in front of the east wall W441 (Fig. 12: BK180001; BK180003; BK180005; BK180006). The horses are ca. 11 cm high and 13 cm long and the riders are ca. 4.7 cm wide and 9.5 cm high (in their remaining parts). There are a lot of horse and rider figures in the Near East (cf. Pruß 2010). However, no comparable figure for this time period was found up to now.

The building R182 was restored twice and in the second phase, the Scythian animal styled bone object was found on the floor of the room R181 (see above and Fig. 3).

The citadel wall W11 was first identified together with Ottoman buildings which were constructed on the citadel wall which served as a foundation. Since then, the citadel wall had been reused each period as the outer wall of the settlement. In 2016, we reached the bottom of the citadel wall in the area of the grid N3W5 and found out the building R182 which was first used with the citadel wall (see Fig. 9, 10). Under the outer floor of this building, there is a debris, possibly filled at the same time with the construction of the citadel wall, since there is a lot of wooden beam fragments in the debris which were remnants used for constructing the citadel wall.

In grid N4W2, a part of the citadel wall W11 was removed to understand its construction technique, and its section was observed in 2017 (Fig. 13). The citadel wall was built on the slope, not on the flattened surface, and was constructed according to the form of the land. In consequence, its height differs from place to place. Today, its width is ca. 2.9m and its height is 5m at the highest point. However, the original top surface of the stone wall is unknown. A mud-brick wall must have been on the stone foundation, although it leaves no trace at present.

In the wall, there are 5 horizontal layers of wooden logs which are laid parallel to each other, and at right angles to the wall. Between the layers of wooden logs, there is a stone wall of ca. 1m in height. Wooden logs were laid possibly for reinforcing the wall (Fig. 14)[6]. Each wooden log protrudes 25–30 cm horizontally from both

6 Such technique is also observed on the Hittite Empire's wall at Büklükale.

the outer and inner wall face. They were not cut at the point of the wall face, because the stone wall was buried under soil.

Outside of the citadel wall, a lot of unstable one-row walls appeared, they were built orthogonally to the citadel wall (see Fig. 9). They were built for filling the outside of the citadel wall with soil. In this way, possibly, filling the soil in was made easy. They would not have been able to stand alone. After constructing a ca. 1m height of stone wall, wooden logs were laid, and outside of the citadel wall was filled by soil by making and using an unstable fragile wall of one-row of stones one after another. In this way, the citadel wall was constructed to such a height.

In the grid N 6W5, inside of the citadel wall W11, a stone staircase was found and its bottom level where the staircase ends is same as the floor level of the contemporary building, R182 (see Fig. 10).

Buiding Period 5 (BP 5), Period of Pit Houses: IA 15

In this period, pit houses (with niches built in a stone wall for pillars) appeared. This type of construction technique is unique in Büklükale and is supposed to be peculiar for this period. At the southwestern corner of the grid N5W4, the room R194 was found and its northeast and southeast walls are partly revealed (Fig. 15, 16). In front of walls, a bench of 50 cm wide and 30 cm in height is constructed with stones and also plastered. As far as it has been excavated, the northeast wall is 3.4 m long and the southeast wall is 0.65 m in height. The preserved stone wall is 0.88 m high from the bench. Moreover, there is a difference: there is a space in a shape of a niche for inserting possibly a wooden post.

In Büklükale, one more pit house with post hole in the stone wall was found (R126) in the grid N2W2. There is a niche for a post in the southeast wall. The size of the house is 4.64x3.52m and the preserved wall is 84 cm in height from the floor. Although there is no direct stratigraphical connection between two pit houses, both are supposed to belong to the same period because of their construction technique. The house R126 was found directly above the layer of the Karum period in the grid N3W2 and above it, there is a late Iron Age layer. Accordingly, there is no contradiction stratigraphically.

Such pit houses are known at Kaman-Kalehöyük in the IIc that is the Middle Iron Age and IIb periods. Especially, pit houses in the IIc Period have benches (e.g., Omura 2003: Fig. 63–4). In this period at Kaman-Kalehöyük, pit houses co-exist with the so called Alişar IV painted pottery. However, unlike the example in Büklükale, there is no post hole.

At Büyükkale II, Boğazköy, pit houses were also found and several wooden posts were built in a stone wall (see Neve 1982: Abb. 75). Neve dated the Building period (die älter-phrygische Bauperiode), according to the destruction level at Gordion which is supposed to have been caused by the Cimmerian attack in ca. 680 B.C. (Neve 1982: 147). However, now the dating of the destruction level at Gordion has been brought back to ca. 800 B.C. (DeVries *et al.* 2003). And thus, this building phase should be dated 810 B.C. or earlier. Pit houses are known also other Central Anatolian sites like Kültepe, Alişar, and Alacahöyük, although no such site shows wooden posts in the wall (See Özgüç 1971: Figs. 1 and 2; Osten 1937: Figs. 348 and 358; Koşay and Akok 1966: 7, Lev. 65–67).

Important is the co-existence of pit houses and Alişar IV-style painted pottery which is characterized primarily by silhouette animals amidst concentric circles and other geometric designs. The Alişar IV-style painted pottery is relatively abundant at sites such as Alişar Höyük, Kültepe, Maşat Höyük, and Büyükkale II of Boğazköy in Central Anatolia (see Matsumura 2005: 514–523; Bossert 2000: 41–52).

At Gordion, the style is rare, with about a dozen examples known from (Gordion excavations' former director) Young's excavations, mostly from Middle Phrygian contexts (Sams 1994:163). At Gordion, three of the vessels represented come from the pre-destruction (YHSS 6B), dated now to around the middle of the 9th century, although the lower temporal limit for production of the style and its variants in the east remains are unclear (Sams 2011: 72–73).

The construction of pit houses is typical for Gordion from beginning of Early Iron Age when Phrygians migrated into Anatolia and established a settlement at Gordion (Voigt and Young 1999: 236). Also, pit houses seem to have been used from the Middle Phrygian to the Late Phrygian period. However, there were some modifications between the two periods. The pit house in the Middle Phrygian period (YHSS 5) has wooden posts which seem to combine with stone walls similar to those in Büklükale and Büyükkale II of Boğazköy (eg. Voight & Young 1999: 205, Fig. 9, 10). However, in the Late Phrygian period (YHSS 4) post holes were situated in the front of walls (eg. Voigt & Young 1999: 227, Fig. 28, 32).

According to the new chronology in Gordion, YHSS 4 (Late Phrygian) is the period under the Persian rule, and YHSS 5 (Middle Phrygian) is the period after the Destruction Level (810 B.C.) under Lydian rule (Ross 2012: 2). Pit houses with in-wall postholes appeared in the Middle Phrygian period. This period includes the time when the king Midas appeared in Assyrian documents.

It is significant that the Alişar IV painted pottery (BK190516; Fig. 17) was revealed from the layer that covers BP 5 at Büklükale. First, the Middle Iron Age layer is not yet identified at Büklükale, although some Alişar IV painted pottery sherds were found. Now, its appearance indicates that BP 5 might belong to the Middle Iron Age. Of course, finds might be older than the layer where they were found, and they are never found from the layer which is older than the finds themselves. In this respect, the layer might be newer than the date of the sherd. On the other hand, the Alişar IV painted pottery was in use during the destruction level at Gordion which is dated to the end of 9th century B.C.

Some Remarks on Finds: Fibulae in Büklükale

Up to 2019, a total of 69 fibulae were found from Büklükale. Their find-spots were distributed from BP 5 to BP 1, which means they existed from the beginning of the Iron Age. Some of them are of importance in connection with the dating of the Building Periods.

Two fibulae were found from BP 5 and one of them is typical Phrygian fibula (BK190068; Fig. 18), type XII.14 of Blinkenberg's classification (Muscarella 1967: 24–25). It indicates that the influence of Phrygian culture is visible already in the BP 5.

A Lydian type fibula was found from the pit which cut into the burnt layer of BP 2 (BK180118; Fig. 18). An attempt to classify Lydian fibulae was first made by Muscarella (1967: 44) and their main characteristic is a milled arc (Muscarella 1967: 13–14; cf. Boehmer 1972: 66–7)[7]. It must be considered that it might belong to one of older layers. It is also important that the Lydians are supposed to have dominated Central Anatolia before Achaemenid rule, and that BP 2 in Büklükale is situated under the layer of the Achaemenid period.

In addition, one fibula of the type XII.9 (BK130137; Fig. 18) was found at Büklükale. Unfortunately, it was found in the pit P172 which cut into the Early Bronze Age layer, and P172 is situated under the room R50 of which the stratigraphic position in the late Iron Age is at present difficult to comprehend. Type XII.9 fibulae have a semi-circular arc which is thick, flat, and rectangular in section, comparable to type XII.7. However, its significant difference is that hollow hemispherical studs are attached to the arc by means of pins of studs (Muscarella 1967: 19). This type of fibula is represented by 50 examples from Tumulus MM (dated to 740 B.C.) and it continues to be attested in the Mamaderesi Tumulus (ca. 720 B.C.), the South Cellar (ca. 700 B.C.) and in K-III (ca. 780 B.C.) (Sams 2011: 64).

Accordingly, this fibula indicates that there is a settlement in the latter half of the 8th centu-

7 Caner dates this type of fibulae to the end of 8th to beginning of 7th century B.C. (Caner 1983: 165–6). However, he classifies this kind of fibula to the Type III. 3 of Blinkenberg's classification and tries to recognize the relationship with fibulae from the northern Syria (cf. Stronach 1959: 189).

ry B.C. in Büklükale. At the moment, the oldest Iron Age occupation is BP 5. Therefore, it is plausible to suppose that BP 5 is probably dated to the late 8th century B.C.

Bronze Socketed Arrowheads:

The so-called 'Scythian' arrowheads (the socketed arrowheads) first appeared in the Andronovo culture in the middle of the 2nd Millennium B.C., and since then, spread to the grassland in Eurasia (Yukishima 1998: 183). They spread throughout the Near East by the seventh and sixth centuries B.C. and were adopted very quickly throughout the region. Many scholars have attributed the introduction of socketed arrows or their presence in general in the ancient Near East to the Scythians (Derin and Muscarella 2001: 197)[8].

Up to now, 114 bronze socketed arrowheads were found at Büklükale. They appear in almost all Iron Age layers except the oldest building period BP 5. It is worth noting that no Scythian arrowhead was found from the Destruction Level at Gordion and they only appeared in the layers after the destruction level (Derin and Muscarella 2001: 195). It is also possible that because of the limited area of excavation, no arrowhead was found from BP 5 so far. Moreover, it should be noted that 5 of 6 arrowheads found from the BP 4 are barbed bilobate (one is uncertain) (Fig. 19).

Six trilobates were found at Büklükale so far (Fig. 20) and five are from the layers of BP1 (Achaemenid period) or later, and one from IA 7. According to Derin and Muscarella's research, they dominate in Iranian sites and all the ten pre-Achaemenian sites they analyzed have trilobates in their destruction levels (Derin and Muscarella 2001: 196). The most important finds are more than 3600 trilobates from Persepolis (Schmidt 1957: 97–99). Moreover, Baitinger who analyzed weapons from Olympia, labeled trilobates with a rhombus-shaped wing as "Persian" type, and found that they appear in all places where Greeks fought against the Persia (Baitinger 2001: 23). Such results are in accord with the distribution of the trilobates from Büklükale.

There are some almond-shaped arrowheads which are supposed to be associated with the Lydians (BK120009, BK120010, BK120011, from BP3; Fig. 21). It is a bilobate arrowhead and the shape of the wing is almost oval and has a dull point, rather round, with and without barb. The barb is normally attached at the end of the socket. At Büklükale, they are found in the BP3 (large pits). Similar examples are found mainly from Central Anatolia and West Anatolia, such as Boğazköy (Boehmer 1972, Taf XXX, 900, Taf XXXI, 930), Kerkenes Dağ (Schmidt 1929: Fig. 69, K73, K33), Gordion (Young 1953: 166, Fig. 10), Sardis (Haufmann & Detweiler 1961: 4, Fig. 4; Waldbaum 1983: Pl. 3, 18), and Kumkale (Przeworski 1939: Taf. XVIII, 3). Especially in Gordion and Sardis, they are dated to the middle of the 6th century B.C. and are related with the collapse of Lydia. On the other hand, almost no such example is seen in Transcaucasia or in Iran (Yukishima 1992: 93).

Conclusion

In the first part of this article, written texts on horse-riding peoples in Anatolia were overviewed at first, and it was concluded that Scythians played no important role, but that it was Cimmerians who served a crucial role in West and Central Anatolian history. Then the so-called "Scythian Animal styled" artifact from Büklükale was discussed in terms of its stratigraphical setting.

Iron Age occupations have been recognized in Büklükale up to now, which are placed from the period after the Destruction Level in Gordion to the Achaemenid rule, that is, from ca. 800 to 540 B.C.

8 Although Ivantchik made a point clearly that such arrowheads do not prove the existence of the Scythians or the Cimmerians (Ivantchik 2001: 57), there is no evidence in the Near East for the existence of socketed arrowheads before the 7th century B.C., and very often they are from post-650 B.C. contexts (Derin and Muscarella 2001: 197).

The Achaemenid layer was already assessed in a previous article (Matsumura 2017) and is ascribed to BP 1, that is 540 to 333 B.C.

It is reasonable to suppose there were Lydian layers below the Achaemenid layer according to the analysis of written texts. The history of this region, the period under the Lydian rule might be the time span from the Lydian reconquest of Sardis (619 B.C.) to their defeat at the hands of the Achaemenids (540 B.C.). That to say, it is logical to suppose that after the defeat of the Cimmerians, Lydian influence emerged and gained momentum. As a result, layers under Lydian control must be situated in the BP 2 and 3, that is above the BP 4 of Büklükale where Cimmerian (Scythian) influence was recognized. If this is the case, then what do the burnt layers of BP 2 and the large pits of BP 3 imply? They might be related with the Lydian activities, for example the military conflict dubbed as Battle of the Eclipse or the Battle of the Halys against Media in the early 6th century B.C.

On the other hand, the period when the Cimmerians ruled over the region around Büklükale might be from the beginning of 7th century to 619 B.C. (recapture of Sardis), because the Cimmerians already controlled territories in Central Anatolia when they attacked Gordion. The possible oldest Cimmerian layer is therefore supposed to be around the Cimmerian attack on Gordion. Berndt-Ersöz proposed the alternative date of short after 645/4 B.C. for both the Cimmerian attack on Gordion and the death of Midas (2008: 30). Given this perspective, it is suggested that the BP 4 of Büklükale, the period related to the Cimmerians, begins with a date at the middle of the 7th century B.C.

For that matter, the appearance of the pit houses, which show the influence from the Phrygians before the Cimmerian arrival, might represent the period when the king Midas of Phrygia increased his power at the end of the 8th century. Mita of Muški (Midas) first came to be mentioned in Assyrian texts on the removal of Kiakki of Šinuḫtu in 718 B.C., and Midas appears for the last time as an ally to Sargon II in 709 B.C. In the period between c. 718–709 B.C., the Phrygians were supposed to have wielded strong power over Anatolia. Consequently, such timespan is the most probable time when the Phrygians occupied Büklükale. Taking all these into account, it is reasonable that Büklükale BP 5 is the period of Phrygian occupation and is dated to the end of the 8th century B.C.

In this article, Iron Age history was discussed according to the stratigraphical sequence in Büklükale. It is hoped that this article will bring up the Cimmerian problem in Anatolia again and will motivate further discussions on the horse-riding peoples.

Acknowledgements

I am grateful to Selim Ferruh Adalı for discussions and reading through various drafts of the article and offering comments and suggestions. Mark Weeden is to be always thanked for proofreading and valuable comments. Further thanks are due to Çiğdem Maner for her encouragement and patience.

Bibliography

Adalı, S. F.

- 2017a "Cimmerians and the Scythians: The Impact of Nomadic Powers on the Assyrian Empire and the Ancient Near East," in H. Kim, Jin, F.J. Vervaet and S. F. Adalı (eds.), *Eurasian Empires in Antiquity and the Early Middle Ages: Contact and Exchange between the Graeco-Roman World, Inner Asia and China*, Cambridge, Mass, pp. 60–82.
- 2017b "The Anatolian and Iranian Frontiers: Analyzing the Foreign Policy," in Drewnowska, O. and M. Sandowicz (eds.) *Fortune and Misfortune in the Ancient Near East: Proceedings of the 60th Rencontre Assyriologique Internationale Warsaw, 21–25 July 2014*, Philadelphia, pp. 307–324.
- 2018 "The Scythian State in the Ancient Near East during the Seventh Century B.C.: Interpreting the Assyrian Sources," in N. V. Kozlova (ed.) *Proceedings of the International Conference Dedicated to the Centenary of Igor*

Mikhailovich Diakonoff (1915–1999), St. Petersburg, pp. 214–232.
- 2020 "Iron Age Kültepe and its Region in Light of Tabal's History," in F. Kulakoğlu, C. Michel, G. Öztürk (eds,) *Integrative Approaches to the Archaeology and History of Kültepe-Kaneš. Kültepe, 4–7 August 2017*, KIM 3 (Kültepe International Meetings 3), Subartu 45, Turnhout, pp. 225–237.

Berndt-Ersöz, S.
- 2008 "The Chronology and Historical Context of Midas," *Historia: Zeitschrift Für Alte Geschichte* (H. 1), pp. 1–37.

Bossert, E. M.
- 2000 *Die Keramik phrygischer Zeit von Boğazköy: Funde aus den Grabungskampagnen 1906, 1907, 1911, 1912, 1931–1937 und 1952–1960*, Boğazköy-Ḫattuša XVIII. Mainz am Rhein.

Brown, S. C.
- 1986 "Media and Secondary State Formation in the Neo-Assyrian Zagros: An Anthropological approach to an Assyriological Problem," *Journal of Cuneiform Studies* 38(1), pp. 107–119.

Bryce, T.
- 2009 *The Routledge Handbook of the Peoples and Places of Ancient Western Asia: The Near East from the Early Bronze Age to the Fall of the Persian Empire*, London and New York.

Bryce, T. and T. R. Bryce
- 2012 *The World of the Neo-Hittite Kingdoms: A Political and Military History*, Oxford.

Çilingiroğlu, A.
- 2018 "Ayanis Fortress: The Day After the Disaster," in A. Çilingiroğlu *et al.* (eds.) *Urartians: A civilization in the Eastern Anatolia*, İstanbul, pp. 13–26.

Cogan, M. and H. Tadmor
- 1977 "Gyges and Ashurbanipal: A Study in Literary Transmission," *Orientalia* 46(1), pp. 65–85.

Derin, Z. and O. W. Muscarella
- 2001 "Iron and Bronze Arrows," in A. S. Çilingiroğlu, and Salvini, S. (eds.) *Ayanis I Ten Years' Excavations at Rusahinili Eiduru-kai 1989–1998*, Roma, pp. 189–217.

DeVries, K.
- 2012 "Textual Evidence and the Destruction Level," in C. B. Rose and Darbyshire, G. (eds.) *The New Chronology of Iron Age Gordion*, Philadelphia, pp. 49–57.

DeVries, K., P. I. Kuniholm, G. K. Sams and M. M. Voigt
- 2003 "New Dates for Iron Age Gordion," *Antiquity Project Gallery* 77(296): http://antiquity.ac.uk/projGall/devries296/

Godley, A. D. (ed.)
- 1928 *Herodotus: Histories (Books 3–4)*, Revised ed., William Heinemann Ltd.; G. P. Putnam's Sons, London, New York.
- 1975 *Herodotus: Histories (Books I–II)*, Revised ed., Cambridge, Mass.; London.

Goldman, B.
- 1957 "Achaemenian Chapes," *Ars Orientalis* 2, pp. 43–54.

Grayson, A. K.
- 1980 "The Chronology of the Reign of Ashurbanipal," *Zeitschrift für Assyriologie und Vorderasiatische Archäologie* 70(2), pp. 226–245.
- 1996 *Assyrian Rulers of the Early First Millennium B.C. II (858–745 B.C.)*, RIMA 3. Toronto–Buffalo–London.

Greenewalt, C. H., A. E. M. Johnston and T. V. Buttrey
- 1973 "The Fifteenth Campaign at Sardis (1972)," *Bulletin of the American Schools of Oriental Research* (211), pp. 14–36.

Greenewalt Jr, C. H., N. D. Cahill, H. Dedeoğlu and P. Herrmann
- 1990 "The Sardis Campaign of 1986," *Bulletin of the American Schools of Oriental Research. Supplementary Studies*, pp. 137–177.

Hanfmann, G. M. A. and A. H. Detweiler
- 1961 "From the Heights of Sardis," *Archaeology* 14(1), pp. 3–11.

Hawkins, J. D.
- 1982 "The Neo-Hittite States in Syria and Anatolia," in *The Cambridge Ancient History*, vol. 3, Cambridge, pp. 372–441.
- 2000 *Corpus of Hieroglyphic Luwian Inscriptions, Volume I: Inscriptions of the Iron Age. Parts 1, 2, and 3*. Berlin.

Kimura, M., M. Matsunaga and I. Nakai
- 1998 "Chemical Study of White Materials in the Pits, Soil Materials, and Mud Bricks from Kaman-Kalehöyük," *Anatolian Archaeological Studies* VII, pp. 305–324.

Koşay, H. Z. and M. Akok
- 1966 *Alaca Höyük Kazısı 1940–1948'deki Çalışmalara ve Keşiflere Ait İlk Rapor/Ausgrabungen von Alaca Höyük Vorbericht über die Forschungen und Entdeckungen von 1940–1948*, Ankara.

Kuhrt, A.
- 1990 "Lygdamis" in *Reallexikon der Assyriologie*, Band 7, De Gruyter, pp. 186–9.

Lanfranchi, G. and S. Parpola
- 1990 *The Correspondence of Sargon II, Part II: Letters from the Northern and Northeastern Provinces*, State Archives of Assyria Vol. V, Helsinki.

Leichty, E.
- 2011 *The Royal Inscriptions of Esarhaddon, King of Assyria (680–669 B.C.)*, Penn State University Press.

Makhortykh, S.
- 2020 "The Scythians and Urartu (in Russian)," *Archaeology and Early History of Ukraine* 36(3), pp. 79–90.

Matsumura, K.
- 2017 "A Hopper-Rubber or Olynthus Mill from Büklükale: Its Stratigraphical Setting and Dating," in I. A. Adibelli *et al.* (eds.), *Barış Salman Anı Kitabı*, İstanbul, pp. 127–140.

Mellink, M. J.
1991 "The Native Kingdoms of Anatolia," in *Cambridge Ancient History*, vol. III/2, Cambridge, pp. 619–665.

Millard, A.
- 1968 "Fragments of Historical Texts from Nineveh: Ashurbanipal," *Iraq* 30(1), pp. 98–114.
- 1975 "The Scythian Problem," in J. Ruffle, Gaballa, G. A. and K. A. Kitchen (eds.) *Glimpses of Ancient Egypt: Studies in Honour of H. W. Fairman*, Warminster, pp. 119–122.

Muscarella, O. W.
- 1967 *Phrygian Fibulae from Gordion*, London.

Neve, P.
1982 *Büyükkale. Die Bauwerke. Grabungen 1954–1966*. Boğazköy-Ḫattuša. Ergebnisse der Ausgrabungen 12, Berlin.

Omura, S.
- 1993 "1992 Yılı İç Anadolu'da Yürütülen Yüzey Araştırmaları," *AST* XI, pp. 311–336.
- 2003 "Preliminary Report on the 17th Excavation at Kaman-Kalehöyük (2002)," *Anatolian Archaeological Studies* 12, pp. 1–35.
- 2007 "Preliminary report of the general survey in Central Anatolia (2006)," *Anatolian Archaeological Studies* 16, pp. 45–83.

Osten, H. H. v. d.
- 1937 *The Alishar Hüyük. Seasons of 1930–32, Part II*, OIP 29, Chicago.

Özgüç, T.
- 1971 *Kültepe and its Vicinity in the Iron Age*, Ankara.

Parpola, S.
- 1987 *The Correspondence of Sargon II: Letter from Assyria and the West*, State Archives of Assyria, Vol. I, Helsinki.

Pruss, A.
- 2010 *Die Amuq-Terrakotten: Untersuchungen zu den Terrakotta-Figuren des 2. und 1. Jahrtausends v. Chr. aus den Grabungen des Oriental Institute Chicago in der Amuq-Ebene*, Turnhout.

Przeworski, S.
- 1939 *Die Metallindustrie Anatoliens in der Zeit von 1500–700 vor Chr: Rohstoffe, Technik, Produktion*, Leiden.

Rose, C. B.
- 2012 "1. Introduction: The Archaeology of Phrygian Gordion," in C. B. Rose (ed.) *The Archaeology of Phrygian Gordion, Royal City of Midas*, Gordion Special Studies 7, Philadelphia, pp. 1–20.

Sams, G. K.
- 1994 *The Early Phrygian Pottery. The Gordion Excavations, 1950–1973: Final Reports IV.* University Museum monograph 43, Philadelphia.
- 2011 "4. Artifacts," in C. B. Rose and G. Darbyshire *(eds.) The New Chronology of Iron Age Gordion*, Philadelphia, pp. 59–78.

Schmidt, E. F.
- 1929 "Test Excavations in the City on Kerkenes Dagh," *The American Journal of Semitic Languages and Literatures* 45(4), pp. 221–274.
- 1957 *Persepolis II: Contents of the Treasury and Other Discoveries*. OIP 69. Chicago.

Spalinger, A. J.
- 1978 "The Date of the Death of Gyges and its Historical Implications," *Journal of the American Oriental Society*, pp. 400–409.

Starr, I.
- 1990 *Queries to the Sungod: Divination and Politics in Sargonid Assyria*, State Archives of Assyria, Vol. IV, Helsinki.

Takahama, S.
- 1999 "Bone Ornaments with Bird Head Design Excavated from Kaman-Kalehöyük (in Japanese)," *Anatolian Archaeological Studies* VIII, pp. 167–178.

Tuplin, C.
- 2004 "Medes in Media, Mesopotamia, and Anatolia: Empire, Hegemony, Domination or Illusion?," *Ancient West and East* 3(2), pp. 223–251.

Voigt, M. M. and T. C. Young, Jr.
- 1999 "From Phrygian Capital to Achaemenid Entrepot: Middle and Late Phrygian Gordion," *Iranica Antiqua* 34, pp. 192–240.

Waldbaum, J. C.
- 1983 *Metalwork from Sardis. The Finds Through 1974*. Cambridge, Mass.

Weeden, M.
- 2010 "Tuwati and Wasusarma: Imitating the Behavior of Assyria," *Iraq* 72, pp. 39 – 61.

Wittke, A.-M.
- 2004 *Mušker und Phryger. Ein Beitrag zur Geschichte Anatoliens vom 12. bis zum 7. Jh. v. Chr.*, Beihefte zum Tübinger Atlas des Vorderen Orients, Reihe B, Nr. 99, Wiesbaden.

Young, R. S.
- 1953 "Making History at Gordion," *Archaeology* 6, pp. 156–166.

Yukishima, K.
- 1992 "Scythian Bronze Arrowhead from Kaman-Kalehöyük (in Japanese)," *Anatolian Archaeological Studies* I, pp. 89–100.
- 1998 "Metal Arrowhead at Kaman-Kalehöyük (in Japanese)," Anatolian *Archaeological Studies* VII, pp. 183–204.
- 2008 *The History and Archaeology of Scythian Horse-Riding Nomadic Country (in Japanese)*, Tokyo.

Zaitseva, G., S. *et al.*
- 1997 "A tree-ring and 14C chronology of the key Sayan-Altai monuments," *Radiocarbon* 40(1), pp. 571–580.

Fig. 1. Büklükale: Aerial photograph.

Fig. 2. Turkey Map showing related sites.

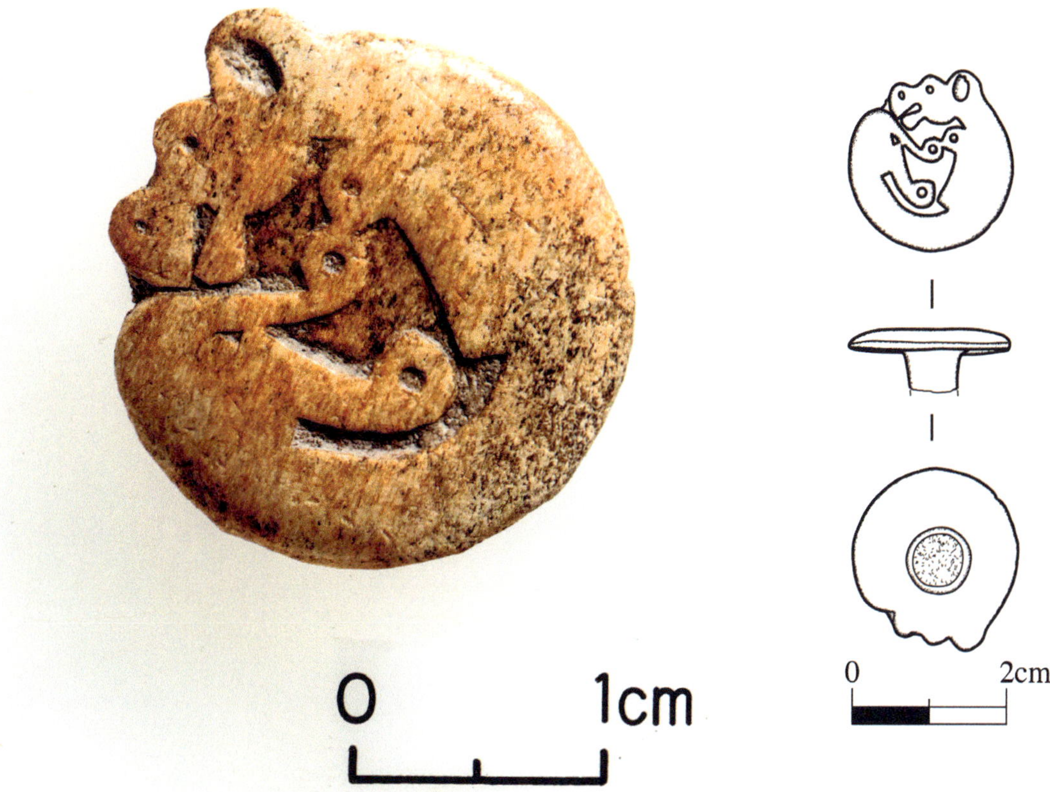

Fig. 3. Bone object with Scythian animal style from Büklükale.

Fig. 4. Bone objects of Scythian stele (a. Ayanis, b. Sardis).

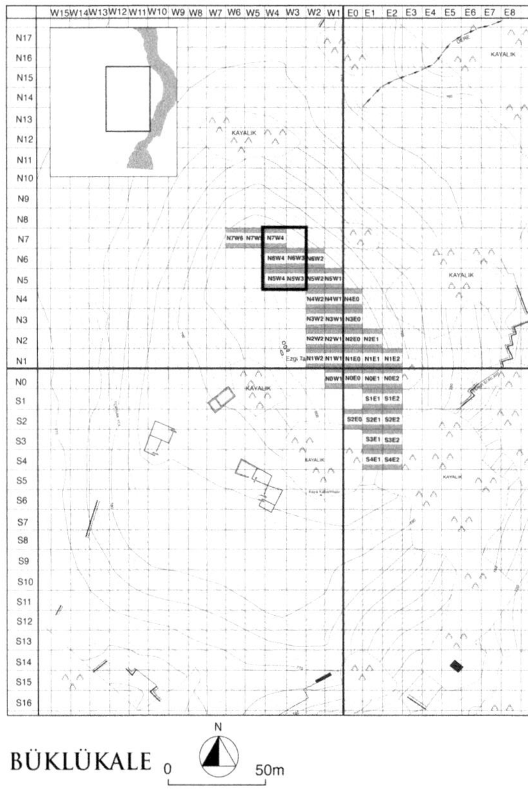

Fig. 5. Büklükale: Grid plan and aerial photograph of the excavated area.

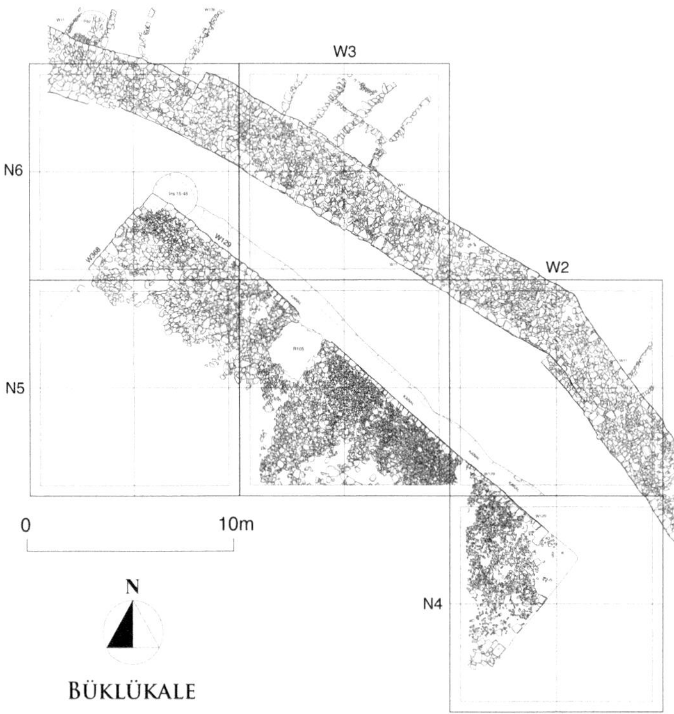

Fig. 6. Büklükale: Building Period 1.

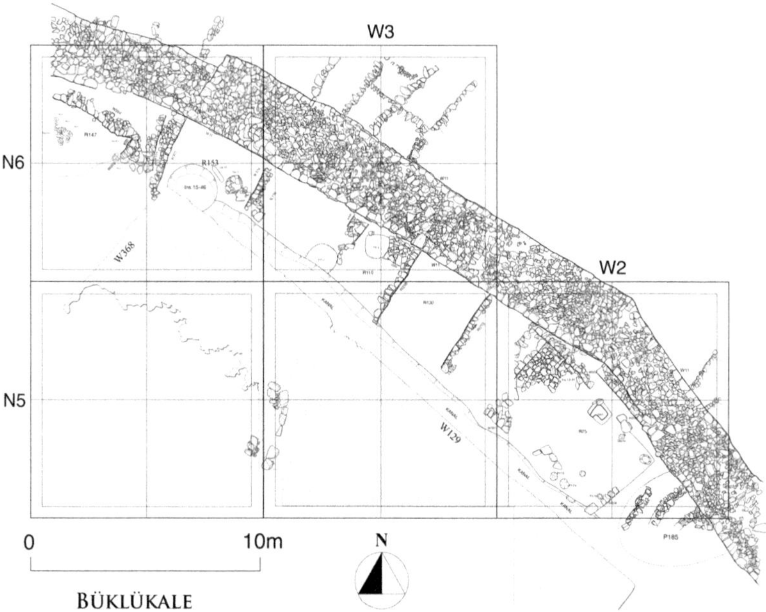

Fig. 7. Büklükale: Building Period 2.

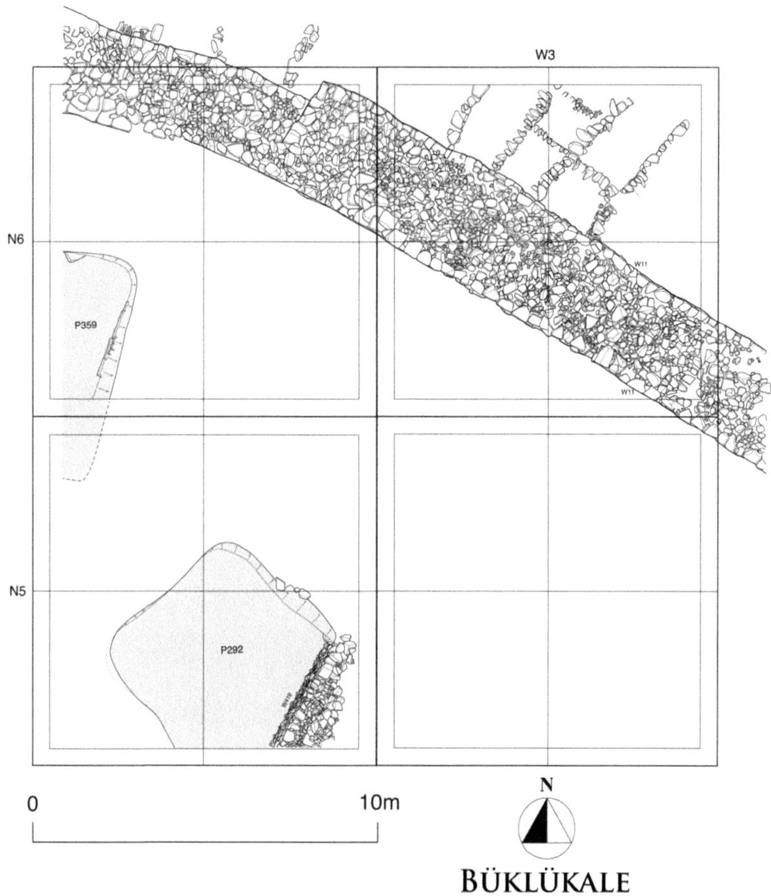

Fig. 8. Büklükale: Building Period 3.

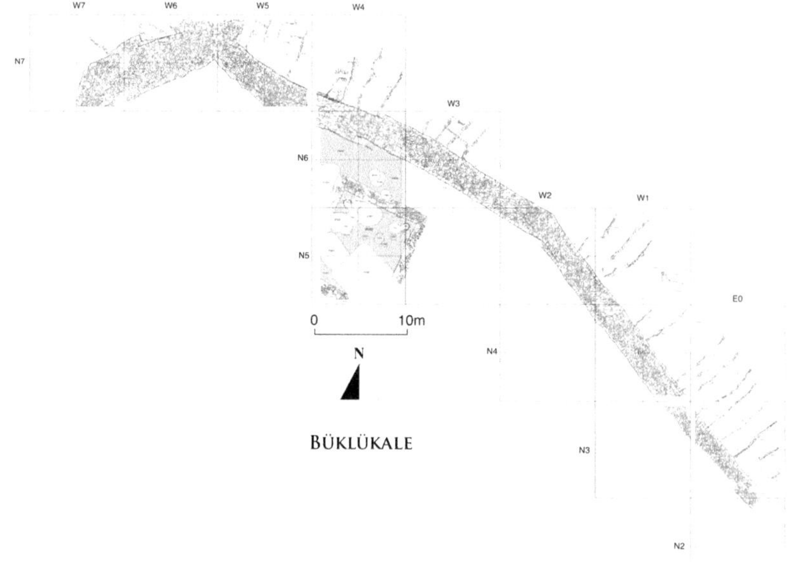

Fig. 9. Büklükale: Building Period 4 with Citadel Wall W11.

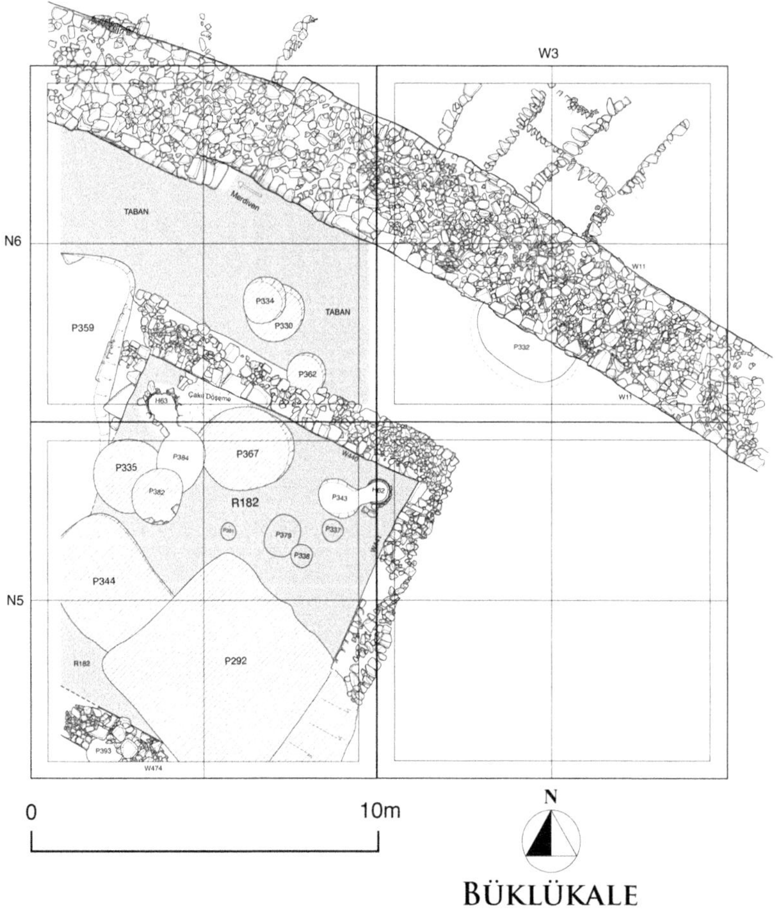

Fig. 10. Büklükale: Building Period 4.

Fig. 11. Hearths in R181.

Fig. 12. Figures of two horses with riders from Büklükale.

Fig. 13. Citadel Wall W11. Section.

Fig. 14. Citadel Wall W11. Exterior, and laid wooden logs.

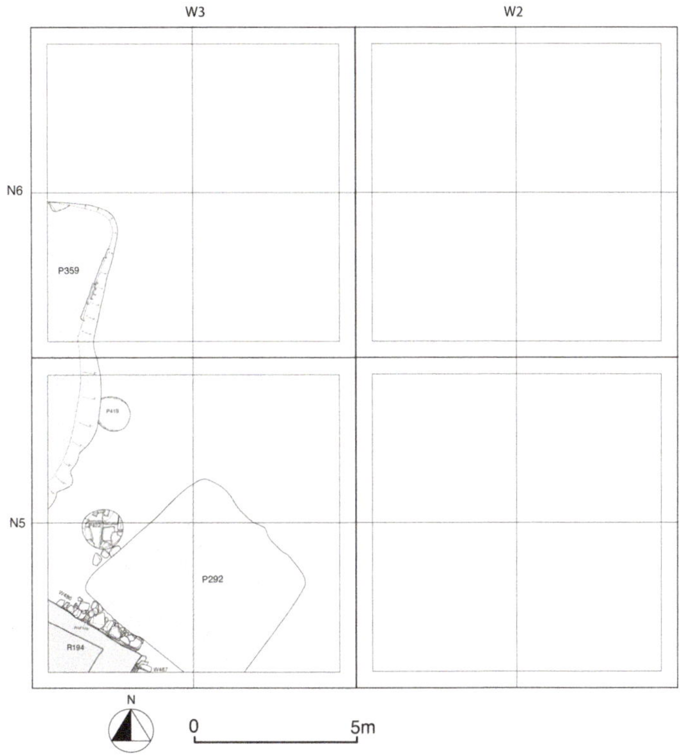

Fig. 15. Büklükale: Building Period 5.

Fig. 16. Pit House R194 (BP 5).

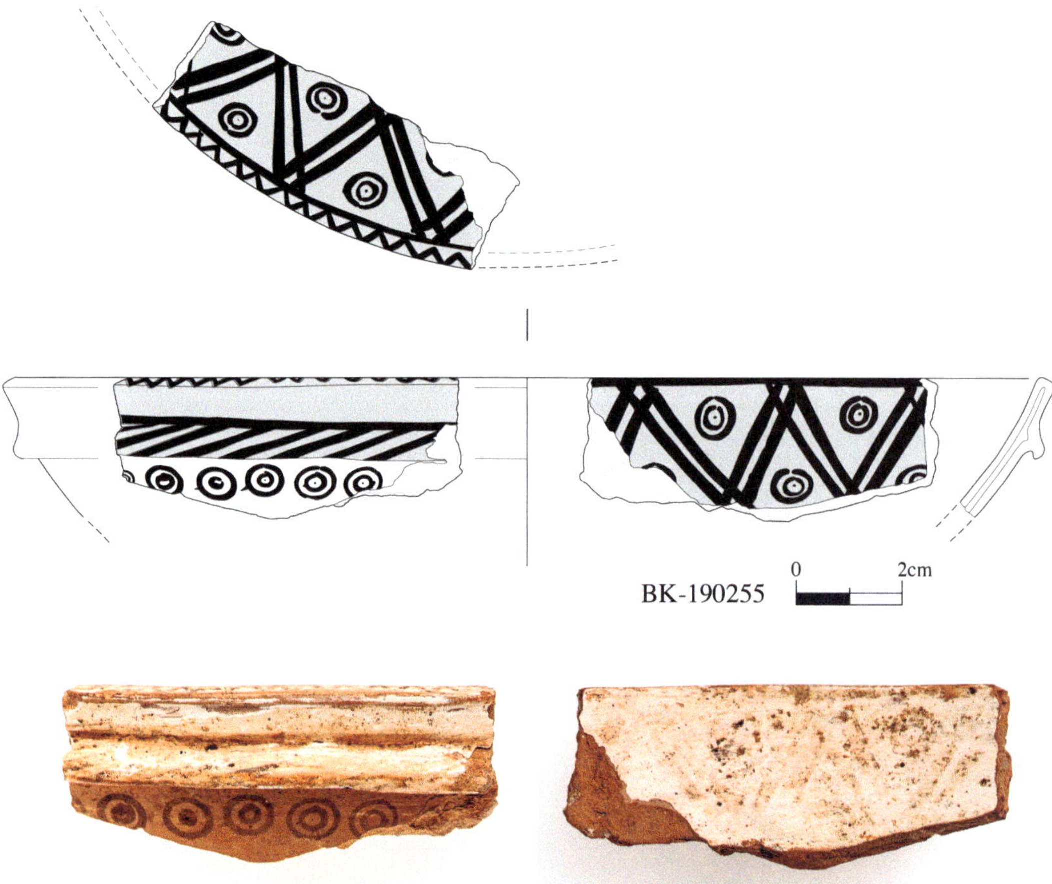

Fig. 17. Alişar IV style painted pottery sherd.

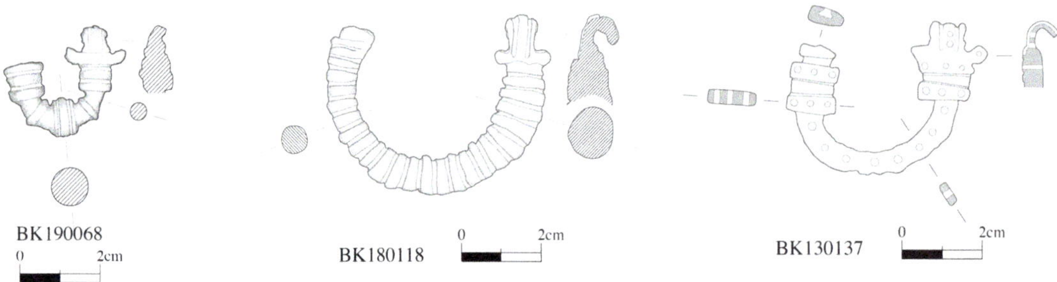

Fig. 18. Fibulae from Büklükale.

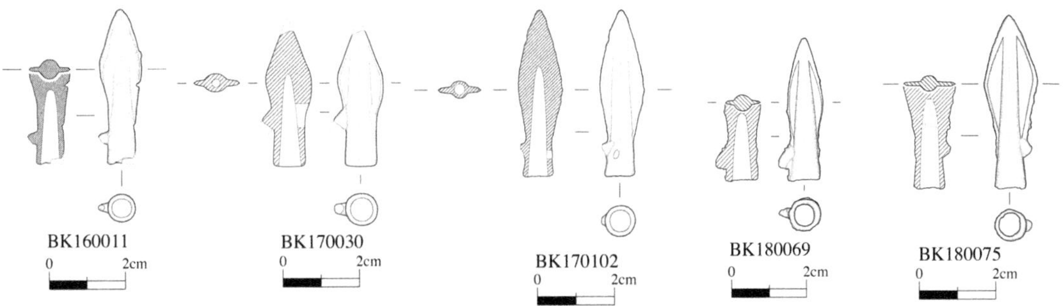

Fig. 19. Bilobate arrowheads from Building Period 4 of Büklükale.

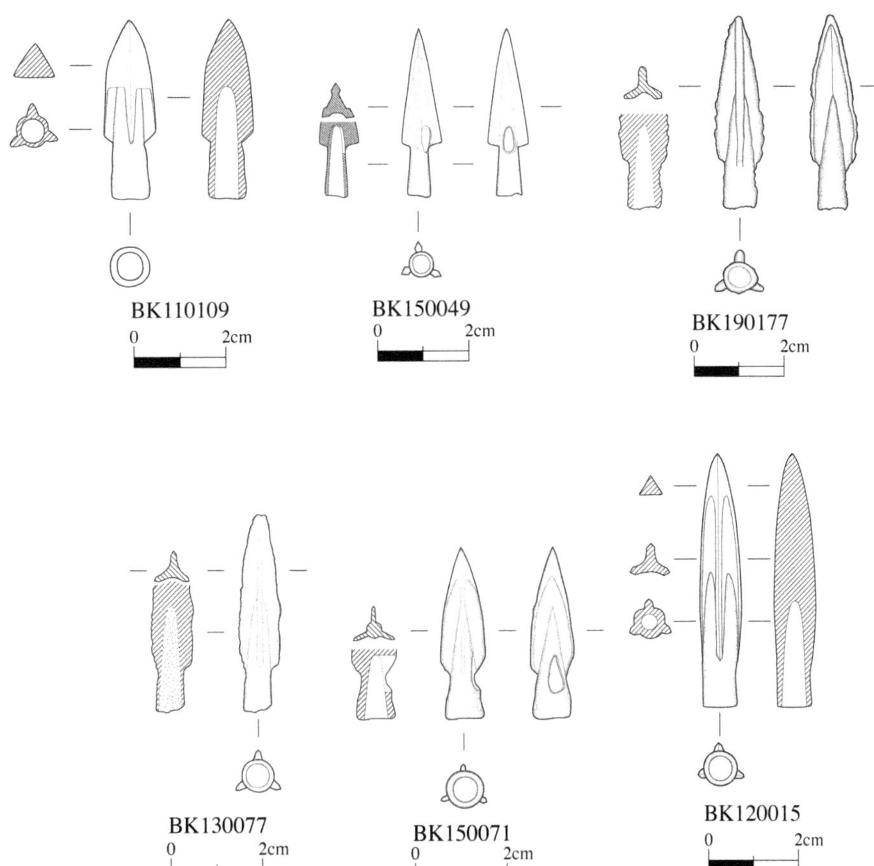

Fig. 20. Trilobate arrowheads from Büklükale.

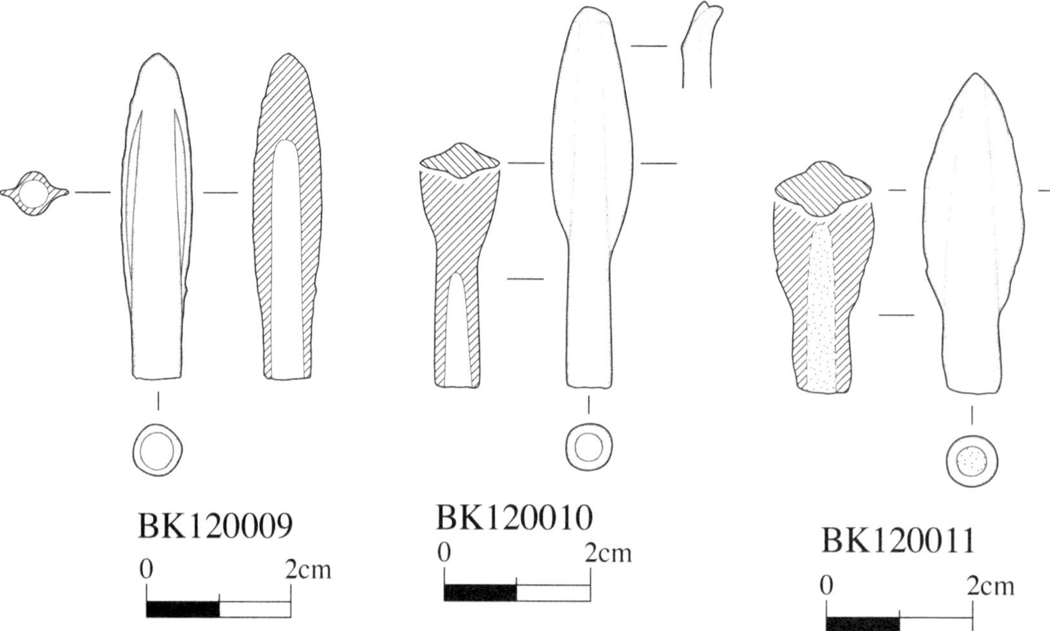

Fig. 21. Willow-leaf arrowheads from Büklükale.

Fig. No	Find No.	Date(yymmdd)	Grid	Provisional L	Structure	Period	Name	Material	Dimension	Note
Fig. 3	BK180085	180625	N5W4	119	R181 Floor	BP 4	Bone ornament	Bone	2.1 x 0.8 cm	1.6g
Fig. 12	BK180001	180605	N5W4	100	R182	BP 4	Human Figure	Clay	9.6 x 4.6 x 2 cm	61.4g
	BK180003	180605	N5W4	100	R182	BP 4	Horse Figure	Clay	13 x 11 x 4.5 cm	195.2g
	BK180005	180605	N5W4	100	R182	BP 4	Human Figure	Clay	8.0 x 4.7 x 2.5 cm	52.9g
	BK180006	180605	N5W4	100	R182	BP 4	Horse Figure	Clay	10.3 x 14.2 x 3.9 cm	
Fig. 16	BK190255	190516	N5W4	139	R182 Floor remove	BP 4-5	Painted Pottery sherd	Clay	Diam. 6.5cm Thick. 0.4cm	Out: 2.5YR5/4 In: 10YR8/2 Sec: 7.5YR6/2 Paint: 5YR4/2
Fig. 17	BK190068	190502	N5W4	129	W441 of R182 remove	BP 5	Fibula	Cu/Cu alloy	2.6 x 3.1 x 1.0 cm	
	BK180118	180706	N1W1	55	P376	BP 3 (<IA2)	Fibula	Cu/Cu alloy	4.3 x 5.4 x 1.3 cm	
	BK130137	130611	S3E1	55	P172	Iron Age	Fibula	Cu/Cu alloy	3.6 x 4.9 x 0.5 cm	
Fig. 18	BK160011	160507	N4W1	29	W11 remove	BP 4	Arrowhead	Cu/Cu alloy	4.0 x 1.1 x 0.7 cm	
	BK170030	170621	N6W4	77		BP 4	Arrowhead	Cu/Cu alloy	3.4 x 1.1 x 0.8 cm	
	BK	170707	N6W4	81		BP 4	Arrowhead	Cu/Cu alloy	4.2 x 1.2 x 0.8 cm	
	BK180069	180622	N6W4	99		BP 4	Arrowhead	Cu/Cu alloy	3.6 x 1.1 x 0.8 cm	
	BK180075	180620	N5W4	116	P353	BP 4	Arrowhead	Cu/Cu alloy	4.4 x 1.4 x 0.8 cm	
Fig. 19	BK110109	110609	N0E1	16		Ottoman	Arrowhead	Cu/Cu alloy	3.8 x 1.2 x 1.0 cm	
	BK150049	150609	S2E1-S1E1	1		Surface	Arrowhead	Cu/Cu alloy	3.6 x 0.9 x 0.7 cm	
	BK190177	190618	S2E1	21		Hellenistic	Arrowhead	Cu/Cu alloy	4.2 x 1.1 x 1.1 cm	
	BK130077	130601	N5W2	24		BP 1	Arrowhead	Cu/Cu alloy	4.1 x 1.1 x 0.9 cm	
	BK150071	150611	N6W4	31		BP 1	Arrowhead	Cu/Cu alloy	3.7 x 1.0 x 0.9 cm	
	BK120015	120525	N0E0	106		BP1-2	Arrowhead	Cu/Cu alloy	5.3 x 0.9 x 0.85 cm	
Fig. 20	BK120009	120424	N0E1	51		BP 3	Arrowhead	Cu/Cu alloy	4.25 x 1.0 x 0.8 cm	
	BK120010	120424	N0E1	52	P52	BP 3	Arrowhead	Cu/Cu alloy	5.1 x 1.1 x 0.6 cm	
	BK120011	120427	N0E1	52	P52	BP 3	Arrowhead	Cu/Cu alloy	4.3 x 1.4 x 0.7 cm	

Table 1. Finds list

Note on the Chronology of the Early Iron Age in South-Central Anatolia

Lorenzo d'Alfonso *

Abstract

The archaeological survey in central Anatolia and the archaeological excavations at Kaman-Kalehöyük led by Dr. Omura from the 1980s are now a milestone of archaeological research in the preclassical periods of this region. This is particularly true for the reconstruction of the early Iron Age in south-central Anatolia. Comparing and discussing specific issues on the stratigraphy of the sites of Kaman-Kalehöyük, Niğde-Kınık Hoyük, and Porsuk-Zeyve Höyük, the paper aims at reassessing absolute dating and key elements of the Early Iron Age in south-central Anatolia. It is confirmed that reorganization of socio-political complexity and urban organization took place in this microregion around 1000 B.C. that is much earlier that the 8th century maintained by early and conservative literature. On the other hand, it underscores evidence of strong discontinuity in the 12th–mid-11th century BC, which was not properly understood until very recently.

Öz

Orta Anadolu'daki arkeolojik yüzey araştırması ve 1980'lerden itibaren Dr. Sachihiro Omura başkanlığında yürütülen Kaman-Kalehöyük arkeolojik kazıları, bu bölgenin klasik öncesi dönemlerine ilişkin arkeolojik araştırmalarda bir dönüm noktasıdır. Bu durum özellikle Güney-Orta Anadolu'da erken Demir Çağı'nın yeniden inşası için geçerlidir. Kaman-Kalehöyük, Niğde-Kınık Höyük ve Porsuk-Zeyve Höyük yerleşmelerinin tabakalanmasına ilişkin belirli konuları karşılaştıran ve tartışan bu makale, Güney-Orta Anadolu'daki Erken Demir Çağı'nın kesin tarihlemesini ve temel unsurlarını yeniden değerlendirmeyi amaçlamaktadır. Bu mikro bölgede sosyo-politik karmaşıklığın ve kentsel yapılanmanın yeniden düzenlenmesinin M.Ö. 1000 civarında, yani erken ve geleneksel literatürün iddia ettiği MÖ 8. yüzyıldan çok daha önce gerçekleştiği doğrulanmaktadır. Öte yandan, MÖ 12. yüzyıldan 11. yüzyılın ortalarına kadar olan ve yakın zamana kadar tam olarak anlaşılamayan güçlü kopuşun kanıtlarının da altını çizmektedir.

The excavations of the site of Kaman-Kalehöyük (K-KH), the foundation of the Japanese Institute of Anatolian Archaeology, the tumulus-shaped archaeological museum and the beautiful garden associated to them have all become a reference point in Turkey for research in archaeology, archaeometry and cultural heritage; for all these great achievements Dr. S. Omura must be acknowledged and thanked for a life devoted to Ancient Anatolia.

Among the many results that surveys and excavations led by Prof. Omura[1] have achieved, one of the most significant is the excavation of an uninterrupted Iron Age (IA) stratigraph-

* ISAW, New York University / Dept. of Humanities, University of Pavia

1 Preliminary reports of the survey in central Anatolia published by Dr. Omura appeared regularly from 1989 until 2015 on *Araştırma Sonuçları Toplantısı* in Turkish and from 1995 in this journal (first papers in Japanese, in English from 2000 onwards). Besides them see (Omura 1996, 1998). Excavations reports published by Dr. Omura (early on in association with T. Mikami or M. Mori); appeared regularly on *Kazı Sonuçları Toplantısı* in Turkish from 1988 onwards, and in the journal Anatolian *Archaeological Studies* from 1995 onwards. On the results of the excavations Dr. Omura published several other contributions, and for the IA of particular significance are (Mori and Omura 1995; Omura 2011, 2016)

ic sequence at K-KH covering the timespan from the late 2nd millennium B.C. to the early Hellenistic period. Today this stratigraphic sequence has become a reference point for all works on IA Central Anatolia.

Among the different levels of that sequence, Level IId 1–3 were particularly important in providing substantial evidence of political complexity dating to the Early Iron Age (EIA), in the form of infrastructure – citadel fortifications -, and labor specialization – wheel-made ceramic production. Researchers studying the IA history and archaeology of Central Anatolia have referred to these two sets of evidence, and the second in particular, as evidence for defining a peculiar regional development for south-central Anatolia (SCA) during the EIA, characterized by the coexistence of elements of continuity and elements of innovation with regards to the former Hittite period. I am pleased to contribute this short and preliminary note on the EIA in SCA to the director of the field project that so strongly contributed to establish a new narrative of this period of transition in inner Anatolia after the fall of the Hittite empire.

Open Questions on the EIA in SCA

The EIA developments of SCA are today considered to be different from those taking place elsewhere in the rest of the Plateau, particularly in north-central Anatolia and west-central Anatolia (Pl. 1, Fig. 1). The latter are characterized by a much stronger social and political transformation, whereas the former present evidence of continuity with the previous Hittite period, besides elements of change and innovation (Genz 2003; Matsumura 2005, 2008; Mora and d'Alfonso 2012; d'Alfonso 2020; Massa *et al.* 2020). Despite a general acceptance of the evidence for a specific EIA trajectory of post-Hittite SCA, some aspects of it need further clarification. For example, a recent paper by G. Summers has correctly called for a more careful definition of the precise timespan assigned to EIA of SCA: "... there is the question of the date of these earliest Iron age levels at Kaman-Kalehöyük. Perhaps there is a need for caution in placing them as early as the eleventh century" (Summers 2017, p. 267). Moreover, the evidence from K-KH Level IId 1–3 show strong comparisons with the evidence of Porsuk-Zeyve Höyük (P-ZH) Level IV, dated by O. Pelon and S. Dupré to the EIA. In a number of recent contributions, however, members of the French-Turkish team excavating at P-ZH from 2000 to 2016 have questioned the existence of an EIA Level IV at their site, thus leaving the EIA horizon of K-KH IId1–3 without clear parallels (see below § 3). This note aims at specifically reconsidering this issue, namely the evidence and the periodization of the EIA developments of SCA, comparing recent results from the excavations at Niğde-Kınık Höyük (N-KH) with those of the two aforementioned sites, with particular emphasis on ceramic production and fortifications.

The EIA Occupation at Kaman-Kalehöyük

The occupation dating to the EIA at K-KH has been extensively excavated, and its stratigraphy and materials are known thanks to the contributions of Dr. Omura (lastly Omura 2016, with bibliography therein), and the PhD thesis of Dr. K. Matsumura (Matsumura 2005). While originally all phases of Level IId were thought to date to the post-Hittite period, more recent work could show that the earliest phases of this level, namely phases IId4–6, likely date to the LBA II. Therefore, only phases IId1–3 are now assigned to the EIA (Omori and Nakamura 2007). Above Level IId1–3, Level IIc corresponds to the earliest part of the Middle Iron Age (MIA). It is meaningful to remember that fragments of vessels belonging to the Alişar-IV ceramic set from K-KH were exclusively found in deposits belonging to Level IIc (Matsumura 2005, p. 70; for the definition of the set see d'Alfonso *et al.* 2022).

In 2007, T. Omori and T. Nakamura published the calibrated modeled dates from a wide set of analyses of ^{14}C samples from the site of K-KH (Omori and Nakamura 2007). After their results, it was clear that Level IIc roughly covers the timespan of the 9th c. B.C. Four dates were provided for Level IId, referring to a more ancient (second/lower) building level and a first/earlier building level. While it remains unclear whether the IId second/later phases also extended back into the 11th century, the dating to the 10th century is secured by the modeled, calibrated results offered by the authors. The passage from IId to IIc is set in the first decades of the 9th century B. C. (Omori and Nakamura 2007; Matsumura and Omori 2010).

The dating of IId1–3 is particularly important because these phases are associated with the earliest geometric painted wheel-made IA pottery from Central Anatolia. Most of the motifs and vessel shapes of this early production continue in the wheel made, Dark-Monochrome Geometric Painted (DMGP) ware characteristic of the MIA, thus supporting Matsumura's suggestion that DMGP may directly derive from this SCA EIA production (Matsumura 2008). Distinctive features of this EIA production vs. the later Level IIc DMGP ware are, among others, distinct vessel forms such as the kraters with outer thickened, either squared or rounded rim, the presence of bichrome, red and black, painted decoration, the wide of occurrence of thick parallel straight or wavy lines on the shoulder of closed vessels .

While these features of the ceramic production are characteristic of all three phases IId1–3, the presence of fortification walls is only attested in the latest phase IId1. Because of several episodes of spoilage and reconstructions, only the 4.5 m wide foundations of the walls are preserved, consisting in the remains of two stone side-walls with a core of smaller stones and rubble (rubble masonry: Matsumura 2005, pp. 76–81). This implies that the bichrome wheel-made ceramic production precedes the fortifications at the site, and that for a substantial time after the end of the LBA the site remained unfortified.

EIA at Porsuk-Zeyve Höyük?

In the 1983 final report devoted to the LBA and IA ceramics from P-ZH, S. Dupré published an assemblage assigned to Level IV, dated to the EIA (Dupré 1983). Information on the stratigraphic contexts emphasize the better preservation of Level IV contexts in the easternmost portion of the site, Chantier IV than in any other trench. Materials associated with a burnt layer are mentioned by Dupré (Dupré 1983, p. 15). Pelon instead emphasized the presence in Chantier IV of a construction phase of the citadel walls dated to the EIA and built directly on top of the LBA walls (Pelon 1991, 1994). On Chantier II, however, Pelon assigns to Level IV the storeroom with *in situ* jars and scattered painted ceramic fragments occupation built into the corridor of the LBA postern gate, after the latter was walled from the outside (Pelon 1972, p. 308).

The results of the 15 years of excavations led by D. Beyer and A. Tibet have brought substantial evidence for a revision of the LBA-IA continuity of occupation at the site. In particular, ^{14}C analyses as well as a reconsideration of the ceramic assemblage could show that that the site was likely abandoned around 1350 B.C. (Beyer 2015). Besides this, the EIA dating of the Level IV assemblage published by Dupré has been put into question.

Even before the new team started works at P-ZH, A.S. Crespin suggested that the date of Level IV ought to be substantially lowered (Crespin 1999). Basically, she critically revised the main elements brought by Dupré for an early dating of the ceramic assemblage of that level. Such elements were the comparanda of specimens from Level IV with EIA ceramics from Tarsus imitating sub-Mycenaean ceramics – in particular geometric painted kraters (Pl. 2, Figs. 3–4) –, and with the EIA "mugs" from Thrace (Pl. 3, Fig. 5, the 'hole-mouth juglets' in the definition adopted by Sams 1994). Crespin noted that the sub-Mycenaean pottery from Tarsus did not have a clear stratigraphic context and could in fact be assigned to the very final LBA levels of that site. They would be erroneously associated with Level IV by Dupré and could instead originally belong to Level V at Porsuk. In contrast, the EIA "mugs" had clear comparanda with the hole-mouth juglets from the Destruction Level (DL) at Gordion and Level

IV at Alişar Höyük, both dated (at the time) in the 8th century B.C. Thus, these mugs called for a much lower dating of part the Level IV assemblage published by Dupré, making it coeval with Level III.

In a series of papers that appeared from 2010 onwards, Beyer and other members of the French-Turkish team added some skepticism on stratigraphy and architecture associated with Level IV (e.g. Beyer 2010, 2015). No mention is made by them of the burnt layer excavated in Chantier IV by Pelon and mentioned by Dupré (see above). In contrast, a re-examination of the phases of the fortifications of the site and a ^{14}C date of a beam dated in the 8th c. B.C. were brought against Pelon's reconstruction of the existence of EIA fortifications in Chantier II, and by extension at the whole site. Beyer notes that during the excavations held under his lead there was a substantial lack of evidence of Level IV occupation both in Chantier II and in Chantier IV (Beyer 2015). While not entirely denying the possibility of the existence of a Level IV at the site, these contributions give the sense of the lack of confidence in the conclusions produced by Pelon and Dupre on this specific occupation period.

The comparison with the results presented above for the site of K-KH offer, in fact, support to the stratigraphy and dating offered by the earlier French team, Pelon/Dupré, on the existence of an EIA level with geometric monochrome and bichrome painted, wheel-made ceramics dating to the 10th century and possibly earlier, and a MIA level with Alişar-IV vessels dating to the 9th–8th cc. B.C. (Table 1). Moreover, the doubts casted by Crespin on the reliability of the Tarsus EIA comparanda for P-ZH Level IV kraters (Fig. 3:3–4), are now dissipated by the publication of a number of EIA assemblages from excavations in the northern Levant, particularly Tell Tayinat and Çatal Höyük (Janeway 2017; Pucci 2019). While the bichrome painting does not emerge as a diagnostic feature in terms of dating, the shape of the rim and the body of the kraters, as well as their basic geometric decorations confirm Dupré's reconstruction of a genetic derivation from the region south of the Tauros. Punctual comparanda are evident in particular for the kraters with squared/rectangular rims (Pl. 3 Figs. 1–4). Janeway's careful analysis could show that both types are likely LBA northern Levantine shapes to which monochrome and bichrome painting typical of the Aegean painted ware added in the EIA I. Wavy lines, bands, pending-semi-circles are adopted but none of the grammar of the sub-Mycenaean decoration was imitated on these kraters, thus characterizing them as a typical EIA local production of the northern Levant. The concentration of these types in the earliest levels of the EIA at Tayınat and elsewhere in the Levant (Janeway 2017, pp. 68–71), strongly support a very high EIA dating for comparanda with the kraters published by Dupré as a main component of the Level IV assemblage, and for the Level itself.

Also, the other main criticism raised by Crespin needs revision. She showed that the *tasses* (hole-mouth jugs/juglets) of Level IV at Porsuk found convincing parallels in the DL at Gordion. However, the DL of Gordion together with YHSS6A are now dated some 120 years earlier than previously thought, thus in the late 9th century B.C. (e.g. Rose and Darbyshire 2011; Kealhofer, Grave, and Voigt 2019; see Table 1). But the same type of mugs characteristic of Level IV at P-ZH, are present in pre-9th century deposits of Level IId1–3 at K-KH (Pl. 3 Fig. 6), and can be compared with similar wheel-made buff ware mugs from the EIA Burned Reed House of Gordion (Pl. 3, Fig. 7), part of YHSS7A (Kealhofer *et al.* 2022, pp. 144–148: YHSS7A has been radiocarbon dated to cover the mid-11th – early 9th cc. B.C., as per Kealhofer *et al.* 2019, pp. 508–509). This might well indicate the fortune and spread of this type as drinking vessel in late EIA Central Anatolia, around 1000 B.C. If this new evidence are considered, the lower dating of the ceramic assemblage of P-ZH Level IV suggested by Crespin no longer appears compelling. The lack of architectural remains associated with this Level at P-ZH remains a major issue. One

Table 1: Comparative chronology of Early Iron Age occupation at key SCA archaeological sites (Gordion added. The presence of political complexity at urban sites indicated by factors such as fortifications and wheel-made, workshop-produced ceramics are marked bold at each site

Period	Dates	A-Ovaören	K-KH	N-KH	P-ZH	YH-G
Early Iron Age I	ca. 1175–1000	YH8	IId3	KH-P VB	---	YHSS7B
Early Iron Age II	ca. 1000–900	YH7	IId2 **IId1**	**KH-P VA**	**Level IV**	**YHSS7A**
Middle Iron Age I	ca. 900–800	**YH6**	**IIc**		**Level III**	**YHSS6**

might consider that the imposing construction activity of the MIA (Level III), might have required the removal of the underlying archaeological deposits in the process of moving earth within the site as a preset for the new construction phase. This seems to be, for instance, the case at N-KH.

EIA at Niğde-Kınık Höyük

More evidence in support of the regional dimension of the EIA horizon from K-KH come from the survey and excavations at N-KH.

The strongest element in support of an EIA reorganization of SCA after the fall of the Hittite empire in terms of political complexity is the construction of the citadel walls of N-KH dating between ca. 1050 (*terminus post quem*)[2] and 1000 (*terminus ante quem*)[3] B.C. (on the ^{14}C dataset from N-KH and the specific contexts of these dates belonging to Kınık Höyük occupation period KH-P VA see d'Alfonso and Castellano 2018; d'Alfonso, Matessi and Mora 2021). While fortification walls around the mounds were equally found at the site of K-KH and – with growing uncertainty (see above) – at the site of P-ZH, only the walls of the mound of N-KH offer a well-defined time frame for their edification. Contemporary, or a little later than the building of the EIA walls, large silos were also constructed inside of the citadel of N-KH (d'Alfonso, Gorrini and Mora 2016; Castellano 2018). Both types of infrastructure required for their construction and their use are evidence of territorial organization and centralized administration. The period characterized by the presence of these two types of infrastructure is labeled KH-P VA at our site (Table 1).

Ceramics classes characteristic of the EIA Level IV assemblage of P-ZH and those of the EIA Level II d1–3 of K-KH have been found also at N-KH. In 2012, together with C. Mora we have published some of these ceramic materials collected during the 2006–2009 intensive survey at the site (Mora and d'Alfonso 2012). After 10 years of excavations several fragmentary vessels belonging to these classes have been brought to light. Unfortunately, no good primary context of the KH-P VA occupation has been exposed so far. The best contexts are the make-up layers of accumulations forming the MIA northern rampart of the site. These accumulations contain a mixed collections of LBA, EIA and early MIA ceramics in the deposits ^{14}C dated ot the 9th century and set above an outer surface associated with the EIA citadel walls, from which a ^{14}C dating to around 1000 B.C. was extracted (d'Alfonso, Gorrini and Mora

2 KIN15C2526s19 (UBA-30441), charcoal – broadleaf in.le, 2878 ± 43 uncal. BP (95.4% probability: 1065.5 ± 137.5 BCE); KIN15C2543s24 (UBA-30442), Charcoal – monocotyledon, 2901 ± 35 uncal. BP (95.4% probability: 1101.5 ± 113.5 BCE); KIN18C3403s43 (TUBITAK-0393), Seeds – Cerealia, 2889 ± 27 uncal. BP (95.4% probability: 1092.5 ± 108.5 BCE). Calibration software: OxCal 4.4.3; Calibration data set: intCal20, update of all dates provided here by L. Castellano, 03/16/2021.

3 UBA-28268, indeterminate wood charcoal, 2834 ±37 uncal BP (95.4%probability 1009 ± 102 cal BCE).

2016; d'Alfonso and castellano 2018; Lanaro *et al.* 2020).

While the context is not primary and the collection mixed, some diagnostics find comparanda exclusively in the EIA assemblages from K-KH and P-ZH. Once again, the case of the kraters with outer thickened rims (rounded or squared) and monochrome or even bichrome (red and dark) painting are the best example (Pl. 2. Figs. 1–2). Standard decorations consist of large horizontal bands on the outer surface under the rim, wavy lines and semicircles on the neck or walls, and a ladder motif running all around the flattened top of the rim. This type of kraters belong to the same class with those found at P-ZH Level IV and K-KH Level IId1–3 (Pl. 2, Figs. 3–6) that they are to be considered a specific EIA subgroup shared by the three sites. While the 12th and 11th century kraters with rectangular rim and monochrome decoration from the northern Levant are slightly different in size and some details (Pl. 3, 1–4), the similarity between the two compared to other types fo kraters is unescapable, and offer fresh support to the suggestion by K. Matsumura that this EIA ceramic horizon with its typical decoration is at least partly derived by the adaptation of monochrome and bychrome painted northern Levantine and Cilician decorations inspired by sub-Mycenaean pottery but associated with some typically local shapes (Matsumura 2005; idem, 2008). This does not imply that the DMGP ware of MIA central Anatolia should exclusively derive from the south, but it makes extremely unlikely that it exclusively emerged from the centuries-long tradition of (north-) central Anatolia, as was suggested by H. Genz and J. Seeher on the basis of the EIA materials from Böğazköy (Genz 2005; Seeher 2010).

The main question that can be addressed at N-KH concerns the period between the end of the Bronze Age and the reconstruction of the urban infrastructure during the second half of the 11th c. B.C. The 2020 excavations in the Deep Sounding C4 explored the deposits under the EIA walls in Operation C. Because of the restrictions set in place by the General Directorate, we could not send any ^{14}C sample to the Marmara lab to ascertain the date of these deposits, but the samples collected from strata immediately under the EIA walls in another deep sounding (C3) only 20m away from Sounding C4 are the ones dating around the first half of the 11th century (see footnote 2). It appears therefore safe to maintain that the deposits excavated in Sounding C4 in 2020 should date to that same time or earlier. Sounding C4 shows that before the building of the EIA walls, a significant work of razing earlier structures, of extraction of building material, and of movement of earth and terracing took place at the site (for a detailed presentation of this stratigraphy see d'Alfonso, Matessi and Mora 2021). A similar conclusion was reached also after the excavation of the fortification walls in Operation A (Mantovan and d'Alfonso 2020). In Sounding C4, these deposits were eventually sealed by a hard packed yellowish mud-brick, make-up layer with a thickness varying between 0.20–0.30 m, which has been interpreted as a terrace laid as preparation for the construction of the EIA walls. This mud-brick layer sealed a sequence of brown soft soil deposits rich in charcoal. The ceramic collection from these deposits is characterized by a mixed wheel-made and hand-made production fairly different from the IA materials so far excavated at N-KH (the collection is presented in the appendix to d'Alfonso, Matessi and Mora 2021). Within a collection of 472 fragments, the majority of the fragments are simple ware (Pl. 1, Fig. 2), with only 11 sherds of fine ware, and only 3 painted sherds (less than 1%). Almost half of the fragments are hand-made. While the former datum is different from any IA context at the site, the latter datum is unexpected for a LBA context. Together, however, they are in line with transitional ceramic collections from sites in NCA such as Böğazköy (Genz 2004), Çadır Höyük, but even K-KH, whose Level IId1–3 EIA collection is characterized by a mixed wheel-made and hand-made collection. Within the hand-made collection, a ware group stands out as it is not known from earlier or later productions. It features a coarse brown fabric, and dark-brown polished outer surfaces (only open vessels inner surfaces bear the same treatment and color). 26 fragments of this dark-brown polished hand-made ware were collected, unfortunately with no diagnostic sherds. The 19 diagnostic fragments from this collection display a preliminary distribution of old and new features in the assemblage. Table wares are characterized by a marked discontinuity from the LBA central Anatolian ceramic production. On the other hand, storage/kitchen wares appear to be more conservative as to LBA traditions both for being wheel-made and for showing shapes very similar to those of the LBA horizons.

The study of this new context is still very preliminary, it is stratigraphically secure but not linked with an absolute dating, and as usual with small soundings it is possible that the context is not representative of the assemblage of the occupation period it refers to; the presence of a larger quantity of storage vessels may very much be the result of such a bias. All these questions notwithstanding, Sounding C4 confirms that also at the site of N-KH the beginning of the EIA was marked by some significant discontinuity. The new excavations in Sounding C4 suggests that the mound remained without defensive structure for a period of time that goes down to the mid-11th century B.C., and during that time the ceramic assemblage was not the one characterized by wheel-made pottery with monochrome and bichrome simplified geometric decoration, but rather a mixed hand-made / wheel-made assemblage partly still related to the LBA tradition, partly adopting new shapes and new appearance (color/treatment of the visible surfaces). Infrastructure and geometric-painted ceramics would start sometimes later, during the second half of the 11th c. B.C.

Conclusions

A re-examination of the Porsuk Zeyve Höyük evidence and a summary of the recent results from the excavations at Niğde-Kınık Höyük support the existence of an EIA horizon typical of SCA characterized by wheel-made, monochrome and bichrome painted pottery and by the presence of infrastructure. While the comparanda from the northern Levant may suggest a very early EIA date for the ceramic assemblage excavated at Porsuk-Zeyve Höyük, the recent results from Sounding C4 at Niğde-Kınık Höyük appear to imply that the adoption of this painted ceramic tradition in SCA at least at this site started not before the second half of the 11th century BCE. Furthermore, the reorganization of political complexity at the site started some good time after the end of the LBA, while before that time a different phase characterized by no defensive infrastructure and a mixed transitional ceramic assemblage is attested. While this is still a preliminary report, and the evidence from a small sounding might not be representative of the situation of the entire site, let alone the region around it, we may tentatively conclude that the EIA horizon typical of SCA might have developed at different times on a site-by site basis, but at some sites, such as Niğde-Kınık Höyük and – possibly – Kaman-Kalehöyük, it started some 100–150 years after the fall of the Hittite empire (Table 1). At least for Niğde-Kınık Höyük, the suggestion by G. Summers that this EIA horizon is not as early as the immediate post-Hittite period appears tenable. At the same time, ^{14}C dates from Niğde-Kınık Höyük and comparanda for Porsuk Zeyve Höyük Level IV and Kaman-Kale Höyük Level IId1–3 suggest that the spread of the reorganization in terms of political complexity (infrastructure) and the ceramic assemblage typical of this horizon took place between the end of the 11th and the beginning of the 10th c. B.C. Recent data from Ovaören, shows that the reorganization of that site into a major urban center may date to the mid-10th century B.C. (Şenyurt *et al.* 2023). It is very much telling that the resumption of political complexity in the whole region is coeval with the one of Yassı Höyük Gordion, in spite of the rather different material culture there (Kealhofer *et al.* 2022, pp. 136–170). While the recently produced wealth of data contributes to define a new understanding of the early phases of the Anatolian IA before the 8th century, the foundation for this new line of research is one of the legacies of the work led by the scholar honored in the present volume, Dr. Omura.

Bibliography

Beyer, D.
- 2010 "From the Bronze Age to the Iron Age at Zeyve Höyük / Porsuk: a Temporary Review," in L d'Alfonso *et al.* (eds.), *Geo-Archaeological Activities in Southern Cappadocia – Turkey*, StMed 22, Pavia, pp. 97–109.
- 2015 "Quelques nouvelles données sur la chronologie des phases anciennes de Porsuk, du Bronze Moyen à la réoccupation du Fer," in D Beyer *et al.* (eds.), *La Cappadoce méridionale: de la préhistoire à la période byzantine*, Istanbul, pp. 101–110.

Castellano, L.
- 2018 "Staple Economies and Storage in Post-Hittite Anatolia: Considerations in Light of New Data from Niğde-Kınık Höyük (Southern Cappadocia)," *Journal of Eastern Mediterranean Archaeology and Heritage Studies* 6/4, pp. 259–284.

Crespin, A-S.
- 1999 "Between Phrygia and Cilicia : the Porsuk Area and the Beginning of the Iron Age," in A. Çilingiroğlu and R.J. Matthews (eds.), *Anatolian Iron Ages 4. Proceedings of the Fourth Anatolian Iron Ages Colloquium*, London, pp. 61–71.

d'Alfonso, L.
- 2020 "An Age of Experimentation: New Thoughts on the Multiple Outcomes Following the Fall of the Hittite Empire after the Results of the Excavations at Niğde-Kınık Höyük (South Cappadocia)," in S. De Martino and E. Devecchi (eds.), *Anatolia between the 13th and the 12th century BCE*, Eothen, Florence, pp. 95–116.

d'Alfonso, L. and L. Castellano
- 2018 "Kınık Höyük in South Cappadocia," *Altorientalische Forschungen*, vol. 45, no. 1, pp. 84–93.

d'Alfonso, L., M. E. Gorrini and C. Mora
- 2016 "The Early Iron Age and the Hellenistic Period at Kınık Höyük, South Central Anatolia. Report of the 5th Campaign (2015)," *Athenaeum* 104/2, pp. 598–612.

d'Alfonso, L, A. Matessi, and C. Mora
- 2021 "Kınık Höyük and South Cappadocia After the End of the Hittite Empire: New Results and a Reassessment," *News from the Land of Hatti* 3, pp. 59–95.

d'Alfonso, L., E. Basso, L. Castelano, A. Mantovan and P. Vertuani
- 2022 "Regional Exchange and Exclusive Wine Drinking Rituals in Iron Age Central Anatolia: Dating, function and Circulation of the 'Alişar-IV ware," *Anatolian Studies* 72, pp 37–77.

Dupré, S.
- 1983 *Porsuk I: La céramique de l'age du Bronze et de l'âge du Fer*, Paris.

Genz, H.
- 2003 "The Early Iron Age in Central Anatolia," in B. Fischer *et al.* (eds.), *Identifying changes: the transition from Bronze to Iron Ages in Anatolia and its neighbouring regions: proceedings of the International Workshop, Istanbul, November 8–9, 2002*, Istanbul, pp. 179–191.
- 2004 *Büyükkaya I. Die Keramik der Eisenzeit: Funde aus den Grabungskampagnen 1993 bis 1998*, Mainz am Rhein.
- 2005 "Thoughts on the Origins of the Iron Age Ceramic Tradition in Central Anatolia," in A. Çilingirolu and G. Darbyshire (eds.), *Anatolian Iron Ages 3*, London, pp. 75–84.

Janeway, B.
- 2017 *Sea Peoples of the Northern Levant? Aegean-Style Pottery from Early Iron Age Tell Tayinat*, Eisenbrauns, Winona Lake, Indiana.

Kealhofer, L., P. Grave, and M.M. Voigt
- 2019 "Dating Gordion: The Timing and Tempo of Late Bronze and Early Iron Age Political Transformation," *Radiocarbon* 61 (2), pp. 495–514.
- 2022 *Ancient Gordion*, Cambridge.

Lanaro, A., L. Castellano, N. Highcock, A. Mantovan and L. d'Alfonso
- 2020 "South-Central Anatolia during the Iron Ages: a Diachronic View from Kınık Höyük (Niğde)," in A. Otto et al. (eds.), *Proceedings of the 11th International Congress on the Archaeology of the Ancient Near East*, Wiesbaden, pp. 215–228.

Mantovan, A. and L. d'Alfonso
- 2020 "Le fortificazioni di Kınık Höyük di Bronzo Tardo: nota relativa agli scavi del settore A-walls," in M.E. Balza *et al.* (eds.), *Città e parole, argilla e pietra. Studi offerti a Clelia Mora in occasione del suo 70° compleanno da al-*

lievi, colleghi e amici, Bibliotheca di Athenaeum 65, Bari, pp. 325–341.

Massa, M., Chr. Bachhuber, F. Şahin, H. Erpehlivan, J. Osborne and A. J. Lauricella
- 2020 "A Landscape-Oriented Approach to Urbanisation and Early State Formation on the Konya and Karaman plains, Turkey," *Anatolian Studies*, vol. 70, pp. 45–75.

Matsumura, K.
- 2005 *Die eisenzeitliche Keramik in Zentralanatolien aufgrund der Keramik in Kaman-Kale Höyük*, FU Berlin.
- 2008 "The Early Iron Agea at Kaman-Kalehöyük: The search for its roots," in H. Kühne et al. (eds.), *Fundstellen: Gesammelte Schriften zur Archäologie und Geschichte Altvorderasiens ad honorem Hartmut Kühne*, Wiesbaden, pp. 41–50.

Matsumura, K and T. Omori
- 2010 "The Iron Age Chronology in Anatolia Reconsidered: The Results of the Excavations at Kaman-Kalehöyük," in P. Matthiae et al. (eds.), *Proceedings of the 6th ICAANE*, Wiesbaden, pp. 443–450.

Mora, C. and L. d'Alfonso
- 2012 "Anatolia after the End of the Hittite empire. New Evidence from Southern Cappadocia," *Origini*, vol. 34, pp. 385–398.

Mori, M. and S. Omura
- 1995 "A Preliminary Report on the Excavations at Kaman-Kalehöyük in Turkey (1989–1993)," *Bulletin of the Middle Eastern Culture Center in Japan*, vol. 8, pp. 1–42.

Omori, T and T. Nakamura
- 2007 "Radiocarbon Dating of Archaeological Materials Excavated at Kaman-Kalehöyük: Second Report," *Anatolian Archaeological Studies* 16, pp. 111–123.

Omura, S.
- 1996 "A Preliminary Report of the General Survey in Central Anatolia (1994)," *Bulletin of the Middle Eastern Culture Center in Japan*, vol. 9, pp. 135–192.
- 1998 "An Archaeological Survey of Central Anatolia (1995)," *Bulletin of the Middle Eastern Culture Center in Japan*, vol. 10, pp. 78–131.
- 2011 "Kaman-Kalehöyük: Excavations in Central Anatolia," in S. Steadman, and G. McMahon (eds.), *The Oxford Handbook of Ancient Anatolia, 10,000–323 B.C.E.*, Oxford, pp. 1095–1111.
- 2016 "Kaman-Kalehöyük Kazıları," in Kültür ve Turizm Bakanlığı, and Tanıtma Genel Müdürlüğü (eds.), *Kırşehir Arkeoloji Çalışmaları*, Ankara, pp. 7–28.

Pelon, O.
- 1972 "Rapport préliminaire sur la deuxième et la troisième campagne de fouilles à Porsuk-Ulukīsla (Turquie) en 1970 et 1971," *Syria*, vol. 49.3–4, pp. 303–317.
- 1991 "Occupation hittite et debut de l'age du Fer a Porsuk," in Br. Le Guen-Pollet and O. Pelon (eds.), *La Cappadoce meridionale jusqu'a la fin de l'epoque romaine. Etat des recherches*, Paris, pp. 15–18.

1994 "The site of Porsuk and the beginning of the Iron Age in southern Cappadocia," in A. Çilingiroğlu, and D. H. French (eds.), *Anatolian Iron Ages 3*, , Ankara, pp. 157–162.

Pucci, M.

2019 *Excavations in the Plain of Antioch III: Stratigraphy, Pottery and Small Finds from Chatal Höyük in the Amuq Plain*, OIP 143, Chicago.

Rose, C. B. and G. Darbyshire (eds.)
- 2011 *The New Chronology of Iron Age Gordion*. Philadelphia.

Sams, K. G.
- 1994 *The Early Phrygian Pottery*, Philadelphia.

Seeher, J.
- 2010 "After the Empire: Observations on the Early Iron Age in Central Anatolia," in I. Singer (ed.), *Ipamati Kistamati Pari Tumatimis. Luwian and Hittite Studies Presented to J. David Hawkins on the Occasion of His 70th Birthday*, Tel Aviv, pp. 220–29.

Summers, G. D.
- 2017 "After the Collapse: Continuities and discontinuities in the Early Iron age of Central Anatolia," in A. Schachner (ed), *Innovation versus Beharrung. Was macht den Unterschied des hethitischen Reichs im Anatolien des 2. Jahrtausends v. Chr.?*, Byzas 23, Istanbul, pp. 257–274.

Şenyurt, S. Y., A. Akçay and A. İlkay
- 2023 "Ovaören-Yassıhöyük Kazıları ve Orta Anadolu Demir Çağı Mimarisinde Gelişim ve Değişime Kronolojik Bir Bakış," Höyük, vol. 11, pp. 41–63.

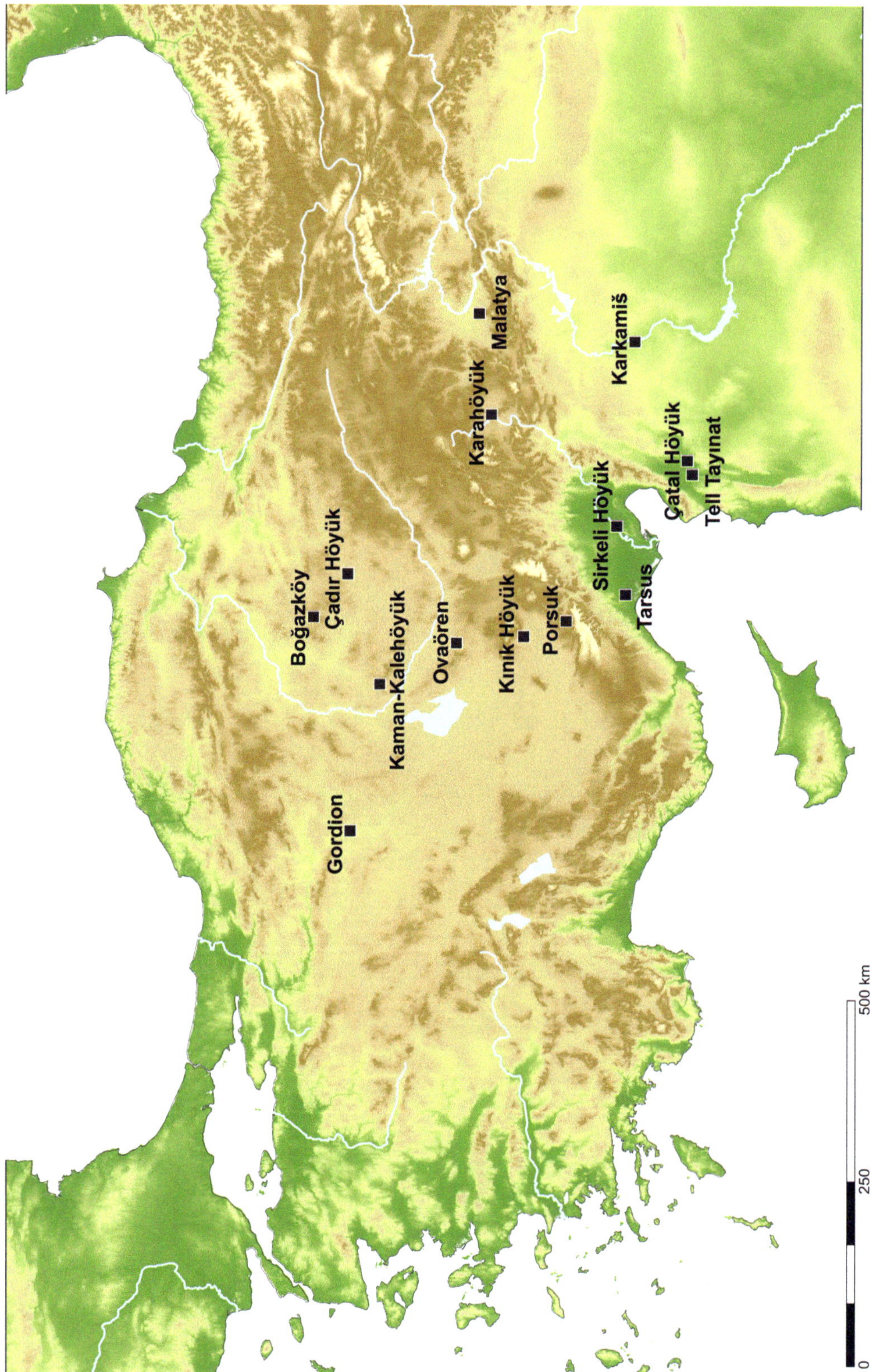

Fig. 1. GIS map of Anatolia and north Syria during the Early Iron Age. Showing the position of the main sites of the time for the regions discussed in the paper (graphics by L. Castallano).

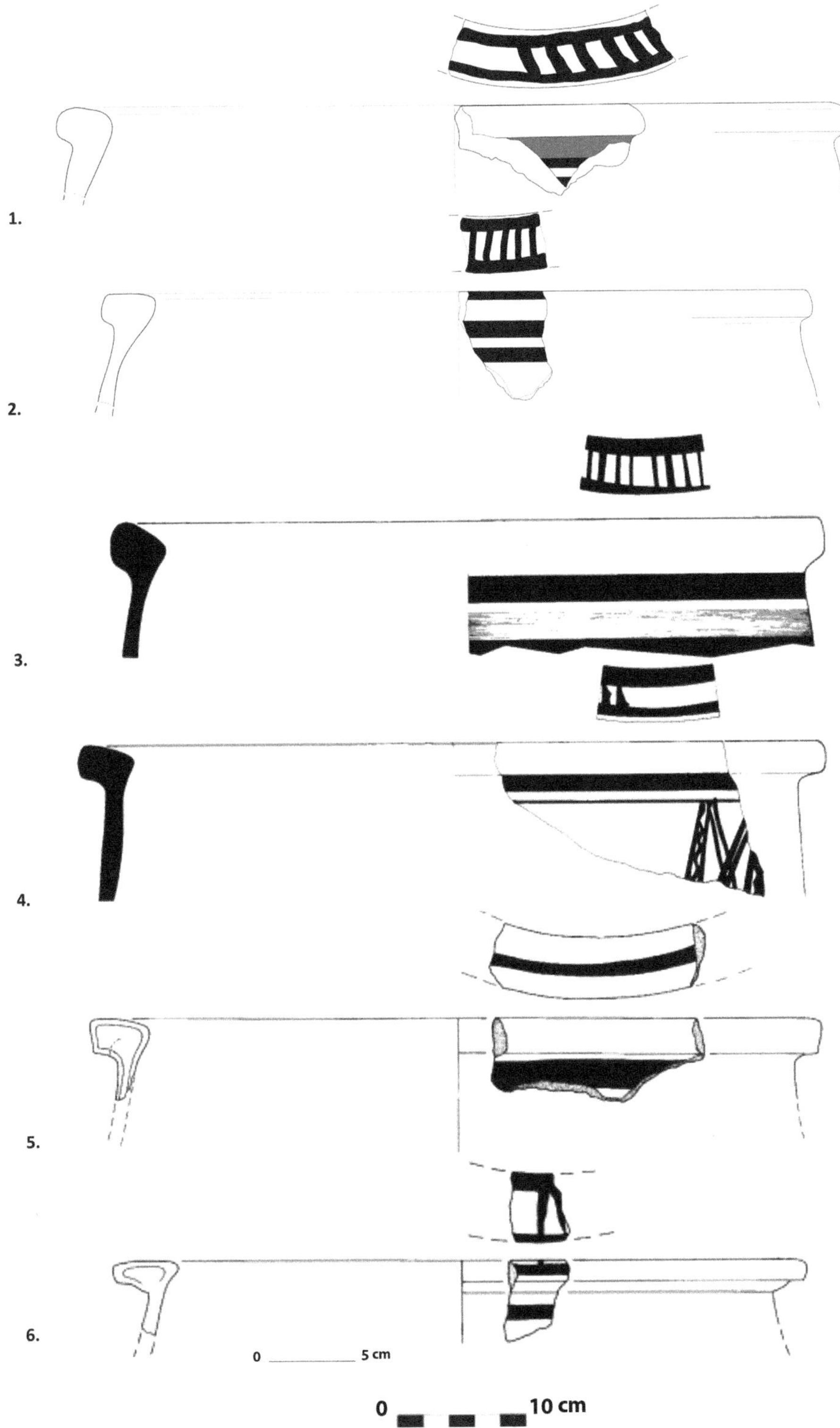

Fig. 2. Monochrome dark painted and bichrome dark and red painted kraters with rectangular rim and vertical or slightly convex walls from south-central Anatolia. Fig. 1–2: krater fragments from N-KH (KIN14A1806.4; KIN14A1801.1), Fig. 3–4: krater fragments from P-ZH (Dupre 1983: Tab. 55 n. 78; Tab. 58, n. 91); Fig. 5–6: krater fragments from K-KH (Matsumura 2005: Tab. 82, KL90.164; Tab. 84, KL92.M37).

Fig. 3. EIA monochrome geometric painted kraters with thick, squared or rounded, everted inward slanting rim and straight slightly inward-slanting shoulders from the northern Levant (Amuq) (1:3): Fig. 1) red painted krater from Çatal Höyük, Phase 5N Late: 119860 (Pucci 2019, Pl.156); Fig. 2) red painted krater from Çatal Höyük, Phase 2M Late: 116409 (Pucci 2019, Pl.61); Fig. 3) dark painted krater from Tell Tayınat, Phase 5a: TT06.G4.55.I78.2 (Janeway 2017, Pl.10); Fig. 4) Dark painted krater from Tell Tayınat, Phase 5a: TT06.G4.65.68.1 (Janeway 2017, Pl.10). EIA II mugs (1.3): Fig. 5) DMGP mug from P-ZH Level IV, Porsuk I nr. 51 (from Dupre 1983, Pl. 51); Fig. 6) DMGP mug from K-KH Level IId1-3: KL90-2012 (from Matsumura 2005, Taf. 102); Fig. 7) buff ware mug from Yassı Höyük Gordion, YHSS7A (from Kealhofer et al. 2022 Fig.6e).

Fig. 4. EIA assemblages from Sounding C4 at N-KH. In the upper row are the two collections of diagnostic sherds from two SUs below the mud-brick terracing; in the lower row the non-diagnostics from the same SUs. In the four images the very limited number of painted material and the appearance of the brown burnished ware is immediately visible.

A Sealing of Innara the Scribe from Kaman-Kalehöyük

Mark Weeden *

Abstract

The following essay presents a sealing that was found at Kaman-Kalehöyük during the 2016 excavation season and collects examples of similar sealings in order to establish its date and broader context and meaning. The seal which made this sealing is of a type that is found a number of times at Boğazköy, and in one possibly comparable case there is a radiocarbon-dated context to its find-spot, which should allow us to posit a similar date for the example found at Kaman-Kalehöyük in 2016. Some of the symbols on the sealing are also considered in the light of recent discussions. It is hoped that the honorand will enjoy reading this as a meagre expression of my gratitude for being able to participate in the excavations at Kaman-Kalehöyük over the last 20 years, an experience that has proven extremely important for my work and personal development.

Öz

Makalede 2016 kazı sezonunda Kaman-Kalehöyük'te bulunan bir mühür baskısı sunulmakta ve tarihini, daha geniş bağlamını ve anlamını belirlemek amacıyla benzer mühür baskı örneklerini bir araya getirmektedir. Bu mühür baskısını yapan mühür, Boğazköy'de birkaç kez bulunan türdendir ve bulunduğu yerde radyokarbon tarihlemesi yapılmış bir bağlamda bulunması, Kaman-Kalehöyük'te 2016'da bulunan mühür için de benzer bir tarih önerilmesine olanak tanımaktadır. Mühür baskısı üzerindeki bazı semboller de son dönemdeki tartışmalar ışığında değerlendirilmektedir. Son 20 yıldır katıldığım Kaman-Kalehöyük kazısı, hem kişisel gelişimim hem çalışmalarım için olağanüstü önemli bir deneyim teşkil etmektedir. Onur'a sunulan bu makale, Kaman-Kalehöyük'teki çalışma ve araştırmalara katılabildiğim için minnettarlığımın bir ifadesidir ve okumaktan keyif alacağını umuyorum.

Introduction

Large numbers of sealed clay lumps have been recovered from Kaman-Kalehöyük, particularly from the stone-lined pit referred to as Round Structure 1 in the North Sector.[1] Most of these date to the end of the 15th/beginning of the 14th century. They are mostly impressions on irregularly shaped clay lumps. Only a few of the conical bullae that constitute the majority of sealing-carriers from the royal archives at Hattusa are found, although there are some.[2] A number of sealings that are Old Hittite (OH) in style, meaning that they roughly correspond in style to those dated to Boğazköy Unterstadt 3 or Büyükkale IVc[3], are found in Round Structure 1, or near it, but other ones have also been found scattered around the site, as well as a small concentration in North sector VII.

The sealing 16000108 (KL 16–1026) was excavated in the South trench, sector XXXI Grid 6 at Provisional Layer 6 on 20/07/2016. The archaeological context has not yet been published, but it corresponds to Late Iron Age

* UCL, Department of Greek and Latin.

1 Yoshida 1999; 2006. A full publication of the sealings from Round Structure 1 is in preparation by the author and D. Yoshida. I am very grateful to Dr. Omura for making this material available to me.

2 Out of 1545 sealings excavated at Kaman-Kalehöyük until 2015 I note the following 14 conical or even roughly conical bullae – not counting Old Assyrian specimens: 90000262 O(ld) H(ittite); 90000730 OH; 92000234 Empire period; 93000005 OH; 93000008 OH; 95000467 (RS 1); 95000471 (North VII, OH); 97000810 (RS 1); 98001068 (North 30, OH); 99000846 (RS 1); 99000876 (RS 1); 00000129 (RS 1, OH); 00000664; 02000302.

3 Boehmer and Güterbock 1987; Weeden 2018.

stratum IIc. As we will see, this means that the find-spot must have been secondary. The artefact is made of baked clay and is shaped like a squat cone. It is likely to have been used as a bulla, meaning that it could have been attached to documents, although attachment to something else is of course also possible. That it was attached to something via a cord of some kind is indicated by indentations on the conical underside. The object measures 1.7cm in diameter and 0.9cm in height.

On the flat side of the cone there is a seal-impression which covers all of its surface (see photo Fig. 1 and drawing Fig. 2).[4] The seal-face is divided into two sections. An outer ring contains guilloche patterning consisting of interweaving strands that overlap three times in each pass. Each strand consists of three threads. It seems that the complex guilloche band must have been carved after the circular central reservation, which appears to be on a raised disc of clay, into which the guilloche has been cut. It is at first unclear whether this was simply part of the manufacturing process of the seal that made this impression, or whether that seal had in fact been re-cut in order to apply the guilloche band, perhaps replacing an earlier decorative border. The former is suggested by the fact that another seal of this construction with the same name was found at Boğazköy (see below).

The circular central reservation contains four signs in relief: The antler CERVUS$_2$+*ra/i* (i. e. L. 103+383), alongside the triangle (L. 370), conventionally transcribed BONUS$_2$ "good (luck)", the "two-legged" Ankh (L. 369), conventionally transcribed as VITA ("life"), and the sign for "scribe" (L. 326), conventionally transcribed as SCRIBA, about which there has been some debate in recent times (see below). The antler can be read in two ways: Kuruntiya or Innara, being two names for the god or gods represented as a stag, sometimes referred to as a "protective deity" due to the fact that these names can be written with the logogram ^{d}KAL in Hittite cuneiform, corresponding to the writing of the divine name ^{d}LAMMA (the same sign as KAL) in Mesopotamian cuneiform (Weeden 2011: 263–268). Given that the sign has the phonetic complement +*ra/i* (L. 383) it is more likely that its reading is Innara rather than Kuruntiya. Theoretically, the name Innara can either be a human name[5] or it could be a divine one, referring to the stag-god Innara, whose name is usually written ^{d}LAMMA(-ri) in Hittite cuneiform (van Gessel 1998/II: 681–714).

Usually we would be quick to assume that this is a personal name, especially when accompanied by the sign for scribe and that this indicated a functionary of some kind. Such would be a perfectly justified conclusion if we were dealing with an Empire-period sealing (ca. 1350–1200 B.C.). However, I hope to show that the small group of sealings of this type probably belongs to an earlier historical period, likely the 16th century B.C. At such an early stage of the use of hieroglyphs it would be unwise to assume that later conventions applied. It should not be excluded that the god's name could instead be employed as a sign of good luck, much like the ankh and the triangle. This is less applicable to the sign for scribe, however, which should indeed indicate that we are dealing with a person.

The *Innara*-Seals and Their Dating

This kind of complex guilloche decoration is not typical for stamp-seals of the pre-Hittite period in Central Anatolia, although a looser guilloche pattern woven out of two strands is already attested at Kültepe and Konya Karahöyük in combination with other motifs.[6] The more

4 A photo of this sealing was already published as a photo in the front matter of *Anatolian Archaeological Studies* 20 (2017): 5. I am grateful to K. Matsumura for providing me with photographs and registration details.

5 Laroche 1966: 79 no. 454.

6 Level I at Konya-Karahöyük is conventionally held to date to a period prior to the establishment of the Hittite state. A more complex guilloche is found on some cylinder-seals from Konya-Karahöyük Alp 1968: Taf. 11/23; 34/88, as is the simpler one. The simpler Guilloche on stamp-seals is found at Alp 1968: Taf. 46/110; 49/113; 50/114–117; 53/128; 54/130–

complex guilloche pattern comes into use from the Old Hittite period, i.e. the second half of the 17th century B.C. This decorative pattern either continues in use until or experiences a renaissance in the 15th century B.C. (Dinçol and Dinçol 2008: 14; Weeden 2018: 64).

There are two sealings found at Boğazköy that have a similar arrangement including CERVUS$_2$+*ra/i* with VITA, BONUS$_2$, SCRIBA in the circular central reservation and some form of guilloche border, although they are not exactly the same as the sealing from Kaman-Kalehöyük. Moreover both of these sealings are found on squat conical bullae that are quite similar to the sealing from Kaman-Kalehöyük. Given the small number of exemplars, this makes it more likely that there is some kind of relationship between the sealings.

In 1975, Hans Gustav Güterbock published the sealing with the excavation number 71/28 (later re-published as BoHa 14.123), which had been excavated in House 5, room 5 of area J/19 in the Lower City at Boğazköy (see Fig. 3, Fig. 4).[7] Few other sealings were found in connection with this multi-roomed building, but two which were belonged to an older style, dated by Boehmer and Güterbock to the Old Assyrian period. However, they were both found in fill from later levels and are therefore are of no relevance for the dating of 71/28 (Boehmer and Güterbock 1987: 26 no. 49, Taf. V, no. 59, Taf. VI). The sealing has a loose, two or three-stranded Guilloche decorative band, that may have led to some confusion in attempts to date it. The seal-face also contains a circular relief dividing line between the Guilloche border and the internal reservation. The signs in the centre are the same as on the sealing from Kaman-Kalehöyük, but they are arranged in a different order (see Fig. 4). They are also not as well executed as the signs on the sealing from Kaman-Kalehöyük.

For the purposes of dating, Güterbock at the time (1975) compared the seal he had previously published as SBo 2.191 in 1942, which shares a similar guilloche band, and he followed Thomas Beran in assigning this to Beran's "Gruppe XI" with a dating to the "Zeit des mittleren und frühen Neuen Reiches"[8], although Beran himself dated this group as "alt-und mittelhethitisch" (Beran 1967: 27 no. 106, 61, Tafel II). It is unclear to me whether Güterbock meant by this that 71/28 should be dated to that period alongside SBo 2.191, or whether he was just talking about SBo 2.191. By the time Boehmer and Güterbock re-published sealing 71/28 in 1987 as BoHa 14.123, it was ordered with the other sealings of the Old Hittite period, as indeed it should be.[9]

At any rate, the sealing SBo 2.191 is not comparable, given that it has two or three extra signs, and shares with 71/28 (= BoHa 14.123) only the sign L. 103, the antler, along with the triangle BONUS$_2$ and Ankh-like sign VITA, which are very common signs. There is no mention of a scribe. On the basis of the arrangement of the signs on the seal-face, with BONUS$_2$ VITA upright and to the side of the main sign-group, as well as the appearance of the sign ASINUS$_{2A}$, Güterbock's dating to the "time of the Middle or Early New Empire", however, seems entirely plausible for SBo 2.191 (= BoHa 5.106). The loose form of double-stranded Guilloche on both sealings is somewhat comparable however, which should be explained rather by the (albeit sporadic?) persistence of this decorative feature from the time of Kültepe Ib right through into the 15th century B.C. rather than by a hypothesised contemporaneity of the two sealings.

Then in the year 2000 another sealing was excavated at Boğazköy, which might have had a decisive influence on the question of the dating, but which is unfortunately damaged to the

131; 56/136–137; 142/436. For a more complex Guilloche band on a stamp-seal at Konya-Karahöyük see Alp 1968: Taf. 139/427–428, but this is rare.

7 Güterbock 1975: 64, 66, no. 29; Boehmer and Güterbock 1987: 46 no. 123, Tafel XII.

8 Güterbock 1975: p. 66; Beran 1967: no. 106.

9 Boehmer and Güterbock 1987: p. 46 no. 123, p. 33 "Althethitische Zeit (Zeit der Unterstadt 3)".

point where one cannot speak of certain proof.[10] Bo. 2000/02, published by Susanne Herbordt, is another quite squat conical bulla, which has a clear series of signs in common with both Kaman-Kalehöyük 16000108 and BoHa 14.123 (BONUS$_2$, VITA, SCRIBA), and also seems to share the remaining sign as well, although this is broken: CERV[US$_2$+*ra/i*]. The signs are organised in a different way on the seal-face, however (see Fig. 6). There are two guilloche borders on Bo. 2000/02, as opposed to the one on the sealing from Kaman-Kalehöyük: one is triple-stranded as the Kaman-Kalehöyük one is, the other double stranded. It furthermore appears from the drawing that the central reservation on Bo. 2000/02 is also situated on a raised clay disc, that has presumably been formed by cutting away the guilloche after the hieroglyphs of the central area had been incised on the seal. This again seems very similar to the style of the Kaman-Kalehöyük example. It is possible but not necessary that BoHa 14.123 is a little later than both of these.

The importance of Bo. 2000/02 lies in the fact that it was found in the insulating fill of a chamber that formed part of the silo-complex adjacent to the postern wall on Büyükkale. This particular chamber, no. 14, went out of use during the 16th century due to a fire and was not used again (Seeher 2006: 69–70, 74). It is thus quite likely that the dating of the chamber can be used to date the sealing, as the fill in which it was found was functional for the storage-use of the construction. This dating would be likely to also be valid for the example from Kaman-Kalehöyük. If Herbordt is right in thinking that BoHa 14.123 from House 5 in J/19 in the Lower City "certainly" belongs to the same scribe as Bo. 2002/20[11], then is this also going to be the case for the exemplar from Kaman-Kalehöyük? The shape of the bullae to which the sealings are attached might support this being the case.[12] So either there is a fashion for producing similar looking sealings with invocations of the deity Innara for good luck at both Boğazköy and Kaman-Kalehöyük in the 16th century B.C., a rather unlikely possibility given the vast majority of attested sealing practices, or we have the same person, a government official or scribe, if it is meaningful to distinguish between the two, who is active at both sites.

This is of interest given the facts that Bo. 2000/02 was found in the context of a 16th century B.C. chamber in the grain silo complex on Büyükkale, and that one of the main architectural features of Kaman-Kalehöyük during stratum IIIb is the large stone-lined pit referred to as Round Structure 1, which may well have been used for grain storage.[13] Even if the Kaman-Kalehöyük example comes from a secondary context in a later level (Iron Age stratum IIc), the fact that this datable item has been found at the site is of importance for understanding the site's occupation during the 16th century B.C. It is difficult to establish the date at which the Round Structure 1 was inaugurated at Kaman-Kalehöyük archaeologically with any precision. If Innara's presence in the city is at all connected with the Round Structure, then at least we have a time before which the huge pit must have been dug. Very speculatively, Innara may have been an official from the capital who was either visiting or ful-

10 Herbordt 2006: 96–97, with Abb. 4a. See comments of Weeden (2018: 62).

11 Herbordt 2006: 96 "sicherlich".

12 It has not been possible to obtain a photo of the shape of the conical bulla Bo. 2000/02, but Jürgen Seeher has kindly sent me a sketch of its profile from his personal excavation records. The profile does look quite like that of Bo. 71/28 (= BoHa 14.123), for which see Fig. 5, as well as resembling the shape of 16000108 from Kaman-Kalehöyük. The record sent to me by Dr. Seeher also indicates that there are two string holes in the bulla.

13 Fairbairn and Omura 2005; Omura 2011. It should of course be noted that just because Innara's sealing was found (discarded) in the insulating fill of a chamber of the silos, this does not necessarily mean that he had anything to do with the management of the silos. It is however a coincidence that should be mentioned if a sealing of his is then also found at Kaman-Kalehöyük.

filling a function at Kaman-Kalehöyük in connection with the storage facilities. Such officials were referred to in cuneiform texts by the title ^{LÚ}AGRIG (Singer 1984). During the reign of Telipinu in the late 16th century B.C. there was some re-organisation of the activities of these officials, after evidence for malfeasance had become apparent.

On the other hand, the name I(n)nar(a) is known from the Old Hittite period. The Edict of Telipinu mentions a chief cup-bearer called Inara who is part of a conspiracy to commit acts of violence against the previous king, whom Telipinu had ejected from the throne, without the king Telipinu's knowledge (Edict of Telipinu § 25, line 33, Gilan 2015: 147). Although Inar is not mentioned among them in the following paragraphs, the men of violence are not killed by Telipinu, but they have their weapons taken from them and are made into "simple farmers" (Edict of Telipinu § 26, Gilan 2015: 148).

It is possible that this Inara is the same as Inar, the "chief of the [x]-men", who also received one of the earlier land-donations from an anonymous king (Rüster, Wilhelm 2012: 92–97, no. 3). The earliest land-donations are dated by Gernot Wilhelm to the reign of Telipinu or slightly before, i. e. in the mid-to-late 16th century (Wilhelm 2005). As has been previously remarked, this document is in fact not a land-donation so much as the protocol of two trials over 5 years during which 5 men try to take Inar to court over land granted to him by the father of the present king in the town of Zitalkissuwa (Rüster and Wilhelm 2012: 94; Bilgin 2018: 140). The current king confirms his father's gift and further promotes Inar to the rank of "Scribe on Wood of the House of Hattusa in Sarissa". [14] This is of course rather similar to the title "scribe" with which I(n)nara appears on the three seals from Boğazköy and Kaman-Kalehöyük. This would presumably have been a high governmental position, rather than being simply someone who just did writing.[15]

If these I(n)nar(a)s are identical, then one might consider that Kaman-Kalehöyük might be the settlement of Zitalkissuwa, the object of the land-donation, but this does not have to be the case. The "land-donation" text stipulates the confirmation of Inar's ownership of Zitalkissuwa with the following words: "(25) he (the king) took up Inar together with his towns, his house and his property" (Rüster and Wilhelm 2012: 92, no. 3, obv. 25–26). This makes it clear that Zitalkissuwa is only one of the "towns" where Inar has property.

There is a problem in combining all this evidence, in that the carbon-14 data from the chamber in the grain silo where Bo. 2000/02 was found were thought by the excavator to probably indicate a date in the earlier 16th century B.C., although it is emphasised that this is not certain (Seeher 2006: 74). If Inna[ra]'s sealing from the silo-complex on Büyükkale is indeed to be dated to the earlier 16th century B.C., then this is likely to exclude Inara the chief cup-bearer or the Inar of the Land-Donation from being the Innara of the seal-impressions, due to the fact that Telipinu's reign is more likely to be dated to the end of the 16th century B.C. So we have several possibilities: (1) if the Innara of the sealings is to be dated to the early 16th century B.C. on the basis of the probable interpretation of the radiocarbon data from Chamber 14 of the silo at Büyükkale, then this is presumably someone different, but quite possibly not unrelated to the later Inar. The Inar of the land-donation who is made into "scribe on wood of the house of Hattusa in Sarissa" and Inara the chief cup-bearer from the Edict of Telipinu could in this case be the same people, or they could also be different. (2) Perhaps the three seals of Innara belong to two people, with the sealing from Lower City J/19 House 5 (71/28) perhaps being a little later than the other two.

14 Rüster and Wilhelm 2012: 92, no. 3, obv. 26–7. The institution of the "House of Hattusa in Sarissa" appears in a number of the early land-donations. It is not entirely clear what it means in concrete terms.

15 For discussion of the sign L. 326 SCRIBA, see van den Hout 2020.

In this case the later Innara might be identical with either Inar or Inara from the cuneiform texts or with both. (3) If we are prepared to grant more latitude to the interpretation of the radiocarbon data and to conceive that the three sealings with two slightly different styles could have existed within the same lifetime, then it is possible that we could combine all of these Inar(a)s and Innaras from perhaps the middle to the later 16th century B.C. It is indeed the case that Inar of the land-donation must have been an official at the very least under the reign of Telipinu's father as well, if we are convinced by Wilhelm that the early land-donations date to Telipinu or slightly earlier. He may thus have been already at that stage quite elderly, or at least belonging to a prior generation.

At the very least then, this assemblage of data points to Kaman-Kalehöyük being tightly bound into the state bureaucracy in this early period, at the time when a centralised state starts being formed in the central Hittite area. If the association of Innara with the grain silos in Hattusa is thought to be convincing, possibly he is part of the early administration of Round Structure 1 in Kaman-Kalehöyük, which gives us a date by which it must have been in operation, either the early 16th century B.C. or perhaps a little later in the 16th century B.C. This seems quite different to the situation we find among the over 500 sealings that were dumped into Round Structure 1 in the late 15th or early 14th century B.C. after it had gone out of use, perhaps around 1500 B.C. Very few of these, if any, present any possible onomastic overlap with contemporary sealings from Hattusa, many of them show differences in style, and indeed seem to indicate rather different organisational structures, as evidenced for example by a collective seal with multiple names, and multiple sealings by women. It would thus appear that the relationship between Kaman-Kalehöyük and the central authority at Hattusa could have been different at various times in Hittite history.

Bibliography

Alp, S.
- 1968 *Zylinder- und Stempelsiegel aus Karahöyük bei Konya*, Ankara

Beran, Th.
- 1967 *Die hethitische Glyptik von Boğazköy 1 Die Siegel und Siegelabdrücke der vor- und althethitischen Perioden und die Siegel der hethitischen Grosskönige*, WVDOG 76/Boğazköy-Ḫattuša 5, Berlin.

Bilgin, T.
- 2008 *Officials and Administration in the Hittite World*, SANER 21, Boston/Berlin

Boehmer, R. M. and H. G. Güterbock
- 1987 *Glyptik aus dem Stadtgebiet von Boğazköy. Grabungskampagnen 1931–1939, 1952–1978*, Boğazköy-Ḫattuša 14, Berlin.

Dinçol, A. M and B. Dinçol
- 2008 *Die Prinzen- und Beamtensiegel aus der Oberstadt von Boğazköy-Ḫattuša vom 16. Jahrhundert bis zum Ende der Grossreichszeit*, Boğazköy-Ḫattuša 22, Mainz am Rhein.

Fairbairn, A. and S. Omura
- 2005 "Archaeological Identification and Significance of ÉSAG (agricultural storage pits) at Kaman-Kalehöyük, central Anatolia," *AnSt* 55, 15–23.

Gessel, B. H. L. van
- 1998 *Onomasticon of the Hittite Pantheon 1–2*, Leiden – New York – Köln.

Gilan, A.
- 2015 *Formen und Inhalte althethitischer Literatur*, Texte der Hethiter 29, Heidelberg.

Güterbock, H. G.
- 1975 "Hieroglyphensiegel aus dem Tempelbezirk," in K. Bittel, H. G. Güterbock, G. Neumann, P. Neve, H. Otten and U. Seidl, *Boğazköy V. Funde aus den Grabungen 1970 und 1971. Ausgrabungen der Deutschen Orient-Gesellschaft und des Deutschen Archäologischen Institutes*, AbhDOG 18, Berlin, pp. 47–76.

Herbordt, S.
- 2006 "Hethitische Stempelsiegel und Tonbullen aus den Grabungen am mittleren Büyükkale-Nordwesthang 1998–2000," in J. Seeher (ed.), *Ergebnisse der Grabungen an den Ostteichen und am mittleren Büyükkale-Nordwesthang in den Jahren 1996–2002*, Boğazköy-Berichte 8, Mainz, pp. 95–97.

Laroche, E.
- 1966 *Les Noms des Hittites*, Études Linguistiques 4, Paris.

Omura, S.
- 2011 "Kaman-Kalehöyük Excavations in Central Anatolia," in S.R. Steadman, and G. McMahon (eds), *The Oxford Handbook of Ancient Anatolia 10,000–323 B.C.E*, Oxford, pp. 1095–1111.

Rüster, Chr. and G. Wilhelm
- 2012 *Landschenkungsurkunden hethitischer Könige*, StBoT Bh. 4, Wiesbaden.

Seeher J.
- 2006 "Der althethitische Getreidesilokomplex," in Seeher, J. (ed.), *Ergebnisse der Grabungen an den Ostteichen und am mittleren Büyükkale-Nordwesthang in den Jahren 1996–2000* (Boğazköy-Berichte 8), Mainz am Rhein, 45–84.

Singer, I.
- 1984 "The AGRIG in the Hittite Texts," *AnSt* 34, pp. 97–127.

Van den Hout, Th.
- 2020 *A History of Hittite Literacy: Writing and Reading in Late Bronze Age Anatolia*, Cambridge.

Weeden, M.
- 2011 *Hittite Logograms and Hittite Scholarship*, StBoT 54, Wiesbaden.
- 2018 "Hieroglyphic Writing on Old Hittite Seals and Sealings? Towards a Material Basis for Further Research," in S. Ferrara and M. Valério (ed.), *Paths into Script Formation in the Ancient Mediterranean*, SMEA NS Supplemento 1, Rome, pp. 51–74.

Wilhelm G.
- 2005 "Zur Datierung der älteren hethitischen Landschenkungsurkunden," *Altorientalische Forschungen* 32, pp. 272–279.

Yoshida, D.
- 1999 "Hethitische Hieroglyphensiegel aus Kaman-Kalehöyük," *Bulletin of the Middle East Cultural Centre of Japan* 11, pp. 183–197.
- 2006 "'Mittelhethitische' Siegelfunde von Kaman-Kalehöyük," *Anatolian Archaeological Studies* 15, pp. 151–162.

Fig. 1. Drawing of Seal face of 160000108.

Fig. 2. Photo of Seal face of 160000108.

Fig. 3. Photo of Seal face of Bo. 71/28 (= BoHa 14.123). Photo by author.

Fig. 4. Drawing of Seal face of Bo. 71/28 (from Boehmer, Güterbock 1987, © Deutsches Archäologisches Institut).

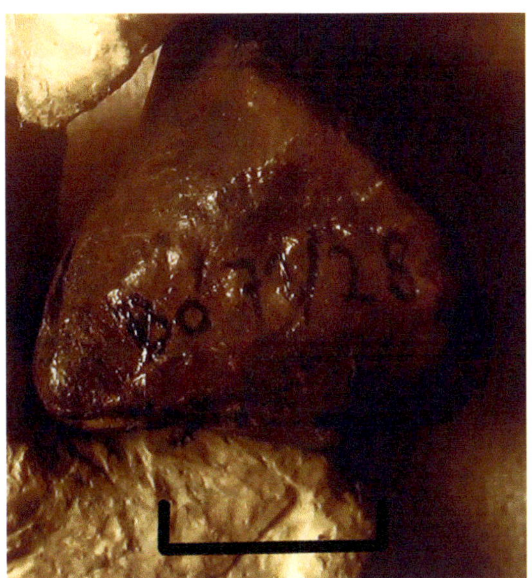

Fig. 5. Underside of conical bulla on Bo. 71/28.
Photo by author.

Fig. 6. Drawing of Bo. 2000/02 by S. Herbordt
from Herbordt 2006.

Seals and Seal Impressions Found in the Lower City and on the Mound of Yassıhöyük

*Masako Omura**

Abstract

Yassıhöyük mound is stratified from the Early Bronze Age to the Late Iron Age and annexed by a lower city settlement at the northern foot of the mound dated to the Period of Assyrian Trade Colony Period. Stratum II on the mound is thought to be contemporary with the Lower City. The seals and the seal impressions excavated in the Lower City and in Stratum II on the mound are representative of the Anatolian style; this is a style that had been established by interpreting the styles and iconographies of the newly imported glyptic art and transforming them into a distinct Anatolian style with some local characteristics. Therefore, it is possible to date the seals of Yassıhöyük and its Lower City after the period when the cylinder seals in Assyrian style were popular in Level II of Kültepe-kaniš *karum*, and even after the period when the cylinder seals in the Anatolian style with influences of Assyrian style were used. That is, the seals unearthed in Yassıhöyük so far are dated to the later phase of the Period of Assyrian Trade Colony Period. However, it is not so late as the time when Pithana and his son Anitta conquered Kaniš and occupied the Waršama palace.

Öz

Yassıhöyük, İlk Tunç Çağı'ndan Geç Demir Çağı'na kadar olan kültür tabakalarından oluşmaktadır. Höyüğün kuzey eteğinde, Asur Ticaret Kolonileri Çağı'na tarihlenen aşağı şehir yerleşimi bulunmaktadır. Höyük üzerindeki II. Tabakanın da Aşağı Şehir ile çağdaş olduğu tahmin edilmektedir. Höyük üzerindeki II. Kat'ta ve Aşağı Şehir'de ortaya çıkarılan mühürler ve mühür baskıları, M.Ö. 2. binin başında ithal edilen gliptik sanatının üslup ve ikonografilerinin yorumlanarak bazı yerel özellikler katılarak, Anadolu'nun kendi üslubuna dönüştürülmesiyle oluşturulan Anadolu üslubunu temsil etmektedir. Bu nedenle Yassıhöyük ve Aşağı Şehir'e ait mühürler; Kültepe-kaniš karum'un II. tabakasında Asur üslubundaki silindir mühürlerin popüler olduğu dönemden sonraya ve hatta Anadolu üslubundaki silindir mühürlerin, Eski Asur üslubunun etkileri ile yapıldığı dönemden sonraya yerleştirilebilirler. Yani bugüne kadar Yassıhöyük'te ortaya çıkarılan mühürler, Asur Ticaret Kolonileri Çağı'nın geç safhasına tarihlenebilir. Ancak bu dönem, Pithana ve oğlu Anitta'nın Kaniš'i zaptettiği ve Waršama Sarayı'nı işgal ettiği zaman kadar geç değildir.

Yassıhöyük and its Lower City

Yassıhöyük is found on the northern edge of national Route 260, which connects Ankara, Kayseri, and Adana. It is 160 km southeast of Ankara, 20 km north of the center of Kırşehir City, and about 25 km east of Kaman-Kalehöyük. It is in Çayağız Village in Kırşehir Prefecture. Its latitude: 39°19'18"N and longtitude: 34°04'29"E.

Yassıhöyük is a relatively large elliptical mound with dimensions of 500 m north-south, 625 m east-west, and 13 m high above the surrounding ground level. A Lower City settlement is spread out at the northern foot of the mound. Yassıhöyük has been known as a mound site since the middle of the 20th century,[1] while the Lower City was detected by ground penetrating radar surveys (GPR) in 2013–2015 (Fukuda-Kumagai 2016, Fukuda *et al.* 2013). Excavations have been conducted

* Japanese Institute of Anatolian Archaeology, m.omura@jiaa-kaman.org.

1 Meriggi 1966: 106, 109, Pl.XXXIX/Fig. 7; Mikami and Omura 1987: 126, res.16, 17, 37, 53/8–13; Omura 2001: 43; Omura 2003: 53.

at the top of the mound since 2009 and in the Lower City since 2018 (Omura 2016).

We have identified the stratified cultures on the top of the mound (Area 1) as Stratum I: Iron Age, Stratum II: Middle Bronze Age, and Stratum III: Early Bronze Age. It is thought that Stratum II on the mound is contemporary with the Lower City, which is dated to the Period of Assyrian Trade Colonies. In this article we discuss the seals and seal impressions excavated in Area 1 and the Lower City together with those found during a general surface survey at the site in 1986. The seals and impressions are thought to date to the early 2nd millennium B.C.

Excavations in the Lower City in 2018 and 2019 revealed four building levels dated to the Period of the Assyrian Trade Colonies (Fig.1). The architectural remains of the 1st (uppermost) building level (I-1) consist of multi-roomed buildings. In some structures of the 1st building level are traces of later rebuilding (I-1a). Below the 1st building level, the 2nd building level (I-2) is represented by partially preserved flat stone pavements. The 3rd building level (I-3) consists of a group of multi-room buildings, and the 4th building level (I-4) revealed partial walls.

Each of the settlements of the upper three building levels was associated with a road approximately 3 meters wide that passes from west to east at the northern edge of the excavated area. This road can be linked with high probability to a lane detected in the 2015 GPR survey further west. The road appears to have been built and used in four separate layers. The fourth layer of the road is contemporary with the structures of the 3rd building level. It is made of round stones that are smoother and more tightly packed than those of the upper three layers of the road, with adherent filling. Traces of wheel ruts on the road show that it could have been one of the main roads on which carts/wagons passed. In addition, the road covers a large area and is likely to be the main road used in the Lower City. Its extension connecting the Lower City with the Yassıhöyük citadel is expected to be uncovered in future excavations.

Finds of Seals and Seal Impressions

Several seals and seal impressions have been found at Yassıhöyük. During excavations in 2018 and 2019 in the Lower City, three stamp seals were unearthed: two made of copper/copper alloy, 190112 (YH19-5) and 190121 (YH19-6); and a pyramid shaped stamp seal made of pumice, 190041 (YH19-4). Impressions of seals have been found on three handles of jugs or jars: 190042 (YH19-3), 190051 (YH19-2), 190125; on a crescent loom weight: 180047 (YH18-19); and on three fragments of bullae: 180066 (YH18-1), 190133, 190154. Excavations in Area 1 at the top of the mound have produced a copper/copper alloy stamp seal, 110121 (YH11-57); and seal impressions on a potsherd, 160001 (YH16-1); and on bullae fragments 110074 (YH11-58), 110135 (YH11-59), 150032, and 150321. Several other bullae that seem to have borne seal impressions were unearthed both in the Lower City and on the mound, but they are so faint that they are not discussed here. Seal impressions were also found during the general surface survey conducted in 1986: on a jug handle, 860001 (YH86-1); and on a crescent loom weight, 860002 (YH86-2), although the impression on the latter (Pl. 2/Fig. 8) is too faint to discuss here.

Seals

1) 190112 (YH19-5):
Lower City (LC) I8/c6, I-2 ㊷, W 1.7 cm, L 1.65 cm, H 2.9 cm, H of the base 0.3 cm, copper/copper alloy (Fig. 2)

This stamp seal has a thin, square seal base and a stalk handle that ends with a thin round penetrated thread hole. The stalk handle is decorated with horizontal grooves. On the square seal face, vertical and horizontal lines are engraved around a central knot.

Many stalk-handled seals are found among the finds of Kaniš Karum Ib, Alişar, Boğazköy, and other sites, made of ivory, stone, and baked clay.[2] An example from Boğazköy Unterstadt

2 Özgüç 1968: Pl. XXX/1, XXXI/1, XXXVIII,

and another from Alişar made of copper/copper alloy most resemble the Yassıhöyük example. The one from Alişar in particular has a similar seal design with short lines in the square seal face, though that of Yassıhöyük is rougher.[3]

2) 190121 (YH19-6):
LC I8/b6, I-3 ⑲, D. 1.8 cm, H. 0.9 cm, H. of the base 0.25 cm, copper/copper alloy (Fig. 3)

This small, round stamp seal has a loop type grip with a thread hole. The grip made of a wide band with thick edges is welded to the thin round base. It is hard to find parallels of this type of grip among copper/copper alloy stamp seals, but they can be found among baked clay stamp seals such as those found in Kültepe Kaniš Karum Ib.[4] On the seal face is depicted a double-headed bird of prey capturing a pair of animals (antelopes) which are seated back-to-back and turning their heads back, and a seated monkey on each side of the double-headed bird.

The heraldic double- or single-headed bird is a favorite motif depicted on stamp seals in the Period of the Assyrian Trade Colonies in the early 2nd millennium B.C.[5] In many cases it is combined with antelope-like animals captured in its talons and is also standardized as one of the representative motifs of the Old Anatolian style in that period.[6] This motif in the Period of the Assyrian Trade Colonies seems to be a rather simple graphic. After that period it became more schematized, and then combined with tight loop or guilloche borders which are commonly seen in the finds from Konya Karahöyük.[7] At Kültepe-Kaniš the developed heraldic double-headed bird encircled in a tight loop or guilloche can be seen among the finds from the Waršama Palace (late Palace) which is contemporary with Kaniš Karum Ib.[8] Some contain a bird-head and a lion-head in the place of double bird heads.[9]

3) 190041 (YH19-4):
LC I8/b6, I-1b ⑪ R15, W. 2.4 cm, L. 2.4 cm, H. 2.5 cm, pumice (Fig. 4)

This pyramid-shaped stamp seal has an off-center peak and a wide thread hole penetrated horizontally. On the roughly square seal face, some animal figures appear to be engraved but they are not clear.

4) 110121 (YH11-57):
Area 1 E8/f10, 62 P34, D. 2.15 cm, H. 2.3 cm, H. of the base 0.6 cm, copper/copper alloy (Fig. 5)

This stamp seal has a conical grip over the disc base. The grip is decorated with horizontal grooves and ends with a knot that has a string hole penetrated horizontally. Because of the corroded condition, it is hard to recognize the exact design on the seal face. Two birds with an animal head between them and two or three animals or birds below them seem to have been engraved inside of a simple guilloche.

This type of stamp seal is one of the standard shapes found in many examples among the seals from Level Ib of Kültepe-Kaniš Karum and contemporary phases of Boğazköy-Unterstadt, Alişar, and other sites.[10] Most are made of stone

XXXIX/1–3; Boehmer and Güterbock 1987: Taf.I/1, 2.

3 Osten 1937: 213, Fig. 250/d747; Özgüç: 1968, Pl. XXXVII/2, XL/3, 4; Boehmer and Güterbock 1987: Taf. I/2.

4 Özgüç and Tunca 2001: Pl. 17 St 32 (Kt ş/k12), St68 (Kt 85/k59); Osten 1937: 212, Pl. 249/c385, d2216; Boemer and Güterbock 1987: Taf. VI/57, 61.

5 1937: 212, Fig. 249/d2081, 1140, 2307, 2310, 2970, 1523; Özgüç 1968: Pl. XXXIII/1–5; 2001, Pl. 30 St71 (Kt 90/k498); Boehmer and Güterbock 1987: Taf. II/24, IV/44A.

6 Özgüç and Tunca 2001: Pl. 17 St 32 (Kt ş/k12), St68 (Kt 85/k59); Osten 1937: 212, Pl. 249/c385, d2216; Boemer and Güterbock 1987: Taf. VI/57, 61.

7 Boehmer and Güterbock 1987: 34–37, Abb. 21/e, f, 23/a; Alp 1972: 169–175, Ş. 71–84, Lev. 68/178–77/204.

8 Özgüç 1968: Pl. III/2; 2001, Pl. 9 /St13 (Kt f/t397), 18/St 39 (Kt v/t 22, 43); Özgüç 1999: Pl. 71/2.

9 Özgüç and Tunca 2001: Pl. 4/ St4 (Kt. b/k 25), 9/St14 (Kt g/t280); Özgüç 1999: Pl. 74/2.

10 Özgüç, N. 1968, Pl. XXX/2, XXXI/2, XXXII, XX XIII/1,2,4,5, XXXIV/1, XXXVI/1–4, XXXVII/6, XL/5; Boehmer and Güterbock 1987: Taf. I/5, 8,

but some are copper/copper alloy, and a gold one from Kaniš Karum is well known (Özgüç: 1968, Pl. XXX/2). The gold seal and some seals from Kültepe, Boğazköy, and Alişar show a very similar profile and decoration to this Yassıhöyük seal.[11]

Although this seal 110121 (YH11-57) is among the disturbed finds discovered when excavating the fill of a pit (P34) dated to the Middle Iron Age, it shares a feature of seals dated to the later phase of the Period of the Assyrian Trade Colonies – a conical grip with a round knotted end. This feature distinguishes seals of this period from the hammer headed seals dated to the Old Hittite period.

Seal Impressions

Seal Impressions on Pottery

1) 190042 (YH19-3):
LC I8/c7, I-1b ⑦, W. 5.6 cm, L. 10.8 cm, T. 3.8 cm (Fig. 9)

A fragment of a red-slipped jug handle bears an impression of a stamp seal at the bottom of the handle.

Impression of a stamp seal: Round, d. ca. 1.6 cm. In the round seal face, a lion attacking a gazelle or antelope is depicted. There may be some dots and a bird-head-like motif filled in among the animal figures.

The lion hunting scene or the lion attacking a smaller animal is commonly depicted on Anatolian style cylinder seals as the main theme of an animal frieze or animals in the field with a god or a hunter, or as the secondary scene beside worship or reception scenes.[12] The motif of the lion attacking an animal is "borrowed" from cylinder seal scenes and used independently on stamp seals, as is the bird of prey attacking an animal.[13] These dynamic iconographies gradually became static and heraldic or symbolic iconographies in Old Hittite glyptic art.[14]

2) 190051 (YH19-2):
LC I8/b7, I-1b ⑩, W. 6.9 cm, L. 8.8 cm, T. 4.4 cm (Fig. 10, 11, 12)

This fragment of a wide, thin handle of a jar is red-slipped and wet-smoothed. Its fabric is medium fine with a small amount of impurities. It bears two impressions of a cylinder seal (A) and one of a stamp seal (B).

A. *Impression of a cylinder seal*: h. ca. 1.6 cm, w. ca. 3 cm (Fig. 11).

In the cylinder seal impression, two friezes depicted in Anatolian style are placed upside down relative to each other. One frieze shows a lion hunting scene (①), and the other seems to express a scene of (the end of) a battle (②). Usually, seals with two friezes in Anatolian style express a procession of animals or a field of animals including lions attacking other animals,[15] and some show the combination of a frieze of an animal procession with a frieze of a hunting scene (human) (Özgüç 2006: Pl. 12/CS316 (Kt d/k34B) or worship/reception scene (Özgüç 2006: Pl. 12/CS317 (Kt d/k34C). The combination of a frieze of animals with a frieze of a battle scene/field is not known except in this Yassıhöyük example at present.

① Lion hunting frieze: Two lions attack three antelopes which follow a seated monkey in front of a fish placed vertically under a disc in a crescent. Among the figures are a bird, an animal head, a fish, a plant, two stars, and a dot. This frieze is engraved in typical Anatolian

9, 12, 14, II/25,III/38, V/50, VI/58,59, VII/68, VIII/82–84; Osten 1937: 212, Fig. 249; Omura 1996.

11 Özgüç 1968: Pl. XXX/2, XXXI/2; von der Osten 1937: Fig. 251/d1906.

12 For examples see Özgüç 1965: Pl. IX/25, X/28, XII/34, XVI/47, XXVII/81, 82; 2006, Pl. 16/CS339 (Kt c/k1634C), 37/ CS481 (Kt n/k1779B).

13 For examples Özgüç 2006: Pl. 4/ St88 (Kt d/k12E), 13/ St100 (Kt d/k38), 14/ St103 (Kt d/k48A), 15/ St104 (Kt d/k48B); Boehmer and Güterbock 1987: Taf. VII/68, 69; Omura 1995: Fig. 17/4.

14 For examples KL94–1: Omura 1995: 29, Fig.17/3, frontispiece; Boehmer and Güterbock 1987: 33ff.

15 For examples Özgüç 2006: Pl. 2/CS262 (Kt d/k9B, 6/ CS285 (Kt d/k17C, 18C, 19B), 9/CS298 (Kt d/k26A), 10/CS301 (Kt d/k28A), 11/CS313 (Kt d/k32D).

style which can find many parallels in Level II of Kültepe-Kaniš Karum.[16]

② Battle scene frieze: This probably depicts a scene of the end of a battle. A man with a saw-toothed sword (the god Šamaš) on a one-horse chariot is led by a man holding a spear, a kneeling man holding a spear with both hands, and another man facing another kneeling man with a spear. One body in front of the man on the chariot and two bodies behind him are laid on the ground. The heads are detached from the bodies and missing. Between the figures are two stars, a human head, and uncertain shapes which could be parts detached from the bodies.

The motifs of the one-horse chariot and the bodies without their heads are factors of interest on this seal. Observing the seals of Kültepe Kaniš Karum, a four-wheeled chariot drawn by four horses (Özgüç 1965: Pl. III/9 (Kt a/k318), a two-wheeled chariot drawn by two boars (Özgüç 1965: Pl. VIII/24b (Kt a/k200, b/k65, b/k833), and a four-wheeled chariot drawn by two horses[17] are found among the Anatolian style seals in Kaniš Karum Level II, though the number is small. Figures laid on the ground which are thought to be dead bodies are also found among the Anatolian style seals in Kültepe Kaniš Karum Level II. They are inserted in divine scenes or worship/reception scenes,[18] in friezes of animals (Özgüç 2006: Pl. 56/CS617 (Kt n/k1840C), and in secondary scenes as subsidiary schematized motifs.[19] These examples show the bodies as whole including the heads, which is different from this example from Yassıhöyük.

B. *Impression of a stamp seal*: Square, 2.9 cm × 2.9 cm (Pl. 3/Fig. 12). The square seal face is divided into four parts and an individual motif is depicted in Anatolian style in each part: two birds placed back to back on their legs; a whorl with four bird heads with a dot at the center; a seated antelope turning its head back in a circle; and an animal head under the arch of possibly a snake. At the center of the seal where the four parts intersect is a small shape like a distorted circle or crescent. The strongly engraved outlines of animal figures and their large eyes clearly illustrate the characteristics of the Anatolian style. Seals with a square face are found among the seals in Levels II and Ib of Kültepe-Kaniš Karum, and some examples have a four-divided seal face with an individual motif in each part.[20]

3) 190125:
LC I8/c5, I-3 ㉒, W. 4.0 cm, L. 6.2 cm,
T. 2.3 cm (Pl. 27)

A fragment of a red-slipped and burnished jug handle bears one half of an impression of a stamp seal at the bottom of the handle. This impression of a rectangular stamp seal bears two lines of short horizontal grooves.

4) 160001 (YH16–1):
Area 1 E9/g1, W. 3.5 cm, L. 4.6 cm,
T. 1.6 cm (Fig. 13)

A small red-slipped and burnished potsherd made of fine buff paste was discovered in the soils that covered the burnt soils of Stratum III. The sherd bears two cylinder seal impressions, but it is not certain whether they were made by the same seal or by two different seals. One impression (A) was rolled vertically and the other (B) horizontally. They intersect each other at a right angle. Probably A was rolled before B, for A was damaged at the intersection.

Impression A: The lower parts of probably a human and an animal figure and fish and plant-like motifs are faintly preserved over a ground line.

16 For examples see Özgüç 1965: Pl. XXX/94, 95; 2006, CS300 (Kt d/k27D), CS339 (Kt c/k1634C), Özgüç 1986: Pl. 122/94, 95.

17 Özgüç 1965: CS970 (Kt g/k397E, 91/k126C).

18 Özgüç and Tunca 2001: Pl. 8/CS49 (Kt. c/k1578, g/k407A); 2006, Pl. 58/CS627 (Kt n/k 1844D, g/k410, 91/k392B).

19 Özgüç and Tunca 2001: CS49 (Kt g/k407A, 94/k1037); 2006, CS627 (Kt g/k410, n/k1884D91/k392B); CS990 (Kt g/k407C). Unpublished seals Kt 91/k395A and Kt 92/k167 also bear this kind of motif.

20 St113 (Kt e/k188A), Özgüç, N. and T. Özgüç 1953: Lev. LV/526; 1968, Pl. XXXIX/3.

Impression B: h. ca. 1.8 cm. A lion hunting scene consisting of three animal figures standing on their hind legs is engraved with emphasized outlines in the Old Anatolian style: a lion attacking a kid or gazelle-like small animal turning its head back, which is running after another animal in the same posture between two lines on both edges.

5) 860001 (YH86–1):
survey find, W. 5.4 cm, L 9.4 cm,
T. 3.4 cm, preserved height of the seal ca. 1.6 cm (Fig. 14)

A fragment of a jug handle was found in the surface survey in 1986. The red-slipped burnished ware is made of fine fabric and fired hard. Part of an impression of a cylinder seal is preserved on it.

Impression of a cylinder seal: Two friezes are divided with a line. One frieze is an animal frieze consisting of a lion attacking a maned animal following another animal of which only a hind leg is preserved, and two birds' heads. In the second frieze is a row of standing figures which are connected, with one arm of each schematized figure raised and the other lowered. The strongly emphasized outlines of animals with large eyes clearly illustrate the characteristics of the Anatolian style, as in the stamp seal impression of 190051 (YH19–2)B, while the row of schematized figures has some Syrian comparisons. A similar example of the row of human figures connected to each other was found on a bulla unearthed in Stratum IIIc at Kaman-Kalehöyük (Omura 1996: 197, Pl. III/1, Fig. 4). These seals are thought to have been engraved in the Old Anatolian style with interference from the Syrian Popular style which has been identified at Kültepe-Kaniš Karum and other sites.[21] To give a distant precedent, the row of schematized human figures resembles the motif in impressions on Early Bronze Age vessels discovered in Palestine and suggest that the motif was transmitted from the 3rd millennium to the 2nd millennium B.C., though the finds treated by Ben-Tor do not seem to come from a clear stratigraphic context (Ben-Tor 1978: 11, Fig. 9/60, Pl. 9/60, 44–45).

Seal Impressions on Crescent Loom Weights

1) 180047 (YH18-19):
LC I8/d7, I-1b ⑥, W. 4.8 cm, L 10.0 cm,
T. 2.8 cm (Fig. 6)

A half fragment of a crescent loom weight bears an impression of a stamp seal, although it is very faded and a part around the edge is missing.

Impression of a stamp seal: Round, D. 1.4 cm. It appears that an animal turning its head back and a fish and an animal head may be depicted in the round seal face, though the impression is too faded to restore the exact shapes.

Seal Impressions on Clay Bullae

1) 180066 (YH18-1):
LC I8/c5, I-1 ①, W. 1.9 cm, L. 2.5 cm,
T 1.2 cm (Fig. 15)

This fragment of a conically shaped token has a hole for string at the top which is broken away. A stamp seal was impressed on the round bottom.

Impression of a stamp seal: Round, D. 1.9 cm. The round seal face is divided into four parts and decorated with dots. The edge is also decorated with dots.

2) 190133:
LC I8/c5, I-3 ㉒, W. 4.0 cm, L. 4.5 cm,
T. 2.4 cm (Fig. 17)

This bulla fragment has six impressions of a round stamp seal. One of the impressions at the center is complete and the other five are partially preserved. On the back side is an impression of a thick string.

Impressions of stamp seal: Round, D. 1.6 cm. Although the impressions are too faded to understand the design clearly, probably a lion attacking an animal turning its head back is depicted in a circle. A dot and a bird head-like motif are inserted behind the animals.

21 Özgüç 1958: p..11, Fig. 10; 1968 p. 56, Pl. V/3; 19, 3, pp. 175–178; Osten 1937: 205–210, Fig. 246/d2987. B1000; Porter 2001.

3) 190154:
LC I8/b7, I-4 ㉗, P11, W. 2.4 cm, L. 2.9 cm, T. 1.3 cm (Fig. 16)

This bulla fragment gets thinner from one side where two impressions of string are found, toward the other side. Two thirds of an impression of a stamp seal is preserved on the upper face, and traces of some figures of a cylinder seal impression and the fringe of a stamp seal impression are faintly preserved on the back face but it is not enough to restore.

Impression of a stamp seal on the upper face: Round, D. 2.8 cm. Possibly a small figure seated under a disc attended by an animal seems to face others. There may be a dot and other filling motifs.

4) 150032 (YH15-60):
Area 1 E9/f1, W. 2.3 cm, L. 2.8 cm, T. 1.2 cm (Fig. 18)

This bulla fragment bears an impression of a stamp seal. On the back of the bulla some impressions of strings in a circle are visible.

Impression of a stamp seal: Square, ca. 1.7 cm × 1.7 cm. The square seal depicts a geometric motif like a variation of a meander.

5) 150321:
Area 1 E9/f1. W. 1.9 cm, L. 3.4 cm, T 1.3 cm (Fig. 19)

This half fragment of a bulla bears an impression of a stamp seal which is also half broken. The thin disk shape and the hole penetrated along the diameter, with impressions of string visible at the broken edge, suggest that this bulla could have been used as a label.

Impression of a stamp seal: Round, D. 2.5 cm. The diameter of the half-preserved impression is almost the same as that of the bulla itself. Depicted on the round seal face surrounded by a circular line is what appears to be a naked hero struggling with a lion placed upside down (this part is broken away) and also a seated monkey inserted behind him and a leg of an animal below him. These motifs are seen as secondary elements within the various main scenes of cylinder seals[22] but they were transferred onto stamp seals as the main theme in Anatolia (Omura 2019). Traditionally, a hero struggles with a lion, bull, or bull-man, but in the Anatolian style he is most often depicted struggling with a lion placed upside down, or sometimes with a lion standing on its hind legs.

6) 110074 (YH11–58):
Area 1 E8/d10 ㉝ W. 2.4 cm, L. 2.3 cm, T. 10 cm (Fig. 20)

Two pieces of a bulla with a flat back bear two almost complete stamp seal impressions and the edge of a third impression. There are two impressions of string on the edges of the bigger piece.

Impressions of a stamp seal: Round, D. 1.6 cm. The design consists of a whorl with four bird heads around a concentric circle. Each bird head has a large beak and a large eye and is decorated with short diagonal lines.

The whorl motif consisting of birds' heads was one of the favorite motifs in the Anatolian style from the period of Level II at Kültepe-Kaniš Karum, just as was the heraldic double-headed bird motif of 190121 (YH19–6).[23] The number of bird heads varies from four to ten and possibly more. A combination of bird and animal heads can be observed in examples from Kültepe-Kaniš Karum (Özgüç 2006: Pl. 81/St112 (Kt n/k1946B).

7) 110135 (YH11-59):
Area 1 E8/d10 ㊸. W. 3.5 cm, L. 3.1 cm, T. 1.0 cm (Fig. 21)

This fragment of a bulla bears three partial impressions of a stamp seal. It has an impression of

22 For the examples see Özgüç 2006: Pl. 10/CS149 (Kt d/k29B etc.), 45/CS538 (Kt n/k1807A, etc).

23 Boehmer and Güterbock 1987: 25, Taf. IV/44B; Osten 1937: 224, Fig. 249/d2952, c2656; Kaman-Kalehöyük: Omura 1997: 121, Fig. 11, 12 ; Kültepe: Özgüç and Tunca 2001: Pl. 21/St65 (Kt 82/k 136B), 22/St67 (Kt83/k250); 2006, Pl. 3/St86 (Kt. d/k10D), 6/St36 (Kt.d/k18A, t/t10), 9/St98 (Kt d/k27B, 48A), 78/St111 (Kt n/k1933A), a very schematized wheel with four bird heads is depicted as a second motif.

string at the side edge and its back side is severely damaged. Two of the seal impressions overlap each other.

Impressions of a stamp seal: Round, D. ca. 2.4 cm. The design of the seal is composed of a whorl with bird heads with a long beak centered around a small whorl with spokes. Each bird is decorated with lineal chevrons.

Summary of Seal and Impression Characteristics

The characteristics of the seals and seal impressions discussed above can be summarized as follows.

1) All the seals found in the Lower City and on the mound of Yassıhöyük are stamp seals in shapes characteristic of the Period of the Assyrian Trade Colonies. In particular, the copper alloy seals 190112 (YH11-5) and 110121 (YH11-57) are regarded to represent the standard shapes of that period. Although the stamp seal with a loop grip 190121 (YH19-6) is not a common shape among copper/copper-alloy seals, a similar shape can be found among clay and ivory seals. Stamp seals dated to the Period of the Assyrian Trade Colonies show a rich variety of forms as observed at Kültepe-Kaniš Karum, Bogazköy, Alişar, Kaman-Kalehöyük, and other sites.[24] The pyramid-shaped seal 190041 (YH19-4) is one of those varied forms.

2) Most of the seal impressions were found on pottery shards and clay bullae. Unfortunately, no textual material accompanying and dating the seals and seal impressions has yet been discovered at Yassıhöyük.

3) Most of the impressions are from stamp seals, and only three are from cylinder seals.

4) All the designs of the seals and impressions found to date are engraved in the Anatolian style.

5) The designs and motifs of the stamp seals and impressions are classified as follows:

- 5-1. Animal figures within a simple circle (180047, 190042, 190133, 190154, 110121). Two of these include a lion attacking a smaller animal (190042, 190133). Although it is hard to restore the corroded design of 110121, a copper/copper alloy stamp seal, it is thought to represent bird motifs within a simpler guilloche fringe.
- 5-2. A whorl with bird heads (190051B, 110074 and 110135).
- 5-3. Heraldic double-headed eagle (190121).
- 5-4. A square seal with independent animal motifs in quarters including a whorl motif with four bird heads (190051B).
- 5-5. A hero probably struggling with a lion turned upside down (150321).
- 5-6. Geometric motifs: meander (150032), grooved short lines and other (190112, 190125), dots (180066).

Elements 5-1, 5-2, and 5-3 are popular motifs of Anatolian stamp seals in the later phase of the Period of the Assyrian Trade Colonies, although the number of examples found in Kaniš Karum II, which is the earlier phase of the period, is not small. Element 5-4 seems similar to clover-shaped stamp seals with the seal face divided into three parts which are also popular in that period. Element 5-5 is a good example of the motifs taken from the scenes of cylinder seals and transferred onto stamp seals (in the same way as the lion hunting motif), a common characteristic in Anatolian stamp seals (Omura 2019).

6) Three impressions of cylinder seals with restorable designs were discovered: 190051A, 160001 and 860001. All were rolled on potsherds.

- 6-1. Two have two tiers of freezes of different scenes: 190051 consists of a frieze of animals and a scene of battle, and 860001 consists of an upper frieze of animals and a lower frieze of human figures connected to each other. Another cylinder seal 160001 presents one animal frieze. All three friezes of animals contain the motif of the lion attacking another animal.

24 Omura 1997: 115ff.; Boehmer and Güterbock 1987: Taf. I–IX; Özgüç and Özgüç 1953: Lev. LV/513–526; Osten 1937: 211ff., Fig. 248–252.

- 6-2. All three cylinder seals were engraved in Anatolian style. However, they can be divided into two groups. The animal figures on 160001 and 860001 are similar to those of 190051B with the engravings with emphasized large eyes and beaks and deep outlines bearing the local taste.
- 6-3. On the other hand, the figures of 190051A are engraved in more delicate style which is observed among the Anatolian style seals from Kültepe-Kaniš Karum Level II. The battle scene of 190051A is more narrative than the animal friezes. And the motifs of the chariot carrying a god and the bodies laid on the ground on 190051A are remarkable. They have some parallels in the seals from Kültepe-Kaniš Karum Level II, and the motif of the body can be found on later seals of the Tyskiewicz group (Boehmer and Güterbock 1987: 37–39). However, bodies without their heads laid on the ground are not found in other examples, while what appear to be detached human heads are seen on cylinder seals from Kaniš Karumu II to the Old Hittite period.
- 6-4. Additionally, a row of schematized human figures in the lower frieze of 860001 brings to mind Syrian influence, while no influences of Assyrian style are seen.

Probable Dating of the Lower City

Sorting the seals and seal impressions according to their find spots in the building levels of the Lower City does not indicate or suggest any major change of style or new turn of glyptic art at Yassıhöyük. The evidence of the seals and impressions indicates that four building levels were settled within a certain period belonging to the same culture, with short time lags.

If we try to date the settled period of the Lower City of Yassıhöyük based on glyptic art without any dated literature evidence, we have to refer to examples from other dated sites such as Kültepe Kaniš. Kültepe Kaniš is a benchmark site of the Period of the Assyrian Trade Colonies according to the chronological context stratified as Level II and Level Ib which are distinguished from each other by a destruction layer caused by a conflagration. The glyptic art of the era is also divided into the early phase and the later phase, parallel to levels II and Ib. However, it is difficult to precisely distinguish the Anatolian style seals of the early phase from those of the later, because Anatolian style seals seem to have appeared during Level II and continued in Level Ib. At least, we can say that Anatolian style seals influenced by Assyrian or Mesopotamian styles are observed much more in Level II, and Syrian influences in style and motifs and local tastes increased in Level Ib. And observing the seals from Waršama Palace on the citadel of Kültepe-Kaniš, which is contemporary with Karum Ib, the characteristics of Old Hittite seals began to appear. One of these Old Hittite characteristics is the favored use of the tight loop or guilloche. The evidence indicating the time when this favored use began can be found through examination of the seal impressions on documents notarized by the kings who ruled and conquered Kaniš (Inar, Waršama, Pithana, Anitta, and Zuzu, in chronological order), which were unearthed in Kaniš Karum Level Ib. It is noteworthy that examples of the stamp seal impressions decorated by the tight loop, guilloche, and spiral are observed on documents notarized by Anitta and Zuzu and the impression of the seal of Zuzu (Özgüç 1996: Fig. 6D, 6E, 7, 8C, 9). However, the seal impressions on documents notarized by the earlier kings Inar, Waršama, and Pithana do not favor this kind of decoration, while their cylinder seal impressions exhibit the Syrian style and its influences (Özgüç 1996: Fig. 1–3). One of the Syrian style of cylinder seals which is said to have been developed in the reign of Samsuiluna is found on a document notarized by Pithana, and the guilloche dividing the two friezes may be a precedent of the tight loop or guilloche of Anatolian stamp seals. And the tight loop or guilloche encircling animal or human figures came to be popular in Old Hittite seals (Boehmer and Gütterbock 1987: 33ff., Taf. X–XV).

A number of features of the Yassıhöyük seals indicate that these seals could have been used in the later phase of the Period of Assyrian Trade Colonies that is almost contemporary with Kaniš Karum Ib period. These features are: stamp seals are dominant; all the seals are engraved in Anatolian style; motifs on the stamp seals are mostly considered to have been transferred from scenes on cylinder seals; the cylinder seals show Syrian style influences but not Assyrian style influences.

However, because the animal figures and the heraldic double-headed eagle motif of the Yassıhöyük seals are not so schematized and not as symbolic as those of Waršama Palace (the late palace) of Kültepe-Kaniš (Özgüç 1999: 64–68, 134–136), and the tight loop or guilloche characteristic of the impressions on documents notarized by Anitta and Zuzu cannot be found among the Yassıhöyük seals, this indicates that the seals found in the Lower City of Yassıhöyük are not so late as the time of Anitta and Zuzu, and probably date before the conquest of Pithana.

According to dendrochronological analysis by Newton-Kuniholm, Waršama palace is estimated to have been constructed after 1835/1832 B.C. and restored after 1810 B.C. and after 1774/1771 B.C. (Newton and Kuniholm 2004: 167). And according to Barjamovic, Hertel and Larsen, based on the revised eponym list of the Old Assyrian period and the middle chronology, it is thought that 1835/1832 B.C. coincides with the gap between the last dated texts from Level II and the earliest dated text from Ib of Kaniš Karum, the reign of Waršama began in 1775 and the Palace could have been used until Kaniš ended, then Pithana of Kuššara conquered Kaniš around 1750 B.C. and his successor Anitta burned Hattuš around 1730 B.C. [25]

In conclusion, the seals and seal impressions discovered in the Lower City and in Stratum II on the mound of Yassıhöyük are probably dated to the period from the later half of the 19th century B.C. to the first half of the 18th century B.C.[26]

Bibliography

Alp, A.
- 1972 *Konya Civarında Karahöyük Kazılarında Bulunan Silindir ve Damga Mühürleri*, TTKY V/26, Ankara.

Barjamovic, G.
- 2011 *A Historical Geography of Anatolia in the Old Assyrian Colony Period*, Copenhagen.

Barjamovic, G., T. Hertel and M. T. Larsen
- *2012 Ups and Downs at Kanesh. Chronology, History and Society in the Old Assyrian Period*, Leiden.

Ben-Tor, A.
- 1978 *Cylinder Seals of Third-Millennium Palestine*, Bulletin of the American School of Oriental Research Supplement Series No. 22, Cambridge.

Boehmer, R. M. and H. G. Güterbock
- 1987 *Glyptik aus dem Stadtgebiet von Boğazkoy*. Boğazköy-Hattusa XIV, Berlin.

Fukuda *et al.*
- 2013 "Geophysical Survey at Yassıhöyük," *AAS* XVIII, pp. 1–14.

Fukuda, K. and K. Kumagai
- 2016 "Ground Penetrating Radar Survey at the Surroundings of Yassıhöyük Mound -Vestiges of Ancient Lower City," *AAS* XIX, pp. 73–79

Koşay, H. Z.
- 1951 *Türk Tarih Kurumu Tarafından Yapılan Alaca Höyük Kazısı 1937–1939'daki Çalışmalara ve Keşifelere Ait İlk Rapor – Ausgrabungen von Alaca Höyük. Vorbericht über die Forschungen und Entdeckungen von 1937–1939*, Ankara.

Mazzoni, S.
- 1975 "Tell Mardikh e una classe glittica siroanatolica del periode di Larsa," *ANNALI a cura dei professori ufficiali dei Seminari di Studi Asiatici e Africani*, 35, pp. 21–43.

Meriggi, P.
- 1966 "Quinto Viaggio Anatolico," *OrAnt* V-1.

Newton, M. W. and P. I. Kuniholm
- 2004 "A Dendrochronological Framework for the Assyrian Colony Period in Asia Minor,"

25 Barjamovic, Hertel and Larsen 2012: 35–40, Appendix 1.

26 Özgüç 1999: 64–65, 134–136; Barjamovic, Hertel and Larsen 2012: 29.

Türkiye Bilimler Akademisi Arkeoloji Dergisi 7, pp. 165–176.

Omura, M.

- 1996 "Cylinder Seals and Seal Impressions Excavated at Kaman-Kalehöyük, *BMECCJ* IX, pp. 193–207.
- 1997 "The Seals and Seal Impressions from Kaman-Kalehöyük: Seals and Seal Impressions dated in the Period of Assyrian Trade Colonies," *AAS* VI, pp. 115–133.
- 1998 "The Seals and Seal Impressions from Kaman-Kalehöyük: A stamp Seal and Seal Impressions Dated in the Old Hittite Period," *AAS* VII, pp. 159–172.
- 2008 "Archaeological Surveys at Yassıhöyük," *AAS* XVII, pp. 97–169.
- 2016 "Yassıhöyük Excavations: First Five Seasons 2009–2013," *AAS* XIX, pp. 11–71.
- 2019 "A Study on the Turning Point of Glyptic Art in Anatolia Based on the Finds from Kaman-Kalehöyük," Nakata, I. *et al.* eds., *Prince of the Orient. Ancient Near Eastern Studies in Memory of H. I. H. Prince Takahito Mikasa*, pp. 67–86.

Omura, S.

- 1995 "A Preliminary Report on the Ninth Excavation at Kaman-Kalehöyük," *AAS* IV, pp. 1–48.
- 2001 "Preliminary Report of the General Survey in Central Anatolia (2000)," *AAS* X, pp. 37–86.
- 2003 "Preliminary Report of the General Survey in Central Anatolia (2002)," *AAS* XII, pp. 37–88.

Osten, H.H. von der

- 1937 *The Alishar Hüyük. Seasons of 1930–32*, Pt. II, OIP XXIX, Researches in Anatolia VIII, Chicago.

Özgüç, N.

- 1965 *Kültepe Mühür Baskılarında Anadolu Grubu: The Antolian Group of Cylinder Seal Impressions from Kültepe*, TTKY V/22, Ankara.
- 1968 *Kaniş Karum Ib Katı Mühürleri ve Mühür Baskıları: Seals and Seal Impressions of Level Ib from Kaniş Karumu*, TTKY V/25, Ankara.
- 1996 "Seal Impressions on Kültepe Documents Notarized by Native Rulers," in H. Gasche, H. and B. Hrouda (eds.), *Collectanea Orientalia. Histoire, Arts de l'Espace et Industrie de la Terre. Etudes offertes en hommage à Agnès Spycket*, Paris, pp. 267–278.
- 2006 *Kültepe-Kaniš/Neša Yerli Peruwa ve Aššur-ımittī'nin Oğlu Assur'lu Tüccar Uşur-ša-Ištar'ın Arşivlerine ait Kil Zarfların Mühür Baskıları – Seal Impressions on the Clay Envelopes from the Archives of the Native Peruwa and Assyrian Trader Uşur-ša-Ištar, son of Aššur-iımittī*, TTKY V/50, Ankara.
- 2015 *Acemhöyük – Burušhaddum I: Silindir mühürler ve Mühür Baskılı Bullalar–Cylinder Seals and Bullae with Cylinder Seal Impressions*, Ankara.

Özgüç, N., Ö. Tunca

- 2001 *Kültepe Kaniš: Mühürlü ve Kil Yazıtlı Bullalar – Sealed Clay Bullae*, TTK Yayınları V. Dizi – No. 48, Ankara.

Özgüç, N. and T. Özgüç

- 1953 *Türk Tarih Kurumu Tarafından Yapılan Kültepe Kazısı Raporu 1949 – Ausgrabungen in Kültepe. Bericht über die im Auftrage der Türkischen Historischen Gesellschaft, 1949 durchgeführten Ausgrabungen*, Ankara.

Özgüç, T.

- 1999 *Kültepe-Kaniš/Neša Sarayları ve Mabetleri – The Palaces and Temples of Kültepe-Kaniš/Neša*, Ankara.

Öztan, A.

- 1995 "Acemhöyük'te Bir Silindir Mühür," in A: Erkanal and H. Erkanal, *Metin Akyurt, Bahattin Devam Anı Kitabı: Eski Yakın Doğu Kültürleri Üzerine İncelemeler*, Istanbul, pp. 287–288.

Porter, B.A.

- 2001 *Old Syrian Popular Style Cylinder Seals*, Ann Arbor.

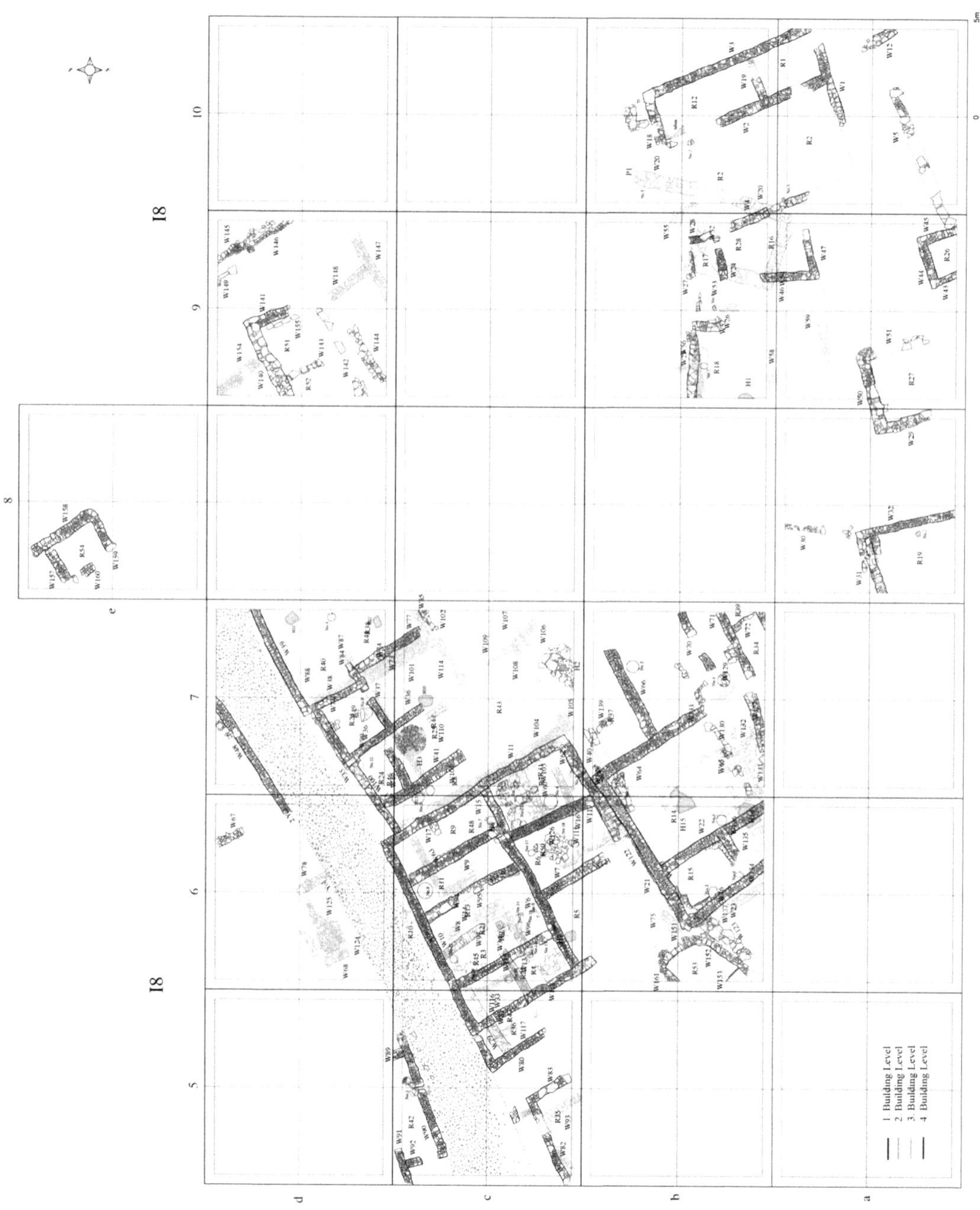

Fig. 1. Plan of Lower City, Yassıhöyük.

Fig. 2. Stamp seal 190112 (YH19-5).

Fig. 3. Stamp seal 190121 (YH19-6).

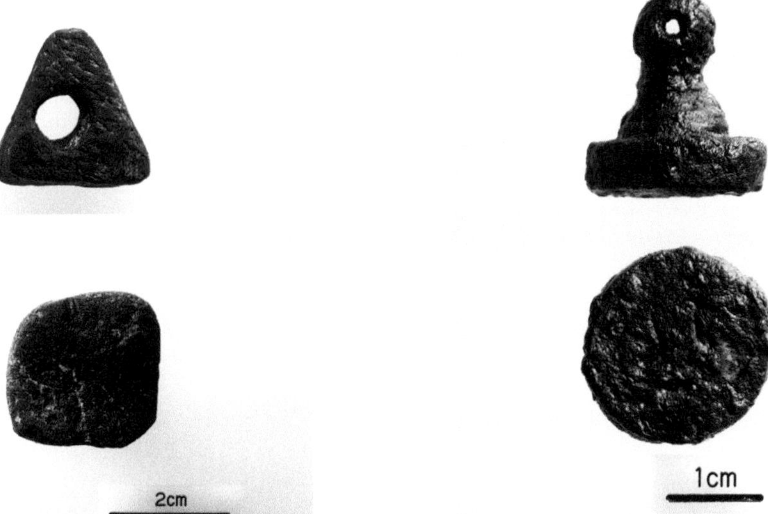

Fig. 4. Stamp seal 190041 (YH19-4).

Fig. 5. Stamp seal 110121 (YH11-57).

Fig. 6. Crescent loom-weight 180047 (YH18-19).

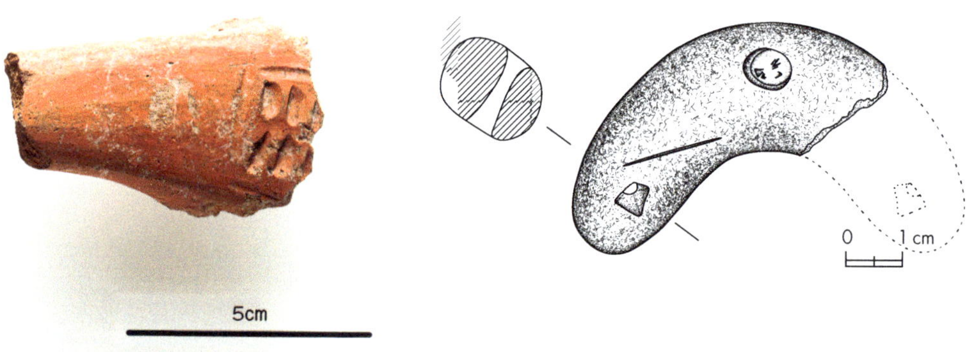

Fig. 7. Handle of a jug 190125.

Fig. 8. Crescent loom weight 860002 (YH86-2).

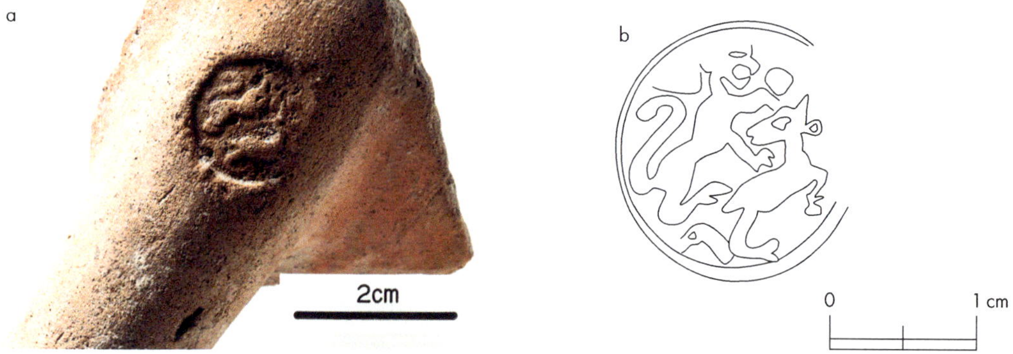

Fig. 9. Handle of a jug 190042 (YH19-3).

Fig. 10. Handle of a jar 190051 (YH19-2).

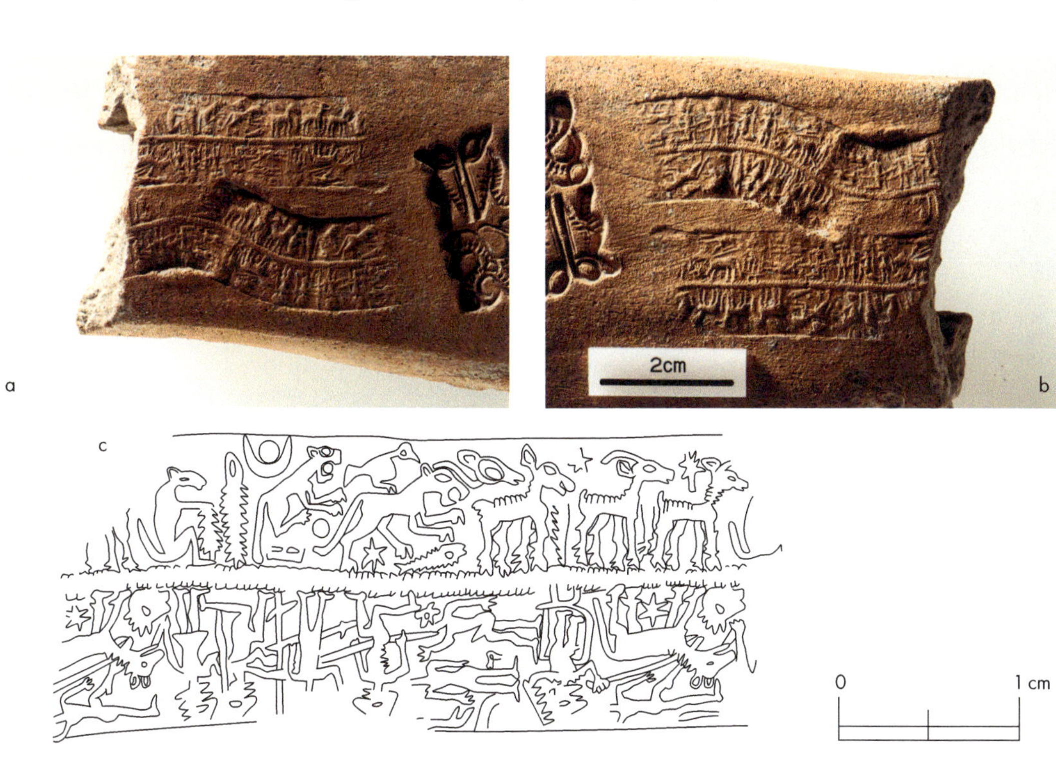

Fig. 11. Cylinder seal impressions on 190051 (YH19-2).

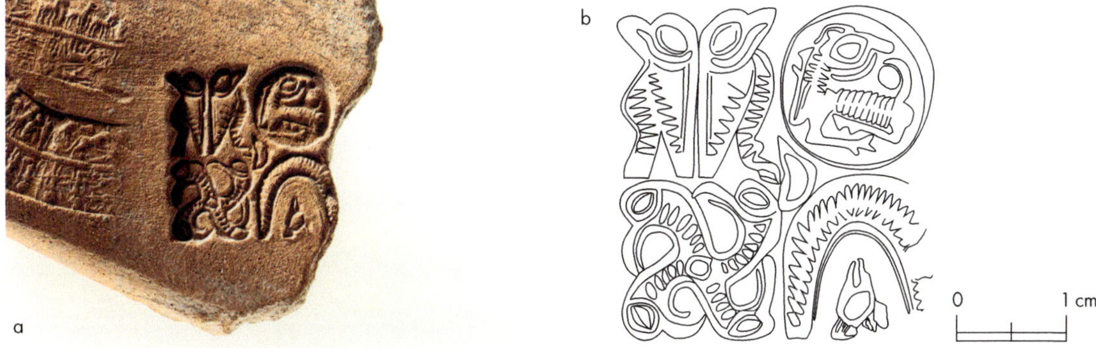

Fig. 12. Stamp seal impression on 190051 (YH19-2).

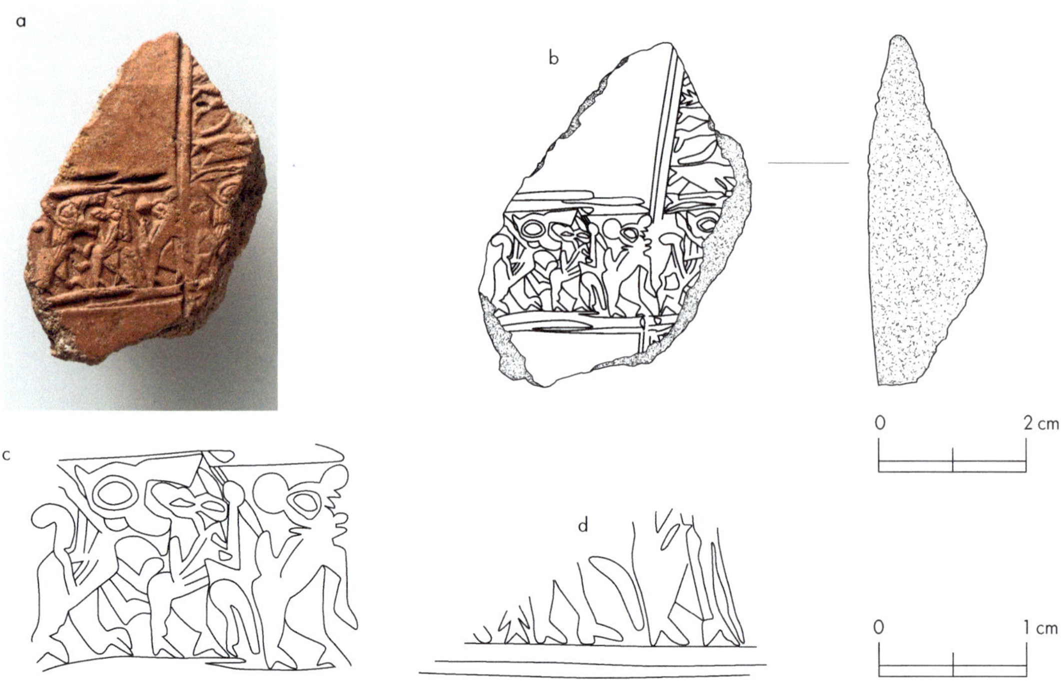

Fig. 13. Cylinder seal impressions on a potshard 160001 (YH16-1).

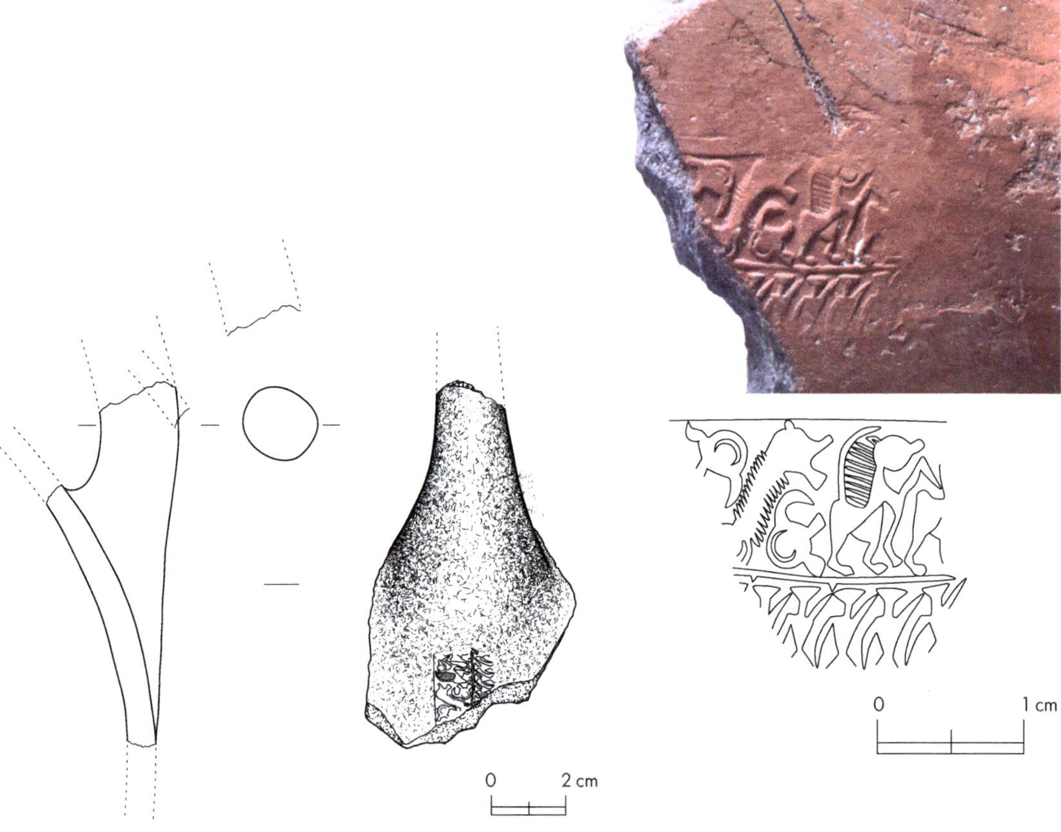

Fig. 14. Cylinder seal impression on a handle 860001 (YH86-1).

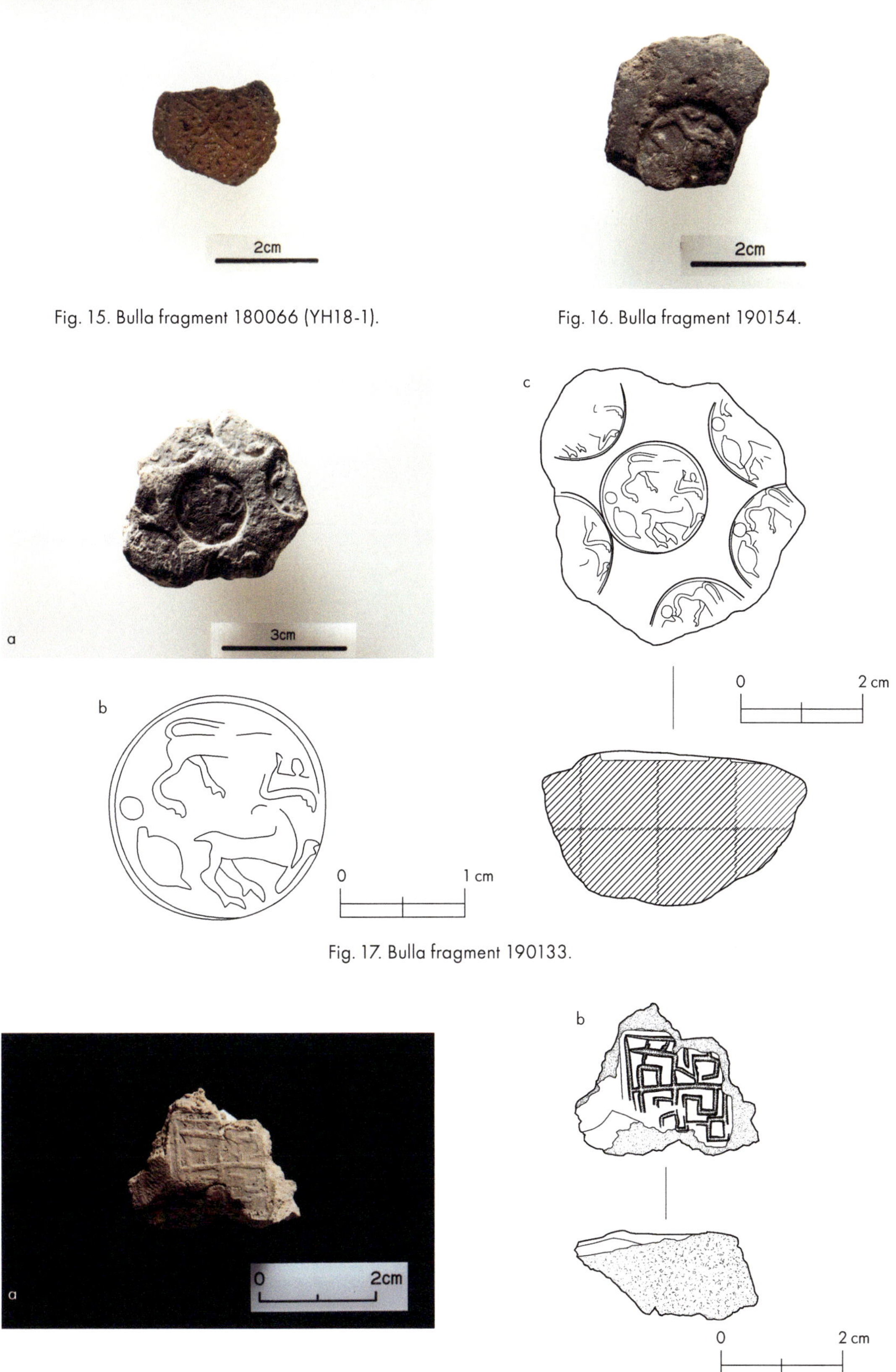

Fig. 15. Bulla fragment 180066 (YH18-1).

Fig. 16. Bulla fragment 190154.

Fig. 17. Bulla fragment 190133.

Fig. 18. Bulla fragment 150032.

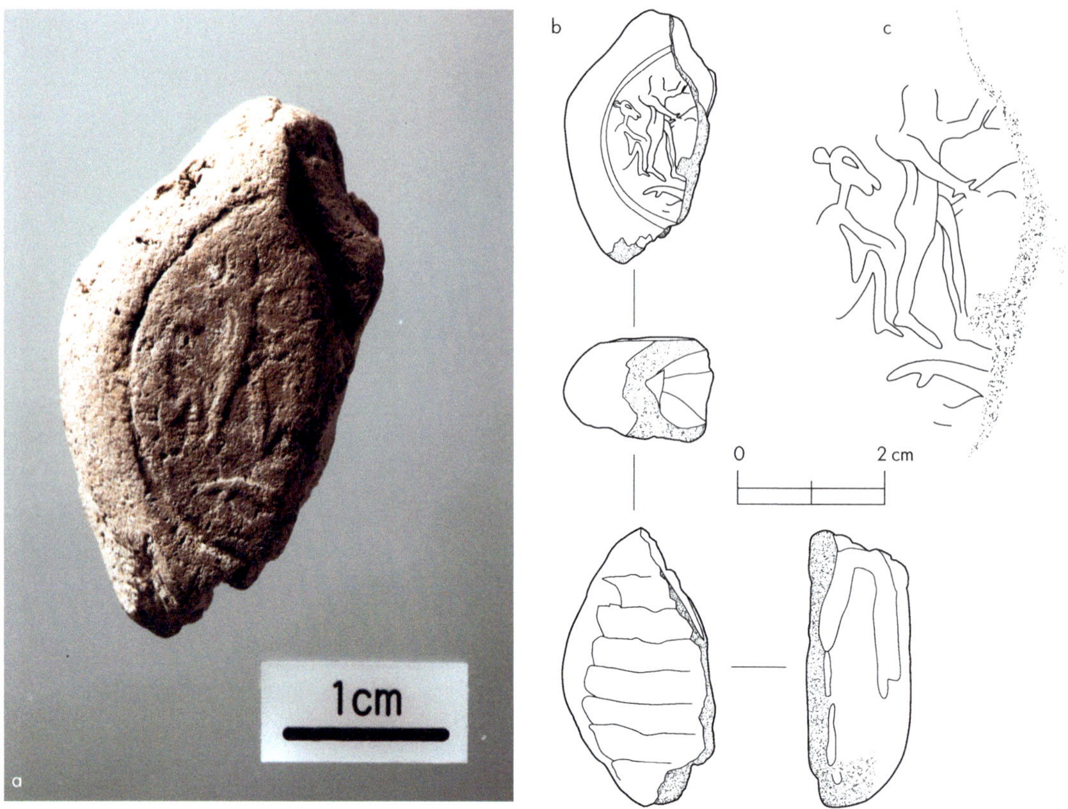

Fig. 19. Bulla fragment 150321.

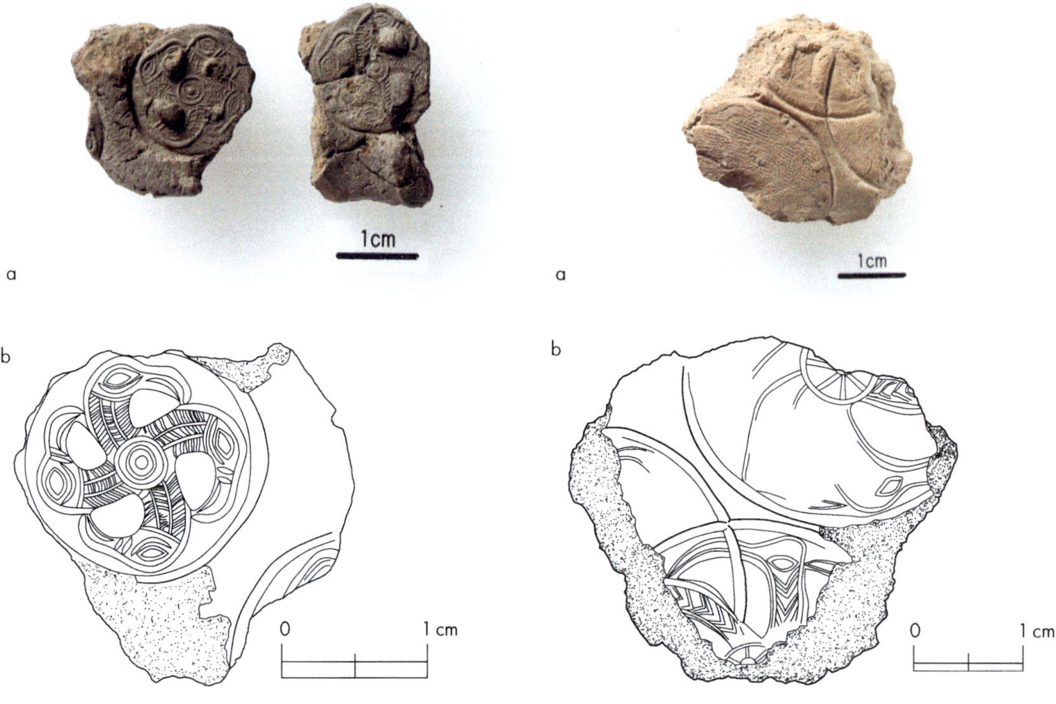

Fig. 20. Bulla fragments 110074 (YH11-58).

Fig. 21. Bulla fragment 110135 (YH11-59).

Cultural Transformations in Central Anatolia Leading to the Emergence of Urban Centres

Mehmet Özdoğan *

To Sachihiro Omura, a genuine friend dedicated to the cultural heritage of Anatolian plateau, wholeheartedly endeavouring to institutionalize archaeological research in the Anatolian heartland.

Abstract

In archaeological context we tend to consider all ancient settlements with those of the present-day ones either as villages, town, cities or as regional centers; however, socioeconomic set up of settlements during later prehistory are different than of present, not making possible to differentiate between a village from a town. For a settlement to be denoted as a village, there must be another settlement with different modalities to be termed as a town. Accordingly, all settlements of the Neolithic era, regardless of being small or big, are just settlements that are different from any we know of later periods. The paper will present a conspectus of changing modalities of Anatolian settlements during later prehistory in comparison with those of Mesopotamia.

Öz

Geçmiş dönemleri incelerken saptadığımız bütün yerleşimleri günümüzün toplumsal ve ekonomik ölçütleri ile köy, kasaba, kent ya da Merkez olarak görerek değerlendirmekteyiz. Ancak tarih öncesi dönemin koşullarını göz önüne aldığımızda, günümüzün yerleşimlerini birbirinden ayıran, köy ya da kent olarak tanımlamamızı sağlayacak ölçütlerin var olmadığını görürüz; dolayısı ile Neolitik Dönem yerleşimleri ister büyük ister küçük olsun, günümüz tanımlarıyla köy ya da kent olarak tanımlayamayız. Yazıda, Anadolu yerleşimlerinin gelişim ve değişimi, Mezopotamya kentleri ile karşılaştırmalı olarak irdelenecektir.

Preamble – Some Introductory Notes

Despite the increase in the pace of research, our knowledge on the early cultures of Central Anatolia is still far being complete, presenting an unbalanced picture, particularly for the Chalcolithic period. Extensive research had been taking place in Central Anatolia since the Early Republican times because the excitement triggered by the outcomes of early excavations at Alişar and Alacahöyük had led to the excavations of several other sites in the northern parts of Central Plateau. In spite of the interest in the region, until recently, most of the work on the cultural sequence had been set under the strong bias disregarding the presence of any pre-Bronze Age occupation on the Anatolian plateau. The bias persisted considerably jeopardizing developing a mutual understanding of the region, particularly its connections with Near East and Southeast Europe (Özdoğan 1996). The well-stratified cultural deposition of Alişar justifiably was taken as the yardstick of Central Anatolian chronology, though pressing the almost 16 meters thick cultural deposition underlying EBA III layers to fit into a time slot of a thousand years. Here, it is of interest to note that the biases in working with short chronology in Central Anatolia endured even after the

* İstanbul University, c.mozdo@gmail.com.

large-scale implementation of absolute dating methods in other regions. This is best reflected in previous attempts to bring order to the cultural sequence of Central Anatolia during late prehistory, ending up in depicting a rather casual or even desultory picture (Orthmann 1963; Yakar 1985).

Nevertheless, recent work at sites such as Çamlıbeltarlası, Çadırhöyük, Karaoğlan and others have already begun drawing a new picture (Bertram 2008; Bertram and Bertram 2020, 2021; Schoop 2011a, 2011b; Steadmann 2011; Summers 1991, 1993); in this respect, the most critical new information has been emerging from Güvercinkayası on the growing interest of the Mesopotamian cultures towards the western parts of Anatolian peninsula, taking place as early as Obeid Period (Çaylı 2020; Demirtaş 2018; Gülçur 2012; Gülçur et al 2018). In earlier years, there was very little and scanty evidence on eastern connections of Central Anatolia during the Chalcolithic Period, reserved to the recovery of some Obeid sherds at Fraktin (Özgüç 1956) and sporadic presence of Uruk related wares (Esin 1982). In this respect, the findings of Güvercinkayası, also now supported by the strong presence of Obeid related assemblage at Yumuktepe (Caneva et al 2012) further widen the picture. The picture now emerging on the later prehistory of Central Anatolia is so different from what we knew before that some more time would be necessary for all these new data to sink in. Notwithstanding all the exciting novel discoveries, here we shall restrict ourselves to presenting an overview to what distinguished Anatolian settlements from those of Syro-Mesopotamia.

Here we consider of first priority looking at problems of terminology in classifying various types of settlements before any comparative categorisation of distinct settlement types at a supra-regional level. The time period that would be necessary to scrutinize would be the 4th and early 3rd Millennium B.C., which regrettably remain as the most questionable times of the Central Anatolia. Inevitably any query on this line would also necessitate looking at the changing modalities in the spheres of cultural interaction among different regions by considering the recent evidence emerging from different parts of the Anatolian peninsula. However still, problems that are of critical importance can only be resolved by attaining solid knowledge of the Central Anatolian basin.

The Problem of Definitions: Settlement – Village – Megasite – Town – Regional Centre

In the course of last few decades, our knowledge of the early settlements of Anatolia and of the surrounding regions has greatly increased, making it possible to develop suggestive models in newly emerging fields such as settlement archaeology and landscape archaeology. However, despite the growing interest in those fields, there are still certain bewilderments in use of phrases selected to define or to categorise settlements. The problem in this respect is due both to ad hoc use of terms or in employing present-day terms such as "village" or "town" that had been devised to feature the socio-economic status of settlements. None of the modalities connoted to those terms applies to the past. The biases in this respect hamper attaining a consensus either in categorisation or in supra-regional comparative studies. Thus, here we consider as useful to retrospect to some earlier discussions on the use of these terms.

Living permanently at the same location, or giving up mobility to settle took place in different parts of the World at different time periods, developing due to several different reasons. In our region, it had been associated with the beginning of farming during the Early Neolithic period. Nevertheless, now we know, at least in the primary core region such as Southeast Anatolia that sedentary life began before farming at the time period of the so-called Proto Neolithic. Moreover, as will be somewhat elaborated further below, the earliest sedentary sites, as exemplified by Göbeklitepe, are far more complex than ever envisaged previously. However, the deeply rooted generalizations featured during the second half of the last century on linear evolutionary models persist, though now beyond context. Most of these models were structured by rationalizing progressive stages from simple to complex. In this respect, the most pertinent model on the emergence and the developing stages of early farming communities had been that of Braidwood, which he devised soon after World War II (Braidwood 1946). Braidwood tried to overrun traditional jargons, suggested a new terminology that would denote socioeconomic modality of the settlements. Braidwood, by simple reasoning, envisaged the early settlements as simple communities striving to survive with no possibility of any social complexity, thus denominated them as incipient farming villages, Jarmo standing as the type-site of this definition (Braidwood 1960). Braidwood's model was challenged by Kathleen Kenyon's excavations at Jericho, which took place almost in the same years Jarmo was being excavated. Braidwood's model, besides denoting a very simple social structure was also considering that the Early Neolithic was a very short period of time. Excavations at Jericho firstly demonstrated that the Early Neolithic period was of considerable duration going through at least two cultural stages, denominated as A and B. Even more striking was the recovery of a monumental tower over 8 m high inciting Kenyon to address the site as a Neolithic "town"; this triggered an interesting discussion between Kenyon and Braidwood, however, neither convincing the other on the usage of terms (Braidwood 1957; Kenyon 1957, 1959). Almost simultaneously, excavations at Çatalhöyük revealed the presence of an exceedingly large settlement with exceptionally sophisticated finds once more stirring the discussion whether Neolithic settlements that are larger than conventional villages were actually "towns" or not. On line with this discussion, Mellaart first defined Çatalhöyük as a city (Mellaart 1965), soon after, as a town (Mellaart 1967) and later presenting an extended overview commented that neither present-day terms such as village or town arises out of any relevance to an early period (Mellaart 1987), nevertheless, the discussion whether Çatalhöyük was a town or a big village sustained up to present, to which Braidwood had remained unconcerned.

By the turn of the century, archaeologists working in the Levant became aware that some of the Pre-Pottery sites were exceedingly large, much larger than anticipated. In this respect, there is a marked controversy between the core area of neolithization in the north and the core in the Southern Levant. While settlements in the former zone are bigger during the early stages of the Pre-Pottery Neolithic, that is at the time of PPNA, those of the Southern Levant were bigger towards the end of the Pre-Pottery Neolithic Period, during PPB and early PPNC. Soon a new concept emerged naming the large sites of the Southern Levant as" mega-sites of PPNB" (Bienert et al 2004; Bogaard and Isaakidou 2010; Gebel 2002, 2004a, 2004b; Hole 2000; Rollefson et al 1992); several interpretative models were suggested to explain why they are big, ranging from them being regional centres, to demographic build-up, to gatherings due to environmental stress (Bocquet-Appel 20008; Guerrero et al 2008; Harris 2002). Even though sites in the North were not considered as mega-sites, their size and the complex structure was ascribed occasionally as them being trading or religious centres, markers of regional administrative centres or even as of meeting place of groups of shared identities (Dietrich et al 2012; Hayden 2014; Schmidt 2008; Watkins 2015). However, as the number of excavated Early Neolithic sites increased, now numbering 37 in the northern core area, all such interpretations turned out inept or unseemly, as every excavated site of that cultural setting distinguished from all others by particular features of its own and at least none of them, including Göbeklitepe, attained a central position either of social, religious or of economic activities, pointing to the need to reconsider terminology in addressing these settlements. Even a brief look to the sites in the northern core area, all signify as "important" though neither connoting being a centre, nor the periphery of any other site. It all leads to say that the settlements of the Neolithic era are "different" from any type of settlement of our times, and during the historic periods there is nothing comparable. Thus, for the time being, we should call them simply as "settlements"; through time, as we develop a better understanding of the period it will be possible to devise an appropriate term.

Cultural Transformations Consequential to the Dispersal of Neolithic Communities

Defining the core area of primary neolithization had been one of the prime questions of prehistoric archaeology. For almost over a century there had been an array of suggestions, however, without reaching consensus. Intensified research mainly on the highlands of Anatolia has, in general terms, resolved the problem in plotting the core areas of primary neolithization; even if there are still problems in drawing exact boundaries, we can now define least four distinct core areas (Fig.1) (Özdoğan 2017, 2019). Even if these core regions touch and at places merge, they differ from each other in their social and economic setting as reflected both in the way of living and in the structuring of their settlements. Nevertheless, it is of interest to note that in spite of the apparent differences, there was intensive interaction and exchange of commodities among different parts of the region with no indication of "stress" through the entire span of Pre-Pottery Neolithic Period. Along with the growing interest in the Pre-Pottery Neolithic Period, we are now far more aware of the diversities, not only in the setup of settlements but in all other aspects of cultural buildup; however still, big or small neither of them would comply with the definition of a village or a town, they are just different from any type of habitation we know from later periods.

The first half of the 7th Millennium B.C. marks the collapse of Neolithic cultures in areas east of Central Anatolia, possibly taking place earlier in Southern Levant than other regions. The causes leading to Neolithic collapse are multifarious ranging from social turbulence to environmental deterioration to climatic events (Bar Yosef 2009; Goring Morris and Belfer-Kohen 2010; Rollefson 1996; Rollefson and Rollefson 1989; Özdoğan 2014c) are far beyond the concern of this paper; however, what is of importance in the context of this paper are the developments that took place consequential to the collapse, marked by the dispersal of Neolithic farming communities in every possible direction (Rowley-Conwy 2011). Here, we find it useful in presenting conspectus on some of the modalities of Neolithic expansion (Özdoğan 2005; 2011, 2014b). Firstly, the expansion of the Neolithic way of living was not an organised migratory movement but took place under different modalities through a diversity of routes. In early stages, it must have been more of sporadic wandering or scouting groups going to and fro, stimulating small bands to look for new prospects, through time inciting more massive endemic movements. In most cases the groups on the move were segregated on the way to join others, occasionally forming new clusters as evidenced though the presence of mixed assemblages at newly settled areas (Özdoğan 2010). It is evident that in a relatively short period of time, Neolithic farmers on the move covered most of the western parts of the Anatolian peninsula, the Aegean, Greece and Southeast Europe up to the Danube, following different trajectories both through the land and sea. The movement of Neolithic communities lasted almost up to 5600 B.C., establishing hundreds of settlements in regions that were previously totally devoid of habitation or had a light presence of semi-mobile Mesolithic communities; developing as new or secondary cores for the regions further beyond.

Neolithic dispersal should not only be taken as the transfer of Neolithic package from the primary cores to peripheries or to exteriors; as the Neolithic communities began moving into habitats that are radically different from their place of origin, modalities of the culture also changed, getting adapted to the prevailing conditions of the newly inhabited regions. Thus, as the Neolithic way of living globalised "different Neolithics" emerged, some through adapting to new conditions, some consequential to the merging with local authentic communities. As it is not possible even to list the scope of different neolithization processes in this paper, here we shall briefly present a comparative look at the settlements of two distinct regions, those in the western parts of the Anatolia plateau and those that moved south along the Euphrates basin to the semi-arid regions of Syro-Mesopotamia.

The original northern core area as we now call it the "region of Göbeklitepe Culture" is in general a region of environmental possibilities with low risk of drought, where farmers could live on dry farming. Likewise, the same holds for most of the Anatolian peninsula, where even in case of a dry year, the environment is rich and varied enough to provide alternative possibilities. Accordingly, surplus food for storage was not an absolute necessity. On the other hand in the semi-arid desert-like habitats of Syro-Mesopotamia, irrigated farming is a must for survival. In this respect irrigated farming, thus providing surplus food to be used as an asset of surplus economy, necessitates intensive labour. In the early stages when farming was introduced to this arid region, either by transfer of knowledge or by endemic movements, farmers must have been facing considerable difficulties. However, once organised to practice irrigated farming, seemingly by the very end of the Halaf period, if not certainly during early Obeid times, the surplus economy set the bases of other developments. Surplus food was the realm of necessity, but it took place in a region where there are no other resources, lacking diversity in vegetation, fauna, minerals and in rocks; the inevitable consequence was organised trade based not on simple exchange of commodities but actual profit-making trading by a professional tradesman. The need for extensive labour to harvest and for digging, maintaining drainage channels necessitated a labour force, which had to be fed controlled and resided. The result was crowded settlements with workers quarters in settlements that necessitated protection, administration and bureaucracy. The conspectus we presented here, transformed settlements of the Neolithic times to a new format what now can justifiably be termed as towns or urban centres.

Almost simultaneously Neolithic settlers had covered most of Anatolia with the possible exception of northern parts along the Black Sea littoral; irrigated farming was not a necessity anywhere in those regions (Bogaard et al 2017). The innovativeness of Neolithic background seems to have given way to conservativeness, settlements continued almost in the same modalities as before on staple economy without developing complex social and economic institutions (Frangipane 2011). Trade remained at the level of barter. Without organised trade striving to attain surplus food was a useless effort. Nevertheless, this does not imply as if nothing changed, evidently, they changed, both in architectural practices employed and as well in the layout of settlements. However, neither, big or small, had the markers of "surplus economic structure, such as workers quarters, extensive storage facilities, indicators of bureaucracy or domineering monumental buildings. Accordingly, as we had noted before, Chalcolithic settlements on the Anatolian peninsula, no matter how large they may be they do not fit the indices either of a village or of town.

The Early Bronze Age marks the beginning of a new era on the Anatolian peninsula bringing in change and social complexity. Firstly, there is a clear increase in the number of settlements in the western parts of the peninsula. Hundreds of small settlements almost mushrooming all over western Anatolia by the beginning of the Early Bronze Age. Through the period there seems to be a sudden economic revival, seemingly consequential to the products of the "Secondary Revolution" as defined by Sherrat (Çevik 2007; Özdoğan 2021; Richmond 2006; Sherrat 1981, 1986,; Şahoğlu 2005) most prominent among them being the introduction of the plough, efficient use of pack animals, complex metallurgy and alloys, weaving and textiles becoming an industry as woolly sheep become widespread. Clear implications of such novelties became clearly readable during the Early Bronze Age II. Small settlements clustered to form central administrative units, thus for the first time becoming possible on the Anatolian peninsula to differentiate "villages" and "towns". However, here it should be made clear that the Anatolian towns of the Early Bronze Age are fundamentally different from their contemporaries in Syro-Mesopotamia. As briefly noted above Near Eastern towns are crowded, dominated by monumental temples, with extensive storage places, workshops, bureaucratic installations and professional fighters, workers. On the other hand, even the biggest settlements on the Anatolian plateau such as Seyitömer (Bilgen 2015) are incomparably smaller than the Mesopotamian towns. Anatolian central settlements feature with an enclosure wall, showy entrances and not having much within their enclosed area. Anatolian Early Bronze Age towns 5 (Fig.3) are more like symbolic citadels (Fidan 2021, Sarı 2013); this is what we had defined as the "Anatolian town model" (Özdoğan 2006). Their small size is best exemplified by the Kanlıgeçit citadel, only 65 meters in diameter, encircled by an enclosure wall, entered through a monumental gate, having only four megarons and a courtyard with some hearths within the walled area (Özdoğan and Parzinger 2012), nevertheless, they cleary stood as regional centres.

Communities that had moved south, to desert-like habitats were in constant change during the Chalcolithic Period, as they became more complex and wealthier by the surplus economy, their need for raw materials and other resources aggrandized; during the Obeid and Uruk periods they had their focus on the region of the old core area in Southeast Turkey, particularly on the East Taurus Range and to the intermountain belt running along its northern foothills, the regions extremely rich in all kinds of natural resources including copper (Fig.2). Regional centres in areas rich in natural sources soon developed their bureaucratic system, manipulating and controlling the trade, at best evidenced at Arslantepe (Frangipane 2012b). Likewise sites such as Tepecik, Norşuntepe, Tülintepe and Değirmentepe had established close relations with the south through Obeid and Uruk periods. However still, all of the settlements in the north differed considerably from those of Mesopotamia, not only in size and not having workers quarters, but also in the social structuring. Mesopotamian towns are dominated by the temple, seemingly clergy being the most efficient social group in administration; however, in the northern settlements the temple is embedded into the palatial complex with clear indicators of strong bureaucracy in keeping records (Frangipane 1993, 2009, 2012a, Gülçur 2000; Oates et al 2007). Intensive interaction between the South and North sustained up to the end of the Uruk cultural stage,, to be seriously interrupted by the end of the 4th Millennium with the massive intrusion of migrating Kura Araxes groups leading to the collapse of the centres of power. Prevalence of unstable conditions taking place in the traditional interaction zone of Mesopotamian cultures must have forced them to look for alternative connections. It is possible to postulate that early contacts mentioned previously as evidenced at Güvercinkayası and at Yumuktepe, with the stimulus of now having pack animals Mesopotamian traders targeted west also opening up to maritime trade. Anatolian towns were rather quick to adapt and change in accordance with organised trade by the Early Bronze Age III, which is best exemplified at Kanlıgeçit in Eastern Thrace, the most remote site in Anatolian town model, becoming the terminal station of the caravan route coming the east (Özdoğan 2021).

Some Concluding Words

The initiative taken by Dr. Omura in 1986 as a modest undertaking to carry out archaeological excavations at Kaman-Kalehöyük had, through time developed as an extensive research project, now to stand as an institute of multifarious activities providing mass amounts of new data on the early cultures of Central Anatolia. In going through the regularly published annual reports of the JIAA, we were startled by realizing how little was known of the region before the activities of the JIAA. Along with the emerging new picture of Central Anatolia during the Bronze Ages, there is now a growing amount of subtle concrete evidence that was not available previously, making it possible to feature the role played by this region in the cultural interaction among different geographical entities. Procurement of new data on the cultural setting of Central Anatolia was not only restricted to the efforts of the Kaman-Kalehöyük team; almost simultaneously, there have been several other research groups working in the region, though each having their particular agendas providing ample new evidence on a diversity of issues.

In view of new data pouring in from the region, we considered as it is the time to go through some of what we had prospected in earlier years on the role played by this region in the processes leading to the emergence of urban centres in the western parts of the Anatolian peninsula. Actually, in earlier years at several occasions we had touched on various issues related to this problem; however still, the pace of research necessitated on several occasions to revise what we had previously commented (Özdoğan 2002, 2006, 2007, 2014a, 2018). We are aware of the drawbacks of generalizations on the supra-regional level as the benchmarks defining the criterion to be employed in each region would vary considerably; nevertheless, this paper should also be considered as a renewed attempt to contemplate the changing spheres of interaction playing a major role in the emergence of incipient urban centres in the western parts of the peninsula.

Bibliography

Bar-Yosef, O.
- 2009 "The Collapse of the Levantine PPNB and Its Aftermath," in J. M. Burdukiewicz, K. Cyrek, P. Dyczek, K. Szymczak (eds.), *Understanding the Past. Papers offered to Stefan K. Kozlowski*, Warsaw, pp. 29–35.

Bertram, J.-K.
- 2008 "Ahlatlıbel, Etiyokuşu, Koçumbeli – Zur Neubewertung der Ankara – Gruppe," *TÜBA-AR Türkiye Bilimler Akademisi Arkeoloji Dergisi* 11, pp. 73–84.

Bertram, J.-K. and G. İlgezdi Bertram
- 2020 "The Alişar 7M-11M / Ahlatlıbel / Çayyolu III- Horizon in Central Anatolia. A Reminiscence to H.H. von der Osten's "Copper Age," in G. Yalçın and O. Stegemeier (eds.), *Metallurgica Anatolica. Festschrift für Ünsal Yalçın anlässlich seines 65. Geburtstags*, İstanbul, pp. 99–110.
- 2021 *The Late Chalcolithic and Early Bronze Age in Central Anatolia*, Istanbul.

Bienert, H.-D., H. G. K. Gebel and R. Neef (eds.)
- 2004 *Central Settlements in Neolithic Jordan*, Berlin.

Bilgen, A. N. (ed.)
- 2015 *Seyitömer Höyük I*, İstanbul.

Bocquet-Appel, J. P.
- 2008 "Explaining the Neolithic Demographic Transition," in: J. P. Bocquet-Appel and O. Bar-Yosef (eds.), *The Neolithic Demographic Transition and its Consequences*, United Kingdom, pp. 35–55.

Bogaard, A., D. Filipoviç, A. Fairbairn, L. Green, E. Stroud, D. Fuller and M. Charles
- 2017 "Agricultural Innovation and Resilience in a Long-Lived Early Farming Community: The 1500-year Sequence at Neolithic-Early Chalcolithic Çatalhöyük, Central Anatolia," *Anatolian Studies* 67, pp. 1–28.

Bogaard, A., and V. Isaakidou
- 2010 "From Mega-Sites to Farmsteads: Community Size, Ideology and the Nature of Early Farming Landscapes in Western Asia and Europe" in B. Finlayson and G. Warren (eds.), *Landscapes in Transition: Understanding Hunter-Gatherer and Farming Landscapes in the Early Holocene of Europe and the Levant*, London, pp. 192–207.

Braidwood, R. J.
- 1946 "Terminology in Prehistory," in R. J. Braidwood and L. Braidwood (eds.), *Human Origins (An Introductory General Course in Anthropology) Selected Series II*, Chicago, pp. 127–143.
- 1957 "Jericho and its Setting in Near Eastern History," *Antiquity* XXXI, pp. 73–81.
- 1960 "Levels in Prehistory: A Model for the Consideration of the Evidence," in S. Tax (ed.), *Evolution After Darwin: Vol. II, The Evolution of Man*, Chicago, pp. 143–151.

Caneva, I., G. Palumbi and A. Pasquino
- 2012 "The Ubaid Impact on the Periphery: Mersin-Yumuktepe during the Fifth Millennium B.C.," in C. Marro (ed.), *The Post-Ubaid Horizon in the Fertile Crescent and Beyond*, Paris, pp. 353–389.

Çaylı, P.
- 2020 "Tarihöncesinde Ürün Depolama, Mimari Düzen ve Sosyal Yapı Üzerine Bir

Değerlendirme," *APAD Anadolu Prehistorya Araştırmaları Dergisi* 6, pp. 149–174.

Çevik, Ö.
- 2007 "The Emergence of Different Social Systems in Early Bronze Age Anatolia: Urbanisation Versus centralisation," *Anatolian Studies* 57, pp. 131–140.

Esin, U.
- 1982 "Die kulturellen Beziehungen zwischen Ostanatolien und Mesopotamien sowie Syrien anhand einiger Grabungs- und Oberflächenfunde aus dem oberen Euphrattal im 4. Jt. v. Chr.," in H. J. Nissen and J. Renger (eds.), *Mesopotamien und seine Nachbarn. Politische und kulturelle Wechselbeziehungen im alten Vorderasien vom 4.bis 1. Jahrtausend v. Chr. (Berliner Beiträge zum Vorderen Orient Band I)*. Berlin, pp. 13–21.

Demirtaş, I.
- 2018 "Güvercinkayası 2 'Coba' Tipi Tarazlı Kaseleri," *OLBA* XXVI, pp. 1–30.

Dietrich, O., M. Heun, J. Notroff, K. Schmidt and M. Zarnkow
- 2012 "The Role of Cult and Feasting in the Emergence of Neolithic Communities. New evidence from Göbekli Tepe, South-Eastern Turkey," *Antiquity* 86 (333), pp. 674–695.

Fidan, E.
- 2021 (in print) Urbanism in the Western Anatolian Early Bronze Age. In Proceedings of the Bronze Age Conference. Buffalo, pp. 129–144.

Frangipane, M.
- 1993 "Local components in the Development of Centralized Societies in Syro-Anatolian Regions," in M. Frangipane *et al.* (eds.), *Between the Rivers and over the Mountains. Arceologica et Mesopotamica Alba Palmieri Dedicata*, Roma, pp. 133–161.
- 2009 "Non-Urban Hierarchical Patterns of Territorial and Political Organisation in Northern Regions of Greater Mesopotamia: Tepe Gawra and Arslantepe," in P. Butterlin (ed.), *A Propos de Tepe Gawra, Le Monde: Proto-Urbain de Mésopotamie (Subartu XXIII)*, Turnhout, pp. 135–148.
- 2011 "Trade versus Staple Economy: Some Remarks on the Background of Mesopotamian Urbanization (Algaze's Ancient Mesopotamia at the Dawn of Civilization: The Evolution of an Urban Landscape)," *Current Anthropology* 52 (2), pp. 300–301.
- 2012a "Fourth Millennium Arslantepe: The Development of a Centralised Society without Urbanisation," *Origini* XXXIV, pp. 19–40.
- 2012b "The Collapse of the 4th Millennium Centralised System at Arslantepe and the Far-Reaching Changes in 3rd Millennium Societies," *Origini* XXXIV, pp. 237–260.

Gebel, H. G.K.
- 2002 "The Neolithic of the Near East. An essay on a 'Polycentric Evolution' and other current research problems," in A. Hausleiter, S. Kerner and B. Müller-Neuhof (eds.), *Material Culture and Mental Spheres. Rezeption archäologischer Denkrichtungen in der Vorderasiatischen Alterumskunde*, pp. 313–324.
- 2004a "Central to What? The Centrality Issue of the LPPNB Mega-Site Phenomenon in Jordan," in H.-D. Bienert, H.G. K. Gebel and R. Neef (eds.), *Central Settlements in Neolithic Jorda)*, Berlin, pp. 1–19.
- 2004b "Lithic Economic Systems and Early Sedentism," in K. von Folsach, H. Thrane and I. Thuesen (eds.), *From Handaxe to Khan. Essays Presented to Peder Mortensen on the Occasion of His 70th Birthday*, Aarhus, pp. 55–65.

Goring-Morris, N. and A. Belfer-Cohen
- 2010 "Great Expectations," or the Inevitable Collapse of the Early Neolithic in the Near East," in M.S. Bandy and J.R. Fox (eds.), *Becoming Villagers: Comparing Early Village Societies*, Tucson, pp. 62–77.

Guerrero, E., S. Naji and J. P. Bocquet-Appel
- 2008 "The Signal of the Neolithic Demographic Transition in the Levant," in J.P. Bocquet-Appel and O. Bar-Yosef (eds.), *The Neolithic Demographic Transition and its Consequences*, United Kingdom, pp. 57–80.

Gülçur, S.
- 2000 "Norşuntepe, die chalkolithische Keramik (Elazığ Ostanatolien)," in C. Marro and H. Hauptmann (eds.), *Chronologies des pays du Caucase et de L'Euphrate aux IVth–IIIrd millenaires (Varia Anatolica XI)*, Paris, pp. 375–418.
- 2012 "The Chalcolithic Period in Central Anatolia Aksaray-Niğde Region," *Origini* XXXIV, pp. 221–234.

Gülçur, S., P. Çaylı, I. Demirtaş, B. Eser and V. İndere
- 2018 "Güvercinkayası und frühe Urbanisierung in Anatolien," *Der Anschnitt Anatolian Metal* VIII, pp. 43–56.

Harris, D. R.
- 2002 "Development of the Agro-Pastoral Economy in the Fertile Crescent during the Pre-Pottery Neolithic Period," in R. T. J. Cappers and S. Bottema (eds.), *The Dawn of Farming in the Near East (Studies in Early Near Eastern Production, Subsistence, and Environment 6)*, Berlin, pp. 67–83.

Hayden, B.
- 2014 "Competitive Feasting before Cultivation? A Comment on Asouti and Fuller," *Current Anthropology* 55 (2), pp. 230–231.

Hole, F.
- 2000 "Is Size important? Function and hierarchy in Neolithic settlements," in I. Kuijt (ed.), *Life in Neolithic Farming Communities: Social Organization, Identity and Differentiation*, New York, pp. 191–209.

Kenyon, K. M.
- 1957 "Reply to Professor Braidwood," *Antiquity* XXXI, pp. 82–84.
- 1959 "Some Observations on the Beginnings of Settlement in the Near East," *Journal of the Royal Anthropological Institute* 89 (I), pp. 35–43.

Mellaart, J.
- 1965 *Çatal Hüyük, A Neolithic City in Anatolia*, London.
- 1967 *Çatal Hüyük. A Neolithic Town in Anatolia*, London.
- 1987 "Common Sense vs Old Fashioned Theory in the Interpretation of the Cultural Development of the Ancient Near East," in L. Manzanilla (ed.), *Studies in the Neolithic and Urban Revolutions*, Oxford, pp. 261–269.

Oates, J., A. McMahon, P. Karsgaard, S. Al Quntar and J. Ur
- 2007 "Early Mesopotamian Urbanism: A New View from the North," *Antiquity* 81 (313), pp. 585–600.

Orthmann, W.
- 1963 *Die Keramik der Frühen Bronzezeit aus Inneranatolien*, Berlin.

Özdoğan, M.
- 1996 Pre-Bronze Age Sequence of Central Anatolia: An Alternative Approach. In U. Magen and M. Rashad (eds.), *Vom Halys zum Euphrat*. Münster, pp. 185–202.
- 2002 "The Bronze Age in Thrace in Relation to the Emergence of Complex Societies in Anatolia and in the Balkans," *Anatolian Metal* II (der Anschnitt 15), pp. 67–76.
- 2005 Westward expansion of the Neolithic way of life: what we know and what we do not know. In C. Lichter (ed.), *How Did Farming Reach Europe? Anatolian-European relations from the second half of the 7th through the first half of the 6th millennium cal B.C. (Byzas 2)*. İstanbul, pp. 13–27.
- 2006 Yakın Doğu Kentleri ve Batı Anadolu'da Kentleşme Süreci. In B. Avunç (ed.), *Cultural Reflections. Hayat Erkanal'a Armağan*. İstanbul, pp. 571–577.
- 2007 "Amidst Mesopotamia-Centric and Euro-Centric Approaches: The Changing Role of the Anatolian Peninsula Between the East and the West," *Anatolian Studies* 57, pp. 17–24.
- 2010 Westward Expansion of the Neolithic Way of Life: Sorting the Neolithic Package into Distinct Packages. In P. Matthiae *et al.* (eds.), *Near Eastern Archaeology in the Past, Present and Future. Heritage and Identity, Volume)*. Wiesbaden, pp. 883–897.
- 2011 "Archaeological Evidence on the Westward Expansion of Farming Communities from Eastern Anatolia to the Aegean and the Balkans," *Current Anthropology* 52 (4), pp. 415–430.
- 2014a Anatolia: From the Pre-Pottery Neolithic to the End of the Early Bronze Age (10,500–2000 B.C.E). In C. Renfrew and P. Bahn (eds.), *The Cambridge World Prehistory Vol:3 West and Central Asia and Europe*. Cambridge, pp. 1508–1544.
- 2014b "A new look at the introduction of the Neolithic way of life in Southeastern Europe. Changing paradigms of the expansion of the Neolithic way of life," *Documenta Praehistorica* 41, pp. 33–49.
- 2014c The Neolithic Collapse, or the Transition from the Pre-Pottery Neolithic to the Pottery Neolithic. In B. Finlayson and C. Makarewicz (eds.), *Settlement, Survey, and Stone. Essays on Near Eastern Prehistory in Honour of Gary Rollefson*. Berlin, pp. 169–175.
- 2017 The Archaeology of Early Farming in Southeastern Turkey. In Y. Enzel and O. Bar-Yosef (eds.), *Quaternary of the Levant. Environmenst, Climate Change and Humans*. Cambridge, pp. 723–731.
- 2018 The Konya Plain in Supra-Regional Context: The Outlook for Correlating the Eastern and Western Parts of the Anatolian Peninsula. In Ç. Maner (ed.), *CROSSROADS, Konya Plain*

from Prehistory to Byzantine Period. İstanbul, pp. 13–24.
- 2019 An Alternative Look at the Neolithisation Process of Western Anatolia: From and Old Periphery to a New Core. In M. Brami and B. Horejs (eds.), *OREA Vol. 12: The Central/ Western Anatolian Farming Frontier*. Vien, pp. 143–158.
- 2021 (in print) Earliest Organised Trade Joining the East with the West. An Overview on Its Consequences in Thrace. In K. Leshtakov and M. Andonova (eds.), *Galabovo in South-east Europe and Beyond. Cultural Interactions during the 3rd–2nd Millennium B.C.* Sofia.

Özdoğan, M. and H. Parzinger (eds.)
- 2012 *Die frühbronzezeitliche Siedlung von Kanlıgeçit bei Kırklareli*. Studien im Thrakien-Marmara-Raum 3, Archäologie in Eurasien 27. Darmstadt.

–Özgüç, T.
- 1956 "Fraktin Kabartması Yanındaki Prehistorik Ev," *Anadolu* I, pp. 59–64.

Richmond, J.
- 2006 "Textile Productions in Prehistoric Anatolia: A Study of Three Early Bronze Age Sites," *Ancient Near Eastern Studies (ANES)* 43, pp. 203–238.

Rollefson, G. O.
- 1996 The Neolithic Devolution: Ecological Impact and Cultural Compensation at 'Ain Ghazal' Jordan. In J. D. Seger (ed.), *Retrieving the Past. Essays on Archaeological Research and Methodology. In Honor of Gus W. Van Beek*. Mississippi, pp. 219–229.

Rollefson, G. O. and I. Köhler-Rollefson
- 1989 The Collapse of Early Neolithic Settlements in the Southern Levant. In I. Hershkovitz (ed.), *People and Culture in Change*. Oxford, pp. 73–89.

Rowley-Conwy, P.
- 2011 "Westward Ho! The Spread of Agriculturalism from Central Europe to the Atlantic." *Current Anthropology* 52 (4), pp. 431–451.

Sarı, D.
- 2013 The Cultural Development of Western Anatolia in the Third and Second Millennia B.C. and Its Relationship with Migration Theories. In A. Mouton, I. Rutherford and I. Yakubovich (eds.), *Luwian Identities. Culture, Language and Religion between Anatolia and the Aegean*. Leiden, pp. 305–327.

Schoop, U.-D.
- 2011a "Çamlıbel Tarlası, ein metallverarbeitender Fundplatz des vierten Jahrtausends v. Chr. im nördlichen Zentralanatolien," *Anatolian Metal* V (Der Anschnitt), pp. 53–68.
- 2011b The Chalcolithic on the Plateau. In S. R. Steadman and G. McMahon (eds.), *The Oxford Handbook of Ancient Anatolia (10,000–323 B.C.E.)*. New York, pp. 150–173.

Sherratt, A.
- 1981 Plough and Pastoralism: Aspects of the Secondary Products Revolution. In I. Hodder, G. Isaac and N. Hammond (eds.), *Pattern of the Past. Studies in Honor of David Clarke*. Cambridge, pp. 261–305.
- 1986 "Wool, Wheels and Ploughmarks: Local Developments or Outside Introductions in Neolithic Europe," *Bulletin of the Institute of Archaeology* 23, pp. 1–15.

Steadman, S. R.
- 2011 The Early Bronze Age on the Plateau. In S. R. Steadman and G. McMahon (eds.), *The Oxford Handbook of Ancient Anatolia (10,000–323 B.C.E.)*. New York, pp. 229–259.

Summers, G. D.
- 1993 The Chalcolithic Period in Central Anatolia. In P. Georgieva (ed.), *The Fourth Millennium B.C. (Proceeding of the International Symposium Nessebur, 28–30 August 1992)*. Sofia, pp. 29–48.

Summers, J.
- 1991 "Chalcolithic Pottery from Kabakulak (Niğde) Collected by Ian.Todd." *Anatolian Studies* XLI, pp. 125–131.

Şahoğlu, V.
- 2005 "The Anatolian Trade Network and the Izmir Region during the Early Bronze Age," *Oxford Journal of Archaeology* 24 (4), pp. 339–361.

Watkins, T.
- 2015 "Who Built Göbekli Tepe?," *Actual Ar chaeology Magazine* 15, pp. 50–59.

Yakar, J.
- 1985 *The Later Prehistory of Anatolia, The Late Chalcolithic and Early Bronze Age*. Oxford.

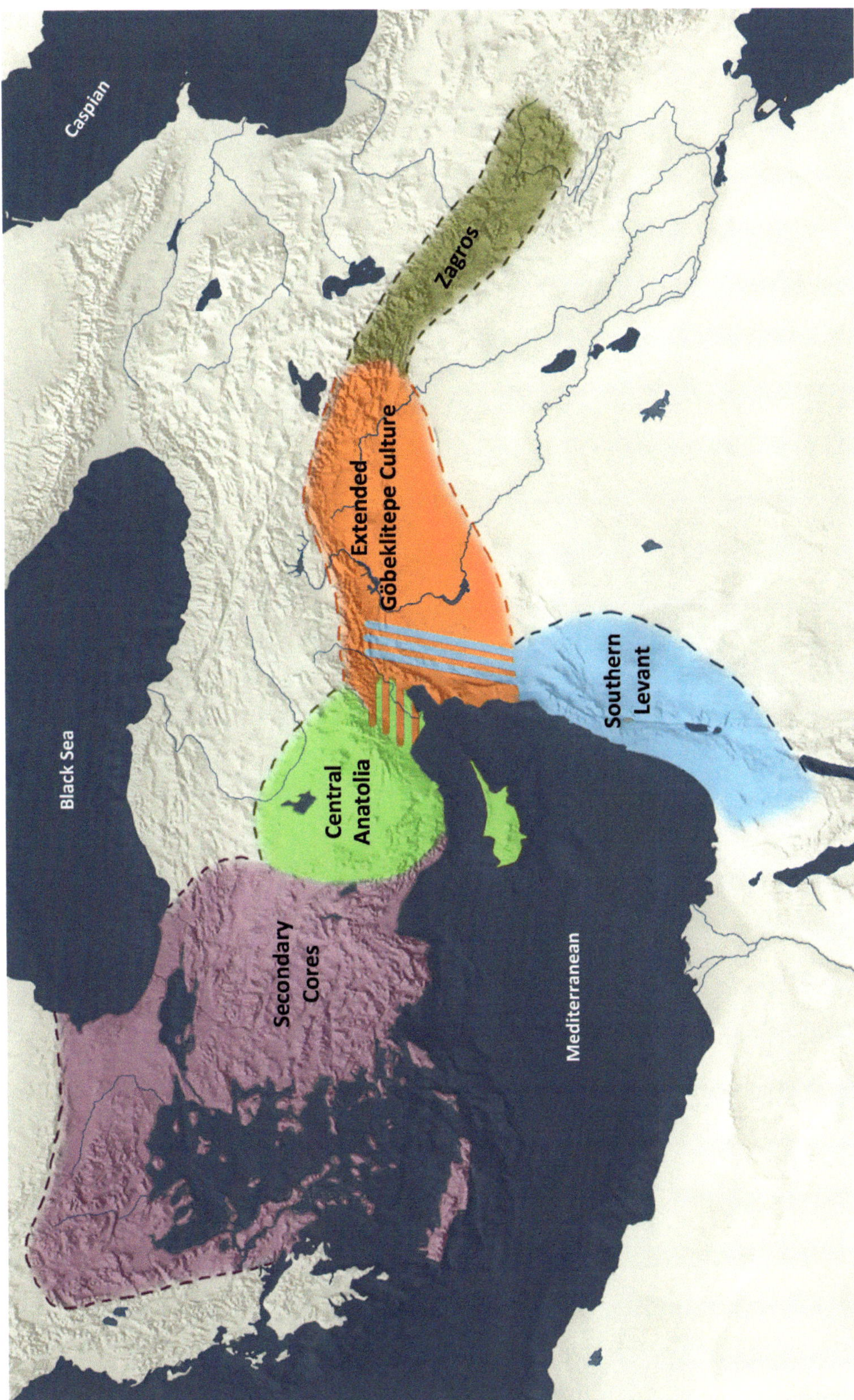

Fig. 1. Main Core Areas of Primary Neolithic Formation, also depicting the transitional regions and secondary cores in newly settled areas.

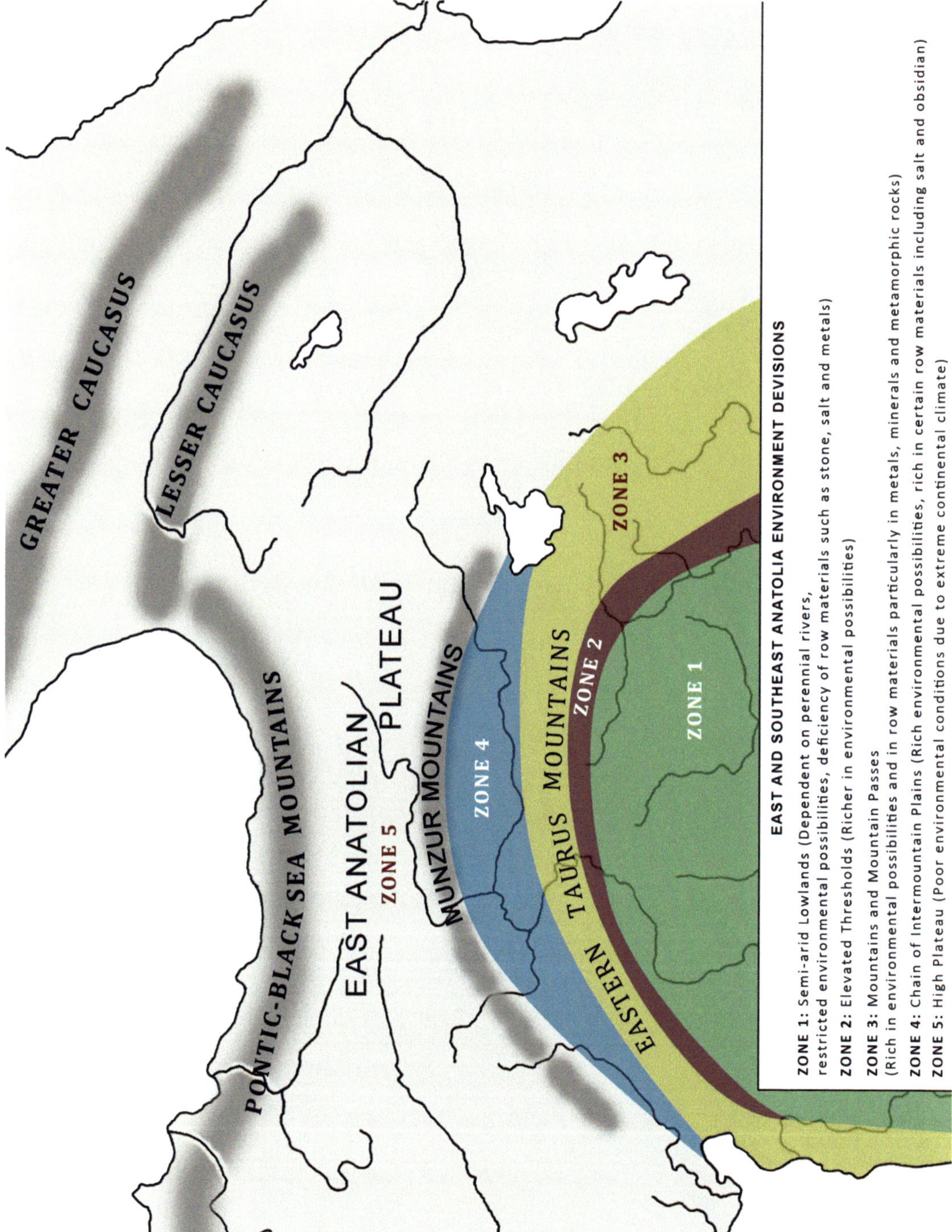

Fig. 2. Major ecological zones of southeast Anatolia, North Syria and Iraq.

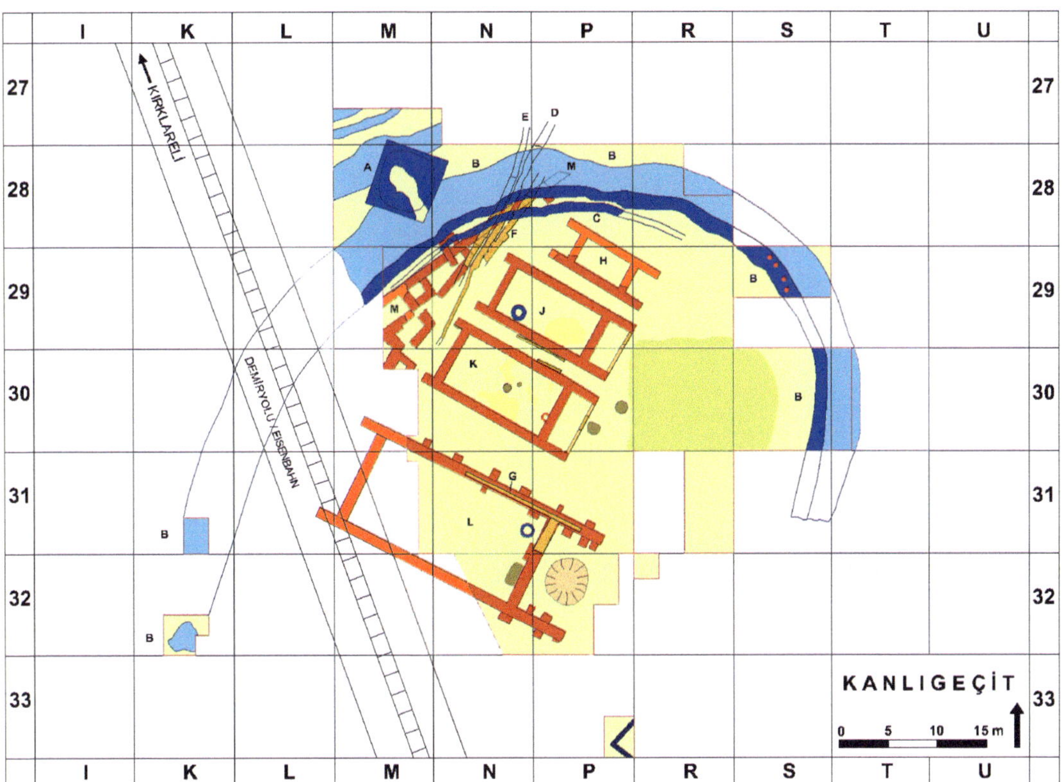

Fig. 3. Kanlıgeçit citadel during Early Bronze Age III.

Exploring the Evidence for the Early Bronze Age Iron Production at Kaman-Kalehöyük

Nurcan Küçükarslan, Tsutomu Ota, Christian Potiszil and Katsura Kobayashi *

Abstract

Iron production represents a technological advance over bronze production, requiring more extreme and better controlled conditions during smelting than for bronze. Therefore, the development of iron production must have been undertaken over an extended period of time prior to the Iron Age. However, exactly when the earliest iron production took place remains a mystery. Here two slag samples and one fragment of an iron object were investigated in order to assess the availability of adequate technology for iron production during the Early Bronze Age in Central Anatolia. The iron object and slags were excavated from the Stratum IV (the late phase of Early Bronze Age, c. 2100–1930 BCE) in the stratigraphy of Kaman-Kalehöyük. Microtextures, chemical compositions, and spectroscopic features of the artifacts were analyzed using scanning electron microscopy, energy dispersive X-ray spectroscopy, and Micro-Raman spectroscopy. Partially reduced hematite ore grains were discovered in the slag samples. The hematite ore grains were encompassed by a network-like structure, which contained relict metallic iron. Also, traces of mm-sized iron and steel formations were recognized in the slag samples. These findings demonstrate that the reduction of iron ore to metallic iron was most likely achieved on a small scale during this period. Moreover, the variable iron and steel structures in the slags and the high carbon content of the iron object suggest that carbon was sporadically adsorbed into metallic iron during smelting of these materials as a result of unstable

Öz

Demir üretimi, bronz üretimine göre daha zorlu ve daha iyi kontrol edilmesi gereken koşulları gerektirdiğinden, bronz üretimine göre teknolojik bir ilerlemeyi temsil ettiği söylenebilir. Bu nedenle, demir üretiminin gelişimi Demir Çağı'ndan önce uzun bir zaman diliminde gerçekleştirilmiş olmalıdır. Ancak, en erken demir üretiminin tam olarak ne zaman gerçekleştiği bir sır olarak kalmaya devam etmektedir. Bu çalışmada, Orta Anadolu'da Erken Tunç Çağı'nda demir üretimi için yeterli teknolojinin olup olmadığını değerlendirmek amacıyla iki cüruf örneği ve bir demir obje parçası incelenmiştir. Demir obje ve cüruflar, Kaman-Kalehöyük stratigrafisinde Tabaka IV'teki (Erken Tunç Çağı'nın geç safhası, yaklaşık MÖ 2100-1930) kazı çalışmalarında açığa çıkarılmıştır. Eserlerin mikro iç yapıları, kimyasal bileşimleri ve spektroskopik özellikleri, taramalı elektron mikroskobu, enerji dağılımlı X-ışını spektroskopisi ve mikro-Raman spektroskopisi kullanılarak analiz edilmiştir. Cüruf örneklerinde kısmen indirgenmiş hematit cevheri taneleri keşfedilmiştir. Hematit cevheri taneleri, metalik demir kalıntıları içeren ağ benzeri bir yapı ile çevrelenmiştir. Ayrıca, cüruf örneklerinde mm boyutunda demir ve çelik oluşumlarının izleri tespit edilmiştir. Bu bulgular, demir cevherinin metalik demire indirgenmesinin bu dönemde büyük olasılıkla küçük ölçekte gerçekleştirildiğini göstermektedir. Ayrıca, cüruflardaki değişken demir ve çelik yapıları ve demir objenin yüksek karbon içeriği, fırındaki değişken redoks koşullarının bir sonucu olarak izabe sırasında metalik demire ara sıra karbon emiliminin olduğunu düşündürmektedir.

* Nurcan Küçükarslan, Chiba Institute of Technology, Institute for Geo-Cosmology, nurcan.kucukarslan@p.chibakoudai.jp; Tsutomu Ota, Pheasant Memorial Laboratory for Geochemistry and Cosmochemistry, Institute for Planetary Materials, Tottori, Okayama University, Japan, tsutom@pheasant.misasa.okayama-u.ac.jp; Christian Potiszil, Pheasant Memorial Laboratory for Geochemistry and Cosmochemistry, Institute for Planetary Materials, Tottori, Okayama University, Japan, cpotiszil@okayama-u.ac.jp; Katsura Kobayashi, Pheasant Memorial Laboratory for Geochemistry and Cosmochemistry, Institute for Planetary Materials, Tottori, Okayama University, Japan, katsura@pheasant.misasa.okayama-u.ac.jp.

redox conditions in the furnace. Thus, the techniques utilized during smelting might have led to unintentional carburization. Therefore, the Early Bronze Age slags of Kaman-Kalehöyük likely represent some of the earliest by-products of extractive iron metallurgy in Central Anatolia.

Bu nedenle, izabe sırasında kullanılan teknikler, birincil (planlanmamış) karbürizasyona yol açmış olabilir. Tüm bu buluntular sonucunda, Kaman-Kalehöyük'ün Erken Tunç Çağı cürufları, Orta Anadolu'daki ekstraktif demir metalurjisinin en erken yan ürünlerinden bazılarını temsil etmektedir.

Introduction

Kaman-Kalehöyük is an ancient mound, situated near Kaman town, which is about 40 km northwest of Kırşehir city at Türkiye. The mound is located on a circular area 280 m in diameter and 16 m in height (Omura 2011). The excavation of the ancient mound was commenced by the Japanese Institute of Anatolian Archaeology (JIAA) in 1985. The systematic excavation has been conducted under the direction of Dr. Sachihiro Omura since this time. Three main areas have been excavated on the mound: the North Trench, the South Trench and the City-Wall Trench (Omura 2011) (Fig. 1). On the North Trench, since the main purpose of the excavation was to find out the overall stratigraphy of the site, a narrow area was excavated to a great depth (Omura 2011). Based on the stratigraphy established by the excavation team, there are four main strata: Stratum I – Ottoman Empire and Byzantine Periods; Stratum II – Iron Age; Stratum III – Hittite Empire (IIIa), Old Hittite Period (IIIb) and Assyrian Colony Period (IIIc); Stratum IV – Early Bronze Age (EBA).

Since the beginning of the excavation and research, iron was one of the ancient materials to which Dr. Omura and his team attached great importance. Therefore, many iron-rich artefacts from Stratum I – Ottoman Empire (Geçkinli 1995), Stratum II – Iron Age (Akanuma 2000, 2001, 2002, 2004, 2006; Masubuchi 2005, 2008, 2016a, 2016b, 2017; Yukishima 2001), Stratum III – Middle and Late Bronze Age (Akanuma 2002, 2003, 2004, 2005, 2006, 2007; Masubuchi 2017) and Stratum IV (Akanuma 2008) were studied from different perspectives and disciplines.

In 2015, a team from the Pheasant Memorial Laboratory (PML), Institute for Planetary Materials (IPM), Okayama University (Japan) under the supervision of Prof. Eizo Nakamura, started the collaboration with JIAA to explore the early history of iron in central Anatolia. The first group of artefacts, on which the team focused, included the earliest iron-oxide-rich oval-shaped artefacts, which were excavated from the stratigraphic layers dated to the EBA in Kaman-Kalehöyük and Yassıhöyük. Accordingly, the team undertook a provenance study of this group of samples through geochemical methods (Kucukarslan *et al.*, in preparation). After the provenance study, the second group of artefacts that were studied in this collaborative project was a group of Fe-rich slags and objects from Strata III and IV in Kaman- Kalehöyük (Kucukarslan *et al.* 2023). The main purpose was to understand the availability of technology for iron production during the Middle and Early Bronze Ages by re-examining the artifacts from the previous studies in terms of their microstructure, mineral phases, chemical composition, and the C content, and distribution within the artifacts.

In this paper, two slag samples and one iron object fragment, which were excavated from the Stratum IV-EBA in the stratigraphy of Kaman-Kalehöyük, are examined to investigate the availability of adequate technology for iron production during the Early Bronze Age in Central Anatolia. To answer this question, the analyses were undertaken to reveal the microstructure and chemical composition of the artefacts and thus to elucidate any preserved evidence of technology relating to extractive iron metallurgy.

Iron Production Process

The process of iron production is outlined in this section prior to moving to the iron artefacts in this study. There are three major steps in the production of iron (Tylecote 1992; Yahalom-Mack and Eliyahu-Behar 2015): (1) **smelting** iron ore to reduce it to metallic iron by liquefying the gangue (valueless) contents and unreduced iron oxide to form slag and obtain bloom (metallic iron-containing component), (2) **primary smithing** to consolidate the iron, purify it from some attached smelting slags by hammering the bloom into a bar, and thus generate a semi-product, and (3) **secondary smithing** to shape the object by annealing and forging, and thus manufacture a final product.

During the step of smelting (1), slag piles up on the furnace floor, which might block the bottom of the furnace. Therefore, the slag accumulated at the bottom of the furnace should be cleaned to smelt with a better iron yield (Bayley *et al.* 2001; Pleiner 2000). Accordingly, there would have been a hole in the bottom of the furnace wall where the slag could be removed. ***Tap slag*** can be tapped from this hole if it is sufficiently liquid and heated (Bayley *et al.* 2001). A flowing pattern on a smooth surface could be recognized especially on tap slags. However, some slag pieces— commonly referred to as ***slag cake*** or ***furnace slag***—may still be found at the bottom of the furnace (Paynter 2007; Veldhuijzen and Rehren 2007). The clusters of partially reduced ore grains and the entrapped bulk of metallic iron in the furnace slags could be recognized as distinctive features.

During the step of primary smithing (2), the spongy bloom is refined by removing pores and slags (Tylecote 1992). Primary smithing is hammering continuously while the bloom is still hot. Since primary smithing and smelting may be performed in the same location, the slags produced as a ***by-product*** after these steps could also be discovered together (Paynter 2007). A ***semi-product***, like a bar or billet, is produced after primary smithing (Blakelock *et al.* 2009; Hedges and Salter 1979; Serneels and Perret 2003).

The step of secondary smithing (3) is performed on the semi-product to give the final shape by a series of hammering and heating steps in an open-hearth with a relatively more oxidizing atmosphere, than in the furnace. The oxidizing conditions can result in the formation of a skin of oxidized iron, also known as ***scale*** or ***hammerscale*** (Dungworth and Wilkes 2009; Unglik 1991). Adding a flux, like sand or clay, could help remove the oxidized scales by reacting with the oxidized iron and forming slag (Serneels and Perret 2003). The ***final product*** could be shaped in different forms.

However, metallic iron is soft, and one method of hardening iron is to form an alloy with carbon (an alloy with c. 0.02-2 wt.% C content is called ***steel***). This process is known as ***carburization (secondary carburization)*** and is generally considered to be a more sophisticated technological process that is practiced during secondary smithing. Nonetheless, steel can be formed during smelting, known as ***primary carburization*** (Scott 1989; Scott and Eggert 2009; Yahalom Mack and Eliyahu-Behar 2015), when a carbon-rich environment is created in the furnace.

Materials

Archaeological context

All the artefacts, an iron object and two slags (Fig. 2, Table 2), were excavated in the North Trench, but from different sectors. The sectors represent areas of 10m x 10m in size and compose at a grid system on the topographic map of the excavation site. The sectors can be viewed in Fig. 1. Here, we describe the archaeological context of the artefacts.

The iron object O1 was excavated from a deposit in Sector IV. This deposit was uncovered after the architectural remains of the room R248 were removed. Furthermore, a radiocarbon analysis (Atsumi *et al.* 2008) was conducted on the charcoal samples collected from a deposit, which was contemporary with R248. Radiocarbon dating supplied the 1σ ranges of 2120–2025, 2140–2080, and 2070–2020 cal.

BCE for this deposit (Atsumi *et al.* 2008). The results of the radiocarbon dating thus validate that the deposit, which is contemporary with R248, could be dated to the EBA. Since the iron object O1 was excavated from beneath R248, the object must be older than the dates obtained from radiocarbon dating. This also confirms that the iron object could securely be dated to the EBA.

The slag sample S1 was unearthed from a deposit in Sector III. Based on the stratigraphy, the slag is dated to the Stratum IV (EBA). Although their purpose of use is not yet known, the remains of several hearths (furnace?) were excavated from the deposits (R287 and its vicinity) which are contemporary with the deposit where S1 was found (Fig. 1).

The slag sample S2 was excavated from a deposit in Sector V. Based on the stratigraphy, this deposit is much older than the above-mentioned deposit that was radiocarbon dated. Such a relationship validates that the slag sample S2 could be firmly dated to the EBA. Moreover, based on the archaeological archive, the grey ash soil deposit, where the slag S2 was found, contained abundant ash and charcoal. It is also worth noting that a hematite stone fragment (Akanuma 2007) was uncovered from a deposit contemporary with the deposit where S2 was found.

We emphasize the importance of the slag samples in this paper. Erb-Satullo (2019) reviewed the history of iron in the ancient Near East, and mentions a *corroded lump* which was excavated from the Stratum III (Middle Bronze Age) in Kaman-Kalehöyük (Akanuma 2007). In this review, the corroded lump artefact is described as having a dendritic structure of possibly metallic iron or wüstite and it is proposed that it could be the *"earliest example of iron metallurgical debris"*. Based on the overall stratigraphy of the ancient mound (Omura 2011) and the results from the radiocarbon dating (Atsumi *et al.* 2008), the EBA slag samples in this study are much older than the metallurgical debris, which is mentioned in Erb-Satullo (2019).

Morphology and sample conditions

The slag S1 has an irregular shape with a length of 2 cm at most (Fig. 2). The slag S2 has a roughly flat/convex shape with a length of 4.5 cm in maximum. Both the samples were heavily corroded. Therefore, the current morphology of slag samples could not help us distinguish from which iron production stage they must have been formed: smelting, primary smithing, or secondary smithing. Therefore, the textural and mineralogical analyses will be helpful for enabling the elucidation of the possible steps in which they were formed.

The iron object O1 was found as a fragment with a length of less than 2 cm. The object was also severely corroded; hence, it is difficult to identify the original shape from the outside. However, based on its X-ray photography of O1, Akanuma (2008) recognized that the object O1 had a prismatic bar shape.

Methodology

Sample preparation

All of the sample preparation and analyses were carried out in the Pheasant Memorial Laboratory, Institute for Planetary Materials, Okayama University at Misasa, Japan (Nakamura *et al.* 2003).

The minimally invasive approach, which was explained in detail in Kucukarslan *et al.* 2023, was utilized for the sample preparation of the iron artefact O1. Dry-polishing with a 3M™ Al2O3 lapping film was applied on the surface of O1, which was exposed by cross-sectioning of the sample in the previous research, to eliminate the thin layer of corrosion and cut marks from the previous cross-sectioning. For the slag artefacts, a thin slice of the sample, up to 2 cm in length, was taken from the slags, and mounted in epoxy resin. After the resin mount had cured, it was then polished.

After all the sample preparation was finished, the artefacts were analyzed in terms of archaeological context, morphology, chemical compositions of dominant mineral phases, concentration and the distribution of C, using a JEOL JSM-7001F, field-emission scanning electron microscope (FE-SEM), and a Thermo Fisher DXR Raman microscope (Kucukarslan et a., 2023). The samples were analyzed without carbon-coating because they were conductive enough that severe electric charging did not occur.

Quantitative analysis

The artefacts were studied using an FE-SEM, equipped with an Oxford, INCA X-act energy dispersive X-ray spectrometer (EDS), with a silicon drift detector and a Be window. The processing of the data obtained was undertaken using the Oxford Aztec software. The quantitative analyses were performed under the following operating conditions with an accelerating voltage of 15 kV, beam current of 5 nA and a working distance of 10 mm. The results of the point analyses were calculated using the elements C, O, Na, Mg, Al, Si, P, S, Cl, K, Ca, Ti, Cr, Mn, Fe, Co, Ni, and Cu, and normalized to 100% in total.

In this research, nickel and cobalt were investigated to evaluate whether or not the iron object O1 was made from a material of a meteoric source. Copper was also examined to assess whether or not the iron-rich slags S1 and S2 were formed after copper smelting. The concentrations of Fe, O, and C were analyzed to decipher their dominant phases such as metallic iron, iron oxides in corrosion products, and iron carbide compounds. The results are shown in weight percentages (wt.%) in Table 1. To assess the analytical results, standard error (wt.% sigma) is acquired from the EDS software. Each individual analysis has its own wt.% sigma deviation. Thus, there is a range of wt.% sigma values for each element, which were obtained from the series of spot analyses (Table 1). If the element concentration is lower than wt.% sigma deviation, it is not included in the data set and it is shown as '–' in Table 1.

Assessment of C content and distribution

The microstructures of the slag samples and iron object were analyzed thoroughly by using FE-SEM and Raman microscope in order to identify any region with pearlite/cementite relics. This would help us to estimate the iron/steel compositions in the object and also to identify if the slag samples contain any iron/steel components.

The C content can be calculated using image analysis by comparing the proportion of the areas containing pearlite remnants to the overall sample surface area. The remnants of pearlite are visible in a lamellar structure with cementite layers that were either significantly lighter or darker compared to the former ferrite layers on the corroded portions of the iron artefacts (Knox 1963; Scott 1989; Notis 2002). In this study, the image processing software NIH ImageJ, 1.52a was used by following the same estimation method in Kucukarslan *et al.* (2023). A set of image analyses (with 5–6 analyses for each artifact, based on the size and condition of the sample section) were conducted using the estimation approach.

Result and Discussion

Slags from copper or iron metallurgy

Fe-rich slag could be obtained from not only an iron metallurgical process but also copper smelting (Miller and Killick 2004; Pleiner 2000; Severin *et al.* 2011). Therefore, the precise analysis and observation of Fe-rich slags is necessary, especially for those from the Bronze Age, in which copper metallurgy was the most common metallurgical process. There is also a debate concerning the minimum threshold for Cu concentration to determine whether the slag sample was a by-product of iron or copper smelting.

Based on the results of EDS analyses (Table 1), which were obtained from 61 spot analyses on the slag samples, Cu concentrations (< 0.0 wt.%) are very low, being below the detection limit of the instrument. Moreover, no Cu-rich phases such as CuO or CuS were not detected. Thus, it is unlikely that the EBA slags of Kaman-Kalehöyük were formed after copper smelting because the by-products of copper smelting includes at least 0.3–0.5 wt.% Cu (Miller and Killick 2004; Pleiner 2000; Severin *et al.* 2011).

Meteoritic Source

Another source of iron, particularly during the Bronze Age, is meteoric iron (Bjorkman 1973, Jambon 2017; Photos 1989; Rehren *et al.* 2013; Yalçın 1999), because there would not be an excessive effort to refine the terrestrial iron ore by smelting if there was an access to the source of meteoric iron (Tylecote 1992).

Since the primary composition of meteoric iron is an Fe-Ni alloy, a high Ni concentration in the range of c. 6–20 wt.% is expected in an iron object, which was manufactured from a meteoric source (Yalçın 1999). Therefore, high Ni concentration is a crucial factor in identifying the origin of the source. On the other hand, Jambon (2017) suggested that the weathered iron artifacts had a small amount of Ni in the corroded areas but a large amount of Ni in the uncorroded areas. Additionally, in the aforementioned study, the weathered iron meteorites demonstrated a comparable Fe:Ni:Co ratio to the weathered iron artefacts from the Bronze Age. Hence, it is essential to analyze the Fe, Co, and Ni contents from various areas of the artefact (Jambon 2017).

In this study, EDS analysis was performed on the corroded sections and any area with metallic iron if preserved in the samples. Based on the EDS results (Table 1) of 110 spot analyses (49 from the iron object and 61 from the slags), the concentrations of Ni (< 0.0 wt.%) and Co (0–1.5 wt.%) in the iron artifacts were extremely low, mostly falling below the detection limit of the instrument. Thus, the EBA iron artifacts from Kaman-Kalehöyük are unlikely to have been manufactured from meteoric iron sources.

Dominant Phases

Although most of the phases observed under SEM-EDS, such as metallic iron, wüstite, or corrosion products, were similar between the samples (Table 3), the dominant phases in each sample were examined individually to discuss the state of the samples separately. Accordingly, the dominant phases of each sample will be discussed in detail below.

Slag Sample S1

Based on the SEM-EDS results, four main phases were identified in this slag sample: (1) wüstite, (2) metallic iron, (3) corrosion products, and (4) partially reacted iron oxide grains.

The sample is mainly composed of wüstite grains, which are globular or dendritic in shape in the glassy silicate matrix. Their sizes range from a few µm to approximately 100 µm. A group of bright metallic iron grains, which are mostly anhedral, were identified from a few µm to 100–150 µm in size (Fig. 3). However, there was also another group of anhedral grains, which were present as a grey phase under SEM observation. These grains vary in size from a few µm to approximately 400 µm. Their chemical composition corresponds to goethite which is usually a corrosion product (Bellot-Gurlet *et al.* 2009; Grevey *et al.* 2020; Neff *et al.* 2004, Neff *et al.* 2005). Regions of relict metallic iron were also detected in these grains. The presence of relict metallic iron regions and their composition of iron hydroxide could indicate that they were originally reduced iron but were subsequently corroded. This observation suggests that the formation of reduced iron extends up to approximately 400 µm in size.

More interestingly, a cluster of subhedral grains, which vary in size from 0.25 mm to 1.5 mm, was detected in the slag sample. Their chemical composition is comparable with the composition of hematite (Fig. 4). When the largest grain in the cluster was observed at finer scale, another structure, which was represented by the grey phase mentioned above, was recognized. This structure encircles the whole grain forming a network (Fig. 4). The chemical composition of the network-shaped phase encircling the whole grain corresponds to the composition of goethite, which is mostly a corrosion product. More importantly, some relics of metallic iron were identified in this network-shaped phase, which is mainly composed of goethite (Fig. 4). Therefore, these relicts of metallic iron might demonstrate that this network-shaped phase encircling the hematite grain was formerly metallic iron. Considering that the composition of subhedral grains is comparable with hematite and that these grains were formerly surrounded by metallic iron, the hematite ore grain might have started to react partially on its outer edge while being in the process of reduction. Also, the reduction process might not have been completed because of the abrupt changes in the redox conditions in the furnace. As such, the partially reacted hematite grains, which were in the process of reduction, could suggest that the slag sample S1 was a furnace slag from smelting or a slag that was discarded from the bloom during primary smithing.

Such *partly reduced ore fragments* were identified in the furnace slags that resulted from the smelting experiment conducted by Stepanov *et al.* (2022). It was reported that the furnace slags in the experiment remained inside the furnace rather than flowing out of the furnace. More significantly, metallic iron was found to be enclosing the *partly reduced ore fragments*. According to Stepanov *et al.* (2022), this could illustrate the direction of the reduction process, which starts from the margin to the interior parts of grains. Such unreduced or partially reduced ore grains were identified in ancient furnace slags from the Iron Age and later periods, in which iron smelting was a prevalent metallurgical operation (Erb-Satullo and Wharton 2017; Georgakopoulou 2014; Veldhuijzen 2005).

For instance, some furnace slags, from the Iron Age in the Levant, have been found to contain both preserved/corroded metallic iron grains with unreduced/partially reduced ore grains (Erb-Satullo and Wharton 2017; Veldhuijzen 2005). Moreover, a hematite ore fragment was found with bloom pieces and the corroded iron artifacts together (Eliyahu-Behar *et al.* 2013, Erb-Satullo and Wharton 2017; Veldhuijzen and Rehren 2007). On the other hand, Erb-Satullo and Wharton (2017) discuss the possibility of determining whether such slags were furnace slags from smelting or slag from smithing. However, the study concludes that it is quite unlikely to observe both the partially reduced ore grains and the formation of reduced iron in a slag from smithing. Therefore, the hypothesis that the slag sample S1 could be a furnace slag from the EBA is supported by the results of the iron studies from the Iron Age (Eliyahu-Behar *et al.* 2013; Erb-Satullo and Wharton 2017; Georgakopoulou 2014; Veldhuijzen 2005;) and the experiment (Stepanov *et al.* 2022).

Slag Sample S2

Two areas, represented by bright and grey phases respectively, were recognized on back-scattered electron (BSE) images (Fig. 5). The bright areas were found to be composed of three phases: (1) wüstite, (2) Ca-rich olivine, and (3) metallic iron. Meanwhile, the grey areas were found to be composed of two phases: (4) corrosion product and (5) pearlite. Therefore, five main phases were determined in total in this slag sample (Table 3).

The bright areas under SEM observation were dominated by wüstite in a glassy silicate matrix (Fig. 5). The group of wüstite grains were globular or dendritic in shape. They ranged in size from a few a few µm to approximately 150–200 µm grains. In the silicate matrix, Ca-rich olivine grains, which were planar or angular in shape, were also observed. Their chemical composition, determined using SEM-EDS, is shown in Table 1. Some small grains of metallic iron, up to 50 µm in size, were also identified in the sample.

The grey areas on the BSE image (Fig. 5) were found to be mainly composed of an iron oxide phase. The results of the EDS analyses show that the composition is close to that of goethite, which is a corrosion product (Bellot-Gurlet *et al.* 2009; Grevey *et al.* 2020; Neff *et al.* 2004, Neff *et al.* 2005). Therefore, these areas were formerly reduced iron, which were then corroded. They illustrate an approximately 5 mm-sized network that is rather loosely connected. Only a few grains of glassy silicate and wüstite remained in these areas (Fig. 5). At finer scales, another structure with a lamellar was identified. Based on the results of the EDS analyses, these lamellar structures have a higher C content than the surrounding matrix, which is composed of formerly reduced iron (Fig. 6). Since these structures have a lamellar pattern and a high C content, they represent the corroded residues of pearlite, which is the main feature of steel (Scott 2011, references therein). More interestingly, the iron/steel compositions vary greatly in the slag sample: iron, low-C steel compositions with fewer pearlite residues, and high-C steel compositions with widely dispersed pearlite remnants (Fig. 7). Consequently, the SEM-EDS results indicated that the EBA slag sample included iron and steel structures up to 5 mm in length.

Iron Object O1

Based on the analyses using SEM-EDS and Raman spectroscopy, four main phases were detected: (1) metallic iron, (2) corrosion products, (3) slag inclusions, and (4) cementite (Table 3). Since the object is entirely corroded. The metallic iron grains were extremely small - between 2.5 and 5 μm in size.

Two sub-phases, which were represented by grey and light grey phases on the BSE images, were identified on the corroded areas of the sample (Fig. 8c–d). These two sub-phases were compared with the compositions of common corrosion products such as goethite, maghemite or magnetite (Bellot-Gurlet *et al.* 2009; Grevey *et al.* 2020; Neff *et al.* 2004, Neff *et al.* 2005) (Fig. 8a). After this comparison, it was recognized that the results of EDS analyses were found to be distributed over a particular range instead of precisely corresponding to the ideal ratios (see Kucukarslan *et al.* 2023, for further details). Thus, Raman spectroscopy was performed to investigate these grey and light grey phases by identifying the iron oxide phases on the corrosion products more precisely. The results of the Raman analyses indicated that the grey phase was mainly controlled by goethite (Fig. 8e, No. 1), and the light grey phase was dominated by the mixture of the magnetite and maghemite phases (Fig. 8e, No. 2).

The iron object O1 also contains slag inclusions, which usually have a round form and vary in size from a few μm to a few ten μm in width. The results of SEM-EDS analyses indicated that slag inclusions are mostly comprised of wüstite and silicate glass, despite the interferences from enclosing iron oxide matrix (Stepanov *et al.* 2018).

In the iron object, the C-rich phases with cementite or pearlite features were identified in lamellar structures. Cementite or pearlite textures can be detected in three forms (Knox 1963; Notis 2002; Scott 1989): (1) with their initial composition and microstructure, (2) with the original microstructure substituted partially by corrosion products, and (3) entirely corroded but with the initial microstructure preserved. The EDS point analyses were performed to investigate the bright lamellar structures in the first and second forms (Table 1).

The bright and dark lamellar structures in all the three forms were examined using Raman spectroscopy. The results of EDS analyses showed that the bright lamellar structures have a significantly higher C content than the surrounding iron oxide matrix (Fig. 8b). The broad G and D band peaks observed in the Raman spectra (Fig. 8e, No. 1–2) indicate the presence of C in the lamellar structures. The results of both the Raman spectroscopy and SEM-EDS analyses thus demonstrated the presence of carbon in the lamellar structures.

These results confirmed the presence of cementite and pearlite remnants in the iron object, which suggests the formation of steel. Therefore, it is crucial to find out if the object was deliberately made as steel during those early periods by determining the carbon content and its distribution within the object. Accordingly, image analyses were undertaken. As a result, this bar-shaped iron object from the EBA had a high C content, up to 0.6–0.8 wt.%. The presence of such a high C content in a bar-shaped object is interesting because the bar must have been highly brittle for a further smithing process to give the final shape (Kucukarslan *et al.* 2023). Therefore, an intentional carburization seems unlikely to occur. On the contrary, it is more likely to have such a high C content due to the abrupt changes in the redox conditions within the furnace, which might lead to the sporadic intake of carbon into the bloom during smelting; then, this bloom might be later shaped into a bar. Therefore, carburization might have occurred unintentionally during smelting (Scott 1989; Yahalom Mack and Eliyahu-Behar 2015).

Evidence for extractive iron metallurgy in the Early Bronze Age

The slag sample S1, which includes the partially reacted ore grains encircled by the phase that was formerly metallic iron, could be strong evidence to show for extractive iron smelting. Although further analyses are necessary to distinguish whether the sample S2 was slag from smelting or smithing, the presence of iron/steel formation, up to about 5 mm, could be promising evidence that the EBA ancient smelters achieved the high temperature and highly reducing atmospheric conditions in the furnace to reduce iron ore to metallic iron. On the other hand, various iron/steel compositions observed in the same slag could indicate that the redox conditions in the furnace were variable. This is probably because it must have been difficult to keep the ideal conditions throughout the iron production. Consequently, the slag S1 was a furnace slag, and the slag S2 was another by-product, such materials would be the earliest evidence of iron production in the EBA in central Anatolia.

Connections between the slags and the iron object in terms of technological condition

The slag sample S2, as a by-product, exhibits distinct iron and steel compositions ranging from low to high C content (Fig. 7) and potentially illustrates the initial compositions formed during smelting or primary smithing while consolidating bloom. The hypothesis, that unintentional carburization caused the high C content in the bar-shaped object O1, could be supported by the SEM-EDS results showing the high C-steel compositions in both the slag S2 and the object O1 (Fig. 7c–d). More significantly, the different stages of iron metallurgy, which generate the slag samples -as a by-product- and iron object -as a final product- in the EBA, indicate a close connection in terms of technological skills for iron production.

Conclusion

In this study, two slag samples and one iron object, which were excavated from Stratum IV in Kaman-Kalehöyük, were examined to find out the availability of adequate technology for iron production in the EBA at Central Anatolia. The samples were analyzed using SEM-EDS, and Raman spectroscopy to identify their microstructure and chemical composition. The Cu, Ni, and Co concentrations of the slag samples are very low (< 0.0 wt.%), being below the detection limit of SEM-EDS. The Ni and Co concentrations of the iron object O1 are also very low, mostly being below the detection limit of SEM-EDS. Therefore, it is unlikely that the slag samples S1 and S2 were a by-product of copper metallurgy, and it is also unlikely that the iron object O1 was manufactured from a meteoric source.

In the slag sample S1, the presence of partially reacted hematite ore grains, which are surrounded by a network-like structure of formerly metallic iron, could indicate the earliest evidence for extractive iron metallurgy in the Early Bronze Age. Such a finding could also support the hypothesis that S1 was a furnace slag. Moreover, the trace of mm-sized iron and steel formations was detected in another slag sample S2. The variety of iron and steel compositions, which range from pure iron to high-C steel, were identified in this slag sample. This observation could indicate that it was likely that iron ore was reduced to metallic iron in the EBA, even if such manufacturing was undertaken on only a small scale.

Furthermore, the high C content of the iron object and the variable iron and steel structures in the slags could suggest that an unintentional carburization might have resulted from a random absorption of C due to the unstable conditions in the furnace. Consequently, the EBA slags of Kaman-Kalehöyük are one of the strongest candidates for being the earliest by-product of the extractive iron metallurgy in Central Anatolia, although it is an open question whether these slags are furnace slags or slags from primary smithing.

Acknowledgments

We would like to express our sincere thanks to Dr. Sachihiro Omura, the director of the Japanese Institute of Anatolian Archaeology, for his encouragement to undertake the analyses reported here on the iron-rich artifacts from Kaman-Kalehöyük, and the JIAA members, especially Mr. Zinnuri Çöl, for providing the stratigraphic data during the research. We also would like to extend our special thanks to Prof. Eizo Nakamura, the founder of the Pheasant Memorial Laboratory, for his invaluable support throughout the research.

Bibliography

Akanuma, H.
- 2000 "Manufacture and Use of Iron in the Cultural Period of Stratum II at Kaman-Kalehöyük: Archaeometallurgical Analysis of Iron Objects from That Site," *AAS* IX, pp. 217–228.
- 2001 "Iron Objects from Stratum II at Kaman-Kalehöyük Correlation between Composition and Archaeological Level," *AAS* X, pp. 181–190.
- 2002 "Iron objects from the architectural remains of stratum III and stratum II at Kaman-Kalehöyük: correlation between composition and archaeological levels," *AAS* XI, pp. 191–200.
- 2003 "Further Archaeometallurgical study of 2nd and 1st millennium BC iron objects from Kaman-Kalehöyük, Turkey," *AAS* XII, pp.137–150.
- 2004 "The Significance of the composition of excavated iron fragments taken from stratum III at the site of Kaman-Kalehöyük, Turkey," *AAS* XIII, pp. 163–174.
- 2005 "The Significance of the composition of excavated iron fragments taken from stratum III at the site of Kaman-Kalehöyük, Turkey," *AAS* XIV, pp. 147–158.
- 2006 "Changes in iron use during the 2nd and 1st Millennia B.C. at Kaman-Kalehöyük, Turkey: composition of iron artifacts from Stratum III and Stratum II," *AAS* XV, pp. 207–222.
- 2007 "Analysis of iron and copper production activity in the central Anatolia during the Assyrian Colony Period," *AAS* XVI, pp. 125–140.
- 2008 "The significance of Early Bronze Age iron objects from Kaman-Kalehöyük, Turkey," *AAS* XVII, pp. 313–320.

Atsumi, S., Yoneda, M., Shibata, Y. and I. Nakai
- 2008 "中央アナトリア,カマン・カレホユック遺跡における青銅器時代の放射性炭素年代による編年 (Radiocarbon chronology on Bronze Age at Kaman-Kalehöyük in the central Anatolia)," 考古学と自然科学 (Archaeology and Natural Science) (57), pp. 37–53, in Japanese.

Bayley, J., Dungworth, D. and S. Paynter
- 2001 *Archaeometallurgy*. English Heritage, London.

Bellot-Gurlet, L., Neff, D., Réguer, S., Monnier, J., Saheb, M. and P. Dillmann
- 2009 "Raman studies of corrosion layers formed on archaeological irons in various media," J. *Nano RES-SW* 8, pp. 147–156.

Bjorkman, J. K.
- 1973 "Meteors and meteorites in the ancient Near East," *Meteoritics* 8, pp. 91–132.

Blakelock, E., Martinon-Torres, M., Veldhuijzen, H. A. and T. Young
- 2009 "Slag inclusions in iron objects and the quest for provenance: an experiment and a case study," *J. Archaeol. Sci.* 36, pp. 1745–1757.

Dungworth, D. and R. Wilkes
- 2009 "Understanding Hammerscale: the use of high-speed film and electron microscopy," *Historical Metallurgy* 43(1), pp. 33-46.

Eliyahu-Behar, A., Yahalom-Mack, N., Gadot, Y. and I. Finkelstein
- 2013 "Iron smelting and smithing in major urban centers in Israel during the Iron Age," *J. Archaeol. Sci.* 40, pp. 4319–4330.

Erb-Satullo, N.
- 2019 "The innovation and adoption of iron in the Ancient Near East," J. *Archaeol. Res.* 27, pp. 557–607.

Erb-Satullo, N. and J. T. Walton
- 2017 "Iron and copper production at Iron Age Ashkelon: Implications for the organization of Levantine metal production," *J. Archaeol. Res.15*, pp. 8–19.

Fushimi, K., Nakagawa, R., Kitagawa, Y. and Y. Hasegawa
- 2019 "Micro- and nano-scopic aspects of passive surface on pearlite structure of carbon steel in ph 8.4 boric acid-borate buffer," *JES* 166 (11), pp. C3409–C3416.

Geçkinli A. E.
- 1995 "Characterization Studies of Kaman-Kalehöyük Slags: A Preliminary Report," *AAS* IV, pp. 151–177.

Georgakopoulou M.
- 2014 "*Metallurgical remains from regional surveys of 'non-industrial' landscapes: The case of the Kythera Island Project,*" *J. Field Archaeol.* 39(1), pp. 67–83.

Grevey, A.L., Vignal, V., Krawiec, H., P. Ozga, Peche-Quilichini, K., Rivalan, A. and F. Mazière
- 2020 "Microstructure and long-term corrosion of archaeological iron alloy artefacts," *Herit. Sci.* 8(1), doi: 0.1186/s40494-020-00398-9

Hedges, R.E.M. and C.J. Salter
- 1979 "*Source Determination of Iron Currency Bars through Analysis of the Slag Inclusions,*" *Archaeometry* 21(2), pp. 161–17.

Jambon A.
- 2017 "Bronze Age iron: meteoritic or not? a chemical strategy," *J. Archaeol. Sci.* 88, pp. 47–53.

Knox R.
- 1963 "Detection of iron carbide structure in the oxide remains of ancient steel," *Archaeometry*, doi:10.1111/j.1475-4754.1963.tb00578.x

Kucukarslan N.
- 2023 "*Early Efforts for Iron Production in Central Anatolia: Geochemical Analysis of Iron-rich Stones, Slags and Metal Objects from the Bronze Age in Kaman-Kalehöyük (Turkey),*" Institute for Planetary Materials, Okayama University, Ph.D. dissertation.

Kucukarslan N., Ota T., Kobayashi K., Nakamura E. and S. Omura
- 2023 "Early Efforts to Smelt Iron in Central Anatolia: Analysis of Iron Artefacts from the Bronze Age in Kaman-Kalehöyük," *MMA 12*, pp. 289–305.

Miller, D. and D. Killick
- 2004 "Slag Identification at Southern African Archaeological Sites," *JAA* 2(1), pp. 23–47.

Masubuchi M.
- 2005 "Scientific Characterization of Metallurgical Slag Excavated from Kaman-Kalehöyük (1)," AAS XIV, Scientific Characterization of Metallurgical Slag Excavated from Kaman-Kalehöyük (1)," *AAS* XIV, pp. 183–194.
- 2008 "A Metallographic Study on Iron and Steel Arrowheads from Kaman-Kalehöyük Stratum II," *AAS* XVII, pp. 281–293.
- 2016a "*Diachronic Changes in Iron and Steel Production and Cultural Transitions in Central Anatolia, 1650–550 BC, in Light of a New Archaeometallurgical Investigation of Iron and Steel Objects at Kaman-Kalehöyük,*" Institute of Archaeology, University College of London, Ph.D. dissertation.
- 2016b "A study on the beginning of the Iron Age at Kaman-Kalehöyük," *AAS* XIX, pp. 111–122.
- 2017 "The Chemical Characterization of Iron And Steel Objects from Kaman- Kalehöyük," *AAS* XX, pp. 51–62.

Nakamura, E., Makishima, A., Moriguti, T., Kobayashi, K., Sakaguchi, C., Yokoyama, T., Tanaka, R., Kuritani, T. and H. Takei
- 2003 "*Comprehensive geochemical analyses of small amounts (< 100mg) of extraterrestrial samples for the analytical competition related to the sample return mission MUSES-C,*" *The Institute of Space Astronautical Science Report SP* 16, pp. 49–101.

Neff, D., Reguer, S., Bellot-Gurlet, L., Dillmann, P. and R. Bertholon
- 2004 "Structural characterization of corrosion products on archaeological iron. An integrated analytical approach to establish corrosion forms." *J. Raman Spectrosc.* 35 (8–9), pp. 739–745.

Neff D., Dillmann P., Bellot-Gurlet L. and G. Beranger
- 2005 "Corrosion of iron archaeological artefacts in soil: characterisation of the corrosion system," *Corros. Sci.* (47), pp. 515–535

Notis M. R.
- 2002 "A Ghost Story: Remnant structures in corroded ancient iron objects." *MRS Online Proceedings Library Archive* 712, pp. 259–267

Omura S.
– 2011 "Kaman-Kalehöyük excavations in central Anatolia." in Steadman, S.R., and McMahon, J.G. (eds.), *The Oxford Handbook of Ancient Anatolia (10,000–323 BCE)*, Oxford University Press, Oxford, pp. 1095–1111.

Paynter R.
– 2007 "Romano-British Workshops for Iron Smelting and Smithing at Westhawk Farm, Kent," *Historical Metallurgy 41(1)*, pp. 15–31.

Photos E.
– 1989 "The question of meteoritic versus smelted nickel-rich iron: archaeological evidence and experimental results," *World Archaeol. 20*, pp. 403–421.

Pleiner R.
– 2000 *Iron in Archaeology: The European Bloomery Smelters*. Archeologický Ustav AVČR, Praha.

Rehren, T., Belgya, T., Jambon, A., Káli, G., Kasztovszky, Z., Kis, Z., Kovács, I., Maróti, B., Martinón-Torres, M., Miniaci, G., Pigott, V.C., Radivojević, M., Rosta, L., Szentmiklósi, L. and Z. Szőkefalvi-Nagy
– 2013 "5,000 years old Egyptian iron beads made from hammered meteoritic iron," *J. Archaeol. Sci. (40)*, pp. 4785–4792.

Scott, B.G.
– 1989 "The retrieval of technological information from corrosion products on early wrought iron artefacts" in Janaway R., Scott B. (eds.), *Evidence Preserved in Corrosion Products: New Field Studies in Artifact Studies*, Proceedings of a Joint Conference Between UKIC Archaeology Section and the Council for British Archaeology Science Committee, Leeds 1983, pp. 8–14.

Scott, D. A. and G. Eggert
– 2009 *Iron and Steel: Corrosion, Colorants, Conservation*. Archetype Publications, London.

Serneels, V. and S. Perret
– 2003 "*Quantification of smithing activities based on the investigation of slag and other material remains*," in *Archaeometallurgy in Europe*, Associazone Italiana di Metallurgia, Milan, pp. 469–478.

Severin, T., Rehren, T. and H. Schleicher
– 2011 "*Early metal smelting in Aksum, Ethiopia: copper or iron?*," *EJM 23(6)*, pp. 981–992.

Stepanov, I., Sauder, L., Keen, J., Workman, V. and A. Eliyahu-Behar
– 2022 "*By the hand of the smelter: tracing the impact of decision-making in bloomery iron smelting*," *Archaeol. Anthropol. Sci. 14*:80, https://doi.org/10.1007/s12520-022-01516-3

Stepanov, I., Weeks, L., Franke, K., Cable, C., Overlaet, B., Magee, P., Händel, M., Al Aali, Y., Radwan, M. and H. Zein
– 2018 *Methodologies for the investigation of corroded iron objects: examples from prehistoric sites in South-eastern Arabia and Western Iran*. Sci. Technol. Archaeol. Res., 3(2), 270–284.

Tylecote, R.F.
– 1992 *A History of Metallurgy, Second Edition*. Maney Publishing, UK.

Unglik H.
– 1991 "Observations on the Structures and Formation of Microscopic Smithing Residues from Bixby Blacksmith Shop at Barre Four Corners, Massachussetts, 1824–55," *Historical Metallurgy* 25(2), pp. 92–98.

Veldhuijzen H.A.
– 2005 "*Early Iron Production in the Levant, Smelting and Smithing at Early 1st Millennium BC Tell Hammeh, Jordan, and Tel Beth-Shemesh, Israel*," University of London. Unpublished Ph.D. thesis.

Veldhuijzen, H.A. and T. Rehren
– 2007 "Slags and the City: Early Iron Production at Tell Hammeh, Jordan, and Tel Beth-Shemesh, Israel" in LaNiece, S., Hook, D. R., Craddock, P.T., (Eds.), *Metals and Mines: Studies in Archaeometallurgy*. Archetype/British Museum, London, pp. 189–201.

Yahalom-Mack, N. and A. Eliyahu-Behar
– 2015 "The transition from bronze to iron in Canaan: chronology, technology, and context," *Radiocarbon*. 57(2), pp. 285–305.

Yalçın Ü.
– 1999 "Early iron metallurgy in Anatolia," *Anatol. Stud.* 49, pp. 177–187.

Yukishima, K.
– 2001 "Iron arrowheads from Stratum II at Kaman- Kalehöyük," *AAS X*, pp. 111–118.

Sample No.	Phase		C	O	Na	Mg	Al	Si	P	S	Cl	K	Ca	Ti	Cr	Mn	Fe	Co	Ni	Cu
	wt.%Sigma (min-max)		0.3-0.9	0.1-0.8	0.07-0.20	0.04-0.13	0.04-0.11	0.03-0.09	0.04-0.1	0.03-0.09	0.03-0.09	0.04-0.10	0.04-0.10	0.05-0.12	0.05-0.13	0.1-0.2	0.3-1.0	0.17-0.38	0.1-0.3	0.3-1.0
O1	metallic iron	avg (n=3)	-	2,9	-	-	-	-	-	-	-	-	-	-	-	-	96,2	-	-	-
		std	-	0,5	-	-	-	-	-	-	-	-	-	-	-	-	1,4	-	-	-
	bright-lamellar	avg (n=11)	4,8	25,2	-	-	-	0,2	-	0,16	-	-	-	-	-	-	69,7	-	-	-
		std	1,3	2,7	-	-	-	0,1	-	0,03	-	-	-	-	-	-	2,0	-	-	-
	light grey	avg (n=16)	-	34,1	-	-	-	0,3	-	0,18	-	-	0,16	-	-	-	65,1	1,5	-	-
		std	-	0,9	-	-	-	0,1	-	0,07	-	-	0,05	-	-	-	1,6	0,2	-	-
	grey	avg (n=19)	1,0	42,1	-	0,29	-	0,5	-	0,15	0,11	0,10	0,17	-	-	-	55,9	1,2	-	-
		std	0,2	1,2	-	0,25	-	0,4	-	0,04	0,02	0,03	0,04	-	-	-	1,9	0,2	-	-

Sample No.	Phase		C	O	Na	Mg	Al	Si	P	S	Cl	K	Ca	Ti	Cr	Mn	Fe	Co	Ni	Cu
	wt.%Sigma (min-max)		0.28-1.38	0.19-0.64	0.05-0.16	0.04-0.08	0.03-0.06	0.03-0.19	0.03-0.06	0.03-0.06	0.03-0.05	0.03-0.07	0.04-0.25	0.04-0.07	0.05-0.08	0.07-0.12	0.22-1.53	0.13-0.26	0.1-0.22	0.26-0.8
S1	metallic iron	avg (n=9)	-	0,7	-	-	-	0,1	-	-	-	-	-	-	-	-	99,3	-	-	-
		std	-	0,2	-	-	-	0,1	-	-	-	-	-	-	-	-	0,3	-	-	-
	corrosion	avg (n=5)	-	39	-	0,2	0,10	2	-	0,2	0,5	0,4	0,6	-	-	-	57	-	-	-
		std	-	1	-	0,1	0,00	2	-	0,1	0,3	0,1	0,3	-	-	-	2	-	-	-
	wustite	avg (n=7)	-	24,7	-	0,8	0,4	0,15	-	-	-	0,1	0,3	0,2	-	-	74	-	-	-
		std	-	0,5	-	0,1	0,1	0,04	-	-	-	0,1	0,1	0,2	-	-	1	-	-	-
	unreduced iron ore	avg (n=6)	-	32	-	-	-	1,0	-	0,09	-	0,11	0,3	-	-	-	66	-	-	-
		std	-	1	-	-	-	0,3	-	0,00	-	0,01	0,1	-	-	-	1	-	-	-
S2	metallic iron	avg (n=2)	-	-	-	-	-	-	-	-	-	-	-	-	-	-	99	-	-	-
		std	-	-	-	-	-	-	-	-	-	-	-	-	-	-	1	-	-	-
	corrosion	avg (n=12)	-	36	-	0,12	-	0,5	-	-	0,6	0,13	0,19	-	-	-	63	-	-	-
		std	-	3	-	0,00	-	0,1	-	-	1,1	0,03	0,05	-	-	-	3	-	-	-
	lamellar structure	avg (n=7)	2	35	-	0,10	0,11	0,7	0,10	-	0,2	0,18	0,3	-	-	-	61	-	-	-
		std	1	3	-	0,00	0,02	0,4	0,02	-	0,1	0,04	0,1	-	-	-	3	-	-	-
	wustite	avg (n=9)	-	25	-	0,5	0,3	0,09	-	-	-	-	0,2	0,14	-	-	73	-	-	-
		std	-	2	-	0,1	0,1	0,01	-	-	-	-	0,1	0,02	-	-	2	-	-	-
	Ca-rich olivine	avg (n=4)	-	41	-	1,0	0,14	14,7	0,2	-	-	-	18,8	-	-	-	25	-	-	-
		std	-	1	-	0,1	0,04	0,2	0,1	-	-	-	0,3	-	-	-	1	-	-	-

Table 1. The average chemical compositions (wt.%) of the dominant phases in the iron object O1, and the slag samples S1 and S2.

Sample No.	Sample	Excavation Archive No.	Trench	Sector	Provisional Layer No.	Context	Chronology	Stratum
O1	object	01000854	North	IV	73-c	-	Early Bronze Age	IV
S1	slag	99001690-1	North	III	82	hearths from contemporary deposits	Early Bronze Age	IV
S2	slag	13000319	North	V	162	high amount of ash and charcoal	Early Bronze Age	IV

Table 2. Information about the archaeological context and chronology of the iron artefacts in the study.

Sample No.	Sample	Dominant Phases						
		unreduced/partially reduced ore grains	Ca-rich olivine	wüstite	relics of metallic iron	formerly iron/steel but corroded	cementite/pearlite remnants	slag inclusions trapped inside formerly iron/steel
O1	object	-	-	√ (as slag inclusions, from a few μm to a few ten μm)	√	√	√(up to 0.6-0.8 wt.%)	√
S1	slag	√ (0.25 mm to 1.5 mm)	-	√ (a few μm to c. 100 μm)	√	√ (up to 400 um)	-	-
S2	slag	-	√	√(a few a few μm to c. 150-200 μm grains)	√	√ (up to 5 mm in a loosely connected network)	√(variety from low to high C-steel composition)	√(glassy silicate and wüstite grains)

Table 3. Dominant phases for the slag samples S1, S2 and the iron object O1.

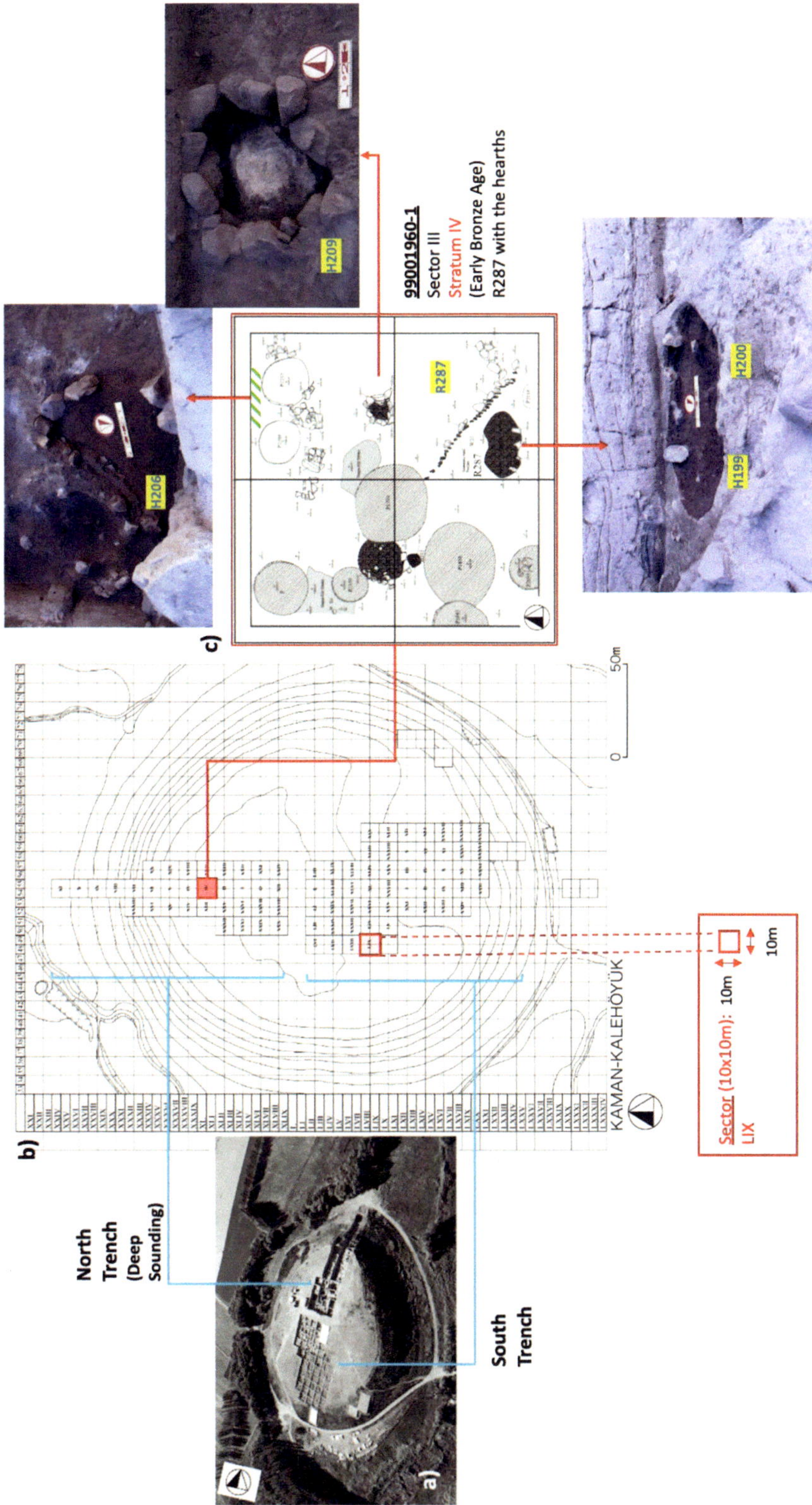

Fig. 1. a) A bird's eye view of Kaman-Kalehöyük (Omura 2011), b) A topographic map with the grid-excavation system, c) A sketch of the Sector III showing the deposit, in which the slag sample S1 was excavated, along with the hearths from the contemporary deposits (The photos from *JIAA archive*, this figure is adapted from Kucukarslan *et al.* 2023: Figure 16).

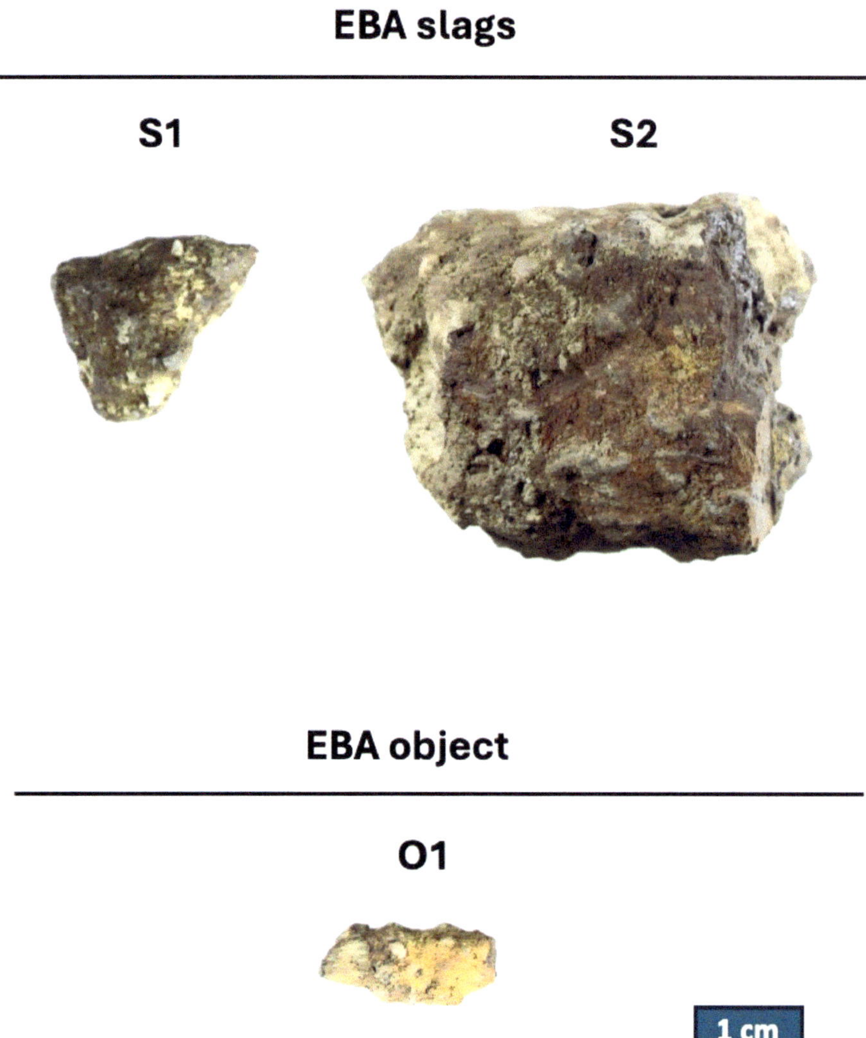

Fig. 2. Photographs of the samples from the Early Bronze Age (EBA), including two slags (S1 and S2) and one object (O1).

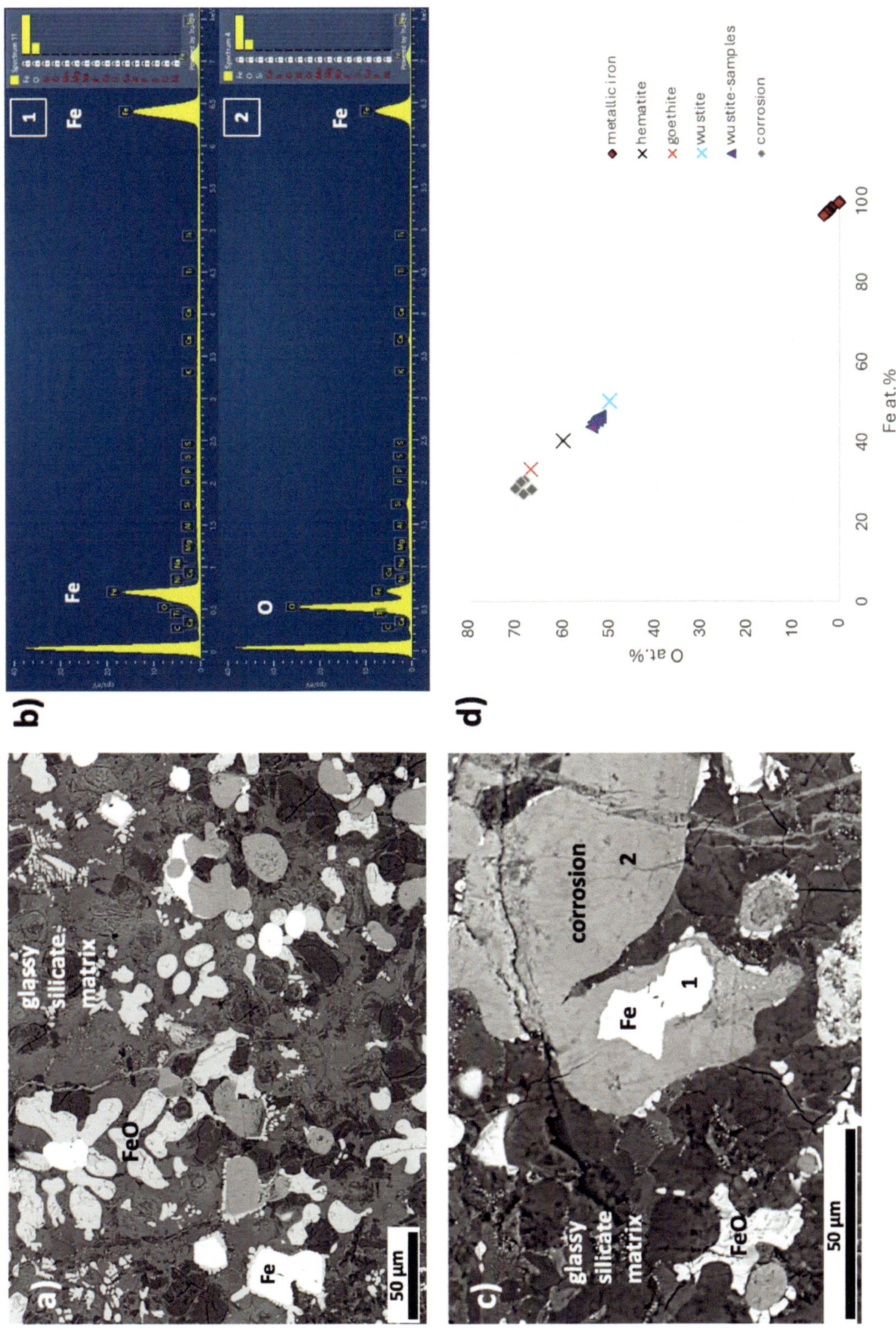

Fig. 3. a) A Back-scattered electron (BSE) image of the slag S1 displaying the dominant phases, b) The EDS spectra acquired from the spot analyses on a metallic iron grain, which is partly corroded, c) A BSE image of a metallic grain which is partly preserved, d) The iron and oxygen contents (at. %) of the dominant phases in S1. (This figure is adapted from Kucukarslan 2023: Figure 33).

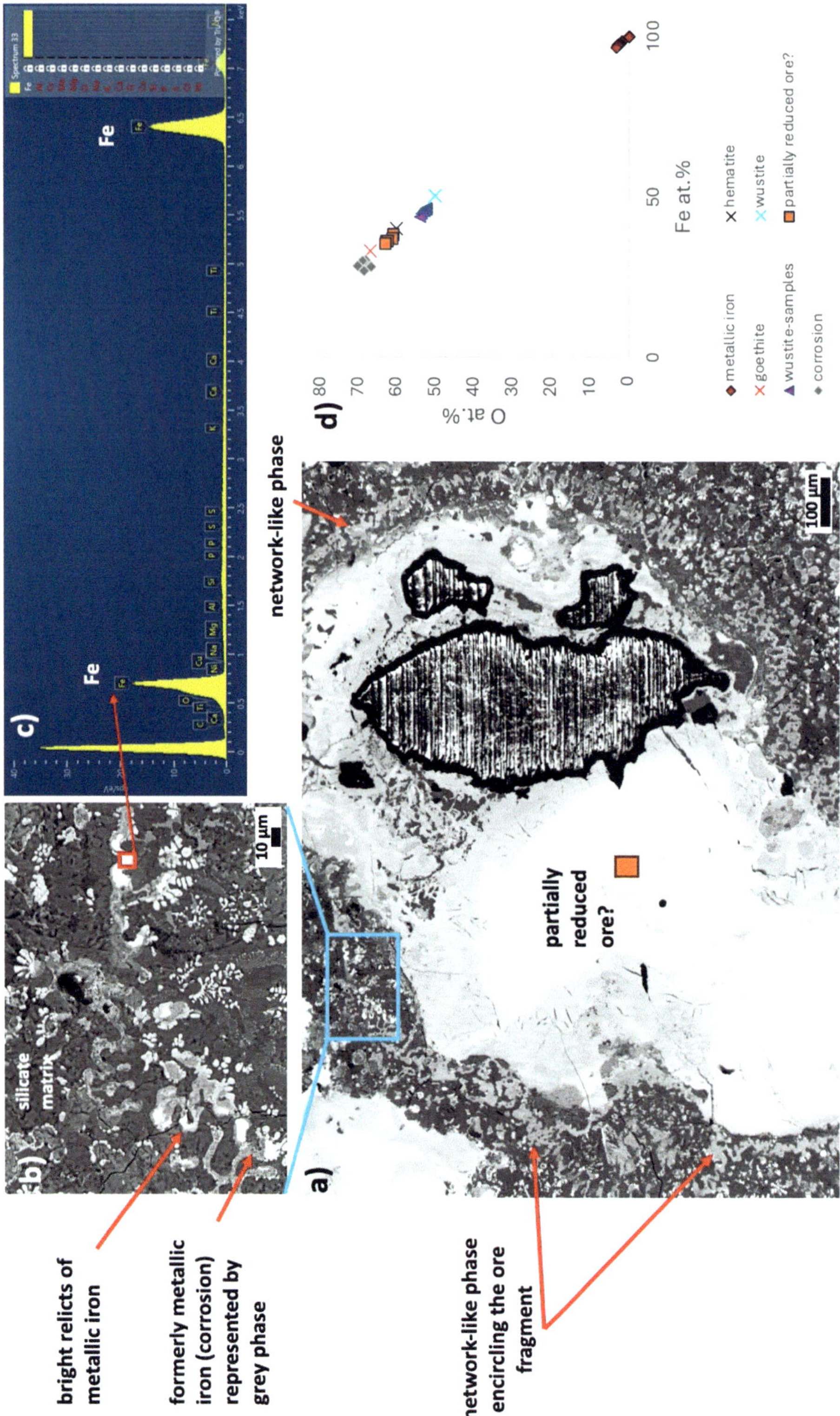

Fig. 4. a) A BSE image of the slag S2 depicting a possibly partially reacted ore fragment which is encircled by a network-like phase, b) A close-up view of the rectangle in (a) showing the relicts of metallic iron in the network-phase encircling the ore fragment, c) The EDS spectrum acquired from a relict of metallic iron, d) The iron and oxygen contents (at. %) of the dominant phases in S1. (This figure is adapted from Kucukarslan 2023: Figure 34).

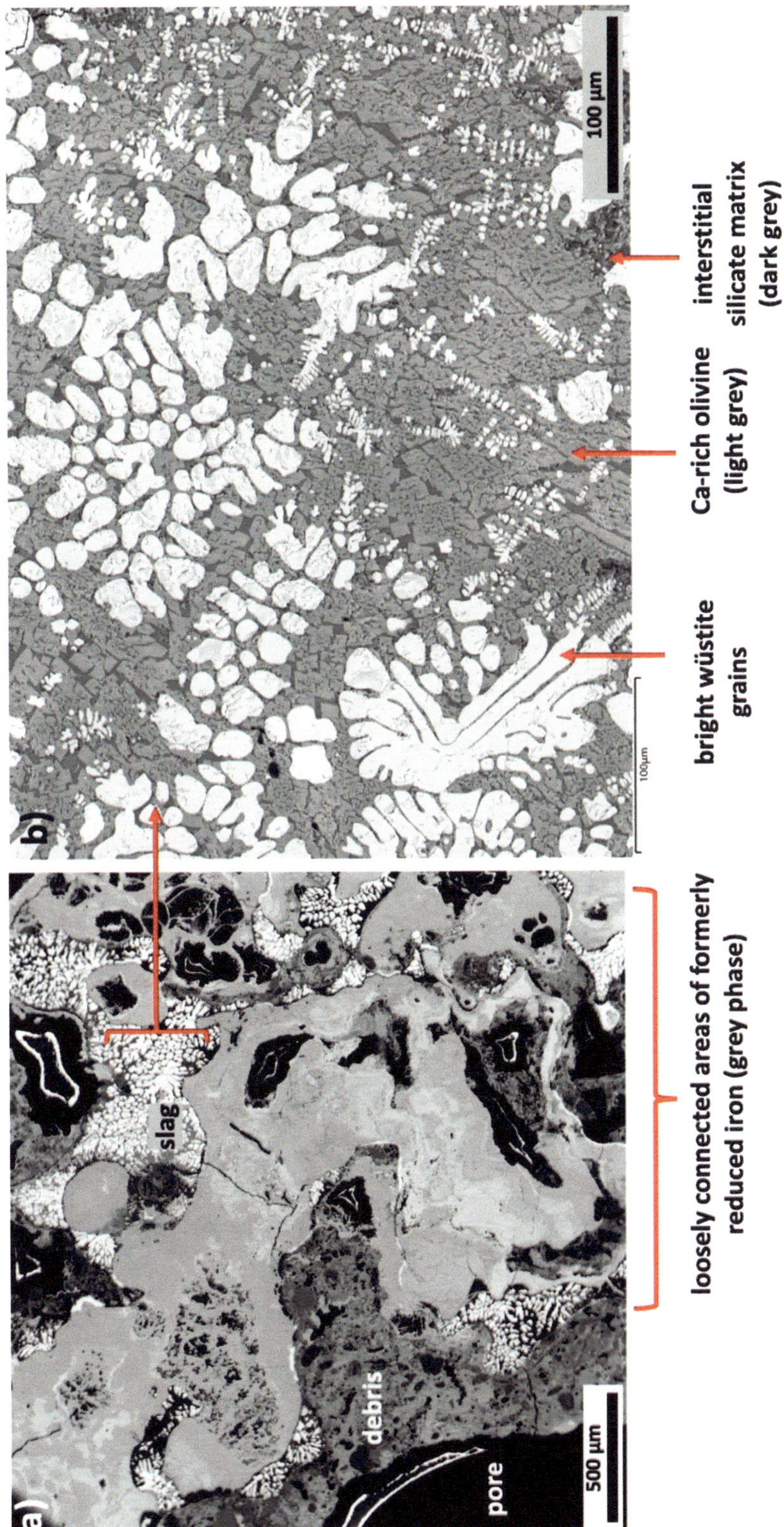

Fig. 5. a) A BSE image of the slag S2. The bright areas represent the slag components of the sample, and the loosely connected areas are the formerly reduced iron that has already corroded, b) The major phases in slag: wüstite grains (bright) and Ca-rich olivine grains (light grey) in the interstitial glassy silicate matrix (dark grey). (This figure is adapted from Kucukarslan 2023: Figure 35).

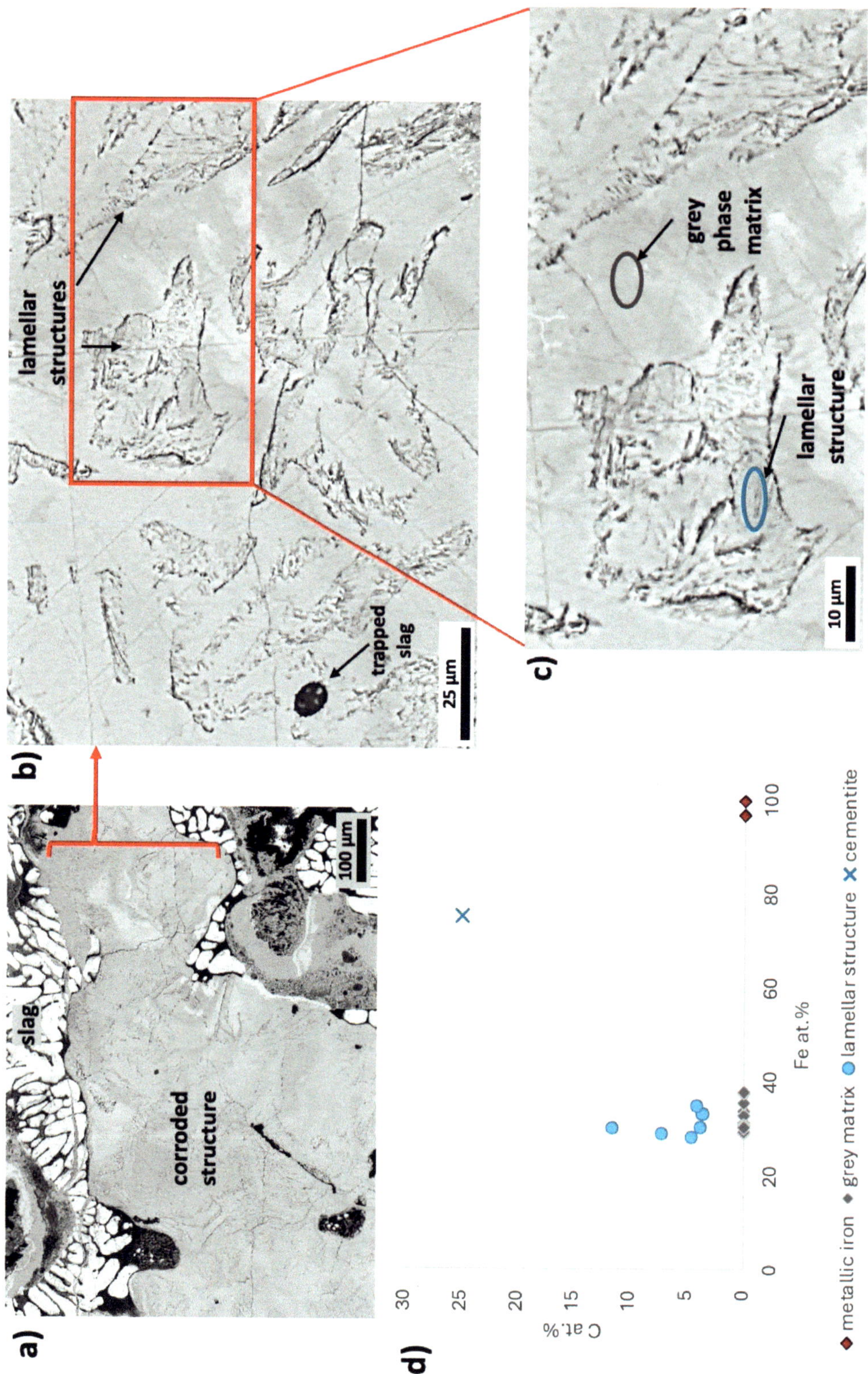

Fig. 6. a) A BSE image of the slag S2. The areas, which are represented by the grey phase, are corroded, b) The structures in lamellar pattern, c) A close-up view of the lamellar pattern area from (b). The circles show the areas, from which the EDS spectra were acquired in the lamellar structure and grey phase matrix, d. The iron and carbon content (at. %) of the dominant phases in the corroded structure. (This figure is adapted from Kucukarslan 2023: Figure 36).

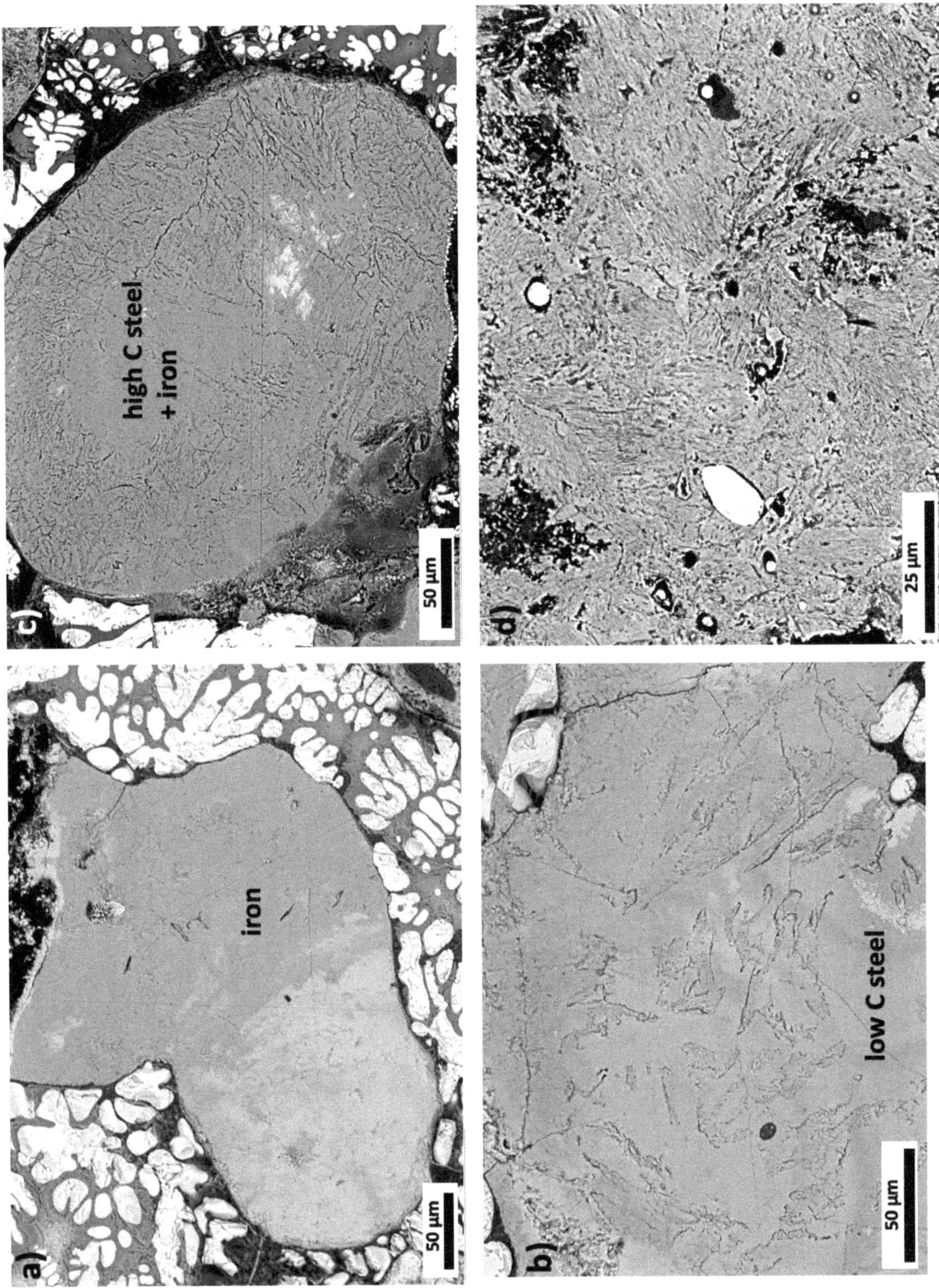

Fig. 7. BSE images of the slag S2, which show the variation in iron/steel compositions: a) iron, b) low C-steel, c) high C-steel, d) A BSE image of the iron object O1, which demonstrates the high C-steel content through densely distributed pearlite structures and bright wüstite inclusions.
(This figure is adapted from Kucukarslan 2023: Figure 37 and Kucukarslan *et al.* 2023: Fig. 8c).

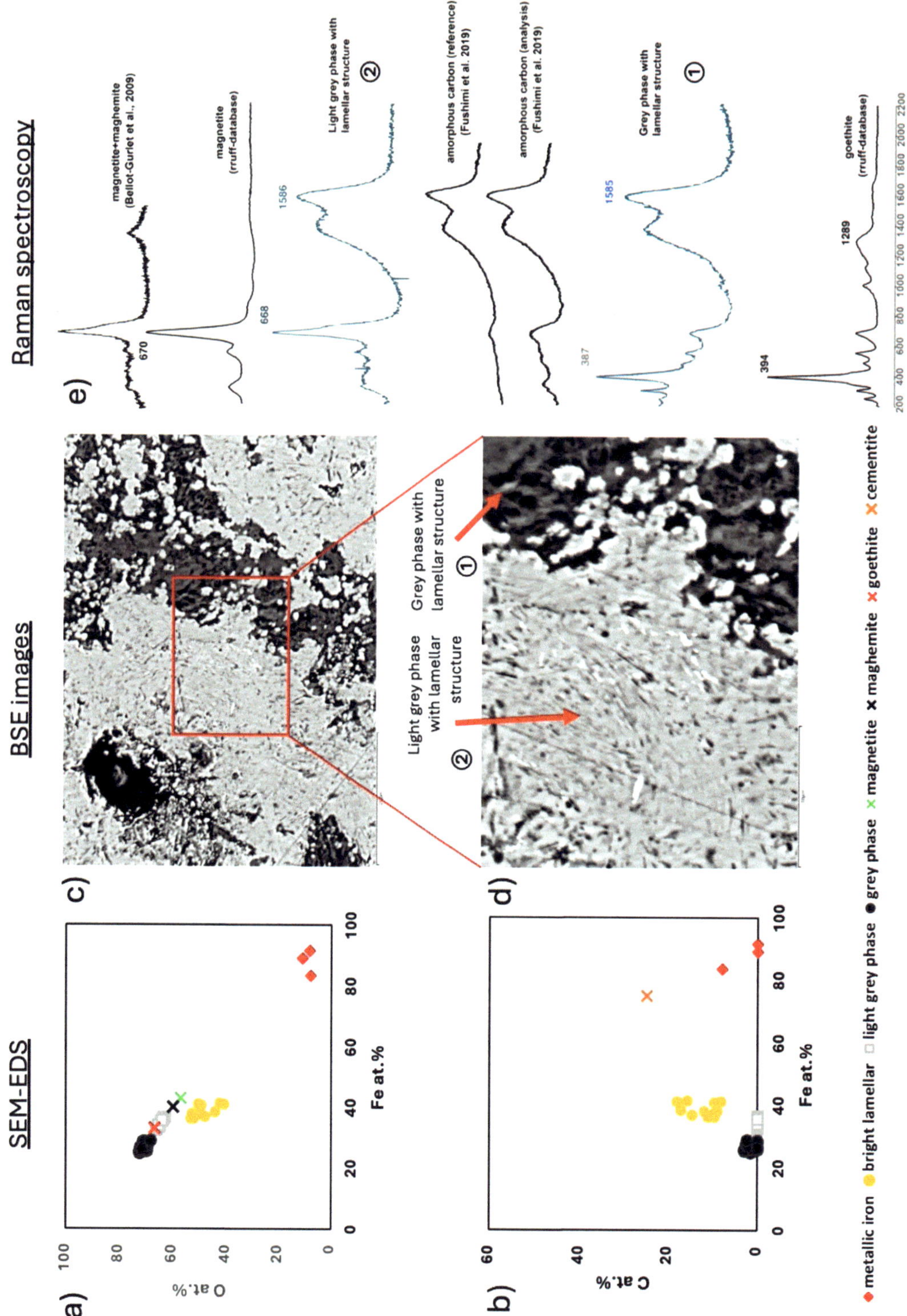

Fig. 8. a) The iron and oxygen contents (at. %), and b) Iron and carbon contents (at. %) of the dominant phases in the sample O1, c) A BSE image, which shows the grey and light grey phases with lamellar structures, d) A close-up view of the rectangular area in (c), e) Interpreted Raman spectra of the grey phase (number 1) and the light grey phase (number 2) with lamellar structures. (This figure is adapted from Kucukarslan *et al.* 2023: Fig. 5–7).
(This figure is adapted from Kucukarslan et al. 2023: Fig. 5–7; the references from the RRUFF database (http://rruff.info/))

Two New Arslantepe Type Short Swords of Unknown Origin

*Önder Bilgi**

I am very pleased to have been invited to contribute an essay to a Festschrift in honour of Dr. Sachihiro Omura, Director of excavations at Kaman-Kalehöyük. We have been colleagues and also close friends since his postgraduate student years at Ankara University.
As always, I offer him my best wishes for his future work and research in Anatolia.

Abstract

Two recently acquired short swords made of arsenical copper indicated that short swords uncovered at excavations at Arslantepe are not limited to the Malatya region. The Arslantepe swords cannot be dated to Late Chalcolithic/Early Bronze Age I period, because arsenic copper alloy metallurgy and the use of moulds in the production of large-sized sophisticated weapons did not occur before the Early Bronze Age II period. Spearheads with a long butt found together with the swords were a late development in the weapon industry and were widely used in the Near East geography after 2400 B.C. Moreover, the plaque with four spirals is another metal object found together with the swords, which should definitely be dated to Early Bronze Age III period since 14 of them were obtained at Samsun-İkiztepe from male burials of a grave belonging to the last quarter of the 3000 B.C.

The arsenic used in the Arslantepe weapons and plaque with four spirals may have originated from the Central Black Sea Region near the town of Durağan located in the Sinop city area rather than from Transcaucasia as proposed by the Director of excavations at Arslantepe. This rich arsenic mineralization discovered in 1997 should be acknowledged as a main arsenic source for the use of Anatolian smiths.

Öz

Son zamanlarda ele geçirilmiş bulunan iki adet ve Venedik'te bir manastırın müzesinde yer alan bir adet arsenikli bakırdan yapılmış kısa kılıcın, ilk defa Arslantepe kazılarında ortaya çıkartılmış bulunanlara dayanarak Malatya bölgesinin yerel ürünleri olmadıklarına işaret etmişlerdir. Arslantepe'de bulunmuş olan kısa kılıçların Geç Kalkolitik/Erken Tunç I dönemlerine ait olamayacakları, Erken Tunç Çağı II dönemi öncesi Anadolu ve komşu coğrafyalarda arsenikli bakır alaşımı ve kalıplar kullanılarak büyük boyutlu gelişmiş silah üretiminin henüz başlamamış olduğu henüz örneklerine rastlanılmamış olmasından anlaşılmaktadır. Arslantepe'de kılıçlar ile birlikte bulunmuş olan uzun boğumlu mızrak uçlarının ise geç dönem gelişmiş silah endüstrisinin ürünleri oldukları ve MÖ 2400 yılları sonrasında Önasya coğrafyasında yaygın olarak kullanılmış oldukları geniş dağılımlarından bilinmektedir. Ayrıca, kılıç ve mızrak uçları ile birlikte ele geçen dört sarmallı metal plakanın Erken Tunç Çağı III dönemininin tipik bir ürünü olduğu Samsun-İkiztepe'de MÖ 3. bin yılının son çeyreğine tarihlenen mezarlıktaki 14 adet erkek gömüsünde ele geçirilmiş olmalarından da bilimsel olarak ortaya konmuştur.

Arslantepe'de silahlar ile birlikte ele geçirilmiş olan dört sarmallı plakada kullanılmış olan arseniğin, Anadolu ve özellikle İkiztepe metal ustalarının, 1997 tarihinde keşfedilmiş olan Orta Karadeniz Bölgesi Sinop ili Durağan ilçesi yakınında saptanmış bulunan ana kaynaktan elde edilmiş olması büyük olasılıktır.

* Retired academic of the University of Istanbul and Ex-Director of excavations at Ikiztepe.

Presented here is a so-called hilted short sword whose date and original location are unknown, which is currently kept in the private Haluk Perk Museum[1] in Istanbul (Fig. 1). This sword which is made of arsenical copper alloy is the second of two unstratified examples. The other was recently published[2] and is kept at Tokat Museum[3] (Fig. 2). The analysis[4] of the Perk Museum sword shows that the flat hilt was moulded separately from the blade and made of arsenical copper alloy. The pointed blade was also moulded. The two pieces were then connected to each other via the crescent-shaped terminus which was hot-forged. The hilt features a distinct semi-circular shape which, if used, had to be inconveniently gripped tightly due to the shortness of the handle.

This sword together with the recently published Tokat example does not represent a new weapon type among Anatolian Prehistoric Age armories. Years ago, two bundles of weapons consisting of nine short swords (Fig. 4), 11 spearheads of butted type (Fig. 5) and a four-spiralled plaque (Fig. 6) were uncovered at the Arslantepe – Malatya excavations. These items were found lying in two separate bundles on the earthen floor of a room in a partly destroyed building of mudbrick construction (Klaunzer 2017: Fig. 2; Palmieri 1981: 104 Pl. XIVb). Three of the nine swords differ from the others by having silver inlaying decoration on the hilts. Two of these decorated swords are inlaid with a small triangle, and the third one has three horizontal independent alternating bands filled in with grooved zig-zag motifs on the hilt (Palmieri 1981: 109 Fig. 3.2–3).

As for the period of the Arslantepe swords, they are attributed to the last quarter to the Late Chalcolithic Age/ Early Bronze Age I, which was reported in an article along with a series of 14C dates (Palmieri 1981: 102) for "The Temple" complex from 2620 to 2470 years B.C.[5] The article reported the MASCA corrected dates as from 3350–3150 to 3450–3230 B.C., the latter of which referred to the date of weapons in question. Later, these dates were repeated in a second article on metalwork in the Near East (Frangipane 1985: 215–228). These latter dates for the period of The Temple Building Complex of Layers VII-VIA corresponding to the the end of Late Chalcolithic and Early Bronze Age I cultures are convincing enough as they are contemporary with Late Uruk and the following Jemdet Nasr period of Mesopotamia. These dates are in line with the pottery and an especially large number of the typical bullae of the period (Palmieri 1981: 104).

The essential issue here is that dating nine swords together with twelve spearheads with straight tangs and a plaque with four spirals found on a floor is not certain. Spectral analyses showed that all these metal items were produced with arsenical copper alloys and were reportedly cast in open and closed moulds, as reported (Palmieri 1981: 109). Later on, scientists interested in archaeometallurgy at Arslantepe examined the group of metal weapons and came to the conclusion that the metallurgical craftsmanship was highly developed and differed from other metal objects, mainly simple tools recovered in earlier or contemporary layers. Significantly, these tools were classed as undeveloped. There was then a stark contrast between the composition and craftsmanship of the metal hoard and other presumed contemporary metalwork.

One thing is clear and that is at Arslantepe almost from the beginning of its metallurgical activities, arsenic was used to obtain an alloy of

1 I am grateful to Mr. H. Perk who allowed me to publish this remarkable sword. Also, I would like to thank Dr. P. de Jesus, who not only kindly undertook the proofreading of the text, but also supplied me with relevant publications which I had not seen before or were out of my reach.

2 Zimmermann *et al.* 2011: 1–7 and 2015: 58–61.

3 This sword is also made of arsenical copper alloy (Cu 89.5, As 9.9) and 44.1 cm in length and weights 411.5 gr

4 The slightly corroded sword is 53.4 cm in length and 748 gr in weight and has a different percent of copper and arsenic in the hilt (Cu 70.3, As 11.4) and in the blade (Cu 68.7, As 14) and tip of the blade (Cu 79.1, As 13.3).

5 According to T = 5568 4420 + 50 to 4570 + 60 BP.

arsenical copper with the intent of producing stronger and more durable metal objects. One lingering question is how was this alloying technology initiated? A simple explanation of how this was done relates to the process of smelting copper ores. It is quite possible that there was a small percentage of arsenic in the copper ore when metallurgists smelted it in the kilns, resulting in an unintentionally natural arsenical copper alloy. This view is shared by a number of researchers who cite numerous cases of unintentional arsenic copper alloys in different areas of Anatolia and the Aegean (Caneva and Palmieri 1983: 637–654; Gale *et al.* 1985:143–173).

The problem with this theory is that it is not possible to explain copper with high arsenic percentages, particularly when used in the production of the above-mentioned swords, spearheads and the four-spiralled plaque. At the time when the Arslantepe hoard was first reported the existence of a source of arsenic ores was not known in Anatolia. Thus, the Director of excavations at Arslantepe attempted to solve the problem by speculating on arsenic sources then known where arsenic sources could have been obtained. She focused on eastern Anatolian and adjacent regions of the Transcaucasus. Having identified in the Caucasian region the existence of arsenic mines, she claimed that arsenic metal was most probably obtained from there. Relying on the research carried out by Selimkhanov (1962) and by Kushnareva and Chubinisvilli (1970), a compelling solution was found. What was lacking in this claim was the absence of any cultural links between Arslantepe and the Caucasus (Schaeffer 1948; Schachner 2002: 115–130). As it turns out, there is no archaeological evidence to indicate any kind of trade links between Arslantepe and Transcaucasia apart from simple tools and a few long-butted spearheads with straight long tangs which were widespread in Southeast Anatolia and Northern Syria and Mesopotamia (Bilgi 1987: 77–108).

Because of a lack of hard evidence, it is not possible to shed any light on how the high arsenical percentages in metal weapons of Arslantepe were obtained. What one can be assured is that routine arsenical copper technology was practised earlier than Early Bronze Age II (before 2800 B.C.) in Anatolia and within the large circum-pontic region[6]. Thousands of arsenic-alloyed copper objects have been acquired in the course of work at scientifically excavated sites as well as from illicit excavations or by chance in the northern Central Anatolia and in the Central Black Sea region. It is not just by coincidence that this region yields rich metalliferous ores.

This question was clarified in 1997 when rich arsenic ore mines were located in the Central Black Sea region in Anatolia by a team headed by H. Özbal from Boğaziçi University-İstanbul and his colleagues (Özbal *et al.* 1997: 47–54). Two different kinds of rich arsenic sources were located at two different locations in this region. The first is on Tavşandağ south of the town of Vezirköprü in Samsun region. It is on the slopes of Peynir Çayı-Bakacak Tepesi (Pırasakaya) north of Bakırçay containing a massive arsenopyrite deposit (Figs. 7a–b). At this site four ancient galleries were also located. The second is along the north banks of Kızılırmak river (Halys) near Gökdoğan village at Ağu (poison) Boğazı where the Gökırmak stream joins the Kızılırmak river (Fig. 8a–b) five km west of the town Durağan in the region of Sinop city. Intensively orange-coloured realgar (Fig. 9a) and red-coloured orpiment (Fig. 9b) mineralization can be found at these locations.[7]

Because of these discoveries the source of arsenic and the production of a large number

6 Chernykh 1992: 54–96 and Chronological Scheme of the Production and use of copper and arsenical copper p. 14 Fig. 6; Evgeny, *et al.* 2002: 83–100.

7 Özbal *et al.* 2002: 44. Actually, these arsenic ore deposits were known from the Roman Period in Anatolia. Strabo, an ancient historian born in Amasya city, mentions in his book Geography Vol XII the existence of arsenic ore around Ilgaz Dağı. Most probably when he described the location of arsenic deposits, he made a mistake of indicating Ilgaz Dağı instead of Tavşan Dağ around 100 kms north of it. See Strabo 1987: 50.

of the over 1500 arsenical copper objects consisting of tools, jewellery, weapons and symbols obtained during the scientific excavations at İkiztepe[8] can now be considered, and without any hesitation, as a regional activity. These objects were logically produced by acquiring arsenic from the above-mentioned sources and copper from the massive metallurgical activity in the Bakırçay valley that contains around million tons of copper slag heaps lying all along the banks of the stream flowing downwards as far as Köprübaşı (Özbal *et al.* 2002: 43).

Among the weapons of İkiztepe there is only one spearhead with a long butt, which is a distinctive feature (Bilgi 1990: 82 Fig. 11), but it has a tang with a curved tip like most of the other butted spearheads. A tang with a curved tip is a feature that appears at İkiztepe throughout Early Bronze II[9] (2800–2400 B.C.), and is especially common in Early Bronze Age III[10] (2400–2100 B.C.). It persists until the beginning of the Middle Bronze Age (2100) when usage of tin copper begins to replace arsenic-copper alloy in Anatolia.[11]

Among the symbolic objects unearthed at İkiztepe there are plaques with four spirals, which comprise a group containing 14 pieces (Bilgi 1984: 271–277 Fig. 18; Bilgi 1990: 439–445 Fig. 1). All of these were obtained from the burials of the Early Bronze Age III graveyard. They were found only in the male burials, generally next to the finger bones of the skeleton which were laid down supine with legs extended. With one exception they are formed of arsenic copper alloy by hot and cold forging. The odd one was cast in a closed mould and has a very high percentage of arsenic giving it a silvery appearance (Bilgi 1984: 277).

An arsenical copper plaque with four spirals (Fig. 5), proposed to be a belt buckle, was also found at Arslantepe together with weapons (Palmieri 1981: Fig. 3.5). This one, in fact, is almost a replica of the İkiztepe examples (Bilgi 1990: 441 Fig. 19). As the weapons were found together with the plaque inside a small room of a damaged mud brick building, which is part of the so-called temple, their date was attributed to the Late Uruk/Jemdet Nasr period by the Director. Judging from the sophisticated appearance and a unique form of the swords it is hard to date them to production of Late Uruk or Jemdet Nasr date when there are no arsenic ore deposits of any kind known.

As there are no known arsenic ore deposits surrounding the area of Arslantepe in Anatolia, Director A. Palmieri turned her investigations towards north-eastern Anatolia and beyond, geographies where arsenic was said to be used to alloy with copper to produce arsenical copper objects in the publications on Transcaucasian lands. In her research she managed to find a few publications as indicated here in footnotes 14 and 15. So she proposed that arsenic used in the swords might have been obtained from the metalliferous mountains of Transcaucasus. However, she did not explain or mention who might have brought arsenic to Arslantepe from those lands, nor did she ask whether sufficient metallurgical technology was known and practised there. As seen from these inadequate data, these Arslantepe swords together with spearheads and a quadruple plaque do not belong to the Late Uruk or Jemdet Nasr period. According to the current Director, the metal hoard mentioned above was wrapped in two bundles, which apparently hung on one of the walls of a room which was part of the Temple Complex. However, in the illustrated photo provided there was no wall high enough to hang them on (Palmieri 1981: Pl.XIVb). Moreover, a mud

8 Most of the metal objects unearthed at İkiztepe were published by the writer in two articles respectively: Bilgi 1984: 31–96; Bilgi 1990: 119–219, Bilgi 2001: 1–35. The rest were announced in the *Kazı Sonuçları Toplantıları* which were held yearly from 1989 to 2011.

9 Butted spearheads of this period were found jumbled on the clay floor of a burned log-house type dwelling.

10 The remainder of spearheads with a butt were recovered from earthen burials of the graveyard at Mound I; see Bilgi 1984: Fig. 12, 33–36; Bilgi 1990: Fig. 10, 70–75 and Fig. 11, 76–81

11 This chronology is based on Kültepe/Karum – Kayseri stratigraphy and supported by written documents. See Addendum below

brick wall would not be strong enough to bear two bundles of heavy weapons. In the past in the Near East and especially in Anatolia valuable goods would be buried to keep them safe. There are many incidents which show that weapons or coins were put in baked clay pots for safe keeping (Bittel 1940: 183–205). In the case of the Arslantepe hoard the weapons were found together as if ready to be carried away for a long-distance journey by a tradesman. It might be possible that they were buried for the sake of safe keeping from the upper layer belonging to the Early Bronze Age II or III into the level of a layer dated to Early Bronze Age I or Late Chalcolithic Age. It is more likely that the Arslantepe hoard dates to a time when trade within the Anatolian territory began to be very active, especially for metal barter. In the following Middle Bronze Age covering the Assyrian Trade Colonies period this metal barter developed to an international level between North Mesopotamia and Anatolia as well as within Central Anatolia under the control of the leading city at Kültepe/Kanish Karum.

The four-spiralled plaque found together with the hoard indicates the Early Bronze Age III without any question since it shares common features with one of the same type plaques acquired from a burial of the graveyard at İkiztepe (Bilgi 1984: 274 Fig. 18). Also, the damaged clay sealing bearing the shape of a metal plaque with four spirals indicates an Early Bronze Age III date as it was found in a pit belonging to one of the upper building levels (Palmieri 1981: Fig. 10,2). Moreover, a baked clay cylindrical pot stand (Fig. 10) is a common form at Arslantepe (Palmieri 1981: p. 112 Fig. 7.6) and at İkiztepe (Alkım *et al.* 2003: 89 Pl. XL,7, CXXXIII,202) where it was found in a grave dating to the Early Bronze Age III period. They have a white paste filled grooving of different geometric patterns.

Elsewhere, spearheads obtained together with swords indicate an Early Bronze Age III date between the 24th to 21st centuries B.C. They have a straight tang with a butt and a blade and were a common and preferable weapon type as stated above in Caucasus[12], Iran[13] and South[14], South-East[15] and Central[16] Anatolia and from North Syria[17] down to Mesopotamia[18] during the Sumerian Early Dynastic period II. Accordingly, the long-butted spearheads are a late development. In the earlier versions, spearhead butts were short and rather thick. When throwing at a target the spear would be gripped along the wooden shaft, whereas gripping spearheads on the elongated butt is handier and provides a well-balanced throw. This type of spearhead, which was found in the settlement area, was also unearthed in a burial evaluated as a Royal Tomb[19] together with other funerary gifts.[20] Among the other gifts there is pottery with red and black slipped specimens[21]. At İkiztepe highly burnished and black slipped and red and black slipped vessels appeared for the first time in Early Bronze Age II (Fig. 11) and continued to be produced in the following Early Bronze Age III[22]. As examples of this type of pottery were found in the Royal Tomb[23] together with the spearheads they should be dated to the Early Bronze Age III, where variously formed bowls were unearthed especially in women's graves as a burial item[24] at İkiztepe.

12 Bilgi 1987: Fig. XXVIII (Tbilisi), Fig. XXIX (Georgia); Evgeny 2002: Abb.2,4 (Achslziche), Abb.2,5 (Ospirisdi), Abb.2,7 (Zarzis Gora).

13 Bilgi 1987: Fig. XXVI (Tepe Giyan), XXVII (Tureng Tepe).

14 Bilgi 1987: Fig. VII (Soli-Pompeopolis), Fig. VIII (Silifke) and Fig. XV (Tell el Cüdeyde).

15 Bilgi 1987: Tülintepe (Harmankaya 1992: Fig. 1–3), Fig. XI (Hassek), Fig. XII,1–5 (Karkamış), Birecik Dam Cemetery (Sertok 1999: Fig. 10A-B), Başur Höyük (Sağlamtimur 2018: Fig. 8).

16 Bilgi 1987: Fig. I,17 (İkiztepe), Fig. III,1–2 (Horoztepe), Res.V (Kültepe).

17 Bilgi 1987: Fig. 13 (Hammam), Fig. XIV (Kara Hasan), Res.XIX (Til-Barsip), Fig. XXII (Mari), Fig. XXI (Tell-Brak).

18 Bilgi 1987: Fig. XXIV (Ur).

19 Frangipane, et al 2001: 105–139.

20 Frangipane, et al 2001: Fig. 18,1–7 and 10–11.

21 Frangipane, et al 2001: 107 and 113.

22 Alkım, et al 2003: CXLVI,259.

23 Palmieri 1981: 106 and 113; Frangipane, et al 2001: 107.

24 Bilgi 1984: Fig. 18, 278; Bilgi 1990: Fig. 20, 446–451.

In the Royal Tomb an arsenical copper dagger[25] with a solid heft shares common features with the one from İkiztepe[26] (Fig. 13), and it appears to have been produced by a mould of the same form as the one from the Arslantepe tomb.

The sword illustrated in Dr. Frangipane's 2001 report on the Royal Tomb is shown with a short tang[27] instead of a massive hilt. This sword is either an incomplete one or lost its hilt before being placed into the tomb. There are no rivet holes on its tang for a hilt of most probably organic material. The first alternative is a more reasonable option and indicates that the Royal Tomb, which also contains long-butted spearheads is contemporary with the hoard that contains swords in addition to the long-butted spearheads. The shared feature of long-butted spearheads from two different locations at Arslantepe inevitably indicate their contemporary date.

In view of the evidence provided above, the short swords of Arslantepe cannot be conveniently dated to the Late Chalcolithic or the Early Bronze Age I. Most importantly, the metallurgical technology to alloy arsenic with copper and use of moulds to produce objects was simply not known.[28] Moreover, so far, no metal object has yet been shown to have been produced by using a mould as early as the Late Chalcolithic Age or Early Bronze Age I.

On current evidence arsenic was intentionally alloyed from Early Bronze Age II onwards, and this alloy was used to produce large sized objects cast from moulds[29]. In the following Early Bronze Age III arsenical copper alloys and moulding technology were widely used especially throughout the Central Black Sea and Northern regions of the Central Anatolia.[30]

During this later Bronze Age, covering the last quarter of the 3rd millennium B.C. a new trend emerged. Arsenical copper objects begin to be decorated with silver inlay to render their appearance more attractive. The three swords of Arslantepe are decorated with silver inlay similar in technique to the stags from Early Bronze III graves at Alaca Höyük.[31] In fact, although silver is known long before Early Bronze Age II it is more widely used during the last quarter of the 3rd millennium B.C. as sophisticated and unparalleled types of objects in quality and in number reflect the skill of the silver smiths at Alaca Höyük. The silver mining operations at Gümüşhacıköy[32] produced tons of silver slags on the İnegöl Dağları. In the Central Black Sea region lie deposits of copper and at Durağan there is arsenic. These can be considered the main source for the smiths at Alaca Höyük. Because of the proximity of these rich metal sources of copper, arsenic and silver, a solid tradition in metallurgy and smithing skills could have contributed to a pioneering development in silver work at the settlement of Alaca Höyük. Simple silver objects, small in number and quality which were said to be found in the Late Chalcolithic Age settlement at Korucutepe in the Elâzığ region north of Arslantepe, do not shed much light on silver metallurgy. Neither silver metallurgy nor the existence of silver illuminate the date of the swords at Arslantepe, which are said to be indicative of the Late Chalcolithic Age.

After viewing the two hilted short swords[33] of unknown origin presented here (Figs. 1 and 2) it becomes clear that the Arslantepe swords are not limited to Arslantepe or the Malatya region. Almost the same arsenic percentage in their alloy with copper indicates the Central

25 Frangipane, et al 2001: Fig. 18,14.

26 This dagger was also found in a grave of Early Bronze Age III date: Bilgi 1990: Fig. 14,181 and Bilgi 2004: the fourth one in p. 50.

27 Frangipane, *et al.* 2001: Fig. 18,8.

28 Bilgi, Özbal and Yalçın 2004: 15–17.

29 Bilgi, Özbal and Yalçın 2004: 15–17.

30 Bilgi 2004: 48–73.

31 Bilgi 2004: 69.

32 Bilgi, Özbal and Yalçın 2004: the last photo in p. 33.

33 The existence of a third one (Fig. 3) has just been reported from Italy. An exactly identical short sword was found at the museum of a Venetian monastery on the island of San Lazzaro degli Armeni in Italy. It is 43 cm in length, also produced with arsenical copper alloy with 1 % percentage of arsenic.

Black Sea as a regional characteristic and it is here where copper and arsenic mineralizations were located. The richest and most accessible arsenic deposits located up to the present day are without question in Anatolia and not in the territory of Transcaucasia.

In the coastal and inland zones of the Central Black Sea region, including adjacent areas of Northern Central Anatolia to the south are where thousands of arsenical copper objects[34], dating after the Early Bronze Age I period, were acquired. This claim is supported by Ufuk Esin's painstaking work using spectral analyses on various objects.[35] Recently a fragment of orpiment-realgar ore acquired in the Resuloğlu excavations points to arsenic deposits in the inland Central Black Sea region.[36] It is quite possible that the Arslantepe swords together with the funerary spearheads found in the Royal Tomb were produced somewhere in these mountainous and metalliferous regions, and the arsenic used in sword production was obtained from the inland Black Sea region. From Malatya (Arslantepe) it is easier to reach the rich arsenic deposits by following the Kızılırmak River than to go to Transcaucasia. One needs only follow the Kızılırmak valley starting in the Sivas region just north of Malatya and travel as far as the town of Durağan where the arsenic deposit was located.

Arsenic ore mineralization (realgar or orpiment) is very easily crushed into powder. In that form it is much easier to transport as opposed to another type of arsenic ore, such as arsenopyrite. Arsenic alloying was a highly sophisticated process and should be viewed as a major feature of metallurgical processing that adopted high standards. This technology that dominated in the Central Black Sea region merits close consideration as an industrial zone with İkiztepe at its centre from 2800 B.C. onwards in Anatolia[37]. Its inhabitants were mainly engaged in metallurgical activities in addition to textile production as over 4000 baked clay loom weights indicate. In this respect the people should be considered as industrialists, not farmers or herdsmen. They obtained ample nutrition by fishing in the nearby lagoons and hunting games in the forest surrounding the settlement.

Because of their convenient access to food, the people of İkiztepe presumably had more than enough time to devote themselves to metallurgical activity, its development, and the production of high-quality objects. Mild climate and abundant fuel from the forest along the coastline of the Central Black Sea were surely other advantages of their lifestyle. The Kızılırmak River which flows to the sea through a long valley provided a natural route to reach inner lands and metal sources.

Lastly it can be said without any hesitation that in the last quarter of the 4th millennium B.C. in Anatolia a new type of weapon, namely hilted short swords, emerged together with two already existing main weapons: spearheads and daggers. The Arslantepe specimens, and the three swords suggested here could be used specifically in close combat. The numbers of examples of this new weapon will surely increase in time as new excavations are carried out in the future in the vast area south of Central Black Sea extending from the vicinity of Tokat in the East to Sinop in the West and to Çorum in South, encompassing of course the arsenic mines.

Addendum

During the last decade, a number of written works in connection with the archaeological excavations at İkiztepe appeared in different years. A few of them are subjects of dissertation theses[38], others are correlations based on arsenical copper objects with the other Anatolian

34 Bilgi 1984: Fig. 18, 271–277; Bilgi 1990: Fig. 1, 439–445; Bilgi 2001: Tables 1–28

35 Esin 1969: 121 (Ahlatlıbel), 122–123 (Alaca Höyük), 124–127 (Alişar Höyük), 134 (Horoz Tepe), 135 (Kayapınar), 141 (Mahmatlar); Perk 2014.

36 Dardeniz 2020: Fig. 8.

37 Özbal *et al.* 2001: 29–40; Özbal *et al.* 2002: 43–46.

38 Selover 2015; Welton 2010.

settlement's specimens[39], and the rest are on the Early Bronze Age III graveyard and its skeletons from osteological (Özdemir *et al.* 2010: 1–9), genomic[40] and pathological[41] perspectives. First of all, one should know that all the items unearthed, and their disclosed illustrations are under the copyright protection act according to International and Turkish legislation and royalties. They should not be copied or used in any event, even if they have been published, without the written permission of the Director of excavations at İkiztepe. Just to give a short reference or a note from where they were copied is not authorization allowing anyone to use them. Moreover, the data and results, which were obtained from the excavations and deduced evaluations, belong to the Director according to "intellectual property rights" by law and should not be used without any citation or permission.

Despite, the above-mentioned copyright and intellectual property rights acts, the owners/writers who are responsible in their written work, mentioned in footnote 2 did not obtain any written permission or acknowledgement from the Director Önder Bilgi to use data and visuals obtained at the İkiztepe excavations carried out between 1974 and 2016. Moreover, these people boldly altered the date of the graveyard from Early Bronze Age III at Mound I to Late Chalcolithic Age/Early Bronze Age I period without giving specific reasons or explanations in their work. It is very clear that they did not bother to read the published yearly reports on İkiztepe, and papers read at symposiums and later published with relevant details. It is obvious that they engaged in this wrongdoing intentionally to profit from scholarly or academic benefits and to promote their misleading theories. No one, either a researcher or an academic, has the right to alter the data obtained scientifically from excavations such as İkiztepe. Surely, one can legitimately put forward critical views so long as they are based on valid interpretations and refer to publications. However, no one has the authority to change stratigraphical facts.

Because of this irresponsible attitude, this addendum is intended to notify these writers that they should remain respectful of scientific fieldwork and review their results and evaluations based on facts, not theories.[42] Their erroneous claims should not serve as a basis of wrong data and concepts for future researchers who wish to study İkiztepe's history.

This addendum seeks to clarify the chronology of specific periods established during 40 years of excavation at Ikiztepe's prehistoric settlement. The chronological scheme at İkiztepe is based on a carefully studied stratigraphy of succeeding cultural layers that equate with an accepted time frame for Anatolian prehistory. At İkiztepe the stratigraphical sequence was established by deep soundings on three different mounds out of four. Accordingly, at "Mound I" the earliest period lying on the virgin soil dates to the Early Bronze Age I layer. Immediately on top of this layer there are the Early Bronze Age II period remains.

Around 650 simple earthen burials in different depths of a graveyard of nearly 2 metres in thickness belonging to the Early Bronze Age III period lay on top of the previous Early Bronze Age II layer and below the later overlying layer of the Middle Bronze Age. The Middle Bronze Age layer contained fast-wheel-made pottery slipped in pale red or buff colour (so-called Hittite ware), and typical of the Old Assyrian Trade Colonies Period in the four Karum building levels at Kültepe-Kanesh.

At Mound II, the second highest and excavated down to virgin soil, revealed that the earliest layer is Late Chalcolithic. The succeeding periods are Early Bronze Age I and II, followed by the Middle Bronze Age like at Mound I. At Mound III only cultural remains of two peri-

39 Klaunzer 2017 141–150.

40 Skourtanioti *et al.* 2020: 1198–1175.

41 Irvine *et al.* 2019: 253–263; Key *et al.* 2020.

42 Anyone who has any doubts regarding the stratigraphy at İkiztepe, which correlates with the current chronology for Anatolian prehistory, can visit the settlement to see with bare eyes the very well-preserved stratification on the northern wall section of Trench "M" as seen in the visual illustration in Fig. 14.

ods were identified. The first one is Early Bronze Age II that sits on the virgin soil, and the second one is Early Bronze Age III immediately on top of the first.

Based on this stratification, a Late Chalcolithic Age settlement was located only on Mound II, while Early Bronze Age I settlements are attested on Mounds I and II. Early Bronze Age II settlements were revealed on Mounds I, II and III (Fig. 14), and an Early Bronze Age III settlement is encountered only at Mound III. The latest Middle Bronze Age settlements are at Mound I and II. With the support of pottery and to a certain extent some 14C dates[43] the periods of these settlements are dated as follows: Late Chalcolithic Age 4300 – 3200 B.C., Early Bronze Age I 3200 – 2800 B.C., Early Bronze Age II 2800 – 2400 B.C., Early Bronze Age III 2400 – 2100 B.C. The Middle Bronze Age 2100 – 1700 B.C. covers the chronological sequence of four layers at Kültepe/Kanesh-Karum. Here historical written documents have supported their dates.

Excavations suggest that the occupants of the burials that contained especially personal metal belongings in the graveyard located at Mound I below the Middle Bronze Age layer appear to have lived at Mound III. The earliest deceased individuals were buried in the latest building level of the Early Bronze Age II period. Before the Early Bronze Age III period deceased individuals were buried intra-murally under the earthen floors inside buildings. No graves other than a few pot-burials for infants/babies have been detected belonging to Late Chalcolithic or following Early Bronze Age I settlement at İkiztepe.

Using established chronology at İkiztepe, the quadruple spiral plaque of arsenical copper acquired together with the weapons of spearheads and swords at Arslantepe should be dated to Early Bronze Age III, that is the last quarter of the 3rd Millennium B.C., as 14 of these plaques were found in burials of Early Bronze Age III date at İkiztepe. These quadruple spiral plaques were found only with male adult and child graves, and hence, they did not belong to warriors as some researchers recently proposed (Klaunzer 2017: 144). As discussed above in the main pages there are other objects which share common features. Among them are the red and black polished bowls found only in female burials at Ikiztepe. The earliest examples of this kind of vessel appeared for the first time in the beginning of Early Bronze Age II period at a time when the high quality of especially cast weapons started to appear and were found inside the buildings scattered randomly on floors.

In the light of the evidence provided above one cannot logically date the İkiztepe quadruple plaques to the Late Chalcolithic/Early Bronze Age I period. These unique objects have been proposed as symbols of power (Bilgi 2019: 6–7) of local rulers and were clearly local products. Their superior manufacture and quality underscore their role as elite family objects. If they are dated to the Late Chalcolithic/Early Bronze Age I period, as at Arslantepe, people living at Mound I during this time would have to go forward into future, to upper Early Bronze Age III time, bury a deceased habitant with a plaque and come back down to original period. As this action is impossible to carry out, it is likewise not acceptable to date the İkiztepe burials earlier than Early Bronze Age III. In Turkish there is a saying; you cannot put the horse behind the cart and expect the cart to function properly.

Other evidence which supports the impossibility of dating the quadruple plaque to Late Chalcolithic or Early Bronze Age I layers is a potsherd from Ikiztepe depicting a standing female figure in relief. This potsherd was found in the early horizon of Early Bronze Age I at Mound I. The figure is shown frontally with a disc over her head decorated with cross lines and surrounding stubbed dots running around the disc border (Fig. 15). The most significant feature of the figure is her head in the shape

43 Alkım *et al.* 2003: 143–144. The dates reported there obtained at Ankara ODTU and Hacettepe Universities and Berlin Akademie der Wissenschaften der DDR Zentral-Institut für Alte Geschichte und Archäologie.

of a triangle (Bilgi 2014: 151 Fig. R15). In this respect she recalls the female figure drawn with multi-colour paints on either side of the main gate leading to the Temple entrance at Arslantepe dated by the excavators to the Late Uruk period, that is to Late Chalcolithic/Early Bronze Age I (Frangipane 1993: pp. 54–55). She is presumed to be in a seated posture, but her most relevant feature is her triangular head (Fig. 16) as in the İkiztepe example.

In addition to the above, four circular clay structures with a central pit were constructed on well-plastered rectangular clay platforms which are particular to İkiztepe and share common features with the one example unearthed in a large room of a mudbrick building at Arslantepe (Frangipane 2014: Figs.1 and 5a). At İkiztepe these circular structures, which belong to the end of Early Bronze Age I/beginning of Early Bronze Age II were unearthed in log-house type buildings. One of them yielded a baked clay cup in its central pit, which might be taken as an indication of a cult ceremony or a simple libation activity. Similarly, the Arslantepe circular clay structure might also have been constructed for serving at a similar cult procedure during the building VIB1 time of the Early Bronze Age and suggests a cultural link with that of social life at İkiztepe.

In the Early Bronze I layer at İkiztepe, contemporary with the female figure, just simple copper tools and pins were found. It is only some 600 years later in time that types of very sophisticated weaponry such as spearheads and daggers make their appearance, as they did at Arslantepe's settlement of the Temple layer. All this leads to a major conclusion. The short swords together with long-butted spearheads and the quadruple spiral plaque of Arslantepe (which can be equated with the appearance of similar examples from İkiztepe) cannot be dated to the beginning of the 3rd millennium B.C. Rather, they belong to a period after the middle of the 3rd millennium B.C., somewhere in the neighbourhood of 2400 B.C.

The high plateau in the Black Sea region bordered by mountains in the north and extending parallel to the coastline of the Black Sea is rich in arsenic and copper deposits. It is here where various types of unparalleled and sophisticated arsenical copper spearheads were produced, and it is this region that should also be considered the homeland of the recently acquired three short swords.

Bibliography

Alkım. U. B., H. Alkım and Ö. Bilgi
- 1988 *Ikiztepe I*, Ankara.
- 2003 *Ikiztepe II*, Ankara.

Bilgi, Ö.
- 1984 "Metal Objects from İkiztepe-Turkey," *Beiträge zur Allgemeinen und Vergleichenden Archäologie* 6, Bonn, pp. 31–96.
- 1985 "Boğumlu Mızrak Uçlarının Dağılışının Işığı Altında Anadolu Mezopotamya İlişkileri," *XXXIV Assiroloji Kongresi*, İstanbul, pp. 377–382.
- 1990 "Metal Objects from İkiztepe-Turkey," *Beiträge zur Allgemeinen und Vergleichenden Archäologie* 9–10, Bonn, pp. 119–219.
- 2001 "Orta Karadeniz Bölgesi Protohistorik Çağ Maden Sanatının Kökeni ve Gelişimi," *Belleten 242*: pp. 1–35 Ankara
- 2004 *Anatolia, Cradle of Castings*, Istanbul.
- 2014 *Anthropomorphic Representations in Anatolia Before the Classical Age*, İstanbul.
- 2019 "Gücün Sembolü," *Aktüel Arkeoloji* 68, pp. 6–7.

Bilgi, Ö., H. Özbal and Ü. Yalçın
- 2004 *Anatolia, Cradle of Castings*, Istanbul.

Bittel K.
- 1940 "Der Depotfund von Soli-Pompeiopolis," *Zeitschrift für Assyriologie und Vorderasiatische Archäologie 12 (Band 46)*, pp. 183–203.

Caneva, C and A. Palmieri
- 1983 "Metal work at Arslantepe in Late Chalcolithic and Early Bronze I: Evidence from Metal Analysis," *Origini 12,2*, pp. 637–654.

Chernykh, E. N.
- 1992 *Ancient Metallurgy in the USSR*, Cambridge.

Dardeniz, G.
- 2020 "Why Did the Use of Antimony-Bearing Alloys in Bronze Age Anatolia Fall Dormant After the Early Bronze Age? A Case from Resuloğlu (Çorum, Turkey)," PLoS ONE 15(7):

e0234563. https://doi.org/10.1371/journal.pone.0234563
Esin, E.
- 1969 *Kuantitatif Spektral Analiz Yardımıyla Anadolu'da Başlangıcından Asur Kolonileri Çağına Kadar Bakır ve Tunç Madenciliği. Cilt I:* Kısım I ve II, Istanbul.
Evgeny, N. *et al.*
- 2002 "Metallurgy of the Circumpontic Area: From Unity to Disintegration," in Ü. Yalçın (ed.), *Der Anschnitt 15, Anatolian Metal II*, Bochum, pp. 83–100.
Frangipane, M
- 1985 "Early Developments of Metallurgy in the Near East," in *Studi di Paletnologia in onore Salvatore Puglisi*1, Roma, pp. 215–228.
- 1993 *Arslantepe, Hierapolis, Iasos, Kyme, Marsilio*, Rome.
- 2014 "After Collapse: Continuity and Disruption in the Settlement by Kura-Araxes-Linked Pastoral Groups at Arslantepe-Malatya (Turkey)," *Paléorient 40,2*, pp. 162–189.
- 2019 "Arslantepe. The Rise and Development of a Political Centre: From Temple to Palace to a Fortified Citadel," *Proceedings of the 1. International Archaeology Symposium 2018*, Malatya, pp. 71–104
Frangipane, M., *et al.*
- 2001 "New Symbols of a New Power in a Royal Tomb from 3000 B.C. Arslantepe, Malatya (Turkey)," *Paleorient: 27,2*, pp. 105–139.
Harmankaya, S.
- 1992 "Tülintepe Höyüğü (Elazığ) Maden Buluntuları," *Arkeometri Sonuçları Toplantısı VII*, pp. 369–379.
Irvine, B., Y. S. Erdal and M. P. Richards
- 2019 "Dietary habits in the Early Bronze Age (3rd millennium B.C.) of Anatolia: A multi-isotopic approach," *Journal of Archaeological Science Reports* 24, pp. 253–263;
Key, F. M. *et al.*
- 2020 "Emergence of Human-Adapted Salmonella Enterica is Linked to the Neolithization Process". *Nature Ecology & Evolution*, https://doi.org/10.1038/s41559-020-1106-9
Klaunzer, M.
- 2017 "A New Player in the game? An Archaeological and archaeometallurgical approach in detecting long distance relations in Late Chalcolithic Anatolia". The TITaK conferences 2013–2014: Raw Materials, Innovations, Technology of Ancient Cultures". Der *Anschnitt 34*, pp. 141–150 Bochum.
Kushnareva, K. and T. Chubinisvilli
- 1970 *Drevnie kulturi yuzhnogo Kavkaza (The Ancient Cultures of Southern Caucasus)*, Leningrad
Özdemir, K., Y. S. Erdal and Ş Demirci
- 2010 "Arsenic Accumulation on the Bones in the Early Bronze Age Ikiztepe Population, Turkey". *Journal of Archaeological Science* 30, pp. 1–9
Özbal, Ö., A. M. Adriaens, B. Earl and B. Gedik
- 1999 "Samsun, Amasya, Tokat İlleri Yüzey Araştırmaları," *Uluslararası Kazı, Araştırma ve Arkeometri Sempozyumu 21*, pp. 47–54.
- *2000 Arkeometri Sonuçları Toplantısı 16*, pp. 29–40.
Özbal, H. *et al.*
- 2001 "Durağan ve Bakırçay Arsenik Cevherleşmesinin Jeolojik, Mineralojik ve Kimyasal İncelenmesi," *22. Uluslararası Kazı ve Arkeometri Sempozyumu*, pp. 29–40.
Özbal, H., A. Adriaans, B. Earl and B. Gedik
- 2002 "Metallurgy at Ikiztepe," ib Ü. Yalçın (ed.), *Der Anschnitt 15* Anatolian Metal II, Bochum, pp. 39–48.
Palmieri, A.
- 1981 "Excavations at Arslantepe (Malatya),"*Anatolian Studies 31*, pp. 101–119.
Perk, H.
- 2014 *The Anatolian Early Bronze Age Collective Founding in the Haluk Perk Museum Collection*, Istanbul.
- 2014 *Proceedings of International Conference; Problems of Early Metal Age Archaeology of Caucasus and Anatolia*, Tbilisi.
Sağlamtimur, H. and M. G. M. Massimino
- 2018 "Wealth Sacrifice and Legitimacy: The Case of the Early Bronze Age Başur Höyük Cemetery (South-eastern Turkey," in *Proceedings of the 10th International Congress on the Archaeology of the Ancient Near East*, Wien, pp. 25–29.
Schachner, A.
- 2002 "Zur Entwicklung der Metallurgie im östlichen Transkaukasien (Azerbaycan und Nahcivan) wahrend des 4. Und 3. Jahrtausends v. Chr, *Der Anschnitt 15* Anatolian Metal II, Bochum, pp. 115–130.
Selimkhanov, I. R.
- 1962 Spectral Analyses of Metallic Articles from Archaeological Monuments of Caucasus,

Proceedings of the Prehistoric Society 28, pp. 68–79.

Selover, S. L.

– 2015 *Excavating War: The Archaeology of Conflict in Early Chalcolithic to Early Bronze in Central and Southeastern Anatolia*, Unpublished Dissertation, University of Chicago.

Sertok, K. and R. Ergeç

– 1999 "A New Early Bronze Age Cemetery," *Anatolica 25*, pp. 87–107.

Skourtanioti, E., Y. S. Erdal, M. Frangipane, P. W. Stockhammer, W. Haak and J. Krause

– 2020 "Genomic History of Neolithic to Bronze Age Anatolia, Northern Levant, and Southern Caucasus," *CELL 181,5*, pp. 1198–1175

Strabo

– 1987 *Coğrafya, Anadolu Kitap XII*, İstanbul (Çeviren A. Pekman)

Welton, M. L.

– 2010 *Mobility and Social Organization on the Ancient Anatolian Black Sea Coast: An Archaeological, Spatial and Isotopic Investigation of the Cemetery at İkiztepe, Turkey*, Unpublished PhD thesis, Univ. of Toronto.

Zimmermann, T. *et al.*

– 2011 "Ein neues Schwert vom Typus, Arslantepe" – Frühmetallzeitliche Waffentechnologie zwischen Reparation und Rituali," *PZ* 86, pp. 1–7.

– 2015 "Arslantepe" Tipinde Bir kılıç ve Altın-Zümrüt Yüzük," *Aktüel Arkeoloji* 45, pp. 58–59.

Fig. 1. Sword of Perk Museum, Ö. Bilgi archive.

Fig. 2. Sword of Tokat Museum; Zimmermann et al 201. Abb.1e.

Fig. 3. Sword of the Monastery Museum on San Lazzaro degli Armeni-Venice; Ca' Foscari University of Venice/ Andrea Avezzù.

Fig. 4. Arsenical copper short swords of Arslantepe; Palmieri 1981. Fig. 3,1–4.

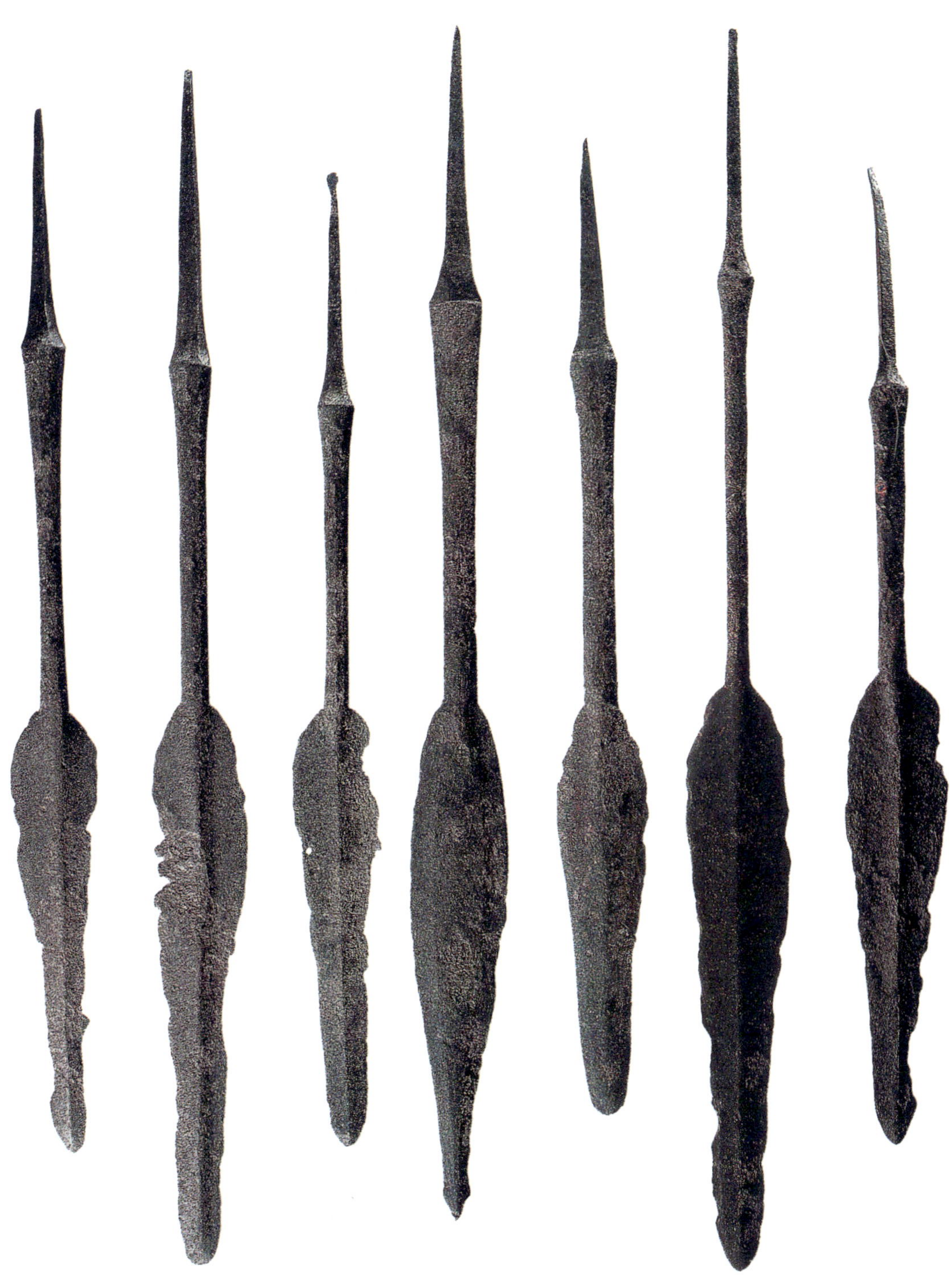

Fig. 5. Arsenical copper long-butted spearheads with straight tangs of Arslantepe; Palmieri 1981. Fig. 4.

Fig. 6. A male burial of Early Bronze Age III with an arsenical copper quadruple plaque at Ikiztepe; Ö. Bilgi archive.

Fig. 7a. Arsenopyrite source at Bakacıktepe/Tavşandağ-Merzifon; H. Özbal archive.

Fig. 7b. Arsenopyrite ore from Bakacıktepe/Tavşandağ-Merzifon; H. Özbal archive.

Fig. 8a. Arsenic mineralization near Gökdoğan/Durağan – Sinop; Ö. Bilgi archive.

Fig. 8b. Arsenic mineralization near Gökdoğan/Durağan – Sinop; Ö. Bilgi archive.

Fig. 9a. Arsenic ore (realgar) from Gökdoğan/Durağan source; Ö. Bilgi archive.

Fig. 9b. Arsenic ore (orpiment) from Gökdoğan/Durağan source; Ö. Bilgi archive.

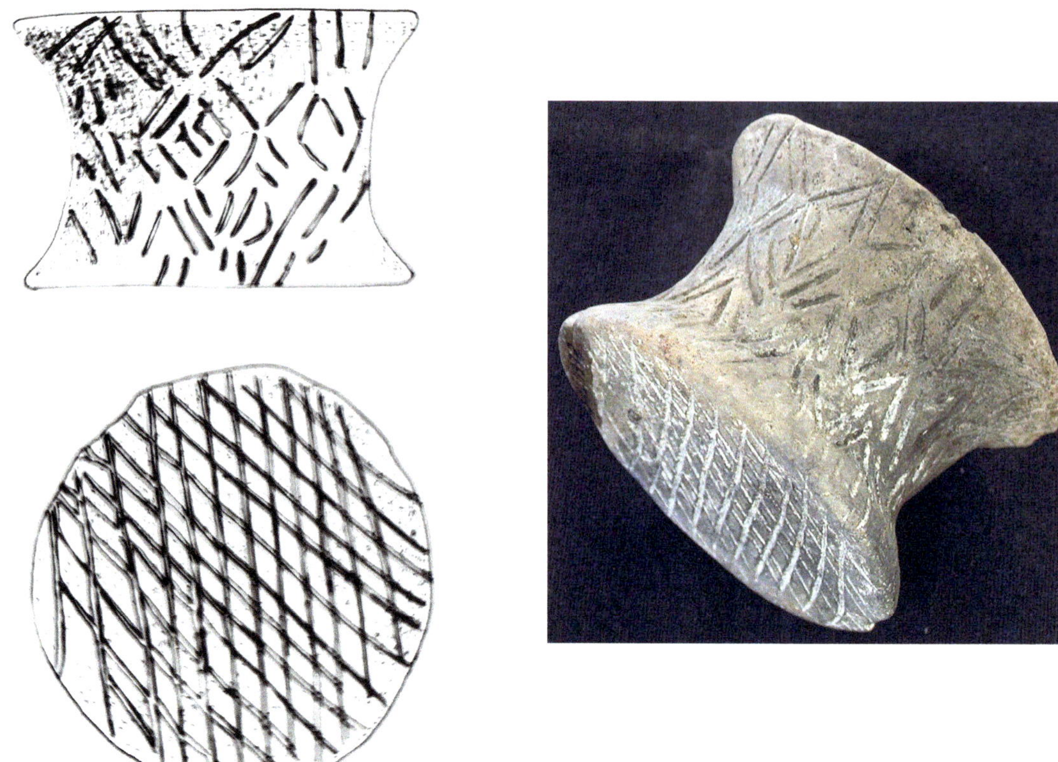

Fig. 10. Baked clay pot stand from Ikiztepe; Ö. Bilgi archive; Ö. Bilgi archive.

Fig. 11. Black slipped and highly burnished baked clay jug with a high neck; Ö. Bilgi archive.

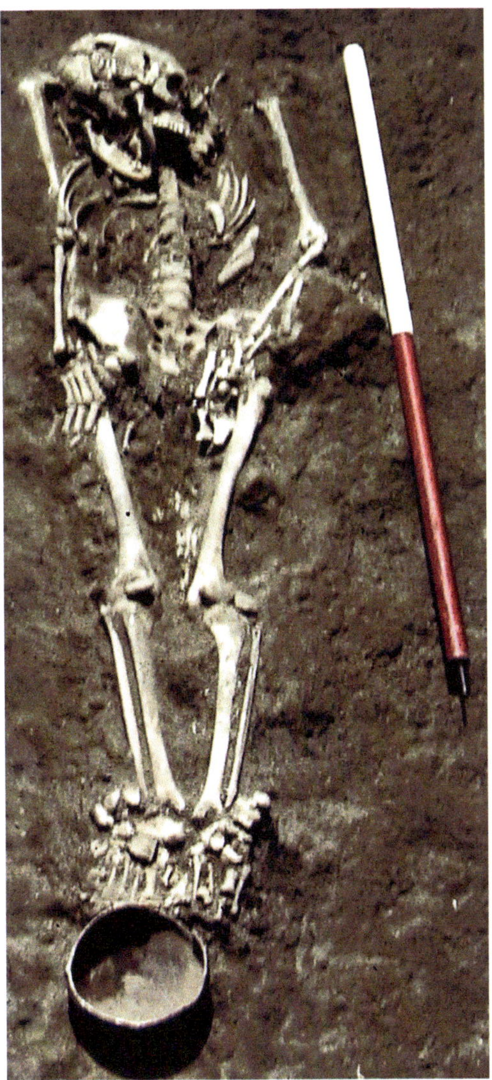

Fig. 12. An Early Bronze Age III burial of a woman with a black-red slipped bowl; Ö. Bilgi archive.

Fig. 13. Arsenical copper dagger from İkiztepe; Ö. Bilgi archive.

Fig. 14. İkiztepe stratigraphic structure of the Early and Middle Bronze Age layers on northern wall section of the Trench "M" at Mound I; Ö. Bilgi archive.

Fig. 15. Female Figurine relief from İkiztepe, Ö. Bilgi archive.

Fig. 16. Wall Painting from Arslantepe; Frangipane 1993. pp. 54–55.

Fig. 17. Sacred place in the form of a clay plastered circular structure with a central pit for a vessel at İkiztepe Mound II, Alkım, et al 2003. Pl. CXXX, p. 186.

Mountain Cult in Hittite Cuneiform Texts

*Özlem Sir Gavaz**

With my regards and respect to dear Dr. Sachihiro Omura, who contributed much to Anatolian Archaeology by all scientific studies he carried out and excavations he led until today ...

Abstract

It is concluded from Hittite texts that there was a very busy annual festival calendar. The rituals and esoteric cults performed during the ceremonies were of paramount importance to please and relieve the gods. These ceremonies also allowed the Hittite King to prove his power and authority, and the king made a show of strength for both his own people and enemy states. In the Hittite period, most of the feasts were performed in temples located in various cult centers, especially in the capital Hattusa. Some of the feasts were celebrated outdoors by a river, at a road junction, in a forested area or on a mountain top. In the Hittite world of belief, mountains symbolise power, magnificence, potency, eternity, immortality accordingly divinity. In this article, Hittite texts were examined, and an evaluation was made on god-mountain perception and king-mountain relationship. In addition, a few examples were shared on the fact that some special rituals performed during the Hittite period still survive in Anatolia.

Öz

Hititçe metinlerden, yıllık bayram takviminin çok yoğun olduğu anlaşılmaktadır. Bayramlar sırasında icra edilen ritüeller ve ezotorik kültler, tanrıları memnun etmek ve yatıştırmak için son derece önemlidir. Bu merasimler aynı zamanda Hitit kralına gücünü ve otoritesini ispatlama fırsatı da vermekte, kral hem kendi halkına hem de düşman ülkelere karşı bir gövde gösterisi yapmaktadır. Hititlerde bayramların çoğu, başkent *Hattuša* başta olmak üzere çeşitli kült merkezlerinde bulunan tapınaklarda gerçekleştirilir. Bayramların bir kısmı ise açık havada bir nehir kenarında, bir yol kavşağında, ormanlık bir alanda ya da bir dağ tepesinde kutlanmaktadır. Dağlar, Hitit inanç dünyasında, gücü, ihtişamı, kudreti, sonsuzluğu, ölümsüzlüğü ve dolayısıyla tanrısallığı simgelemektedir. Makalede örnek Hititçe metinler incelenerek, tanrı-dağ algısı ve kral-dağ bağlantısı üzerine bir değerlendirme yapılmıştır. Ayrıca Hititler zamanında yapılan bazı özel ritüellerin, Anadolu'da hala uygulama alanı bulduğuna dair de birkaç örnek paylaşılmıştır.

Mircea Eliade argues that "*A meaningful world is a result of a dialectical process which is called the reflection of the holy*" (Eliade 2015: 13). In this regard, the existence of God becomes meaningful for an ancient human being when it appears in any shape and condition and makes its presence felt. In other words, God may appear sometimes in the middle of an awe-inspiring ritual, during a ritual sacrifice, after a purification ritual performed by a river, on a holy stone or at a holy tree, at a cult ceremony performed on a mountain peak. Thus, the closer a human being gets to God, the more meaningful his/her life becomes. Therefore, the Hittites wished to become closer to Gods, to satisfy them, to protect themselves and their country from evils and disasters when performing the festivals, which were covering almost more than half of a year (Sir Gavaz 2012: 39; Ünal 2003: 92). In addition, there were a number of important religious activities to prove the absolute authority of the king and to announce the permanent

* Ankara University, Department of Hittitology.

power of the state to the whole world, especially to its own people. Hittite kings, who are believed to be the representative of God while living and to have become deities after death, become integrated with God during these rituals they perform for gods. Drinking ceremonies performed during feast ceremonies are one of the methods to integrate with God, and kings believe that they are equipped with some power and authorities as if they were reborn after these rituals (Sir Gavaz 2017: 87; cf. Heffron 2014: 165–185).

"*[Kin]g drinks [Ašga]šipa mountain from its standing lion (shaped) golden BIBRU (ryton). [Singer]s sing songs. Mag[ici]ans sing. The Kit[a] man calls. A cupbeare[r] brings a sacrificial bread from the door.*" (KUB 1.17 rev. V 28'–34'; Badali 1991: 16). As understood from this text, the king performs a drinking ceremony by standing, and drinks *Ašgašipa* mountain from its lion shaped drinking cup. The holiness and divinity attributed to the *Ašgašipa* mountain is seen clearly. As the king drinks it (in his honour), he is almost integrated with it. In addition, other activities performed at that time, namely the singing of the singers, the awe-inspiring shouts of clergies and the presentation of the sacrificial bread show that the ritual is performed as a whole. In a similar part of the text, the queen and the king drink *Piškurunuwa* Mountain God: "*[The king (and) the queen drink the God Piškurunuwa (Mountain)] by [sitting].*" (KUB 25.6+2 rev. V 2'-3'; Badali 1991: 31).[1]

On the other hand, the fact that King "wears a god's dress" during ceremonies indicates that he has probably assumed a divine function (Ardzinba 2010: 71): "*When it is dawn, the King wears 'the God's cult clothes, cloak (jacket?) and a dressing (shirt?) and wears its belt in Nerik.*"[2] (Bo 2839 obv. III 24'-28'; Haas 1970: 260–61; KUB 58.33 see Košak 1990: 147). Thus, the king symbolises the "God" not only after death but also during rituals. Unfortunately, there is not a sufficient amount of evidence on this issue. However, the ceremonies performed for the gods consist of a number of special rituals to be closer to the God/gods and to integrate with them. In this respect, the rituals performed by going up to the roof (šuhha-) of temple or *halentuwa* and the rituals performed on mountains should relate to the wish to establish a direct connection with the gods (Ardzinba 2010: 84).

In Hittite texts, the following words "Hit. *kalmar-, /kalmara-* Hur. */pappenna-/ papan-/ pappi*" stand for "mountain". What is more, "HUR.SAG", which is frequently observed in texts, is a determinative used before mountains and mountain names in Sumerian Language (Rüster and Neu 1989: 325; Ünal 2016: 251, 393, 672). Among the Hittites, most of the feasts were performed in temples located in various cult centres, especially in the capital *Hattuša*. Some of the feasts were celebrated outdoors by a river, at a road junction, in a forested area or on the top of a mountain. Therefore, some cult cities were called after the mountains located nearby. For example, *Zippalanda* city is called by *D/Taha* Mountain while *Arinna* city is called by *Hulla* Mountain[3]. The rituals performed on top of mountains and the mountain gods in the pantheon (Haas 1994: 461.) show the holiness attributed to mountains. Moreover, Hittite Kings have the names of the *Arnuwanda*, *Ammuna* and *Tuthaliya* (Fig. 1) mountains (De Martino 2019: 206). According to the Hittite texts, mountains were either gods themselves or cult places where gods lived or gathered. God-mountains are frequently mentioned in oath sections of state agreements, and

1 29' [...$^{HUR.SAG}$*Ga]ši-pa-an e-ku-zi* Badali, 1991: 16. The mountain mentioned here should be *Ašgašipa* Mountain, see Monte and Tischler, 1978: 47; Monte 1992: 15.

2 A different suggestion for translation: "*As soon as it dawns, in the city of Nerik they open (the royal wardrobe) and the king puts on the divine clothes, the shirt and the festive garb and fastens (them) by means of a belt*" Thank you to Ahmet Ünal for this suggestion.

3 For Hittite text sections mentioning about $^{HUR.SAG}$*Hulla/Hula* Mountain, see Monte and Tischler 1978: 114; Monte 1992: 40; *Hulla* is a holy mountain in *Arinna* region. In addition, *Hulla* Mountain is seen in the list of gods of *Arinna* city in KBo 9.98 obv. I 1ff. Popko 2009: 33.

some mountain gods are seen to be the servers of the Storm God (Bryce 2003: 163). The most known ones of these are described at the main stage of Chamber A in Yazılıkaya. The Storm God is located above the mountain gods, which are assumed to be (*Tešup*) *Namni* and *Hazzi*[4] (Seeher 2011: 65)[5] (Fig. 2). The Hittites believed that mountains carried Hittite gods on their backs and they enabled the establishment of relationships between gods and human beings. This is observed clearly in *Hattuša*. In this regard, the actual Hittite settlement was established not in the valley, but on the slope above, that is, in the mountainous part. The upper city founded here is entirely dedicated to religious purposes (for commentary see Roller 2004: 60; see Mellink 1991: 130).

Thought to be very close to the capital *Hattuša, Tapala* Mountain[6] is included in the cult route, covering the places visited by Hittite King during some feasts. When the king goes to the mountain, he performs a number of ceremonies inside the tent, prepared before, and celebrates the arrival of spring: "When king goes to *Tapala mountain in spring, tents are set up beforehand. When the king arrives at the Tapala mountain, he goes into the tent*" (KUB 20.85 obv. I 1–6; Sir Gavaz 2012: 188). In the text numbered KBo 30.69 in which AN.TAH.ŠUM feast is described, a ritual performed with the participation of the king and queen on the *Tapala* Mountain is mentioned: "*Queen sits. King offers (drinking) in a cup for the Tapala Mountain and the Tapala Mountain God, God Maliya, Guardian God of the Seven Gods and God Wašuma named after kurtalli*[7] *by standing up. The singers from Kaneš sing songs. Cupbearer takes the thick sacrificial bread and gives it to the oracle. The oracle puts it on its place.*" (KBo 30.69 rev. III 22–30; Popko and Taracha 1988: 84; Haas 1994: 813, f.n. 219)[8]. As it is seen, drinking and bread are offered to many gods, especially the God of *Tapala* Mountain, in the celebrations held on top of the mountain with the participation of king and queen.

During the AN.TAH.ŠUM feast, one of the frequent destinations of king while going over *Tahurpa* to *Hattuša* is *Tippuwa* mountain[9]. It is also mentioned in the text about a tent set up on a mountain (Sir Gavaz 2012: 99). What is more, a god statue placed inside a tent is mentioned: "*If the king came to Hattuša from Tahurpa for the feast of* AN.TAH.ŠUM *in the spring, the stele was placed in the tent before he arrived in Tippuwa.*" (KUB 10.18 obv. I 1–5; Badali 1991: 37).

These sections of the text show that mountains were used as cult places and a number of cult activities were performed sometimes outdoors and sometimes inside the tents set up. In KBo 2.1 rev. III 13, *huwaši* stone of the Šaluwanta[10] mountain was mentioned (Carter 1962: 56). We think that *huwaši* stones are one of the signs of gods on the earth. It is known from the texts that these stones were offered sacrifices, drinking libation was conducted, gods' statues were placed on them, and the Hittite kings showed respect to these stones (Sir Gavaz 2020: 178). Erected in different places generally during feast celebrations, these stones play an important role in ceremonies. In Hittite texts, *huwaši* stones are generally described in an outdoor forested land, by a river or a mountainside as specified in the sample text above. Although no mountain name is provided in some parts of the text, it is understood that these holy stones are also consecrated on high hills and thus above mountains by means of the following expressions: "*when king approaches city, he does not*

4 The mountains, mentioned in oath sections of agreement texts with the Storm God and its bulls Šeri and *Hurri, Namni* and *Hazzi*. Güterbock 1943: 280.

5 For these mountain gods, see KUB 33.108; Haas 1994: 463.

6 For Hittite text sections mentioning about $^{\text{HUR.SAG}}$*Tapala* Mountain, see Monte and Tischler 1978: 397; Monte 1992: 158.

7 *kurtalli-* "a god's name" see Ünal 2016: 300.

8 See also Bo 5480 4–1; Popko and Taracha 1988: 86.

9 For Hittite text parts mentioning $^{\text{HUR.SAG}}$*Tipuwa* Mountain, see Monte and Tischler 1978: 427. Monte 1992: 170.

10 For Hittite text parts referring to $^{\text{HUR.SAG}}$Šaluwanta Mountain, see Monte and Tischler, 1978: 337; Monte 1992: 136.

go to city, but meets with the Storm God's huwaši stones by going through upper road." "King gets in his chariot and climbs to the Storm God's huwaši stones" (Müller-Karpe and Müller-Karpe 2013: 220–221), *"and he (the king) rides on a horse, goes up to the huwaši stone of the god Anziliya."* (KUB 7.25 obv. I 6–7; Ertem 1965: 38). In addition, in one more part of the sample text and in KUB 7.24 obv. 4, the following is stated: *"And they place his huwaši stone in Tuhniwara city on a rock."* (Carter 1962: 116).

On the other hand, it is mentioned about the temple of the Guardian God *Kurša*, located on *Piškurunuwa* Mountain[11], during the *nuntarriyašhaš* feast: *"When Majesty goes to Piškurunuwa Mountain, a goat from the house of ABUBITUM men is given on the same day. The grain storehouse of the temple of God Kurša?"* (KUB 22.27 IV 30–32; Sir Gavaz 2015: 199).

In the route texts covering ceremonial trips of king, it is seen that *Piškurunuwa* mountain is included within the places to be visited: *"The journey is specified. They add Piškurunuwa Mountain (to the cult trip). King spends the night in the city of Haitta on the following day. They carry God* NISABA *up to the mountain. King and queen go up the mountain on the following day. And it becomes his festival."* (KBo 10.20 IV 5–9; Alp 1983: 144).

In another part of the text, it is expressed that the king went to the *Piškurunuwa* mountain during the AN.TAH.ŠUM feast and the cult activities performed there are mentioned. *"The king gets out of the chariot. The king sits. A dancer turns around himself/herself and then stands in front of a deer. The cupbearer libates to the deer with a cup of gold tapišana"* (KUB 25.18 II 6–11; Alp, 1983: 338). As seen in the texts, there is also a temple[12] of the guardian god *kurša* on the mountain and the mountain is told by the deer, the symbol of the guardian god. This reveals the guardian character of *Piškurunuwa* Mountain. What is more, the performance of a ritual involving deer indicates the presence of a fenced place on the lands of the temple where sacred deer are also protected (Popko 2009: 102). In addition to this information, the importance of the cult of this mountain in religious life of the Hittites is provided in the Hittites texts mentioning the festival of *Piškurunuwa* Mountain (*ŠA* EZEN $^{\text{HUR.SAG}}$*Piškurnuwa*; KUB 44.4 I 18) and great feast (*A-NA* $^{\text{HUR.SAG}}$*Piškurnuwa* EZEN$_4$ [G]AL ; KUB 55.1 IV 16).

D/Taha Mountain[13], located around the *Zippalanda* City and becoming the holy mountain of the city, is an important religious centre. In the texts, *Daha* Mountain (Fig. 3) is specified referring to Guardian God of *Daha* Mountain (^{D}LAMMA), the Pleiades of *Daha* Mountain (^{D}IMIN.IMIN.BI) and Guardian God of Prairies (^{D}LAMMA.LÍL) (Popko 1994: 38; Sir Gavaz 2012: 124). In the text on the celebration of *purulli* feast, sacrifices are presented to the Storm God of Zippalanda City and *Daha* Mountain: *"S/he presents sacrifices to the Storm God of Zippalanda City and Daha Mountain. Sings song with lyre. Palvatalla officer applauds. Kita man shouts. They celebrate purulliyaš festival."* (Bo 5045 rev. V 5'–10'; Popko 1994: 204–205.). As seen in the text, a sacrifice is offered to *Daha* Mountain during the *purulli* feast, and the feast is celebrated, possibly by performing some cult activities on *Daha* Mountain. In another part of the text, the relationship between *the Storm God of Zippalanda City and Daha Mountain* is described in an interesting manner: "*The [m]an of the Storm God tells: "the Storm God of Zip<pa>l[anda] wake from your nice sleeping! Look! the tabarna, Kin[g], Sun Goddess of Arinna, mother's priest will take you to your beloved at Daha Mountain*" (A. KUB 41.29 B. IBoT 4.92 =A. III obv. III 6'–11'; Popko 1994: 216)

11 For Hittite text parts mentioning $^{\text{HUR.SAG}}$*Piškurunuwa* Mountain, see Monte and Tischler 1978: 324–25; Monte 1992: 128.

12 In addition, a mountain is said to have a cult for the Guardian God *Zithariya* in KUB 11.23 rev. V 6ff. Popko 2009: 102.

13 For Hittite text parts mentioning $^{\text{HUR.SAG}}$*D/Taha* Mountain, see Monte and Tischler 1978: 374; Monte 1992: 151.

It was indicated that a running race was held in the *Tippuwa* Mountain as part of the festival celebrations during AN.TAH.ŠUM festival: *"The king and queen go to Hattuša the following day. On Mount Tippuwa, a troop of guardsmen and palace boys compete."* (KBo 10.20 I 19–21; Alp 1983: 136; Güterbock 1960: 80). The races were probably carried out to calm down and cheer the gods (Ardzinba 2010: 102)[14].

The Hittite Texts mention festivals celebrated for Horse God *Pirwa*. *"Pirwa and (his) horses in the middle of a mountain"* are written about in a Hittite cuneiform text (KBo 41.68 obv. 1ff). On the other hand, "*horse*" is used with the verb of *kuer-* "to cut, cut off, strike off" in KUB 39.56 1ff (Ünal 2007: 354). These expressions in the texts point to Pirwa's having a cult-place in the mountains and a horse sacrifice being carried out for him (Ünal 2013: 50)[15]. Today, the ritual, performed by the residents of Mehmet Dede Tekke and Mehmet Dede Obruk villages in Dodurga District, Çorum Province by climbing Kızıltepe Mountain located near their villages (Fig. 4), is characterised as welcoming spring, rainmaking and fertility ritual. In addition to food and drinks, the villagers carry the horses they will sacrifice, to the hill and perform a ceremony on the hill. Before sacrificing the horses, a wrestling ceremony is carried out on top of the mountain. This is followed by sacrifice prayer. Horses are sacrificed along with the awe-inspiring shouting and prayer gestures of the villagers. Horses are cut in half and granted to nature. Later on, the food they have brought is eaten, gratitude prayers are made and then they return to the village. After a while, scouting flights of raptors begin in the area of sacrifice. It is believed that this is a sign of acceptance of the villagers' prayers (Sir Gavaz 2016a: 83). As it is seen, this horse sacrifice ritual performed today reminds us of the rituals performed by the Hittites for God *Pirwa*. On the other hand, the wrestling ceremony performed by villagers on top of the mountain is very interesting and is very similar to a part in a Hittite text: *"The cities around the mountain bring all the bread (and) beer. Thick bread they break. The rhytons they fill. They eat. They drink. The cups they fill. In the presence of the god (there is) wrestling. They step into a fight. They (their Gods) entertain."*[16] (KUB 25.23 I 19–22; Carter 1962: 155, 165). As it is understood, the people living in the cities around the mountain meet on the mountain and present the sacrifice materials they have brought to gods. Next, at the banquet tables set up in the presence of the gods, meals are eaten, drinks are drunk, gratitude prayers are made and wrestling was performed before the gods. The banquet tables established during these rituals do not only cover presenting what has been brought by villagers. These rich tables were probably established to set up a relation between gods and humans. The peace of society was ensured by appeasing the gods (Ardzinba 2010: 98). In KBo 11.14 I 24–25 subjecting a mythos, the festival of Sun God is mentioned where all gods and the dead were invited. On the other hand, the richness, abundance and plenty of the banquet tables set up should represent the wealth of a country.

The text dealing with the *Karahna* City Cult Inventory provides information on various feasts performed. Of these festivals, festivals for the *Kantahuya/Kantariya* Mountain[17] and Šakudunuwa Mountain[18] are mentioned: *"every year, a rain festival, an eššai festival, a Kantariya mountain festival, a vine-harvest festival are performed. The Šakadunuwa mountain is performed every three years. The food granted to god in every year is as follows: seven cattle?*

14 In addition, see KUB 25.23 I 20–22; Archi 1973: 26.

15 For detailed information, see Ünal 2013; in addition, on this subject, see Sir Gavaz 2016a.

16 cf. Ünal 2019: 177: "*They divide loaf bread and fill animal-shaped cups with drink. They eat, drink. They fill glasses and, everyone performs a boxing match one by one before the God and everyone has fun one by one.*"

17 $^{\text{HUR.SAG}}$*Kán-ta-hu-ya-aš* for the part mentioning this mountain see Monte and Tischler 1978: 171. For translation $^{\text{HUR.SAG}}$*Kantariyaš* see Darga 1973: 21.

18 For the Hittite part mentioning $^{\text{HUR.SAG}}$Šak(u)tunuwa Mountain, see Monte and Tischler 1978: 331; Monte 1992: 133.

sheep one hundred fifty-five half measure tarša-[19] *(sacrificial material), half scale wine...... a lunar festival and three...*" (KUB 38.12 obv. I 22–26; Darga 1973: 8,14). The foods offered to the god were probably carried to the mountain. EZEN$_4$ HUR.SAG-*i pedummaš* used in Hittite texts are associated with "*festival of the carrying to the mountain*" (KBo 2.1 I 43; Carter 1962: 37). On the other hand, in another part of the text, it is mentioned about the god statue being carried to the *Halwanna*[20] Mountain: *nu* HUR.SAG *Halwannan* HUR.SAG-*i* UGU *pitinzi "And they carry (the image of) Mountain Halwanna up to the mountain.*" (KUB 25.23 I 11') When the god arrives at the mountain, he is set on or near his *huwaši* stone, and there worshipped (see Carter 1962: 37). In KUB 58. 108+[?] KUB 51.23 obv. II. 19'–22', the sacrificial material presented to Šarpa Mountain is referred: "*1 cattle of (mountain) Šarpa the town delivers regularly[ ] 9 sheep, of which 3 sheep of (mountain) Šarpa (and) 6 sheep the town deliver[s] regularly [ ] 18 PARĪSU (and) 3 SŪTU of wheat (and) corn, of which 13 PARĪSU of wheat (and) corn of the threshing floor... × PARĪSU of flour of (mountain) Šarpa......*" (For transcription and translation see Hazenbos 2003: 104, 106).

"The Rain Festival" found as EZEN$_4$ *hewaš-* / EZEN$_4$ *ZUNNU* in Hittite texts is one of the festivals that must be celebrated for the existence and richness of Hittite state. Rain is requested from god through performing it because the rainfall throughout the year is very important for the Hittite State, which had to cope with drought and famine from time to time. It is understood by the texts that the rain festival is celebrated in various settlements. In addition, there are also records indicating that rain was requested from some other mountains. "*Zaliyanu mountain is the first of all. When it grants rain to the city of Nerik, the sceptre-bearer brings the loaves of bread from Nerik. He brings loaves of bread (by sacrificing them and praying) and expects rain from Mount Zaliy[anu].*" (KBo 3.7 obv. II 21–29; Laroche, 1965: 8–9/ 68–69; Karauğuz, 2015: 53). This part of the text indicates that the rain festival of *Nerik* City is celebrated on *Zaliyanu* Mountain. On the other hand, *Zaliyanu* Mountain is associated with *Kaštama*[21] City in the Hittite texts (Haas 1994: 462–63). In Çorum, Alacahöyük residents perform a rain-making ceremony every year in the spring. The villagers climb a hill/mountain near the village by taking their sacrificial materials, food and drink. Visiting the Tekgone Tomb (Fig. 5) located there, the villagers perform a rain prayer, then eat the foods they have brought and request rain by sacrificing animals next to the tomb (Source person, Nazım Kaplan, Farmer, 59 years old). In Anatolia, many rain-making rituals are still carried out on the mountains or hills located near the settlements (Sir Gavaz 2016b).

One of the practices performed in Hittite texts during the festivals is the opening and closing of cereal containers. While opening containers (EZEN$_4$ ^{DUG}*harši-/haršiyalli*) refers to the beginning of spring and rainy season, closing the containers by filling them (EZEN$_4$ ^{DUG}*harši šuhhuwaš*) points out that autumn has come (Sir Gavaz 2016b: 578). In the text numbered KBo 2.7 obv. 6, a ritual about filling the food festivals in autumn: "*If they fill the container in autumn for Šidduwa mountain*[22]*, they divide a dannaš bread*" (Sir Gavaz 2016b: 579). On the other hand, in a different passage, permission is obtained from the Šidduwa mountain in order to cut a *eia* tree, having an important place in Hittite cult life and which is the equivalent of a pine tree: "*He breaks* LABGA *bread into pieces and [cities li]ke this. Šidduwa mountain! Look! We will take this* ^{GIŠ}*eia tree to decorate it.*" (KUB 12.19 rev.III 18–21; Ertem

19 *tarša-* "measuring cup, unit of measure, sacrificial material to be given or the number and quantity of animals" Ünal 2016: 523.

20 For the Hittite part mentioning $^{HUR.SAG}$*Halwanna* Mountain see Monte and Tischler 1978: 74–75.

21 For localization of *Kaštama* City, see Erkut 1999.

22 For Hittite text parts including Šidduwa/ Šituwa Mountain, see Monte and Tischler 1978: 362. Monte 1992: 147.

1987: 113). As it is understood from the text, a vow is offered to the mountain. In a different part of the text, the *eia* tree cut on the Šidduwa mountain is carried by back (KBo 15.33 rev. III 33ff.). This means that this mountain is also the protector of holy *eia* trees.

In a magic ritual about the removal of blood and tears of evil, the king asks the mountains for help: "*The king addresses the mountains as follows: "Huge mountains [...] Why did I come? Why did I struggle? A human being was sent to the [barn] behind fences [like cattle]. And you mountains, [help me!]" The mountains [res]pond as follows: Do not be afraid! We [will] help you.*" (KUB 30.33 obv. I 12–15; Melzer and Görke 2017). In this ritual, the King's call to the mountains and asking them for help is highly significant in terms of understanding the god-mountain perception in the Hittites.

In a different part of the text, the depiction of a mountain god is told as the description of a man standing on a lion (Güterbock, 1943: 280): "*In the past, Mountain (God) Malimaliya*[23]*did not have a god description (cult object). My sun Tuthaliya <made> it as an iron statue of a male and in a half hand span tall. His eyes are gold and he stands on an iron lion. They brought it to the temple of Kukumuša*[24] *Mountain God*"[25] (KUB 7.24 obv. 1–4; Carter 1962: 116, 119; Darga 1992: 112)[26]. We can understand in this part the extent to which the mountain gods in the pantheon are important and that there were special temples. The same text mentions the vow ceremony in the temple of *Kukumuša* Mountain God: "*1 PA of spelt (and) 1 PA of wine they pour into the harši vessel (that is) in the temple of Mountain Kuškumiša*". (KUB 7.24 obv. 5; Carter 1962: 116, 119) In a different part of the text, it is reported about a silver plated statue made for *Hapidduini* Mountain[27]: "*Sun God of the city of Durra, God Hatipuna, [...] Hapidduini Mountain, god Hašuma, [....]: Three statues of Fate Gods*[28]*: God Allinalli, God [....], God Iyaya. A total of nine gods, they were thrown away. Later on, new silver-plated statues were made for (them). And seven temples were built for them.*" (KUB 28.12 rev. III 7–13; Darga 1973: 16). In some Hittite texts, the mountain gods were depicted to be a ^{GIŠ}TUKUL[29] "Weapon, weapon of war, mace" on which male depictions were available (Ünal 2016: 547) while the river and spring goddesses were described as female depictions: "*City of Mamnanta: the Storm God's bull of iron, (and) Arnuwanda Mountain* ^{GIŠ}TUKUL *(as mace), on which is a statue of iron, they make. Huranašša Mountain* ^{GIŠ}TUKUL *(as mace), an iron statue is made iron which is a statue of iron, (and) White Mountain* ^{GIŠ}TUKUL *(as mace) on which is a statue of iron they make...*" (KBo 2.13 obv. 21–22; Güterbock 1943: 280, f.n. 22; Carter 1962: 107, 112). The mountains (divine mountains) we have mentioned so far in all parts of the Hittite texts are proof of the importance of mountains in Hittite cult life. In addition, mountains played an active role in the pantheon, not only as cult places where rituals for gods

23 For Hittite text parts subjecting $^{\text{HUR.SAG}}$*Malimaliya* Mountain, see Monte and Tischler 1978: 256; Monte 1991: 99.

24 For Hittite text parts mentioning $^{\text{HUR.SAG}}$*Ku(n)kumi/ uša* Mountain, see Monte and Tischler 1978: 223; Monte 1992: 85.

25 cf. "*Mountain Malimaliya: formerly there were no divine images. My Sun, Tuthaliya, <made> his (the deity's) statue of iron, 1 ½ sekan (in size), its eyes of gold. On a lion of iron he (the statue) stands. Into the temple of Mountain Kukumuša they carry it.*" See for translation Carter 1962: 119.

26 Haas, mentions about the statues of *Arwaliya* Mountain, *Taliya* Mountain, *Halalazipa* Mountain, Šummiyara Mountain and *Ziwana* Mountain gods in addition to *Malimaliya* Mountain and pointed out that although these cult figures did not constitute a uniform iconographic style, they still showed various similarities. He also stated that they were depicted with a lion or an eagle by adding that these mountain gods were male figures.. Haas 1994: 461.

27 For Hittite text passages concerning $^{\text{HUR.SAG}}$ *Hapidduini/ Hapituni*, see Monte and Tischler 1978: 82; Monte 1992: 27–28.

28 ^{D}MAH= ^{D}*kunuštalluš*- "God of Destiny" Ünal 2016: 294, 329.

29 ^{GIŠ}TUKUL: "mace" For the commentary and similar examples of the mace accompanying the mountains and depictions of the mountain gods associated with the Storm God, see Güterbock 1943: 280; Savaş 2002: 116.

were performed, but also as gods, for which shrines were built, their statues were made and which were depicted with some special symbols. In addition to philological data, archaeological data also show the existence of the mountain god and sacred-mountain motif in Hittite life. In Hittite art, depictions of mountain gods are seen clearly since the 13th century B.C. It is seen that mountain gods are more common in the Hittite pantheon since Hattušili III and his wife Puduhepa, when Hurrian influence was felt intensely. The Hurrian effect reflected on the rock reliefs of the Empire period is significant, and the effect of mountain god motifs known to be of Hurrian-Mitanni origin in this period (Darga 1992: 181) is of paramount importance in terms of the perception of divine mountain perception. The Storm God (*Tešup*) stands on two mountain gods in the main stage in the Yazılıkaya Chamber A. In addition, Tuthaliya IV stands on two stylized mountains in the king relief, which is also found in Yazılıkaya Chamber A[30] (Fig. 6). In the Fasıllar monument, the young god Šarruma (?) stands on the Mountain God. On the other hand, mountain gods and bulls are depicted on the rock relief in Hanyeri-Gezbel. The bull is depicted stepping on the shoulders of a mountain god with its front legs outstretched. In the Imamkulu rock relief (Fig. 7), three mountain gods carry the Storm God with his carriage with a bull (Güterbock, 1943: 282). In addition to these, the ivory mountain god statuette uncovered in Boğazkale gives an original mountain god iconography (Darga 1992: 110) (Fig. 8). These examples may be multiplied. The main point attempted to be indicated is the effect of the concept of mountain on Hittite religious and social life.

The text passages provided are important for the mountain-god-king perception. The expression of "*When my Grandfather Šuppiluliuma reached/went to the Mountain*" (*Als Šuppiluliuma, mein Großvater, den Berg erreichte*: see Haas 1994: 216.) mentioned in KBo 1.8+KUB 3.8+ 408/u obv. 7 are shown as the place where mountains, kings go after they die, that is, after they become god. In this respect, mountains symbolise divinity because of their power, magnificence, might, eternity and immortality. In fact, the Hittites did not only worship their gods, but also proved the permanent authority of the king and the permanent power of the state by means of the rituals they performed on high mountain peaks. Therefore, besides the god-mountain perception, the king-mountain connection should be read correctly. The Hittites were very successful in using religious activities as political arguments. On the other hand, similar practices such as welcoming spring ceremonies, fertility ceremonies, rain-making rituals, which are still performed on mountain hills in Anatolia, show that Hittite religion continues as the beliefs, traditions and customs of the public[31].

Bibliography

Akurgal, E.
- 1961 *Die Kunst der Hethiter*, München.

Alp, S.
- 1983 *Beiträge zur Erforschung des Hethitischen Tempels. Kultanlagen im Lichte der Keilschrifttexte*, Ankara.

Archi, A.
- 1973 "Fêtes de printemps et d'automne et réintegration rituelle d'images de culte dans l'Anatolie Hittite," *UF* 5, pp. 7–27.

Ardzinba, V.
- 2010 *Eskiçağ Anadolu Ayinleri ve Mitleri*, çev: Orhan Uravelli, Ankara.

Badali, E.
- 1991 *Strumenti musicali, musici e musica nella celebrazione delle feste ittite*, TH 14/1, Heidelberg.

Bittel, K.
- 1976 *Les Hittites*, Paris.

Bryce, T.
- 2003 *Hitit Dünyasında Yaşam ve Toplum*, çev. Müfit Günay, Ankara.

30 For the reliefs of the mountain god in Yazılıkaya and detailed information, see Seeher 2011: 33–85.

31 A detailed study on this subject is prepared by the author.

Carter, C. W.
- 1962 *Hittite Cult Inventories*, Chicago.

Çekmek A.
- 2016 *Hititçe-Türkçe, Türkçe-Hititçe Büyük Sözlük*, Ankara.
- 2019 *Hititçe Dilbilgisi. Çivi Yazısı İşaret Listesi ve Çok Sayıda Okuma Parçalarıyla Birlikte*, Ankara.

Darga, M.
- 1973 *Karahna Kült Envanteri (Keilschrifturkunden aus Boghazköi XXXVIII 12)*, İstanbul.
- 1992 *Hitit Sanatı*, İstanbul.

Erkut, S.
- 1999 "Hitit Kenti Kaštama'nın Yeri Üzerine," *12. Türk Tarih Kongresi Bildirileri*, (12–16 Eylül 1994 Ankara), pp. 129–131.

Ertem, H.
- 1965 *Boğazköy Metinlerine Göre Hititler Devri Anadolu'sunun Faunası*, Ankara.
- 1987 *Boğazköy Metinlerine Göre Hititler Devri Anadolu'sunun Florası*, Ankara.

Eliade, M.
- 2015 *Dinin Anlamı ve Sosyal Fonksiyonu*, çev. Mehmet Aydın, İstanbul.

Güterbock, H. G.
- 1943 "Eti Tanrı Tasvirleri ile Tanrı Adları," *BELLETEN* CVII (26), pp. 273–293.
- 1960 "An Outline of Hittite AN.TAH.ŠUM Festival," *JNES* 19, pp. 80–89.

Haas, V.
- 1970 *Der Kult von Nerik. Ein Beitrag zur hethitischen Religionsgeschichte*, Roma.
- 1994 *Geschichte der hethitischen Religion*, Leiden.

Hazenbos, J.
- 2003 *The Organization of the Anatolian Local Cults During the Thirteenth Century B.C.*, Boston.

Heffron, Y.
- 2014 "The Material Culture of Hittite 'God-drinking,," *Journal of Ancient Near Eastern Religions* 14, pp. 164–85.

Karauğuz, G.
- 2015 *Hitit Mitolojisi*, Konya.

Košak, S.
- 1990 Popko M., "Rev. of: Keilschrifturkunden aus Boghazköi 58 hethitische Rituale und Festbeschreibungen, (KUB 58) Berlin," *ZA* 80, pp. 146–151.

Laroche, E.
- 1965 *Textes Mythologies Hittites en Transcription*, Paris.

Martino, de S.
- 2019 "Din ve Mitoloji," in M. D. Alparslan and M. Alparslan (eds.), *Hititler. Bir Anadolu İmparatorluğu*, İstanbul, pp. 410–429

Mellink, M. J.
- 1991 "Archaeology in Anatolia," *American Journal of Archaeology* 95, pp. 123–53.

Melzer, S. and S. Görke
- hethiter.net/: CTH 401.2 (ExPl. A, 20.04.2017).

Monte, del G. F. and J.Tischer
- 1978 Die Orts und Gewäsernamen der hethitischen Texte, *RGTC* VI.

Monte, del G. F.
- 1992 Die Orts und Gewässernamen der hethitischen Texte, *RGTC* VI/2.

Müller-Karpe, A. M. and V. M. Müller-Karpe
- 2013 "Kuşaklı-Šarišša," in M. D. Alparslan and M. Alparslan (eds.), *Hititler. Bir Anadolu İmparatorluğu*, İstanbul, pp. 220–225.

Popko, M. and P. Taracha
- 1988 "Der 28. und der 29. Tag des hethitischen AN.TAḪ.ŠUM-Festes," *AoF* 15, pp. 82–113.

Popko, M.
- 1994 *Zippalanda: Ein Kultzentrum im hethitischen Kleinasien*. Texte der Hethiter, vol. 21, Heidelberg.
- 2009 *Arinna. Eine heilige Stadt der Hethiter*, Wiesbaden.

Roller, L. E.
- 2004 *Ana Tanrıça'nın İzinde. Anadolu Kybele Kültü*, çev. Betül Avunç, İstanbul.

Rüster, C. and E. Neu
- 1989 *Hethitisches Zeichenlexikon/Inventar und Interpretation der Keilschriftzeichen aus den Boğazköy-Texten*, Wiesbaden.

Savaş, Ö. S.
- 2002 "Hititlerde "Fırtına Tanrısı" İle "Boğa Kültü" Üzerine Bazı Gözlemler ve Yorumlar," *Archivum Anatolicum* 5, pp. 97–170.

Seeher, J.
- 2011 *Taşa Yontulu Tanrılar Hitit Kaya Tapınağı Yazılıkaya*, İstanbul.

Sir Gavaz, Ö.
- 2012 *Hitit Krallarının Kült Gezileri. Ayinler, Ziyaret Merkezleri, Yollar ve Lokalizasyonla İlgili Yeni Gözlemler*, Çorum.
- 2015 "Hititçe Metinlerde Geçen $^{HUR.SAG}$Piškurunuwa Üzerine," *5. Çorum Kazı ve Araştırmalar Sempozyumu* (10 Aralık 2015, Çorum), pp. 195–204.

- 2016a "MÖ. 2. Binyıl Bazı Gelenek ve Halk Motiflerinin Günümüze Yansıyan Örnekleri," *TÜBA-AR* 19, pp. 79–91.
- 2016b "Hititlerden Günümüze Yağmur Duası," *Uluslararası Bütün Yönleriyle Çorum Sempozyumu* (28–30 Nisan 2016), pp. 573–585.
- 2017 "Hititçe Metinlerde Geçen 'šalli ašeššar' ve İşlevi," Çeşm-i Cihan Tarih, Kültür ve *Sanat Araştırmaları E-Dergisi* C.4, S.2, pp. 83–93.
- 2020 "Hititlerden Günümüze Anadolu Halk İnanışlarına Yansıyan Taş Kültü," in B. Gür and S. Dalkılıç (eds.), *Anadolu Prehistoryasına Adanmış Bir Yaşam: Jak Yakar'a Armağan*, Ankara, pp. 177–190.

Ünal, A.
- 2003 *Hititler Devrinde Anadolu* II, İstanbul.
- 2007 *Multilinguales Handwörterbuch des Hethitischen/ A Concise Multilingual Hittite Dictionary/Hititçe Çok Dilli El Sözlüğü*, Hamburg.
- "Eski Anadolu'da At, Hititçe Kikkuli At Eğitimi Metinleri ve "Tavlaya Çekmek"le İlgili Teknik Bir Ayrıntı," *Çorum Kültür Sanat* II, pp.40–66

Fig. 1. Seal impression of the Great King Tuthaliya IV (as the Mountain God). Bittel, 1976. 172, Fig.193.

Fig. 2. Yazılıkaya, Chamber A. Main scene. Bittel, 1976. 209, Fig.239.

Fig. 3. Kerkenes Mountain (in Yozgat) = *Daha* Mountain?
Source: http://www.kerkenes.metu.edu.tr/kerk1/02images/photos/2009/pg2009.html

Fig. 4. Kızıltepe Mountain, Dodurga, Çorum, Ö.Sir Gavaz.

Fig. 5. Alacahöyük, Tekgone Mountain and Tomb. Foto courtesy: Ö. Sir Gavaz.

Fig. 6. Yazılıkaya, Chamber A, Tuthaliya IV. Bittel, 1976. 214, Fig.249.

Fig. 7. Imamkulu relief. Bittel, 1976. 182, Fig.203.

Fig. 8. The ivory mountain god figurine. Bittel, 1976. 213, Fig. 248.

Sticky Stratigraphy and Cranky Chronology: Adventures at Çadır Höyük on the North Central Plateau

Sharon R. Steadman, T. Emre Şerifoğlu and Gregory McMahon *

Abstract

Anyone who has worked on a höyük, tell, or tepe, knows the challenges such archaeological settings can present. The 30 meter-high Çadır Höyük mound is no exception. Over our 27 years of work at the site we have been presented with numerous stratigraphic and chronological challenges. This contribution offers us the opportunity to describe how we have (sometimes) overcome these challenges, and certainly how they have allowed us to better understand our site. Among the topics discussed are the various spatial usages of the mound over time, resulting in stratigraphic sequences with enormous gaps, though we know the mound was occupied elsewhere during those gap periods. We also address the series of Early Bronze Age C14 dates in the middle of our Iron Age trench, and how the burial of a Byzantine woman ended up in the middle of our Bronze Age fortification wall. The mystery of what is both the stratigraphic and chronological position of our entire western slope excavations is explored. Finally, the conundrum of massive piles of fist-sized stones in three distinct areas of the mound is also considered. It is such stratigraphic and chronological mysteries that make the excavation of a höyük a joy, an adventure, and a headache at any given moment of the season!

Öz

Bir höyükte, "tell"de ya da tepede çalışan herkes bu tip arkeolojik alanların sunabileceği zorlukları bilir. 30 metrelik Çadır Höyük de bu konuda bir istisna değildir. Yerleşimdeki 27 yıllık çalışmamız esnasında karşımıza sayısız stratigrafik ve kronolojik zorluk çıkmıştır. Yayına bu katkımız bize bu zorlukları (bazen) nasıl aşabildiğimizi ve daha kesin olarak yerleşimimizi daha iyi anlamamıza nasıl vesile olduklarını açıklama imkanı vermiştir. Tartışılan konulardan biri ilgili boşluk dönemlerinde höyüğün başka kısımlarının iskan edilmeye devam ettiğini bilsek de stratigrafik silsilelerde çok büyük boşluklarla neticelenen höyüğün zaman içindeki çeşitli alansal kullanımlarıdır. Demir Çağı açmamızın ortasından elde edilen Erken Tunç Çağı Karbon-14 tarih serileri ve bir Bizans kadınının mezarının Tunç Çağı savunma duvarımızın ortasında nasıl karşımıza çıktığı ele alınan diğer konulardır. Tüm batı açması kazılarımızın hem stratigrafik hem de kronolojik durumunun ne olduğu gizemi de tartışılmıştır. Son olarak yumruk büyüklüğündeki taşlardan oluşan ve höyüğün üç farklı yerinde bulunan büyük yığıntılar muamması değerlendirilmiştir. İşte bu tip stratigrafik ve kronolojik gizemler bir höyük kazısını bir keyfe, bir maceraya ve sezon esnasında herhangi bir anda bir baş ağrısına dönüştürmektedir!

Çadır Höyük (Fig. 1) is a steep-sided mound on the north central plateau, situated between the major Iron Age site of Kerkenes Dağı and multi-period Alişar Höyük, within the curve of the Kızılırmak. Under the direction of Ronald L. Gorny a 1994 intensive surface survey of the mound was followed by excavations launched in the same year; directorship transitioned to Gregory McMahon and Sharon R. Steadman in 2010, and later to T. Emre Şerifoğlu. Steadman now directs the project. Çadır began life as a salvage project due to the anticipated inundation by Gelingüllü Lake, a fate that never came to pass. Our quarter century of work at the site has demonstrated an occupational history

* SUNY Distinguished Professor and Chair, Department of Sociology/Anthropology – Independent Scholar – University of New Hampshire, Department of Classics, Humanities, and Italian Studies

spanning over six millennia (ca. 5200 B.C. to final abandonment in the 14th century A.D.), revealed in no fewer than 42 10 × 10 m trenches spread across the summit, terrace, and all four slopes of the mound (Fig. 2). Our earliest extant horizontal exposure dates to the early 4th millennium B.C. (Steadman *et al.* 2019a, b); excavations have also produced a substantial 2nd millennium occupation (Ross *et al.* 2019a; Steadman and McMahon 2015, 2017), a nearly complete Iron Age sequence (Ross 2010; Ross *et al.* 2019b), and an extensive Byzantine settlement (Cassis 2009; Cassis *et al.* 2019; Cassis and Steadman 2014). Our Deep Sounding has demonstrated that occupation stretches back to at least the Middle Chalcolithic (Steadman *et al.* 2007, 2008). A mounded site with such an extensive, unbroken, occupation is bound to be rife with stratigraphic and chronological problems, and Çadır is certainly up to the task of providing these. The following sections outline some of our most vexing issues, only some of which have we resolved.

STICKY STRATIGRAPHY

We begin this section by outlining the first cruel stratigraphic blow at Çadır Höyük: residents through the ages did not live one on top of another. In 1994, anticipating soon-to-be site destruction, we opened a 2 × 20 "Step Trench" on the east side of the mound to obtain a stratigraphic sequence; we also opened two 2 × 2 m soundings, one at the base of the mound on the north, one mid-slope on the south slope (see Figure 2). The Step Trench provided a marvelous stratigraphic sequence spanning the Middle Bronze to the Late Iron Age period, though minus the Early and Middle Iron Ages. On the eastern slope, Late Iron Age occupation rests directly on the later Hittite Empire remains. Just north of the mound, the 2 × 2 m sounding yielded Classical period ceramics, but not a single iota of Classical architecture. The biggest surprise was the Late Chalcolithic ceramics appearing in the southern slope 2 × 2 m sounding within 30 cm of the surface (Gorny *et al.* 1995). Over the next years, excavations on the southern slope revealed that the Early Bronze I occupation rests beautifully on the Late Chalcolithic; above the Early Bronze is an Old Hittite and Hittite Empire occupation (with no intervening Early Bronze III or II at all). The mystery of the Byzantine occupation and its Iron Age underpinning, sans any Classical between, is discussed below. While it is common to have significant lacunae in occupation, this is not the situation at Çadır where we have the "missing bits" (Early/Middle Iron Age, Early Bronze III and II, Classical) well represented, just not where one would expect them. The residents through the six millennia at Çadır simply refused to occupy the site in a uniformly stratigraphic manner, which would have created a perfect "layer cake" of the site for us. Instead they hopped around, picking and choosing certain areas, and leaving the others defunct. Welcome to archaeology on a steep höyük.

A Rolling Stone Gathers No....Stratigraphy

In this section we detail three other specific stratigraphic migraines: three piles of stones, in three distinct locations across the Çadır mound, which have given us years of angst trying to explain their function and placement.

The "Untomb" on the Mound Summit

The first pile of stones appeared in 2000 on the mound summit in SMT 19 (Figs. 3a, b). It rested above a very fine Byzantine plastered courtyard next to a large storage building. We did not yet know of the courtyard and building when we came upon the stones. These mostly fist-sized, with a few head-sized, stones had been placed in a pile with a diameter of approximately 5 meters in a rough circle. Our best inference at the time was that it was a grave, possibly of Iron Age date, or even earlier. We had yet to conduct excavations on the summit; our survey had indicated Byzantine occupation there, but such a grave was not of Byzantine style. We photographed and drew the feature, and then began a careful excavation, expecting to find a tomb beneath. What we did find was....nothing. The stones rested on a thin layer of fill above the fine plastered courtyard, suggesting that someone placed them there not too long after use of the courtyard ceased (thus, probably in the late 12th or 13th century A. D.). Who made this pile of stones? There were two modern robber pits on the summit, but both were some distance from this pile, and both had the debris heaped next to the pits. Recent excavations suggest that the last inhabitants at Çadır may have not been the Byzantine population, but rather a brief stay by Turkic/Selçuk groups (Steadman *et al.* 2017; Steadman and McMahon 2017). However, these groups simply used the existing architecture without dismantling or changing the Byzantine footprint. Did some post-Selçuk temporary habitation occur on the summit, leaving no trace but a pile of stones? After three decades of work on the summit, as yet we have found no evidence of a dismantled Byzantine building in the area; where then did the stones come from? Thirty Years later the mystery of the summit pile of stones remains and will likely never be solved.

The ST 2 Stones: Hittite, Iron Age, Neither, or Both?

A second pile of stones made its appearance in 2013 in the eastern slope "Step Trench," specifically in trench ST 2 (Fig. 4a). The majority of the thus far excavated eastern slope occupation dates to the 2nd and 1st millennia B.C. We have our most robust Late (?) Bronze Age/Hittite architecture here, and a good bit of Iron Age material as well. We opened trench ST 2 in 2013 in order to expand our Hittite/Late (?) Bronze Age exposure. Excavations began in the westernmost, and highest, portion of ST 2. Within just a few centimeters we came upon a well-built stone feature, F2 (Fig. 4b). With only approximately 1 m of it jutting from the western baulk we could not identify its function. However, excavations in the adjacent ST 1 trench in 2017 revealed that F2 is a (Bronze/Iron Age) staircase leading staircase leading up the mound to the summit. This staircase rests on a clay and mudbrick platform supporting it on the steep slope. The 2013 excavations proceeded, leaving F2 in place on a pedestal. Approximately 30 cm of fill/slopewash lay beneath the clay/mudbrick platform underneath F2. And then came the pile of stones (F3). Once again, we encountered an extensive deposit of gravel and fist-sized, along with a few head-sized, stones, with a fair amount of mudbrick crumble amidst the stones (Fig. 4c). We dutifully photographed and drew F3. The nearly 2-meter tall strapping trench supervisor was nearly moved to tears when the Field Director (Steadman) informed him he had to draw F3 (Fig. 4d). He has since left the field of archaeology, entering the field of education followed by politics. F3 may have caused the loss of an excellent archaeologist, but it also helped to produce a gifted educator.

As excavations proceeded we expected to find something underneath F3 that would explain its function. Instead, we found another 20–30 cm of fill/slopewash below F3 followed by significant mudbrick and stone architecture belonging to the second millennium Hittite occupation. The F3 stone pile measured 3 m on its north-south axis, and extended 2.5 m from the western baulk; at least another meter or so probably extends into the baulk. This pile of stones appears to be "floating" within the slopewash between the Iron Age and 2nd millennium deposit. If it was meant to serve as drainage for the F2 staircase, why was there slopewash deposit between F2 and F3? Who put that pile of stones there and why? Many years later F3 still stares out at us from the ST 2 western baulk. Our only recourse will be to continue excavations in ST 1, and eventually reveal the entirety of F3. We doubt that this will shine any more light on the function of F3, but at least we will be able to excavate the remainder of the feature and it will no longer haunt us from the western baulk.

The Stone Migration: The Western Slope

Our work on the western (WSS) slope had a relatively late start, in part due to the fact that this is the steepest side of the mound (Fig. 5a). It seemed far easier, especially working on our knees, to address the many mysteries in other areas of the mound. Nonetheless, Şerifoğlu took on the WSS excavations in 2015 in order to glimpse activity on that side of the mound, and revealed a stratigraphic sequence going as deep as the Middle Bronze Age level. Work began in WSS 15, excavating what we can call a tiny step trench. Almost immediately, we were greeted by a strange stratigraphic sequence, beginning with a thick and hard lime and clay layer, below which rested a sandy layer, and then pebbles and gravel, and finally fist-sized river stones at the bottom (Fig. 5b).

Upon first discovery we ran through the possible functions, thinking drainage system, or perhaps spare construction materials. We then turned our attention to the Step Trench. Could it be related to the ST 2 pile of stones beneath the ST 1 staircase architecture? Our tendency was to link the WSS engineering project to the Step Trench, as WSS 15's features very much resembled those. However, we were stymied by the nearly complete absence of identifiable accompanying archaeological material; it was never possible to date this feature with any certainty. Further, the F3 stone pile in the Step Trench rested over 8 meters higher than those in WSS 15. Could this "stone piles" occupation "tilt" by that much? By the end of the 2015 season the WSS stone pile remained unexplained.

Excavations in WSS continued in following seasons, and soon after, a north-south aligned wall (Fig. 5c) made its appearance just to the east of the original WSS 15 features, revealing that other architecture existed on the western slope. Further team discussion resulted in the suggestion that the WSS 15 stone pile could relate to construction associated with a Byzantine period drainage system. An actual drain in the Byzantine defensive wall system was located east of the WSS area, on the mound summit. Succeeding seasons of excavations revealed Middle Iron Age material in the lower phases and Late Bronze Age material in layers beneath this complex. Further investigations along the massive wall revealed that in fact it has a better constructed lower layer, so our current tendency is to date the original wall, which probably had a defensive purpose, to the Middle and Late Iron Ages, with later Byzantine additions made to it, integrating it to a larger engineering project Thus, as of the 2020 season, mainly based on the pottery types and the general construction techniques of the architectural remains, the top WSS 15 stratigraphy could indeed be Late or Middle Iron Age in date, or it could also be Byzantine... or anything between these two periods. Remarkably, the western slope stratigraphic complexities have not driven the WSS team, including Şerifoğlu, to other areas of the mound. We retained our optimism that the identity of the WSS 15 stones will someday be revealed.

The Wild World of WSS Stratigraphy

Our work in the larger WSS area focused on revealing the rest of the north-south aligned wall in the following years. This work allowed us to understand that this almost 2 meter wide wall, stretching across the top part of WSS 15 and into WSS 14, had a lower layer built with dressed stones, larger and placed more regularly than what was revealed in the upper part of the wall. The excavations around this lower phase of the wall provided a mixture of Iron and Late Bronze Age sherds (along with a few Middle and Early Bronze Age sherds) but were predominantly Middle Iron Age in date; we have therefore dated the wall to this period. The wall seems to have buttresses at regular intervals on its west side and may well have functioned as a substantial fortification wall that encircled the mound in that period (Fig. 6).

The excavations conducted just to the west of and below the wall revealed a burnt floor below thick debris dating to the Late Bronze Age based on the pottery, and a bronze pin with general characteristics typical of that period (Steadman *et al.* 2017: 230). Below this layer we uncovered the remains of a burnt mudbrick wall at the western edge of WSS 15, which we provisionally identified as a continuation of the Middle Bronze Age fortification wall found in the "Step Trench" many years ago. Over the last half decade our work in the WSS area has shown that in spite of its steepness, or perhaps because of it, the stratigraphic formations are as, or more, complicated than anywhere else on the mound. The active Çadır residents continuously reshaped the mound here based on the needs of the ages in which they were living.

Florence of the Byzantine Bronze Age

The 2013 excavations in trenches ST 8 and ST 3, in the Step Trench on the eastern slope (Fig. 7a), were enormously important in helping us understand the Bronze Age stratigraphy here, which includes three phases of defensive architecture spanning the Middle Bronze Age to the Hittite Empire period (Fig. 7b), including a Hittite tower built within the wall (Steadman and McMahon 2015). The supervisor for these trenches revealed a vast array of stone and mudbrick architecture which he meticulously articulated, allowing us to understand the complicated stratigraphy. Ceramics and subsequent C14 dates placed the architecture firmly in the 2nd millennium B.C. spanning the periods noted above. On the second-to-last day of excavations, a day really devoted to small jobs to clean up for final photos, a small mound of dirt in the NE corner of ST 3 was removed to "neaten up" this area which rested at the foot of a massive Hittite stone and mudbrick wall. Just a few centimeters below the mound of dirt we discovered human skeletal remains. We spent the rest of the day revealing the burial, which we believed must date to the Hittite period. Was it a worker who perished while building the wall or a soldier defending it? Was it an attacker repelled by fierce defenders of Çadır? The burial was quite interesting as it was only the second adult burial found at Çadır; most of our burials to date are in the form of infant jar burials in the Late Chalcolithic and Early Bronze Age (Yıldırım *et al.* 2018).

The small team who stayed most of the (hot) day to excavate the skeleton contained one person with physical anthropology training. She identified the burial as likely female, which later turned out to be the case (Steadman *et al.* 2015); the excavation team nicknamed her Florence. She was therefore likely not a builder, defender, or attacker. One interesting aspect of the burial was the large stone that had been laid over Florence's neck, presumably by those who buried her there (Fig. 7c). The even bigger surprise was the vessel placed as a burial good with Florence, which our Byzantinist identified as clearly of Byzantine date. Not only was Florence not a Hittite wall builder or defender, she was not even Hittite. We were left to answer the questions of who buried Florence, and why at the foot of the Middle Bronze/Hittite defensive wall?

It took some time to try and answer these questions, and we should note that not long after the 2013 season, before the following interpretation came together, the ST 3 trench supervisor changed his focus to South American archaeology. We hope that Florence did not drive him away. Our interpretation of Florence's fate takes us to some of the last days of the Çadır occupation. At some point in the late 11th or possibly the early 12th century A.D., Çadır appears to have been abandoned, at least for a short time, possibly not long after the Byzantine defeat at Manzikert by Selçuk forces. Livestock were locked in a pen on the mound summit, ostensibly because they would have slowed down departure (Cassis *et al.* 2019). It seems likely that residents believed they could return in time to retrieve their livestock, but that was not to be the case. Byzantine residents did eventually return, only to abandon the site for good some time in the following century. After this second abandonment a temporary occupation by Turkic/Selçuk peoples ensued. Physical anthropological analysis identified Florence as an adult female with some physical anomalies that may have impeded her mobility, perhaps even rendering her unable to walk (Steadman *et al.* 2015). The lack of trauma to her mostly complete remains suggests that she did not die from an injury. Was she left behind during one of the abandonments, and then carefully buried by "invaders" who may have found a disabled, possibly starving woman at Çadır? Did they place a rock on her neck to symbolically keep her in her grave, and place a vessel from "her people" to comfort her in the next world?

The choice of burial location would make sense if those who buried her were temporarily inhabiting the mound summit. Placing her at the foot of ancient visible massive stone walls, far from their tents, might have seemed wise. We will likely never know when Florence died and who buried her. She shall, therefore, remain our Byzantine woman of the Bronze Age.

CRANKY CHRONOLOGY

Building chronologies is not only the lifeblood of archaeological work, but also a terror-inducing process. We are certain that we are not the only archaeologists who hold our collective breaths when sending carbon samples for laboratory tests. Will the results confirm what we believe, and often have already published, about that stratum?

Early Bronze Pits in Iron Age Workshops

Our "Iron Age Trench," USS 4 on the Upper Southern Slope, has been very carefully excavated since 2001; during the majority of these years it was under the gifted supervision of our Associate Director Jennifer Ross. In many ways USS 4 is one of our most important trenches on the mound. It provides an *unbroken* sequence from the Hittite Empire period to the Late Iron Age, based on both ceramic analysis and radiocarbon dates. One of the most important aspects of this trench was that it allowed for the close investigation of the transition from the Hittite Empire period to the Early Iron Age, a period fraught with controversy about what was taking place on the plateau (Hawkins 2002; Omura 2011; Seeher 2001; Voigt 1994, 2013). We were eager to describe the Early Iron Age occupation at Çadır as it emerged from the Hittite imperial collapse. Our excavations demonstrated that the USS 4 trench consisted of workshops. Middle Iron Age inhabitants engaged in wool-working and general textile production (Ross et a. 2019a). As excavations proceeded we discovered a range of fascinating Early Iron Age features in this trench, including semi-circular, possibly covered, "work huts," a well-built rectangular ash/charcoal pit, and heavily-plastered concave pits (Fig. 8).

With tremendous anticipation we sent a number of carbon samples for analysis to document what we believed to be an Early Iron Age felt-making operation (Ross *et al.* 2019b). Imagine our horror when some of our radiocarbon dates came back dating the context to ca. 3000–2500 B.C.: Early *Bronze* Age? Stratigraphically, this was utterly impossible, as this layer was absolutely sandwiched between the Middle Iron just above it, and a Hittite wall below it. Fortunately, most of the other dates brought back stress-reducing dates ranging from 1210–970 B.C. The Early Bronze dates were based on carbon samples from the ash/charcoal pits. We believe that the intrepid Early Iron folks, who needed to heat water in order to steep the felt, traveled a few meters down the slope to the abandoned Early Bronze I structures and scarpered back up the mound with some of the wooden beams (some already burned) they found lying around. Why go out into the surrounding countryside to cut a tree when there is kindling nearly at your fingertips? This was not the only time Çadırites reused readily available materials from earlier times (Steadman and Ross 2020). It is, however, the only example that gave us heart palpitations regarding our stratigraphic control at the site.

Wherefore Art Thou Romans?

We frequently describe Çadır as a site featuring "6000 years of uninterrupted habitation" in our publications. When we are being exceedingly careful, we also note that evidence for substantive occupation in the Classical period is lacking. As noted above, our 1994 North Terrace sounding (see Fig. 2) offered up Classical-period sherds but refused to reveal any architecture. In 2006, when investigating the northern slope of the mound, excavations of a Late Iron Age wall perched atop the Hittite wall coughed up a beautiful Greek Black Figure sherd with the word *kalos* written on it. Yes, it was indeed beautiful. Based on these two sets of data, we can confidently say that Greeks and Romans may have been walking across Çadır dropping sherds from their pockets.

Our best evidence comes from our horizontal excavations on the North Terrace, reported on in a number of publications (Cassis *et al.* 2019; Cassis and Steadman 2014; Steadman and McMahon 2015). A collection of Byzantine structures here, which surely sat near the agricultural fields, yielded two radiocarbon dates that fell in the 1st century A. D., retrieved from the lowest levels of excavation. It is quite likely that a Roman-period manor house rests below the Byzantine structures on the North Terrace. In fact, our Byzantinist, Marica Cassis, is quite confident that there might be more than a manor house in that area, which is not suitable for cultivation because of all the large rocks probably belonging to Roman structures.

There is no reason to doubt that there was a small to medium size Roman settlement stretching across the flat landscape below the mound making use of the fertile agricultural fields and numerous water sources present here, likely safeguarded by a watch tower or a small castle on the mound's summit. Besides the high potential this area has for sustaining large populations, its location close to the major routes makes it a good candidate for a Roman settlement. Roman regional roads linked Ancyra (Ankara) and Tavium (Büyüknefes, Yozgat) to Sebastopolis (Sulusaray, Tokat) and Sebaste (Sivas); major roads also connected this part of Anatolia to Caesarea (Kayseri) and to Cappadocia, making it strategically important (French 2016: 13–14, map 2b, table 1).

This region was and is still famous for its natural warm water pools which are believed to have curative powers. The Roman baths in Sarıkaya (Yozgat) (Aquae Sarvenae/Basilica Therma), which was added to the tentative list of world heritage sites of the United Nations Education, Scientific and Cultural Organization (UNESCO) in 2018 (https://whc.unesco.org/en/tentativelists/6350/), is located relatively close to Çadır (Şenyurt 2016), and it is rather appealing to imagine that Roman legions and citizens traveling from north central Anatolia to Caesarea stopped in Sarıkaya to have a bath after they passed by Çadır Höyük and Alişar during their long journey. Many intrepid souls seek to take over the responsibility to uncover the yet mysterious Hellenistic and Roman settlements lying under the fields surrounding Çadır Höyük, and their work will hopefully shed light on a long forgotten period of northern Anatolian history.

THE JOYS, AGONIES, AND HEADACHES OF WORKING ON A HÖYÜK

The following offers a few comments from each of the authors about their experiences working on the wonderful Turkish höyük called Çadır.

Sharon Steadman, Field and Project Director

As Field Director, I clocked numerous kilometers and attained enviable aerobic workouts each season traveling between trenches all over the mound including, by my count, 14 complete trips from mound summit to the North Terrace trenches in one day in 2013. My greatest joy over the years has been working with our incredible team who have become like family. Two field tasks stick in my mind as both the most difficult, and in many ways, the most enjoyable of my entire tenure working at Çadır Höyük.

In our earliest field seasons field photography was conducted by our former director, Ron Gorny. In 2001, due to an injury to Ron's hand, field photography was ceded to me since I had been an amateur photographer in my college days. Taking clear, effective, and edifying field photographs on a steep höyük is not for the faint of heart; edging up to a trench with a deep baulk, on the down slope, can be as exhilarating as it is frightening (Fig. 9a). I will admit that in recent years, as knees and balance have become more unsteady, I often ask one of my colleagues to stand behind me grasping my shirt! In 2008, long before the advantage of drone photography, we had the bright idea of asking the Sorgun fire department to bring out their hook-and-ladder truck for our final photos. Both Sharon and Greg went up in the bucket (Fig. 9b), making joint decisions about placement and taking dual photos so as not to miss this golden opportunity. The photos we acquired were spectacular and have been used many times in publications. The photo of us in the bucket (Fig. 9c) shows the calm bucket operator, and Greg, who enjoyed every minute of the undertaking, attempting to shout down to our team to move even further back from the trenches. What is harder to see in this photo are my closed eyes! For the entire ride up, and back down, I had eyes closed and silently asked the spirits of Çadır Höyük to ensure a safe return to earth. I only looked out on the incredible expanse around us, at the highest point, to take our pictures. This was an event I will never forget, and will likely never repeat!

The other task I will note here involves working with the total station. While several team members (Anthony Lauricella, Jennifer Ross) are skilled total station operators, they are also valuable area supervisors. Often the task of checking points and laying out new trenches (and revising the topographical map as we deposited or took away sections of the mound) fell to the Project Director (McMahon) and the Field Director. Greg describes his love/hate relationship with the total station below. I was the "prism operator." The joys of this task included the pleasure of working with Greg and the sense of accomplishment when the corners of a new trench were flagged with precise measurements, or a contour was adjusted for our topographical map. The agonies and aches derived from two things: a steep-sided mound and the fact that the slopes of the mound sit enough degrees off of magnetic north to be confusing on a slope. Normally I am a pretty good judge of distance and placement, but due to the attitude of the mound vis-à-vis north/south, laying out a 10 × 10 m trench on the slope was sometimes... agonizing. From the total station Greg would advise me, over the walkie talkie, to move something like 7 cm north, which I would do, only to be told to move 12 cm north after the next measurement because I had actually moved west! Occasionally a time out, in order for me and the prism to come to terms with one another (Fig. 9d), was necessary to turn the tide.

Gregory McMahon, Former Project Director

The 2008 ride skyward in the fire truck bucket was indeed a highlight, so much more effortless than trudging up the east side slope with my friend and colleague Ron Gorny to discuss stratigraphy (Fig. 10a). I also enjoyed my time with the total station. However, in 1994, when we drilled and placed our metal rod for the mound datum into the largest visible rock on the southeast corner of the summit (Fig. 10b-c), I often wished we'd chosen another location. Excavations revealed that this was a rock in the Byzantine defensive wall. Beyond the problem of having our datum *within* an archaeological feature, attempting to level the total station's tripod on a rocky wall over the last 25 years has been, to say the least, a challenge. However, perhaps my most enduring memories after a quarter century are the non-fieldwork experiences that are associated with the archaeological pursuit.

As everyone who digs in Turkey knows, one major reason why working on an excavation in Anatolia is so satisfying is the people, culture, (and food) that one encounters and enjoys. For me as Associate Director and then Director of the excavation, an unexpected benefit of our work was the cultural experience, the opportunity to live in a village and get to know our neighbors, getting to know our workers, mostly local villagers who came back to work in the same trenches year after year, and sharing our passion for studying the past with them. The first two seasons of our project we lived in Sorgun, our market town, and thus many of my contacts in those early years were there in Sorgun.

During our first season in 1993, it became clear that we needed reliable hardware support, which is how I made my first friend in Sorgun, Muzaffer. From him I learned the depth of possibilities in forging a relationship which was both business and friendship. Regardless of how strange the requests of the yabancı, he was always gracious and resourceful in making sure we had what we needed to do our work.

That first season, in 1993, we had borrowed a flotation machine from Mark Nesbitt, and I was assigned the task of building a replica of it so we could return the original to Mark. Explaining what we wanted, and how it worked, to Muzaffer was really beyond my Turkish skills, but he grasped the idea, and he immediately put me in his truck and we went racing around Sorgun scrounging a steel drum for the machine. He knew everyone in town, and eventually he found an old friend whom he talked into giving us a drum. Of course he also knew a blacksmith who would be patient enough for me to explain, haltingly, the modifications that would turn the drum into a flotation machine. The bubbler and other plumbing fittings for the machine Muzaffer insisted on doing himself; he had promised me he would make the machine work, and he invented on the fly a combination of plumbing fittings that did exactly what they needed to. That flotation machine over the last quarter century (Fig. 10d) has processed thousand of samples and works just as smoothly now as it did the day Muzaffer delivered it in his truck. I think of him with fondness at the beginning of every season when we haul it out of storage and I try to remember how to set it up and run it.

We have been working at Çadır Höyük so long that I now deal with Muzaffers' son Mehmet, who was a very young and deeply unwilling shop assistant in the early summers of our project. He is just as gracious, knowledgeable, and actively helpful as his father. I came to Çadır Höyük for the archaeology, to learn from people who lived thousands of years ago. What I did not know when we started was how much I would also learn from the people who still live there.

T. Emre Şerifoğlu, Former Project Director

Until I joined the Çadır Höyük team as the assistant director in 2013 I had not worked in this part of Anatolia; I had only conducted projects in Cilicia and the northwestern Black Sea coast. My knowledge of local archaeology and culture was limited to that in publications and what I encountered in visits to various sites and museums as a young, enthusiastic archaeologist. I knew that my involvement in the project would be the beginning of a new phase in my career and that I would work with this wonderful team for many years to come, but I had no idea that I would one day end up taking over the project as the new director, which happened in 2020. Every season had its surprises, and besides the joys of archaeological excitement, every year there was more to learn about the local culture, village politics, numerous challenges related to project management, and technical or methodological difficulties that we had to overcome.

I've spent most of my seven years at Çadır Höyük on the quiet west side of the mound, the only area that had not been investigated (Fig. 10e), due mainly to the steep topography and extensive remains on other parts of the mound. I started my investigations with an intensive micro-survey of the fields below, discovering that the archaeological material mostly dated to the Bronze and Iron Ages; this work was followed by excavations in deep soundings around the mound and some geophysical investigations. One of my roles at the project was to take the aerial photographs of the mound with a drone for the last five years, which provided us with beautiful images not only of the höyük but also of our team working hard on the mound and the wonderful scenery surrounding Çadır Höyük.

Probably my most interesting experience was the final two weeks of the 2015 season when I and a very small team began excavations on the western slope after the larger team had left. With this small team we not only excavated, but also cooked, cleaned the house, shopped and worked day and night even when it rained heavily. I was amazed by the level of commitment of this small group of students and researchers, members of which walked back and forth from the site, carrying all the equipment, excavating until noon, then also carrying the finds back to the dig house to be washed, drawn and photographed, and finally working together to cook and clean. It was truly an exemplary communal life that we managed to sustain which proved to be efficient although very tiring. This launched our investigations in the WSS trenches where we found the mysterious feature filled with river stones and rocks, and the massive wall that marked its edge. Our small team revealed what will likely be, in future excavations, important stratigraphy from the Middle Bronze Age to the Iron Age.

My experience with the locals and villagers has always been positive. From our site guards and the workmen from Peyniryemez, Yazılıtaş, and Sorgun to the mayors and *kaymakams* of the district, I have met so many people, and every year I have made many new friends. They were always very helpful and did their best to make everything pleasant and easier for us as foreigners not accustomed with the local ways of "doing things." One year the village residents expressed an interest in using our compound for their own activities. We invited them to use it off-season, but they themselves finally decided that its location at the edge of the village made it an unfavorable place for their activities. Our dig house complex with all the trees, living and working quarters, and pleasant open spaces to meet and eat, have been a place we all enjoyed living in and is a piece of heaven located in a beautiful landscape bearing all the elements of the north central Anatolian nature and environment.

The project has now moved into its fourth phase after my directorship, after many years of service by Ron Gorny and Gregory McMahon as directors, and now to Sharon Steadman as director. This latest phase, which is being conducted by a new, energetic administrative team, will see the continuation of the excavations, lots of restoration work, and the designing of the surrounding area, including the mound, as a visiting spot for anyone interested in the history, culture and archaeology of the region. We also intend to conduct numerous local, national, and international activities to make the results of our work even more visible and more accessible for anyone to learn from and enjoy. The local governors and academic collaborators are very enthusiastic to work with us and willing to be a part of this final phase, and Çadır Höyük is destined to become one of the top attractions for anyone who will visit this part of Turkey in the future.

Bibliography

Cassis, M.

– 2009 "Çadır Höyük: A Rural Settlement in Byzantine Anatolia," in T. Vorderstrasse and J. Roodenberg (eds.) *Archaeology of the Countryside in Medieval Anatolia*, Leiden, pp. 1–24.

Cassis, M., A. J. Lauricella, K. Tardio, M. von Baeyer, S. Coleman, S. E. Adcock, B. S. Arbuckle and A. Smith

– 2019 "Regional Patterns of Transition at Çadır Höyük in the Byzantine Period." *Journal of Eastern Mediterranean Archaeology and Heritage Studies* 7.3, pp. 321–49.

Cassis, M. and S. R. Steadman

– 2014 "Çadır Höyük: Continuity and Change on the Anatolian Plateau," in S. Stull (ed.), *East to West: Current Approaches to Medieval Archaeology*, Newcastle upon Tyne, pp. 140–154.

French, D. H.

– 2016 *Roman Roads and Milestones of Asia Minor. Volume 4: The Roads Fasc. 4.1, Notes on the Itineraria*. London.

Gorny, R. L., G. McMahon, S. Paley and L. Kealhofer

– 1995 "The Alişar Regional Project: 1994," *Anatolica* 21, pp. 68–100.

Hawkins, J. D.

– 2002 "Anatolia: The End of the Hittite Empire and After," in E. A. Braun-Holzinger and H. Matthäus (eds.), *Die nahöstlichen Kulturen und Griechenland an der Wende vom 2. zum 1. Jahrtausend v. Chr. Kontinuität und Wandel von Strukturen und Mechanismen kultureller Interaktion*, Möhnesee, pp. 143–151.

Omura, S.

– 2011 "The Stratigraphy of Kaman-Kalehöyük in Central Anatolia," in S. R. Steadman and G. McMahon (eds.), *Oxford Handbook of Ancient Anatolia*, Oxford, pp. 1095–1111.

Ross, J. C.

– 2010 "Çadır Höyük: The Upper South Slope 2006–2009," *Anatolica* 36, pp. 67–87.

Ross, J. C., G. McMahon, Y. Heffron, S. E. Adcock, S. R. Steadman, B. S. Arbuckle, A. Smith and M. von Baeyer

– 2019a "Anatolian Empires: Local Experiences from Hittites to Phrygians at Çadır Höyük,"

Journal of Eastern Mediterranean Archaeology and Heritage Studies 7.3: pp. 299–320.

Ross, J. C., S. R. Steadman, G. McMahon, S. E. Adcock and J. W. Cannon
- 2019b "When the Giant Falls: Endurance and Adaptation at Çadır Höyük in the Context of the Hittite Empire and Its Collapse," *Journal of Field Archaeology* 44.1, pp. 19–39.

Seeher, J.
- 2001 "Die Zerstörung der Stadt Hattuša." In G. Wilhelm (ed.), *Akten des IV. Internationalen Kongresses für Hethitologie. Würzburg, 4.–8. Oktober 1999.* Studien zu den Boğazköy-Texten 45, Wiesbaden, pp. 623–34.

Şenyurt, H. K.
- 2016 "Sarıkaya Roma Hamamı Tarihçesi ve 2010–2015 Yılı Kazı Çalışmaları Sonuçları" in K. Özköse and M. Fidan (eds.), *I. Uluslararası Bozok Sempozyumu, 5–7 Mayıs 2016*. Yozgat, pp. 110–21.

Steadman, S. R. and J. C. Ross
- 2020 "The Old Becomes New: Material Culture and Architectural Continuity on an Anatolian Höyük," in A. Blanco-González and T. Kienlin (eds.), *Current Approaches to Tells*, Oxford, pp. 47–55.

Steadman, S. R., G. McMahon, T. E. Şerifoğlu, M. Cassis, A. J. Lauricella, L. D. Hackley, S. Selover, B. Yıldırım, B. S. Arbuckle, M. von Baeyer, Y. Heffron, K. Tardio, S. Adcock, E. Dinç, G. Özger, B. Selvi, S. Offutt and A. Hartley.
- 2019a "The 2017–2018 Seasons at Çadır Höyük on the North Central Plateau," *Anatolica* 45, pp. 77–119.

Steadman, S. R., L. D. Hackley, S. Selover, B. Yıldırım, M. von Baeyer, B. Arbuckle, R. Robinson and A. Smith
- 2019b "Early Lives: The Late Chalcolithic and Early Bronze Age at Çadır Höyük," *Journal of Eastern Mediterranean Archaeology and Heritage Studies* 7.3, pp. 271–298.

Steadman, S. R., T. E. Şerifoğlu, S. Selover, L. D. Hackley, B. Yıldırım, A. J. Lauricella, B. S. Arbuckle, S. E. Adcock, K. Tardio, E. Dinç, G. McMahon and M. Cassis
- 2017 "Recent Discoveries (2015–2016) at Çadır Höyük on the Anatolian North Central Plateau," *Anatolica* 43, pp. 203–250.

Steadman, S. R. and G. McMahon
- 2017 "The 2015–2016 Seasons at Çadır Höyük on the North Central Anatolian Plateau," in S. R. Steadman and G. McMahon (eds.), *The Archaeology of Anatolia: Recent Discoveries (2015–2016). Volume II*, Newcastle upon Tyne, pp. 94–117.

Steadman, S. R. and G. McMahon
- 2015 "Recent Work (2013–2014) at Çadır Höyük on the North Central Anatolian Plateau," in S. R. Steadman and G. McMahon (eds.), *The Archaeology of Anatolia: Recent Discoveries (2011–2014). Volume I*, Newcastle upon Tyne, pp. 69–97.

Steadman, S. R., G. McMahon, J. C. Ross, M. Cassis, T. E. Şerifoğlu, B. S. Arbuckle, S. E. Adcock, S. Alpaslan Roodenberg, M. von Baeyer and A. J. Lauricella
- 2015 "The 2013 and 2014 Seasons of Excavation at Çadır Höyük on the Anatolian North Central Plateau." *Anatolica* 41, pp. 87–124.

Steadman, S. R., J. C. Ross, G. McMahon, and R. L. Gorny
- 2008 "Excavations on the North Central Plateau: The Chalcolithic and Early Bronze Age Occupation at Çadır Höyük." *Anatolian Studies* 58, pp. 47–86.

Steadman, S. R., G. McMahon, and J. C. Ross
- 2007 "The Chalcolithic at Çadır Höyük in Central Anatolia," *Journal of Field Archaeology* 32.4, pp. 385–406.

Voigt, M. M.
- 1994. "Excavations at Gordion 1988–89: The Yassıhöyük Stratigraphic Sequence, " in A. Çilingiroğlu and D. H. French (eds.), *Anatolian Iron Ages 3: The Proceedings of the Third Anatolian Iron Ages Colloquium Held at Van, 6–12 August 1990*, London, pp. 265–293.

Voigt, M. M.
- 2013 "Gordion as Citadel and City," In S. Redford and N. Ergin (eds.), *Cities and Citadels in Turkey: From the Iron Age to the Seljuks*, Leuven, pp. 161–228.

Yıldırım, B., L. D. Hackley and S. R. Steadman
- 2018 "Sanctifying the House: Child Burial in Prehistoric Anatolia," *Near Eastern Archaeology* 81.3, pp. 164–173.

Fig. 1. View of Çadır Höyük in 2013 looking north.
Inset map shows location of Çadır Höyük on the north central plateau.

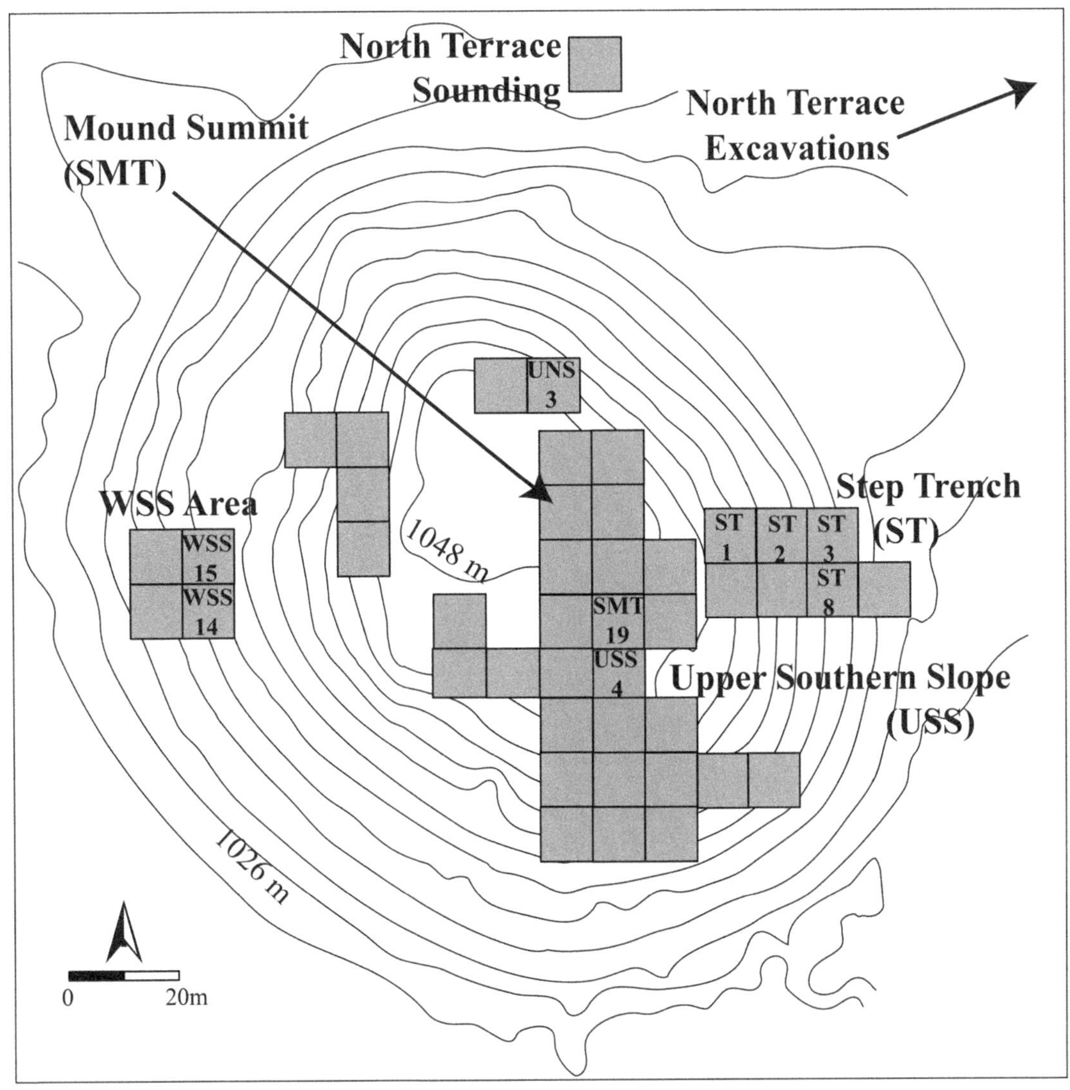

Fig. 2. Topographical plan of Çadır Höyük showing locations of open excavations (grey), noting areas and specific trenches discussed in the text.

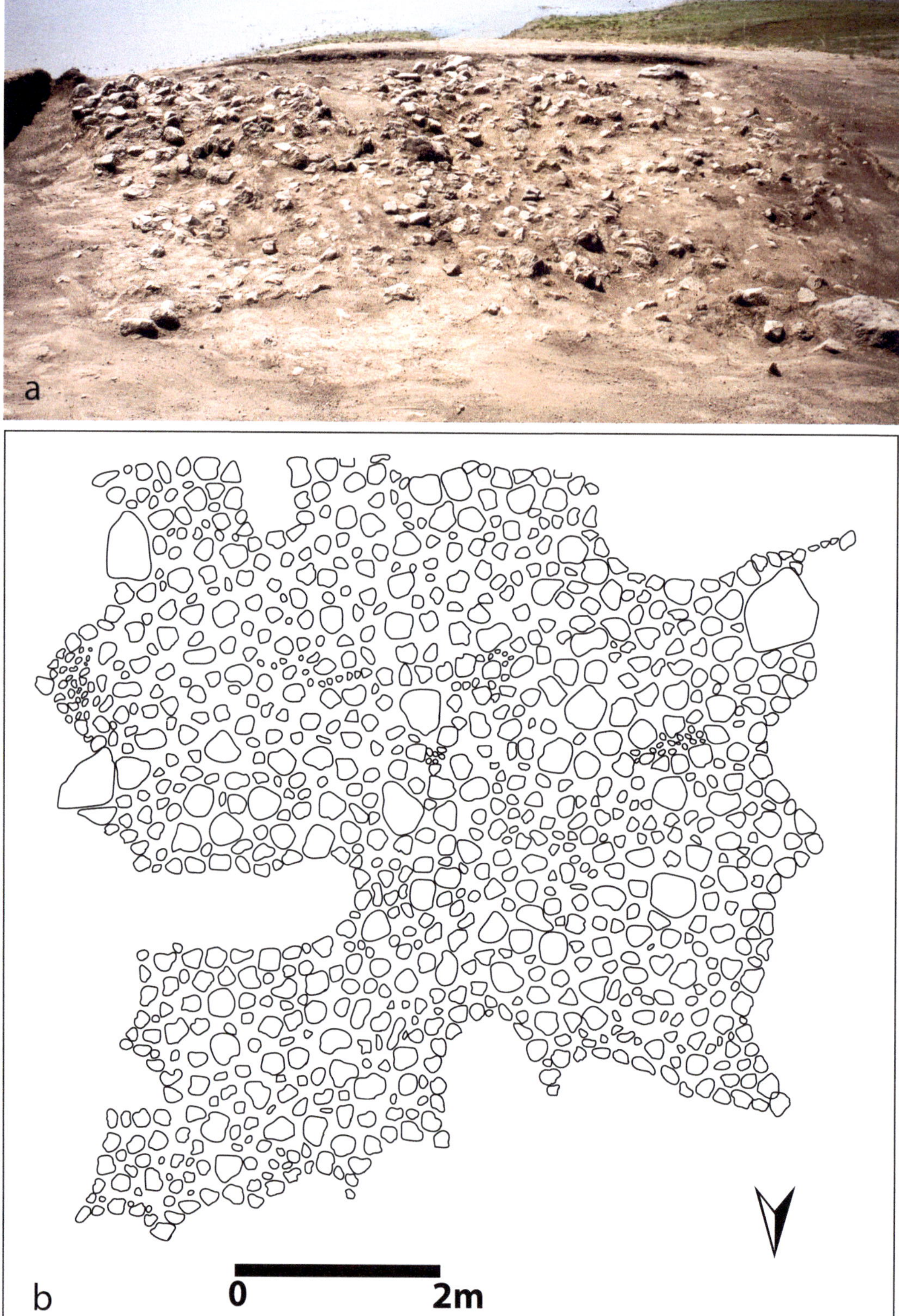

Fig. 3. The "stone pile" in SMT 19 which turned out to be nothing more than a stone pile.

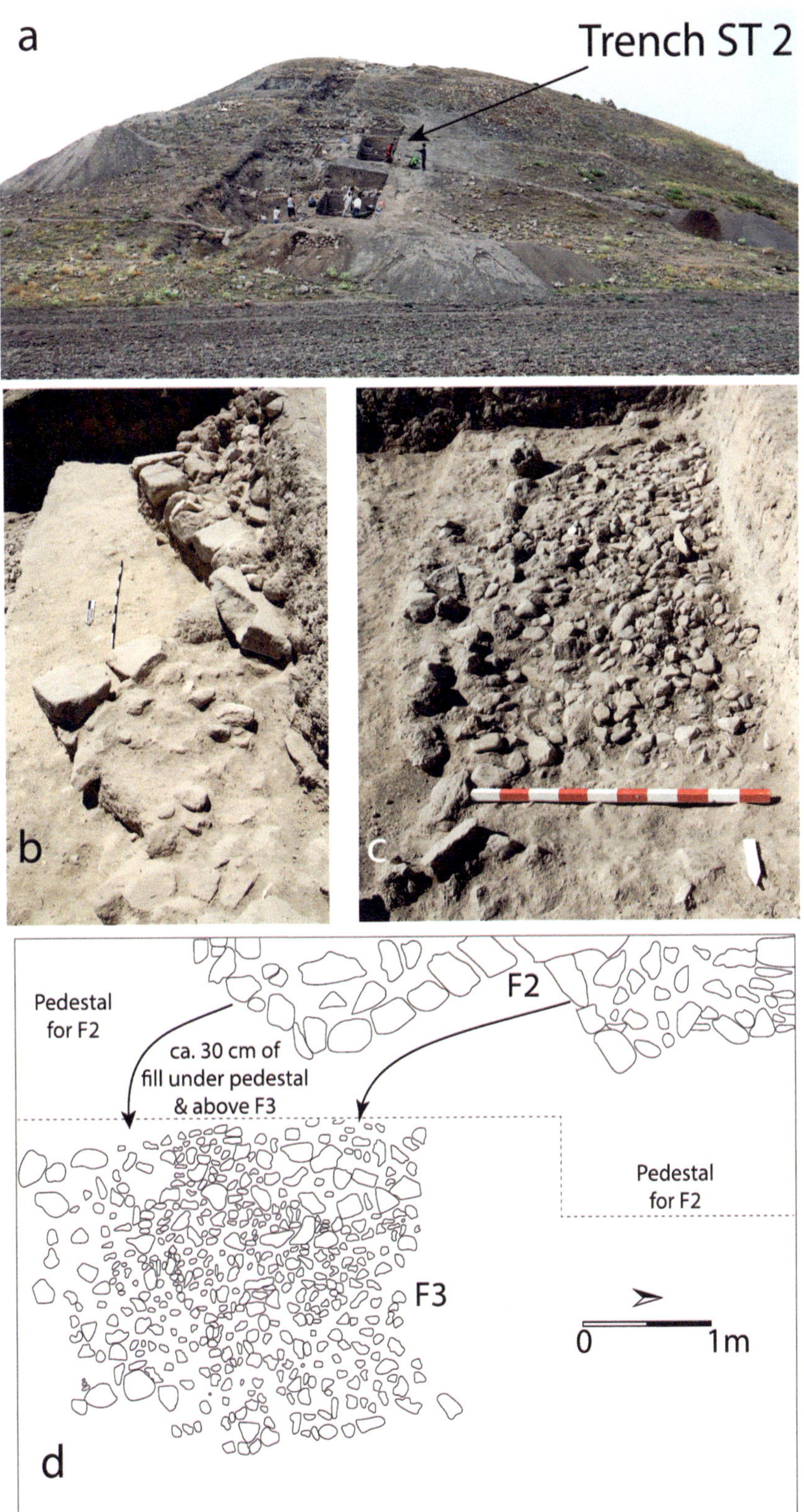

Fig. 4. a: View of Step Trench on eastern slope of mound; b: photo of F2 in trench ST 2 (looking south); c: photo of F3 in trench ST 2 (looking south); d: plan of drawings made by trench supervisor H. Kanzler showing juxtaposition of F2 and F3, separated by ca. 30 cm of mudbrick crumble and natural (slope wash) fill.

Fig. 5. a: Aerial view of mound showing location of the WSS trenches on steep western slope; b: photo of the very top of the "rock pile" in WSS 15 which included a layer of gravel and river stones; c: north-south wall in WSS 14 with baulk section (left side of photo) showing location of 5b rock pile in stratigraphy.

Fig. 6. Photo of WSS 14 buttress attached to the WSS 15 north-south aligned wall (see Fig. 5c).

Fig. 7. a: 2014 aerial view of mound with arrow showing location of ST 3 (and Step Trench) on eastern slope; b: 2014 aerial view of trenches ST 8 and ST 3 showing extensive Middle Bronze and Hittite stone and mudbrick architecture; c: burial of "Byzantine Florence" with arrow showing her burial location amidst the Middle Bronze architecture in Fig. 5b. A Byzantine partial vessel rests on "Florence's" hip in Fig. 5c.

Fig. 8. Photo of the types of USS 4 plastered Iron Age pits that yielded charcoal dating to the Early Bronze Age.

Fig. 9. a: Steadman perches (precariously) at the edge of a trench for a field photo in 2004; b: the Sorgun Fire Department hook-and-ladder truck at the 2008 final photos near its highest point; c: McMahon (left), Steadman (center), bucket operator (right) at highest point; d. Steadman and prism have a chat at the top of the mound overlooking Gelingüllü Lake.

Fig. 10. a: Ron Gorny (left; director of project from 1993–2009) and G. McMahon (right) in steep eastern slope Step Trench at beginning of 2001 excavations; b: the 1994 "perfect placement" of the summit datum point before excavations (datum point turned out to be the Byzantine defensive wall); c: G. McMahon balancing precariously at the total station on the excavated Byzantine wall (2017); d: the flotation device built by project friend Muzaffer, workmen share in the joy of the first gush of water from the pump in 2000 (it continues to work!); e: T. Emre Şerifoğlu excavating the WSS trenches.

Between Syria and Anatolia: The Many Aspects of a Long-Lasting Interaction

*Stefania Mazzoni**

As a toast to Sachihiro Omura, remembering friendly discussions between Ebla, Tokyo, Kaman-Kalehöyük and Uşaklı Höyük.

Abstract

The retrieval of an Old Syrian fragment of a basalt stele in a later context at Tell Afis provides the opportunity for a reappraisal of the pattern of trade and cultural interaction between North West Syria and Anatolia during the first part of the 2nd millennium B.C. After an in-depth stylistic and iconographic analysis of the monument, considerations about different types of objects (seals, vitreous materials, metal finds) are also offered to illustrate the complexity of contacts between the two areas at different levels of society.

Öz

Tell Afis'te MÖ 2. bin yılın ilk yarısına tarihlenen bazalt stelinin daha geç bir bağlamda bulunması, Kuzeybatı Suriye ile Anadolu arasındaki ticaret ve kültürel etkileşim modelinin yeniden değerlendirilmesi için fırsat sağlamaktadır. Anıtın derinlemesine üslup ve ikonografik analizinin ardından, toplumun farklı düzeylerinde iki bölge arasındaki ilişkilerin karmaşıklığını göstermek için farklı türdeki nesnelere (mühürler, camsı malzemeler, metal buluntular) ilişkin düşünceler de sunulmaktadır.

Introduction

Connections between Syria and Anatolia have always been a vital component of the social and economic developments of both regions. Movements of people and goods were easy along the banks of the many riverine valleys that crossed mountains and highlands, and constituted natural routes of communication: the Euphrates and its tributaries, the Khabur and Balikh and the rivers draining the Amuq from the north, Afrin and Kara-su from the south, and the Orontes in the northern sector of the Rift Valley. The western system of riverine routes was certainly used from the Halaf-Obeid and Late Chalcolithic periods on, as documented by the diffusion of common cultural traits (stamp seals, pottery, architecture) and the rise of a network of rural villages exploiting the most fertile plains on both sides of the Taurus range. The emergence of political centers with rulers, who could manage more or less vast territories and accumulate food and resources, had the beneficial effect of increasing productivity, consumption, work and specialised crafts in the shadow of the administrative organisations of the economic hubs of the period: palaces and temples. Economic and political relations between kingdoms were expanded along various trajectories crossing the inner zones, inland Syria, and Anatolia, as indicated in the course of the Early Bronze Age by the diffusion of various materials; objects such as seals, weapons, jewels, and special vessels for official display and use in the institutional sphere. Toward the end of the third millennium, during the period of primacy in Mesopotamia of the Ur III dynasty,

* Università degli Studi di Firenze.

merchants and messengers travelled regularly across the entire Near East, with Byblos and Ebla included in the Neo-Sumerian network of exchange. Inner Anatolia started to interact directly with Mesopotamia, as is documented by recent findings in the late 3rd millennium levels of the acropolis of Kültepe/Kanesh, where the presence of a palace gives evidence of a centralised power.[1] The emergence of political powers with their economic wealth, rich native resources, heavy metal ores, and specialized production of metal artefacts[2] attracted the interest of the more powerful kingdoms of the period; a trading organization was created in Ashur that founded commercial outposts in several Anatolian towns – the Cappadocian *karums* – in Middle Bronze I, contemporary to the Old Assyrian and archaic Old Syrian periods.

Contacts between Syria and Anatolia increased in this period in the wake and in the orbit of the Old Assyrian colonial organisation, and were characterized by distinct dynamics which included political and cultural interaction as well as economic exchanges. This process is documented by the circulation in Syria and Anatolia of various materials and the creation of a shared repertoire of images with their symbolic significance and specialised use. This second case can be represented by the group of the "Syro-Anatolian cursive linear style" seals, often made of clay and showing rows of figures alternating between symbols and animals, engraved in a linear style well identifiable by the schematic rendering of the body details by use of the drill and disc.[3] Seals of this group have been found in many sites of the Levant, Syria and Anatolia; two impressions and their original seal from Tell Hammam et-Turkman on the Balikh, and two impressions from Tell Biʿa (ancient Tuttul) on the Euphrates,[4] were used in specific activities and maybe owned by officials or merchants as a part of a guild operating in the major towns of the area. A further impression on a jar stopper (or a sealing of a box or a sack) found at Beth Shean[5] attests to the movement of goods imported, probably from northern Syria, is tentatively and cautiously identified in the area of the Khabur on the basis of the petrographical analysis.

While these seals are indicative of the diffusion of common cultural traits and social affinities between Syria and Anatolia, other materials, valuable goods and precious objects were exchanged over long-distances within the framework of diplomatic and political interplay and accordingly betray a shared ideological and religious background, and related ritual and official performances with their material paraphernalia.

1 Kulakoğlu 2017. See the numerous bullae found at Kültepe in the recent excavations: Kulakoğlu, Öztürk 2015, Fig. 4; and particularly a lapislazuli cylinder seal from a Level 11B grave underneath Temple 1, and consequently dated to the final EB III showing a presentation scene of Ur III style: Öztürk 2019: 54–55, Fig. 6.

2 Recent researches have revealed evidence of extraction of tin and metal working near to Kültepe at Hisarcik on the foothills of the Erciyas montain dominating with its high profile the plain of Kayseri. Yener *et alii* 2015.

3 Mazzoni 1975; 1995, 407, no. 250. B. Porter (2001: 171–181) re-considered in detail and implemented this group of seals that she defined as schematic seals and a subset within the Oòd Syrian Popular Style. Many seals of this group have been found in the excavations in Syria and Anatolia that increase the list given in 1975 and 2001, and help to support the hypothesis of a distinct social role of their owners in the context of the trade system; as for the date, the seals found in primary context suggest a quite long life between the 19th–18th cent. B.C. i.e. between Kültepe IB and the end of Mardikh IIIB, but with antecedents of a similar style found in Kültepe II; however, considering the possibility of re-use, a date to MB I and early MB II for their original diffusion seems more appropriate (Mazzoni 1995: 407, no. 250; Porter 2001: 180). New specimens from Anatolia, at Kaman-Kalehöyük: Omura 2005: 26, Fig. 61; Büklükale: Matsumura 2014, p. 429, Fig. 9.Fig. 9.

4 Meijer 1995 (for the Tell Hammam et-Turkman seals and impressions); Otto 2004: 88–89, no. M 91, Pl. 93, 2a–e (for the impression of Tell Biʿa).

5 Amihai Mazar (2018) gives a suggestive interpretation of the detail of the "hunchback" detail of the body characterizing many seals of this group as a rendering of sacks carried by the figures and illustrating their activity as traders. For the petrographical analyses see Goren 2018.

A Fragment of a Stele from Tell Afis and the Avanos/Akarca Monument

A fragment of an Old Syrian stele[6] (Fig. 1a–b) was found in a layer constituted by numerous basalt flakes, pieces of sculptures, and carved pieces of basalt among which there was a fragment of an Aramaic inscription:[7] this layer covered the structures of the entrance hall of the Iron III temple AI on the summit of the acropolis of Tell Afis. Temple AI was the latest of a sequence of sacred buildings documented by the excavations, which date from Iron Age I (10th cent. B.C.: temples AIII.1–2), Iron II (9th–8th cent.: temple AII) and Iron III (final 8th–7th cent.: temple AI).[8] Sculptures, and reliefs were probably part of the decoration of the Iron II–III temples which suffered lengthy and extensive spoliation in classical and medieval times when the latest monumental building became a quarry for extracting building materials such as basalt and limestone blocks that constituted the massive foundations and bases of the Iron II–III buildings.

The Old Syrian stele may have been installed in the hall at the entrance, or have been inserted in a wall as an ancient sacred monument, probably preserved from an earlier Middle Bronze Age temple lying under the Late Bronze and Iron Age strata; buildings and structures of the MB periods are well documented in the western and eastern areas of the acropolis.[9]

The stele shows, at the top, the astral symbols; the moon is clearly preserved and below it a crouched bull lies mid-air in the field. On the left margin the point of a peaked cap of a personage looking right is the only visible element of the original figure; on the right margin we can recognize the rounded cap of another figure facing left.

The image of the relief, although only preserved in a small fragment, can be easily identified as a presentation or homage scene; on the right the round cap belongs to a personage facing left towards the figure wearing the peaked cap. This personage is well known and documented in various scenes of presentation and ritual offerings in different media – stone sculpture and seals – and can be identified with the king of Ebla on the basis of his presence in the scenes carved on the face of the stone basins from Ebla and in seals and seal impressions from Kültepe II and IB, two of which are inscribed with the name Eb-Damu, king of Ebla.[10]

6 TA.03.A.290: Mazzoni 2005: 10, Fig. 8.2; D'Amore 2005: 19, Fig. 15.1; Mazzoni 2013: 211, Fig. 10; 2016: 309–310, Fig. 12.

7 D'Amore 2005: 18–19, Fig. 18. For the inscription see Amadasi 2009, 2014: 54–55, Fig. 2.

8 Soldi 2009; Mazzoni 2012, 2019.

9 The outer town and the acropolis of the Middle Bronze Age I–IIA were walled by a complex system of fortifications excavated in Areas B (northern lower town), E (western acropolis) and N (eastern acropolis; a domestic quarter was built inside the walls in Area E: Mazzoni 2013: 209–212. For Area N, see now Di Michele 2021.

10 The association of the figure wearing the peaked cap in the Kültepe impression with the figure represented in the upper register of the face of the basin from Temple D of Ebla has been first suggested by Edith Porada (1980: 386 (2c. Der Kolonial-Syrische Stil); Porada 1985: 94). Beside the basin TM.65.D.226 (Matthiae 1966: 113–129, Pl. XLIV) also a second basin in the Museum of Aleppo (found in the site before the start of the Italian excavations) shows the figure with the peaked cap (see *ibidem*, p. 115, note 55, and Matthiae 1965: 71–73, Pl. LXX). Matthiae associated this figure to the one represented with a similar cap in two seals of Syrian style and identified the headgear as a Syrian royal thiara (1965: 78, note 54; 1966: 126, note 106; see discussion in Porter 2001: 270–273). Later B. Teissier (1993) investigating the provenance of ten seal impressions (five from the Adad-sūlūli archive of Karum II, a few showing the peaked cap figure, compared with the figure of the Ebla basins (and a golden leaf plaque from Byblos) supported an attribution to north-western Syria. Teissier (1994: 58) has then published the impressions nos. 529a–b (a: with an inscription of Eb-damu mekim Eb-la; reading by K. Veenhof), 530, 533, 536. D. Owen (1990, p. 120, footnote 50) related the epithet Mekum of the inscription of the torso of Ibbit-Lim of Ebla with the epithet of the Kültepe impression, and M.V. Tonietti (1997: 225) offered a thorough analysis of the title of Mekum in the literary sources. P. Matthiae (2003: 390) aknowledged this identification and added further arguments; cf. also N. Marchetti (2003), and L. Peyronel (2017: 199–200). See now a full discussion of the data

We could, therefore, suggest that the scene originally carved in the Afis fragment may have represented the homage of an overseer, probably of Afis, to the king of Ebla. Ebla was the capital of north-western Syria during the MB I–II period (19th–18th cent. B.C.), and maintained its importance as a religious center when Yamkhad, alongside Aleppo, was the leading kingdom of the region. Afis was certainly in the political orbit of Ebla in MB I–IIA, being an important walled town very rich in agriculture, exploiting a fertile alluvial plain to its north, and also controlling the strategic crossroads that connected Aleppo with the Mediterranean. Furthermore, two Old Syrian cylinder seals from Afis (Figs. 2a–b, 3a–b) showing the peaked cap personage,[11] offer another relevant document of the respect paid to this figure in Afis. It is worth noting that one of them (Fig. 3a–b) representing the peaked cap personage seated in front of a jar and an altar with a bull, was found in the area of Temple I; it constitutes a further testimony of the connection of the peaked cap figure with the cult of the Storm-god.

A good comparison for understanding the original composition of the scene represented in the Afis fragment comes from a Syro-Cappadocian seal with the figure with the peaked tiara seated on the left, and the officer standing and facing him from the right.[12] When I first published this fragment I had suggested that the astral symbols topping the scene and the crouching bull in the field could have hinted at the presence of the Storm-god, who might have been represented standing and smiting in a register of the monument not preserved. However, as an impression from the Adad-ṣūlūli archive from Kültepe II[13] gives the closest comparison for the bull appearing in mid-air in front of the ruler with the peaked tiara making a libation to a god with the rays issuing from his shoulders, I could not exclude for the Afis fragment the presence of another god, such as the Sun-God. Certainly, the possible presence of the Storm-god, also proposed in the case of the impression of Eb-damu, ruler of Ebla,[14] seems to be particularly appropriate for the fragment from Afis, found, albeit in a secondary context, in the Iron Age temple probably dedicated to a local Storm-god. A further element connecting the Afis stele to Ebla is the representation of the astral symbols that appear on top of a fragmentary basalt stele found re-used in the village of Mardikh (Fig. 4); under the symbols is preserved the high conical tiara that identifies the personage wearing it as a ruler well known in Old Syrian seals of MB II On this basis this fragment is certainly later than the Afis fragment.[15] The astral symbol appears on two other Old Syrian stelae, one from Hama, re-used as the entrance threshold over the court B in Batiment II of the citadel of level E destroyed in the 8th cent. B.C., and a second one from the Collection Alsdorf.[16]

in Matthiae 2020: 158–159, 224–229, Figs. 1.9, 9.2, 11.16; Pl. XXII.1, Fig. 11.16.

11 TA.99.E.185: Mazzoni 2000: 17–18, Fig. 13.1; 2005: 10, Figs. 8.2–3. TA.03.A.33: Soldi 2005: 27–28. Fig. 21.1.

12 Teissier 1993: 610–611, no. 12, from private collection.

13 Teissier 1993: 609, Fig. 1.

14 Teissier 1993: 609, Fig. 4 = Teissier 1994, no. 629a: the bull appears over the inscription behind the god, who cannot, again, be identified by specific attributes. P. Matthiae (2003: 390–391) identified the god wearing a headdress with a plume and holding a mace or a flamed weapon, or a snake, near the nude goddess (identified as the Ishtar of Ebla), with the Storm-god in the group of seals of the peaked cap ruler.

15 TM.85.S.450: Matthiae 1993, p. 390, note 13, Pl. 69: 2. A basalt stele from Tell Afis found in the modern cemetery at the eastern border of the lower town represents only a similar astral symbol and may date to a later period on the basis of its shape and smaller dimensions: Mazzoni 1998; see p. 11 for a comparison with TM.85.S.450.

16 Riis and Buhl (1990, no. 48: 56–58, Fig. 26) compared the astral symbol with the Hittite "signe royale." See Pinnock 1992 and her comments for the astral symbol at p. 116. It is interesting that this stele represents a banquet and the double-headed eagle under the astral symbol; see pp. 115–116. The Aldsorf stele has been analysed by Di Paolo 2006 (for the astral symbols see pp. 147–148).

The best comparison for interpreting the Afis fragment comes now from a basalt stele found at Avanos-Akarca in central Anatolia.[17] The stele is preserved in nearly all of its upper part, and is completely carved on four sides by individual scenes depicting rituals and images belonging to the cultic sphere. An in-depth stylistic and iconographic analysis has enabled us to date the stele to the archaic Old Syrian period and propose a provenance from north-western Syria. The scene carved on the face (Obverse: A) represents the personage with the peaked tiara standing and receiving the homage of two figures approaching him; on the top appear the astral symbols, a crouching goat, and a star. The fragments of Afis and Ebla correspond to parts of this scene with minor variants: the bull instead of the goat in the Afis fragment, and the tall tiara in the Ebla fragment (Fig. 5). The other main scene in the Avanos monument shows a banquet on the reverse side (C) and, on the lateral sides, a winged bearded god (B) and the Storm-god riding his bull over the mountains (D); the scale pattern representing the mountains decorates the stele pervasively, especially the upper field of the scenes with the gods and represents the base as a natural landscape on which the Storm-god and his bull move.

The direct comparisons with the many representations of the peaked cap ruler in the monuments of Ebla, and the impressions from Kanesh, provided the documentary base for the attribution of the monument to north-western Syria. E. Genç and U. Yanar have proposed that the Avanos stele reached Anatolia as war booty of the kings of the Old Hittite Kingdom after their conquest of northern Syria. The practice of taking captive also the images and statues of gods and kings is well documented in the Near East and Anatolia by literary sources, as rightly pointed out by these authors.[18] This is certainly an attractive hypothesis and can help to situate our fragments in the same historical context. We can suggest that the Afis stele may have been destroyed when Afis fell to the powerful Hittite army, but Afis seems to have been abandoned in an earlier phase of MB II, while Ebla (Mardikh IIIB) was instead destroyed in the late MB II, final 17th cent. B.C. probably at the time of the raid into northern Syria by Murshili I, and possibly by a Hurrian chief.[19] We can therefore maintain the hypothesis that the fragment belonged to a stele still preserved at Afis in the Iron Age temple.

The Avanos-Akarca stele representing the king of Ebla may have been installed originally in Ebla itself[20] but also in other centers that may have acknowledged its authority and housed the cult to a Storm-god connected to the sacred mountain of his epiphany: some elements, such as a certain flavor of *horror vacui*, the representation of the Storm-god on his bull on the mountains, the winged god seem to refer to a more norther cultural milieu.[21] Apart from Aleppo,

17 Genç and Yanar 2019 have offered a detailed description and an in-depth interpretation of the scenes represented on the stele, and supplyed a large set of comparisons.

18 Genç and Yanar 2019, p. 81.

19 Wilhelm 2001 has given a convincing translation of the "Chant of the Release; P. Matthiae (2020, p. 163–166, XXVI–XXVII) considering that that the expedition of Khattusili I in northern Syria mentions the destruction of Alalakh and that the pottery of Mardikh IIIB is later than the pottery of Alalakh VII attributed the destruction of MB IIB Ebla after the raid of Khattusili I and to the conquest by a Hurrian chief mentioned in the "Chant of the Release."

20 It is true that the rich iconographic cultic context of the Avanos monument can be found only in the Ishtar stele of Ebla, as correctly stressed by Genç and Yanar (2019: 79–81, Fig. 12); the clear division in registers may be indicative of a date of the Ishtar stele in a mature phase of MB II, later than the Avanos one, reflecting a more archaic style. Matthiae dates the Ishtar stele to around 1800 B.C.(Matthiae 2020: 238–243, Fig. 11.25, Pl. XXIII)

21 The image of the Storm-god on his bull appears in the Anatolian group of seal impressions from Kültepe, with their complex cultic iconographic repertoire of Akkadian derivation: Özgüç 1965: 63–64, Pl. XI.31, XXIII.70, XXIV.71 (type a); XXIII.68 (type d). The transmission of the Akkadian model in northern Syria and in the Hurrian milieu of Urkish can be appreciated in an impression showing a god and an animal moving on the high mountains: G. Buccellati and M. Kelly-Buccellati 1997, p. 93, figure top right)

the main center of the Storm-god,[22] other towns conquered by the Hittite king Khattusili (Ikakali and Hashshu, beside Urshu which lie more to the north) can be proposed.[23] There is no doubt, however, that the historical scenario has to be better understood and documented by further sources.

The Afis stele can be properly interpreted in a regional background in the frame of the veneration of the Storm-god and the sacred mountains, specifically Mount Hazzi/Saphon/Casius (Jebel el 'Aqra) which is well visible from Tell Afis on clear days as a remarkable landmark.[24] Furthermore, if the scene represented the homage to a deceased king of Ebla, it belongs to the funerary ideology and cult of ancestors which, from the 3rd millennium on, was an important components of the legitimation of the Ebla dynasty. The kings of Ebla recognized, in fact, their origins and anchored their territorial power in the area north of Tell Afis, which included the towns of Neirab and el Athareb, where funerary pilgrimages and rituals were performed.[25] In this area, Afis was the main MB settlement which controlled the route to the Mediterranean and Aleppo, consequently playing a role in the ancestral territory of the Ebla kingdom. Afis was, moreover, the seat of the Storm-god cult at least from the 2nd millennium. The route connecting Syria and Anatolia, and linking Ebla and Kanesh by way of Afis, Aleppo and other centers, was not only a commercial route, but may have also represented a cultic trajectory into the mountainous landscape of the Storm-gods.

Precious Objects and Gift Exchange

Diplomatic, as well as commercial exchanges were probably a significant factor in the development of political and economic interaction between the kingdoms, as is well attested by the circulation of precious objects in official milieu, palaces, and temples from the 3rd mill. B.C. Excavations in the area of the *karum* have produced extensive evidence of the circulation of goods managed by private traders who belonged to the orbit of their institutional patrons. However, some single documents could hint at a different, probably official, level of exchange. The presence of materials of Anatolian provenance in Syria is documented at Ebla and has been analysed in detail, as in the case of the bronze pans found in a MB II grave with a cylinder seal showing the double lion-headed eagle,[26] or in the case of metals, such as ingots, balance-weights, lead figurines and stone moulds for figurines.[27] Many of these materials are documented in the MB I–II burials lying at

suggested that it may have represented Silver, the son of Kumarbi, the patron god of Urkish, roaming on the mountains in search of his father.

22 For the importance of the 3rd millennium Storm-god of Aleppo see Archi 2010. The temple of the Middle Bronze Age has been identified under the Iron Age monumental building: Kohlmeyer 2013, p. 184–192, Fig. 5; see the Old Syrian fragmentary reliefs from the area of the temple, Figs. 9–10.

23 We know that Hashshum and Ikakali were under the political orbit of Ebla in 3rd millennium B.C. and we may suppose that some of them may have recognized the protective role of the king of Ebla still at the very beginning of 2nd millennium around 1900–1850 B.C. in MB I. We also know that Ebla kept prisoners the leaders of Ikakali according to the "Chant of Release" (above, nt.19), at the time of Khattushili I and Murshili I. For the towns taken by Khattushili I see De Martino 2003: "Annali di Khattusili I", pp. 34–36 (Alalakh, Ikakali, Urshum), 50–53 (Hashshu). Urshu can be identified with Gaziantep: Archi 2020, p. 33–34. Aleppo was not taken by Khattushili I but by Murshili I, while Ebla is not mentioned

24 Mazzoni 2016: 311, Fig. 14. Hazzi was the seat of the Hurrian Teshub, Saphon of the Ugarit Baal and Casius of Zeus, see the image of the Storm-god striding over two peaks in Old Syrian cylinder seals and Yazilikaya, identified as Mounts Hazzi and Namni, the Jebel el 'Aqra and the Amanus. See Yasur-Landau 2017, p. 133–134; Healey 2020.

25 This is the plain of the Jazr: Mazzoni 2020: 348–352; Matthiae 1980 for the identification of Athareb with Darib: this was one of the places in the region connected to the cult of the ancestors of the Ebla dynasty: Archi 2012.

26 Mazzoni 2000b, 2011; for the seal see also 1995: 407, no. 249. Peyronel 2017 re-considered these and other materials in the context of the Ebla-Kanesh interconnections; see p. 204 for the pans.

27 Peyronel 2017: 200–201.

the base or on the lower slopes of the acropolis of Ebla and seem to belong to artisans; this was suggested for the grave containing two andesite stone casting moulds for Syrian fenestrated axes,[28] while the seal and the pans of the other grave perhaps belonged to a tradesman connected to Anatolia.

Another find discovered among the many and precious grave goods in the "Tomb of the Princess" is a glazed pottery vase which was certainly an import to Ebla (Figs. 6, 7.1). The vase[29] has an elaborate shape, a sort of deep carinated bowl or chalice with pointed base and slightly grooved body; the original elliptical handles are missing but they would have curved upwards. The body is completely covered by a thick glaze and is decorated with vertical lines of blackish paint on the neck and body. The vase is unique, but we have to admit that other single glazed vases and objects are documented at Ebla which seem to belong to a local production and can, in fact, be compared with local types. The most notable is the cup with a female mask and Hathoric headdress, with comparisons to a similar glazed vase from Alalakh; they can be dated to late MB II and constitute the antecedents of the well known female chalices especially documented at Ugarit.[30] In any case, the shape of the vase from the Tomb of the Princess finds no parallels in the local MB pottery horizon; two similar vases made of rock crystal and two made of obsidian (Fig. 7.2–3) from the Palace of Serikaya in Acem Höyük (and found in the same room as the group of ivories that joined those in the MMA Pratt collection) offer the most direct comparison.[31] These stone chalices were certainly produced in Anatolia, as no doubt indicated by the use of local materials such as rock crystal, and especially obsidian. Vessels of the same type are documented at Acem Höyük and Kültepe by Burnished Ware specimens.[32] It is clear that these chalices, with their distinct fluted decoration and pointed base, were manufactured in central Anatolia and reflect the mastership and creativity of the local craftsmen, well documented by the many ritual vessels and their great variety of shapes.

The production of glazed materials and faience is considered to have been not well diffused in Anatolia in the earlier 2nd millennium, as in Syria and Mesopotamia where the presence of glazed pottery vessels is represented in a small percentage alongside the far more frequent personal ornaments (beads, amulets) in the 3rd millennium B.C.[33] However, a re-consideration of faience objects, mostly female figurines and small vessels, from Kültepe Ib, Alişar Höyük level 10 (compared to specimens from Ras Shamra niveau II), and Alaca Höyük (all of MB I–II date) has provided documentary evidence of objects in faience and also vessels and cups in glazed pottery.[34] Some of these have been considered imports from Syria or Mesopotamia and consequently the possibility of local manufacturing centres has been variously debated.[35] A few other objects found in

28 *Ibidem*: 202–203, Fig. 9.

29 TM.78.Q.150: H.12,2; diam. opening 8,2/5,4; diam. body: 7,5. Tomb of the Princess, Hypogeum Q.78. A. Mazzoni 1995, p. 456, no. 369, dated to BM I–II, ca. 1825–1775 B.C. See the vase in place in Matthiae 1985: 270–271, Pl. 71. Matthiae 2020: 270–271, Fig. 14,39.

30 Mazzoni 1987: 66, Fig. 1; 1995, p. 457, n. 370 (see here also nos. 368,371); Matthiae 2020: 271, Pl. XXVI.

31 Özgüç 1966: 42, 48–49, Figs. 4–6, Pl. XXIII.1 (rock crystal); XXIII.2,3a–b (obsidian); these, out of 5 specimens, could be restored. See other similar shapes from Kültepe in obsidian with fluted body, pointed base and vertical handles: Özgüç 1986: 50 (Kt.82/K 261, Pl. 95.7; three fine specimens in red and dark grey polished ware from level II show similar fluted decorations and were considered as metal imitations: 56, Pl. 111.2–4.

32 Emre 1966, Pl. XXXV.1.

33 Moorey 1994: 171–175.

34 Özgüç 1986: at p. 207 noted the limited number of vases in faience from Anatolia; Moorey 1995, p. 176 analyzed in detail the published faience from Anatolia and discussed its date in MB I–II.

35 Foster 1979: 46 followed the attribution of the Kültepe and Alişar specimens to northern Syria. Özgüç 1986: 205, 207, defended the existence of indigenous Anatolian faience workshops, mostly on the basis of the diffusion of stamp seals, The presence of workshops in southern Anatolia in the final phase of MB may also have been favoured by contacts with Syria,

Kültepe and Ebla are strictly comparable; this is the case of the miniature couple seated from the two sites, which could also come from a unique centre. However, in this case as well it is not easy to understand from which workshop they were produced between Syria and Anatolia.[36]

The case of the chalice from Ebla can be more easily attributed, as mentioned above, to an Anatolian workshop; form and decoration belong to a local tradition of luxury vessels made of precious materials and technologically sophisticated craftmanship for ritual or official commensality, in the tradition of the two-handled bowls, such as the *depas* and tankard of the 3rd millennium B.C. This attribution apparently corroborates the hypothesis of an Anatolian manufacture of glazed materials in local workshops, which may be at the base of the development of a more sophisticated glass technology which is now documented at Büklükale.[37]

It is important at this point to examine the context of the Ebla chalice and its association with the grave goods of a woman. Among these goods there were four jugs of the North-Syrian Cilician Painted Ware of early MB IIA date; jugs of this group are also known from Kültepe (II), where they were imported;[38] the specimens date the "Tomb of the Princess" to 1825–1775 B.C. The faience chalice represents, however, a unique document from central Anatolia, and attests to connections existing between the centers of this period, though it is of course difficult to say whether such connections between the courts were direct or mediated. However, as we know that Ebla tradesmen were active in the *karum* of the earlier period, and the king of Ebla acknowledged by his image and title, the hypothesised direct relations between the two kingdoms seems plausible. It is then possible to suggest that the chalice may have constituted an example of gift exchange; we may speculate whether it was a precious object that had belonged to the deceased and was buried with her, as were the earring and jewels decorating her arm, maybe her wedding goods, following a practice known from sources dating from the 3rd millennium.[39]

We may also suppose that the chalice could have been sent for the funerals with its content of ointments or perfumes. The fact that it was carefully placed above the other grave goods, and opened (Fig. 8), could indicate that the aromatic substances contained therein were to perfume the burial. The custom of sending gifts for the funerals of members of the courts is also documented by historical sources.[40]

Conclusions

The objects here examined attest to the cultural and economic interaction connecting Syria and Anatolia in the first half of the 2nd millennium, as well as to different levels of exchange established by tradesmen and between the courts and elites. On one side, there was a consistent

and Anatolian artisans, with the possible assistance of Syrian itinerant craftsmen who may have produced faience.

36 Özgüç 1986: 204–205, Ill. 10a–b, from a pot grave of level Ib was compared with one from Assur; Mazzoni 1987: 66–69, Fig. 2.

37 Matsumura 2018, Henderson et alii 2018, Matsumura 2020. See for the earliest examples from Tell Açana/Alalakh, level VII: Dardeniz 2018; Gries, Schmidt 2020: 243, discussing the relevant Assur Late Bronze production.

38 Nigro 2009: 125–129. Pl. XII–XV; Peyronel 2017: 197–198, Fig. II; Matthiae 2020: 273: 353 for the date of the tomb.

39 For the bracelets see Matthiae 2020: 261–262, Fig. 12.10–11. Textual sources from third millennium Ebla indicate that "the clothes and jewels which these ladies (from the royal family) received on their marriage or their ordination as priestesses were exactly the same as those destined to adorn them on their burial. They were not, however, the objects that they had used when alive": Archi 2002: 178–79.

40 In the texts of Ebla, personal objects were listed among the expenditure for the burial: the same object could not be cited twice among the lists of expenditure which were drawn up for the many occasions celebrated in the palace. As a consequence, there were funerary goods and gifts intended to be worn and used by the deceased in the afterlife. Neo-Assyrian funerary inscriptions (Nasrabadi 1999: 25–31) cite funerary gifts or personal ornaments to be worn on the occasion of the internment, as a part of the funerary rite.

flow of goods and raw materials resulting from commercial interaction and there was a group of agents and officials regulating the transactions in the various centers, probably using their own type of seal (the Syro-Anatolian linear cursive style). Furthermore, craftsmen and traders circulated in both regions and their funerary goods attest to their activity in life, as we can suggest for the tomb of the owner of the two bronze pans and his seal. There was a further and higher level documented by rare and precious objects in the context of institutional gift exchange between the courts of this period, and these were more probably sent for various occasions, strengthening political agreements with their economic value, or constituting presents to honour inter-dynastic marriages or funerals of personages recognized for their social position. Exotic imported objects belong to this sphere of interaction. That the kings of Ebla and their officials were active counterparts of the Anatolian trade networks is documented by the presence and use of seals showing the peaked cap personage who was the king of Ebla receiving homage, probably as a deified ancestor, or instead performing rituals to the gods. This brings us back to the ritual basins of Ebla, the Afis fragment and seals, and the Avanos stele. If this last was taken to Anatolia as booty from northern Syria (we may suppose besides Ebla, Afis and Aleppo, also Ikakali and Hashshu), this can only indicate that the images represented were understood in their political significance and religious value. The diffusion of images and monuments celebrating rituals and the cult of the main protective gods, particularly the Storm-god, as an act of legitimacy of the power, identifies a further level of interaction between Syria and Anatolia that pertains to the political sphere of communication.

Bibliography

Amadasi, M.G.
- 2009 "Un fragment de stèle araméenne de Tell Afis," *Orientalia* 78, pp. 336–347.
- 2014 "Tell Afis in the Iron Age: the Aramaean Inscriptions," *Near Eastern Archaeology* 771, pp. 54–57.

Archi, A.
- 2002 "Jewels for the Ladies of Ebla," *Zeitschrift für Assyriologie* 92, pp. 161–199.
- 2010 "Hadda of Halab and its Temple in the Ebla Period," *Iraq* 72, pp. 3–17.
- 2012 "Cult of the ancestors and funerary practices at Ebla," in P. Pfälzner, H. Niehr, E. Pernicka and A. Wissing (eds.), *(Re-)Constructing Funerary Rituals in the Ancient Near East, Proceedings of the First International Symposium of the Tübingen Post-Graduate School "Symbols of the Dead" in May 2009*, Qatna Studien Supplementum 1, Wiesbaden, pp. 5–31.

Archi, A.
- 2020 "Linguistic and Political Borders in the Period of the Ebla Archives," K.A. Yener and T. Ingman (eds.), *Alalakh and its Neighbours. Proceedings of the 15th Anniversary Symposium at the New Hatay Archaeological Museum, 10–12 June 2015*, åAncient Near Eastern Studies. Supplement 55, Leuven, Paris, Bristol, pp. 31–40.

Buccellati G. and M. Kelly-Buccellati
- 1997 "Urkesh.TheFirstHurrianCapital",*Biblical Archaeologist* 60:2, pp. 79–86.

D'Amore ,P.
- 2005 "Area A1: il settore centrale," in "Tell Afis – Siria 2002–2004," *Egitto e Vicino Oriente* 28, pp. 17–21.

Dardeniz, G.
- 2018 "The Preliminary Archaeological and Scientific Evidence for Glass Making, Hatay, Turkey," *Anatolian Archaeological Studies* 21, p. 95–110.

De Martino, S.
- 2003 *Annali e Res Gestae antico ittiti* (Studia Mediterranea 12), Firenze.

Di Michele, A.
- 2021 *Tell Afis (Syria). Excavations Seasons 2001–2007. Phases XI–I Middle Bronze Age – Iron Age I. Stratigraphy, Architecture and Pottery*, Studi di Archeologia Siriana 7, Firenze.

Di Paolo, S.
- 2006 "The Relief Art of Northern Syria in the Middle Bronze Age: The Alsdorf Stele and Some Sculptures from Karkemish," in F. Baffi, R. Dolce, S. Mazzoni and F. Pinnock (eds.), *Ina Kibrat Erbetti, Studi di Archeologia Orientale Dedicati a Paolo Matthiae*, Roma, pp. 139–163.

Emre, K.
- 1966 "The Pottery from Acemhöyük," *Anadolu* 10, pp. 99–153.

Foster Polinger, K.
- 1979. *Aegean Faience of the Bronze Age*, New Haven and London..

Genç E. and U. Yanar
- 2019 "An Old Syrian Period stele from Avanos. Karca, Anatolia," OLBA 27, pp. 61–96.

Goren, Y.
- 2008 "Appendix: Material Examination of the Cylinder Seal Impression from Beth Shean," I.1, J.R. Chadwick, L. Hitchcock, A. Dagan, Ch. McKinny and J. Uziel (eds.), *Tell it in Gath. Studies in the History and Archaeology of Israel. Essays in Honor of Aren M. Maeir on the Occasion of his Sixtieth Birthday*, Ägypten und Altes Testament, 90, Münster, pp. 164–166.

Gries H., Schmidt K.
- 2020 "The Core-Formed Glass Vessels from Middle Assyrian Aššur," *Zeitschrift für Assyriologie und Vorderasiatische Archäologie* 110/2, pp. 242–275

Healey, J.
- 2020. "The Sacred Mountains of Ugarit and Alalakh? Mount Kasion and Related Issues," in K.A. Yener and T. Ingman (eds), *Alalakh and its Neighbours. Proceedings of the 15th Anniversary Symposium at the New Hatay Archaeological Museum, 10–12 June 2015*, Ancient Near Eastern Studies. Supplement 55, Leuven, Paris, Bristol, pp. 307–316.

Henderson, J., S. Chenery, S. Omura, K. Matsumura and E. Faber
- 2018 "Hittite and Early Iron Age Glass from Kaman-Kaleh.yük and Büklükale, Turkey: Evidence for Local Production and Continuity?," *Anatolian Archaeological Studies* 21, pp. 70–84.

Kohlmeyer, K.
- 2013 "Der Tempel des Wettergottes von Aleppo," in K. Kaniuth, A. Löhnert, J. L. Miller, A. Otto, M. Roaf and W. Sallaberger (eds.), *Tempel im Alten Orient. 7. Internationales Colloquium der Deutschen Orient-Gesellschaft 11.13. Oktober 2009, München*, Colloquien der Deutschen Orient-Gesellschaft 7, Wiesbaden, pp. 179–218.

Kulakoğlu F. and G. Öztürk
- 2015 "New Evidence for International Trade in Bronze Age Central Anatolia. Recent Discovered Bullae at Kültepe-Kanesh," *Antiquity* 89, Issue 343.

Kulakoğlu, F.
- 2017 "Early Monumental Bronze Age Structures," in F. Kulakoğlu and G. Barjamovic (eds), *Movement, Resources, Interaction KIM 2. Proceedings of the 2nd Kültepe International Meeting, Kültepe July 2015*, Subartu XXXIX, Turnout, pp. 217–226.

Marchetti, N.
- 2003 "Notes on an Old Syrian Seal Impression from Sippar," *Iraq* 65, pp. 161–169

Matsumura, K.
- 2014 "Büklükale Kazisi 2012,"35. *Kazı Sonuçları Toplantısı* 3, Muğla 2013, pp. 428–430
- 2018. "The Glass Bottle and Pendant from Büklükale and Their Dating," *Anatolian Archaeological Studies* 21, pp. 11–29.
- 2020 "Glass Production Centre in Central Anatolia? Büklükale in Relation to Alalakh and Mesopotamia," K.A. Yener and T. Ingman (eds.), *Alalakh and its Neighbours. Proceedings of the 15th Anniversary Symposium at the New Hatay Archaeological Museum, 10–12 June 2015*, Ancient Near Eastern Studies. Supplement 55, Leuven, Paris, Bristol, pp. 103–116.

Matthiae, P.
- 1965 "Le sculture in basalto," in A. Davico, M. Floriani Squarciapino, M. Liverani, P. Matthiae, P. Minganti and F. Pericoli Ridolfini (eds.), *Missione Archeologica Italiana in Siria. Rapporto preliminare della Campagna 1964*, Roma, pp. 61–80.
- 1966 "Le sculture in pietra," in G. Castellino, S.M. Cecchini, A. Davico, M. Floriani Squarciapino, P. Fronzaroli, M. Liverani, P. Matthiae and G. Matthiae Scandone (eds.), *Missione Archeologica Italiana in Siria. Rapporto preliminare della Campagna 1965 (Tell Mardikh)*, pp. 103–142.
- 1980 "Appunti di iconografia eblaita, II," *Studi Eblaiti* 2: 41–47.
- 1985. *I Tesori di Ebla*, Bari: Laterza.
- 1993 "A Stele Fragment of Hadad from Ebla," in M. Mellink, E. Porada and T. Özgüç (eds.),

Aspects of Art and Iconography: Anatolia and its Neighbors. Studies in Honor of N. Özgüç, Ankara, pp. 389–397.
– 2003 "Ishtar of Ebla and Hadad of Aleppo: Notes on Terminology, Politics and Religion of Old Syrian Ebla," *Semitic and Assyriological Studies Presented to Pelio Fronzaroli by Pupils and Colleagues*, Wiesbaden, pp. 381–397.
– 2020 *Ebla. Archaeology and History*, Cities of the Ancient World.

Mazar, A.
– 2018 "Middle Bronze Syro-Anatolian Cylinder Seals and Impressions from Tel Beth Sheans," in I. Shai, J. R. Chadwick, L. Hitchcock, A. Dagan, Ch. McKinny and J. Uziel (eds.), *Tell it in Gath. Studies in the History and Archaeology of Israel. Essays in Honor of Aren M. Maeir on the Occasion of his Sixtieth Birthday*, Ägypten und Altes Testament, 90, Münster, pp. 153–163.

Mazzoni, S.
– 1975 "Tell Mardikh e una classe glittica siro-anatolica del periodo di Larsa," *Annali dell'Istituto Orientale di Napoli* 35, pp. 21–43.
– 1979 "A proposito di un sigillo in stile lineare-corsivo da Tell Mardikh," *Studi Eblaiti* 1, pp. 49–64.
– 1987 "Faience in Ebla during Middle Bronze Age II," in M. Bimson and I. C. Freestone (eds.), *Early Vitreous Materials*, British Museum, Occasional Papers, no.56, London, pp. 65–77.
– 1995 "Nos. 249–250, 368–370," P. Matthiae, F. Pinnock and G. Scandone Matthiae (eds.), *Ebla Alle origini della civiltà urbana*, Milano, pp. 407, 456–457.
– 1998 "Une nouvelle stèle d'époque araméenne de Tell Afis (Syrie): *Transeuphratène* 16 *Mélanges Jacques Briend III*, pp. 9–18.
– 2000a "Sigilli del Bronzo Medio e Tardo dall'Area E," Tell Afis Siria – 1999, *Egitto e Vicino Oriente* 22, pp. 17–19.
– 2000b "Handled Pans from Ebla and the Evidence of Anatolian Connections," in R. Dittmann , B. Hrouda, U. Löw, P. Matthiae, R. Mayer-Opificius and S. Thürwächter (eds.), *Variatio Delectat Iran und Westen. Gedenschrift für Peter Calmeyer*, Alter Orient und Altes Testament 272, Münster, pp. 403–413.
– 2005 "Tell Afis, the Survey and the Regional Sequence," *Egitto e Vicino Oriente* 28, pp. 5–14.
– 2011 "Bronze Pans from Ebla," in M. Rossi (ed.), *Archaeology for Cooperation. Afis – Deinit and the Museum Of Idlib – Activities in the frame of the MEDA Project*, Studi di Archeologia Siriana 1, Napoli 2011, pp. 107–109.
– 2012 "Temples at Tell Āfis in Iron Age I–III," in J. Kamlah (ed.), *Temple Building and Temple Cult. Architecture and Cultic Paraphernalia of Temples in the Levant (2.–1. Mill. B.C.E.)*, Abhandlungen des Deutschen Palästina-Vereins 41, Wiesbaden, pp. 23–40.
– 2013 "Tell Afis History and Excavations," *Near Eastern Archaeology* 76/4, pp. 204–213.
– 2016 "Storm Gods at Tell Afis and a Syro-Hittite Seal," in J. Patrier, Ph. Quenet and P. Butterlin (eds), *Milles et une empreintes. Un Alsacien en Orient. Mélanges en l'honneur du 65e anniversaire de Dominique Beyer*, Subartu 36, Turnhout, pp. 299–318.
– 2019 "Iron I Temples at Tell Afis," in F. Briquel Chatonnet, E. Capet, E. Gubel and C, Roche-Hawley (eds.), *Nuit de pleine lune sur Amurru. Mélanges offerts à Leila Badre*, Paris 2019, pp. 307–321.

Meijer, J. D.
– 1995 "A Cylinder Seal and some Ramifications," in Th. P. J. Van den Hout and J. De Roos (eds.), *Studio Historiae Ardens: Ancient Near EasternSstudies Presented to Philo H. J. Houwink ten Cate on the Occasion of his 65th Birthday*, pp. 195–203.

Moorey, P. R.S.
– 1994 Ancient *Mesopotamian Materials and Industries. The Archaeological Evidence*, Oxford.

Nasrabadi, B.
– 2010 Untersuchungen zu den Bestattungssitten in Mesopotamien in der *Ersten Hälfte des Ersten Jahrtausends v. Chr.* (Baghdader Forschungen 23), Mainz am Rhein.

Özgüç, N.
– 1965 *Kültepe MühürBaskılarında Anadolu Grubu. The Anatolian Group of Cylinder Seal Impressions from Kültepe*, Ankara.
– 1966 "Excavations at Acem Höyük," *Anadolu* 10, pp. 29–52.

Özgüç, T.
– 1986a *New Researches at the Trading Center of the Ancient Near East*, Ankara.
– 1986b "Glazed Faience Objects from Kanesh," in M.-Kelly-Buccellati (ed.), *Insight through Images. Studies Honor to Edith Porada*, Bibliotheca Mesopotamica 21, Malibu, pp. 201–208.

Öztürk, G.
- 2019 "Post-Akkadian and Ur III Features on Cylinder Seals from Kültepe-Kanesh: An Iconographic and Stylistic Analysis," *Adalya* 22, pp. 45–68.

Omura, S.
- 2005 "Preliminary Report on the 19th Excavation at Kaman-Kalehöyük (2004)," *Anatolian Archaeological Studies* 14, pp. 1–54.

Otto, A.
- 2004 *Siegel und Siegelabrollungen, Ausgrabungen in Tall Bi'a/Tuttul, Bd. 4*, Wissenschaftliche Veröffentlichung der Deutschen Orient-Gesellschaft 104, Saarbrücken.

Owen, D.
- 1990 "Syrians in Sumerian Sources from the Ur III Period," in M. W. Chavalas and J. L. Hayes (eds.), *New Horizons in the Study of Ancient Syria*, Bibliotheca Mesopotamica 25, pp. 121–175.

Nigro, L.
- 2009 *I corredi vascolari delle Tombe Reali di Ebla e la cronologia ceramica della Siria interna nel Bronzo Medio*, Materiali e Studi Archeologici di Ebla 8, Roma.

Peyronel, L.
- 2017 "From Ebla to Kanesh and Vice Versa. Reflections on Commercial Interactions and Exchanges between Northern Syria and Anatolia during the Middle Bronze Age," F. Kulakoğlu and G. Barjamovic (eds), *Movement, Resources, Interaction, KIM 2. Proceedings of the 2nd Kültepe International Meeting, Kültepe 26–30 July 2015*, Subartu 39, Turnout, pp. 197–216.

Pinnock, F.
- 1992 "Una riconsiderazione della stele di Hama6B599," *Contributi e Materiali di Archeologia Orientale* 4, pp. 101–121.

Porada, E.
- 1980 "Kaniš, Karum. C. Die Glyptik," *Reallexikon der Assyriologie*, V/6, Berlin, pp. 383–389.
- 1985 "Syrian Seals from the Late Fourth to the Late Second Millennium," H. Weiss (ed.), *Ebla to Damascus. Art and Archaeology of Ancient Syria*, Washington, pp. 90–104.

Porter, B.
- 2001 *Old Syrian Popular Style Cylinder Seals*, Columbia University, New York.

Riis, P. J. and M. L. Buhl
- 1990 *Les objets de la période dite syre-hittite (Âge du Fer). Hama. Fouilles et Recherches 1931–1938* (NationalMuseets Skrifter Større Beretninger 12), København.

Soldi, S.
- 2005 "Area A1: il settore occidentale," in Tell Afis – Siria 2002–2004, *Egitto e Vicino Oriente* 28, pp. 25–29.
- 2009 "Aramaeans and Assyrians in North-Western Syria: Material Evidence from Tell Afis," *Syria* 86, pp. 97–118.

Teissier, B.
- 1993 "The Ruler with the Peaked Cap and other Syrian Iconography on Glyptic from Kültepe in the Early Second Millennium," in M. Mellink, E. Porada and T. Özgüç (eds), *Aspects of Art and Iconography: Anatolia and its Neighbors. Studies in Honor of N. Özgüç*, Ankara, pp. 601–612.
- 1994 *Sealing and Seals on Texts from Kültepe Karum Level 2*, Publications de l'Institut historique-archéologique néerlandais de Stamboul LXX, Istanbul.

Tonietti, M. V.
- 1997 "Le cas de *Mekum*: continuité ou innovation dans la tradition éblaite eentre IIIe et IIe millénaires?," *Mari Annales de Recherches Multidisciplinaires* 8, pp. 224–242.

Venturi, F.
- 2012 "New Evidence of Cultural Links Between Syria and Anatolia Through Analysis of Late Bronze Age II Tell Afis material culture," *Orientalia* 81.1, pp. 1–31.

Wilhelm, G.
- 2001 "Das hurritisch-hethitisch 'Lied der Freilassung'," in M. Dietrich et *alii* (eds.), *Texte aus der Umwelt des Alten Testaments, Ergänzungslieferung*, Gütersloher Verlag, pp. 82–91.

Yasur-Landau, A.
- 2017 "Twin Peaks: From Mt. Saphon to the Pillars of Herakles,"in B. Halpern, K. S. Sachs and T. E. Kelley (eds), *Cultural Contact and Appropriation in the Axial-Age Mediterranean World. A Periplos*, Leiden/Boston, pp. 129–136.

Yener, A. K., F. Kulakoğlu, E. Yazgan, R. Kontani, Y. Hayakawa, J. Lehner and G. Dardeniz
- 2015 "New Tin Mines and Production Sites Near Kültepe in Turkey: A Third Millennium B.C. Highland Production Model," *Antiquity* 89 345, pp. 596–612.

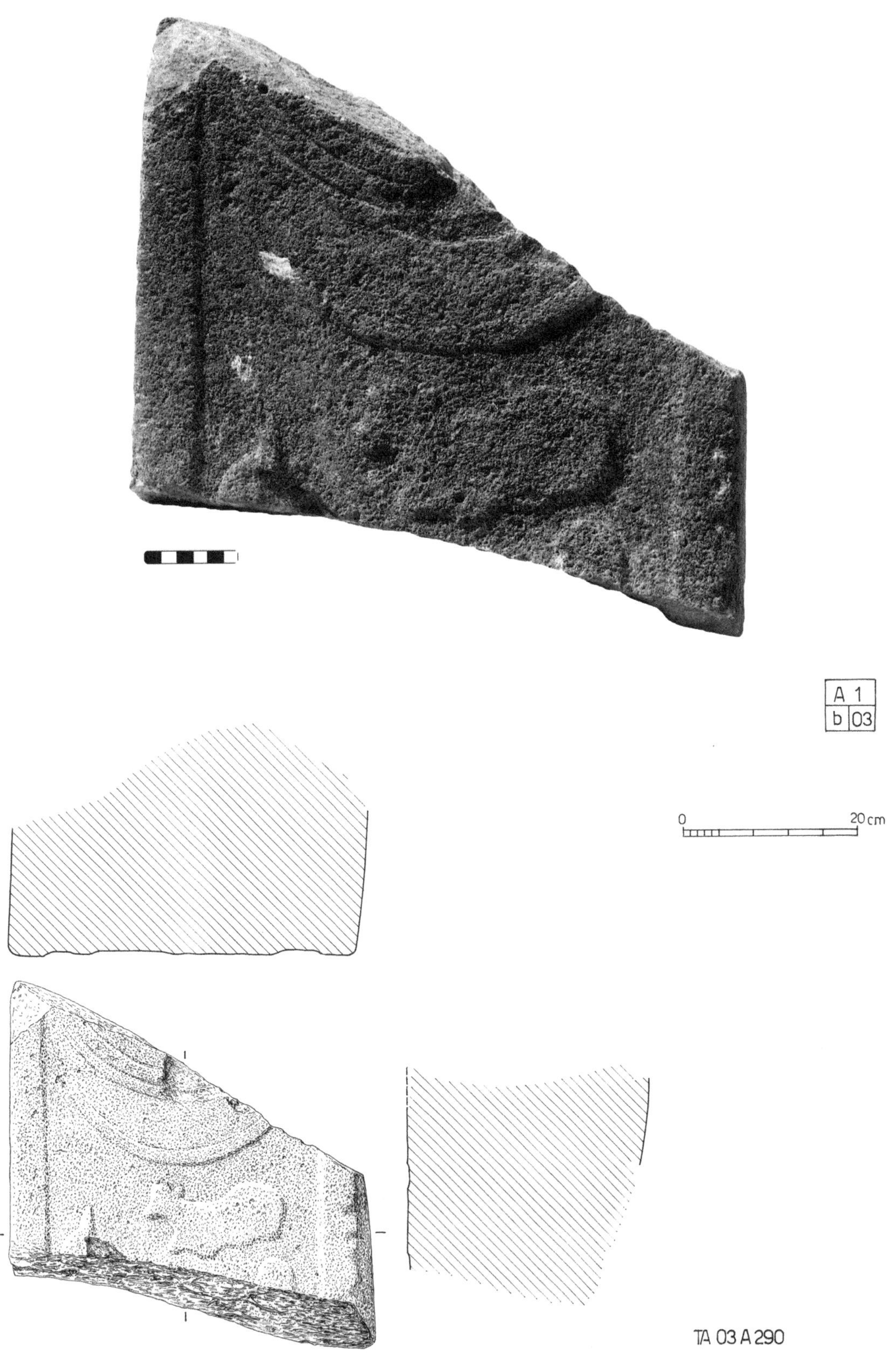

Fig. 1a,b. Fragment of the Old Syrian stele TA.03.A.290, area A, Tell Afis (drawings by Sergio Martelli).

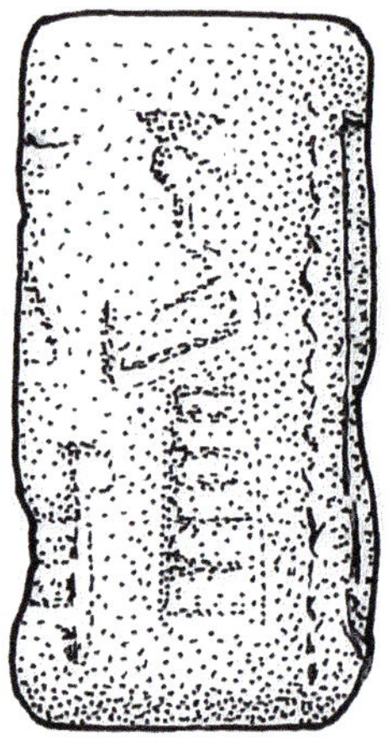

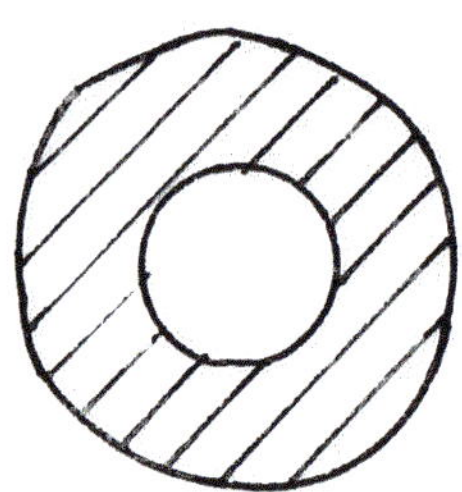

TA 99 E 185

Fig. 2a, b. Old Syrian cylinder seal TA.99.E.185, area E, Tell Afis (drawings by Sergio Martelli).

TA 03 A 33

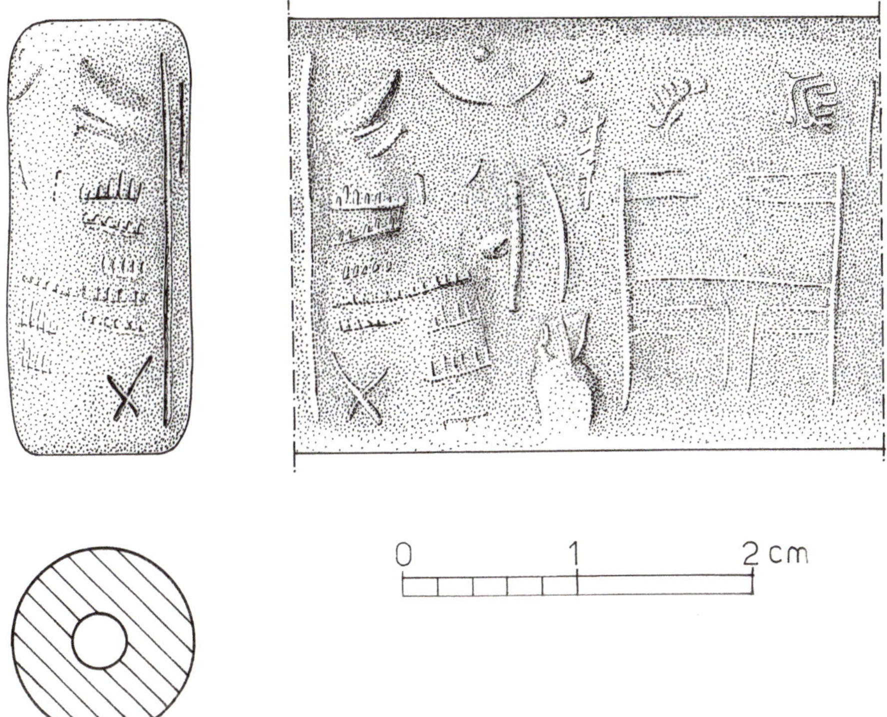

Fig. 3a, b. Old Syrian cylinder seal TA.03.A.33, area A, Tell Afis (drawings by Sergio Martelli).

Fig. 4. Fragment of the Old Syrian stele TM.85.S.450, Tell Mardikh-Ebla

Fig. 5. The stele from Avanos (Turkey) compared with the Tell Afis and Tell Mardikh Old Syrian stele (drawings by Sergio Martelli).

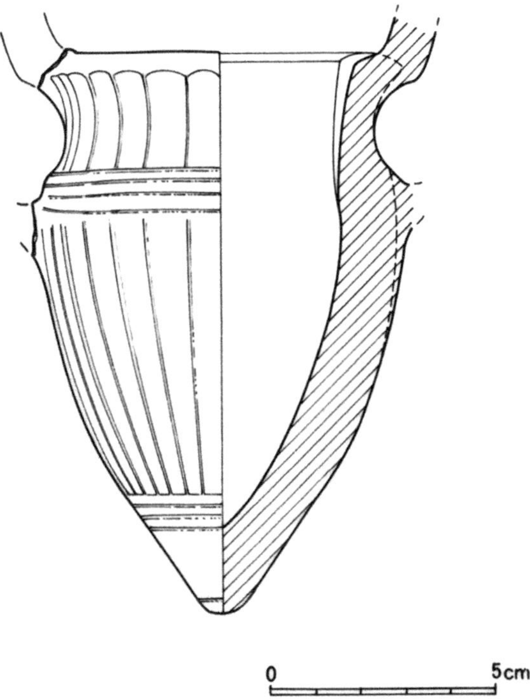

Fig. 6 a, b. Glazed vase TM.Q.150 from are Q, Tomb of the Princess, Tell Mardikh-Ebla (drawings by Sergio Martelli).

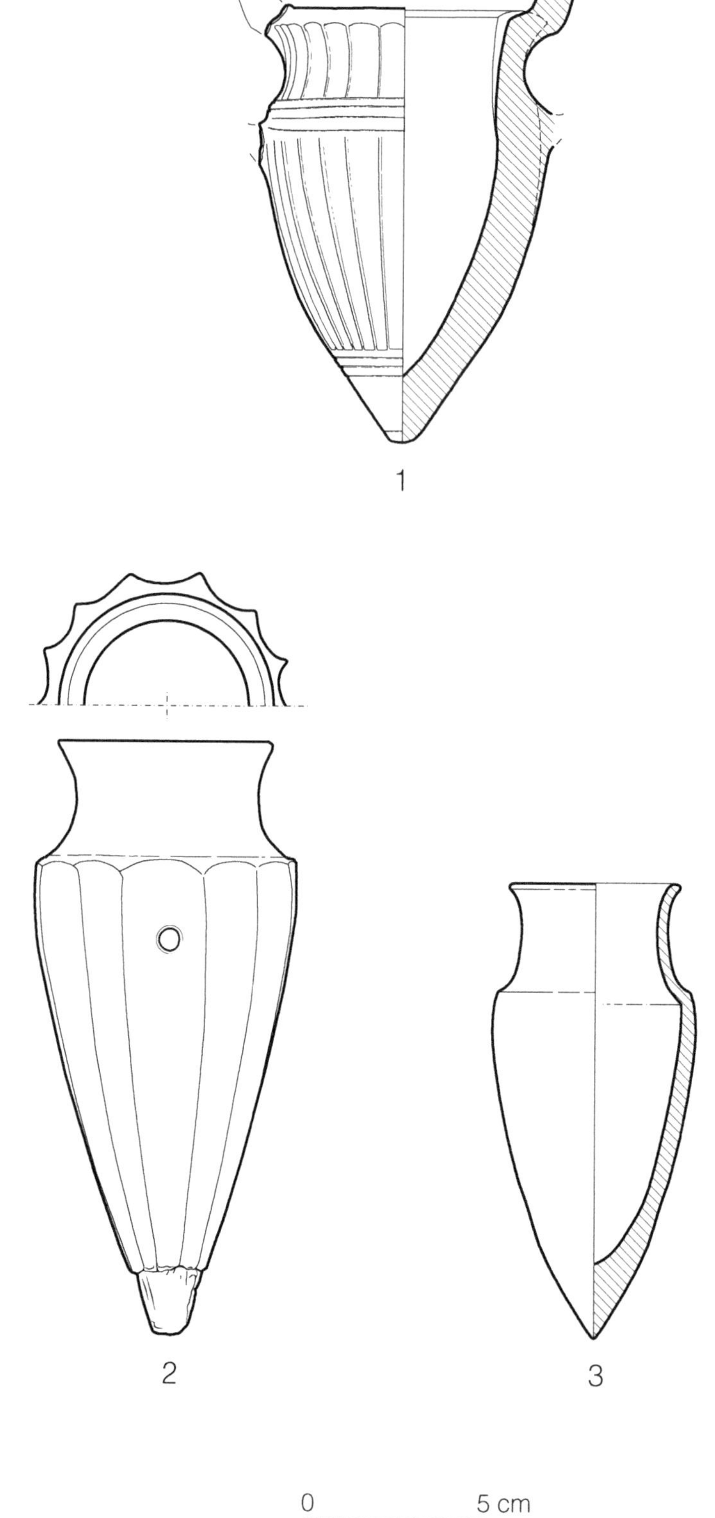

Fig. 7. 1. Glazed vase TM.Q.150 from Tell Mardikh; 2–3. Rock crystal vases from the Palace of Sarıkaya, Acem Höyük (drawings by Sergio Martelli).

The Iron Age in Amasya Province: In the Light of New Evidence From Oluz Höyük and the Harşena Fortress

*Şevket Dönmez and E. Emine Naza-Dönmez**

Abstract

During the collapse of the Hittite Empire, approximately at the beginning of the 12th century B.C., the Thraco-Phrygian migrations, drought and famine that occurred with adverse climate change, as well as the great earthquakes that occurred in the late thirteenth century B.C., led to the Hittites leaving the Land of Hatti and moving to the south and southeast. It might be thought that the Kaška people also played an important role in their retreat to southeastern Anatolia. Similar pottery sherds decorated with dotted triangles, found in the Middle and especially the Late Phase of the Dark Age settlement in Boğazköy-Büyükkaya, were unearthed in Oluz Höyük Architectural Layer 7A, as well as in Eskiyapar, Çorum and Amasya provinces, which constitute the distribution area of this paint-decorated pottery group, which was observed to have emerged just after the Hittites left the region in the Kızılırmak Bend and indicate some new human movements in the 12th century B.C. The place-name Kašku mentioned in Neo-Assyrian sources has a clear relationship with the name Kaška mentioned in Hittite written documents, and it seems quite logical to equate the Land of Kašku with today's Yozgat – Çorum – Amasya – Samsun. Considering that there was an integrity in the pottery tradition and paint decoration in this region during the Dark Ages, it can be seen that these communities took action from north to south in the Early Iron Age, that they played an important role in the Hittite abandonment of the Kızılırmak Bend and it is understood that they settled the region in

Öz

Hitit Büyük Krallığı'nın yaklaşık olarak MÖ 12. yüzyılın başlarında yıkılmasında Thrako – Frig göçleri, olumsuz iklim değişikliği ile birlikte ortaya çıkan kuraklık ve kıtlık, MÖ 13. yüzyıl sonlarında meydana gelmiş olan büyük depremler kadar Hititlerin Hatti Ülkesi'ni terk edip, güney ve güneydoğu Anadolu'ya çekilmelerinde Kaškalar'ın da önemli bir rol oynadıkları düşünülebilir. Boğazköy-Büyükkaya'daki Karanlık Çağ yerleşmesinin Orta ve özellikle Geç Evresi'nde ele geçen, içleri noktalanmış üçgenlerle süslü çanak – çömlek parçalarının benzerleri, Eskiyapar'ın yanısıra, Oluz Höyük'ün 7A Mimari Tabakası'nda da açığa çıkarılmıştır. Kızılırmak Kavsi İçi'nde Hititler'in bölgeyi terk etmesinden hemen sonra ortaya çıktığı gözlenen boya bezekli bu çanak – çömlek grubunun yayılım alanını oluşturan Çorum ve Amasya illeri, MÖ 12. yüzyılda bir takım yeni insan hareketlerine işaret etmektedir. Yeni Assur İmparatorluğu yazılı kaynaklarda yer alan Tabal Kızılırmak Kavsi'nin güneyi ile lokalize edilmektedir. Tabal ile birlikte bazı kaynaklarda pek çok yer adının geçmesi, bu bölge civarındaki topraklarla ilgili tarihsel coğrafya verileri sağlamaktadır. III. Tiglat – Pileser'e (MÖ 745–727) vergi verenler listesinde Kaşku ya da Kaşkili Dadilu'nun adının geçmesi bölgenin tarihsel coğrafyası bakımından önemlidir. Hitit yazılı belgelerinde anılan Kaška ismi ile ilişkisi çok açık olan Kašku'dan yola çıkarak Kašku Ülkesi'ni bugünkü Yozgat – Çorum – Amasya – Samsun ile eşitlemek oldukça mantıklı görünmektedir. Karanlık Çağ'da bu bölgede çanak –çömlek geleneğinde boya bezeme genelinde bir bütünlük olduğu düşünülürse, insan topluluklarının kuzeyden güneye doğru Erken Demir Çağı'nda harekete geçtiğini, Hititlerin Kızılırmak Kavsi İçi'ni terk etmelerinde önemli bir rol oynadıklarını ve Demir Çağı'nda bölgeyi iskân ettikleri anlaşılmaktadır.

* Prof. Dr. Şevket Dönmez, İstanbul Üniversitesi, Faculty of Letters, Department of Protohistory and Near Eastern Archaeology, Beyazıt 34453, İstanbul – Prof. Dr. E. Emine Naza-Dönmez, İstanbul Üniversitesi, Faculty of Letters, Department of Turkish and Islamic Art, Beyazıt 34453, İstanbul.

the Iron Age. The existence of painted pottery pieces with plant and geometric motifs and Scythian-type bronze arrowheads found in the excavations of Harşena Fortress in Amasya city center prove that there was a settlement in the Maidens Palace area, politically under Achaemenid (Persian) rule and traditionally under the influence of Phrygian culture. These findings indicate that a similar and parallel process took place as in Oluz Höyük, located 25 km southwest of Amasya.

Amasya kent merkezindeki Harşena Kalesi kazılarında bulunmuş olan bitkisel ve geometrik motiflerle bezenmiş boya bezekli çanak-çömlek parçaları ile İskit tipi mahmuzlu tunç ok uçlarının varlıkları, Kızlar Sarayı Mevkiinde politik olarak Akhamenid (Pers) egemenliğinde, geleneksel olarak ise Phryg kültürü etkisinde bir yerleşmenin olduğunu kanıtlamaktadır. Bu bulgular, Amasya'nın 25 km güneybatısında yer alan Oluz Höyük ile benzer ve koşut bir süreç yaşanmış olduğuna işaret etmektedir.

Introduction

At the time of the destruction of the Hittite Empire around 1180 B.C. and the retreat of the Hittites to southern and south-eastern Anatolia, the abandonment of their homeland Hatti was caused by the aggression of the *Kaška* people as well as the *Thraco-Phrygian* migrations, drought and famine caused by climate change as well as destructive earthquakes at the end of the 13th century B.C. (see Map 1). As the Büyükkaya excavations at Boğazköy had proven, with the beginning of the Dark Age (1180 – 1050/1000 B.C.) in Central Anatolia, *Hattuša* (Boğazköy), which was the political administrative center of the Hittite Empire, was largely abandoned and only sporadic population centers remained in particular sites. Potsherds decorated with dotted triangles were found in the middle and especially the late period of the Dark Age settlement of Büyükkaya (Genz 2000: 35–56; 2003: 179–191 ; 2004), and similar ones were also uncovered in Eskiyapar (Bayburtluoğlu 1979: 293–303) and Alaca Höyük (Fig.1) located in the Alaca District of Çorum as well as the Architectural Layer 7A of Oluz Höyük (Fig.2) located near the Çorum border of the city of Amasya[1]. Çorum and Amasya provinces constitute the expansion area of this painted pottery group, which is observed to have emerged immediately after the Hittites left the region of the Kızılırmak Bend, and indicates a number of new human movements during the 12th century B.C. In the IId Layer of Kaman-Kalehöyük within the boundaries of Kırşehir province, which is understood to be contemporary with the Boğazköy-Büyükkaya Dark Age settlement, Dark Age potsherds containing both painted ware samples and undecorated pieces were also found (Matsumura 2005: Taf. 40–106).

Tabal is localized around the south of the Kızılırmak Bend in the written sources of the Neo-Assyrian Empire (see Map 2). The mention of many place-names in sources in connection with *Tabal* provides data for the historical geography of the lands around this region. The mention of the name Dadilu of *Kašku* or *Kaški* in the list of tributaries of Tiglat–Pileser III (745–727 B.C.) is important in the scope of the regional historical geography (Sevin 1998b: 188). Up until now Divriği-Kangal[2] or the mountainous region[3] between Malatya and Kayseri were proposed as the *Kašku* Land which was understood to be located near *Tabal*. On the other hand, Veli Sevin states that the *Tabal*, *Muški* and *Kašku* lands were located in the region that can be called Southern *Kappadokia* or Greater *Kappadokia* (Sevin 1998a: 48). It seems quite logical to equate the *Kašku* Land with today's Yozgat – Çorum – Amasya – Samsun area, based on the similarity between *Kašku*, and the name *Kaška*, which was clearly mentioned in the Hittite written documents. When we think that there is a basic unity of painted-ware in the pottery tradition of this region in the Dark Age, we can see that communities have migrated

1 Dönmez and Abazoğlu 2018; 2019.

2 Landsberger 1948: 16, footnote 34.

3 Landsberger 1948: 15–16, footnote 34.

from north to south in the Early Iron Age, thus having an important role in the Hittites' migration from the Kızılırmak Bend and that they have settled the region in the Iron Age. In this context, we can say that Oluz Höyük within the provincial borders of Amasya is an important city of the *Kaška* Land.

Oluz Höyük

Oluz Höyük[4] (see Maps 1–3, Fig.2) is located in an area that has many names in terms of geographical region. The settlement is located in the northern half of the inner region of Kızılırmak (*Halys*) Bend, in the middle of the region referred to as North-Central Anatolia, extending from Çankırı to Sivas, and also in the Yeşilırmak Basin. Oluz Höyük is located on the territory of Gökhöyük Agricultural Operation Directorate (TİGEM) 27 km along the Amasya-Çorum Highway. Oluz Höyük is located in the fertile Geldingen Plain, through which the Çekerek River (*Zuliya* in Hittite texts, classical *Skylax*), one of the important branches of the Yeşilırmak (*Kummešmaḫa* in Hittite texts, classical *Iris*) passes. It is located 2 km northwest of Gözlek Village, approximately 5 km east of Oluz Village and 3 km south of the road in question. Oluz Höyük, with its dimensions of 280 × 260 m and approximate height of 15 m from the level of the plain (478.8 m altitude above sea level) covers an area of 45 acres. Systematic archaeological excavations in Oluz Höyük have been ongoing since 2007, and the existence of 10 architectural layers was determined by evaluating the coins and pottery pieces recovered. Among these, those from the 7th to the 1st Architectural Layer reflect a long Iron Age period.

The architectural remains unearthed during the work carried out in the Architectural Layer 7A (11th–10th centuries B.C.) located over the Layer 7B dated to the Hittite Empire Collapse Period (1180 B.C.) are the first for Oluz Höyük and the Amasya Region. The ruins in question consist of a wall belonging to a mudbrick building built on the slope and a simple hearth (Fig.3)[5]. In *Gordion* layers 7B and 7A (1100–950 B.C.), which date to the Dark Ages, indoor hearths were unearthed[6] in single-roomed, simple residences built with mudbrick and wattle and daub techniques. In the light of the findings of Oluz Höyük, similarities have started to emerge between the Kızılırmak Basin and the west of Kızılırmak in terms of building design in the Dark Ages on the basis of the use of indoor hearths.

The continuation of the painted ware tradition which started at the collapse of the Hittite Empire in Architectural Layer 7B at Oluz Höyük (Figs. 4–5) into the Architectural Layer 7A, despite the change in the decorative programme (Pls. 1–3) and the chronological gap, is a probability we can not ignore. It is observed that the pottery from Oluz Höyük Architectural Layer 6 (Figs. 6 a–b, 7 a–b), dated to the beginning of the Middle Iron Age following these developments of the Early Iron Age, has started to form a tradition of Alisar IV. The pottery of Architectural Layer 6 reflects the Classical Phrygian culture of the Middle Iron Age in its general features. It was also found that some of the painted ware examples encountered in this layer exhibit early features. It is thought that the decorated body fragments belonging to the large krater-type wares (Pl. 4), of a similar type to ones which were found in the Early Iron Age architectural layers of Kilise Tepe, may belong to the end of the Early Iron Age and the beginning of the Middle Iron Age (Postgate 2008: Fig. 4/2). Pottery of Architectural Layer 5 (Fig. 8 a–b), which was excavated in a limited scope, shows typical Middle Iron Age properties just like Architectural Layer 6. Oluz Höyük lived through the Architectural Layer 4 (600–500 B.C.) period as a Late Iron Age settlement under Phrygian cultural influence in the *Kaška* Land. An altar of Kubaba (Fig. 9), along with a cult statuette of Kubaba (Fig. 10 a–b) and a stamp seal with lion-gazelle scene on the stamp face (Fig. 11 a–c), which were uncovered in

4 For Oluz Höyük see Dönmez 2010; 2017.

5 Dönmez and Abazoğlu 2018: Fig. 22.

6 Voigt and DeVries 2011: Fig. 2.8a.

Architectural Layer 4, show a *Phrygian* character. In Architectural Layer 3, which is understood to have run between 500–450 B.C., the continuity of the painted ware tradition, especially on the basis of pottery, and the increase in plant and figural decoration as well as geometric decoration (Fig. 12), shows that the pottery workshops started to be influenced by new cultural elements in Anatolia. The fourth and third architectural layer findings show that Oluz Höyük continued its life in the *Phrygian* culture in *Kašku* Land just like: Alaca Höyük, Eskiyapar, Boğazköy, Maşat Höyük, Ovaören, Yassı Höyük (Kırşehir), Alişar Höyük, Çadır Höyük, Uşaklı Höyük, Kınık Höyük, Zeyve (Porsuk) Höyük, Zank Höyük, Ayvalıpınar Höyük, Oymaağaç Höyük, Kuşsaray and Çengeltepe. The fact that no Achaemenid settlement or building remains were found in any of these Central Anatolian Iron Age cities mentioned above indicates that these settlements continued to live under the Phrygian culture in the Persian period, as opposed to Oluz Höyük, sustaining their cultural characteristics.

However, the presence of a Persian elite that arrived at Oluz Höyük (see Map 3) in 450 B.C., or 5–10 years before this date, reached a level that can be easily monitored on the basis of architecture, small finds, pottery and religious findings in the Architectural Layer 2B (450–300 B.C.). It is known that the Persians, who ruled Anatolia with the satraps they assigned from the center for 220 years from 550 B.C. to 330 B.C., attached great importance to the Satrapy of *Kappadokia* (*Katpatuka*), which included the vicinity of Amasya in Central Anatolia. The evidence unearthed in the systematic archaeological excavations implemented in Oluz Höyük suggests that in this process the Persians brought with them to Oluz Höyük the Fire Cult, which consituted the core of Early Zoroastrianism during the Achaemenid Period[7].

In this period, the Fire Cult, was brought into Oluz Höyük as supported by the findings brought to light by systematic archaeological excavations. Among the architectural remains unearthed in Oluz Höyük, the Colonnaded Hall structure attracts attention with its location next to the *Atashkadeh* (see Plan 1, Fig. 13).

Until the beginning of the 6th century B.C., when the Medes started their conquest, Anatolia was strongly marked by paganism within the framework of different belief systems. Together with the Medes, it is understood that Early Zoroastrianism, which had "Archaic Monotheism" and "Aniconism" at its core, started to be dominant especially in the Kızılırmak Basin and the geography to its east. The archaeological findings that started to come to light related to archaic monotheism and the fire cult in Oluz Höyük probably also point to the settlement of the Medes and their routes of movement. The Oluz Höyük excavations indicate that there is no statue and altar in this new religion, and there is an opposition in thought and action to the glorification or worship of images. Finds related to this new religion, in which visual expression is replaced by fire, and perhaps fire is used as a *qibla*, continue to be revealed in Oluz Höyük. The fact that artifacts with god/goddess figures belonging to the pagan religion and culture of ancient Greece have still not been uncovered during the period of the Architectural Layer 2B (see Plan 1; 450–300 B.C.), which corresponds to the end of the Classical Period and the onset of the Early Hellenistic Period, shows that there was a strict prohibition on figures and idols, namely aniconism, in the Early Zoroastrian religious life at Oluz Höyük which was centered around the fire-cult.

The Harşena Fortress

Amaseia (see Map 3) is one of the important cities of Classical *Pontus*. It could be identified with the city of *Hakmiš* or *Hakpiš* in the Hittite Period. Today it is in the borders of the modern city of Amasya. *Amaseia* had a geographical situation suitable for settlement in almost every

7 Dönmez 2015: 467–473 ; 2018a: 205–230; 2018b: 145–160; 2019: 244–257 ; Dönmez and Abdullaev 2019: 703–729 ; Dönmez and Saba 2019a: 112–121; 2019b: 1–65 ; 2020: 61–69.

period, because it was located at a strategically dominant point in the fertile *Iris* (Yeşilırmak) valley and on the north-south route. Between 281 B.C. and 180 B.C., it was the capital of the Mithridatic Dynasty. Amasya was established on the side of the hill occupied by the Harşena Fortress (Fig. 14), on the slopes rising to the north of the Yeşilırmak for security and defense reasons. Once its security was assured, the settlement expanded to the valley bottom from the slopes. A Late Iron Age potsherd with painted festoon decoration (Pl. 13/3) uncovered on the skirts of the fortress in recent years constitutes the earliest find of the Harşena Fortress thus far. On the other hand, it is thought that Amasya Fortress was initially built in the Hellenistic Period due to certain features which were identified on the city walls. The castle was repaired in the Roman, Byzantine and Ottoman periods. The Harşena Fortress consists of three main parts. These are, from the bottom up, the Lower City; the castle terrace called the Maidens Palace (Basileia) and the Upper Fortress. The part of the Harşena Fortress known as the Maidens Palace is on a terrace leaning against the mountain at the back.

The systematic archaeological excavations[8] initiated by a team under the direction of E. Emine Dönmez in 2009, on behalf of Istanbul University, at the Harşena Fortress have provided new and important findings regarding the Seljuk and Ottoman periods as well as the Protohistorical periods of Amasya. Some of the findings uncovered in the Ottoman layer during the studies on the Upper Fortress and Maidens Palace indicate a pre-urbanization stage, even if they were found in a stratification which does not belong to their period.

The fact that Herodotus (484–420 B.C.), one of the most important ancient writers of Anatolia, did not mention Amasya shows that the settlement centered on Maidens Palace in the 5th century B.C. did not have remarkable features. The fact that Amasya did not attract the attention of an observer and chronicler such as Herodotus who conveyed historical events, personalities and geographic elements in the 5th century B.C., when the magnificent fortress and Royal Rock-Cut Tombs were not yet built, is an important aspect, which indicates the mediocrity of the settlement. The presence of the painted-ware pottery with plant and geometric decoration and the Scythian arrowheads which were uncovered in the excavations implemented under the leadership of E. Emine Naza-Dönmez proves that in the period when Herodotus lived, there was a settlement under Achaemenid (Persian) dominion and with traditional Phrygian cultural identity in the area where the Maidens Palace (Fig. 14) stood. A similar process has been demonstrated in Oluz Höyük, which is located 25 km southwest of Amasya (Dönmez 2013: 103–140).

Inverted rim and carinated bowls (Pl. 5/1–2) are common among Iron Age pottery. Another group of bowls has a slightly inverted rim and a body with a rounded turn (Pls. 6/1–4, 7/1–4). Some of these bowls with an "S" profile (Pl. 8/2–3) are flat-rising (Pl. 8/1) and rim types (Pl.8/4) that are open to the outside. In addition to the buff groups, there are also pieces of pots differing in terms of their technical structure with their paste and undercoat in gray and tones. Some of the gray colored amorphs are undecorated (Pl.9/1), others are incised and decorated with hollow-points (Pl. 9/2). It is observed that the outer surfaces of other gray amorphs are composed of small and round reliefs (Pl. 9/3), notches (Pl. 9/4) and notch (Pl. 9/5–6) decorations. Most of the amorphs are painted. In these amorphs, thick and thin bands of paint are observed in brown tones placed on buff backgrounds (Pl.10/1–6). One of them is the lower part of a pot with a round bottom (Pl.10/5). On another group of amorphs, there are also shades of brown and reddish buff and horizontal thin bands made on buff backgrounds (Pl. 11/1–5). Some of these thin bands were also applied to light-colored ground areas (Pl. 11/5). It is observed that some painted band decorations were

8 Naza-Dönmez 2011: 111–120; 2012: 267–281; 2013: 427–436; 2014: 29–49; Naza-Dönmez and Parlak 2014: 279–291.

also applied vertically (Pl. 11/6–7). Apart from thick or thin bands, irregular brown (Pl. 12/1) or rounded motifs (Pl.12/2) stand out. Cross-character decorations (Pl.12/3–4), and bands filled with short lines (Pl.12/5–6) are also seen in brown or reddish brown. The most characteristic finds of the Harşena Fortress and Maidens Palace Late Iron Age painted-ware are the amorphs characterized by plant motifs. Among these, closely similar examples to the pot fragment (Pl. 13/1) decorated with ivy leaves in reddish brown tones are known from Architectural Layer 2B at Oluz Höyük (450–300 B.C.). There are also other amorphs indicating that the number of vessels decorated with plant motifs is even higher (Pl. 13/2).

Apart from these, a fragment of a terracotta rhyton found during the excavations carried out by the Amasya Museum in the area of Maidens Palace is interesting. The horn-shaped rhyton piece decorated with short lines (Pl. 14/1) must belong to a ram-shaped container. The rhyton fragment in question, which can be dated to the 6th or 5th century B.C., should be considered in the same context as the Late Iron Age pottery. Among the Late Iron Age finds from the Maidens Palace, 2 Scythian-type arrowheads made of bronze (Pl. 14/2–3) are very important. Maidens Palace arrowheads, which are similar to the arrowheads[9] found in the Oluz Höyük Architectural Layer 2B, which is dated to the Achaemenid Period, constitute the strongest findings of the Iron Age settlement, which we could not otherwise identify in any finds other than in pottery.

Conclusion

The architectural remains and small finds and pottery unearthed during the studies carried out in Oluz Höyük (Fig. 2) and the Harşena Fortress (Fig. 14) indicate that the uncertainties regarding Iron Age archaeology within the boundaries of Amasya will decrease and the gaps in the chronological sequence will be filled. Especially in Oluz Höyük, the chronological continuity that can be traced since the Early Iron Age (*Kašku* Period) is characterized by the strong findings of the Middle Iron Age (Phrygian and Scythian periods) and the Late Iron Age (Achaemenid Period). In the Harşena Fortress and the Maidens Palace, no finds dating back to the Late Iron Age (Achaemenid Period) have yet been encountered.

9 Dönmez and Yurtsever Beyazıt 2013: Fig. 13; 2014: Fig. 11.

Bibliography

Bayburtluoğlu, İ.
- 1979 "Eskiyapar Phryg Çağı," *VIII. Türk Tarih Kongresi, Cilt I*, Ankara, pp. 293–303.

Dönmez, Ş.
- 2010 *Amasya Oluz Höyük. Kašku Ülkesi'nin Önemli Kenti. 2007 ve 2008 Dönemi Çalışmaları Genel Değerlendirmeler ve Ön Sonuçlar/The Principal Site of Kašku Land. The Preliminary Reports of 2007 and 2008 Seasons General Evaluations and Results*, Ankara.
- 2013 "Oluz Höyük: Kuzey-Orta Anadolu'nun Kralî Pers Merkezi," in Ş. Dönmez (ed.). *Güneş Karadeniz'den Doğar. Sümer Atasoy Armağanı/Lux ex Ponto Euxino. Studies Presented in Honour of Sümer Atasoy*, Ankara, pp. 103–140.
- 2015 "Achaemenid Presence at Oluz Höyük, North-Central Anatolia," in G. R. Tsetskhladze, A. Avram and J. Hargrave (eds.). *The Danubian Lands between the Black, Aegean and Adriatic Seas (7th Century B.C. – 10th Century AD). Proceedings of the Fifth International Congress on Black Sea Antiquities*. Belgrade, 17–21 September 2013, Oxford, pp. 467–473.
- 2017 *Amasya-Oluz Höyük. Kuzey-Orta Anadolu'da Bir Akhaimenid (Pers) Yerleşmesi. 2009–2013 Çalışmaları Genel Değerlendirmeler ve Önsonuçlar*, Amasya.
- 2018a "Early Zoroastrianism at Oluz Höyük, North-Central Anatolia," in A. Batmaz, G. Bedianashvili, A. Michalewicz, A. Robinson (eds.), *Context and Connection. Studies on the Archaeology of the Ancient Near in Honour of Antonio Sagona*, Leuven, pp. 205–230.
- 2018b "Amasya – Oluz Höyük Ateşgedesi ve Erken Zerdüşt Dini Kutsal Alanı," *TÜBA-AR 22*, pp. 145–160.

– 2019 "The Land of Sacred Fire: Amasya – Oluz Höyük," in G. Tsestskhladze and S. Atasoy (eds.), *Settlement and Necropoleis of the Black Sea and Its Hinterland in Antiquity*, Oxford, pp. 244–257.

Dönmez, Ş and F. Abazoğlu

– 2018 "Kızılırmak Havzası Demir Çağı Çanak-Çömlek Geleneğinin Kökeni Üzerine Düşünceler," *TÜBA-AR 23*, pp. 81–99.

– 2019 "Hitit Sonrası Kuzey-Orta Anadolu: Oluz Höyük'te Karanlık Çağ ile İlgili Yeni Bulgular," in A. Süel (ed.), *IX. Uluslararası Hititoloji Kongresi Bildirileri/Acts of the IXth International Congress of Hittitology*, I. Cilt/Vol. I. Çorum: pp. 237–260.

Dönmez, Ş and K. Abdullaev

– 2019 "Oluz Höyük – Amasya: Discovery of A Site in the North of Central Anatolia/Олуз Хююк – Амасья: открытие памятника на севере Центральной Анатолии," *Journal of Ancient History 79/3*, MOCKBA, pp. 703–729.

Dönmez, Ş and M. Saba

– 2019 "New Discoveries at Oluz Höyük: An Early Zoroastrian Sanctuary in North-Central Anatolia," in S. R. Steadman and G. McMahon (eds.). *The Archaeology of Anatolia. Volume III. Recent Discoveries (2017–2018)*, Cambridge, pp. 112–121.

– 2020 "Güncel Arkeolojik Bulgular Işığında Anadolu'da Erken Zerdüşt Dini," *Arkhe Dergisi 14*, Eskişehir, pp. 61–69.

Dönmez, Ş and A. Yurtsever Beyazıt

– 2013 "Oluz Höyük Kazısı Altıncı Dönem (2012) Çalışmaları: Değerlendirmeler ve Sonuçlar," *Colloquium Anatolicum XII*, pp. 165–192.

Genz, H.

– 2000 „Die Eisenzeit in Zentralanatolien im Lichte der keramischen Funde vom Büyükkaya in Boğazköy/Hattuşa," *TÜBA-AR 3*, pp. 35–56.

– 2003 "The Early Iron Age in Central Anatolia," *Identifying Changes: The Transition from Bronze to Iron Ages in Anatolia and Its Neighbouring Regions*. Proceedings of the International Workshop (Istanbul, November 8–9, 2002), Istanbul, pp. 179–191.

– 2004 *Büyükkaya I. Die Keramik der Eisenzeit, Funde aus den Grabungskampagnen 1993 bis 1998*, Mainz am Rhein.

Landsberger, B.

– 1948 *Sam'al: Studien zur Entdeckung der Ruinenstätte Karatepe*: 1. Ankara, pp. 7–16.

Matsumura, K.

– 2005 *Die Eisenzeitliche Keramik in Zentralanatolien aufgrund der Keramik in Kaman-Kalehöyük* (Freie University, Unpublished Ph.D. Thesis), Berlin.

Naza-Dönmez, E. E.

– 2011 "Amasya – Harşena Kalesi ve Kızlar Sarayı Kazısı 2010 Yılı Sonuçları," *32. Kazı Sonuçları Toplantısı – 4*, Ankara, pp. 111–120.

– 2012 "Amasya – Harşena Kalesi ve Kızlar Sarayı Kazısı 2010 Dönemi Çalışmaları," *33. Kazı Sonuçları Toplantısı – 3*, Ankara, pp. 267–281.

– 2013 "Amasya – Harşena Kalesi ve Kızlar Sarayı Kazısı 2011 Dönemi Çalışmaları," *34. Kazı Sonuçları Toplantısı – 3*, Çorum, pp. 427–436.

– 2014 "Amasya – Harşena Kalesi ve Kızlar Sarayı Kazıları," F. Özdem, *Amasya. Yar ile Gezdiğim Dağlar*, Istanbul, pp. 29–49.

Naza-Dönmez, E. E. and S. Parlak

– 2014 "Amasya – Harşena Kalesi ve Kızlar Sarayı Kazısı 2012 Dönemi Çalışmaları," *35. Kazı Sonuçları Toplantısı – 3*, Muğla, pp. 279–290.

Postgate, J. N.

– 2008 "The chronology of the Iron Age seen from Kilise Tepe," *Ancient Near Eastern Studies 45*, pp. 166–187.

Sevin, V.

– 1998a "Tarihsel Coğrafya," in M. Sözen (ed.). *Kapadokya*, Istanbul, pp. 44–61.

– 1998b "MÖ I. Binyıl: Demir Çağı," in M. Sözen (ed.). *Kapadokya*, Istanbul, pp. 170–193.

Voigt, M and K. De Vries

– 2011 "Emerging Problems and Doubts," in C. B. Rose and G. Darbyshire (eds.), *The New Chronology of Iron Age Gordion*, Istanbul, pp. 23–48.

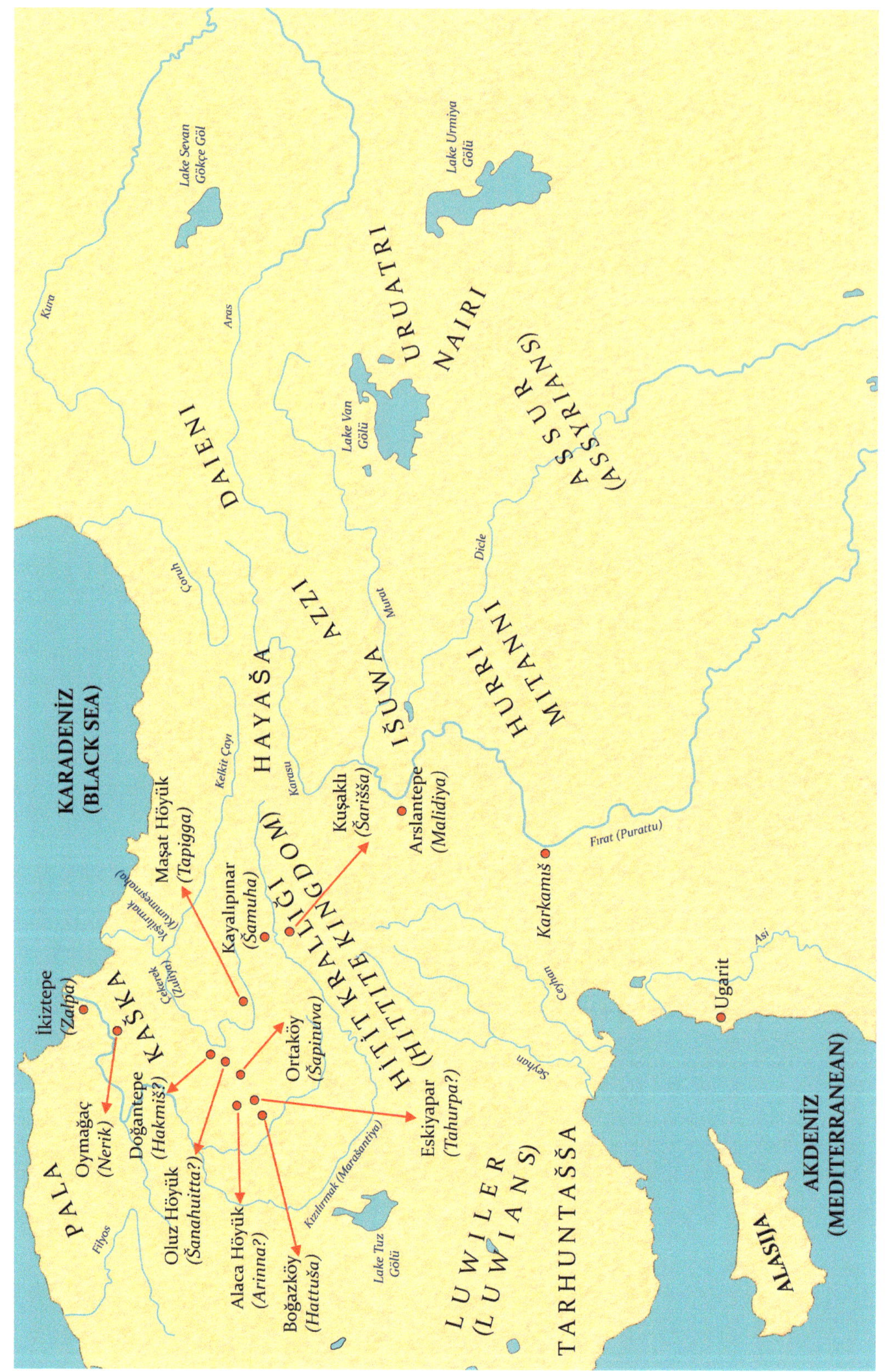

Map 1. Anatolia during the End of Late Bronze Age (Fidane Abazoğlu).

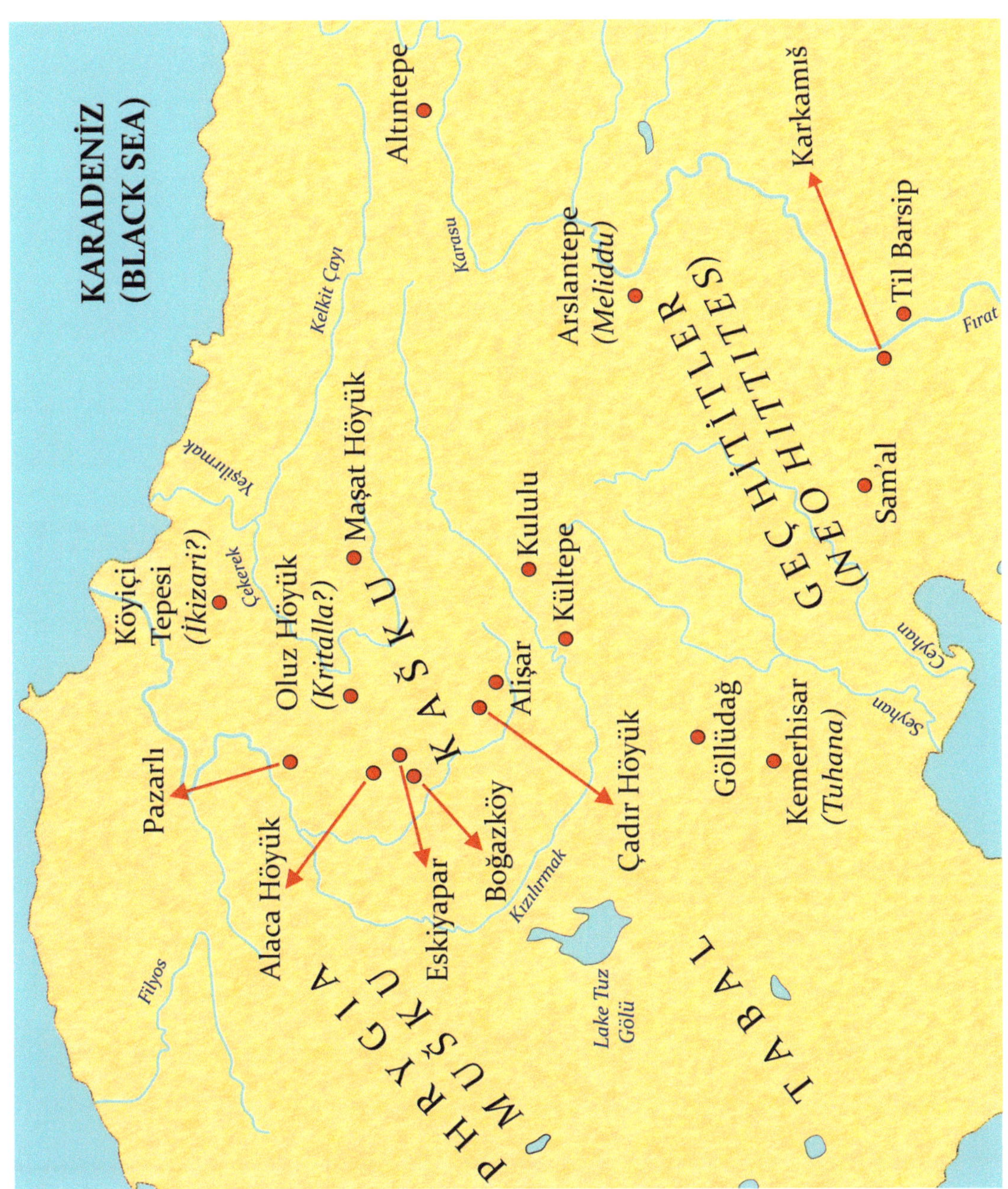

Map 2. Central Anatolia during the Middle Iron Age (Fidane Abazoğlu).

Map 3. North-Central Anatolia during the Late Iron Age (Nurcan Koç).

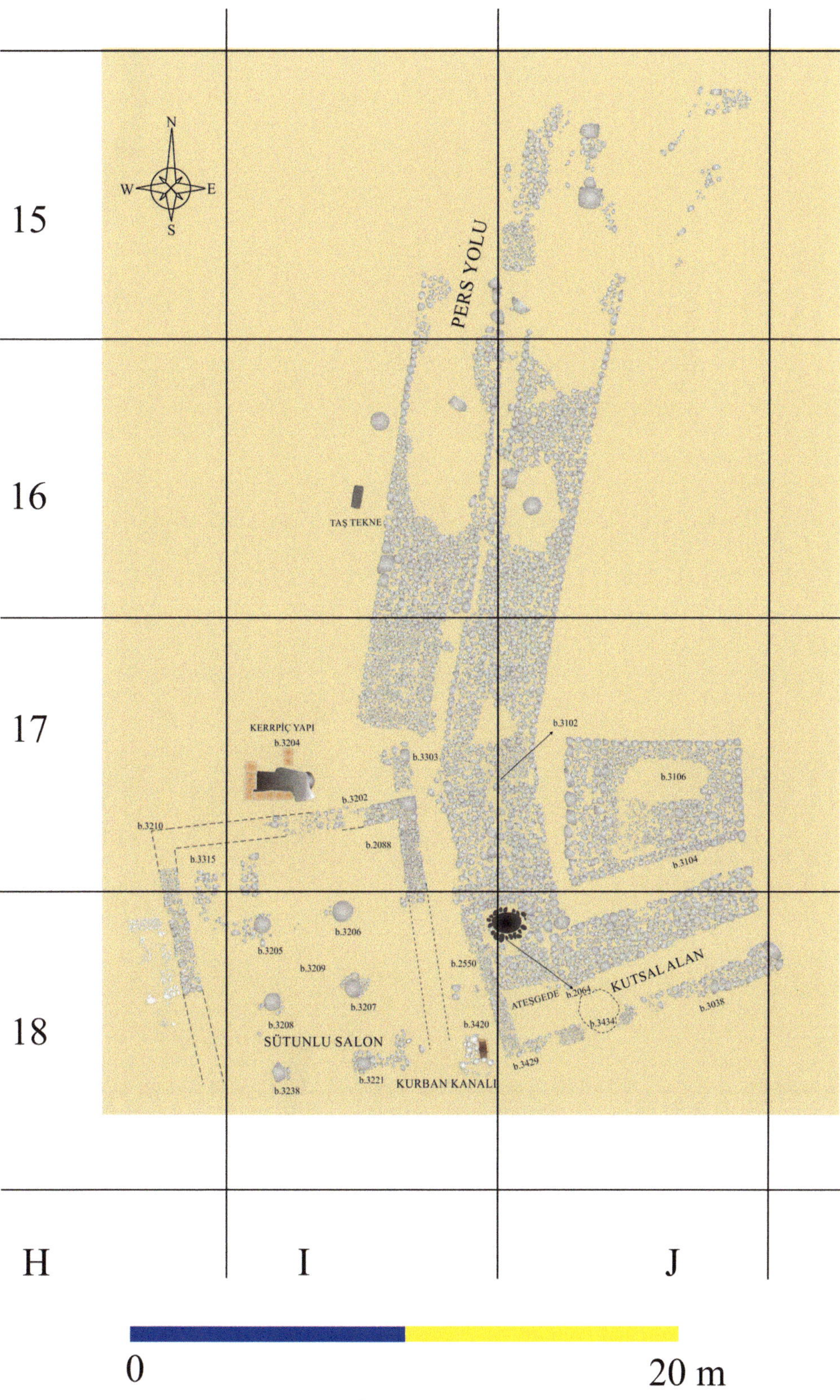

Plan 1. Oluz Höyük Architectural Layer 2B.

Plate 1. Early Iron Age potsherds from Oluz Höyük Architectural Layer 7A.

Plate 2. Early Iron Age potsherds from Oluz Höyük Architectural Layer 7A.

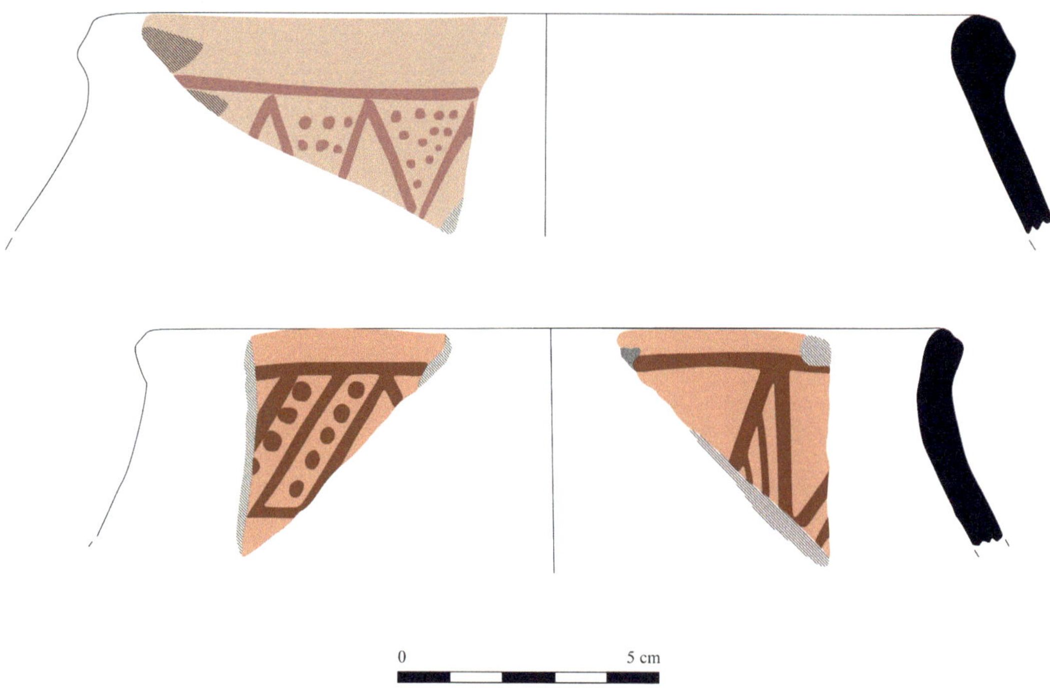

Plate 3. Early Iron Age potsherds from Oluz Höyük Architectural Layer 7A.

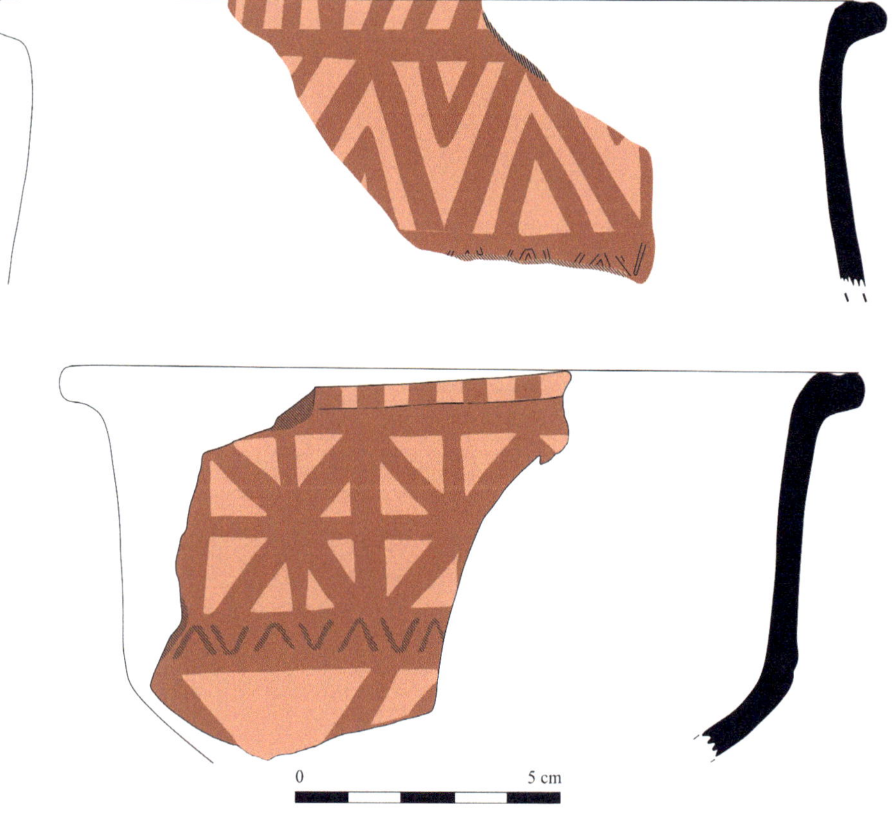

Plate 4. Middle Iron Age potsherds from Oluz Höyük Architectural Layer 6.

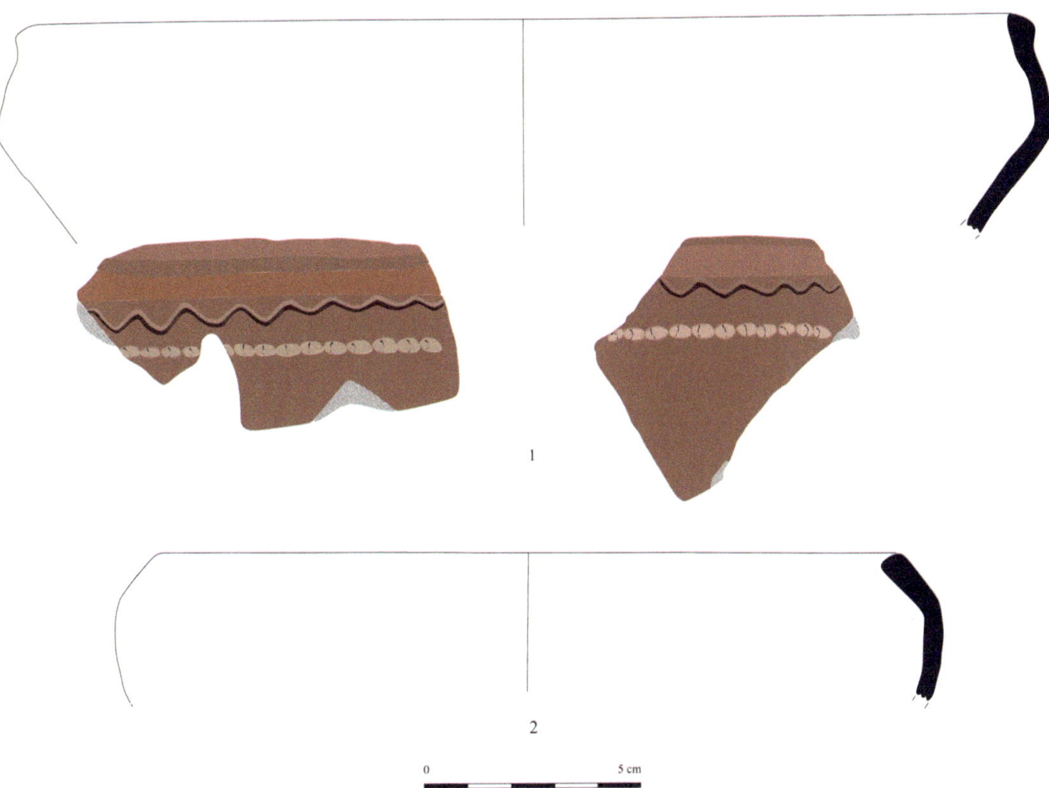

Plate 5. Late Iron Age potsherds from the Harşena Fortress.

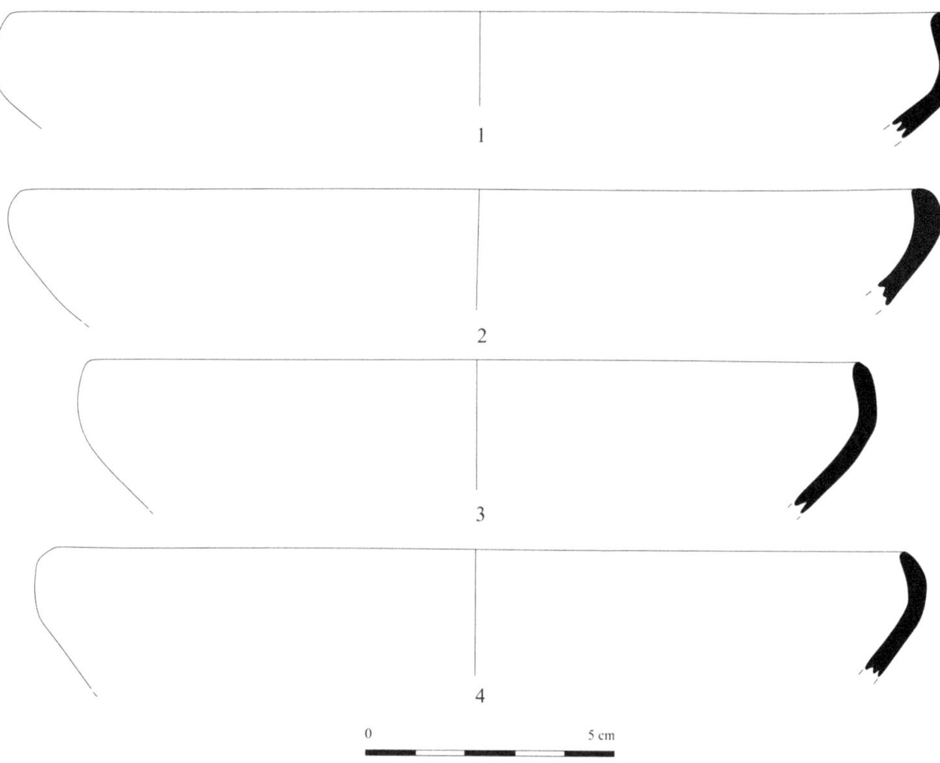

Plate 6. Late Iron Age potsherds from the Harşena Fortress.

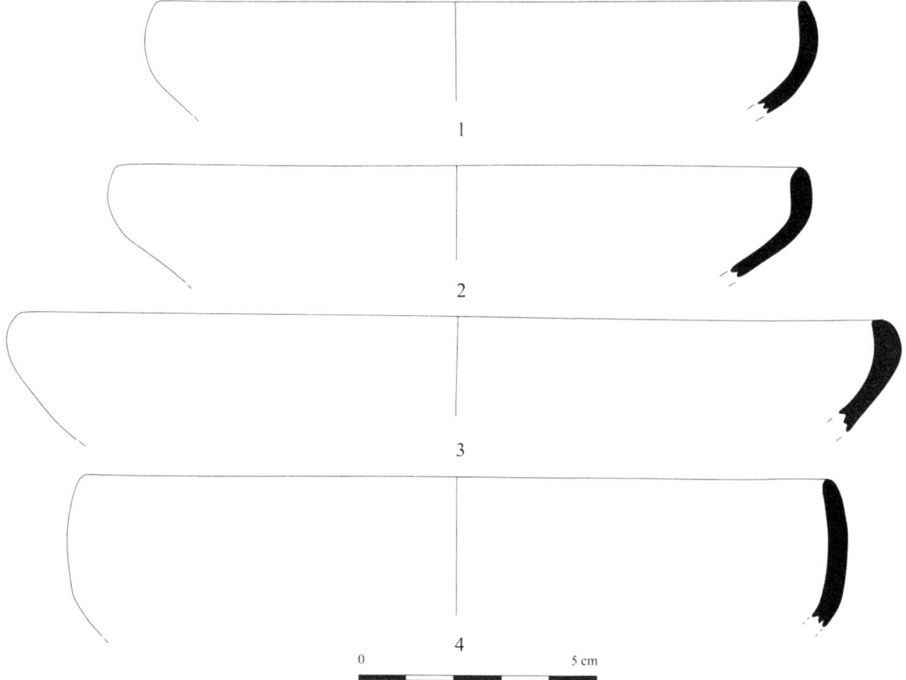

Plate 7. Late Iron Age potsherds from the Harşena Fortress.

Plate 8. Late Iron Age potsherds from the Harşena Fortress.

Plate 9. Late Iron Age potsherds from the Harşena Fortress.

Plate 10. Late Iron Age potsherds from the Harşena Fortress.

Plate 11. Late Iron Age potsherds from the Harşena Fortress.

Plate 12. Late Iron Age potsherds from the Harşena Fortress.

Plate 13. Late Iron Age potsherds from the Harşena Fortress.

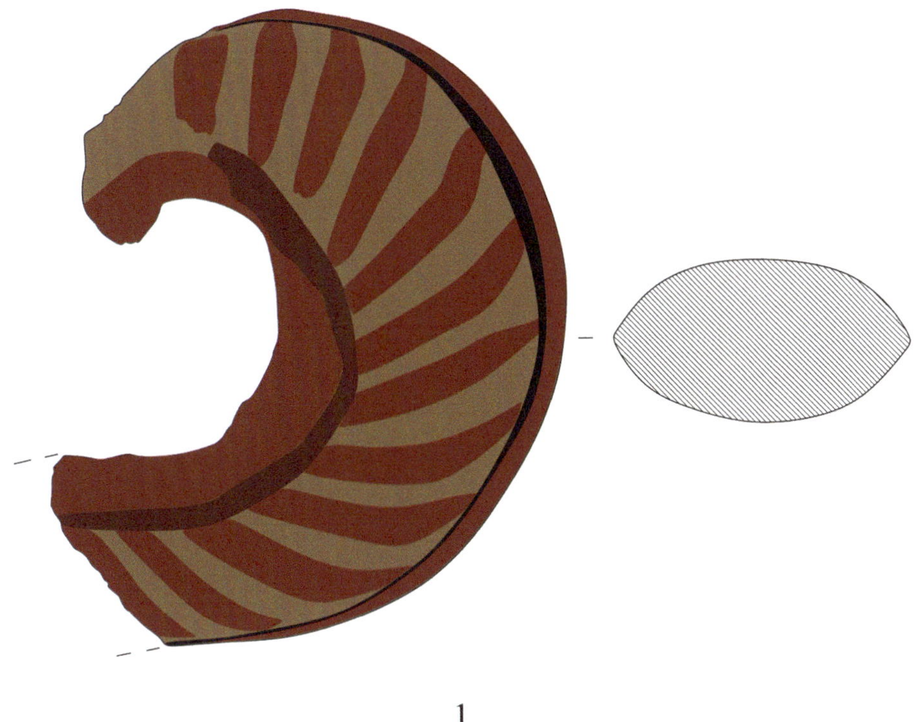

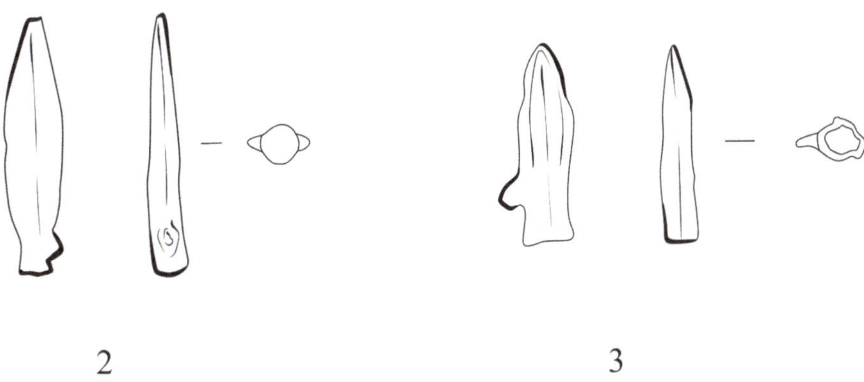

0 5 cm

Plate 14. Late Iron Age rhyton fragment (Baked Clay) and Scythian type arrowheads (Bronze) from the Harşena Fortress.

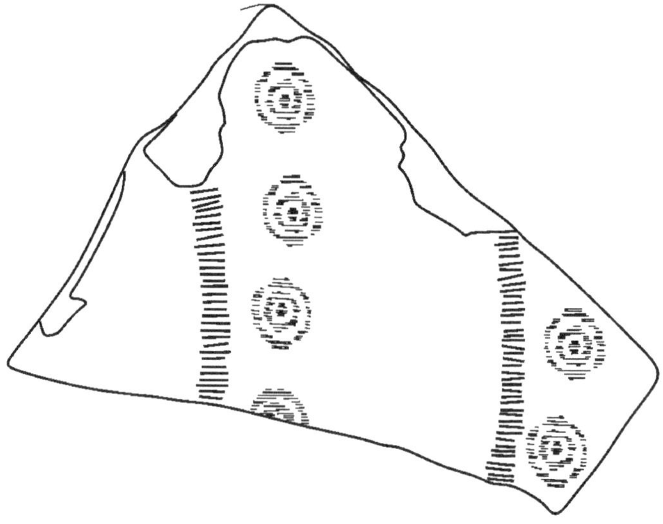

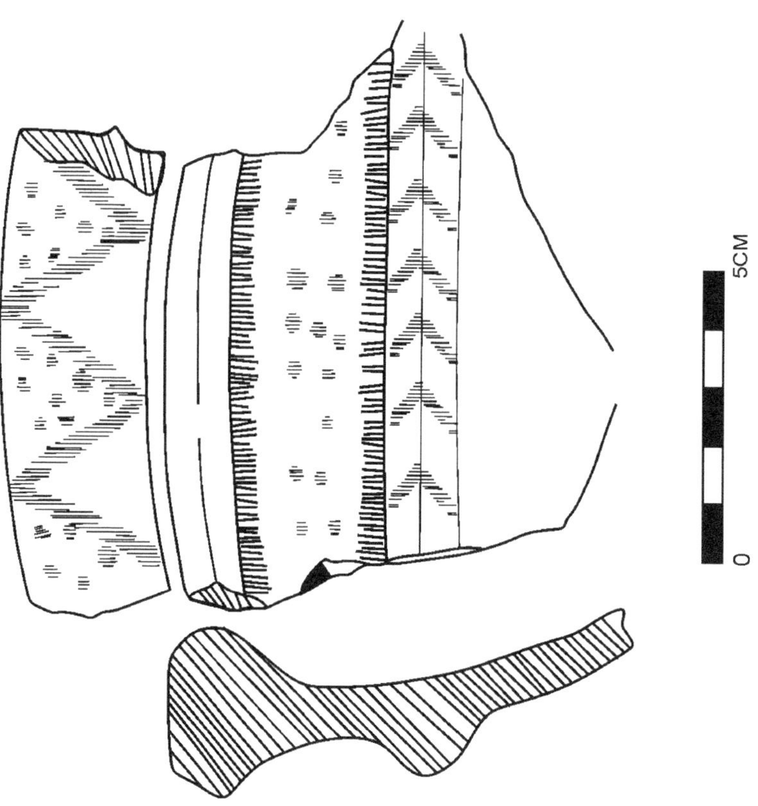

Fig.1. Early Iron Age potsherds from Alaca Höyük.

Fig.2. General view of Oluz Höyük (Şevket Dönmez).

Fig.3. Architectural remains of Oluz Höyük Architectural Layer 7A (Şevket Dönmez).

Fig. 4. Plain potsherds from Oluz Höyük Architectural Layer 7B (Şevket Dönmez).

Fig. 5. Painted potsherds from Oluz Höyük Architectural Layer 7B (Şevket Dönmez).

Fig. 6a–b. Alishar IV Style painted potsherd from Oluz Höyük Architectural Layer 6 (Şevket Dönmez).

Fig. 7a–b. Alishar IV style painted potsherd from Oluz Höyük Architectural Layer 6 (Şevket Dönmez).

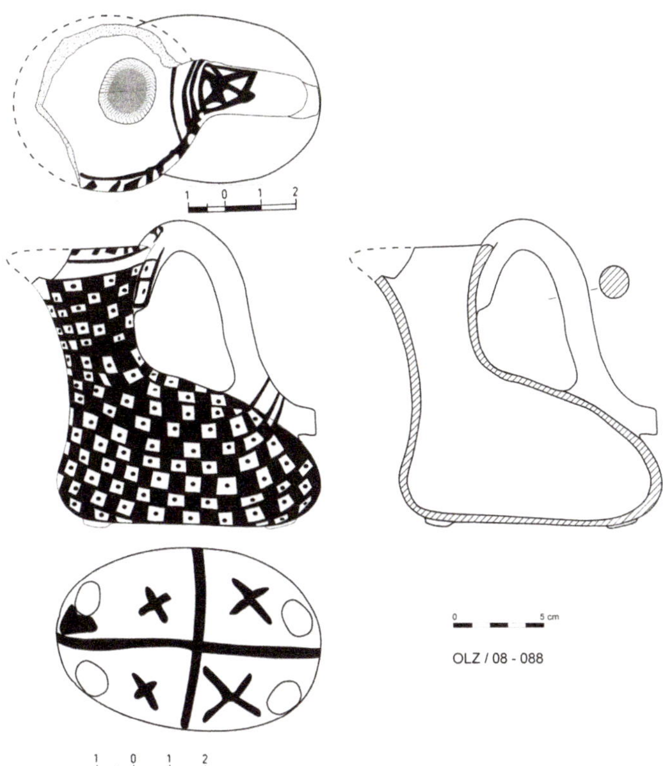

Fig. 8a–b. Phrygian type painted Askos from Oluz Höyük Architectural Layer 5, baked clay (Şevket Dönmez).

Fig. 9. General view of Kubaba altar from Oluz Höyük Architectural Layer 4 (Şevket Dönmez).

Fig.10a–b. Kubaba statuette from Oluz Höyük Architectural Layer 4, stone (Şevket Dönmez).

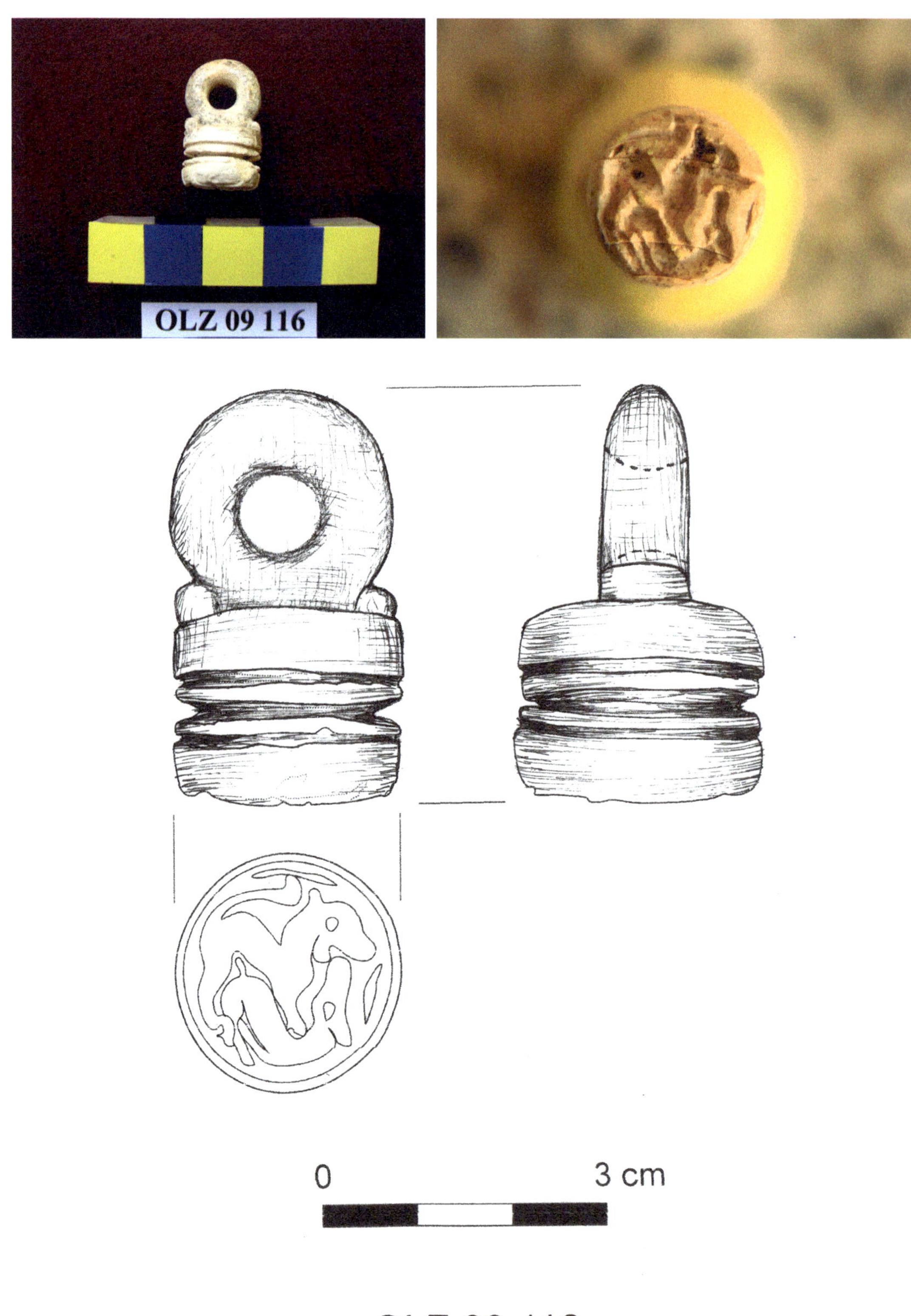

Fig.11a–c. Stamp seal from Oluz Höyük Architectural Layer 4, ivory (Şevket Dönmez).

Fig.12. Painted potsherd from Oluz Höyük Architectural Layer 3 (Şevket Dönmez).

Fig.13. General view of Oluz Höyük Architectural Layer 2B (Şevket Dönmez).

Fig.14. General view of the Harşena Fortress (E. Emine Dönmez).

A Group of Metal Vessels Excavated in the Early Bronze Age Cemetery at Resuloğlu

Tayfun Yıldırım *

I first met Sachihiro Omura in 1987 while working with my professor, Kutlu Emre at Kültepe. Omura is a precious friend, who completed his education in Hittitology and dedicated himself to Ancient Anatolian Archaeology. He was educated under the influence of Professor Tahsin Özgüç's Ecole, and inspired by Japanese Prince Takahito Mikasa's words, "The history of Anatolia is the history of the World." Omura Bey, as his colleagues call him, is a scholar who had a vital role in installing a cultural bridge between Japan and Turkey by means of excavations at Kaman-Kalehöyük under his directorship and his efforts in establishing the Japanese Institute of Anatolian Archaeology and Kaman Museum. I would like to express my happiness in contributing to this Festschrift prepared in honor of Omura, who has a close interest in the Early Bronze Age archaeology of Central and Northern Anatolia alongside the Hittites and Iron Ages. This paper addresses a group of Early Bronze Age metal vessels from Resuloğlu (Çorum) aligning well with Omura's scholarly interests.

Abstract

The excavations at Resuloğlu cemetery and settlement, discovered in 1998, present new information on North Central Anatolian Archaeology. Until today 288 burials have been investigated at Resuloğlu, one of the few Early Bronze Age (hereafter, EBA) sites in the area with coexisting cemetery and settlement areas. A group of metal utensils stand out among the grave goods of Resuloğlu, one of the richest cemeteries of the north. The technical and morphological properties of the metal vessels show that these vessels were produced locally reflecting the fashion of the era. A few examples made of lead were excavated alongside the copper alloy vessels, which constitute the majority of the metal burial gifts. The owners of these metal vessels, which were found as burial gifts, were once the residents of the fortified southeastern settlement dated to the EBA. Metal vessels and many other artifacts unearthed are parallel to examples that were found in the elite burials in levels 5 and 6 at Alaca Höyük. It is understood from the new evidence that the relationship between the settlements got stronger at the beginning of the EBA III.

Öz

1998 yılında keşfettiğimiz Resuloğlu mezarlığı ve yerleşim yerinde sürdürülen kazılar, Orta Kuzey Anadolu arkeolojisi için yeni bilgiler sunmaktadır. Bölgede hem yerleşim yeri hem de mezarlık alanı birlikte kazılabilen az sayıdaki Erken Tunç Çağı (ETÇ) yerleşimlerinden biri olan Resuloğlunda, bugüne kadar 288 mezar araştırılabildi. Kuzeyin zengin mezarlıklarından biri olan Resuloğlunun ölü hediyeleri arasında, bir grup metal kap kacak dikkat çekmektedir. Metal kapların teknik ve biçimsel özellikleri, onların bölgenin yerli işçiliğinde ve dönemin modasına uygun olarak yapıldıklarını göstermiştir. Çoğu bakır alaşımlarından yapılmış kap kacağın az sayıda kurşun örneğine de rastlandı. Mezarlığa bırakılmış metal kapların sahipleri, Erken Tunç Çağı'nda surla çevrildiği anlaşılan güneydoğu yerleşiminin eski sahipleridir. Metal kaplar ve beraberinde ele geçen bir çok eşya Alaca Höyük'te 5. ve 6. mimarlık katına ait seçkin mezarlarda bulunan örneklerle paraleldir. Yeni delillerle bu bağlantıların ETÇ III başında kuvvetlendiği anlaşılmaktadır.

* Prof. Tayfun Yıldırım, Ankara Üniversitesi, Faculty of Letters, Department of Ancient Near Eastern Archaeology.

North Central Anatolia during the 3rd millennium B.C. was one of the rare areas where people knew how to manage underground mining and metallurgy very well and built an organized production chain. Results from the excavations and research conducted in the area since the 1930s indicate that from the Chalcolithic Period onwards communities were dependent on agriculture and animal husbandry. Especially during the EBA, mining became an important line of work (Özgüç 1964: 32). Certainly, the northern regions of Anatolia having rich metal resources had a vital role in the development of both the production of the metal artifacts and the metalworking. During this period, various types of metals were processed and metal processing techniques such as forging, plating, inlaying, and casting were improved. The types of the artifacts cast in the local workshops near the raw material resources reflect the technological advancement and aesthetic values of their craftsmen. The vast amount of excavated metal artifacts in the settlements and burials in the sites located in the North such as Alaca Höyük (Koşay 1944; Koşay 1951; Koşay and Akok 1966; Koşay and Akok 1973), Horoztepe (Özgüç and Akok 1957; 1958; Özgüç 1964), Eskiyapar (Özgüç and Temizer 1993), Mahmatlar (Koşay and Akok 1950), Kayapınar (Temizer 1954: 323–326), Kalınkaya (Mellink 1972: 169–170; Mellink 1974: 109; Zimmermann 2006: 271–311; Zimmermann 2007: 35–42), İkiztepe (Bilgi 1984; 1990), Oymaağaç (Özgüç 1978), Göller (Özgüç 1978; 1980), Balıbağ (Süel 1989: 145–163; 1991: 205–214; 1992: 129–146), Devret Höyük (Türker *et al.* 2018), which were ruled by chiefs, princes or feudalists, are enough to demonstrate the metalsmiths' accomplishments (Map 1). The advancement in metal art, certainly, enhanced the cultural and economic relationships with the surrounding areas. The demand for this area's luxury artifacts increased. Many metal artifacts from the North used as grave goods were the distinguished production of the high culture of Hatti (Özgüç 2002: 400), whose existence is evident in the area in the second half of the 3rd millennium B.C. Excavations in the Resuloğlu settlement and cemetery located at the intersection point of the Delice and Kızılırmak rivers in the North, present new information on personal metal artifacts of the local communities known as Hatti (Yıldırım 2006: 1).

A total of 288 burials of different types; stone or mudbrick cist graves, pithoi and jar graves, and simple inhumation were unearthed. On a high ridge facing the Delice river it was seen that the adults were buried as simple inhumation, pithoi or cist burials, while jars were used mainly for burying children and babies (infants). It was understood that in some cist graves and pithoi burials, two individuals (who were related to each other) were buried together (Yıldırım 2012: 242). A group of massive and elaborate stone cists, belonging to the upper-class or wealthy class, is located in a certain area of the cemetery. This situation may indicate that there is social differentiation in the cemetery area. A small number of grave goods was unearthed in these burials, which were recently disturbed. Until now, three different phases were identified in Resuloğlu Cemetery. The burials in these three phases are approximately dated between 2500–2100 B.C. (Yıldırım 2019: 155).

Grave goods reflecting the admiration of the Resuloğlu population consist of pottery, metal weapons (Yıldırım 2011: 457–464), rich ornaments made of semi-precious stones, or metal and metal vessels. Some of the grave goods representative of the afterlife belief of Resuloğlu individuals are *profane* and were actually utensils of daily use. Other than these, alabaster and stone idols unearthed in pithoi are related to religion and cult.[1] The tradition of placing metal vessels known in numerous burials of the North during the EBA, is visible also in Resuloğlu Cemetery though through a few examples. Different metal vessels made for daily usage such as bowls, cups, vases, pans and spoons

1 The so-called sun disks are known from sites in the north such as Alaca Höyük, Horoztepe, Oymaağaç, Kalınkaya and Balıbağ. These objects were not found in Resuloğlu cemetery.

compose the metal grave goods. No examples of the beak-spouted[2] metal jugs commonly excavated in the region have been unearthed in Resuloğlu. As clay beak-spouted jugs are known in the region, lack of metal ones must be a coincidence. Metal vessels found in graves were situated near the heads, chests and feet of individuals. Textile remains spotted on ornaments and weapons along with the metal vessels indicated that the individuals of Resuloğlu were buried with their clothes (Tütüncüler 2006: 137ff.). Some of the metal cups were left on the right chest or attached to the fingers of the deceased. Many of the metal cups put in the graves were intentionally bent and made unusable. The first example of this tradition was documented in the elite graves of Horoztepe (Özgüç and Akok 1958: 8). The same tradition in the Resuloğlu cemetery was not only applied to metal vessels but also to weapons and pins (Yıldırım 2012: 245). Moreover, some metal vessels were found broken and shattered and were deposited both inside and next to the grave or around the grave covering. It is not clear whether this tradition was a part of the ritual or a precaution against grave robbery.[3] However, examples of complete metal objects next to broken ones support the idea that the act of breaking cups/placing fragments might be related to a burial ritual. The same idea applies to pins. Metal vessels of Resuloğlu were deposited in the graves of both men and women. Thereby, it is understood that metal vessels put in the graves, just as weapons and jewelry, during this period in the north do not identify the gender of the deceased. To date, there has been no metal vessel that was unearthed in the EBA Resuloğlu settlement, especially in the houses of the southeast mound. At the moment it is thought that metal vessels left in the graves were used as grave goods as known in many other northern Anatolian examples. These metal vessels, like jewelry and weapons, must have been the most precious items of their owners. According to their afterlife beliefs, the dead must have taken their belongings with them, which they needed and deserved for the afterlife (Özgüç 1948: 112).

Excavations conducted at Resuloğlu cemetery showed that metal vessels were left only in stone cist, pithoi and jar burials. There has been no metal vessel that was identified in small-numbered inhumations. It is possible to group the Resuloğlu metal vessels as follows:

Bowls

Basic, with omphalos and single-handled bowls constitute two different types of bowls deposited in various graves.

a) Simple Omphalos Bowl

Ro.09/Etd.65, Museum Inventory no (hereafter, Inv. no.): 1237, (Fig. 1)
Height: 8.8 cm, Width: 13.6 cm. M.265, Trench AE 29, II. Level pithos burial
Cu 81.66, **Sn** 17.81, **As** 0.14, **Pb** 0.03, **Ni** 0.15, **Fe** 0.58, **Ag** 0.05 Total **100.42** [4]

Made of a thin layer of bronze by forging. Flared rimmed, depressed globular bodied, thin-walled, flat-based with omphalos in the middle/center. Intentionally bent while it was being put in the grave. Excavated on the chest of an adult's skeleton.

Baked Clay bowls with omphalos were known in various phases of the EBA in central/north-

2 See Koşay 1951: Pl.CXLVII (Alaca Höyük burial D) Arık 1936: Pl.CCXXXV (Alaca Höyük burial RM); Özgüç and Akok 1958: Pl.IV/3 (Horoztepe) ; Türker *et al.* 2018: Fig. 3 (Devret Höyük) for more information on copper-alloy beak-spouted jars.

3 See Durgun 2019: 326, for recent interpretations of the topic.

4 See Dardeniz and Yıldırım 2020: 141- 161; Dardeniz 2020: 12–34. I am thankful to Assoc. Prof. Gonca Dardeniz Arıkan, who conducted portable X-ray fluorescence (pXRF) and lead isotope analysis on the Resuloğlu metal cups. My colleague revised previous works and presented that Resuloğlu metal vessels were made of alloys of copper, copper-tin, copper with arsenic, copper-arsenic-tin, silver-copper, copper with antimony, copper-silver-gold, copper-tin-lead, copper-arsenic-silver-gold, copper-silver-antimony-gold. These results indicate that the metallurgical practices at the region are more diverse than previously thought (Dardeniz 2020).

ern Anatolia; they are documented from settlements such as Ahlatlıbel (Koşay 1933: 53) and Maşat Höyük (Emre 1996: 14, Fig. 55). Clay examples unearthed in Resuloğlu date to the end of the EBA II and the beginning of the EBA III. Further in the South in the Yozgat region, the development of this ware type is known since the Late Chalcolithic.[5] A small amount of the metal bowls, which were among the favorite cup type of the north, have an omphalos. A shallower and more sharply shouldered bowl type with omphalos was identified in Horoztepe[6], among grave goods in Pit A dated to ca. 2100 B.C. An omphalos bowl excavated in treasure A of Eskiyapar[7] is the only silver example found in the north. Further towards the Black Sea region, an example made of copper with arsenic found in İkiztepe was dated to Early Bronze Age III (Bilgi 2001: 65, 97, Fig. 74). The closest examples of omphalos bowls outside of central/northern Anatolia are recorded in Troy, Treasure A.[8] The relationship between these two metal rich regions has been discussed in various publications. During the 1950s, Machteld Mellink related the growing importance of land trade between central Anatolia and Troy to the development of a rich metal industry in both regions. Her argument was based on the similarities between some of the well-known metal artifacts unearthed in the Aegean Region and Troy to Alaca Höyük (Mellink 1956: 54ff.). In 1959, K. Bittel discussed the similarities of the bronze vessels of these two regions in the framework of the omphalos cooking pans (Bittel 1959: 32). Tahsin Özgüç, who introduced the treasure of Eskiyapar to the scholarly community in 1993, explained the cultural relations between northern Anatolia and Troy with numerous examples in the light of various ornaments and metal vessels (Özgüç 1993: 613ff.). Özgüç states that "*These relationships developed not only due to trade but also thanks to the developments in culture and metallurgy easing the contact between two regions, and individuals from both regions took one another's pottery, metal vessels and jewelry as models.*"[9] Like others, we are also evaluating the similarities of the Resuloğlu bowl to examples from Troy within the same framework. Omphalos bowls, which gained popularity in central/northern Anatolia at the end of the 3rd millennium B.C., continued in existence during the Old Assyrian Trade Colonies Period (Özgüç 1986: 68, Pl. 126,1a–b).

b) Single-Handled Bowls

Bases of two examples with thin walls belonging to this group are slightly embossed or with omphalos.

1. Ro.08/Etd.48, Inv.no: 1173, (Fig. 2)
Height: 3 cm, Width: 14 cm, Weight: 26.75 gr, M.217, Trench AB/29 II. Level, pithos burial
Cu 82.46, **Sn** 16.6, **As** 0.71, **Pb** 0.07, **Ni** 0.14, **Fe** 0.6, **Ag** 0.06, **Au** 0.01, Total **100.65**
Made of a thin layer of bronze by forging. The base of the simple rimmed shallow bowl is slightly rounded and embossed. Narrow band handle connected to the rim is bent in a spiral shape throughout the body. Deposited on the chest of a young female's skeleton after having been bent intentionally.

5 Gurney *et al.* 1999: Fig. 13/97 (Çadır Höyük).

6 Özgüç and Akok 1958: Fig. 18.

7 Özgüç and Temizer 1993: 618, Fig. 47, Pl. 116/2.; Toker 1992: no. 41.

8 Dörpfeld 1902: 353, Fig. 285 b, c, Fig. 286.

9 Özgüç and Temizer 1993: 627. Vasıf Şahoğlu defines the period, in which new ideas and technologies influenced people in the area extending from Mesopotamia to Syria, Anatolia, the Aegean, Cyprus and the Balkans, as the "Early Bronze Age Anatolian Trade Network". Especially in the second half of the EBA, the increase in mineral use, mineral trade, the emergence of new vessel forms, long-distance trade, similar ceramic features in a wide geography and the existence of communities with social stratification and urbanism can be explained by this theoretical approach. See Şahoğlu 2005: 339ff.; 2019: 115ff. For trade relations in EBA West and Central Anatolia see Yılmaz 2009: 441ff.

2. Ro.08 Etd.18, Museum Inv. no: Etd.1143, (Figs. 3–4)
Height: 2 cm., Width: 13 cm, Weight: 48.55 gr, M.220, Trench AC/28, II. Level, pithos burial.
Cu 85,54, **Sn** 16.35, **As** 0.12, **Pb** 0.12, **Ni** 0.14, **Fe** 0.3, **Ag** 0.04, **Au** 0.01, Total **102.61**
Made of a thin layer of bronze by forging. The base of the simple-rimmed shallow bowl is slightly rounded and embossed. Narrow-band handle connected to the rim is bent in shape through the body. Deposited under the chest of an adult male's skeleton after being intentionally bent.

The Pithos burials of Resuloğlu showed that metal bowls were mostly left on the right chests of skeletons (Fig. 5, Fig. 10b, Fig. 16). Metal examples of handled bowls constituting the popular ware type of the north were produced out of thin and flat plates. Narrow-band handles are connected only to rims and not to the body. A copper cup unearthed in Alaca Höyük grave H[10] is the closest parallel to the Resuloğlu example. However, as the Alaca Höyük example was smashed and broken; it is not certain if it was embossed. Bases of bronze examples from Gümüşhacıköy[11] and Merzifon-Göller[12] along with the bronze example in Metropolitan Museum of Art, which is thought to originate in Horoztepe,[13] are flat with smaller rim diameters. These examples differ from Resuloğlu's single-handled bowls with their small body shapes and flat bases.

Other various grave goods excavated from the same graves of Resuloğlu bowls made it easier to date the grave goods, which were evidently used in the same temporal frame. Parallels to the carnelian beads which were among the grave goods unearthed with the single-handled bowl in grave no. 217 (Fig. 5), can be seen especially in the elite graves of Alaca Höyük.[14] Flat silver beads with tubular midrib[15] found in the same grave were excavated also in many other settlements situated on the trade routes extending from southern Mesopotamia to Troy in Western Anatolia during the EBA III period, the end of the Early Dynastic and Akkadian periods. The examples in the Level II Resuloğlu graves represent the northmost distribution of this type. Silver grave goods and completely similar carnelian beads to the ones we are familiar with from graves H and L in Alaca Höyük,[16] are important, because they indicate that the metal bowls were used approximately in the same time period.

Cups

Compared to other examples among the Resuloğlu grave goods, metal cups are higher in number. The cups are represented by two different groups: big, semi-globular bodied, omphalos-based and small, shallow, flattened or rounded based.

a) Big, Semi-Globular Bodied, Omphalos cup

Ro.04/Etd.21, Inv. no.: 999, (Figs. 6–7)
Height: 5.5 cm, Width: 13.4 cm., Weight 69 gr, M.86, Trench C/27, Level II. Pithos burial.
Cu 87.41, **Sn** 10.93, **As** 0.08, **Pb** 0.03, **Ni** 0.15, **Fe** 0.72, Total **99.14**
Found on an adult male's skeleton broken in scattered pieces. It was intentionally left in the grave in a broken state. Thickened rimmed, half globular bodied, a circular-section type of handle rises from the rim and bends toward the bottom. Rounded base with omphalos.

10 Koşay 1951: 63, Pl. CXXXIII/H 18.
11 Perk 2014: 27, HPM6818.
12 Toker 1992: 48, no. 20, 21.
13 Tezcan 1960: 15, Pl. 17/Fig. 3; Muscarella 1988: 411, vessel no. 564.
14 Koşay 1951: Pl.CXXXIV/ H 39 (Tomb H); Pl. CLXVII/Al.C/ E.20 (Tomb E) ; Pl. CC/Al.D./ L17 (Tomb L)
15 Yıldırım 2019: 158, Şek.20 M.217/2008. For distribution of these beads (flat beads with tubular midrib): Yılmaz 2019: 173, Fig. 11.
16 See footnote 15.

Smaller examples without omphalos on the bottom belonging to this group are known from Horoztepe.[17]

b) Small and Shallow Cups

Bodies of many small cups get narrower towards the base, while bodies of some examples have hemispherical bodies.

1. Ro.04/Etd.14, Inv. no.: 992, (Figs. 8–9)
Height: 5.5 cm, Width: 13.4 cm, Weight: 29.25 gr. M.80, Trench C/27, Level II. Pithos burial
Cu 89.47, **Sn** 10.08, **As** 0.26, **Pb** 0.02, **Fe** 0.23, Total **100.78**
Made by forging. Slightly thickened rimmed, shallow bodied, a broadband handle connected to the rim of the cup was bent down. Slightly flat based. The body was bent intentionally. The handle is broken. Excavated on the chest of an adult's skeleton.

2. Ro.06/Etd.18, Inv. no.: 7902, (Figs. 10 a,b–11 a,b)
Height: 1.8 cm, Rim Dia: 6 cm, Weight: 42 gr, M.141, Trench A-B/7, Level II. Pithos burial
Cu 65.7, **Sn** 0.04, **Sb** 0.02, **Pb** 0.16, **Ni** 0.1, **Fe** 0.55, **Ag** 25.37, **Au** 0.65 Total **92.59** (Copper-Silver alloy)
Made by forging. Simple rimmed. Band handle rises from the rim bent at an angle towards the body. Body gets narrower from rim to base, connected to the base in a slightly concave shape. Cup was deposited on an adult skeleton's right hand little finger, placed on the chest.

3. Ro.06/Etd.26, Inv. no.: 7910, (Figs. 12–13)
Height: 3.9 cm, Width: 10.5 cm, Weight: 121.45 gr, M.145, Trench A/26, Level II, pithos burial.
Cu 91,49, **Sn** 7,85, **Pb** 0.45, **Fe** 0.06, Total **100.05** (Copper-tin alloy)
Simple rimmed, wide, round-mouthed, shallow-bodied, rounded-based. A single vertical handle connects the rim to the body. Intentionally bent. Deposited between the right shoulder and chest of a young female's skeleton.

4. Ro.03/Etd.05 (Figs. 14–15)
Height: 3.7 cm, Rim Diam: 7.9 cm, M.20, Trench E/28, Level II stone cist burial.
Cu 93.89, **Sn** 6.26, As 0.12, **Fe** 0.17, Total **100.44** (Copper-tin alloy)
Simple rimmed, wide, round-mouthed, globular- bodied. Narrow band handle bent from rim to the body. Half of the cup was partially preserved. Recovered between the cover stones of the stone cist. Intentionally broken.

Cups, which were among the favorite ware types of the north in the Early Bronze Age, are the most common metal grave goods of the Resuloğlu burials with bowls. Bowls were excavated on skeletons' right chests or right hands. This indicates that some examples of them were intentionally broken into pieces and scattered in the burials or between the cover stones of stone covers of the cist graves. All of the excavated examples belong to pithoi and cist burials in level II. Exact parallels for the cup with hemispherical body and single handle unearthed in a cist burial is known from gold and silver[18], gold-plated over silver or bronze[19] examples excavated in Alaca Höyük. There are two copper alloy, fully preserved cups with hemispherical bodies

17 Özgüç and Akok 1958: 13, Fig. 15. ; Özgüç 1964: 5, Fig. 4 (silver, the example without omphalos).

18 Koşay 1951: Pl. CXCVI/Al.D. L4 (burial L); Arık 1937: Pl.CCXXXI/Al.1083, burial R.M.

19 Koşay 1938: Pl. LXXXII/36, burial M.A., Toker 1992: p. 187, no. 18 "Burial A " and no:19 in "Burial K".

in the collection of Merzifon Gümüşhacıköy (Perk 2014: 28ff. HPM6721, HPM5668). The examples from Gümüşhacıköy are slightly different from Resuloğlu with their ornamented round handles. One bronze cup from Çorum/ Yenihayat cemetery (Müller-Karpe 1994: Pl. 92/18), which belongs to the same group as the Resuloğlu cups, is distinguished from them by its sharp body. The shallowest and biggest example (121,45 gr) of the Resuloğlu cups must have been made by casting. Close parallels of other examples with shallow body and flattened base are known from the Göller and Gümüşhacıköy regions.[20] Some of the the Resuloğlu cups were put on the right hand and fingers of the deceased with the mouth of the cup looking up, intentionally without any damage (Fig. 10b). Therefore, it can be thought that there was a ritual practiced during the deceased's passage to the afterlife. However, scientific analysis to understand the type of any liquid inside the cup, is inconclusive at this stage of the work.

This tradition is seen for the first time among the north Anatolian cemeteries. The interesting thing in this situation is the fact that the other single-handled cup deposited on the deceased's chest was intentionally bent.

Vases

One of the two lead examples representing the metal vases of Resuloğlu was excavated in a stone cist burial of level II.

> **Ro.03/Etd.03 (Figs. 17–18)**
> Height: 15.7 cm, Body Width: 17 cm, Rim Diam:16.5 cm, Approx. Weight: 300 gr. Trench D/29, M.28, Level II. Cist burial.
> **Cu** 0.08, **Sn** 0.04, **Pb** 94.7, **Fe** 0.07, Total **94.89** (Lead)

Vases in the 3rd millennium B.C. show the same characteristics in their form as their ceramic counterparts. The closest parallels to the Resuloğlu vase were unearthed in Tokat/ Kayapınar[21] and in Alaca Höyük Burial K (Koşay 1951: CLXXV/2 Al.D.K 6, gold). Lead vases originated from Merzifon-Oymaağaç in the north are mostly beak-spouted.[22] It is known that one lead vase bought along with the other metalware by the Anatolian Civilizations Museum (Ankara) and brought to the museum, originates from Oymaağaç (Silistreli 1976: 30, Pl.XXVI/2). The number of lead vases is also increasing in the Çorum region. My colleague Dr. Önder İpek reported a similar lead vase excavated in Sungurlu/ Aşağı Fındıklı Köyü.[23] The Sungurlu vase unearthed with a metal pin must be a grave good. Lead vases placed in the burials of Demirci Höyük- Sarıket in Eskişehir region during the EBA indicate the existence of authentic vase models produced in different regions of Anatolia (Baykal-Seeher and Seeher 1998: 116ff., Fig. 1–11). I believe that workshops in the northern Anatolia, especially in Merzifon and Tokat regions (Özgüç 1978: 35ff.), must have produced the lead vessels unearthed in Resuloğlu and Oymaağaç.

Cooking Pan

Metal cooking pan represented with a single example in Resuloğlu is poorly preserved.

> **Ro.03/Etd.02 (Fig. 17, 19)**
> Height: 4 cm, Mouth Width: 12.5 cm, M.28, Trench D/29, Level II. Stone Cist burial.
> **Cu** 97.69, **As** 2.67, **Fe** 0.16, Total **100.52** (Copper-arsenic alloy)
> Basic rimmed, wide, round-mouthed, shallow bodied, rounded-flat bodied. The edge of the handle connected to the mouth and a small part of the body is broken and missing. The cooking pan was

20 Toker 1992: 188, no. 20,21; Perk 2014: 27, HPM6818.

21 Temizer 1954: 326, Pl.16a; Toker 1992: 189, no. 27, bronze

22 Anlağan 1990: 68, Pl. 15; Toker 1992: 184, no. 6; Silistreli 1983: 35

23 Çorum Müzesi env.no: Etd. 2000/5. I thank my colleague who informed me about the artifact and helped me to see it.

placed on the shoulder of the skeleton. Intentionally bent.

A bronze cooking pan originating in Merzifon-Göller region bought by the Anatolian Civilizations Museum (Ankara) is an exact parallel to the Resuloğlu example (Toker 1992: 59/no. 36). There is also a small electrum cooking pan from the treasure of Eskiyapar[24] which lacks its handle, which was reconstructed according to examples from Troy IIg. This cooking pan is morphologically different from the examples from Göller and Resuloğlu. The example from Eskiyapar dating to the Early Bronze Age III is the shallowest and smallest example of the cooking pans found in the north. The Eskiyapar cooking pan could have been brought from Northwestern Anatolia to Eskiyapar during the EBA, when the cultural relationships between the Troad region, northern Anatolia and Mesopotamia were strong (Özgüç and Temizer 1993: 626). Resuloğlu's and Göller's cooking pans with flat band handles should be local examples from the north.

Spoon

The only example of a spoon placed in the burials was unearthed with the lead vase and cooking pan in a cist burial belonging to an adult male.

Ro.03 / Etd.01 (Fig. 17, 20)
Length: 9.9 cm, Height: 1.4 cm, Mouth Width: 5.4 cm, M.28, Trench D/29, Level II. Stone cist burial
Cu 93.89, **Sn** 6.26, **As** 0.12, **Fe** 0.17, Total **100.44** (Copper-Tin alloy)
Basic rimmed, ovoid mouthed, shallow bodied. The handle connected to the mouth was twisted. Deposited in the burial after being intentionally bent.

This bronze spoon from Resuloğlu is the third example representing the same group in the north along with examples from Alaca Höyük (Koşay 1951: Pl.CXCVII/Al.D.L. 9) and Gümüşhacıköy (Perk 2014: 35, HPM6720). A parallel example is a silver spoon with gold-plated handle excavated in Tomb L Alaca Höyük indicating that such spoons were in use by the elite. The recently published bronze Gümüşhacıköy spoon with a twisted handle is identical to the Resuloğlu example. They must have been produced in the same workshop. These workshops, which were controlled by chiefs, produced similar types of vase according to the taste of both elites and settlers. A bronze spoon with a long flat handle with semicircle finish originating in Oymaağaç shows the variety of products in the northern workshops (Toker 1992: 60, no. 39).

Pottery, metal weapons and jewelry excavated along with metal vases in Resuloğlu's level II burials of female, male and young adults, are the personal effects of individuals who resided in the southeastern mound, which is 90 m. away as the crow flies. Excavations being conducted since 2010 in the southeastern mound presented a settlement with a feudal-style complex with fortification walls. Houses have rectangular plans and are situated next to silos. Exact parallels to the jugs excavated in the houses were found in the level II burials. Moreover, exact parallels to the daily pottery unearthed in granaries and houses were placed in the level II burials. Exact parallels of black slipped, s-profiled, finely polished jars with stripe designs, which are the imitations of metal vases, are found in Tomb A (Koşay 1938: Pl. LXXXVI/4,5) and Tomb T (Arık 1935: Pl. CCLXXXIX/Al.1074) at Alaca Höyük. Other well-dated examples of black slipped, finely polished cups with dots and stripe designs imitating metal cups unearthed in the level II burials of Resuloğlu[25], are known from excavations at Tokat/ Maşat Höyük. Black slipped and well polished cups from Maşat Höyük belong to the EBA, which are represented by the levels VI and VII of the site, situated right under the level V dated to

24 Özgüç and Temizer 1993: Pl. 117, 3a–b, Figs. 48 a–b, 50.

25 Yıldırım and Ediz 2008: 446, Fig. 7; Yıldırım 2006: 8, Fig. 12; Yıldırım 2011: 18.

the late Old Assyrian Trading Colonies period (Emre 1979. 1ff; Emre 2012: 238). Imported Alişar III ware fragments and depas sherds were found next to the typical monochrome ceramics of the north in the last burned layer. These finds support the dating suggested for Maşat Höyük. As it is well known from the literature, Alişar III pottery was unearthed in the chronologically well-dated layers of the EBA III (the end of the third millennium) at Kültepe (Özgüç 1963: 34; Ezer 2014: 11ff.). There has been no metal, decorated mug from Resuloğlu. However, exact parallels made of pottery found in the level II burials are known from the Eskiyapar treasure dated to the EBA III (Özgüç and Temizer 1993: 617, Fig. 44, Pl. 117/2). Black slipped and burnished pottery with geometric groove design are observed in mugs or vases placed in the level II burials of Resuloğlu. A similar design is noted on a piece of gold-plated silver vase in burial H in Alaca Höyük (Koşay 1951: 63 H.17, Pl.CXXXI/17). On the other hand, similar bronze single-handled bowls are known from burial H. Cups with parallels made of precious metals are known from tombs L, R, A and K. The lead vase of Resuloğlu with a comparandum made of gold from burial K and the bronze spoon with a comparable example made of silver found in burial L are significant, as, they show the chronological synchronization between the Resuloğlu level II burials and Alaca Höyük burials. Jewelry made of gold, silver, bronze and carnelian documented in the level II burials of Resuloğlu along with metal vases are identical to examples especially found in the Tombs B, T, A', C, H, E, K, L and S in Alaca Höyük.[26] It is possible to enhance the parallels between the bronze pins and weapons in the level II burials of Resuloğlu. The dating and stratigraphy of Alaca Höyük have been discussed by many scholars up until now. Burials, according to their depth, were assigned to the layers as follows: Graves A', B, H, R, S, D, T were assigned to Layer 5, which is the last burnt layer of Alaca Höyük. The graves A, C, E were assigned to Layer 6. The graves F, K, L were assigned to Layer 7 (Arık 1937; Koşay 1938; Koşay 1951). Özgüç and Akok, two eminent scholars of Near Eastern Archaeology, wrote their suspicions that three burials (F, K, L), out of six burials (F, K, L, A, C, E) cutting the walls of structures of the Layer 8, should belong to the layer 7. Based on the burial types and similarities between the grave goods (from 6th and 5th layers), they argued that the three burials (F, K, L) should be assigned to the 6th layer (Özgüç and Akok 1957: 208). The Level II burials of Resuloğlu and their metal vases along with other grave goods are exact parallels to Alaca Höyük's 5th and 6th layers. The most important thing which we should emphasize is when exactly in the 3rd millennium B.C. these parallels are fitting in. We stated that the owners of level II burials resided in the houses of the southeastern mound. C 14 results of the carbonized material taken from two-phased houses and silos in the southeastern mound revealed the following dates:[27] for the later phase of the southeastern mound; 3896±28 BP (calibrated 2467–2298 B.C.), 3866±28 BP (calibrated 2464–2278 B.C.); for the earlier phase of the southeastern mound, 4005±29 BP (calibrated 2577–2470 B.C.E), 3993±28 BP (calibrated 2573–2468 B.C.). A charcoal fragment found in a silo excavated at the later phase of the southeastern mound was sent to the laboratory of the University of Zürich by my colleague Ünsal Yalçın. The sample (ETH-42014 – DK-10/101) revealed the date 3960±35 BP (calibrated 2580–2340 B.C.).[28] Accordingly, the level II burials of Resuloğlu, which are contemporary to the later phase of the southeastern mound, are dated approximately between 2500–2300 B.C. Thus, it is clear that the cemetery was used at the beginning of the EBA III. Other than the

26 Jewelry of Resuloğlu is in publication. Detailed descriptions of the Resuloğlu jewelry are far beyond the remit of this particular article.

27 TÜBİTAK MAM report date 7/12/2018, report no: 82325108-125.05-32/7066.

28 I thank my colleague Professor Ünsal Yalçın for sending the sample to analysis.

other relative datings, these datasets also help us to correlate the dates of the Resuloğlu burials to the 5th and 6th layers of Alaca Höyük. In my opinion, the most important issue that needs to be highlighted here is: the graves of Alaca Höyük can not be dated to the beginning of the 3rd millennium B.C. or to the first quarter of the period, as was suggested.[29] Furthermore, it is important to note that Alaca Höyük Tomb L, with its artifact assemblage comparable to Resuloğlu, should belong to the layer 6 of Alaca Höyük, as Özgüç previously stated.

Bibliography

Arık, R.O.
- 1937 *Alaca Höyük Hafriyatı, 1935'deki Çalışmalara ve Keşiflere Ait İlk Rapor,* TTKY, Seri 5, No.1, Ankara.

Baykal-Seeher, A and J. Seeher
- 1998 "Gefäße aus Blei in der Frühen Bronzezeit Anatoliens," in G. Arsebük *et al.* (ed.) *Light on Top of the Black Hill, Studies presented to Halet Çambel,* Istanbul, pp. 115–121.

Bilgi, Ö.
- 1984 "Metal Objects from İkiztepe-Turkey," *Beiträge zur Allgemeinen und Vergleichenden Archäologie* 6, pp. 31–96.
- 1990 "Metal Objects from İkiztepe-Turkey," *Beiträge zur Allgemeinen und Vergleichenden Archäologie* 9–10, pp. 119–219.

Bittel, K.
- 1959 "Beitrag zur Kenntnis Anatolischer Metallgefässe der zweiten Hälfte des Dritten Jahrtausends v. Chr.," *JDI 74*, pp. 1–34.

Dardeniz, G.
- 2020 "Why Did the Use of Antimony-Bearing Alloys in Bronze Age Anatolia Fall Dormant After the Early Bronze Age? A Case from Resuloğlu (Çorum,Turkey)," *PLOS ONE* 15(7), pp. 1–34.

Dardeniz, G. and T. Yıldırım
- 2020 "Resuloğlu (Çorum, Turkey) Updated: Preliminary Results of pXRF Analysis of Metal Artifacts from the Early Bronze Age Cemetery," in F. Kulakoğlu *et al.* (ed.) *SUBARTU, Kültepe International Meeting 3,* Turnhout, pp. 141–161.

Dörpfeld,W.
- 1902 *Troja und Ilion,* Athen.

Durgun,P.
- 2019 "Erken Tunç Çağı Batı ve Orta Anadolu'da Yerleşim Dışı Mezarlıkların Ortaya Çıkışı ve Ölü Gömme Ritüelleri," in A. M. Büyükkarakaya *et al.* (eds.) *Memento Mori, Ölüm ve Ölüm Uygulamaları,* Istanbul, pp. 317–336.

Emre, K.
- 1996 "The Early Bronze Age at Maşat Höyük Seasons 1980–1984," in H.I.H. Prince Takahito Mikasa (ed.), *Essays on Ancient Anatolia and Syria in the Second and Third Millennium B.C.,* Wiesbaden, pp. 1–67.
- 2012 "Maşat Höyük (1945, 1973–1984)," *Dil ve Tarih-Coğrafya Fakültesi 75. Yıl Armağanı, Arkeoloji Bölümü Tarihçesi ve Kazıları (1936–2011) Anadolu/Anatolia Anı-Armağan Serisi Ek* 111.2, pp. 231–236.

Gorny, R. L. *et al.*
- 1999 "The 1998 Alişar Regional Project Season," *Anatolica* 25, pp. 149–171.

Koşay, H. Z.
- 1934 "Türkiye Cumhuriyeti Maarif Vekaletince Yaptırılan Ahlatlıbel Hafriyatı," *TTAED* II, 1–101.
- 1938 *Türk Tarih Kurumu Tarafından Yapılan Alaca Höyük Hafriyatı, 1936'daki Çalışmalara ve Keşiflere Ait İlk Rapor,* Ankara.
- 1951 *Alaca Höyük Kazısı 1937–1939' daki Çalışmalara ve Keşiflere Ait İlk Rapor,* Ankara.

Koşay, H. Z. and M. Akok
- 1950 "Amasya Mahmatlar Köyü Definesi," *Belleten* 14, 55, pp. 481–485.
- 1966 *Türk Tarih Kurumu Tarafından Yapılan Alaca Höyük Kazısı 1940–1948'deki Çalışmalara ve Keşiflere Ait İlk Rapor,* Ankara.
- 1973 *Alaca Höyük Kazısı 1963–1967 Calışmaları ve Keşiflere Ait İlk Rapor,* Ankara.

Mellink, M.J
- 1956 "The Royal Tombs at Alaca Höyük and the Aegean World," in S. Weinberg *et al.* (ed.), *The Aegean and the Near East, Studies Presented to Hetty Goldman on the Occasion of her Seventy-fifth Birthday,* New York, pp. 39–58
- 1972 "Archaeology in Asia Minor," *American Journal of Archaeology 76* (2), pp. 165–178.
- 1974 "Archaeology in Asia Minor," *American Journal Archaeology,* 78 (2), pp. 105–130.

29 Yalçın 2011: 61–62; Yalçın 2011a: 143; Yalçın and Yalçın 2013: 38; Yalçın and Yalçın 2019: 21ff.

Muscarella, O. W.
- 1988 *Bronze and Iron. Ancient Near Eastern Artifacts in the Metropolitan Museum of Art*, New York.

Müller-Karpe, A.
- 1994 *Altanatolisches Metallhandwerk*, Neumünster.

Özgüç, T.
- 1948 *Ön Tarih'te Anadolu'da Ölü Gömme Adetleri*, Ankara.
- 1964 Yeni Araştırmaların Işığında Eski Anadolu Arkeolojisi," *Anadolu 7*, pp. 23–42.
- 1966 "Yeni Horoztepe Eserleri," *Anadolu* 8, pp. 19–25.
- 1978 *Maşat Höyük Kazıları ve Çevresindeki Araştırmalar*, Ankara.
- 1980 "Çorum Çevresinde Bulunan Eski Tunç Çağı Eserleri," *Belleten* 44(175), pp. 459–497.
- 1986 *Kültepe Kaniş II, Eski Yakındoğu'nun Ticaret Merkezinde Yeni Araştırmalar*, Ankara.
- 2002 "Eski Tunç Çağı, Hitit Kültürünün Kaynağı Olarak Hatti Kültürü," *Hititler ve Hitit İmparatorluğu – 1000 Tanrılı Halk*, Stuttgart, pp. 400–401.

Özgüç, T. and M. Akok
- 1957 "Horoztepe Eserleri," *Belleten* 82 (21), pp. 201–228.
- 1958 *Horoztepe Eski Tunç Devri Mezarlığı ve İskan Yeri*, Ankara.

Özgüç,T. and R.Temizer
- 1993 "The Eskiyapar Treasure,"in M.J. Mellink, E.Porada and T. Özgüç (eds.), *Nimet Özgüç'e Armağan, Aspects of Art and Iconography: Anatolia and Its Neighbors. Studies in Honor of Nimet Özgüç*, Ankara, pp. 613–628.

Perk, H.
- 2014 *Anadolu İlk Tunç Çağı Toplu Buluntusu*, Istanbul.

Silistreli, U.
- 1976 Ön Tarih'te Anadolu Mezarlıkları I,II (Unpublished Ph.D.Thesis) Ankara.
- 983 "Göller ve Oymaağaç Eski Tunç Çağı Küp Mezarları," *Bilim ve Teknik* 16–184, pp. 34–36.

Süel, M.
- 1989 "Balıbağı1988 Kurtarma Kazısı," *Türk Arkeoloji Dergisi* 28, pp. 145–163.
- 1991 "Balıbağı1989 Kurtarma Kazısı," *1. Müze Kurtarma Kazıları Semineri*, pp. 205–214.
- 1992 "Balıbağı 1990 Kurtarma Kazısı," *2. Müze Kurtarma Kazıları Semineri*, pp. 129–146.

Şahoğlu, V.
2005 "The Anatolian Trade Network During the Early Bronze Age," *Oxford Journal of Archaeology* 24, pp. 339–361.

Temizer,R.
- 1954 "Kayapınar Höyüğü Buluntuları," *Belleten* 18/70, pp. 317–326.

Tezcan, B.
- 1960 "Yeni Horoztepe Buluntuları," *Anadolu* 5, pp. 13–28.

Toker, A.
1992 *Metal Vessels*, Ankara.

Türker, A. *et al.*
- 2018 "Devret Höyük Ölü Gömme Gelenekleri ve Mezar Uygulamaları, *TÜBA-AR* (Özel Sayı), pp. 107–137.

Tütüncüler, Ö.
- 2006 "Çorum-Resuloğlu Eski Tunç Çağı Mezarlığı'nda Kumaş Kullanımına İlişkin Yeni Bulgular," *Anadolu/Anatolia* 30, pp. 137–148.

Yalçın, Ü.
- 2011 "Alacahöyük İlk Tunç Çağı Kral Mezarları Üzerine," *Çorum Kazı ve Araştırmalar Sempozyumu* 1, pp. 55–64.

Yalçın, Ü and G. H. Yalçın
- 2013 "Reassessing Anthropomorphic Metal Figurines of Alacahöyük, Anatolia," *Near Eastern Archaeology* 76, 1, pp. 38–49.

Yıldırım,T.
- 2006 "An Early Bronze Age Cemetery At Resuloğlu, Near Uğurludağ, Çorum. Preliminary Report at the Archaeological Work Carried out Between Years 2003–2005," *Anatolia Antiqua* 14, pp. 1–14.
- 2011 "Resuloğlu Mezarlığında Ele Geçen Bir Grup Sap Delikli Balta," in A. Öztan *et al.* (eds.) *Karadeniz'den Fırat'a Bilgi Üretimleri, Önder Bilgi'ye Armağan Yazılar*, Ankara. pp. 457–464.
- 2011a "Resuloğlu Kazısı ve Anadolu Arkeolojisi'ne Katkıları," *1.Çorum Kazı ve Araştırmalar Sempozyumu*, pp. 11–22.
- 2012 "Resuloğlu (2003-)," in O. Bingöl *et al.* (eds.), *D.T.C.F. 75. Yıl Armağanı, Arkeoloji Bölümü Tarihçesi ve Kazıları (1936–2011)*, ANADOLU Anı-Armağan Serisi Ek III.2, Ankara, pp. 241–248.
- 2019 "Yeni Araştırmalar Işığında Kuzey Anadolu Erken Tunç Çağı Maden Sanatı ve Çevre Kültürlerle İlişkiler," in V. Şahoğlu *et al.* (eds.) *Kültürlerin Bağlantısı, Başlangıcından*

Roma Dönemi Sonuna Kadar Eski Yakın Doğuda Ticaret ve Bölgelerarası İlişkiler, ANADOLU Ek Dizi. 4, Ankara. s. 147–163.

Yılmaz, D.

– 2009 "Commercial Activities Between West and Central Anatolia Regions During the Early Bronze Age," *SOMA 2007,* Oxford, pp. 441–448.

Zimmermann, T.

– 2006 "A Chalcolithic-Early Bronze Age Settlement and Cemetery in Northern Central Anatolia, First Preliminary Report: The Burial Evidence," *Anadolu Medeniyetleri Müzesi* 2005 Yıllığı, pp. 271–311.

– 2007 "Hatti'den Yeni Haberler: Kalınkaya'nın Kalkolitik ve Erken Tunc Cağı Mezar Buluntuları Hakkında İlk Gözlemler," *Araştırma Sonuçları Toplantısı* 24(2), pp. 35–52.

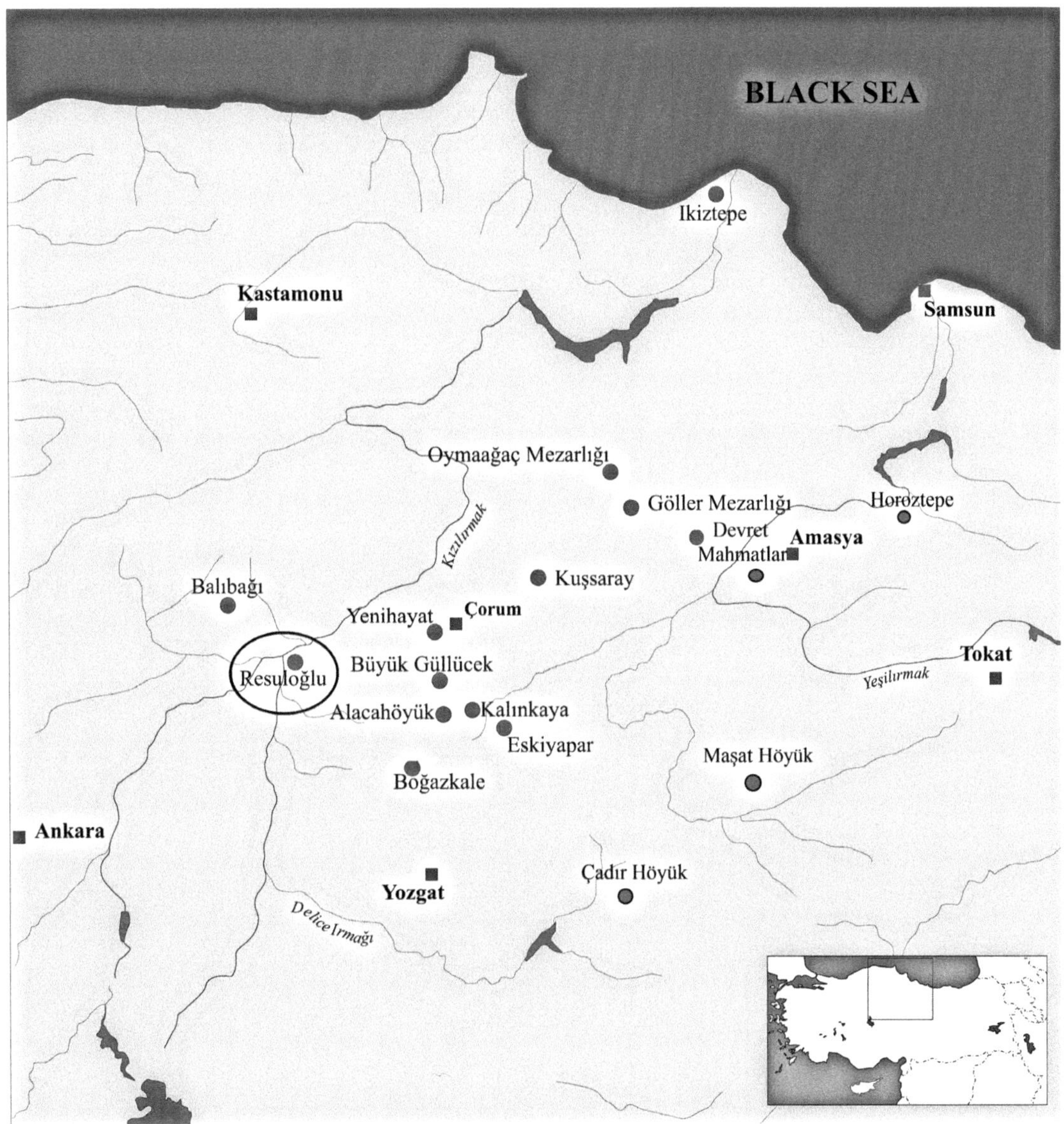

Map 1. Resuloğlu and other EBA cemeteries and settlements.

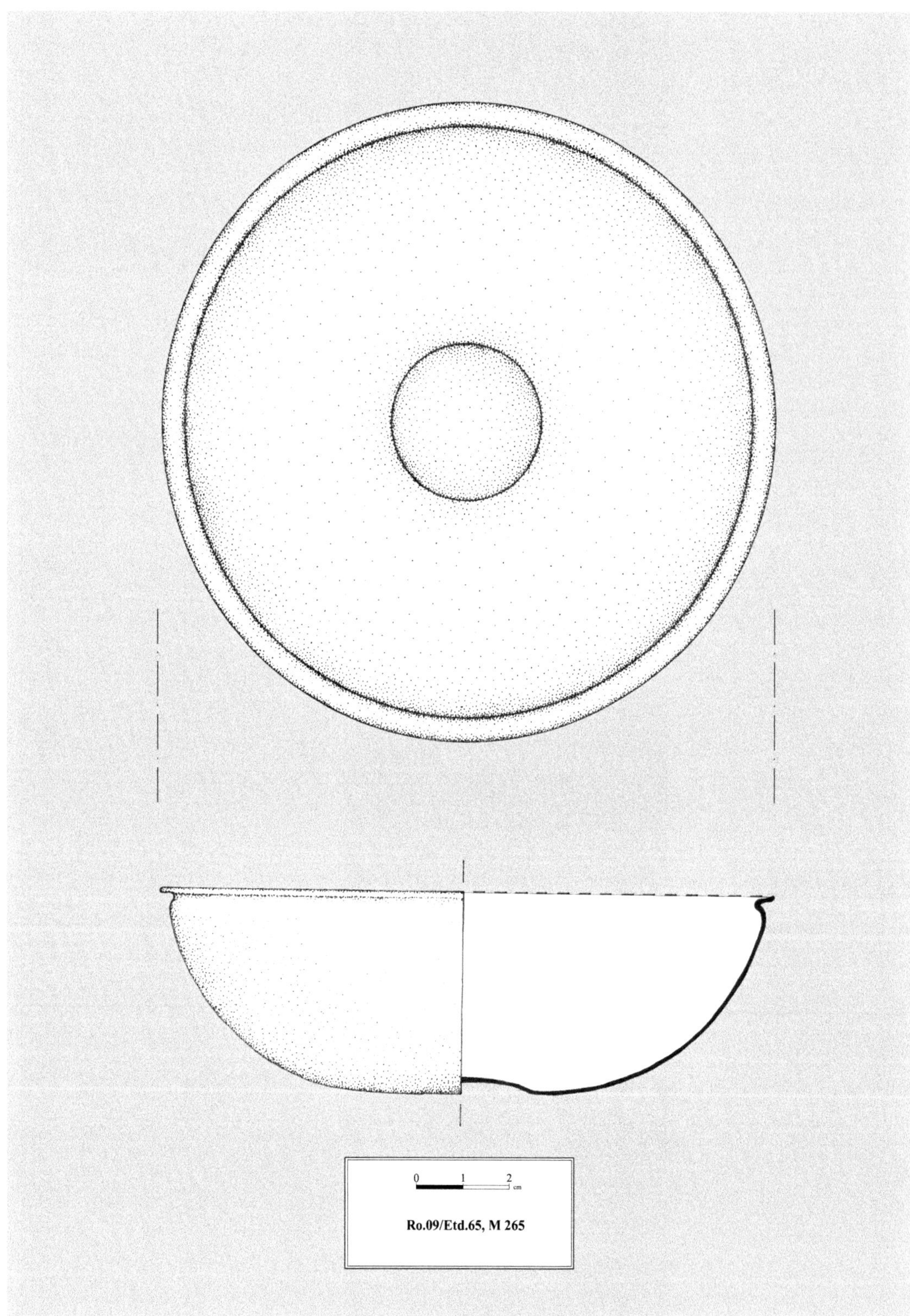

Fig. 1. Bronze bowl from Grave No. M 265.

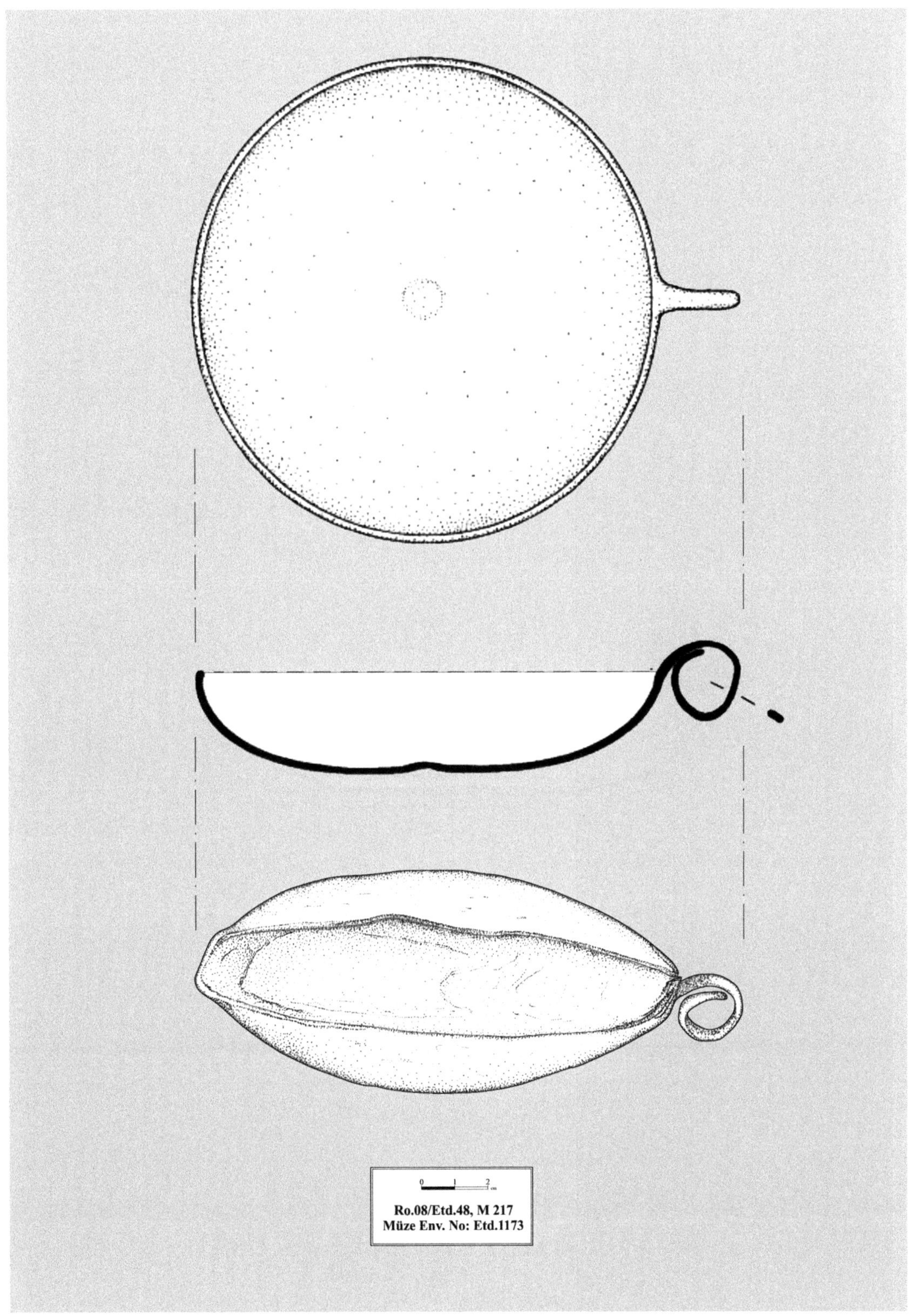

Fig. 2. Single handled Bronze bowl from Grave No. M 217.

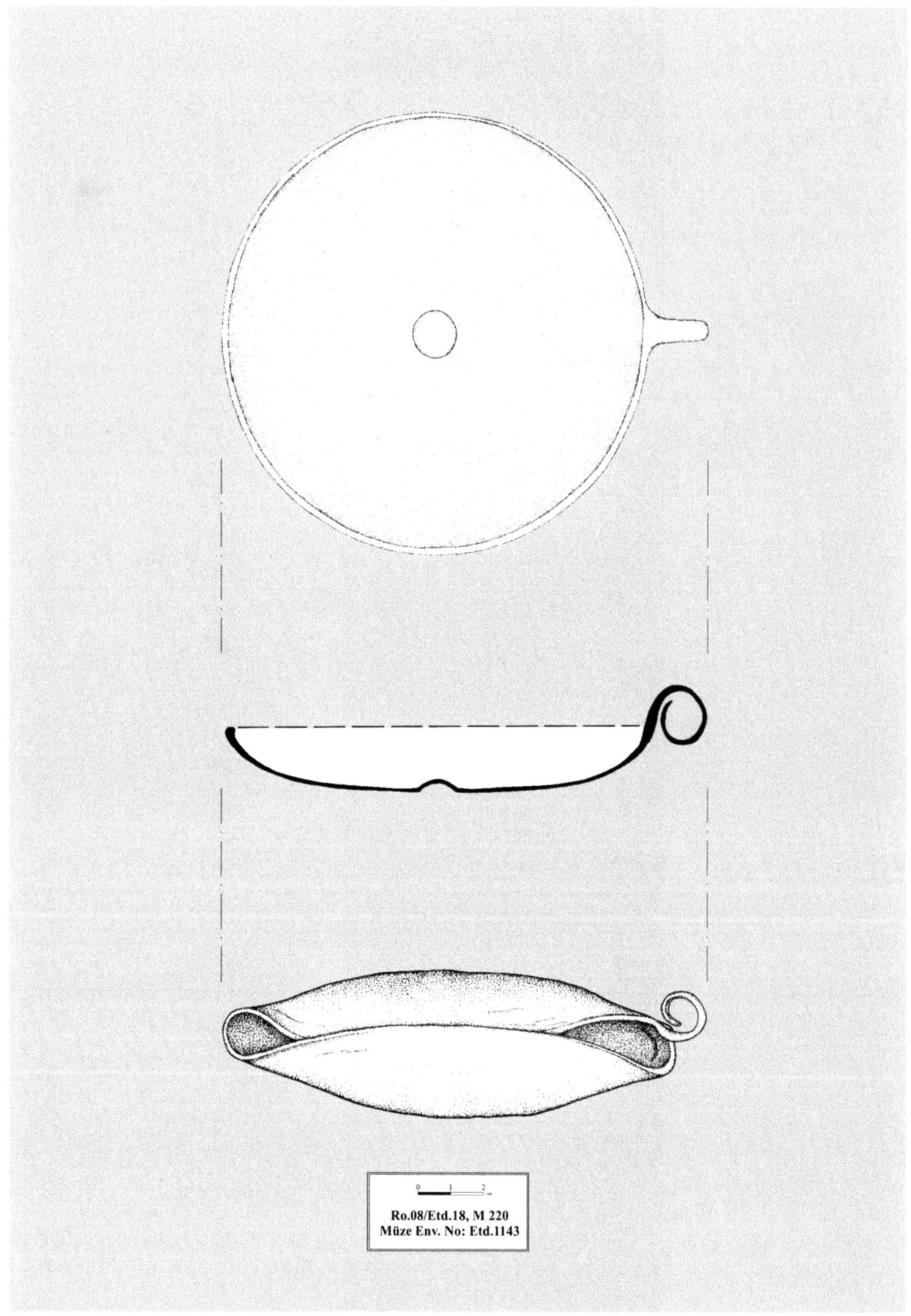

Fig. 3. Single handled Bronze bowl from Grave No. M 220.

Fig. 4. Grave gifts of Grave No. M 220.

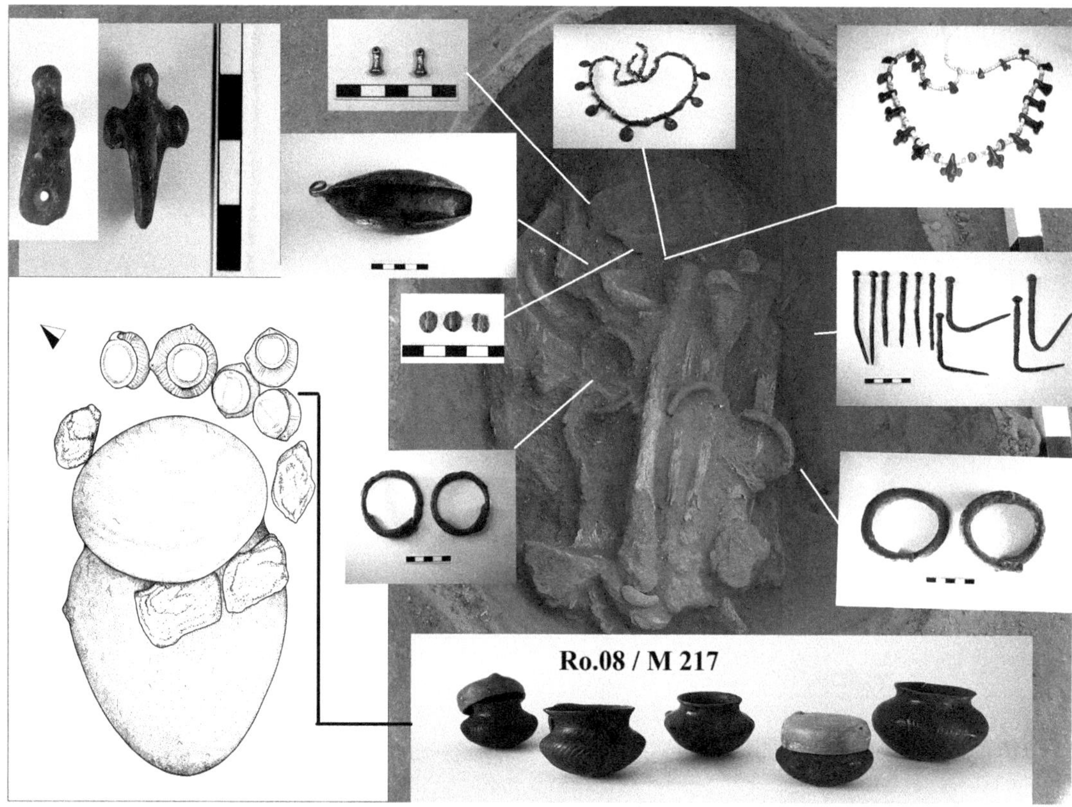

Fig. 5. Grave gifts distribution of Grave No. M 217.

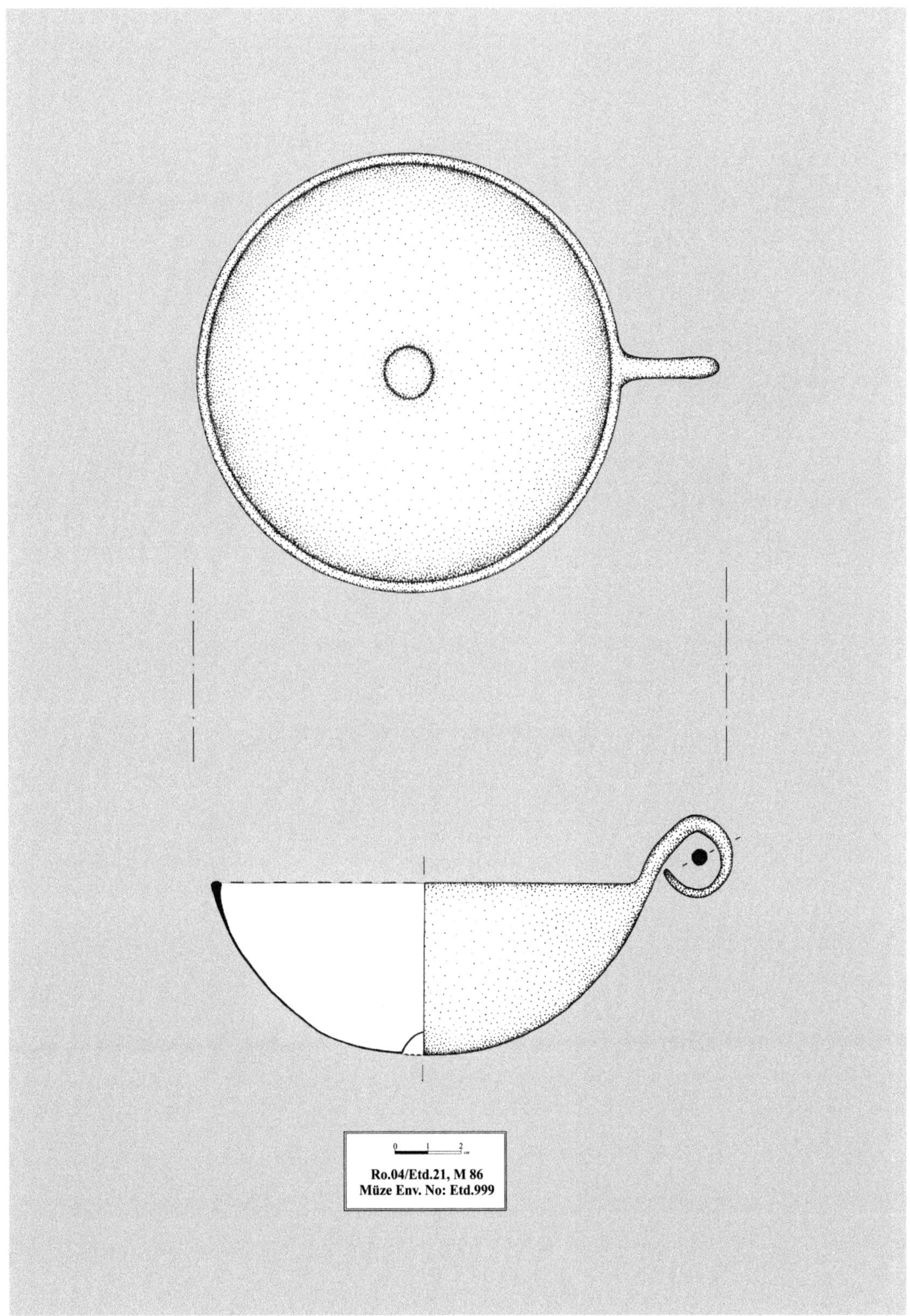

Fig. 6. Bronze cup from Grave No. M 86.

Fig. 7. Single handled cup pieces from Grave No. M 86.

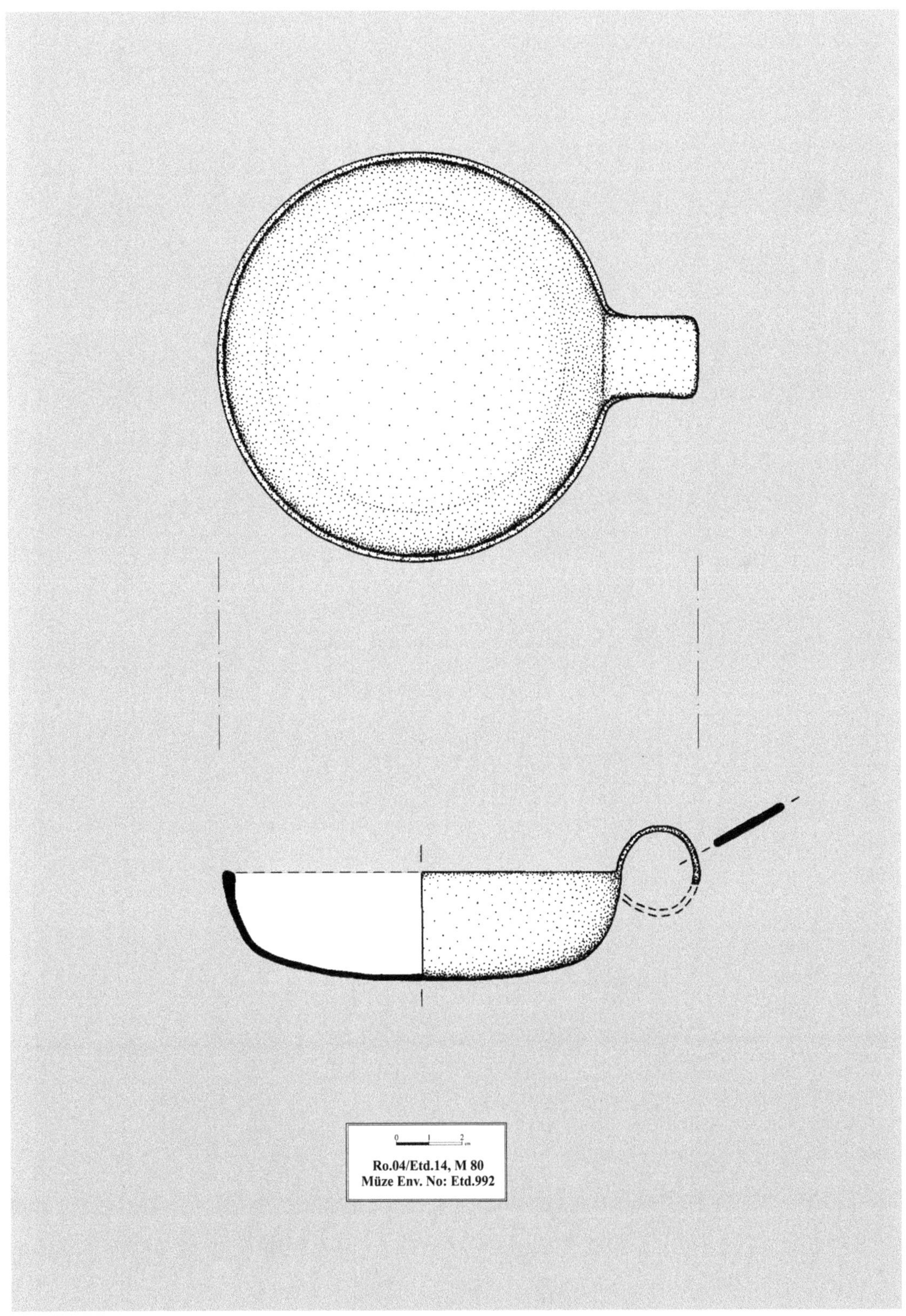

Fig. 8. Bronze cup from Grave No. M 80.

Fig. 9. Bronze cup from Grave No. M 80.

Fig. 10a. Bronze cup from Grave No. M.

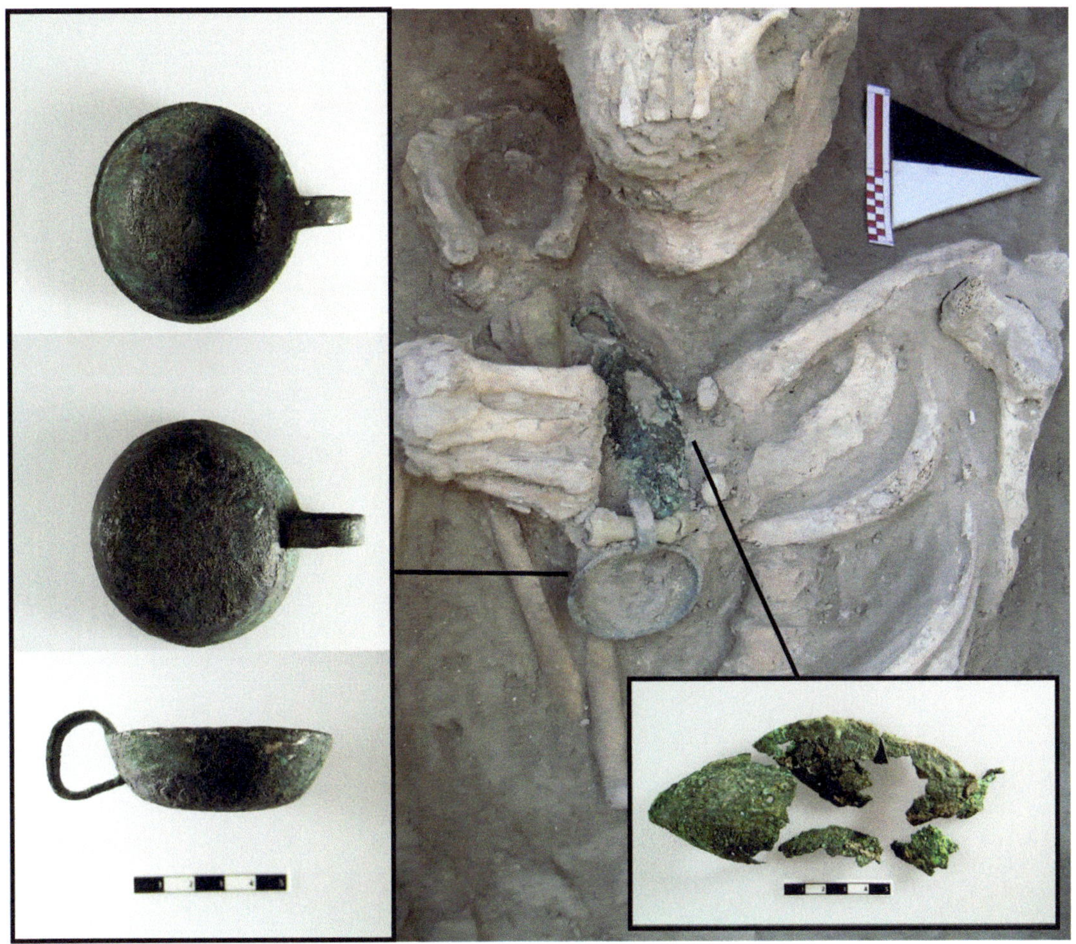

Fig. 10b. In-situ bronze cups from Grave No. M 141.

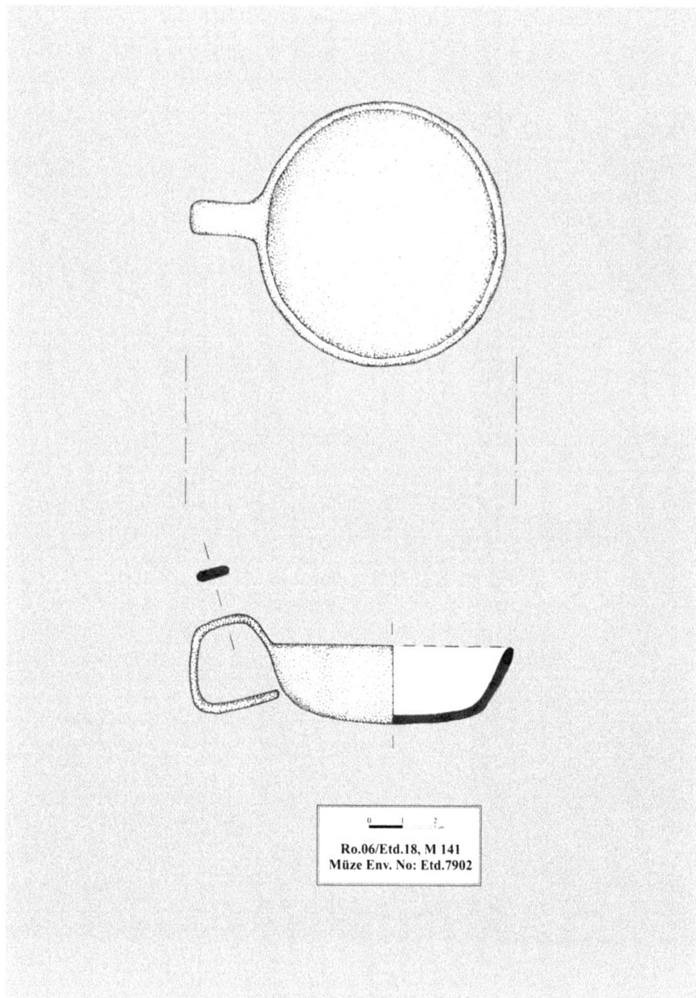

Fig. 11a. Bronze cup from Grave No. M 141.

Fig. 11b. Bronze cup from Grave No. 141.

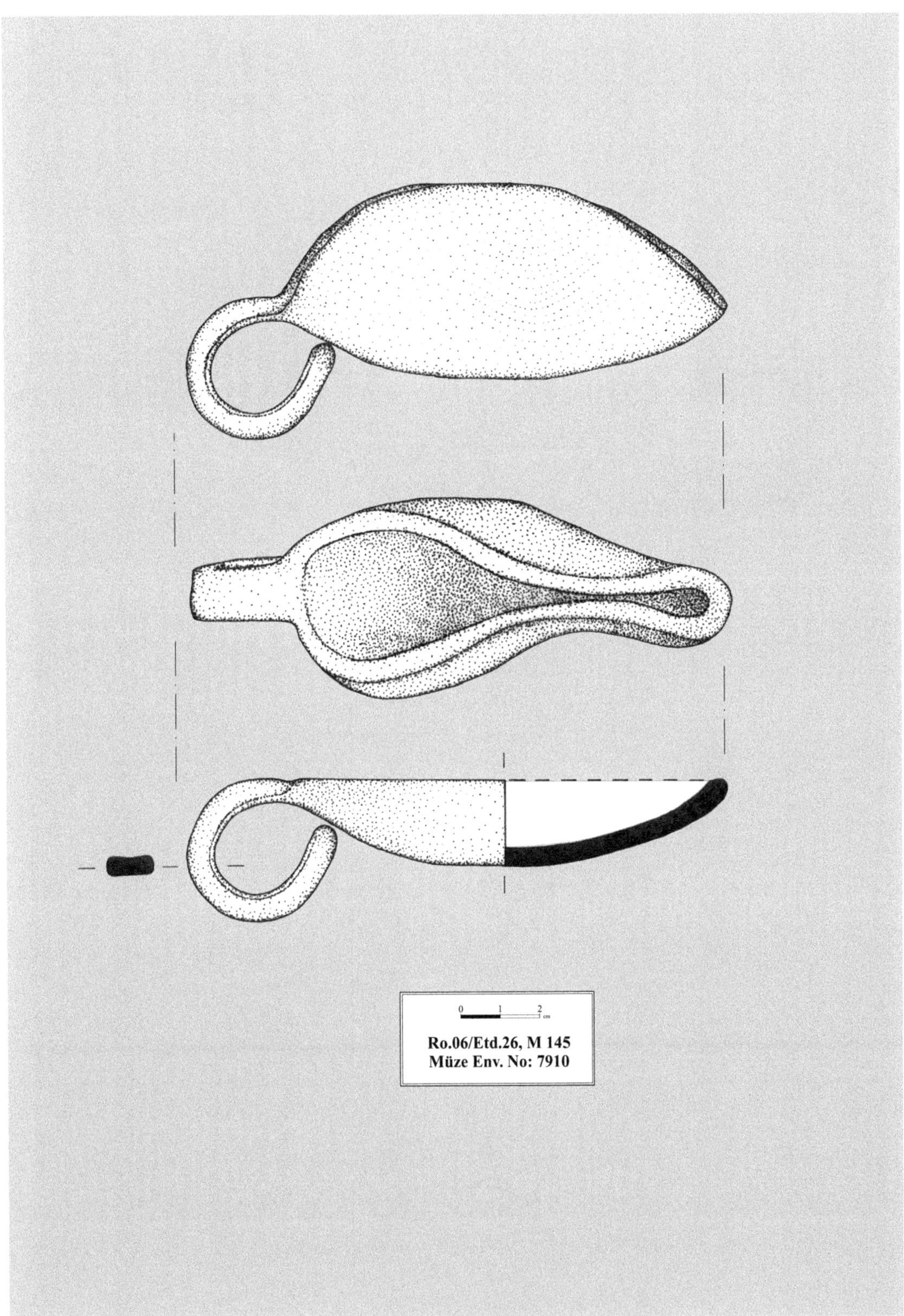

Fig. 12. Bronze cup from Grave No. M 145.

Fig. 13. Bronze cup from Grave No. M 145.

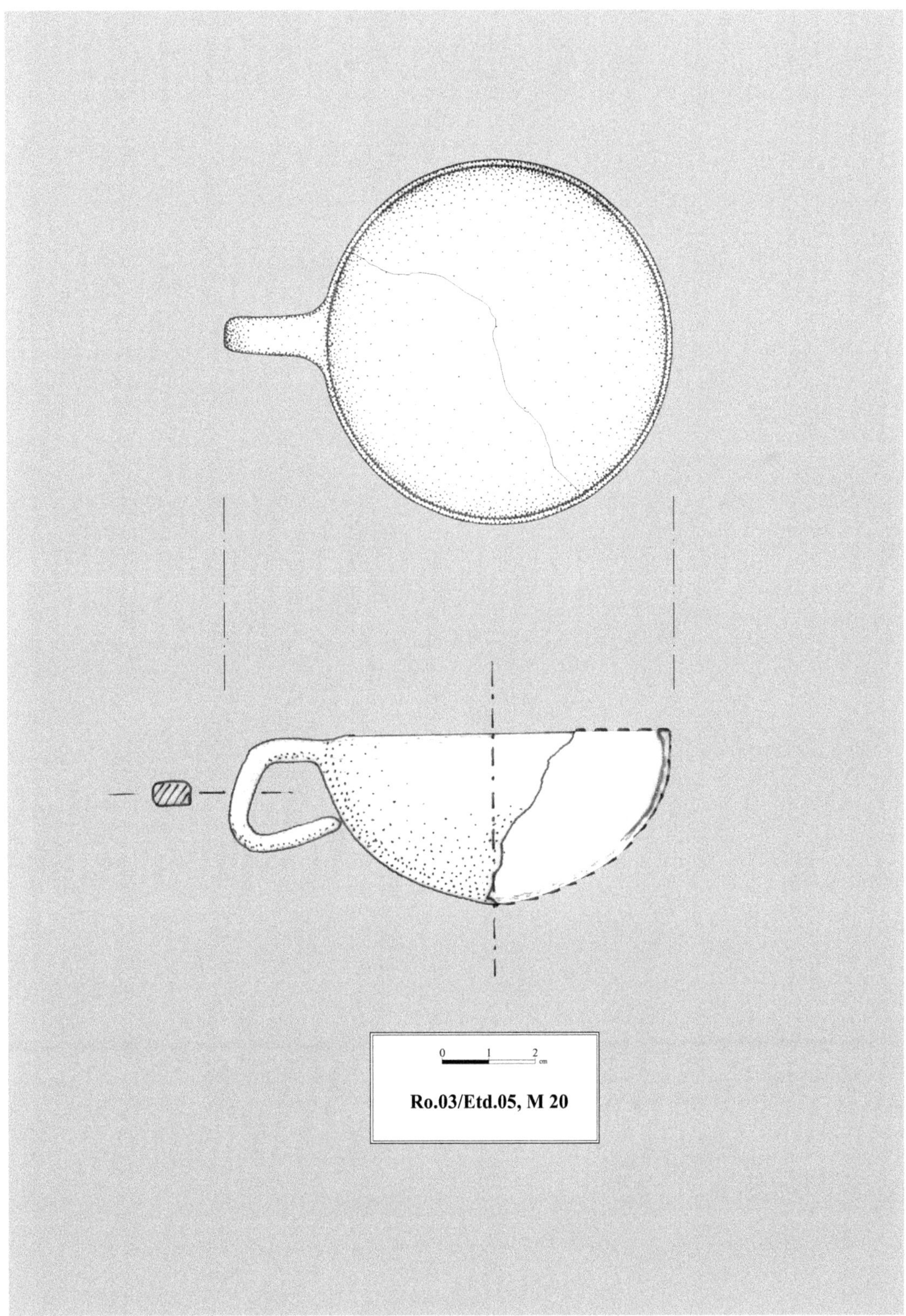

Fig. 14. Bronze cup piece from Grave No. M 20.

Fig. 15. Bronze cup piece photo from Grave No. M 20.

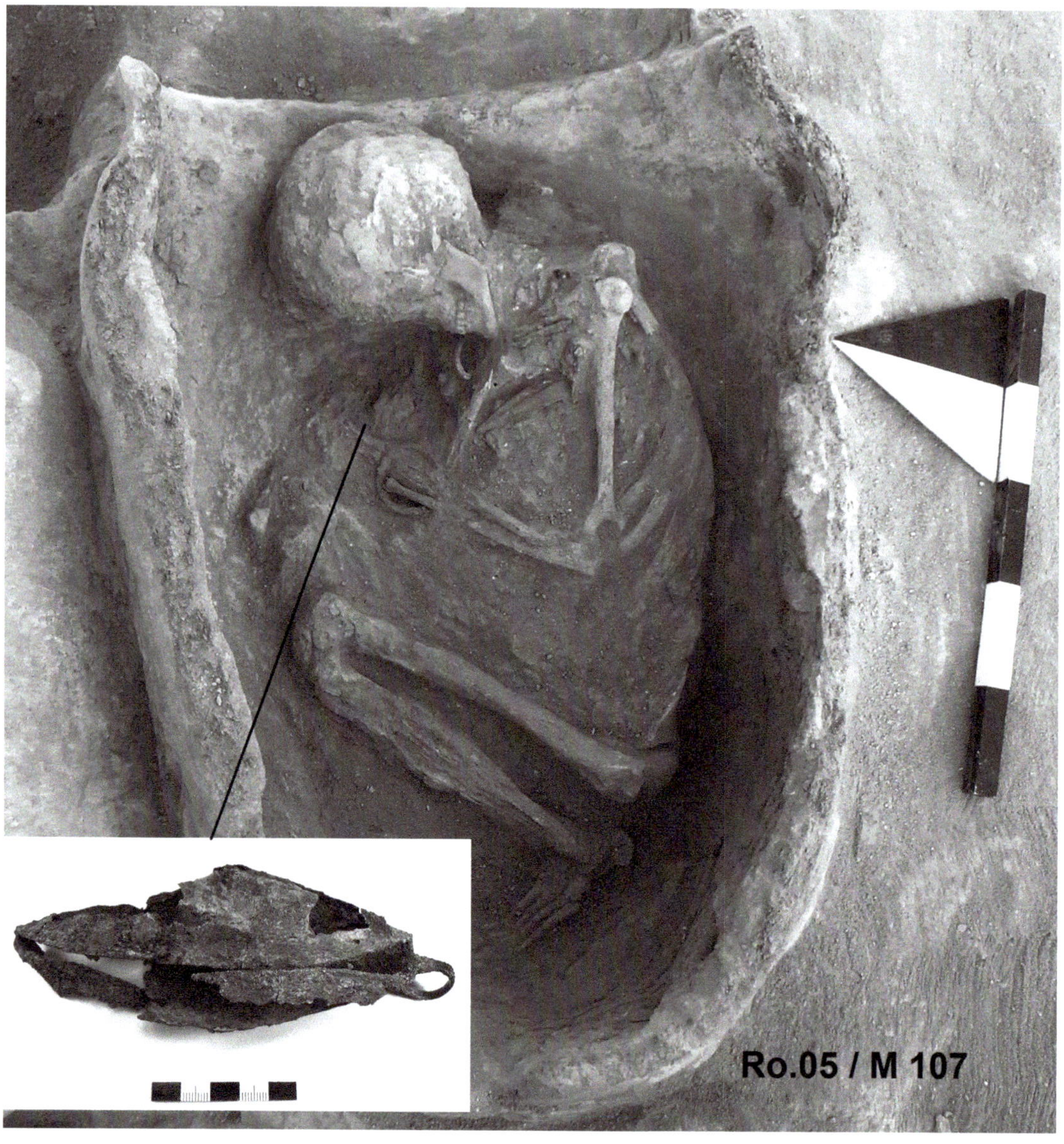

Fig. 16. Bronze cup from Grave No. M 107.

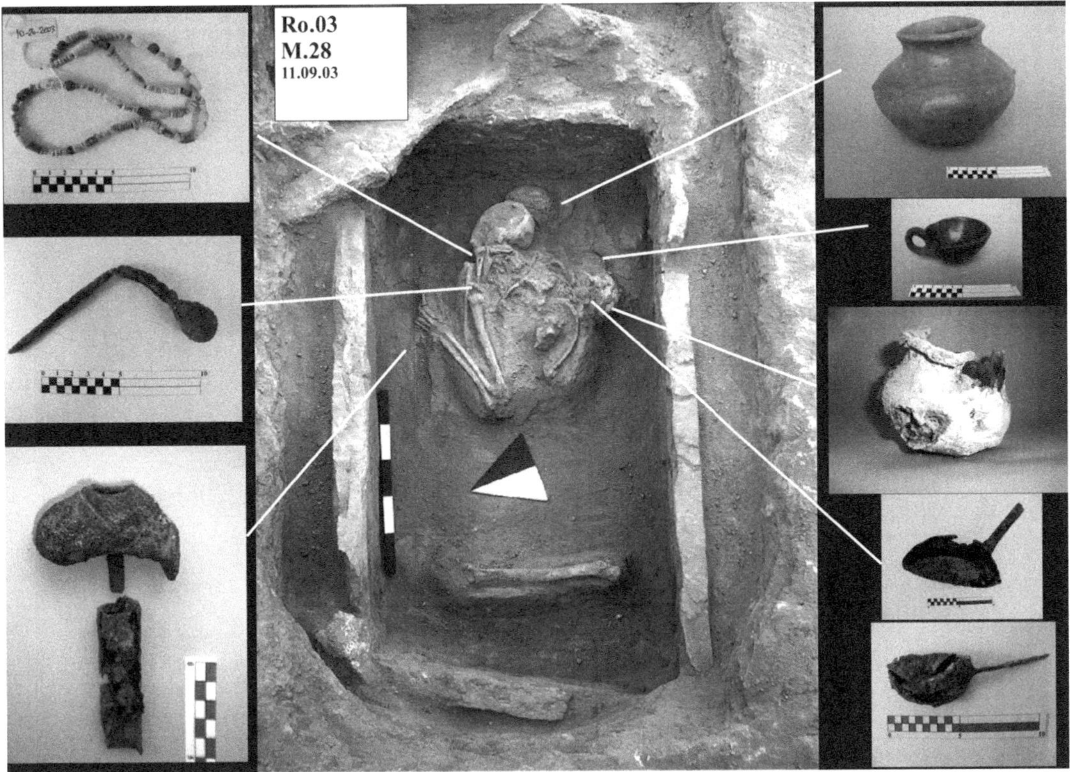

Fig. 17. Grave gifts distribution in cist Grave No. M 28.

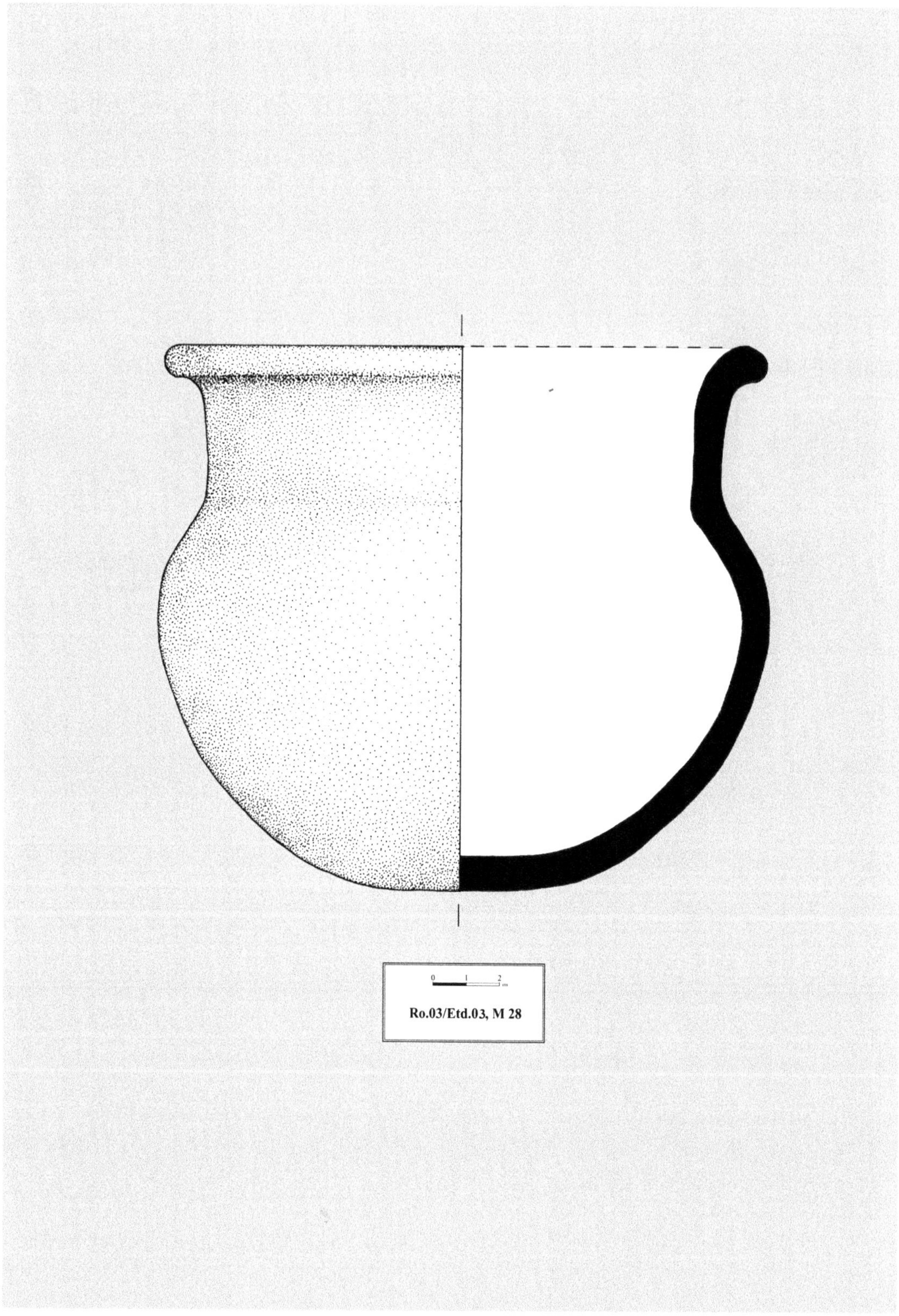

Fig. 18. Lead cup from Grave No. M 28.

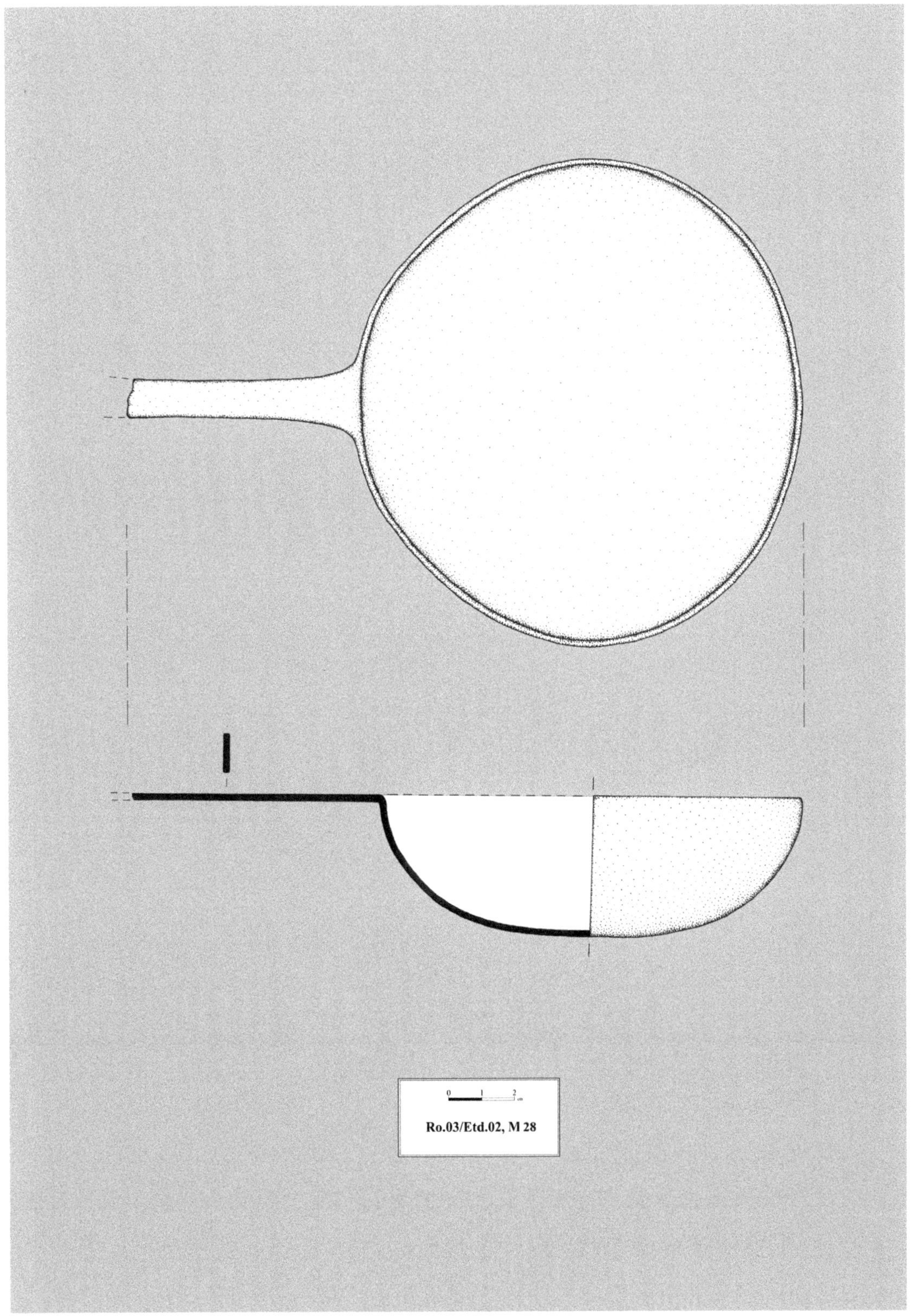

Fig. 19. Bronze pan from Grave No. M 28.

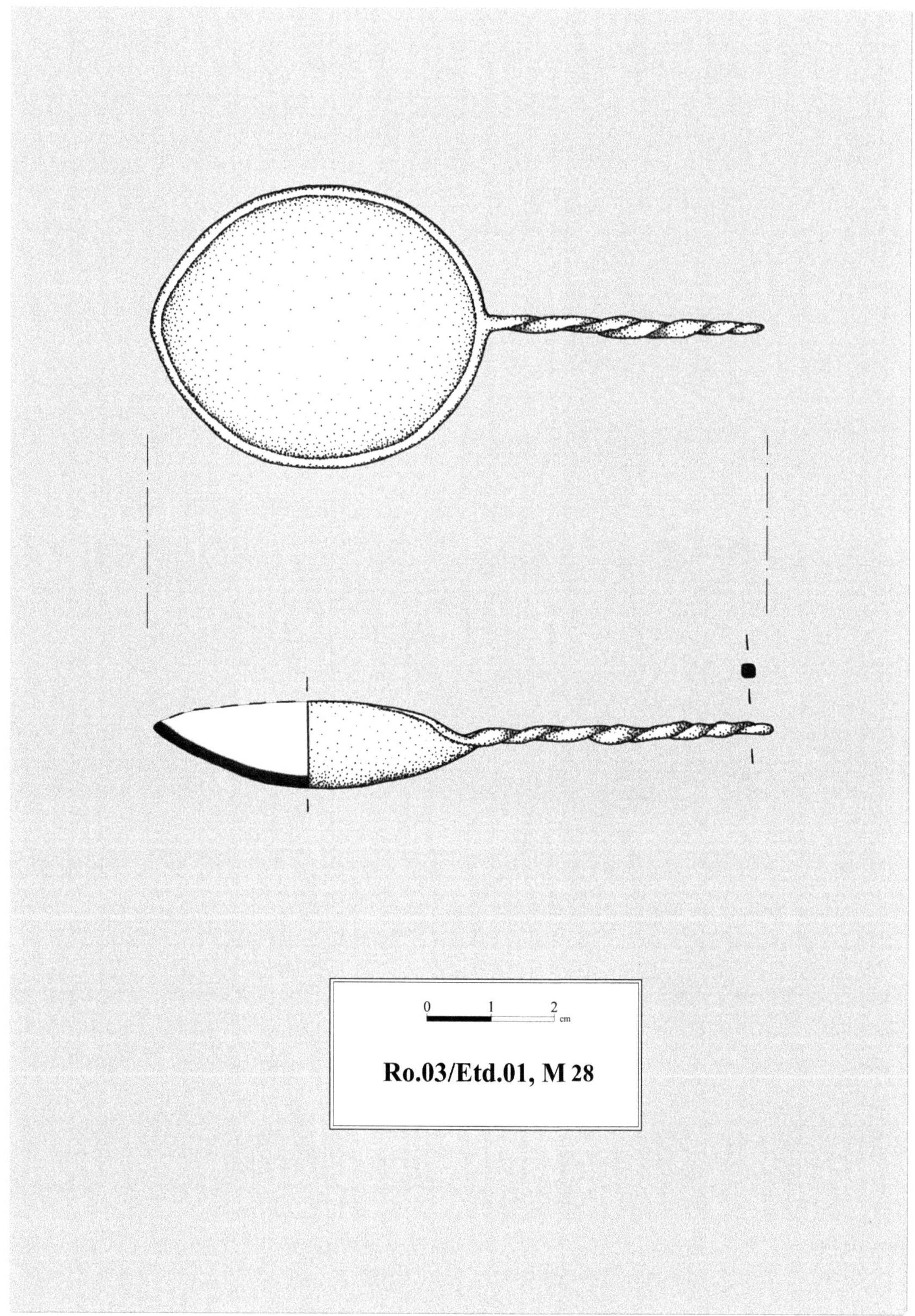

Fig. 20. Bronze spoon from Grave No. M 28.